Judah P. Benjamin

❈❈❈

The Jewish Confederate

To the Katzens,

With best wishes

Eli Evans

Praise for *Judah P. Benjamin: The Jewish Confederate*

". . . Romantic, improbable, and spell-weaving . . . Some of the best history is written by historians with roots deeply planted in the past of which they write. This often means emotional involvement and that can also produce some of the worst history. But if emotions are harnessed not to partisanship or defensiveness but to a passion for understanding and an uncompromising concern for the truth, those dangers can be avoided. Eli Evans has avoided the dangers and gained much from his involvement and emotion. The main part of the past he relates here lies at an anguished juncture in the history of Jews and Southerners. But the past he taps to illuminate that scene, and especially the Jewish role in it, is much older and deeper. It is a past and a theme rarely available to the understanding of non-Jewish historians. For that reason, we are all the more indebted to him for this very fine and moving book."

> C. Vann Woodward
> Sterling Professor History Emeritus
> Yale University
> in the *New York Review of Books*

"Evans has filled a host of voids and in the process of doing so, he has written a thoughtful, easy-paced narrative that is a solid addition to Civil War literature. This is one of those rare studies that will stand unchallenged for decades to come."

> James Robertson
> Miles Professor of History
> Virginia Polytechnic Institute
> in the *Richmond News Leader*

"The story is intriguing and fascinating. Evans' recapturing of it is nothing less than spectacular. He has given Judah P. Benjamin back to the Jews. That, in itself, is a substantial accomplishment. But even more importantly, Evans has restored Benjamin to his significant place in American history."

> Joseph Cohen
> Chairman, Department of Jewish Studies
> Tulane University

"This well-written and well-researched volume replaces Robert Meade's biography (1943) as the standard study and is a significant contribution both to Southern Jewish and Civil War history."

> *Library Journal*

"No writer has really captured this stellar Southern statesman until now. Evans' book tells a remarkable story and is the definitive biography of Benjamin."

> Edward D.C. Campbell, Jr.
> Editor, *Virginia Cavalcade*
> in *Civil War Times Illustrated*

JUDAH P. BENJAMIN

The Jewish Confederate

Eli N. Evans

THE FREE PRESS
A Division of Macmillan, Inc.
NEW YORK

The Free Press
A Division of Macmillan, Inc.
866 Third Avenue, New York, N.Y. 10022

Collier Macmillan Canada, Inc.

First Free Press Paperback Edition 1989

Printed in the United States of America

printing number

1 2 3 4 5 6 7 8 9 10

Library of Congress Cataloging-in-Publication Data
Evans, Eli N.
  Judah P. Benjamin, the Jewish Confederate

  Bibliography: p.
  Includes index.
    1. Benjamin, J.P. (Judah Philip), 1811–1884.
  2. Statesmen—Confederate States of America—Biography.
  3. Confederate States of America—History.
  4. Legislators—United States—Biography. 5. United
  States. Congress. Senate—Biography. 6. Lawyers—
  Southern States—Biography. 7. Lawyers—Great Britain—
  Biography. I. Title.
  E467.1.B4E9   1988   973.7′13′0924 [B]   87-19256
  ISBN 0-02-909911-0

Epigraph: "John Brown's Body" by Stephen Vincent Benét. From *The Selected Works of Stephen Vincent Benét,* Holt, Rinehart & Winston, Inc. Copyright renewed 1955, 1956 by Rosemary Carr Benét. Reprinted by special permission of Brandt & Brandt Literary Agents, Inc.

✻

*To my father, Emanuel J. "Mutt" Evans, who carved out
his own place in Southern Jewish history as Mayor of
Durham, North Carolina, from 1951 to 1963, and
inspired many of the insights in this book*

and

*To the memory of my mother, Sara Nachamson Evans,
who raised her family, even in a small town, to believe
that every Jew walks in the footsteps of history, Southern
Jews especially*

✻

From *John Brown's Body*

BY STEPHEN VINCENT BENÉT

(*1927*)

Judah P. Benjamin, the dapper Jew,
Seal-Sleek, black-eyed, lawyer and epicure,
Able, well-hated, face alive with life,
Looked round the council-chamber with the slight
Perpetual smile he held before himself
Continually like a silk-ribbed fan.
Behind the fan, his quick, shrewd, fluid mind
Weighed Gentiles in an old balance. . . .

    The mind behind the silk-ribbed fan
Was a dark prince, clothed in an Eastern stuff,
Whole brown hands cupped about a crystal egg
That filmed with colored cloud. The eyes stared,
searching.

"I am a Jew, What am I doing here?
The Jew is in my blood and in my hands,
The lonely, bitter and quicksilver drop,
The strain of myrrh that dyes no Gentile mind. . . .
A river runs between these men and me,
A river of blood and time and liquid gold,
—Oh white rivers of Canaan, running the night!—
And we are colleagues. And we speak to each other
Across the roar of that river, but no more.

I hide myself behind a smiling fan.
They hide themselves behind a Gentile mask
And, if they fall, they will be lifted up,
Being the people, but if I once fall
I fall forever, like the rejected stone.

That is the Jew of it, my Gentile friends,
To see too far ahead and yet go on. . . .
It is the Jew, to see too far ahead. . . .

Jefferson Davis, pride of Mississippi . . .
I sent you a challenge once, but that's forgotten
And though your blood runs differently from mine,
The Jew salutes you from behind his fan,
Because you are the South he fell in love with
When that young black-haired girl with the Gentile eyes,
Proud, and a Catholic, and with honey lips,
First dinted her French heels upon his heart . . .

Tell me, you Gentiles, when your Gentile wives
Pray in church for you and for the South,
How do they pray? . . .
You do not have so good a prayer as mine,
You cannot have so good a prayer as mine . . ."

    One day he is there and smiling
The next he is gone as if he had taken fernseed
And walked invisible so through the Union lines.
You will not find that smile in a Northern prison
Though you seek from now till Doomsday. It is too
wise . . .

Contents

❈❈❈

Prologue

❊❊❊

Judah P. Benjamin served as Attorney General, Secretary of War, *and* Secretary of State to the Confederacy from 1861 to 1865. Though historians have routinely called him "the brains of the Confederacy," they knew relatively little about him. Many historians of the Civil War have referred to him as President Jefferson Davis's most loyal confidant. Yet Davis himself, in a laborious 1881 memoir of the war, referred to Benjamin in the most perfunctory fashion, mentioning his name only twice in the 1,500-page, two-volume work. That is especially odd if, as Varina Howell Davis, the First Lady of the Confederacy, testified in a letter written in 1889, Judah P. Benjamin spent ten to twelve hours a day in the office with her husband and was his "right hand," a central figure in events.

I first became curious about Judah P. Benjamin fifteen years ago when I began my research for *The Provincials: A Personal History of Jews in the South.* I was intrigued with the ways in which Jews and Southerners were alike—stepchildren of an anguished history—and yet how different. Whereas the Jewish search for a homeland contrasted with the Southerner's commitment to place, Southern defenders of the Confederacy often used Old Testament analogies in referring to themselves as "the chosen people" destined to survive and triumph against overwhelming odds. Benjamin fascinated me then because of the extraordinary role he played in Southern history and the ways in which Jews and non-Jews reacted to him. He was the prototype of the contradictions in the Jewish Southerner, and the stranger in the Confederate story, the Jew at the eye of the storm that was the Civil War. Objectively, with so few Jews in the South at the time, it is astonishing that one should appear at the very center of Southern history. Benjamin himself avoided his Jewish-

---

*Full information for bibliographic references in the Prologue can be found in the Selected Bibliography.

ness throughout his public career, though his enemies in the Southern press and in the halls of the Confederate Congress never let the South forget it. The virulence of the times, which saw an outpouring of anti-Semitism such as in no previous period in American history, required a symbolic figure as a catalyst for an ancient hostility and perhaps contributed to his intentional elusiveness.

If Benjamin's role in history has been misjudged by historians and was minimized even by participants, much of the responsibility for that lies with Benjamin himself. He chose obscurity early in the war with the unwavering decision that he could best serve the South by serving Jefferson Davis and remaining in the presidential shadow. For reasons that puzzle historians, Benjamin burned his personal papers—some as he escaped from Richmond in 1865, and almost all of the rest just before he died—because he left only six scraps of paper at his death. One historian called him a "virtual incendiary."

Benjamin fled to England after the war and built a second career as a successful international lawyer. He had been known in the U.S. Senate as one of its outstanding orators, but in England he gave no published speeches on the war. He wrote a classic treatise on commercial law in England known even today to law students as *Benjamin on Sales,* but he left no articles, essays, or books about his role in, or any other aspect of the war. Indeed, he made only two public statements in nineteen years involving the war. The first was a three-paragraph letter to the *Times* of London in September 1865, just after he arrived in England, protesting the imprisonment of Jefferson Davis. The second was a short letter in 1883 contradicting the charge that millions of dollars in Confederate funds were left in European banks, under his control. There were no letters, even to family or friends, defending strategy or admitting error; nor does history record any revealing war-related conversations with students or scholars. He spent a few evenings at dinner with Davis when the ex-President visited London five times between 1868 and 1883. Otherwise, he avoided nostalgic encounters with friends from the South. It is one of the enduring mysteries that Benjamin's behavior after the war contrasted so dramatically with his hunger for recognition and fame before the war. He chose to erase all ties to his previous life. In fact, he never even returned to the United States, dying in Paris on May 6, 1884.

Benjamin survives, then, as he willed it: a shadowy figure in Civil War history, widely thought of as a dependable administrator for Jefferson Davis. But a man of his analytical skills and personal dynamism, acknowledged by scholars to have been one of America's most brilliant legal minds and most arresting orators, could never have served merely as "Mr. Davis's clerk" or administrative assistant.

To understand the story behind Judah P. Benjamin requires an exploration of motivation and character extending to other major figures in the Civil War. Chief among them is the President he served. Though the subject of dozens of biographies over the past century, Jefferson Davis, too, still stands as an enigmatic figure in the Confederate adventure—staunch and exhausted, hobbled by physical illness and overwhelming pressures, a restless and arrogant military man trapped at his desk, a political leader who hated politics and politicians. Yet, give Jefferson Davis his due on one level—he was the first chief executive in America to appoint a Jew to his Cabinet, and he confirmed that decision twice more in the face of the storm of controversy surrounding Judah P. Benjamin.

Oddly, Jefferson Davis has grown less heroic with the passage of time, perhaps because of his colorless personality, severe manner, and unsympathetic treatment by historians. Overshadowed by Lee and Lincoln, he remains what Senator Clement Clay of Alabama called him in the beginning, "the Sphinx of the Confederacy," and, in Frank Vandiver's phrase, "a leader without a legend" and "a strangely muffled man." To understand the complexity of the drama that was the Civil War, one must probe the intricate interplay between these two secretive men who controlled the destiny of the South.

Among Jews in the United States, Judah P. Benjamin's acceptance has taken time. He was a neglected figure for almost seventy years after the Civil War. The immigrant generation was not yet secure enough in America to celebrate or even acknowledge ties to the leadership of the Southern states that led a rebellion in behalf of slavery. Although some experts estimated that more than 10,000 Jews fought for the Confederacy, American Jews preferred to celebrate an earlier and safer personality, Haym Salomon of Philadelphia, who helped finance the American Revolution.

In the 1930s, when America began to take a new look at Robert E. Lee and "Stonewall" Jackson and to put the Civil War into perspective, Judah P. Benjamin emerged also in pamphlets, children's books, and patriotic essays, and in American Jewish literature as one of the men in American history who substantiated Jewish claims to American roots. If it was now all right for the non-Jews to accept the South's part in the war as a heroic chapter of the nation's history, it was acceptable for the Jewish community as well.

Pierce Butler in 1907, and Robert Douthat Meade in 1943, wrote

the two standard biographies of Benjamin, pulling together the thousands of Civil War orders and letters to friends and family in England,
France, New Orleans, Charleston, and elsewhere that he was unable
to destroy. Butler interviewed Benjamin's contemporaries, including
Varina Howell Davis. Meade spent twelve years traveling—research-
ing diaries, memoirs, and papers, and interviewing Benjamin's family
members and friends. This book revealed Benjamin, in the words
of others and in his letters to friends and family, both as a gifted
tactician with a philosophical nature and an urbane manner, and as
a gourmet, an inveterate gambler, and a man whom women adored.
Still, it acknowledged a paucity of material.

Meade and Butler were both Southern historians unfamiliar with
American Jewish history. Judaism for them represented strange and
unsteady territory, which they, perhaps too deeply ingrained with
the attitudes of their times, were not prepared to explore. Butler
treated Jewishness as if it were an unpleasant component of his
admiring portrait, one that he was reluctant but duty-bound to include briefly. He referred to Benjamin's father as "that *rara avis,*
an unsuccessful Jew," and described Benjamin in England as "this
wonderful little Jew from America." Meade, writing during the sensitive period of the rise of Nazi Germany just before World War II,
was more circumspect, yet observed that "like so many of Jewish
blood today, Benjamin tended to become cosmopolitan." In the late
1930s, no Southern historian could convey the harshness of the
anti-Semitism surrounding Benjamin without seeming prejudiced
himself.

I have investigated the research papers of both men—Butler's
papers are at Tulane University, and Meade's papers were given to
the University of Virginia in 1978. Both interviewed acquaintances
and surviving relatives who had known Benjamin, but they left out
of their books much material they collected that reflected on Benjamin's Jewishness and other personal matters. I have now attempted
to reinterpret the research they used, for whatever insights might
now be revealed.

Meade and Butler also drew from the research of the spare beginnings of an unfinished biography by Francis Lawley, the Richmond
and Washington correspondent of the London *Times* during the
war, who became, according to Meade, "devoted to Benjamin, who
doubtless helped to color his vivid dispatches with a sympathetic
attitude toward the Confederacy." Benjamin kept up a relationship
with Lawley for the rest of his life, but only six pages of the biography

Lawley planned exist, along with fewer than a dozen letters. Two of the letters, dated 1898, are from Varina Davis to Lawley. They describe in fascinating detail Benjamin's relationship with her husband.

This book is partly an interpretive study of the unusual relationship between Judah P. Benjamin and Jefferson Davis, using a reconstruction of events and personalities pieced together from the shards of evidence. Civil War literature offers to the historian insights, usually unavailable to researchers of other periods, into the social and political atmosphere of another era. Numerous people kept diaries and verbatim accounts of meetings and debates—even of tea parties, balls, banquets, and social events. Many other accounts and reminiscences by Cabinet members, governors, congressmen, senators, and generals, as well as their wives and aides, offer the kind of detail that allows the historian to speculate with more confidence than would normally be the case. More than 60,000 books have been written on the Civil War, and every detail of all manner of things has been collected: clothing, furniture, architecture, religion, food, manufacturing techniques, slave customs. That kind of detail allows the careful writer to recover much of the age without distorting history.

For me, the City of Richmond, Virginia, is a living, breathing thing, with near-human characteristics. There is a rich literature concerning the city during the Civil War period. It was a far more fascinating place than Margaret Mitchell's Atlanta, for it changed from the self-confident capital city of both Virginia and the Confederacy into a teeming campground of raw recruits and black industrial slaves, the scene of gambling dens, a hotbed of political intrigue and espionage. The Union Army and Abraham Lincoln, just 100 miles away, viewed it as a tempting plum on the Confederate cake. For four years, the two armies battled back and forth across Virginia, transforming Richmond slowly into a hospital for the wounded, besetting it with deprivation and hunger, and finally consuming it with fire. Richmond was the great stage for Judah P. Benjamin and Jefferson Davis. But it was more than just their physical home; it was the struggling heart of the Confederacy.

This book undertakes four lines of inquiry which I believe have not been appropriately treated before by historians.

First, it tries to place Benjamin in a Jewish context, to explore and illuminate the profound dilemma of the Jew in the nineteenth-century South. For Jewish scholars of American Jewish history, Judah P. Benjamin has presented complex problems. Subconsciously, as Jews themselves, they may have wanted to put as much distance between him and Jewishness as possible, because he was incomprehensible as a Jewish figure. As a Confederate leader who once owned 140 slaves, he was to those historians part of a failed culture, not a Jew whom scholars of American Jewish history could explain, and therefore it was easier to dismiss him as Jewish than try to probe him and understand him as an integral figure in American Jewish history. Benjamin's story has also been either misinterpreted or overlooked by Southern historians, who cannot be expected to bring an awareness of Jewish experience to Confederate history. For Southern scholars, Benjamin was more of a Rorschach test for personal feelings about Jews than a historical figure. They tended to rely heavily on the statements of his contemporaries, many of whom held anti-Semitic views, for their assessment of him. Contemporary perceptions of his "fatalism," his "exotic" birth, or his "oriental qualities" were repeated over and over, again, embellished and elaborated until transfigured into fact. He was an apparition who from time to time took on human dimension, but then would disappear again into Jewish stereotype.

Judah Benjamin's boyhood was much more steeped in Jewish culture and tradition than either Southern or Jewish historians have acknowledged. It was easy superficially to dismiss him as a Jew. He married out of the faith, had little to do with religious institutions, did not speak or write of his religious beliefs, and failed to keep Jewish laws and to celebrate Jewish holidays. But one cannot judge Jewish identity only by public acts. It is my thesis that to presume him simply a nonbeliever, as historians have, represents a fundamental error in Southern history and has been the main reason for the shroud of mystery that surrounds him.

From the facts of Benjamin's boyhood, another conclusion is more justifiable. He was reared in Charleston, South Carolina, and grew to manhood in New Orleans, two of the largest Jewish communities in the United States in the early nineteenth century. His father was one of the twelve dissenters in Charleston who formed the first Reform Congregation of America. The character of a Jewish boy reared in Charleston by a deeply involved Jewish family would be shaped by that experience the rest of his life. He could stand apart from his Jewishness in public, but he could not run very far from it psychologically. He could try to assimilate, but the powerful would not let him forget his roots. And no Jew can make the leap from a childhood with religious immigrant parents to an assimilated Southern leader in twenty years, without retaining psychological ties to his Jewish past. Thus when newspapers, political enemies, and military leaders ridiculed his Jewishness, attacking and insulting him with stinging phrases of religious prejudice, there had to be demons loosed inside him. In Stephen Vincent Benet's words in *John Brown's Body,* what lay behind the "perpetual smile"?

Part of my fascination with Judah P. Benjamin comes from my own life as a Jewish Southerner. At times, I provide my own insights in the book, because I cannot help but feel that even though our boyhoods were separated by more than a hundred years, Benjamin is not remote. He is somehow familiar because there are certain changeless verities to growing up Jewish in the Bible Belt and passing for white in that mysterious underland of America. The problems Benjamin experienced are not very different from those of other Jews in the South who have had to deal with having power, with race, with religious fundamentalism, with anti-Semitism. As Bertram Korn pointed out in *American Jewry and the Civil War,* the nation both North and South experienced the "greatest outpouring of Judaeophobia in its history" during the Civil War, and Judah P. Benjamin was its most convenient target. Political and internecine passions were unbridled and flared into war. It was a time of primitive attitudes by Southerners toward Jews, and Benjamin was unique as a visible symbol of the mighty; but, illustrious as his life was, he did not escape the hatred. Nor, as we shall see, did other members of the Jewish communities that this book examines in the three cities where he lived—Charleston, New Orleans, and Richmond.

The second line of inquiry builds on the insights into Benjamin's Jewishness to explore his many-sided relationship with Jefferson Davis. It is my view that there were elements in each man that deepened the relationship; that their boyhood, parental attitude, religious heritage, cultural history, and education were so different, yet so similar, that they became, as Varina Davis described them, "two master minds which seemed to be the complement of each other . . . breasting as one man the heavy storm." Davis was rural and physical, the unusual mixture of Southern Baptist and Catholic, with family ties to the American Revolution and to the War of 1812. Benjamin, on the other hand, was urban, intellectual, Jewish, and an immigrant, with parents who did not arrive in the United States until 1813. As their separate and entangled stories unfold, it is apparent that Judah Benjamin becomes as it were a lens through which one can better focus on and understand Jefferson Davis. Like two flintstones in darkness, they make sparks when brought together. To understand one is to explore the other; they are twin pieces of a puzzle, together less of a mystery than apart.

In the beginning, Benjamin and Davis were cool to each other because neither had been raised to trust easily. Benjamin's Jewishness stood in the way of both men, raised as outsiders and bred to suspicion. The presence of a remarkable woman—Varina Howell Davis, the second wife of the President of the Confederacy, who married him at eighteen when he was thirty-seven—was the crucial element that fostered the growth of trust between the two men and made it sustain itself. Author of a two-volume book about her husband and the Confederacy, she was a wise and perceptive woman and, like many women in Richmond during the war, deeply involved in the strategy debates that swirled around the Confederate White House. While most historians dismiss her book as dull and unimportant, her writing contains nuggets of information and insight. She was schooled in politics from her earliest years, and Judah Benjamin was her obvious fascination. At the end of her life, she wrote of Benjamin that his "greatness was hard to measure . . . I loved him dearly." Did Benjamin, caught in the pain of a strange marriage of his own to a New Orleans wife living in Paris, find solace in his affection for Varina Davis? How did Benjamin and Varina Davis interact with the President, who was suffering under intense physical strain and emotional pressure? The story then is three-cornered, a triangle with Varina Davis as the bridge between an ailing President and his Jewish jack-of-all-trades. This book is the first to treat the three of them together.

The third line of inquiry concerns the evolving attitudes of both men toward slavery. We are just beginning to understand in depth the unusual plantation life of the slave communities at Davis Bend, the more than 11,000 acres that belonged to Joseph and Jefferson Davis. Two recent books have explored with great care their slave records still on file in Mississippi: Clement Eaton's 1977 biography of Jefferson Davis, and a 1981 book by Janet Sharp Hermann entitled *The Pursuit of a Dream.* Both reveal that the attitudes of the Davis family on their own plantation, influenced by British utopians, were much more progressive (one might say even democratic) than on perhaps any other plantation in the South.

As for Judah Benjamin, Jewish historians have reacted with revulsion to the fact that he owned slaves at all and have been unable to consider the question of his views on slavery with anything but embarrassed dismay. To understand Benjamin on this score, one must put him into context as a political figure against a backdrop of planter dogmatism and Abolitionist fervor. Such an exploration leads directly to an extraordinary episode of the war in which Benjamin played a central role: the effort to persuade Jefferson Davis to issue a Confederate Emancipation Proclamation, which would promise slaves freedom in exchange for military service. That move, which began to take shape early in the war in the minds of military and political leaders but did not surface until 1864, is usually dismissed as a desperate gamble made at the end of the war to lure the British into the fighting. As the clouds of defeat gathered, Judah P. Benjamin spoke before 10,000 people in Richmond, delivering a remarkable speech in favor of a Confederate offer to free the slaves who would fight for the South—the first major address in four years from a frustrated master orator.

The fourth strand of this book is concerned with Benjamin's personality. It explores the anomaly between his early hunger for recognition and fame and the utter secrecy and privacy of his later life. I shall suggest that the key to understanding his silence after the war is his creation of a Confederate spy ring in Canada, and the subsequent proclamation, conceived by the Union's Secretary of War, Edwin Stanton, and issued by Lincoln's successor, President Andrew Johnson, for the arrest of Jefferson Davis and seven Canadian Confederate spies after the Lincoln assassination. History, by means of the trials of the conspirators, by exhaustive investigations, and by endless inquiries of both scholars and buffs, has absolved both Judah P. Benjamin and Jefferson Davis from any responsibility. But what has not been previously considered is the inner man, the psychological and emotional impact on Benjamin of the long period of hysteria that followed the assassination. It took several years for Northern vengeance to subside: "Wanted for the Assassination of Lincoln" posters dotted the South for Davis and the leaders of the Canadian spy ring, and eventually Davis spent two years in prison under the cloud of charges of complicity in the assassination. Had Benjamin been captured could he, as a Jew, have received a fair trial? Would Northern leaders as ruthless as Stanton, looking for a scapegoat, have been able to resist the opportunity to exploit the explosion of anti-Semitism that would have been released by his capture and the accusation? Four people were hanged, at least one on little evidence. John Wilkes Booth was called the "American Judas." Would Benjamin have been spared?

When the earliest wave of Civil War history was written by its participants, no one in the South knew for certain what to think about Jews—nor were Southern Jews themselves very psychologically self-aware. Newly emancipated from centuries of nonvoting and nonparticipation in public life, most Jews were politically innocent; Christians, especially in the Bible Belt, were inexperienced in dealing with Jewish political accomplishment. Jewish self-consciousness in literature and history has developed as a *twentieth*-century phenomenon. Today, Judah P. Benjamin deserves a new evaluation, a reexamination of the events of his life and times by a contemporary writer aware of Southern Jewish history. It may be that the hidden Jewish experience of this major figure can clarify some of what has been impenetrable about the Confederate story. Significant as well is what Benjamin's rise to prominence says about America.

Judah P. Benjamin achieved greater political power than any other Jew in the nineteenth century—perhaps even in all American history. At the height of his career, when he served as Secretary of War and Secretary of State to the Confederacy, he was at the center of events shaping America, leaving in his letterbooks more than 2,000 official memoranda, letters, and telegrams to the military, ambassadors, political figures, and influential citizens; writing speeches for Jefferson Davis; consulting with the President on almost every decision, large or small; a familiar figure to those on the battlefields and in the legislative halls, known at home and abroad. Yet, he was never permitted by the press or political opponents to forget his Jewishness, and though he was a nonpracticing Jew, he never attempted to deny his faith. Benjamin thus must stand as a symbol of American democracy and its openness to religious minorities. In spite of the bigotry surrounding him, not only was he elected to the U.S. Senate and appointed to three high offices in the Confederacy, but he was also offered an appointment as the Ambassador to Spain and a seat on the U.S. Supreme Court. The nineteenth-century emancipation of the Jews, which began in Europe after the French Revolution, was as great a shock to Jews as were the centuries of persecution that preceded it. Judah P. Benjamin was the main beneficiary of that emancipation and its most visible symbol in America.

In the final years before the war, Benjamin was widely admired nationally in both Jewish and non-Jewish communities for his prestige as a Southern leader and his eloquence as an orator. His election as the first acknowledged Jew in the U.S. Senate was a watershed for American Jews. Because of the war, he became the first Jewish political figure to be projected into the national consciousness. Jews in the South were especially proud of his achievement, because he validated their legitimacy as Southerners. A pivotal figure in American Jewish history, Benjamin broke down the barriers of prejudice to achieve high office. After him, it was more acceptable for Jews to be elected to office and to aspire to service in the councils of national power.

Although Judah P. Benjamin concealed himself in the shadows of his own times, only a fresh effort to understand him, rooted in new perspectives one hundred years after his death, can reveal him in his proper place at center stage in the bitter struggle that shaped this nation.

ELI N. EVANS
Durham, North Carolina
August 1, 1987

1

❧

JEWISH SOUTHERNER

1808–1860

1

Charleston:
Boyhood in the Reformed Society

❁❁❁

Judah Philip Benjamin (1811–84) was descended from the Sephardics, Spanish Jews who flourished for three hundred years on the Iberian peninsula in the "Golden Age." Their name derived from the Biblical reference to "Sepharad," a mysterious place where wandering Hebrews gathered after the Babylonian exile and the destruction of Solomon's temple in Jerusalem.[1] The Moorish conquest of Spain from North Africa in the eighth century caused both Islam and Judaism to gain in power and grandeur. The Moors found among Spanish Jews a respect for learning and culture kindred to their own. Although in 1215 Pope Innocent III tried to hold back the progress of Jews into the professions by forcing them to wear stigmatizing yellow badges, after 1200 the Jews in Spain and Portugal dominated the medical profession and were prominent as judges, architects, writers, scientists, and teachers. The courts of Aragon and Castile relied on them as advisers, ministers of finance, financiers of military expeditions, and royal counselors; as leaders in international commerce and colonial expansion; as merchants; and, in the technical professions, as navigators, mapmakers, and astronomers.[2]

Nowhere in the world did Jewry occupy a more influential place than in the court of King Ferdinand and Queen Isabella. The Queen's

3

confidential secretary was Jewish, as were other court officials and her closest female friend. The general bailiff of Aragon, the grand treasurer, the comptroller general of the royal household, the vice chancellor of the Kingdom of Aragon, and three top military officers under Ferdinand's command all were Jews.

As Moorish power diminished, however, so did the safety of the Jews. Simple envy and jealousy gave way to a far greater danger: Christian suspicion growing into subsequent persecution. In 1479, Ferdinand and Isabella initiated the Inquisition, confining Jews to specific ethnic areas and expelling them from certain cities and provinces. As Jewish properties were seized, the greed of the populace grew. Finally came the Expulsion Edict of 1492: "We order all Jews and Jewesses of whatever age that before the end of this month of July they depart with their sons and daughters and manservants and maidservants and relatives, big and small . . . and not dare to return."[3] Hundreds of thousands of Jews fled in the ensuing few months, prompting the Sultan of Turkey to exclaim, "The King of Spain must have lost his mind. He is expelling his best subjects and [Spain's] wealth."

Thirty of the most prominent Jewish families of Spain escaped to Portugal as a group. One of them bore the name of Mendes.[4] Several generations later a Mendes descendant migrated to the Netherlands, where he married a Dutch Jewish woman. The couple had three daughters; one of them, named Rebecca, would be Judah Benjamin's mother. The family moved to London, ultimately living in suburban Finsbury with the most prosperous class of Jews.

Both of Rebecca's sisters married wealthy West Indian planters and moved to Caribbean islands. Rebecca married a small, intelligent, olive-skinned Sephardic named Philip Benjamin, who soon afterward opened a shop in London in which Rebecca worked selling dried fruit. Later they, too, moved to the British West Indies. Philip's grandmother had lived on St. Eustatius, where she had achieved a local reputation as a doctor and a midwife. (The records state that she allowed her house to be used by worshipers after the local synagogue was destroyed in a hurricane in 1772.) Philip rarely spoke of his ancestors, however—perhaps because of his wife's more illustrious lineage. For an ambitious boy like Judah, who would scale the heights in his newly adopted country, the achievements of the aristocratic Jews of Spain would follow him as part of his family heritage all of his life.

Judah Philip Benjamin was born on August 11, 1811, on the island of Saint Croix, which at the time was part of the British West Indies. He was thus entitled by birth to British citizenship. Although his father was later naturalized in the United States, Benjamin retained a tie to Britain all of his life. Like the religion of his birth, the place of his birth reinforced his status as an outsider: Whereas many American children he would grow up with could claim roots in the American Revolution, his roots would be in English territory, an island possessed by the enemy during the Revolutionary War.

"Judah" was an appropriate given name for a boy who would attain Confederate leadership. In Biblical times, the tribe of Judah, the largest and in many ways the most important of the twelve tribes, gave its name to the Southern Kingdom (also Judea), which split away from Israel in rebellion after the death of King Solomon. The word "Jew" was derived from Judah and, according to Jewish belief, the Messiah would spring from that tribe. Much of the Bible was written in Judah, where most of the prophets lived and wrote. Biblical tradition lent descriptive names to the tribes; Judah was "the lion." Benjamin was another of the twelve tribes. More aggressive than Judah, it was warlike and is referred to in Genesis as "ravenous wolf." Both names imply strength and courage. Clearly Judah Benjamin's name signified intellectual, spiritual, and Biblical roots in Jewish history and tradition.[5]

Judah Benjamin, one of seven children, inherited by fate the legal position of the first-born son. An older brother, also named Judah, had died in infancy. He began life conforming to Sephardic Jewish tradition, which named the eldest son after his paternal grandfather, who circumcised the boy himself. He was raised, therefore, as the oldest son, burdened with all of the family ambition attaching to his favored position.[6] He adored his older sister, Rebecca (whom he called Penny), his brothers Solomon and Joseph, and learned to protect his younger sisters, Hannah (called Harriet or "Hatty") and Judith, and his little brother, Jacob, named after his uncle in America.

Like other Sephardic Jews of London, his parents, Philip and Rebecca, had come to the West Indies searching for a new life but, with better opportunities beckoning them northward, decided to gamble on America. They sailed in 1813 for Fayetteville, North Carolina, on the Cape Fear River, where they stayed with Judah's Uncle Jacob, his mother's brother and the only relative in America with means.[7] But Jacob's small store could not support two families. As more children arrived, the port city to the south looked more promising. Philip's family settled finally in Charleston about 1821. There the family earned a modest income selling fruit in the market on the docks.[8]

Charleston was the first community in the new world to grant Jews the right to vote. Charleston early in its history earned a reputation as a tolerant place where Jews could worship freely, trade openly, own land, leave property in wills, and generally prosper with the community. Historians explain such a unique attitude by the fact that the philosopher John Locke drafted the constitution for the colony at the request of his friend Lord Ashley, one of the eight noblemen to whom Charles II granted the Carolinas. Although the constitution recognized the Church of England as the official faith of the colony, Locke managed to include a provision that "Jews, Heathens," and others should have the chance to acquaint themselves with "the purity of the Christian religion and by good usage and persuasion. . . be won over to embrace . . . the truth." Thus, Charleston from the beginning attracted a diverse population.

Jews had lived in Charles Town, as it was known in colonial times, since 1695, and the Jewish population had grown steadily as the community developed into the largest seaport in the thirteen colonies, trading deerskins, rice exports, and indigo valuable to Jewish merchants in London as dye for the blue uniforms of the British merchant fleet. By 1749, Charleston had a Jewish congregation, Beth Elohim Unveh Shallom (House of God and Mansion of Peace), the fifth Jewish congregation in the United States. By 1800, Charleston had the largest Jewish community in America, five hundred Jews, with more than a thousand in the state of South Carolina. There were only 2,500 Jews in all of the United States at that time, including four hundred in New York and somewhat fewer in Philadelphia. The Jews of Charleston, as it happened, were a part of the cultural center of America. The city boasted two theaters and an opera house, the first paid orchestra in the colonies, frequent concerts by foreign artists, and lecture tours by the leading literary and scientific scholars of the day. There were wealthy Jewish merchants in Charleston, and the trade with the West Indies was brisk enough to furnish Philip Benjamin with information about its opportunities. Jews in Charleston were especially proud of the history of Francis Salvador, the Jewish son of an English merchant, elected as a revolutionary to the first and second Provincial Congresses of South Carolina in 1774, the first Jew in the modern world to be elected by Christians. Less than a month after the adoption of the Declaration of Independence, Salvador was ambushed with a band of patriot militia by a group of British-armed Indians and Tories, and scalped before help could reach him. Francis Salvador died at the age of twenty-one, the first Jew to give his life for the American Revolution.

Though the Jewish community prospered in Charleston, Philip Benjamin was unsuccessful at everything he tried in business. Judah's mother, Rebecca, industrious and hardworking, held the family together financially by running a small fruit shop on King Street near the docks.[9]

According to Barnett Elzas's *Scrapbook,* a memoir of Charleston written at the turn of the century, "As a matter of fact, the Benjamins were not strict Jews. The mother kept her little shop open on the Sabbath and that at a time when strict Sabbath observance was general in Charleston. This was told to me by the late Sally Lopez, who died here in 1902 at the age of ninety-six. . . . This trading on the Sabbath on the part of Mrs. Benjamin was much resented by the old-time Jews of Charleston."[10]

Judah's ambitious mother and less practical father mirrored the differences in ancestral lineage between his mother and father. She ran the house and the shop with a strong and organized presence, while Philip spent an inordinate amount of time reading books and arguing the fine points of Jewish law with his friends. To a realist like Rebecca, the debates between synagogue leaders over tradition must have seemed a waste of time, but Philip was in fact a religious activist, committed to changing Judaism to conform to the realities of the modern world. The boy Judah listened to his father, and Philip took pride in the child's quickness. Judah inherited his love of ideas and books from his father and his ambition to make money from his mother.

Rebecca was a proud woman who always believed she deserved better. Considering herself an impoverished aristocrat, she taught Judah that he came from a proud heritage and at the same time suggested by her attitude that she had married beneath her. Philip, in reaction, withdrew from business affairs and returned to the Talmud and religious activism, to the issues raging in the Charleston Jewish community over Reform Judaism, knowing, that if he could never measure up to the Mendes line in terms of material success, he might achieve status in his own world of Jewish ideas as an outspoken leader.

Judah P. Benjamin's early biographer Pierce Butler interviewed one of Rebecca's granddaughters, who recalled "the stern and severe rule of the old lady, resolved to hold her head high in spite of poverty."[11]

Once when her two rich sisters sent a trunk of linens and other luxuries to them from the West Indies, Rebecca promptly returned the chests unopened. She would take no one's charity, least of all her sisters'. Judah was the hope, the aspiration, the true heir to the Mendes blood, and she had to do everything for him: send him to the finest academies in the South and Yale Law School at fourteen, even if that meant violating her pledge of independence by accepting money from other families in Charleston. If it supported her son's education, she would make an exception.

Judah worked hard all his young life. At the fruit shop after school, he came to know every corner of the exotic market that stretched along the port. He played all over the Charleston market, visiting other shops to see all the wonderful things to buy from the world over. He lived a life of the senses. The Benjamin stand had colors and tastes: oranges from Florida and big, prickly pineapples from Cuba.

We know from historians that there was an eerie quality to the Charleston harbor. The air was permeated at certain times of the day with the smell of decaying fish and rodents left on the mud flats when the water ran out of the harbor at low tide, attracting huge buzzards, which roosted on the tall dead pines and the twisted cypress trees in the harbor. They fed off the remains as well as the carcasses, innards, and spoiled meat that the butchers dumped into the water. They sat on the roofs of the market, and their wings cast ominous shadows when they took flight. The city considered the buzzards so useful that there was a fine of five dollars, a large sum then, for killing one. Two of them were so tame that they crept along the meat market among the feet of the buyers. Though they had blood and flesh on their beaks and represented death to the adults, local historians tell us that children learned to accept them almost as pets.

Judah was raised with slavery all around him. Charleston was the largest port in the nation in 1800 and a prominent center for the slave trade. Although rich Gentiles looked down on the waterfront shopkeepers, records of the time reveal that even as modest a family as the Benjamins owned slaves.[12] The family had owned three house slaves in St. Croix before coming to Fayetteville to live with Uncle Jacob in 1813, when Judah was two. Uncle Jacob, the successful relative, owned a number of slaves, among them a mulatto, Margaret, who took care of Judah and her own child Jacob, named after her master. Uncle Jacob also bought a twenty-six-year-old named Isaac to protect Judah and his younger brother, Solomon. In 1817, Jacob freed Margaret and the child, but she stayed on as a housemaid.

When Judah's last brother, also named Jacob, was born in 1818, Uncle Jacob deeded "the mustee girl slave, Maria, and her future increase" to his namesake "in consideration of natural love and affection" and $10 paid by Judah's father, Philip.

Like many Southerners, Judah Benjamin might have romanticized the warmth he felt for blacks from his childhood. Margaret, his black mammy, had fixed his food and kissed his hurts from the age of five to age eleven; for five years he played with the older Isaac in the fields in Fayetteville. As he grew older, he would spend hours with Hannibal, the Benjamin house slave and later his personal servant, down in Beaufort, South Carolina. There they would harpoon the horned devil fish, which he later recalled as a mighty monster that would drag the boat along for a few hundred yards before coming to the surface exhausted and ready for the kill.

These stories which he told in later years indicate that to the mature Judah Benjamin, as to other white settlers of his time, those household slaves remained vivid personalities from his youth, strong influences in his life, and, in a real sense, part of his family history.

Judah was eleven years old during the dreadful days of Denmark Vesey's attempted slave uprising in Charleston in 1822.[13] A cache of arms was found near the synagogue, to be used, the newspapers claimed, for "murdering all the whites in Charleston, raping the women, robbing the banks, commandeering the ships for Santo Domingo, and burning the city as they left." The militia hanged twenty-two blacks at one time, including a slave who was owned by a member of Beth Elohim. The bodies were left dangling for a week for all to see. The leader, Denmark Vesey, had begun a nightmare come true for Charleston, a potential slave uprising turned into a mass retribution by the whites. As Benjamin's later biographer Robert D. Meade pointed out, "Of such stuff are conservatives made."[14]

Judah's boyhood coincided with a time of change for the Jews newly arriving from Europe, uprooted into a strange land. Immigrants brought with them new ideas of religious practice that were sweeping Europe and that found fertile ground in a turbulent seaport city. As the South became more vigorously Protestant, it was natural that it would become the seedbed for a more assimilated form of Judaism. In November 1824, Philip became one of the forty-seven people at Beth Elohim in Charleston to petition their trustees to shorten the service, to pray in English rather than in Hebrew or Spanish, and to require a sermon or "an English discourse" at each service. When the ruling trustees tabled the request, Philip joined with twelve others of the dissenters to form the "Reformed Society of Israelites."

No longer, they said in their second more far-reaching petition, would they worship as "slaves of bigotry and priestcraft." They would worship as part of an enlightened world. This time they demanded even more radical changes: preferring to call the synagogue "temple," editing their own prayerbook to include contemporary prayers in the service, worshiping with heads uncovered. Philip was elected to the "corresponding committee" of the Reformed Society, which, as described in Article VI of the Society's constitution, was an important leadership committee. Article VI stated that:

> There shall be annually elected from among the resident members
> a committee of five, entitled a Committee of Correspondence,
> for the purpose of conferring and corresponding at all times . . .
> with the several congregations, or respectable individuals, or sections of Jews throughout the United States, Europe, or elsewhere,
> as to any assistance or co-operation, which they may be disposed
> to afford this Society in its future operations.[15]

Charles Reznikoff and Uriah Engleman, in *The Jews of Charleston,* stated that Philip's election "would seem to show that he had ability and was not unrecognized."[16]

By being a leader in such a movement, however, he risked the enmity of most of the Jewish community. Such a bold departure would be bad for business and could cause the children to be ostracized. But he soon alienated even the Reformed Society, which could no more accept his keeping his shop open on the Sabbath than did the traditionalists. Finally, in 1827, the Society expelled him for the same offense. Rejected by both congregations in Charleston, he became deeply embittered.

It is often said by historians that Judah was a nonbeliever, raised without tradition in an assimilated home. It is true that, in rebellion, the family may not have practiced Judaism or kept the Sabbath and the daily rituals. But their nonpractice was activist in character, not lazy or indifferent. Neither was Philip a man bent on blending with the non-Jewish community, seeking out Gentile associations or denying his Jewishness out of shame of his heritage. Philip was an intellectual, well-versed in Jewish law, an assertive and argumentative personality who took matters of custom and practice seriously. Even as a poor man, he had paid a relatively large assessment to the synagogue the year before the dissent, which indicated the priority the family assigned to participation in the religious life of the Jewish community.

So Judah was not raised in ignorance of Jewish law and tradition.

The debate in the Charleston Jewish community between Reform and Orthodox Judaism raged all about him during his formative years, and he was an alert, curious boy. The children of the reformers were involved, for the petition stated that those who signed "cannot consent to place before their children examples which are only calculated to darken the mind and withhold from the rising generation the more rational means of worshipping the true God."[17]

It is difficult in modern times to convey the bitterness that characterized the early divisions of American Jewish history. But Charleston was where the debate began, and Philip helped alter the path of American Jewish history, one of the first Jews in America to challenge centuries of orthodoxy and, in the eyes of the city patriarchs, to dare violate the laws of God. Yet Philip was not a fallen-away Jew in flight from his people. He was a man who cared deeply about his beliefs, a man of principle punished for his views and his willingness to act on them. "Slaves of bigotry and priestcraft," the petition he signed had called the elders—strong words expressing intense emotions, no compromise in language; it was no document for the faint-hearted.

As the son of one of the leaders of the society, Judah understandably would have been deeply affected by the religious divisions. The reform movement was not just for adults; it sought to influence history through the children of its members and the generations to come. "The compilers act only for themselves, [and] for their children," one of the prayers adopted by the Society stated. The Society pledged itself in Article III of its constitution that "it will educate a youth or youths of the Jewish persuasion, classically in the English, Latin and Hebrew languages, so as to render him or them fully competent to perform Divine Service, not only with ability, learning and dignity, but also according to the true spirit of Judaism, for which this institution was formed."[18]

The Society substituted the "confirmation" ceremony for the bar mitzvah, requiring it for all boys who attained the age of thirteen. Its prayerbook laid out in careful detail the character and articulation of the confirmation ceremony and implemented it from the beginning, in 1824, when Judah P. Benjamin turned thirteen years of age. The ceremony was described as follows in the Society prayerbook:

Mode of Confirmation

(Any one born of Jewish parents, not under the age of thirteen, and desirous of expressing his belief in the Jewish faith, may, on any Sabbath, make declaration of the same and be confirmed therein as follows. He advances to the minister's desk, and says:)

YOUTH: Here, in the presence of this congregation, and in the presence of that gracious God whose goodness has endowed me with reason, I desire to declare my firm and religious belief in the Divine origin of the moral law, and in the great Articles of the Jewish faith. I desire to appear in the presence of heaven and earth, an Israelite according to the faith and customs of the Reformed Society of Israelites, in whose temple of worship I now stand.

MINISTER: My son, dost thou act from thine own free will, and is this the wish of thy heart and the conviction of thy understanding?

YOUTH: It is. I have been taught to love the paths of piety and virtue; I hope to follow them. Through God's goodness, I also hope that I comprehend the essential points of our excellent religion, and I shall strive with my best endeavors, to observe and practice through life its moral and pious doctrines.

MINISTER: Repeat, my son, the Articles of that religious creed which thou has adopted, and in which thy parents and guardians, assisted by thine own industry, have happily instructed thee. Repeat them in sincerity and truth; for the offering thou art about to make, must be a free will offering to God. If any compulsion hath been exercised towards thee, the sin of hypocrisy will be thine, in declaring that which is not in thy heart, and the sin of tyranny and impiety on those, who have brought thee hither against thy will. Repeat to me, then, the Articles of our holy faith.

YOUTH: I repeat them freely, with sincerity, and truth. (He repeats the Articles of faith, of the Reformed Society of Israelites.)[19]

Unfortunately, no records of Jewish life in Charleston survived a fire in 1838 which burned the original (1794) Beth Elohim building, so whether young Judah Benjamin was confirmed with such vows cannot be verified. We know, however, that it was customary for members of the society, and expected of its leaders, to obey its constitution and follow its prayerbook. Therefore, it is probable that Judah was one of the first children confirmed in the new Reformed Society. The vows were written to fill those who were confirmed with deep memories and religious resolve. And, indeed, history shows that Judah P. Benjamin would never deny his Judaism or allow the judgment of the orthodox community to convince him that his soul was not worthy or his Judaism unacceptable. He would be the double outsider, however, estranged not only from the non-Jewish world but from the established Jewish world as well.

At the age of thirteen, reliant on his own talent, Judah was cast into the Charleston community where secular influences enticed and confronted him without the certitude and support of his traditional religious group. New winds were blowing, and it was easy to stray from a narrow path. A Gentile schoolmate recalled in later years how he and Judah played together and how he used to sneak slices of ham off his mother's table for his Jewish friend. On the docks, crabs and other unkosher shellfish abounded in the stalls. Because Charleston was a population center, scores of traveling evangelists came to win the souls of the crowds of people who would gather in huge tents for the revivals. Diaries of the times record the fear and isolation felt by Jews during those periods of intense soul-saving. Southern Jews have always confronted a special kind of Jesus: a constant presence perched on the shoulder of every believer. Fearsome to Southern Jewish children is the role of Jews in the prophecy of the Second Coming, calling Jews to return to the fold and atone for rejecting Jesus by converting to Christianity. For every Jewish boy in the South, close Gentile childhood friends worried about the disposition of Jewish souls. And every Jewish child swimming in a sea of Bible Belt fundamentalism that was the nineteenth-century South heard the warnings of the old men around the synagogue: "Be careful of the soul-savers; converting a Jew is a special blessing for them."

Yet Southern Jews yearned to be a part of the Southern way of life and to be accepted as legitimate heirs to its cultural history. After Beth Elohim was rebuilt, Rabbi Gustavus Poznanski revealed an attitude in Charleston that was deeply ingrained in Judah Benjamin's generation of Southerners. "This synagogue is our temple," Poznanski exclaimed to a crowd of Jews and Christians, "this city our Jerusalem, this happy land our Palestine, and as our fathers defended with their lives that temple, that city and that land so will our sons defend this temple, this city and this land."[20]

Judah was sent to the school of the Hebrew Orphan Society (which was also for children of the poor) and grew into adolescence as an earnest boy devoted to his studies and eager to succeed. He plunged headlong into his father's library and scoured the Jewish community for more books. He would memorize long passages and recite them without a flaw, often with dramatic flourishes of rhetoric. His teachers were astonished at his intelligence and absorptive capacities. One friend even recalled that he recited Shakespeare while playing marbles and that at recess he made preparations for the next lesson while other boys were at play.[21] Judah's talent caught the eye of Moses Lopez, one of the Jewish merchants of Charleston, who advised Rebecca and Philip of what they already knew—that their eldest son was extraordinary and must receive the very best education in America. He offered to pay for the boy's education at the finest academies in the South and, at the age of fourteen, to send him to Yale University to study law.

There is no record of any hesitation in Rebecca's decision to send her young son so far away from home. She helped him pack a few possessions, among them a Hebrew Psalter, for the thousand-mile journey to New Haven, Connecticut.

2

Yale:
A Mysterious Departure

✺

Although Yale was far from Charleston, it was a natural choice for those who recognized the mark of excellence in young Judah Benjamin. Yale was known across the South as the "Athens of America," where the Southern gentry sent their sons to acquire the high polish of a gentleman and the disciplined habits of a scholar. The contingent of Southerners at Yale rose from 20 percent to almost 30 percent during Judah's stay, and, after New York, New Haven, and Hartford, Charleston had the fourth largest representation. But admission was not automatic: Judah had to pass entrance examinations in Cicero, Virgil, Greek testament, Latin grammar, and arithmetic.[1] Thus, for the first time in his life, Judah was tossed into the mainstream of competition with the sons of the most noted families in the South and could measure himself and them against the scions of Northern aristocracy as well. He was not the first Jew at Yale, but seventeen years separated him from the last known Jewish student.

Yale, which sought to build a hierarchy based on talent, did much to try to reduce class differences in the student body by mandating a uniform dress code. Judah, only fourteen and so short that he looked even younger, was required to dress in a uniform of black frock coat, black or white pantaloons, cravat, and vest. It was a costume that must have made a young boy look prematurely grave.

Though it was beginning to liberalize its curriculum, Yale still

15

described itself as a seminary. Activities started at daybreak, with morning prayers at six in the winter and five in the summer. Chapel attendance was compulsory in the morning and evening, with no exceptions for Jewish students.[2] Judah arrived at Yale with the Hebrew Psalter in his possession.[3]

A former classmate, W. W. Hoppin, recalled Benjamin's early days at Yale in 1884: "He was a small, bright-eyed boy, of a dark and swarthy complexion, evidently of Jewish blood. . . . He apparently passed his time in sauntering around the college grounds or dropping in at the students' room. . . . Without any attention to his studies, and following out this desultory and vagrant existence, he easily and without dispute, took at once the highest stand in his class, and was acknowledged to be a riddle and prodigy of intellectual power."[4]

This poor Jewish slip of a boy now found himself among the landed Southerners and the arrogant Northern merchant sons, plucked from his plain circumstances in Charleston and deposited into the Gothic ambiance of Yale. He was a Southern provincial woefully out of place. Paralleling the experience of his father in Charleston, he soon was alienated from his community: His Jewishness and his Southernness were a double barrier to acceptance. But he wore a mask of diffidence while working relentlessly to earn acceptance to at least some part of the university. The sons of the rich could ease their way into their family's fortunes after schooling, but Judah would have to strive all his life for every penny he earned and every recognition he was accorded.

The curriculum was rigid and demanding. He studied Horace, the Greek orators, philosophy, and astronomy; the curriculum required him to master logarithms, trigonometry, navigation, surveying, spherical geometry, French or Spanish, and Hebrew. From learning to read the Old Testament in the original, all the rest of his career he would be able to recall it in speeches and writing. Yale so emphasized forensics that he had to debate once or twice a week before instructors and practice declamation in the chapel before the professor of oratory, other faculty members, and students.

Judah's two years at Yale were a glorious confirmation of his brilliance and promise, building his self-confidence and sharpening his orator's wit. During his first and fourth semesters, he averaged 3.3, the highest in his class. In his second and third semesters, his 3.0 tied him for highest in the class. His tutor, Simeon North, reported in a letter to a Mr. Brayton that Benjamin had a "pleasing manner" and that his academic achievements allowed him to be "regarded by his mates as an ornament to the class."[5] He won a Berkeleian Prize, a book inscribed by President Jeremiah Day for excellence in scholarship.

Judah was naturally drawn to the student debating societies, thriving in the atmosphere of repartee and exchange. He argued such questions as, "Are the abilities of the sexes equal?" (answered by the Society, according to the minutes, with a "gallant . . . affirmative"). He also participated in a debate on the question, "Was the confinement of Bonaparte on the island of St. Helena justified?"

Yale was neither isolated nor protected from the turbulence in the nation over slavery, and when a Northerner was elected president of one of the societies, the Southern contingent broke off to form a new group "as a sort of class to themselves," debating issues of interest to the South. They voted down a motion regarding the advisability of meeting with other colleges to assist in the "manumission of slaves."[6] Judah, ready for verbal combat, soon joined his fellow Southerners in the new debating society.

Benjamin learned many things outside of the classroom at Yale. Watching the rich boys carefully, he learned upper-class manners. He worked prodigiously to beat them academically, besting them in debate with crisp analysis and wit. He emulated their best qualities, discarding their foppish tendencies, and steeped himself in art, music, and poetry, the better to mask his humble origins. A lad of limited means cast into the world of America's elite, a country bumpkin with Jewish audacity, he became an eager emulator of the quintessential Yale man. It is likely that he inspired his share of jealousies and resentments when he spouted Shakespeare and Tennyson and bested his older classmates in every arena.

After only two years, Judah Benjamin suddenly left Yale under clouded circumstances that would follow him in the form of gossip and accusations the rest of his life. His departure from Yale became a matter of talk during the Civil War because of an article written thirty-three years after the incident, in 1861, just before he was appointed Attorney General in the Confederate Cabinet. The article appeared in the New York *Independent,* written by Francis Bacon, a member of one of Yale's most illustrious families and a graduate of the law school class of 1831. Coming from a respectable source, the article revived the speculation and made headlines in the Northern press. Although the personalities in the article were thinly veiled, the charges were unusually detailed:

The Early History of a Traitor

BY FRANCIS BACON

The class of 1829 in Yale College (two years in advance of mine) was the finest body of young men that I ever saw in college. There was one of the class whose name cannot be found on the list of graduates, or in any annual catalogue after 1827. He was and still is a handsome little fellow, looking very small in his class, who, with a few exceptions, were of full manly growth. This youth hailed from a great state of the chivalrous South, bright-eyed and dark-complexioned, and ardent as the Southern sun would make him.

In the early part of 1828 there was a mysterious trouble in that class. Watches, breast pins, seals, pencil cases, penknives, etc., etc., etc., and lastly, sundry sums of money lying around loose in students' rooms disappeared unaccountably. The losers looked gloomily at each other and suspiciously at others. Something must be done.

They finally constituted themselves a volunteer detective force, set their trap—baited with thirty-five dollars in good bank notes—and soon caught the thief. He confessed. On opening his trunk in his presence, they found it nearly full of missing valuables—jewelry, pocket cutlery . . . —he begged pitifully not to be exposed; they looked piteously on his handsome young face, and relented at the thought of blasting his opening young life. They agreed not to inform either the city magistrates or the faculty of the university, but ordered him to clear out at once and forever. He went instantly to good President Day, obtained a certificate of honorable dismissal and vanished.

The little thief is now a Senator in Congress, advocating and justifying and threatening the robbery of forts, and the stealing of the military hardware and cutlery generally of the Federal government, without any more color or shadow of pretext than he had for his like operations on his fellow students just thirty-three years ago.

A third of a century has not made and can never make, any change in such an originally inborn rascal. Had these early filchings been a mere boyish escapade, a momentary yielding to temptation while in great want, they would not deserve mention now; but they were systematized theft—long, continued, accumulated, and hoarded pilferings from trusted bosom friends.

Had the fellow not at length reproduced his private morality in public life, I would have allowed the secret of these early times to remain in the hearts of the few who then knew and now remember it.[7]

Since the incident looms so large in Benjamin's boyhood and later life and has drawn the detailed investigation of his biographers, it once again deserves some attention and analysis.[8]

Robert D. Meade and Pierce Butler both point out that *The Independent,* which published it, was an Abolitionist journal, an organ for the views of Henry Ward Beecher and Francis Bacon, who was a well-known Abolitionist spokesman. The New Orleans *Delta,* in defending Benjamin, asserted that "the story was hatched by abolition malice, and the place and time of the incidents were selected with cunning regard to the difficulty of refutation."[9]

Benjamin hired two well-known Northern attorneys to bring suit for libel, but they advised him against any legal steps for fear of fanning the controversy into a still more widely publicized exchange. Benjamin was caught on the horns of a dilemma. After secession, it would have been unseemly for a potential Cabinet member to sue in a Northern court, and Southern courts had no jurisdiction over disputes in the North. So he was stymied by events.

He wrote to friends: "I left college in the fall of 1827, in consequence of my father's reverses rendering him unable to maintain me there any longer." Should he point out the discrepancy of dates in the article, which claimed that the events occurred in 1828, "and get friends that were college mates to state that no such things ever occurred," he would risk a small correction of dates and the "whole affair again goes the round of all the newspapers at the North, with the most malignant comments that can be invented." In a subsequent letter to a friend, he continued that "there is something so inexpressibly loathsome and revolting at the bare idea of having one's name published in the newspapers in connection with so degrading a charge. . . . However, I have determined to yield to the advice of my friends and to let a life-long career of integrity and honor make silent and contemptuous answer to such an attack."[10]

Francis Lawley, the former London *Times* correspondent, investigated the charges in 1901 and received a letter from the only survivor of the class of 1829. The letter said that not long after Judah entered college, "he fell into association with a set of disorderly fellows who were addicted to card playing and gambling, and his abrupt withdrawal from college was understood to be occasioned by difficulties growing out of this practice."[11]

On January 14, 1828, after six painful weeks at home with his parents, Judah wrote to President Day asking for readmission. The letter, because it speaks of "shame" and "improper conduct," seems to confirm that at least some incident of moral turpitude caused his departure and confesses to his father's "pecuniary affairs" as the source of his trouble:

HIGHLY RESPECTED SIR:

It is with shame and diffidence that I now address you to solicit your forgiveness and interference with the Faculty on my behalf. And I beseech you, Sir, not to attribute my improper conduct to any design or intentional violation of the laws of the college, not to suppose that I would be guilty of any premeditated disrespect to yourself or any member of the Faculty. And I think, Sir, you will not consider it improper for me to express my hopes, that my previous conduct in college was such as will not render it too presumptuous in me to hope that it will make a favorable impression upon yourself and the faculty.

Allow me, Sir, here to express my gratitude to the Faculty for their kind indulgence to my father in regard to pecuniary affairs; and also to yourself and every individual member of the Faculty for their attention and paternal care of me, during the time I had the honor to be a member of the institution.

With hopes of yet completing my education under your auspices, I remain, Sir, your most respectful and obedient Servant.

J. P. Benjamin

P.S. May I solicit, Sir (if it is not too troublesome to you) the favor of a few lines in answer to this letter, that I may be able to judge of the possibility of my return to the University?[12]

Benjamin had to swallow much pride to reapply for permission to return. At any rate, after one reads the letter, precisely why he left remains a mystery. There is no record of President Day's having answered his letter. Nor is there anything in other Yale records to indicate why he left or even that the authorities actually asked him to leave. In similar cases, the faculty records usually carefully detail names and offenses of students who are punished, but Judah Benjamin's name does not appear. Those records were kept by Simeon North, his tutor, who told the New York *Times* in 1883 that because of his fondness for Benjamin, he had "closed his eyes to many college pranks."[13]

A letter from Simeon North does confirm, Meade points out, the existence of debts to Yale in the amount of $64.34 and that his parents had been unable to deposit money for expenses. That much seems to confirm Benjamin's version of the story in his Civil War letters. Judah had left, North said, "without the knowledge or the permission of his friends or instructors," but he added a phrase that supports the more serious side of the story "in a manner that justly exposed him to sensure[sic]."[14] There is also evidence that his debating society investigated charges of "ungentlemanly conduct" against him and passed a motion to expel him from the society. "It was requested," the society's minutes stated, "that the charge against Mr. Benjamin be kept a secret." However, the Yale scholar Anson Phelps Stokes was of the opinion that the phrase "ungentlemanly conduct" suggested boyish mischief rather than criminal conduct as the reason for his departure.[15]

Further investigation seemed to deepen the mystery rather than resolve it. Dan A. Oren, the author of *Joining The Club: A History of Jews and Yale,* points out that Bacon may have been mistaken in the original charge and may have confused Benjamin with a student named "Peniman," who "did receive admonishment for playing cards on January 4, 1828 (after Benjamin left Yale), the year used in the Bacon letter."[16] Simeon North reported that when Benjamin became stranded in Rochester, New York, after leaving Yale and losing his pocketbook, students thought enough of him and were concerned enough about his well-being to take up a collection to help him return to South Carolina. Had he been stealing from substantial numbers of students, it is unlikely that fellow students would have responded so generously to his difficulties.

The truth grew more elusive as events unfolded after Benjamin's departure. A week before his letter requesting readmission, John D. Boardman, Benjamin's roommate, sent the faculty an apology "for whatever was done by me contrary to their laws or wishes, in the late affairs."[17] Did the apology refer to subsequent disorders, another incident, or to the Judah P. Benjamin affair? Was Boardman involved in the incident that embarrassed his roommate? Whatever the answer, Boardman remained at Yale and Judah left for New Orleans and a new life before hearing from the college concerning his request for readmission. Meade suggests that he may not have told his father the truth about the reasons he had to leave Yale and wrote the letter at his father's insistence, having already decided to leave for New Orleans. Subsequent events indicate that he saw his father little after leaving, though he managed to see his mother and sisters at least once a year. Leaving Charleston, his boyhood home, was clearly the beginning of a deep estrangement between Judah and his father, which would never heal.

By the age of sixteen, Judah had suffered through years of humiliation, to such an unusual degree that dealing with humiliation would become a significant factor in his later life. His parents had come from the Caribbean with so little that the family had to live with a relative for several years. In Charleston, the family had to be supported by a small shop and the hard work of his mother, who did not let his father forget that dependency; his father had bolted from one congregation and had been expelled from another. The boy had arrived at the aristocratic campus of Yale University, a Southerner and the only Jew; he left Yale under a humiliating cloud of suspicion and returned to Charleston for what must have been the most miserable time of his young life. He was a disappointment to his father, to his mother, to his siblings, to his benefactor, and to himself. Had he stayed in Charleston, he would have been known as a failure, especially to his own family.

He chose to leave all that behind, to leave his family for another city where he was not known and where he could start over. To leave Charleston for New Orleans was to abandon a more traditional and stable Jewish community for one that was then almost nonexistent, freewheeling, and unanchored. Because it was Catholic and French, New Orleans presented the greatest challenge a Jew could have selected; but because it was unstructured socially as a seaport city where a single shipload of rum could make a man rich, a Jew would be less restricted, more able to be judged by his accomplishments, and more likely to prosper by his ability.

Moreover, Charleston by the 1820s had begun to dissolve as a trade center, its growth faltering from the competition in the Northeast boosted by the Erie Canal, discriminatory tariffs, and thermal navigation, which shortened the routes from Europe to Boston and New York. The migration westward had begun to lands unexhausted by yearly cotton crops, away from the epidemics of yellow fever and malaria that had given Charleston such a bad reputation. Contemporaries described the city at this time as a "place of tombs." As its economic base began to shrink, its ruling class became more inaccessible to those born at the bottom of the ladder. For a young Jewish Southerner looking for a brisk economy and a legal career as an apprentice to lawyers needing assistance, the great river port in Louisiana looked far more promising.

3

New Orleans to Bellechasse:
The Climb to
U.S. Senator

❊❊❊

Young Judah P. Benjamin arrived in New Orleans in 1828 with but five dollars in his pocket—a daring young adventurer entering the most permissive, raucous, open, and mystical city in America.[1] It was a colorful place where the classes readily mixed, where fortunes were made and lost over the turn of a card—or the whim of the sea. New Orleans attracted shipping from both the river and the sea, with scores of steamboats, schooners, giant sailing ships, and flatboats loading and unloading at the docks where the muddy Mississippi flowed by on its way into the blue Gulf of Mexico. Passenger ships disgorged sailors, gamblers, travelers, traders—turning the city into a turbulent place where the talk was of land, slaves, cotton, and sugar; and where a man's mind and talent, not his religion or birth, determined his fate.

The richness of life in New Orleans suggested Liverpool or Alexandria: there were spices and silk from China, teakwood from Africa, oils from North Atlantic whales, indigo and rum from Jamaica. New Orleans was growing at a furious pace and would double in population—from 50,000 to 100,000—between 1830 and 1840. Judah Benjamin could not have picked a more promising place or time to start over and to begin a law practice.

By day, New Orleans was a commercial beehive; by night, sheer mystery. The city was laced with narrow streets full of people of every known color, couples who had just met; sailors and sinners gulped down fresh oysters with beer, pockets jingling as they wandered the French Quarter searching for music and watching for roulette tables and dancing girls; belligerent types just looking for a good street brawl for the sheer pleasure of it.

Benjamin worked for a time at odd jobs until he could get settled: in a mercantile house, processing due bills and ledgers, then teaching school part-time. Eventually, he reached the first rung on his ladder of ambition by becoming an apprentice to Greenbury R. Stringer, a notary attached to a commercial law firm. As Benjamin learned his craft, Stringer assigned him increasingly difficult cases. Meanwhile, Benjamin's circle of friends slowly began to spread to other young men of ambition in the city.

Soon after he had departed for New Orleans, Judah's mother and most of the rest of her family moved to Beaufort—known as "Little Charleston," where the rice-planting aristocracy lived.[2] Philip did not move with them: Historians have concluded that he and Rebecca had separated. For more than twenty years thereafter, Philip and Rebecca lived apart, setting an example for their son as to the way a marriage could remain publicly intact yet privately "adjusted."[3]

Each summer, when the New Orleans heat grew oppressive, Benjamin, loaded down with a trunkload of books and gifts, would visit his mother and sisters in Beaufort. The daughter of one of Benjamin's sisters told Pierce Butler how Judah delighted in reading stories to the whole family, that he performed novels with great zest and drama. That niece had no recollections of his father's ever being present on any such occasion.

Much refreshed, Judah would return to New Orleans, ready to plunge back into his law practice and the political activity of the city. He vowed to be a great lawyer, Yale or no Yale. The restrained aggression of the profession attracted him. He loved the courtroom as a self-contained arena of battle with rules and audiences, winners and losers; a place of structured competition where he could thrash his opposition with all the intensity, charm, brilliance, and powers of concentration at his command.

For ambitious young men in New Orleans, a daughter of a wealthy Creole represented the ideal. To marry into one of the Creole families was to marry into a velvet world of influence and money. The Creoles were the premier families of New Orleans, descended from the earliest French settlers. They preserved the characteristic form of French speech and culture. Benjamin's aspirations called for the access, power, and status a Creole connection could provide.

A struggling young lawyer in New Orleans would have to master the Napoleonic Code, which loomed like a mountain of legal tangle before him.[4] Judah Benjamin spoke not a word of French. As fate would have it, Auguste St. Martin, a Creole official of a local insurance company, hired him to tutor his daughter in English. The young upstart accepted—but only on the condition that she would teach him French.[5]

Natalie St. Martin was only sixteen and Benjamin twenty-one, when they met to begin their lessons and the first few months of their courtship. They were the only happy months of their relationship—and perhaps the happiest time of his life.

A painting of Natalie reveals a woman with large, dark, expectant eyes and bare shoulders, her lips curled into a smile perhaps a degree beyond propriety. Her skin was smooth and supple—almost an olive color—and her dark, plentiful hair ran down her back, making wild intricate turns, suggesting a rebellious nature that refused to be controlled by convention or channeled by upper-class expectations. She radiated the anxious sensuality of a Creole princess—undisciplined, selfish, and entrancing. She cast a spell over him like some sorceress.

Their meetings for lessons began to absorb him entirely. She was audacious, unafraid, and decidely experimental, always leading her English tutor into a new and exciting phase of their learning. History records her later indiscretions, but in the beginning she was a restless child-woman with the instinct of a courtesan. His life began to take on new dimensions as he studied at night for the bar and met Natalie to be instructed in French and other cultural nuances of a ripening young girl.

New Orleans in the summer and fall of 1832 experienced the worst plague of mosquitoes from the swamps in its history, spreading a devastating epidemic of yellow fever and Asian cholera. Five hundred people a day were dying, ultimately nearly one-sixth of the city's population. The city fathers lit pots of coals to produce black, acrid smoke to drive the mosquitoes away. Every hour, cannons were fired to stir the air. There was no place to escape, no way to block out the cholera or to avoid stacks of bodies awaiting coffins.[6]

Later in 1832, after the epidemic had passed, Benjamin was admitted to the bar. His relationship with Natalie matured into courtship.

It required a special audacity and self-confidence for a young man who was poor and Jewish to imagine himself marrying into the New Orleans Catholic aristocracy. Religion, in fact, was a problem. Natalie's father wanted Judah to convert to Catholicism for the sake of propriety, even though Auguste St. Martin himself was not a strict Catholic. But church records and later events prove that Benjamin did not convert. He agreed, however, that the couple's children could be raised in the faith of Natalie's mother and grandparents.

That apparently sufficed. Judah and Natalie were married on February 12, 1833, with a onetime justice of the Louisiana Supreme Court as a family witness. Perhaps to deceive the priest so that the marriage could proceed without his formal conversion, the marriage register recorded him as Philip Benjamin. Conforming to the custom of the time, he and Natalie spent their honeymoon in her parent's home. Throughout their marriage, Natalie called him by his French name, "Philippe." He never corrected her; it was her affectation, a name that assimilated him into French New Orleans and helped him submerge what he then thought would be his invisible past.[7]

For three years after their marriage, they lived with Auguste and his wife Françoise, also from a noted Creole family, in their large house on Chartres Street. He endured this with mixed emotions: fine surroundings, but total dependence. For a young man of fierce ambition, the St. Martin household was a daily reminder of his lack of power, of station, and of independent means.

Soon after her daughter's marriage, Françoise had a son, who was named Jules. As much from convenience as sentiment, the baby came to be taken care of more by the childless couple in the house than by the parents. Judah and Natalie taught the child to walk and cuddled the boy over the first ten years of their marriage. Jules St. Martin spent so much of his formative years with his "Uncle Judah" that he almost became the son that Natalie and Judah P. Benjamin never had.

Benjamin worked and saved but could not yet altogether afford a home of his own. When the St. Martins moved to Bourbon Street in the French Quarter, the Benjamins moved into an adjoining house, where Natalie could stand on the wrought-iron balcony and talk to friends in the street below. Thus, for ten years they either lived with or next door to the St. Martins.[8]

Benjamin worked constantly in the early days, late into each evening, eager for further independence, with an even larger dream of land and a home of his own, to make his wife and in-laws proud.

His cases, the records show, were the kind of low-level contracts and complaints that come to struggling young lawyers. Instead of waiting around for clients to show up, his boundless energy and ingenuity led him to begin a book on Louisiana law, which required the analysis of six thousand cases. He worked on the digest of cases with Tom Slidell, who would become a future Chief Justice of the Louisiana Supreme Court. The reference book, written in 1834, when Benjamin was just twenty-three years old, became a standard text for lawyers and judges in the state.[9]

His friendship with the Slidell brothers—the younger Tom became his law partner and John his political mentor—pushed him ever along in New Orleans legal and political circles. John Slidell was also a commercial and maritime lawyer who maneuvered his way into becoming the political "boss" of New Orleans and adopted Judah P. Benjamin as his protégé. Both were new men in the city, challenging traditional Creole leadership, and yet both married into the very Creole power structure they battled. Slidell would later be described as "a wire puller . . . a man who moves the puppets on the public stage." "Slidellian" became in New Orleans politics what "Tammany" was to New York, the city where Slidell was born in 1793, attended Columbia College, began his career, and learned his politics. He was not beyond ballot-stuffing or the manipulation of "repeaters" to get his candidates elected. He himself was elected to the U.S. Senate after running and being defeated twice. New Orleans politics was bitterly divided among many factions, which enabled a man like Slidell, with questionable tactics, to wheel and deal his way to success. His reputation for delivering the state would take him in 1856 to the rare heights of chief patronage distributor for the National Democratic Party during the Buchanan administration. James A. Buchanan later rewarded him with an ambassadorship to Mexico, an experience that placed him in line for a later Confederate appointment to France to conduct sensitive negotiations with Louis Napoleon's court. He looked the polished gentleman—large stature, sharp nose, a twisted mouth. Benjamin trusted him, and he would become ruthless in Benjamin's behalf; they became political colleagues in the Senate and as close as brothers.[10]

The law digest was a success and projected Benjamin in 1835 into association with a group of prominent New Orleans business, political, and professional men who planned to build the first Louisiana railroad. At the time, there were only 9 miles of railroad in the state. The syndicate dreamed of one great railroad extending all the way to Jackson, Mississippi. It required public and private charters, financing, engineering, and Benjamin began to develop a familiarity with railroads that would help his career enormously.

There were great lawyers in New Orleans to fire a young man's ambition, to lift his vision of what was possible: Mazureaum, the outstanding Creole master of the Civil Code; Janin, a Portuguese nobleman who had been a general under Frederick the Great and spoke five languages and was now one of the most noted land lawyers in America; John Randolph Grymes, a Virginia aristocrat who had resigned his office as district attorney to defend the pirate Jean Lafitte for a twenty-thousand-dollar fee; and Roselius, who later turned down a partnership with Daniel Webster because he loved New Orleans.[11] Benjamin would be tilting with some of the great minds in America, and that meant work, careful preparation, more nights with the kerosene lamps. His specialty began to be commercial law, and because of his familiarity with precedents through the digests, he was beginning to be sought to write briefs and to argue more significant appeals to higher courts.

The panic of 1837 caused fourteen banks to fail and paralyzed business, thus setting him back in his practice. But by 1839, his law practice was growing dramatically, and he was handling major appeals to the Louisiana Supreme Court and outside the state as well. In 1839, he appeared in nine cases; in 1841, he won nine of eleven cases; in 1844, he won twenty-three of thirty-five; and in 1846, he or his firm appeared in forty-nine cases. They were, for the most part, civil suits of a technical nature regarding property claims, slavery disputes, mercantile conflicts, or shipping disagreements. His growing reputation as a persuasive advocate and eloquent speaker was drawing him into other arenas, and with John Slidell's encouragement he began attending political meetings, making important friends, and considering the opportunities for elective office.

Two stories from Robert D. Meade's papers give insights into Judah's attitude toward his Jewishness at this period in his life. First, Meade's papers contain a letter from William Cabell Bruce reporting a story given to him by John K. Cowen, General Counsel to the Baltimore & Ohio Railroad:

"On one occasion," Bruce writes, "Benjamin, when in Baltimore, went before a Justice of the Peace to make affidavit to a paper. A blank had been left in the certificate of affidavit for the insertion of the name of the affiant, and, when Benjamin handed the paper to the Justice, he asked him to fill in the blank. Instead of inserting the name 'Judah,' the Justice inadvertently inserted the name 'Judas'; whereupon Benjamin reclaimed possession of the paper and dashed it down with great force on the desk of the Justice, exclaiming, as he did so—'My God, man, is not Judah Jew enough?' "[12]

It was not the first time the question of his name had been raised, according to an interview that Meade had with Mrs. G. G. Myrover, who described her mother-in-law who had once lived near and later boarded with Benjamin's mother in Beaufort and was there during one of Benjamin's visits.

"She knew Benjamin well," Meade reported from his interview. "She said he seemed to hate to be a Jew. He asked his mother why she named him Judah, "and then said she heard Judah say 'You might well have written Jew across my forehead.' "[13]

Those two anecdotes point in an extraordinarily revealing way to Benjamin's discontent and anger toward his Jewishness. The incidents are not dated exactly, but both occurred after he entered the practice of law, perhaps in his mid-twenties or later, and provide a strong indication of a personality ashamed of his roots and in flight. He was not, as he has been portrayed in history, indifferent and uninvolved, assimilated and adjusted to a new identity. Even had he wanted a new identity, it would not have been possible. To Benjamin, Judaism was a burden, an inhibition to advancement, a restraint upon success. It caused him much suffering, especially from Christians who saw in him the personification of a story nineteen centuries old. At least in the struggling early years of his career as a Jew in a Catholic city, much indignation and resentment lay beneath the veneer of affability, self-confidence, and achievement.

But New Orleans was a city growing too fast for anti-Semitism to hold back a young lawyer with talent. There was almost no tradition, and so many young men were caught up in the idle world of whiskey, women, and fine clothes, that an ambitious, hardworking Jewish lawyer could get ahead. Besides, anti-Semitism had never been a strong local tradition. There were a number of prominent Jews whom Judah knew: Henry Hyams, an older cousin, who was Lieutenant Governor of Louisiana, and Dr. Edwin Warren Moise, Attorney General of Louisiana and Speaker of the Louisiana House of Representatives, were two of them.

Just before the Civil War, Salomon de Rothschild of the Parisian branch of the noted banking family met Benjamin, Hyams, and Moise in New Orleans. He called Benjamin "perhaps the greatest mind on this continent" and added in a letter home: "What is astonishing . . . is the high position occupied by our coreligionists . . . who, having married Christian women, and without converting, have forgotten the practices of their fathers . . . and what is odd, all these men have a Jewish heart and take an interest in me, because I represent the greatest Jewish house in the world."[14] Thus, to an informed observer in the late 1850s Judah P. Benjamin appeared to have a "Jewish heart," no easy accomplishment in a city as incorrigible as New Orleans.

Marriage to Natalie took Benjamin far away from the Jewish community in New Orleans, not that it was such a substantial community in the 1830s. Jewish life followed the pattern of general religious observance in a city that was just too busy for worship. There were so many opportunities to pursue that the Jewish community did not really have a congregation until 1829 or take the synagogue seriously until 1840. With a community of seven hundred, only four households did not eat forbidden food, two-thirds of the boys were not circumcised, and almost no one read Hebrew.[15]

How could anybody take old Rabbi Rowley Marks seriously? The clownish self-styled rabbi in New Orleans was a part-time comic actor and fireman, a fake clergyman given to high jinks and ludicrous asides. Once, when a member of the congregation complained of Rowley's conduct during a High Holy Days service, he banged on the podium with his fist and shouted, "By Jesus Christ! I have a right to pray."[16]

The New Orleans congregation changed into a more religious and serious group after German Jews began arriving in large numbers in the 1840s. The Orthodox traditionalism of the newcomers, however, drove Judah as far away as the earlier rowdyism of Rowley Marks.

They just were too insular for him; they lived in the Old World, he lived in the New. Because they had been forced to live together in ghettos in Europe, they clustered together in New Orleans as well. He understood, but his history was linked to the Sephardics of Spain. In New Orleans, the Sephardics were the aristocrats of Judaism and the pillars of the general society; they married into the best Gentile families. Did anyone think they achieved such a position by looking inward?

In his new life, money and fine things seemed to make Natalie momentarily happy. Luckily, Benjamin's law practice allowed her trips, clothes, and jewelry. One can only imagine her reaction to his political friends and to the tiresome discussions of politics.

She must have liked the prestige that his participation in political life brought—the parties and the balls in the Governor's mansion when foreign dignitaries came to call. But she seemed to crave attention as strongly as a child does, especially as her husband's prominence grew. The diaries of the times record the reaction of other wives to her flirtations, beckoning men of all sorts but particularly Frenchmen, who seemed specially attractive to her, as if she were searching for some primal resolution to her Creole culture and her American birth.

Judah P. Benjamin's career blossomed in New Orleans as his marriage shriveled. Natalie resented the price she had to pay for his success, the loneliness, and the neglect of her husband.

Bellechasse was his answer. Money was so plentiful for Benjamin by the 1840s that a plantation near New Orleans, far enough away from Natalie's family, from other men, and from his legal and political involvement, seemed a perfect solution both for him and for Natalie, who could preside over a grand house and elegant parties.

First of all, Bellechasse fitted the thrust of his political career. To be successful in Louisiana politics, a man had to be a successful planter. To own land and slaves was to gain the trust of the propertied class, who cast the only votes that counted. That was especially so for a Jewish lawyer without property or slaves, for whom suspicion would abound, be he married to the best Creole family in all Christendom.

But Bellechasse offered more. His mother was getting old, and he wanted her to see him in the splendor of a Southern fantasy. He would design and build the most beautiful house in all Louisiana, on rich land with massive oaks. Natalie and he would make grand entrances down the spiral staircase, and it would not be just a showplace but a working, thriving plantation alive with slaves and sugar and boasting the riches of his toil and ingenuity.

Benjamin's eyesight had suffered from the late nights and long hours of his law practice. He had to give up and move to Bellechasse, where he sat in darkness for weeks. Characteristically, as he would approach all new challenges throughout his life, when he recovered, he plunged into the work of the plantation, spending hours implementing new ideas and techniques. What was extraordinary, looking back on his life, was that such a cerebral personality could transform himself into a successful gentleman farmer and plantation owner.

He wanted to show the South that sugar cane could be its future.[17] Sugar production was in its infancy in Louisiana, which was using primitive techniques for refining, handed down from father to son. From a trip to France in the early 1840s, Benjamin brought back new varieties of seed and the advanced techniques and inventions of French chemists whom he had interviewed in Paris. He experimented to develop precise drainage and fertilization methods and introduced the principle of boiling cane juice in a vacuum, so that little syrup was wasted and more pure sugar extracted from the molasses. The wife of his partner, Theodore Packwood, recalled that "I never see them riding about the field together without trembling for the consequences. Mr. Benjamin can talk him into buying any newfangled pot or pan he's pleased with for the moment and then Theodore has the worry of trying to make the thing work."[18] He was the fount of ideas, the theoretician, the researcher who combed books and articles for the latest techniques. He wrote and visited inventors and brought back drawings and designs. In Packwood, he had a willing implementer and master tinkerer.

Planters came from all over the state to dinner parties with experts from other countries, as did officials from the Federal government studying the latest refining techniques in Cuba and Louisiana. Having convinced himself of the practicality of his experiments, Benjamin wrote a small book with such clarity that it made the innovative process understandable for less competent planters and accessible to those who might try raising sugar cane for the first time. Even to read it today, it serves as a model of clear exposition to a person altogether unfamiliar with the process. It was distributed widely, adding to Benjamin's reputation statewide and creating a new role for him as a popularizer of new scientific knowledge.[19]

Benjamin's aspiration for Bellechasse required the purchase of 140 slaves. By then, he was in his mid-thirties and had years of travel behind him in the course of his law practice and his search for English and French techniques for his plantation. He was not therefore parochial in his views on slavery and was aware of the views toward it in other countries. Britain, in fact, had abolished slavery in the 1830s. He had felt the sting of the Abolitionists and had certainly discussed slavery abroad with men who did not agree with him.

Since Bellechasse was not a plantation handed down to him by an earlier generation, he came to slaveowning late in life from an urban background. Consequently, he was not steeped in its traditional philosophy. He would acquire an articulated point of view, but without the Biblical justifications that sustained its most extreme advocates. Though he had entered the ranks of the planter class that ruled Louisiana, he never felt that slavery reflected the divine order of things. He was not taken in by distorted theories of the Bible; he never argued that blacks were of a lower order; and he hated the cruelty of the overseers he heard about. Benjamin took care to have a plantation noted for its humaneness and sought to be known across Louisiana as a gentleman who treated his slaves well. According to Pierce Butler, former Bellechasse slaves who were still living in the early twentieth century reported "none but kindly memories and romantic legends of the days of glory on the old place."[20]

But Natalie was miserable in his paradise. Benjamin had moved into a more graceful atmosphere, but once again he was too busy for her. After ten years of marriage, she was pregnant with Ninette. When the child came in 1843, she sank into an immense depression. They were isolated on the plantation, and Benjamin tried to dispel her melancholy with a frantic round of grand parties and dances, constant entertaining of the rich, and frequent trips to New Orleans for amusement and shopping. But it all went stale for her. She missed the variety of urban life and dreamed of the excitement of living in France. Suddenly she announced in 1844 her intention to leave Louisiana altogether and move to Paris.

Benjamin must have been torn over losing his child, if not Natalie, but he had no choice and reluctantly had to acquiesce. They would give it a trial; he would send her money to provide for her needs and would visit as often as he could. Benjamin probably thought she would tire of Paris and would find herself isolated again when the French treated her disdainfully as just another American woman who spoke French. He predicted she would feel a growing loneliness for her friends and a nostalgia for New Orleans. But France and Paris had always held an attraction for her. In vain he hoped that the reality of living there would get it out of her system, and that she would return to him in some new circumstance in a few years.

By marrying into the St. Martin family, Judah P. Benjamin managed to escape the career limitations of his Jewishness, but the marital relationship would cause him lifelong humiliation. A well-positioned Creole family like the St. Martins would never have chosen a struggling

Jewish lawyer had they been given a choice. They took him into their home and must have been kind, but he was forced to live with them for more than three years. Had he moved out of the family house, he could not have afforded to keep their daughter in the grand New Orleans manner. By staying, however, he signaled to the upper classes of New Orleans that he was not a success in his law practice and had to be subsidized by the St. Martins to live in their aristocratic style. He could have relaxed and become the *bon vivant* son-in-law; but he never broke stride from a pattern that would be sustained throughout his life: a pattern of hard work and unbridled ambition. It was as if he were becoming conditioned to accepting humiliation as an incentive to drive and push himself even harder than he otherwise might have. It happened in Charleston and at Yale; it would be the same in New Orleans. That meant nights and weekends at the office; after all, to return to the St. Martins was to be reminded that he was not the master of his own house.

In addition, in a Catholic world couples were expected to have children, yet he and Natalie did not, for ten years. They might have suffered a stigma from that childlessness—if not among the Catholic aristocracy of New Orleans, then surely in the eyes of the St. Martin family. Auguste St. Martin had every right to expect Natalie to continue the family line. When the Benjamins finally did have a child, the failure to do so earlier became his, not his wife's. If that did not call his manhood into question, it certainly reflected on his marriage.

After the Benjamins left the St. Martin home, Natalie's flirtatious and libertine nature brought new embarrassments into Benjamin's life. To outsiders, he not only could not father a child but had a wayward wife as well, facts humiliating enough in the telling to supply the insatiable gossip mill of the New Orleans elite. His instinct and life pattern since Yale and Charleston were to start over, to abandon the past and begin anew against almost impossible odds. Bellechasse was that kind of choice for a Jew raised in urban life and trained to use his mind in the courtroom, not his physical forces on a plantation. And Bellechasse seemed a way to isolate and control Natalie.

But there was more to it. Humiliation can cause a reaction of exaggerated self-sacrifice, which can be a manifestation of honor. A man in the South had to rise to any challenge, had to act honorably, and had to stand tall when others found the burden of the code too weighty to bear. Financial success in the South did not in itself confer honor. That kind of success was a Northern standard. In the South, honor meant adherence to a gentleman's code—perseverance in adversity, disdain for those with a lesser standard, firmness against the winds of chance, unbowed by suffering. Benjamin was trying to change his social class, to become a gentleman of property, to transcend his birth and move into the planter class with its rewards of respectability and public office. That was the true purpose of Bellechasse, and he built it with his own brand of demonic activity.

To marry Natalie St. Martin was both an opportunity and a courting of humiliation. A poor Jew in a wealthy Catholic world could expect nothing less; a man with a faithless wife, notorious and open in her conduct, would have to learn to absorb intense pain. Natalie did not act otherwise than could have been predicted for her at Bellechasse. She could not remain indefinitely in her husband's velvet cage. What was not predictable was the extreme step she would take in reaction: She packed up their only child, almost as if the child was hers alone, sailed to Europe, and left him alone in his empty paradise. He had to accept a marriage of extended separation, similar to the marriage of his parents.

Benjamin did not let Natalie's departure deter him from carrying out the plans he had made to keep her at Bellechasse. He tore down the old house on the plantation and built an even more splendid new one, a square grand mansion surrounded by double balconies supported by twenty-eight square cypress columns. There were twenty rooms, with hallways 16 feet wide running through the house, crystal chandeliers, a marble fireplace, some statues he had purchased in Florence, a spiral mahogany staircase that ran up the middle of the structure, and a veranda around the entire house, so he could look out across his land in any direction and catch the air and a view of the flowing Mississippi River. No detail was overlooked: silver-plated doorknobs, great escutcheons, the finest furnishings.[21]

Bellechasse would be a Louisiana showplace and would add to the Judah P. Benjamin legend. He would be as successful a planter as he had been a lawyer.

But he, too, missed New Orleans. He found that by careful management he could both supervise the plantation and resume his law practice. Without Natalie, the isolation of Bellechasse became intolerable. Benjamin returned to his New Orleans law practice and an even more active life than before, including the consuming world of politics. Since he would live in both city and country, the new Bellechasse would need a mistress. He invited his recently widowed older sister, Penny, and her young daughter, Leah, to come live with him, along with his aging mother, Rebecca. His father, Philip, remained in Charleston, uninvited to Judah's Camelot.

Bellechasse existed until 1935. Photographs show it to be of unusual design, ordered by a man obviously unafraid of innovation. It said to all Louisiana and even to Charleston that Judah Benjamin was a success, that he was rich and landed. The Benjamins had never owned land. When Rebecca arrived to see it she had a perfect view of the glorious mansion below, toward the river on grounds as far as the eye could see, the new shoots of sugar cane pushing up from the black earth, and fine horses grazing in the pasture.

The road into the grounds cut between two giant oaks framing the house, passing a white fence gate with a large silver bell. The bell had been made especially for him by a New York foundry, and Benjamin had provided two hundred silver dollars to be tossed into the molten kettle for clarity. It rang with a great throaty clang so that the noise resounded through the lowlands and signaled the house whenever guests arrived.

Judah P. Benjamin was now a gentleman, and he had made the Mendes-Benjamin name a lasting one by planting its future in the land.

Rebecca died in the autumn of 1847 and was buried in New Orleans, far from her husband and her homes in Charleston and Beaufort. Penny and her younger brother grew even closer than before.[22] To Penny, he was now "J. P." as she called him in all the glory of his maturity and achievement.

At Bellechasse, Penny and her child, Leah, provided Benjamin with a loving family and welcome companionship. Penny was a "sharer of my perplexities," Benjamin wrote, and an excellent manager of the house. Together they entertained with even more enthusiasm than Benjamin had when he was trying to entice Natalie to stay. He could return from the brutal legislative battles in Baton Rouge or the courts in New Orleans and Washington to the utter tranquility of the place. As a lawyer and a rising star in Louisiana politics, he could converse about the attractions of Bellechasse with other planter-politicians. For such men the plantation was an object of reverence, their refuge from the divisive turmoil of political affairs.

In 1846, when Benjamin was thirty-five, a description of him in *Sketches of Life and Character in Louisiana* appeared in New Orleans newspapers and stated that "as a speaker, he is calm, collected, forcible, though sometimes a little too rapid in his elocution. . . . His style is distinguished for its conciseness, and close adherence to the matter at hand. . . . To his many scholarly acquirement he adds the French language, which he speaks with fluency and elegance."

Clearly, Benjamin had come very far in his profession, but he had not managed to assimilate completely into Creole culture. The directory text continued: "Mr. Benjamin is by birth, and as his name imports, an Israelite. Yet how far he still adheres to the religion of his fathers, I cannot tell, though I should doubt whether the matter troubled him much."[23]

Judah P. Benjamin rose to political prominence in spite of the fact that in his young years he never showed himself to be an extremist on the question of slavery either in the cases he took as a lawyer or in the speeches he made as an emerging figure in Louisiana politics. He did not join with the politicians who spoke of reopening the slave trade, who stirred up racial hatreds and fears for personal gain, or who were intemperate in their language in the fist-pounding, red-faced, blowhard defense of it.

Benjamin was a pragmatist. He accepted what he could not change and built his career on issues he could influence: a railroad from Louisiana to the Pacific, for example. Like all Southern politicians, he, too, on occasion, was capable of changing his message on the subject, depending on the time, the place, or the audience. Historians would have defined him as an enlightened Southerner who could be passionately critical of the most inhuman aspects of slavery and could denounce its cruelties with eloquence, yet not be an opponent of the system itself.

In 1842, in one of the most celebrated insurance cases in American history involving slavery, Benjamin represented insurance companies who were being sued by slaveowners to recover the cost of some slaves they had lost because of an uprising at sea on the brig *Creole*. During the voyage from Virginia to New Orleans, nineteen slaves mutinied and forced the captain and crew to take the ship to Nassau. There the authorities arrested the mutinous slaves but let the others go free, because they were now in British territory. The owners brought suit in New Orleans for $150,000 against the insurance companies involved.

Benjamin argued before the Louisiana Supreme Court that the

British did not have to recognize the status of the slaves on the ship:

> The position that slavery is a contravention of the law of nature is established by the concurrent authority of writers on international law and of adjudications of courts of justice, from the era of Justinian to the present day. . . . View this matter as we may, it at last resolves itself into the simple question—does the law of nations make it the duty of Great Britain to refuse a refuge in her domains for fugitives from this country, whether white or black, free or slave? It would require great hardihood to maintain the affirmative as to whites; but the color of the fugitive can make no possible difference. It will scarcely be pretended that the presumption of our municipal law, that blacks are slaves, is to be made a rule of law of nations.

Benjamin had begun his argument using the laws of nature, a classic Abolitionist rationale, and urging the court to make a decision regarding race. He continued insisting that the law of nations shall determine the case:

> It is obvious that the only criterion by which they can be governed is that which is insisted on by the American government, viz.: if the blacks reach there under the control of the whites as their slaves, so consider them; but if the blacks reach there uncontrolled by any master and apparently released from any restraint on the part of the whites, to consider them as free. These are the principles on which by the law of nations Great Britain has the right to regulate her principles.

But Benjamin's boldest argument was that the risk of mutiny was inherent in the slaveowner's decision to pack the slaves so tightly into the ship as to incite a mutiny and that the crew brought the loss on themselves by their cruelty. This passage of his legal brief was reprinted in pamphlets by abolitionists and circulated all over the country:

> What is a slave? He is a human being. He has feeling and passion and intellect. His heart, like the heart of the white man, swells with love, burns with jealousy, aches with sorrow, pines under restraint and discomfort, boils with revenge and ever cherishes the desire for liberty. His passions and feelings in some respects may not be as fervid and as delicate as those of the white, nor

his intellect as acute; but passions and feelings he has, and in some respects, they are more violent and consequently more dangerous, from the very circumstances that his mind is comparatively weak and unenlightened. Considering the character of the slave, and the peculiar passions which, generated by nature, are strengthened and stimulated by his condition, he is prone to revolt in the near future of things, and ever ready to conquer his liberty where a probable chance presents itself.

Benjamin concluded by asking, "Will this court be disposed to recognize one standard of humanity for the white man and another for the Negro?" The Louisiana Supreme Court said no and ruled for Benjamin's clients against the slaveowners. The case became a *cause célèbre,* argued about in Congress and ultimately the object of international arbitration.[24]

Many writers have quoted from the brief in Benjamin's defense as an indication of his true feelings about slavery. But it must be pointed out that he was making the case for a client and he received a substantial fee from the insurance company for winning the case. Advocates of his era often looked for the most persuasive parts of an argument and in drafting their briefs overwrote the strong points to cover the weaker side of a case. Society did not question a lawyer's ethics for taking a case he disagreed with; a lawyer made the best possible case for his client, and society accepted that as part of the workings of the legal system. Moreover, there was not the communication system between courts and the bar that there is today, and briefs were rarely circulated widely. Benjamin was probably embarrassed by the use of his arguments in the pamphlets of the Abolitionists and certainly did not foresee such a use when he was writing his brief.

Still, this was passionate language for a Southerner with political ambition, because no one with such views could be elected to any office in the ante-bellum South. It is testimony to the acceptance of the practice of the legal system that Benjamin, after writing such a brief and in spite of its use by the Abolitionists, could be elected to public office at all.

Like many Southerners, Benjamin would be incensed over the harsh picture of plantation life that Harriet Beecher Stowe painted in *Uncle Tom's Cabin* in 1851, particularly when it was quoted in the Congress and was used as a basis for legislation. He once compiled some controversial figures from government reports to show that slaves were well treated on plantations, and accused a Republican colleague of misleading the people.

"He has read in a novel the authentic fact that Mr. Legree whipped Uncle Tom to death," he would say later in a Senate debate, "and that is a thousand times more satisfactory than any such foolish thing as official documents." Then he attacked the entire criminal justice system, claiming that the Southern way of whipping was more humane than long jail terms.

> If a slave in the South broke open the cabin of another slave and stole his pretty treasure, he would be whipped and there the criminal procedure would end. But if the same event occurred in the North between white persons, the offender would be given a term of years in the penitentiary. If it occurred in philanthropic England, the man . . . I believe, formerly would have been hanged . . . but now he simply will be torn from wife, children, country, home and friends, manacled, and transported to a penal colony of Great Britain in the southern seas.[25]

Although he owned slaves, he vigorously opposed the use of the so-called federal ratio, under which five slaves would be counted as three white men in determining the basis of representation in Louisiana elections. Adopting such a plan would have increased the representation of slaveowners in the legislature.

In the Louisiana Constitutional Convention of 1845, he turned the logic of the slaveholders against their interests:

> Slaves were, by our laws, nothing but property. But, says the delegate from Lafourche . . . we should allow them to form a part of the basis of representation because they are productive labor and labor should be represented. If this argument holds good, then it might, with equal propriety, be argued that we should allow representations to oxen, horses, etc., which are equally productive labor."
>
> If property is to be represented at all, why not all property? Why not houses and land? . . . or if at all, why not make it a qualification for voting?

The convention was talking about counting slaves for purposes of representation, not letting them vote; Benjamin was arguing *against* the planters, and their slave interests who would have gained representation if slaves had been counted, thereby supporting his constituency of white nonslave owners in New Orleans, who would have lost strength had the system of counting slaves been adopted.[26]

Benjamin then was capable of manipulating the slavery issue and serving the voters of New Orleans, who were the bulwark of his rising career, even as he changed from city lawyer to plantation owner from south Louisiana. He was building a formidable coalition as a downstate political personality with the support of the Slidell machine in New Orleans. In 1842 he was elected to his first public office as a Whig member of the Louisiana legislature, and his law office became the meeting place for the party executive committee. He became a Whig delegate to the Louisiana Constitutional Convention, where his tact, courtesy, and ability to find compromises impressed the political elders in all corners of the state. With the outbreak of the Mexican War in 1846, he turned his attention to national and international affairs. Because of his knowledge of Spanish, he was appointed by the Federal government as a California land commissioner to help settle land claims based on Spanish ownership one year after the territory was wrested from Mexico. As a Whig elector in 1848, he traveled to Washington for the inauguration of Zachary Taylor, meeting Cabinet members, Senators, and judges at state dinners and events. Benjamin Perley Poore, the Washington correspondent of the Boston *Journal,* who loved gossip, wrote in his *Reminiscences* in 1886 about "Benjamin, whose features disclosed his Jewish extraction," that "General Taylor had wished to have Mr. Benjamin in his cabinet, but scandalous reports concerning Mrs. Benjamin had reached Washington, and the General was informed that she would not be received in society. Mr. Benjamin then rented a house at Washington, furnished it handsomely, and entertained with lavish hospitality. His gentleman friends would eat his dinners, but they would not bring their wives or daughters to Mrs. Benjamin's evening parties and she, deeply mortified, went to Paris."[27] Poore's gossip about the Cabinet offer cannot be verified, and his sequence of events concerning Benjamin's move to Washington and Natalie's flight to Paris is confused, but it would not be the last time that Natalie's behavior would be reported in a public journal or a book.

Two of Benjamin's most noteworthy cases occurred after he was admitted to the Supreme Court in 1848. In the trials of the Cuban filibusters (an obsolete use of the word to describe Americans fomenting insurrections in Latin America in the nineteenth century), he assisted the United States district attorney in New Orleans in prosecuting a group of revolutionaries who sailed from New Orleans to Cuba to seek to overthrow the Spanish government and annex the island to the United States. The U.S. Government had a difficult task in prosecuting those who had violated the neutrality laws, because the group included John A. Quitman, Governor of Mississippi. Feelings were running so high in New Orleans that when the mission failed and several of its leaders were killed, a mob destroyed the Spanish consulate and abused the Spanish flag.

Benjamin led the case against them by asserting before the jury that they had violated the tranquility of a relatively peaceful and satisfied population:

> Not a single movement has been made in Cuba; not a ripple disturbs the smooth current of the life of that people; not a single proof is given of their dissatisfaction with their lot;—these discontents exist only in the imaginations of our Cuban bondholders. The rich are busily engaged in rolling their sugar cane, gathering in their rich crops; the poor are eating tortillas, smoking cigars, swinging in hammocks, and sucking oranges. They do not appear to be at all troubled by their oppression or disturbed with their lot. Their independence is to be achieved for them by our enterprising young men who rejoice in the outlandish name of Filibuster.[28]

But hung juries resulted in mistrial four times, in spite of the clear evidence, and the government eventually dropped the charges out of frustration. The *Delta* said that Benjamin could not secure a verdict because of "the spirit of the age" and reported that the jury had received from the marshal the following bill of fare:

> *Soup:* oyster and turtle—plenty. *Roasts:* duck and beef—with individual vegetables and separate gravies. *Vegetables:* Irish potatoes, mashed; sweet potatoes, roasted; onions boiled. Tenderloin steak with mushrooms; venison steak with cranberry jelly. Custards, tarts, oranges, raisins, mince pies and bananas. *Liquors:* brandy, Madeira, hock, and whiskey. Dinner for twenty-four, Liquors for forty-eight.[29]

Benjamin was accused by Quitman of receiving a whopping $25,000 fee in secret from the Spanish government and was so incensed by the charge that he answered it publicly, writing in a rare letter to the newspapers on May 22, 1851:

> I observe . . . that Governor Quitman had asserted, in a public speech, that I had received from the Court of Spain a fee of $25,000 (!) for assisting in the Cuban prosecutions. The story is so ridiculous

that I should not have deemed it worth noticing, if coming from a less responsible source. Nor can I now think it possible that a gentleman of Governor Quitman's high position can really have said such a foolish thing. Your correspondent must have misunderstood him. Yet, as there is no limit to the credulity of some people, I beg to say that I have never been employed, directly or indirectly, by any other person than Mr. Hunton (District Attorney), acting under an order from Washington, which was shown to me when he employed me; that I was never promised,—have never received—nor do I expect, to receive, one cent of compensation for my services from any other source than from the government of the United States; and in order that everybody taking an interest in my private affairs may be fully informed on the subject, I will add that I have not yet received one cent of Compensation, even from our own government, and will feel much indebted to any kind gentleman that will take the trouble to procure for me the allowance of a reasonable fee from the authorities at Washington.[30]

The government eventually paid him a $5,000 fee for his work.

Benjamin's other noted case in New Orleans involved a legal battle that lasted four years to break the will of an eccentric millionaire named John McDonogh. McDonogh was a miserly bachelor who had never given money to charity. He had accumulated property holdings that newspapers in New Orleans reported as among the largest in the United States, more than $2 million in New Orleans alone, through a series of questionable business dealings that included brothels and "drunkeries." Though noted for being a skinflint during his lifetime, he left the bulk of this estate to the cities of New Orleans and Baltimore to establish schools for the poor, regardless of race and color. The heirs, living in various states, were represented by Benjamin, and the case went all the way to the U.S. Supreme Court. While the case created a sensation in New Orleans, the argument for upholding the will met with a much more sympathetic hearing in the more distant atmosphere of the Supreme Court, and Benjamin and the heirs lost their appeal. A reporter for the Washington *Union*, who was sympathetic to the cities involved, heard Benjamin's argument and wrote:

Whoever was not in the Supreme Court this morning missed hearing one of the finest forensic speakers in the United States. In the case of the great McDonogh estate, Mr. Senator Benjamin made one of the most truly elegant and eloquent speeches that it was ever my good fortune to hear. His address is refined, his language pure, chaste and elegant; his learning and reading evidently great; his power of analysis and synthesis very great; his argument as logical as the nature of the case will admit; his rhetoric so enchanting as for the time to blind his hearers to the faults in his logic if any. . . . Mr. Benjamin contends that substantially the devise in the Will is not to the cities of New Orleans and Baltimore as beneficiaries, but only as trustees of others; and you can judge of his powers as a debater when I say that I think he carried conviction to most all if not all of his hearers, at least during the time he was speaking. So fascinating was his oratory that his hearers, at least one of them, lost sight of the fact that the City of New Orleans, to which the devise was made was not that spot of earth or physical entity known as, such city, but the community occupying the spot. . . . The man who has the power to render, for even a moment, such a question obscure, must be a finished debater.[31]

Benjamin lost the case but gained renown as an eloquent advocate and a skilled appeals attorney.

The white population of Louisiana exploded again in the decade of the 1840s, growing from 158,457 to 225,491, straining both its political and its economic structures. But the system of canals and railroads in the Northeast was beginning to cut into the supremacy of New Orleans as a port, since the Mississippi River was so much slower as a trade route. Benjamin with others in New Orleans picked up an old idea and propounded a visionary new strategy: to link New Orleans with the North and West by a new system of railroads. He became the chief spokesman for the boldest plan of all—not only to reinstate the previous plan to link to Jackson, Mississippi, and northward, but to build a new line from New Orleans through Mexico across the Isthmus of Tehuantepec to the Pacific Ocean. During the ten previous years, the idea had floundered as a pipedream, but Benjamin would give it life again.

"This straight line of railroad," he said to the Southwestern Railroad Convention in 1852, referring to the plans for the Great Northern Railroad through Jackson, "will stop at New Orleans, but it will not cease there as a line of travel. That line carries us straight across the Gulf of Mexico to the narrow neck of land which divides the

Pacific from the Atlantic, whereon Nature has bestowed every blessing of soil and climate, where she has even lowered the hills as if purposely to point the way for a railroad; then when we cross this Isthmus, this Isthmus of Tehuantepec—what have we before us? The Eastern World! Its commerce makes empires of the countries to which it flows, and when they are deprived of it they are as empty bags, useless, valueless. That commerce belongs to New Orleans."[32]

Such a plan required his planning and drafting state charters, guiding the plans through the state legislature and the Congress, arranging public and private financing, all with a high degree of local, national, and international political acumen. Benjamin became counsel to the Tehuantepec Company and headed the effort to organize the idea. He had to enlist the support of the U.S. government in the persons of Secretary of State Daniel Webster and President Millard Fillmore. He drafted a prospectus to incorporate and arrange financing, which he then implemented through visits to the Governor and the appropriate leaders in the Louisiana State Legislature. A provisional treaty was drawn up with the Mexican government, which, for political reasons, began to pull back out of concern for its self-interest in the details of the plan. Benjamin paid a personal visit to President Fillmore in Washington and then traveled up to Massachusetts to see Daniel Webster at his home. The *Delta* wrote a parody of the visit, which gave some insight into the Benjamin lobbying technique:

> Of course, it would be a breach of official etiquette to introduce the subject to Mr. Webster, in his secluded family mansion, so far away from his bureau, but what objection could there be to the accomplished New Orleans lawyer going there to take a dish of Daniel's farfamed chowder, and incidentally broaching the Tehauntepec subject to him, just while he was waiting for his chowder to cool? We don't see any. In fact, when a thing is well done, we should not be too hypercritical as to the manner of doing it.[33]

Webster threatened to withhold funds, but the Mexican government held firm. Win or lose with Mexico, Benjamin was accumulating powerful friends to help him run for the U.S. Senate and take the Tehuantepec plan into the world of international politics and finance.

At the 1852 Louisiana constitutional convention, Benjamin did a complete flip-flop on the issue of counting slaves for purposes of representation, giving still greater influence to the slave interests and, especially important to his political career, to the Whig planters downstate. He saw the issue in terms of the future of the Whigs and personal opportunism, linked to the popular election of judges and the political necessity to maintain Whig influence over the courts.

One opposition paper attacked him, complaining that "the one hundred slaves of J. P. Benjamin of Plaquemines are made just as good as one hundred citizens."[34] The paper called it "The Negro-good-as-a-white-man Constitution," and another noted that he was just as eloquent on behalf of the provisions as he had been in opposition to them seven years earlier.

Solidly entrenched with various factions in the Louisiana legislature, Benjamin emerged in 1852 as the leading candidate for the U.S. Senate. Benjamin surprised his opposition by being elected by a large majority with the help of the state Democratic machine of John Slidell, which, as the *Delta* reported, helped put together a coalition of New Orleans commercial interests and "the country members who rather preferred a gentleman [who] was a sugar planter and had, therefore, a common interest and sympathy with them." It also pointed out that "Mr. Benjamin made good use" of the advantage "of being a prominent member of the legislature."[35] The newspaper complimented him with the observation that "he not only rendered himself very agreeable to the members of the legislature, but he manifested a zeal, industry and capacity in the preparation of business for the legislature—digesting and framing bills, and drawing up reports, etc.—which produced a most favorable impression as to his great practical talent and usefulness."

The fact that John Slidell managed Judah P. Benjamin's political ascendancy was not without its consequences. Slidell's political enemies were so mystified by his support of a Jew for election to the U.S. Senate that they accused Slidell of being a Jew himself. As additional evidence they could have pointed to the fact that Slidell's niece, the daughter of his sister, had married August Belmont of New York City, a well-known Jewish name in American finance. But Slidell was not Jewish. He was an Episcopalian, and family records indicate ceremonies in the Episcopal Church. But having been born, reared, and educated and having begun his career in New York City, he was much more cosmopolitan than the usual Louisiana political leader. Perhaps because of his perspective as a Northerner, he was able to sense that the state was ready to look beyond religious prejudice and judge its Senate candidates by ability and political preference. He certainly had to weigh Benjamin's religion in his political calculations, and it is to his credit that he was able to support wholeheartedly a Jew for such high office and risk the future influence of his political machine on the outcome of such a consequential state election.[36]

The *Delta,* which had ridiculed Benjamin's candidacy earlier, summed up his career with uncharacteristic praise:

> Though not yet forty, he has reached the topmost round of the ladder of distinction as an advocate and counselor in this state.
> . . . He has a fine imagination, an exquisite taste, great power of discrimination, a keen, subtle logic, excellent memory, admirable talent of analysis. [While attending to a very heavy law practice] he had the time to look after one of the largest sugar plantations in the state, to pay a yearly visit to Paris, to see to the interest of the Great Tehuantepec enterprise, to fulfill all of the duties of an active partisan, of a public-spirited citizen, of a liberal gentleman, with a taste for elegance, the social pleasures and refinements of life.[37]

Philip Benjamin never visited his son in New Orleans or Belle-chasse, but he did live to see him elected to the U.S. Senate. He died a few months later, on June 11, 1852, at the age of seventy-three. He had given up his small shop a few years before and had been living in an undistinguished neighborhood on the outskirts of Charleston. Philip Benjamin was buried in Charleston, far from his wife, Rebecca, who had died five years earlier in New Orleans and was buried in a family plot there.[38]

Soon after his father's death, there were other problems for Judah Benjamin. The flooding Mississippi reached the very steps of the mansion at Bellechasse, and the front yard was filled with cattle, deer, and wild animals from the swamps driven to the high ground to escape the waters. Benjamin's growing crop of sugar cane was destroyed, even the seeds, and he had no time to supervise the replanting and repair of the refining equipment on the spot. To add to his burdens, he had endorsed a note for a friend who could not pay it and had to assume a huge debt. Benjamin was not in financial despair, only financial trouble, forcing him to sell Bellechasse for a sum large enough to enable him to retire the debt, buy a fine house in Washington, and move Penny to an elegant home in a New Orleans suburb. His years as a slaveholding planter were ended.

Historians have recognized the Honorable Judah P. Benjamin of Louisiana as the first acknowledged Jew elected to the U.S. Senate. There was an earlier election in Florida, however, of Senator David (Levy) Yulee, called the "Florida fire-eater" because of his passionate pro-slavery oratory. Levy changed his name to Yulee and renounced Judaism, converted to Christianity after his marriage to the daughter of the Governor of Kentucky, and claimed he was not Jewish at all but descended from a Moroccan prince. Thus, because he acknowledged his Judaism, it can be said that Judah P. Benjamin took his seat in the halls of history as the first Jew in America's most influential legislative institution.

4

Jefferson Davis: *The Education of a Lonely Protestant*

❄❄

The generation that emerged as the leadership of the South in the Civil War was shaped by the great ideas and events of the early nineteenth century, when America feverishly embarked upon the work of nation-building. The Louisiana Purchase of 1803 doubled the size of the country, extending its borders from the Mississippi River to the Rockies; Lewis and Clark returned from their expedition to the Pacific in 1806 with dreams of a nation extending "from sea to shining sea." The War of 1812 stabilized the course of America as an independent and free nation, involving still another generation in a war with Great Britain. The conquest of the West began in earnest, and the nation pulsed with new developments and inventions to enlarge its commerce and shrink its borders—the railroads, the telegraph, the steamboat. The Erie Canal was completed in 1825, and the first wagon train made its way along the Oregon Trail in 1832.

In Europe, Napoleon met his Waterloo in 1815, the same year General Andrew Jackson, unaware of the treaty ending the War of 1812, won the Battle of New Orleans. President James Monroe issued the Monroe Doctrine in 1823, warning European powers to stay out of the Western Hemisphere. Beethoven composed his Pastoral Symphony in 1808 and his Ninth in 1823; Rossini wrote *The Barber of Seville* in 1816. Later in the century, Europeans as well as cultured Americans who traveled to Europe (as did Judah Benjamin) heard Chopin and Liszt play piano concertos, and new works by Franz Schubert. In England, Disraeli was born in 1804, and in Germany in 1815 Mayer Amschel Rothschild, founder of the Jewish banking dynasty, died in Frankfurt.

Eli Whitney's cotton gin (invented in 1792) increased cotton production in the South from several thousand pounds to a phenomenal 35 million pounds by 1800. In the next three decades, King Cotton made slavery immensely profitable in America while Britain abolished slavery throughout the Empire in 1833. John Adams and Thomas Jefferson died on July 4, 1826, both lingering through serious illness to reach the fiftieth anniversary of the Declaration of Independence. Five years later, after a solar eclipse, which he took as a sign, Nat Turner heard voices saying "The last shall be first" and led a slave rebellion. Eighty-five whites and sixty slaves were killed before Turner was captured and hanged.

James Fenimore Cooper won international fame in 1826 with the publication of *The Last of the Mohicans,* popularizing the American Indian all over the world. In 1832, Chief Black Hawk, fighting against overwhelming odds in the Battle of Bad Axe, was captured and accompanied to prison by troops led by Lieutenant Jefferson Davis.

These events, ideas, and personalities shaped the legends of America and the dreams of young men growing to maturity in the nineteenth century. War would shape the lives of every American generation. For Southerners especially the struggle against European domination would give way to sectional conflicts in their homeland.

In 1808, three years before Judah P. Benjamin's birth in the West Indies, Jefferson Davis was born in Kentucky, the last of ten children and the fifth son.[1] His father, Samuel Emory Davis, was a yeoman farmer of Welsh peasant stock; his mother, Jane Cook Davis, was of Scotch–Irish descent. They worked their farm with fewer than a dozen slaves, and, as was customary among the lesser class in the rural South, Samuel worked alongside the slaves, picking cotton under the hot sun. The Davis roots did not touch a noble heritage: Neither parent could point to a family coat-of-arms. Like Andrew Jackson, they were what the South called "one-generation aristocrats."

As a reward for patriotic services in the Revolutionary War, eighteen-year-old Samuel Davis had received land in Georgia. However, he was an impetuous man and a restless spirit to whom prospects always looked better elsewhere, so the family moved to Christian County in the new state of Kentucky. There, at the age of forty-five, Jane Davis bore her last child. They named him after the author of the Declaration of Independence *and* gave him the whimsical middle name Finis. The Davises' other sons all had Biblical names— Joseph, Benjamin, Samuel, and Isaac—and the girls' names strung out like lyrical verse: Anna, Lucinda, Amanda, Matilda, and Mary. They called him "Jeff" and a year after his birth, less than 100 miles away, Abraham Lincoln was born—also in a log cabin. But the Davis cabin had more polish. It was one of the first in rural Kentucky to boast glass windows, and people came from miles around to see it.

Before Jeff was two, the family had moved twice more—to Louisiana; and then, harassed quite enough by that state's deadly mosquitoes, 300 miles north to their permanent home in Mississippi. They lived 20 miles from the big river, on a farm between the rich delta and the poor soil of the pinelands. A man would not get rich there, but he could sweat out a fair living. They called their home "Rosemont," because Jane loved flowers and planted whole hedges of roses to separate the orchard from the garden. Samuel was fifty-six years old and ready to settle down, and it was clear that Jane wanted a home and a place they could count on.

Within a year, all the older sons but Isaac went off to fight in the War of 1812. Jeff slept at the foot of Anna's bed, and the fifteen-year-old girl cared for him. The other sisters nurtured him with love, warmth, and approval.[2]

Jeff grew into a handsome boy with golden hair, a quick mind, and a lighthearted disposition. As the baby of the Davis family, he received an abundance of attention and affection, and his natural charm attracted even more of it. Samuel was not a stern disciplinarian but expressed paternal disapproval by withdrawing into a distant coldness. He was, in Jeff's own words, "a man of wonderful physical activity" who loved riding horses into old age, a "silent, undemonstrative man of action." He was a hard worker in the fields who "talked little and never in general company," and developed the grave demeanor that hard work dictates. Jeff said at the end of his life that Samuel was "a man of deep feeling though he sought to repress the expression of it whenever practicable."[3]

Samuel was a Baptist and a religious man, though never much of a churchgoer. While he was not of the planter class, he was influential in the county and respected for his rock-ribbed integrity.

Thomas Jefferson's name gave Jefferson Davis some attachment to a political heritage that set him apart from the other sons. This boy had an apparent talent, everyone in the family said, and it must be given the chance to blossom, not in the backwood schools of Mississippi, but in the best school to be found. Like Judah P. Benjamin in Charleston, he must be sent away from the South to an outstanding institution that the family knew.

At the age of eight, Samuel decided that he would send the boy back to Kentucky, to a Catholic school called the College of St. Thomas Aquinas near Bardstown, the headquarters of Catholicism in the state. Jane was deeply concerned, because the boy was too young to be sent off so far. Jeff's oldest brother, Joseph, now practicing law in Natchez, joined his father in the decision, mindful of the influence on the boy of his oversolicitous older sisters.

Jane was so heartbroken that Samuel would not tell her when the day of departure would be. Jeff left on his 800-mile journey with Joseph's friend, Major Thomas Hinds, without even a farewell kiss from his mother.

The trip had to be made on horseback with pack mules, because steamers had not yet appeared on the Mississippi. They traveled the wild but beautiful Natchez Trace, teeming with game, where travelers could meet occasional trappers and Choctaw Indians. At night, Major Hinds and the two slaves accompanying them took turns standing watch to protect the camp from panthers and bears.

The highlight of the trip, and an event that Davis would remember always, was a two-week visit to the Hermitage in Nashville, the home of General Andrew Jackson, under whom Major Hinds had fought at the battle of New Orleans. "Old Hickory" received them cordially in his home, and Davis would always recall how impressed he was with a man reputedly so fierce in battle yet so courteous and hospitable in his home.

In the last year of his life, at age eighty-one, Davis began to dictate his life story to his wife Varina, and she preserved the verbatim account in her biography of him. He sensed the end was near, so that the choices of anecdotes and ideas took on a surreal, reflective quality, as if he were sifting through photographs in his mind. His oral history ended after a few weeks, so that all he was able to complete was a disjointed description of his early years. The visit with Andrew Jackson loomed large in the account of his boyhood.[4]

"During that period I had the opportunity a boy has to observe a great man. . . . I have never forgotten the unaffected and well-bred courtesy which caused him to be remarked by court-trained diplomats, when President of the United States, by reason of his very impressive bearing and manner."

Davis recalled Jackson's courtliness in ways uncharacteristic of the Jackson legend: "Notwithstanding the many reports that have been made of his profanity, I remember he always said grace at his table, and I never heard him utter an oath."

For recreation, young Jefferson Davis, the General's adopted son, and other children competed in pony riding and other games, but "he would not allow us to wrestle; for he said, to allow hands to be put on one another might lead to a fight. He was always very gentle and considerate. . . . In me, he inspired reverence and affection that has remained with me throughout my whole life."

Davis was the youngest boy at St. Thomas College and so small that old Father Angier put a little bed for the boy in his own room. Moreover, as the only Protestant in the school, he was cast into an unfamiliar world of new rituals that were part of the value system and upbringing of Catholic boys. But, in addition, he was suddenly taken from a female-dominated household in which he was the center of attention and expectation and placed in a totally male environment where he would have to prove his manhood every day, compete for recognition, and earn the affection and respect that were so abundant at home. Being so young and at a physical disadvantage, it was difficult for him to excel or even compete at games except by pure stubbornness and endurance.

As in all Catholic schools, there were a rigid schedule for every hour of the day and rituals he had never seen before: morning prayers with genuflections and boys crossing themselves, lessons to be recited, catechisms to be memorized, communions to attend, evening prayers and grace before and after meals, and bedtime with final prayers and lights out.

Several incidents stood out in Davis's memory all his life, one of them as laced with humiliation as Judah Benjamin's incident at Yale. One of the incidents involved the priest in whose room he slept. He told Varina:

There was an organized revolt among the boys one day, and this priest was their special objective point. They persuaded me to promise to blow out the light which always burned in the room; so after everything was a quiet, I blew it out; then the insurgents poured in cabbages, squashes, biscuits, potatoes, and all kinds of missiles. As soon as the light could be lit, search was made for the culprits, but they were all sound asleep and I was the only wakeful one. The priests interrogated me severely, but I declared that I did not know much and would not tell that. The one who had especial care of me then took me to a little room in the highest story of the monastery and strapped me down to a kind of cot, which was arranged to facilitate the punishment of the boys; but the old man loved me dearly and hesitated before striking the first blow, the first I should have received since I had been with the monks. He pleaded with me, "If you tell me what you know, no matter how little, I will let you off." "Well," I said, "I know one thing, I know who blew out the light." The priest eagerly promised to let me off for that piece of information and I then said, "I blew it out." Of course I was let off, but with a long talk which moved me to tears and prevented me from cooperating with the boys again in their schemes of mischief.

Jefferson Davis told this story to Varina when he was eighty-one, so that it obviously represented more than just an amusing episode or prank. He confessed to less than he knew to protect the older boys with whom he had conspired to embarrass the priest to whom he was closest. For this eight-year-old boy, 800 miles from home, strapped down to a cot in a lonely room high in a monastery, protecting his friends from punishment, it was his earliest confrontation with absolute authority, with the threat of punishment tempered with mercy, and with the idea of honor. Whatever the lessons he learned, the memory of that incident endured into the last months of his life.

The school taught rigid concepts of right and wrong, the belief in divine inspiration, and the rewards of service and self-abnegation. It demanded respect for authority and taught a hierarchical system of the universe in which all men had a place and obedience to God's will was the first law of entry into heaven. He learned of sin, omnipotence, guilt, confession, and forgiveness.

Finally, unable to endure the unrelenting pressure for conformity "under the influences that surrounded me," Jeff asked to be converted to Catholicism. To his credit, Father Wilson, "the venerable head of the establishment whom I found in his room partaking of his frugal meal . . . received me kindly, handed me a biscuit and a bit of cheese, and told me that for the present I had better take some Catholic food."

This story reveals the early beginnings of a religious feeling that led to a break with his parents and the only life he had known. His request probably reflected a prior emotional and psychological torment over the Catholicism all around him, for he also said: "I was the only Protestant boy remaining, and also the smallest boy in the school. . . . I had been sent too young to school, and far from home, without my mother's knowledge or consent."

One can sympathize with the confusion and guilt he must have suffered at school and wonder at a small boy's reaction to the gentle rejection by the monks, who would not take his request seriously. Had he done something even more wrong? What was expected in morning devotionals? Could he pray with his friends? Was he to believe in the rituals or protect himself from them? Was he a sinner if he wanted in his heart to immerse himself in the Catholicism all around him? Was he being excluded from the true faith because of his parents? And how tolerant were the other boys of his lonely status as a Protestant in an era when tolerance between faiths was not yet a national virtue? A Southern Jew like Judah P. Benjamin could empathize with such loneliness.

Not permitted to convert, yet given no instruction in his own faith, Jefferson Davis remained a hazy Protestant for more than four decades and did not join any church until he was past fifty. He was confirmed in the Episcopal Church on the eve of the Battle of Richmond, just before Varina and their children were sent out of the city, when he did not know whether he or the Confederacy would survive.

As unalike as they were, there were many similarities in the boyhoods of Jefferson Davis and Judah P. Benjamin, which would influence them individually and together in later years.

Both Judah and Jeff were raised in loving homes, strongly influenced by their mothers and sisters. Both their fathers were restless men who struggled for an economic stake in the South, and both fathers were disappointments to their families. Jeff was pushed by his father and older brother and sent from home at an early age to a Catholic school. Judah, too, was sent far from home to Connecticut, where he was the only Jew among upper-class Gentiles. Thus both were poor boys educated among the sons of the rich, and both had to acquire the manners of the well-born from the atmosphere around them.

Both schools required great discipline yet preached systems of belief and values to which neither boy was accustomed. It was a profound change for both of them.

Both schools put enormous pressure on their students to conform. Jeff wanted to convert to Catholicism. Judah married a Catholic. In that sense, both men had a familiarity with Catholicism as a religion. However, like their fathers, both spent most of their lives outside any congregations.

Being a Southern Jew at Yale and a Protestant at St. Thomas created analogous situations and responses. They shared the loneliness of the outsider, the ostracism, the social humiliation, the aching heart that longs to join, to belong, to be accepted. Jeff's punishment for mischief was private, though painful enough to recall. Judah's punishment at Yale was more humiliating because it was more public, so consequential, and we cannot know whether his Jewishness was a factor or whether he considered it a factor. At Yale he too put his religion aside and began to blend in with his surroundings.

While St. Thomas College left Jeff a legacy of religious confusion, it contributed positively to his intellectual development. The British-born Dominicans taught the students Latin and English grammar and emphasized the need to speak well, to enunciate and pronounce clearly. Davis learned to work hard, to be precise, and to prepare his lessons each day. And the school did not disturb his Mississippi social values. Though the friars took individual vows of poverty, the school itself was well-to-do and owned slaves to work on the large estates and care for the crops, the sheep, the cattle, and the flour mill. Here, too, slaves were an accepted part of the order of things.

After two years, Jane Davis could not bear the separation any longer and demanded that her boy be brought home. By now, the early steamboats were chugging the giant Ohio and Mississippi rivers, and little Jeff Davis, not yet ten years old, became one of the first Americans to ride the miraculous new invention and experience the adventure of the varied life of the river banks. The settlements were growing as trading centers for the new river queens, and he could feel the stirring changes wrought by them and absorb the sights of the roustabouts and the showboats, the furs and crops and blankets on the docks, the Indians selling fresh venison. As the steamboat drew closer to home, he could listen for the cries of the bald eagles and the blue cranes, hear the sounds of the steam whistle, the dark stories of river pirates and gamblers.

The boy had grown so tall that he pretended to be a stranger asking for directions, but Jane recognized him easily from her veranda as did Samuel from the fields. His father ran to him, abandoning his austere manner momentarily to smother his son in repeated kisses. "He took me in his arms with more emotion than I had ever seen him exhibit," Davis recalled. "I remember wondering why my father should have kissed so big a boy."

Though he could comfort himself at age eighty-one with the thought that he was sent away without his mother's "knowledge or consent," she, of course, had known he was leaving and had not objected strenuously enough to prevent it. Samuel had sought to spare her the pain of parting, but that may have been a mistake. The absence of his mother from his leave-taking deprived him of solace as his loneliness at school grew and became a painful memory, we know from his autobiography, that remained with him all his life. He would always blame his father. Why else at age eighty-one— did he use the phrase "without my mother's knowledge or consent"— except to absolve his mother? His father's error in judgment and insensitivity to a boy's need shaped him and his attitudes in ways that no amount of rejoicing at his return could heal. Jane had been right: The boy had been too young and they would keep him close to home for the next five years.

The family sent young Jeff to a log cabin school near his home. Looking back on that time, he complained in his dictation to Varina of the ignorance of the teachers, who "used the oil of the birch as a lubricator for any want of intelligence." His impatience with their stupidity shows in his recollection that "after some time, a bright boy could repeat all the rules; but if you asked him to explain why, when he added up a column of figures, he set down the right and carried the left-hand figure, he could give the rule, but no reason for it. And I am not sure that, as a general thing, the teacher could have explained it to him."

When a new county academy opened in a nearby town, Jeff was fortunate to be taught by a "scholarly man," a well-educated Bostonian who remembered him in later years "favorably."

"He was a quiet, just man," Jefferson Davis explained to Varina, "and I am sure he taught me more in the time I was with him than I ever learned from anyone else . . . he was the first of a new class of teachers in our neighborhood, and was followed by classical schol-ars who raised the ability to teach." He added an apology for his other schools and their teachers. "The era of the dominies whose sole method of instruction was to whip the boy when he was ignorant has passed."

He assumed that his exaggerated sense of injustice, already formed in the discipline at St. Thomas, would be more indulged at home, but there were new lessons to be learned. One day his teacher assigned him a piece to memorize that he regarded as excessively long. He protested, but the teacher refused to lessen the assignment and, when he failed to memorize it, threatened the boy with a whipping. Young Jeff simply picked up his books and went home. His father told him simply that he had the choice of going back to school or working in the cotton fields. After two days in the hot sun picking cotton with the slaves, he went back to school. One could not imagine Jeff reacting to the monks at St. Thomas in such a manner. Jefferson Davis at home with his sisters and his mother was simply more self-centered than in Kentucky in a strict Catholic boarding school.

Before the age of ten, Jefferson Davis had traveled overland through the compelling interior beauty of America and returned dramatically by steamboat down its greatest river. He had met Andrew Jackson and caught the wide-eyed spirit of the frontier; he had experienced its need for commerce, highways, and great men with a vision to shape its future. His name had singled him out from the rest of the family for the heroic tradition; a doting family had given him the self-centered confirmation that he was of special stock. The ambitions of his father and brother blessed him with a sense of destiny.

But there were costs as well. His youth had sown the seeds of a divided personality: His happy and free-spirited childhood nurtured by his loving mother and sisters contrasted with the loneliness and stern strictness imposed by the Dominican friars. The school instilled in an eight-year-old boy a strict Catholic love of ritual and authority that would attract him to West Point, a life of discipline, obedience to superiors, and honor. He had survived alone at the school and had learned to be independent. His lonely perseverance would eventually give him a personal code of honor, a belief in hard work, and confidence in his ability.[5]

In 1823, at the age of fifteen, he entered Transylvania College in Lexington, Kentucky, larger than Harvard and the most prestigious institution west of the Appalachians. Transylvania was called the "Athens of the West." Davis would learn to read omnivorously there and would receive an excellent liberal education. He was a freshman with boys who were younger yet ahead of him in their studies.

"My chief deficiency was in mathematics which had been very little taught at the Academy. The professor of mathematics, Mr. Jenkins, kindly agreed to give me private lessons, and I studied under him for the balance of the session and through the vacation, so as to enable me to pass examination as a sophomore."

He participated in the debating society but, because of his discouraging experience at St. Thomas, chose not to compete in athletics. Transylvania attracted the sons of the aristocratic families in the South, some of whom brought slave valets. Thomas Jefferson had preferred it to Harvard because it had "more the flavor of the old cask" and its graduates seemed destined for leadership. (No fewer than six of Davis's contemporaries from Transylvania would join him and Judah Benjamin in the U.S. Senate.) He made up his deficiencies and graduated with honors.[6]

He did not see his family for two years, although his father, Samuel, wrote Jeff a long, sad letter confessing his failure to collect an inheritance from his grandfather that might have made the family "immensely rich." He ended with the advice: "Use every possible means to acquire useful knowledge as knowledge is power, the want of which has brought mischief and misery to your father in old age. That you may be happy and shine in society when your father is beyond the reach of harm is the ardent wish of his heart," and he signed it: "Adieu my Son Jefferson, your father Saml Davis."[7]

The distraught old man who had written from the depth of his soul in this last communication of his ambitions for the boy to "shine in society," had put "Son" in upper case and "father" in lower case.

A year later, Samuel lost his farm and the six slaves as a result of signing a note for his son-in-law. After a quarrel, he impetuously left in an open boat for his son Joseph's plantation, Hurricane, caught malaria, and died. Jefferson received the news at Lexington and wrote a letter home so oddly cold and stiff that Varina felt it necessary to apologize for it in her book. She called it "a quaint, pitiful letter from a bereaved boy. . . . The formal manner of the letter he retained as long as he lived."[8] The letter said: "DEAR SISTER: It is gratifying to hear from a friend, especially one from whom I had not heard from so long as yourself. . . . In my father I lost a parent ever dear to me, but rendered more so (if possible) by the disasters that attended his declining years."[9] It seemed as though Jeff never got over his resentment toward his father for having sent him away to school at so young an age.

Three days after the death of his father, Jefferson Davis accepted an appointment to the U.S. Military Academy, arranged by his brother Joseph through political friends in Mississippi. After all, patriotism and military service had been a family tradition: His father had served four years in the army during the American Revolution, and three of his brothers had fought in the War of 1812. Military traditions ran deep among Southerners, and the constant threat of a slave rebellion had given even the local militia some status born of necessity. Jeff had been set on going to law school like his oldest brother, but Joseph, who had inherited his father's hopes for the boy, persuaded him to try the Academy. Jeff did not even go home to visit the family before he left Lexington for West Point, and he would not come home again for six years. He was putting the cotton fields of Mississippi behind him.

Jefferson Davis's formative years had been shaped by dramatic and frequent changes of milieu, discipline, and values. His character became rigid and rock-ribbed; his family and his experiences in school had shaped a personality embodying extremes: idealism, honor, patriotism; extreme stubbornness, self-importance, and pride.

If honor was the center of the aristocratic tradition he acquired in Kentucky, then he would become the most honorable of Southerners. If toughness was a lesson to be drawn from the violence that marked the Mississippi frontier, he would learn at West Point that unyielding righteousness could dominate men of less certitude. And if loyalty was the measure of the civilized man who devoted his life to the military tradition, then he would be as loyal to family, friends, and superiors as any man who ever lived—and would expect the same from those who served him.

5

Melancholy War Hero

❧❧

"M y oldest brother, who then occupied to me much the relation of a parent," Jefferson Davis told Varina for his autobiography, "notified me that he had received the news of my appointment as a cadet in the United States Military Academy; and fearing the consequences of being graduated at the early age of seventeen, he insisted that I should proceed at once to West Point. Of course, I disliked to go down from the head class of one institution to the lowest of another, but I yielded."[1]

Because Davis was entering late in the term, he had to take a special entrance examination in front of the staff. He almost flunked it. A family friend on the staff saved him from embarrassment by asking beforehand, according to Davis's own account, whether he had learned arithmetic. "To which I had to answer in the negative. . . . He was quite alarmed, and went off and got me an arithmetic, telling me to study as much as I could of fractions and proportion." Fortunately, Davis was asked only one or two questions, and the professor of mathematics was satisfied, "probably thinking that I knew a great deal more than I did."[2]

Cadet Davis arrived at West Point in 1824 a green Mississippian with an apparently good bearing and an eagerness to learn. He joined the generation of soldiers that would later fight in the Civil War— among them Albert Sydney Johnston and Joseph E. Johnston, who became generals in the Confederacy, and Robert E. Lee, who ranked second in scholarship and went through four years without a demerit.

Jefferson Davis accumulated no such record. His biographers report a brief period of rebelliousness in which he received demerits for having long hair at inspection, failing to keep his room in order, spitting on the floor, absence from reveille and from classes, making noise during study hours, firing his musket from the window of his room, disobeying orders, cooking in his room after 8 P.M., using "spiritous liquors," absence from evening parade, and "foul clothes not in clothes bag."[3] It was as if the carefree spirit of his childhood, which had been cut short and bottled up by St. Thomas, erupted once again at West Point.

In his first year, Davis was arrested for patronizing Benny Haven's Tavern and, according to the report, exhibited "extreme embarrassment bordering on weakness" attributable to the consumption of alcohol. He was court-martialed and sentenced to dismissal from the Academy, but the sentence was suspended because of what interestingly was termed his previous good record. He was again arrested, on Christmas Eve, 1826, for attending an eggnog party given against regulations by Southerners, seventy of whom were later involved in a riot against their officers, and of whom nineteen were expelled. Fortunately, Davis missed the altercation—probably only because he had been ordered to his room and had fallen asleep. Nevertheless, he was put under arrest and confined to his quarters for six weeks. He graduated in 1828 with less than an average record, twenty-third out of thirty-two in his class.[4] Had he been less lucky, like Judah P. Benjamin, Davis's boyish pranks might have gotten him expelled from West Point and changed his life. But no such stain followed him, as it did Benjamin: He was commissioned a second lieutenant and ultimately sent to the frontier.

Unhappy from the beginning yet stoic, Lieutenant Davis resolved to see if he could find a home in the army. In 1972, a letter was discovered in Paris, Kentucky, which Davis wrote to his sister after his graduation from West Point. Dated June 3, 1829, the letter was written from his first military post, a frontier garrison established to prevent a war with the Indians. In it he confessed that West Point had made him "a different creature from that which nature had designed me to be." His officers, he said, were "men of light habits both of thinking and acting." He now intended to pursue a course of study, especially of law books, since, should he leave the service, he would prefer the practice of law to any other profession.[5] Yet, straight-backed and mindful of duty, he did not resign from the army for another six years.

The rest of the story was Confederate legend—how the young lieutenant wooed and won Sarah Knox Taylor, the beautiful, blue-eyed daughter of Colonel Zachary Taylor, who was Davis's commanding officer during the Black Hawk War. For two years her father forbade their marriage because he had vowed that his daughter would never marry a military man. Davis considered threatening a duel but finally decided to resign his commission and return as a planter to Mississippi in order to win Taylor's approval and be with the love of his life. At last Taylor acquiesced. But then, just three months after the wedding, malaria in the lower bayou took her from him. For eight years thereafter, Davis brooded alone, a melancholy shadow, leading almost a hermit's life on his brother's plantation, Hurricane. He never visited neighbors or received callers but devoted his time to reading and farming. He was a recluse, letting time heal the deep wound of his lost love.

The light had gone out of his life, and his exaggerated sense of honor and propriety would not let him look at another woman. Davis entered an eight-year period of overwhelming grief that stands as a mysterious chapter in his life. Davis's ascetic existence surely helped mold the solitary and austere personality that emerged from that emotional exile. The mischievous young officer who loved practical jokes turned into the kind of man his father had been: terse, difficult, and dour, a distant figure lost in his own thoughts.

After Sarah Knox Taylor's death, Davis grew closer to his older brother, Joseph, already one of the wealthiest men in Mississippi. Joseph owned a Delta kingdom of 11,000 acres he called Davis Bend, part of which he sold to friends, keeping 5,000 acres of the richest land on the river for himself. From that land, he gave Jeff 800 acres and ten slaves on land so fertile, as Varina later described it, "that golden rod grows large enough for a strong walking-stick."[6] By 1860, Joseph owned more than three hundred slaves, one of only nine men in Mississippi with so large a number.

Under Joseph's influence, Jefferson Davis came to be fired with all the ambition for politics that the older brother possessed for money and property. Joseph was patient with his younger brother's grief and rode with him about the land seeking to engage him in the dreams of a plantation empire. When Joseph saw his brother's fascination with the huge library built as a replica of a Greek Doric temple, he took it as a sign of recovery. Immersed in the writings of Madison, Jefferson, and Locke, Davis was preparing himself for public service in the Southern tradition. He would make up for the poor educational experience of his early years and his lack of achievement at West Point. But the scholastic isolation had to come to an end, and Joseph conceived a second solution, which went right to the nub of things.

Joseph had been watching Varina Ann Howell grow up in Southern Mississippi with all the right social graces and family history required for his younger brother. The Davis family had money, land, and slaves; what Joseph wanted now for the family was blue blood and status, and Varina would bring both. Her father was a Natchez lawyer and the son of the eight-term Governor of New Jersey; her mother was the daughter of a Virginia aristocrat. Since Joseph had been best man at her father's wedding, Varina was brought up to call the elder Davis "Uncle Joe," and he observed her intellectual growth with the pride of a member of his own family.

"By jove, she's as beautiful as Venus," Joseph exclaimed to brother Jefferson. It was not altogether true. Although she carried herself well and combed her dark hair tightly into a plait to emphasize her features, she was attractive but unexceptional. Her eyes were her most notable feature—dark and intelligent, contrasting with her creamy white skin. While Joseph exaggerated her beauty, he was right about her other qualities: "As well as good looks, she has a mind that will fit her for any sphere that the man to whom she is married will feel proud to reach."

From the age of four until she was sixteen and went off to Philadelphia to school, Varina had been tutored by a Mississippi Supreme Court Justice named George Winchester. He had come to Natchez from Salem, Massachusetts, a graduate of Harvard and a classical scholar. He never married and took the little girl like a daughter into his world, teaching her Latin classics, introducing her to English literature, and schooling her in the Whig politics of Natchez, where so many prominent Northerners settled. The Whigs of Natchez were the "nice people" who despised the common folks who supported Andrew Jackson, held the "hillbillies" and the "dirt eaters" in contempt, and looked down on the rough-and-ready Democrats in the lowlands, where the Davises lived. Judge Winchester was one of the overpowering influences in Varina's life; he shaped her character and her mind. Oddly, a portrait of him reveals a strong resemblance to Jefferson Davis. In conversation with Judah Benjamin in later life, she called the Judge by her childhood name for him, "Great-Heart."

Joseph invited seventeen-year-old Varina Howell to Hurricane for the Christmas holidays of 1844, and Judge Winchester accompanied her on the riverboat *Magnolia* up the Mississippi. She wrote her first impression of the tall horseman, now thirty-five, in a letter to her mother:

> I do not know whether Mr. Jefferson Davis is young or old. He looks both at times; but I believe he is old, for from what I hear, he is only two years older than you are. He impresses me as a remarkable kind of man, but of uncertain temper, and has a way of taking for granted that everybody agrees with him when he expresses an opinion, which offends me; yet he is most agreeable and has a particularly sweet voice and a winning manner of asserting himself. The fact is, he is the kind of person I should expect to rescue me from a mad dog at any risk, but to insist upon a stoical indifference to the fright afterward. I do not think I shall ever like him as I do his brother Joe. Would you believe it, he is refined and cultivated, and yet he is a Democrat![7]

From Varina's description, their first extended time together sounded like a storybook romance over the two weeks of the Christmas holidays. They rode about the plantation together, Jeff on his white Arabian and Varina on a bay galloping beside him in a plumed hat and dark blue riding costume. Varina played the piano while Jeff sang his favorite Scottish ballads; they sat reading together by a log fire, played charades, and took long walks through the gardens. Davis even took her to meet some of his slaves, especially Jim Pemberton, who had once nursed Jeff back to health after a serious illness out West and now ran his plantation. "Uncle Joe," as delighted as a mother hen, shooed away all who might interfere with the couple and, whenever he came upon them, found a reason to take his leave.

Varina's mother's objections—the eighteen-year difference in their ages, Davis being a widower, the political differences between the families, Varina's own inexperience—postponed the wedding for more than fourteen months.

His first love letter to Varina was written in an awkward prose that matched the stiffness of his personality. "Ephemeral passion," he wrote, "or accidental preference, is withered by separation; sincere affection is sufficient for its own support, by absence it is not cast down, neither is it heightened, the latter will, however, often seem to be the effect because in losing that which is essential to our happiness we are brought most actively to realize its value."[8]

Finally Judge Winchester spoke up strongly for the match, and Varina made up her mind. On February 26, 1845, they were married in her home on a bluff near Natchez, in a house surrounded by a tangle of hyacinths and a forest of magnolia, oak, and pine trees. Below the bluff was a magnificent view of the riverboats on the Mississippi.

Since the lives of Jefferson Davis and Judah P. Benjamin were intimately bound up in the fatal years of the Civil War and the fate of the Confederacy, it is useful to compare aspects of their early lives as well. Davis was just three years older, and it is important to understand that both men were proceeding in their chosen careers at approximately the same time.

Jefferson Davis's young years have all the elements of a romantic Southern adventure story. With tales of the American Revolution and the War of 1812 all about him, young Jefferson Davis was reared in a military tradition of the Old South that treasured the virtues of love of country, self-sacrifice, and courage. It was natural, then, for his hero to be Andrew Jackson, who a decade after they met would be President. He carried the name Jefferson with a sense of his own destiny. Jackson and Thomas Jefferson were strong male figures, idealized and heroic, role models for his own career and substitutes for a disappointing father.

The Benjamins, on the other hand, were the classic newcomers in the Southern story, overlooked characters on the periphery of Southern history, who arrived in 1813 as new immigrants to Charleston. They were Jews who were excluded from military duty in Europe and in whom patriotism and the sense of participation in American history would require time to take root. Judah P. Benjamin was named after his paternal grandfather, his path less certain, his heroes garnered from books he read rather than from the people he met, but a young man also estranged from his father. Jefferson Davis, shaped by the heroic tradition of the plantation South, could dream of future armies he would command and even the presidency of his country. Like so many children of immigrants, Judah P. Benjamin was raised as a survivor, a Jewish immigrant moving from country to country, with wealth and status as his goal and political power available to him only if he could shed, in the eyes of the Gentiles, the burden of his Jewishness.

Jeff was a lean and athletic boy whose competitive instincts were challenged by his age and size at St. Thomas. Any boy who could ride a pony for 800 miles must have developed the fortitude of a potential cavalryman. Judah was older when he left home, but small for his age, and was dark-eyed and olive-skinned in the race-conscious South. Judah was not admired for his appearance; it was only after listening to him that others began to respect him and be drawn to him. Judah was a city boy, raised in the crowded streets of Charleston, in a market place where the farmers brought their produce and the ships their goods and where traders came to bargain, to cheat, and to gamble. Jeff was a farm boy, raised with a sense of the changing seasons, where physical labor rather than book learning was ingrained and rewarded, where he worked with the slaves alongside his father, and where men trapped and slaughtered animals when the first frost covered the fields. He was a witness to nature's beauties and its cruelties.

Contrast Jeff the adventurer with Judah the intellect. Jeff grew up in a world of physical challenge, an out-of-doors boy who traveled the length of the Mississippi River twice before he was ten years old. His values were shaped by the Deep South, where the ideal of manhood was a military career and a plantation. Judah was raised in a tradition of ideas, under the tutelage of a father who debated beliefs and who could challenge the accepted standard of an entire community. Judah Benjamin's playground in Charleston was the world of commerce, where shrewdness and a quick wit determined profit and a man was measured by the size of his fortune.

Judah's education was superior to Jeff's, for such were the advantages of the Charleston schools, the Fayetteville Academy, and Yale. Jeff complained that methods in his schooling were primitive: "to prescribe the lesson and whip any boy who did not know it." Judah excelled academically, and in every class was at the top, confirming his intelligence and abilities. Jeff struggled with books and was an average student. It is no wonder that Jeff was attracted to the pragmatic career of the military, where he would assume that his other qualities—daring, courage, and leadership—would be better appreciated and would work to his advantage. West Point beckoned him as naturally as the courtrooms of New Orleans called to Judah Benjamin.

After West Point, Davis's rise to prominence and wealth was not wholly earned but was facilitated by his older brother. Joseph was a powerful figure in the Delta, and his plantation gave young Jefferson Davis roots and reputation, a respected name, solidity, and a financial underpinning for a political career.

Judah P. Benjamin, in contrast, had to make his way alone, step by step, without important family connections, beset by religious prejudice, as a brilliant lawyer who by contacts and alliances could accumulate a personal fortune. But his marriage into the St. Martin family gave him an early rung on the ladder, awarding him the status in New Orleans that Joseph provided Jeff in Mississippi.

For Davis, recognition and status were part of the natural order of things. He would lead and others would follow. For Benjamin, the fruit seller's son, every ounce of recognition and status represented a special triumph. His secret was his ability to cultivate others, to prove himself through the law as a faithful servant of the interests of the powerful. For Davis, the military man educated in a Catholic hierarchy, men were to be ordered and were duty-bound to obey. For Benjamin, men were to be persuaded, cajoled, manipulated by self-interest and negotiation, or convinced by sanctions in the law. Jefferson Davis revered loyalty; Judah P. Benjamin was used to serving others loyally and, as a lawyer, profiting from that service.

Fate seemed to be shaping two men whose destinies—in character, personality, and events—would bind them to each other for the stormy years awaiting them.

From the beginning, Jefferson Davis had not hidden his past feelings from his second bride. On their honeymoon he had insisted that they visit Sarah Knox Taylor's grave at Locust Grove Cemetery in Bayou Sara, Louisiana, where Jeff's sister was living in the house where his first bride had died.

Earlier, on his way to Natchez for the wedding with Varina, Davis had had a chance meeting with General Zachary Taylor, a fellow passenger on the riverboat. That encounter had unlocked painful memories for him. Though they had not spoken in ten years, the father of the woman he had loved had shaken his hand warmly in a common bond of sorrow.

A few months after the honeymoon, Davis was out on the hustings campaigning for a seat in the U.S. Congress. He had come out of his plantation retreat and the seclusion of his eight years of mourning with great vigor. In November 1845 he was elected to Congress. Thus, the new bride who had envisioned her life as a plantation wife had to pack for Washington and prepare herself for a far different existence.

Davis seemed a man miscast by history from the beginning, ambivalent about his choices from an early point. Southern custom drew him into the military and back to plantation life, which absorbed him totally. His attraction to politics flowed more from duty and the expectations of the times for planters in the Delta than from personal inclination. He was not happy even as a Congressman who had no executive responsibility, who had only the power of persuasion and his vote. Varina was not happy either. She wrote: "Then I began to know the bitterness of being a politician's wife and that it meant long absences, pecuniary depletion from ruinous absenteeism, illness from exposure, misconceptions, defamation of character, everything which darkens the sunlight and contracts the happy sphere of the home."[9]

That life, too, was short-lived; the upright Mississippian from West Point soon heard a new call to duty. The Mexican War broke out over control of the Rio Grande River, and in June 1846, without first consulting his wife, Davis simply announced to Varina that he had volunteered for the army. He returned to the West, fighting once again under the command of his former father-in-law. The West Point generation that would lead the armies in the Civil War were all fighting together in the Mexican War: Colonel Jefferson Davis, Colonel Robert E. Lee, Captain George B. McClellan, and Lieutenant Ulysses S. Grant. It was at the Battle of Buena Vista that Davis won lasting military fame, devising his famous V-formation that Varina always said "conquered one-half of Mexico and made General Zachary Taylor President of these United States."[10] Davis had to be helped off his horse after leading a charge, his leg bloody and swollen, pieces of brass spur driven into the wound and imbedded there so that his boot filled with blood.

His return to Mississippi with his regiment stirred the nation, and his home state lionized its returning hero. A steamboat was chartered to take the regiment up the Mississippi, stopping to greet cheering crowds at every town along the way. Varina met the boat at Natchez and remembered it in detail:

[T]welve young ladies, holding a garland many yards long, met the regiment at the Bluff and crowned the officers with a wreath. Their banners were also wreathed with bowers . . . speeches by townspeople . . . then, a procession; after which Mr. Davis—who was on crutches—came out in a barouche, nearly hidden with flowers to take me to the steamboat. The journey was one long ovation.[11]

The reception confirmed in his memory the triumph of one of the important moments in his life and left him intoxicated with his image as a brilliant military strategist. It left another lasting memory as well, as Varina wrote:

> Mr. Davis suffered intensely from his wound, as indeed he did for five years, and was unable to dispense with two crutches for two years. The bone exfoliated, and pieces that had been shattered worked out or were extracted by a surgeon, causing dreadful nervous disturbance, not to speak of the physical anguish. Even after the foot was apparently well, for eight or ten years, the slightest misstep gave him pain.[12]

The Davis reputation for rectitude and high-minded adherence to duty began to develop from the stories his men told about serving under him in Mexico. When his men, encamped near a farm, plundered a field of corn "like a drove of mules," Colonel Davis lectured them on private rights and paid the owner for the crop. Though the churches in Mexico were filled with gold vessels and statuary studded with diamonds, rubies, and pearls, Varina proudly reported, the First Mississippi regiment, "from the Colonel down to the last private, returned home without one article belonging to a citizen of Mexico."[13]

When the President of the United States offered Davis a promotion to Brigadier General, he turned it down on the grounds that the Constitution provided that only the states could make such appointments in volunteer regiments. His refusal was vintage Davis: high principle, a reverence for states rights and the Constitution above all, a self-abnegation all the more honorable since personal gain would have resulted from acceptance.

In August 1847, within two months of Davis's return home as the toast of the Delta and the hero of Buena Vista, Governor Albert G. Brown appointed him to fill out the term of a U.S. Senator who had died suddenly. The Mississippi legislature subsequently confirmed the popularity of the choice by electing him unanimously to a full six-year term. In December 1847 Jefferson Davis hobbled on crutches into the chambers of the United States Senate to join such men as Clay of Kentucky, Calhoun of South Carolina, Webster of Massachusetts, and Douglas of Illinois in their great debates.

Judah P. Benjamin would join Davis in the Senate six years later but by a more conventional route characterized less by destiny than by mere determination and political shrewdness. Benjamin had learned politics, not battle.

Jefferson Davis's youthful life as a hunter, a horseman, and a planter commanding a community of slaves drew him back to the frontier world of the military, even in his late thirties, seeking glory on a field of flashing sabers and bravery. Only after the success of Buena Vista did he rationalize public office. It was as if Andrew Jackson had inspired his life: politics only after heroism, service only after sacrifice.

Judah P. Benjamin spent his early career in drawing rooms and offices, in courtrooms and carriages, where he would learn to observe more of human nature in conflict, to watch others and plan his moves sequentially, to be cautious of the opposition, to understand the other party's motives, to learn the intricacies of compromise and the virtue of settlement. He thrived in a world where resolution of differences overshadowed principle and obstinacy could result in an expensive trial for his clients, risking the loss of everything on a judge's idiosyncrasies.

Jefferson Davis's election was a testimony to personal popularity, not the result of the usual deal-making and accommodation of various political interests. Judah P. Benjamin arrived in the Senate in 1853, the product of the political machinery of Louisiana, a man of considerable political and legal acumen as well as oratorical ability. Davis had such a rigid code of honor and was so devoted to the Southern slave interests that he could not desert the Democratic party in the presidential election of 1848 even to support his former father-in-law, Zachary Taylor. Having been appointed to the Senate to the cheers of the populace, he understood little of the process of politics. Benjamin, on the other hand, was the quintessential politician who built bridges to opposing interests, negotiated differences, and won the respect of opponents whom he would need in future fights.

In Washington, Varina had to learn to live with the shadow of Sarah Knox Taylor, as President Zachary Taylor's political and military prominence kept the Taylor presence in her life. After Buena Vista, old "Zeke" had grudgingly said, "My daughter was a better judge of men than I was." The General's rise to the presidency in 1848 was a constant reminder to Varina of what Davis's life might have been had his first wife lived, and she must have imagined that her husband was flooded by those same speculations. Even their home, Brierfield, had been drawn up and built to Sarah Knox Taylor's wishes. It was to have been their paradise. She must have felt deprived of a corner of Jeff's soul and somehow unsure of her ground. Her husband had tasted the deep ecstasy of youth and first love, then had had it snatched from him. She advised another young bride of a widower after the war "not to be content with anything less than the whole of a man's heart."

Although Varina reported that Jefferson Davis grew "pale and ema-ciated" from the damage done to his nervous system by the war wounds, he regained his energy and entered the work of the Senate with enthusiasm as the emerging spokesman for Southern interests. The gold rush to California in 1848 raised the question of the admis-sion of California into the Union, and Davis opposed the Compromise of 1850 that Senator Henry Clay of Kentucky hammered out to balance Southern slave and Northern interests. It admitted California as a free state, organized Utah and New Mexico as territories without mentioning slavery, provided for a tougher fugitive slave law, abol-ished the slave trade in Washington, D.C., and assumed the Texas national debt. Davis's arguments were couched, as they often would be, in Constitutional terms: Since slaves were property under the Constitution, they should therefore be protected as property when transferred into the Federal territories. Congress had no right to discriminate between different kinds of property in the territories, he claimed, and since his position had been endorsed by the Missis-sippi Governor and legislature, he assumed the people of the State of Mississippi supported him.

Davis did not share John C. Calhoun's view that slavery was a permanent condition; from his own plantation experience he argued that it was an "institution for the preparation of that race for civil liberty and social enjoyment." He summoned the scriptures to declare that its origin was in the "divine decree—the curse upon the graceless son of Noah." He advised the North to "leave natural causes to their full effect, and when the time shall arrive at which emancipation is proper, those most interested will be most anxious to effect it."

In 1851 Davis resigned his Senate seat to run for governor and to defend his opposition to the Compromise of 1850. He faced a bitter and slashing attack from his great rival in Mississippi, Henry Foote, who as a Senator had vacillated and then had supported the Compromise. Davis had misread the voters in the South, who reversed their opposition almost overnight out of relief that the slavery contro-versy had finally been settled. Because of prosperity, wealthy planters called the Compromise the "Businessman's Peace." Before the elec-tion, Alabama and Georgia had accepted it. Bad luck had been stalking

Davis. In the heat of the campaign, pneumonia confined him to his room for three weeks, enfeebling his defense of his position, and he was defeated by fewer than a thousand votes.

Events had overtaken Jefferson Davis and sent him back to Brierfield and the life of the plantation gentry.

Clement Eaton, in his 1977 biography of Jefferson Davis, wrote a chapter entitled "Slavery on the Davis Plantation" in which he detailed the paternalistic treatment of slaves over the twenty years of Davis family ownership of Brierfield.[14] By 1860, the manuscript slave schedules in Mississippi recorded that the Jefferson Davis plantation had 113 slaves, 67 female and 56 male. They dwelt in twenty-eight cabins, averaging about four to the cabin. According to Eaton, neighboring plantations had as many as seven slaves in a cabin, and the Davis quarters were more spacious.

According to Janet Sharp Hermann in *The Pursuit of a Dream*, Joseph Davis met the British industrialist and utopian Robert Owen on a stagecoach in the 1820s and was much impressed with Owen's ideas about cooperation and encouragement as superior to harsh rule for increasing the productiveness of workers. He decided to try those notions on his plantation, and Jeff followed the example of his brother at Brierfield.[15]

"The cottages were well-built," Hermann wrote, "with plaster walls and large fireplaces and they contained two large rooms and two shed rooms behind them," a decided improvement over ordinary slave cabins, which usually had one room. "The Davis cottages had front and back galleries, often shaded by fruit trees, and were near a large cistern house from which pure water was readily available." Each cabin had a henhouse in back, from which eggs and chickens were plentiful, and cornmeal was provided for feed.[16]

The Davis plantations provided feasts at wakes, at Christmas, and at other holidays and provided gifts of "astonishing variety," according to Varina, for weddings and births, such as "candy, negro shoes, field implements, new saddles and bridles, fancy plaid linsey or calico dresses for the negro women who needed consolation for a death in their families, guns and ammunition for hunting, pocket knives, nails and screws." She described a slave wake at Brierfield at which mourners received "a large quantity of flour, several pounds of sugar, the same quantity of coffee, a ham . . . and a half dozen or a dozen bottles of claret." For the death of babies they expected less, she reported, but for weddings much more, and a wedding dress.[17]

Not only were the slaves on the Davis plantations physically better off than other slaves, but the Davis brothers also set up a form of self-government unique for its times. Every Sunday, in a Hall of Justice, slave juries heard testimony about misconduct in trials over which one of the Davis brothers presided, allowing the extraordinary procedure of permitting a slave to testify in his own defense.

"No matter who told him anything about his Negroes," Varina wrote, her husband said " 'I will ask him to give me an account of it.' The servant was always heard in his self-defense. Mr. Davis said 'How can I know whether he was misunderstood, or meant well and awkwardly expressed himself?' "[18] Corporal punishment was not permitted, and the Davis brothers often reduced the severity of sentences. A Mississippi historian reported that only one other plantation owner in Mississippi gave his slaves a trial to ascertain guilt or innocence.

The slave juries also heard complaints from overseers, who could not punish anyone without court permission. Consequently, as one former slave pointed out, "the overseers had only partial power," and many left out of dissatisfaction. When Davis departed for Washington, he wrote in his book of instructions for his black overseer and trusted slave, Jim Pemberton, who served from 1835 to his death in 1850, that it was the overseer's duty to provide the slaves with coffee, sugar, molasses, and salt, and no flogging of slaves would be permitted.

Davis cared for the old (as evidenced by the number of old slaves who lived on the plantation), the sick, and the handicapped; employed a dentist to come from Vicksburg periodically for the slaves; and once sent a sick fieldhand to a celebrated doctor in New Orleans because she was "a good girl in every sense of the word." He studied medicine and with Joseph set up a slave hospital with steam-powered machinery for hydrotherapy. Varina made clothes for the slaves with her own hands. Though Davis claimed a Biblical basis for slavery, he did not emphasize religious training on the plantation, because he and Varina were not religious. The plantation was "exceptional in respect to having literate slaves," Eaton wrote, and Davis "was such a mild master that the neighboring planters said that his slaves were spoiled."

Joseph wanted to encourage self-advancement and initiative, so he and his brother allowed slaves to keep all profits beyond their value as fieldhands. Slaves sold chickens, eggs, home-grown vegetables, and wood to the steamboats plying the river and traded with each other. One slave, Ben Montgomery, managed a profitable store, trading with slaves, whites, and the steamboat captains bringing goods to the plantation or taking cotton back to the markets. Montgomery studied engineering, surveying, mechanics, and architecture in the family library; invented a more efficient steamboat propeller; and designed buildings for the property. After the war, Ben Montgomery led the slaves who remained at Brierfield in a cooperative experiment supported by the Freedmen's Bureau. According to Janet Hermann, Joseph wrote after the war that "hc had wanted to free his slaves for more than twenty years but could think of no adequate way of guaranteeing their welfare." Jefferson Davis did not share his brother's ambivalence about slavery, but the plantation he ran was a model for its time.

In defending slavery in the Senate, he could "sincerely present the most favorable side." It was a view he would share with Senator Judah P. Benjamin of Louisiana.

Both Benjamin and Davis were exemplary slaveowners—paternalistic masters who profited from the slave system yet did not abuse their slaves. Davis was not one of the "fire-eaters"; in the context of the times he was a more moderate figure among the Southern spokesmen. Benjamin's history was more complex; as a lawyer he accepted cases that set him both against and for the interests of slaveowners. He never argued that Negroes were of a lower order or that slavery was foreordained by God. He could in a legal brief criticize the harsher aspects of slavery and even speak eloquently against the abuse of slaves; but politically he was pragmatic and was a supporter of slavery in his rise to prominence and in his service in the Senate.

Benjamin came to plantation ownership late in life, taking a rare step for a Jew in the South, far from his roots. He was the first in his family to own a plantation or to deal with large numbers of slaves.

For Jefferson Davis, his brother Joseph was a role model and much more. Joseph was twenty-four years older and the strong guiding, almost paternal influence in his younger brother's life. Jefferson Davis thought of him as a mentor and deeply respected his profession of the law and the fact that he had run for office three times and had helped shape the Constitution of the State of Mississippi. But Joseph could also be overbearing, a quality that Varina resented.

"He, like his brother Jefferson," Varina observed, "could not comprehend anyone differing from him in political policy after hearing the reasons on which his opinion was based, and was prone to suspect insincerity on the part of the dissenter." Varina had produced a telling insight, meant to describe the oldest brother she did not like, but revealing the same quality in her own husband.

While respecting the lineage of the Howells of Natchez, Joseph took deep exception to their Whig politics and looked down on them for their lack of land and possessions. Varina, reared as a city girl, in return considered Joseph rather coarse and uncultured, a man who lacked the gentlemanly and refined qualities of mind of the younger brother. Joseph acted as if he owned everything on his property, but nobody could get away with treating Varina Howell as just another hireling! When Davis was away in the Mexican War, Varina began to supervise the slaves in building a larger house at Brierfield; Joseph insisted that it have two kitchens, to accommodate a widowed sister with a large brood of children, whom Joseph expected to occupy half the house. Varina drew the line: The house would have one kitchen, thank you, and if Joseph invited his sister to live on the plantation, she and her children would have to reside at Hurricane with Joseph, not at Brierfield, where she would be building a family.

When her fourth child was born in May 1859, Varina wanted to name it in honor of her father, but her husband insisted that the child be named Joseph. She wrote her mother: "I cried myself sick" over the insistence that they name their son after "a man whose very name was only suggestive to me of injustice and unkindness from my youth up to middle age." As fate willed it, the boy looked like Joseph—small build, gray eyes, large nose, and black hair—but she prayed that he would grow out of it.

The resentment spilled over into questions about the ownership of Brierfield. Joseph refused to give them a written deed for the property, though it was clearly understood that he had given the land to his brother orally when the young officer returned from the Black Hawk wars to marry Sarah Knox Taylor. Varina suspected that Joseph's motive was to exclude her from any ownership claims or to torment her with a reminder that it was Sarah Knox Taylor's union with Jefferson Davis that he had blessed with the promise of Brierfield, not Varina's. Indeed, Joseph's grandchildren coveted the property as their own, as if it were just another corner of their grandfather's huge plantation, and they seized it back from the ex-slave Ben Montgomery after the Civil War. Davis's high-minded code of honor dictated that such a personal question could not be raised with the patriarch of the Davis family. The tensions boiled over, leading to painful litigation with the Davis relatives many years later.

Varina was sensitive regarding the childless first seven years of her marriage. Her letters reveal that she felt less than a complete woman. She wrote her mother in despair after only six months of marriage that "we both regret to be condemned to live in single blessedness." Women in the South were obligated to bear children in the first year, and society pitied the barren wife. They spent four years in Washington without children when Jeff was in the U.S. Senate the first time. Varina must have blamed both herself and, in weaker moments, the ghost of Sarah Knox Taylor. Varina's mother had gone through eleven pregnancies, and though she too was impatient for a grandchild, she supported Varina with the faith that God in time surely would smile on them.

Their first child, Samuel Emory, was born at one of the happiest times in her life, during that short period of fifteen months in 1852–53 back at Brierfield after Jeff's loss of the governorship of Mississippi to Henry Foote.

Varina described the reaction of the slaves at Brierfield who sensed her relief at long last to mother a child.

When our first child was born, every negro on the plantation, great and small, came up with little gifts of eggs and chickens and a speech of thanks for the birth of a "little massa to take care of we, and be good to we," from the year-old, open-mouthed, glossy little tot, with an egg in his fist, to the old women with a squawking hen, or a dozen large yams in their aprons. The men looked lovingly on at a distance, but the women each took a kiss. One lifted up the little rosy finger and said "De Lord, honey, you ain't never gwine work—your negroes gwine do all dat for you."[19]

Varina proudly took her firstborn home to her mother and sisters, beaming with satisfaction that she at last was a mother but sad that she would never be able to show off her son to Judge Winchester, her "Great-Heart," who had died the year before.

Varina and Jefferson Davis spent that spring riding horses over the Brierfield plantation, cultivating roses and shrubs, grooming horses, sewing, and painting the plantation house they had missed so much. She romanticized the calm between political storms that would toss them in turbulence for the rest of their lives. The spring of 1852 did not mean war, but aromas of wild crabapple and plum blossom, of lotus blossoms floating in the ponds like splashes of sunlight.

"I was a plantation wife," she later remembered warmly, spinning cloth and cooking, while he supervised the plowing, sowing, and reaping of the cotton crop. It was one of the few times she had her husband all to herself without politics or official duty to interfere with their time together.

There were elements of tragedy in the personal lives of both Jefferson Davis and Judah P. Benjamin. Those aspects of their emotional histories and their relationships to women and children would eventually bring them together.

Jefferson Davis and Judah Benjamin were both in love with ghosts—Davis with the memory of a first romance in his youth, Benjamin with the smoldering Creole temptress he first encountered over English lessons in New Orleans. Davis's love was taken by death, Benjamin's by time and events. Davis had found another who cared for him deeply, while Benjamin endured an unhappy marriage long ago shattered, held together only by his wealth and a willingness to accept separation and loneliness.

For Davis, both Sarah Knox and Varina were proper mates, fitting for a man of means and destiny. Natalie was appropriate in station but not in character, leaving a great, desolate hole in Benjamin's life.

Yet one cannot imagine a man like Judah P. Benjamin, a man of gregarious nature, who relished the world around him, retiring to a plantation for eight years to brood over a lost love. Episodes of such extreme reaction as Davis's withdrawal after Sarah Knox Taylor's death, indicating deep depression, raise profound questions about his psychological state during that period. It was an unnatural bereavement, a paralyzing grief for too great a period of time.

Moreover, to travel with his new wife Varina, eighteen years old and on her honeymoon, to the grave of his former wife has a callousness about it. She was nineteen years younger than he, less experienced, eager to please her new husband. One wonders what words were exchanged, what emotions expressed and unexpressed, what memories carried forward by both bride and groom. For a man as considerate of women as Jefferson Davis was said to be, there is a strange and puzzling melancholy to his life, punctuated by his unwillingness to let go of his old love, even on his honeymoon, as if he had to show Varina that he was not giving all of himself to her.

Both Jefferson Davis and Judah Benjamin were childless in their marriages for an unusual length of time. It was not the custom of the times to do so. In the world of an ambitious planter-politician in the Delta, the seven childless years are even more at conflict with a way of life in which large families were expected than in New Orleans, where Benjamin was childless for ten years. That Varina in later life bore him six children testifies to her health and capacity to bear children; her letters to her mother testify to her eagerness from the start to have children. One cannot help but wonder if the years of brooding and the visit to the first wife's grave on the honeymoon were linked psychologically to the seven childless years of marriage. It is as if Davis had lost his way for a decade and a half, unsettled and disturbed, and sought a cure in building a plantation home and in politics. By reattaching himself to people, land, events, and issues, he began to recover his former vitality, his vigorous personality. His marriage to Varina signaled the beginning of his recovery, a return simultaneously to politics, the military, and the adventure in his previous life even as the shadows of his past remained.

Judah P. Benjamin, too, worked feverishly at his law books and at his Bellechasse, building it into a model sugar plantation. The names of their plantations were symbolic of their contrasting attitudes toward life: Brierfield was rugged and difficult; Bellechasse was peaceful, lovely, and French. Both Benjamin and Davis were consumed with their plantations and developed illness from overwork, but Benjamin drew strength from his absorptions, whereas Davis was debilitated by them. In contrast to Davis's isolation, Benjamin's answer to Natalie's desertion to Paris was a return to New Orleans and reinvolvement in its social and political life.

Perhaps Benjamin had a greater capacity for pretense. He pretended all his life that there was no strain in having a wife and daughter in Paris whom he saw one month a year. He seemed to take personal setbacks with equanimity. Davis's wounds penetrated more deeply and took years to heal. He was less flexible than Benjamin, more brittle. Even his return to Zachary Taylor's command for the Mexican War in 1846 seemed to Varina a rash act of escapism. She argued against it and "cried myself stupid" trying to persuade him not to leave Congress to pursue again a military career for which he professed a dislike. Perhaps it represented for him a return to the old and familiar psychological terrain, of fifteen years earlier, when he had met and won the General's beautiful daughter. He was repeating a previous step, as if he were starting life all over again.

Jefferson Davis and Judah Benjamin were not the best of husbands. Davis took long absences from Varina, rejoined the army without consulting her, and seemed to want to keep the past alive in his new marriage. Both men were addicted to their work and became fathers late in their marriages, and both were absorbed in their careers, with few friends or other interests.

Neither man was from the gentry, as one would expect the future leaders of the Confederacy to be. Davis was from yeoman stock and worked on a small farm as a boy. Like Benjamin, he was already a young adult when he came to know plantation life through his brother Joseph. Thus, at the center of the Southern leadership that would meet in Washington in 1852 were two outsiders, struggling for respectability, fighting to preserve a way of life they had attained but to which they were not born.

6

Washington:
Senate Duel

❦

ore than 80,000 people—one of the largest crowds in the capital's history—poured into Washington for the inauguration
of Franklin Pierce on March 4, 1853. Spectators lined Pennsylvania
Avenue in the mush of melting snow, hoping for a glimpse of the
new President. Inside the Capitol at noon, a dozen senators were
sworn in, among them Judah P. Benjamin of Louisiana, Stephen A.
Douglas of Illinois, and Sam Houston of Texas. A new generation
of men was assuming leadership, fiery orators of deep principles to
replace the great compromisers who had died in the previous three
years—Daniel Webster, Henry Clay, and John Calhoun.

Varina and Jefferson Davis attended the inauguration at the insistence of President-elect Pierce, who had hinted in his letter of invitation that he wanted to confer about a possible Cabinet position for
Davis.[1] Davis had spoken on Pierce's behalf during the summer and
fall campaign of 1852, because Pierce, though a former New Hamp-
shire governor and senator, expressed pro-slavery views and had
been nominated by the Democratic Party on the forty-ninth ballot
with Southern support. Davis, a military hero and West Point graduate
with political experience, was an obvious choice as Secretary of
War, and he reluctantly accepted. He was one of two Southerners
in the Pierce Cabinet.

Davis and his wife moved into a twenty-three-room mansion in

Washington. Varina invited her younger brother and sister to live there and pursue an education. The house was rented from Edward Everett, a former U.S. senator from Massachusetts and president of Harvard University (who ten years later would deliver the two-hour main address that preceded Abraham Lincoln's remarks at Gettysburg).

Judah P. Benjamin lived with two other Southern senators in a private home in a fashionable neighborhood near the Treasury, where many Southerners seemed to congregate out of a compatibility of political views and a mutual love of the social scene. Soon after the inauguration, Senator Benjamin received an invitation to attend a dinner at the White House. There he sat with Secretary of War Jefferson Davis and Varina—whose impressions of him are preserved in a long letter Varina wrote in 1898 to London *Times* correspondent Francis Lawley:

> I first met him at dinner at President Pierce's house, and well remember a distinct consciousness of disappointment. His type was decidely Hebrew; he had not a marked line in his face which was boyish in the extreme and was rendered more so by soft black curls about his temples and forehead; he was short and inclined to be fleshy, and had rather the air of a witty bon vivant than that of a great Senator. He seemed to prefer the light society topics rather than to impress upon his audience any grave utterance. He appeared to be, in fact, only an elegant young man of the world, and a past master in the art of witty repartee.

While physically she found him "decidedly Hebrew," she was struck by the sound of his voice and the elegance of his language:

> However, it would be difficult to convey to you the impression his voice made upon me; it seemed a silver thread woven amidst the warp and woof of sounds which filled the drawing room; it was low, full and soft; yet the timbre of it penetrated every ear like a silver trumpet. From the first sentence he uttered, whatever he said, attracted and chained the attention of his audience.

At their first meeting there was some tension between Benjamin and Davis. It continued through many years in Washington:

> Mr. Benjamin and Mr. Davis were too much alike, in many respects, to be at first very good friends. They had the same tireless mental energy, the same quick perception, the same nervously excitable

tempers. They were both quick at repartee and whatever they knew was as ready for reference in the heat of debate as it had been when they first acquired it. They were both ambitious men, and led their party.

"Too much alike"—particularly in competitive aspiration: They were taking the measure of each other, both leaders of the Southern bloc, even at that early point. Neither man had been conditioned by his history to trust easily, each was supremely self-confident, each was respectful but wary.

"Sometime," Varina continued in her letter to Lawley, "when they did not agree on a measure, hot words in glacial, polite phrases passed between them, and they had up to the year of secession little social intercourse; an occasional invitation to dinner was accepted and exchanged, and nothing more."

Still, she came to like Benjamin immensely, finding his charm irresistible. She recalled a dinner table disagreement over a small social point in which she playfully remarked, "If I let you set one stone, you will build a cathedral before I knew it"; to which Benjamin laughed and replied, "If it should prove to be the shrine of truth, you will worship there with me, I am sure."[2]

Judah P. Benjamin's reputation as an orator grew to towering heights over the next few tumultuous years. The South was looking for a spokesman, and the Southern press printed his eloquent speeches with relish.

Soon after his election to the Senate, his career almost took another extraordinary turn. In the fall of 1852, the outgoing President, Millard Fillmore, offered him a seat on the U.S. Supreme Court. It was a seat that had been promised to a Southerner who could represent the Fifth Circuit (consisting of Alabama and Louisiana) held by the late Justice John McKinley. The Democrats in the Senate were not going to approve the nominations of a lame-duck Whig President and rejected three candidates that Fillmore put forward. On February 15, 1853, the New York *Times* reported that "if the President nominates Benjamin, the Democrats are determined to confirm him." It predicted that "Mr. Benjamin, the new Senator, if nominated would properly be confirmed." Fillmore was turning to the leading lawyer in the Senate in the probability that he would be confirmed, since the Senate could not reject one of its own members from the deep South, albeit newly elected. Benjamin turned down the offer, preferring the give-and-take of the Senate and looking forward possibly to representing clients before the Supreme Court.³ It would require another sixty years before the first Jew would sit on the nation's highest court. Fillmore, probably on Benjamin's recommendation, actually nominated two of Benjamin's New Orleans law partners, E. A. Bradford (who would join the firm in a month) and William Micou (already his partner), but neither was confirmed, as the Senate awaited the inauguration of Franklin Pierce. Benjamin would be the ranking member of a law firm of which three partners had been considered for the nation's highest court. If Benjamin preferred the challenge of the political arena, history would not disappoint him.

After Davis was named Secretary of War, his son, Sam, born in 1852, became a favorite of Mrs. Franklin Pierce, who insisted that Varina bring him often to the White House. But in June 1854 the child suddenly came down with yellow fever, and the dread disease claimed a second love from Jefferson Davis's life.

Varina later wrote about the impact of their only son's death on her husband. "For months afterward," she wrote, "he walked around the house half the night, and worked fiercely all day. A child's cry in the street well nigh drove him mad."⁴

Davis was a well-organized Secretary of War, so scrupulous in his duties that he would not even let Varina use his official stationery for a thank-you note. Mrs. Clement Clay, the wife of the Alabama senator and a friend of Varina, wrote that Davis had a reputation as an honest watchdog of such determination that "it would be impossible to cheat the government out of a brass button." He increased the army's strength from 10,745 to 15,752; reorganized the system of forts across the plains; introduced improved muskets and rifles; developed an advanced system of infantry tactics; substituted iron for wood in gun carriages; began the use of the steel ball, which improved the accuracy of guns; and promoted experiments in breech-loading rifles for faster firing and the use of heavy guns in coastal defenses. He commanded the Corps of Engineers and began the surveys for a railroad route to the West to contribute to a political and economic alliance between the South and the West. Interestingly, he opposed the creation of a military academy in the South on the grounds that it was proper for West Point to develop "a national point of view in the young men from different states that attended it." William Lee, a clerk under him, said, "He was one of the best Secretaries of War that ever served."⁵

President Pierce perhaps saw in Davis what others did not: that he possessed an extraordinary capacity for military management and skilled administration. He had made his reputation as a fighting officer, and nothing, not even his plantation career, had prepared him for managing such a large enterprise as the United States Army. Yet, he was a military visionary with a determined interest in shaping the future of the army, whether it concerned weaponry or tactics, and he would seek out the best men to help him.

Davis's admiration for Southern Jews may have had its origins in his interaction with an extraordinary Jewish army officer at West Point and later when Davis served as Secretary of War.

Several years before Davis arrived at West Point, Alfred Mordecai had graduated first in his class at the military academy as an engineer and ordnance expert. Born in North Carolina of German Jewish parents, he was one of the first Jews to graduate from the U.S. Military Academy and was of such rare talent that he was brought back to West Point as a teacher from 1823 through 1825. He taught Cadet Jefferson Davis, who arrived in September of 1824. Mordecai had an illustrious forty-year military career; he was involved in testing, developing, and analyzing the weapons, ammunition, ballistics, and metallurgy of new weapons and reorganizing the production of durable, uniform, and efficient tools of war.[6]

As Secretary of War, Davis tapped Major Mordecai, who had drafted the first U.S. Army *Ordnance Manual* in 1841, to serve on a military commission, all three of whose members had placed first or second in their West Point classes (one of them was the future Union General George McClellan). The commission was ordered to spend six months in Europe observing the Crimean War and studying weapons, method of organization, supply systems, and the command structure of the armies of Britain, France, Austria, and Russia. It was a mission of the utmost importance, in Davis's view, and he asked for detailed reports to help shape the future of the American military. The series of reports was considered so important that the Congress authorized the printing of 20,000 copies of some of the reports, which ultimately influenced the type of weaponry used by the armies of the North and the South. After Mordecai's return from Europe, Secretary Davis kept him as an aide, even while Mordecai sought a more active post.

At the beginning of the Civil War, Davis offered Mordecai the position of Chief of Ordnance for the Confederacy. At the same time, political figures in North Carolina asked Mordecai to become general of the state armies. His North Carolina family pleaded with him to return, and after a long period of deliberation, he decided to resign from the army altogether, to avoid the agonizing choice, and live as a civilian teacher of mathematics in Philadelphia. Mordecai was one of thirty Southern officers in the U.S. Army to take that step, unable to fight for the North against their families or for the South against their flag. Had he accepted, both the Chief of Ordnance and the Secretary of War to the Confederacy would have been Southern Jews.[7]

Varina wrote of him in her *Memoir* that "Major Mordecai was a Hebrew, and one could readily understand, after seeing him, how the race had furnished the highest type of manhood; his mind was versatile, at times even playful, but his habits of thought were of the most serious problems . . . his moral nature was as well disciplined as his mental. . . . He was an 'Israelite without guile.' "[8]

One of the ideas that Davis asked Mordecai and the Commissioners to investigate was "the use of camels for transportation, and their adaptation to cold and mountainous countries," and Davis eventually commissioned a camel corps in the American West.[9] He had been struck by the loss of horses and mules on the wagon trains west to California in the 1850s. So Davis persuaded President Pierce to appropriate thirty thousand dollars to buy and train thirty-three camels a year for two years and the men to use them. They were purchased in Egypt and landed in Indianola, Texas, an exotic moment in history. They were a disaster and a total embarrassment to Varina, who bore the brunt of the teasing from which her husband's office protected him. The animals were afraid to wade streams, for when had a camel seen rushing water? They would wander off to feed on bushes and shrubs and spit at their army riders. The packs would slip off their backs, because their equipment was designed for mules. Horses whinnied all night if the camels were stabled anywhere near them. Finally, they were auctioned off to Mexicans, circuses, or just turned loose by disgusted soldiers to be eaten in the desert by jackals and wolves. The episode remained a well-known comic incident in Davis's otherwise illustrious career.

The Secretary of War extended his interests beyond military affairs; his influence over a weak president grew so strong that a Mississippi newspaper called him "the de facto president" and "the great Mogul." Davis persuaded Pierce to support the Kansas–Nebraska bill in 1854, which broke up the Compromise of 1850, allowing slavery in the territories. The political reaction swept across the country, opening wounds most of the nation thought had been healed and deepening divisions between North and South. It created the Republican Party, summoned Abraham Lincoln back to political life, and started a bloody civil war in Kansas.

In New Orleans the Whigs deserted the Republicans for a know-nothing alternative, and Judah P. Benjamin transferred his allegiance to the Democratic Party and continued to lead the arguments for states rights, claiming he had only "changed name, not principle."

He attacked the know-nothing Whigs for expelling the Louisiana delegation because it was largely Catholic, saying their anti-Catholicism had revealed "hideous features . . . in all their naked deformity." The Whigs, he said, were "held together not by the ties of a common belief in certain principles and measures of public policy, but simply by their preference of themselves as the right kind of men for office holders." Benjamin continued:

> Although the Democratic party is not yet so thoroughly disorganized as the Whig party, it requires no political sagacity to perceive that it cannot maintain itself as a national party. . . . Impressed with these views of public affairs, I shall hold aloof from the present state canvass. I will not even join the attempt to revive the organization of the Whig party. Its ashes alone remain, and the Phoenix is equally a fable in political as in natural history. I shall await the fast approaching time when not only Louisiana but the entire South, animated by a single spirit, shall struggle for its dearest rights, and in defense of that Constitution which is their most precious heritage.[10]

The Washington *Union* called his conversion speech one of the most powerful ever delivered on any subject. "He ought to have been a Democrat long ago," it editorialized, and the *Courier* echoed the phrase.[11] He and John Slidell became leaders of the "Buchaneers," a group that took over the Democratic National Convention in 1856 to nominate James Buchanan for President, and in the election defeated the "Black Republicans" to maintain a "sacred balance," as Buchanan put it, between North and South.

Just before his term as Secretary of War was to end in 1857, Davis decided to run again for his Senate seat in Mississippi. He refused to leave Washington to campaign, stating to a friend that it was a matter of personal honor that he not violate the trust of his Cabinet post. It was an example of his exaggerated pride prevailing over practicalities, which was misinterpreted as arrogance. He carried the Mississippi state legislature by only one vote, the closest election of his career. He had won two elections without electioneering and had drawn from the results false lessons for the future. The gritty reality of politics would be beneath his dignity, wheeling and dealing with local politicians violated his principles, and he had mistakenly concluded that, in politics, high-minded personal honor would carry the day over his opponents.

Davis had already established his reputation as a defender of the South in his earlier Senate term and in his forays into politics as a Cabinet member. But by 1859 the debates were becoming fiercer, with less room for compromise. Still, he broke with the "fire eaters" in his own state by opposing the revival of the slave trade. Other Southerners, including Benjamin, voted with him, but there was only a particle of idealism involved in Davis's case. The influx of additional slaves would have reduced the value of the slaves of the largest planters, and Davis believed that Mississippi had as many slaves as it needed.

Davis's speeches in the Senate were legalistic, not inspiring, yet competent and respected. States rights was his battle cry, and he never budged from the strictest construction of the Constitution, which gave the states absolute authority over their own affairs. He even opposed the Morrill Land Grant Act to establish agricultural colleges on the grounds that the Southern states needed no federal aid. As for the long-term solution to the problem of slavery, he believed that "the slave must be made fit for his freedom by education and discipline and thus made unfit for slavery."[12]

While he had always been a sectionalist, he harbored ambitions of running for President of the United States. Indicative of his national perspective, he advocated a transcontinental railroad to develop the West, but even that idea could be defended at home as providing a new market for Southern products.

Judah P. Benjamin, on the other hand, believed that there were constitutional problems in building a transcontinental railroad without the consent of the states, and other Southerners opposed it as a device to strengthen the political power of the North. But Davis's answer was to construct the railroad before the territories became states. While he was narrow on interpreting the Constitution as to states rights, Davis was always expansionist in foreign policy, advocating the extension of Texas to the Rio Grande and the acquisition of Cuba, as well as the building of the railroad to the West.

Although he was a sectionalist, he was not yet a secessionist eager to found a separate Southern republic. He wished to live in peace and union with the North in a nation extending to the Pacific, but his obsession was to establish the Constitution as a federal compact of states, with limited powers for the Federal government. The union he envisaged included the right to own slaves. Slavery itself was no longer subjected to rational debate; he masked it in doctrinaire legalism.

Various observers noted his poor health during the 1850s. Varina wrote that he entered the Senate in 1850 "pale and emaciated from the nervous pain"[13] and that in 1854 "he had escaped his usual attacks of fever this fall for the first time since he has been in public life."[14] In the campaign for governor in 1851, he was confined to his home for three weeks with pneumonia; at the same time, Varina reported that his eyes were so weakened that he could not read or write and had to wear goggles when he came out of his darkened room.[15] In defending a trip to the North before the Mississippi legislature in 1858, he said he had been ordered by doctors to seek a cooler climate and to escape from tensions and described himself as wasted by "protracted, violent disease."[16] According to one writer, "his brow [was] furrowed and his hair frosted by the passage of time."[17] He was so seriously ill during the winter of 1857–58 that he appeared in the Senate infrequently, "emaciated and head bandaged, leaning on a cane."

Benjamin commented on Davis's poor health in a letter to a friend in New Orleans in 1858, indicating the serious state of his condition: "Poor Jeff Davis is very ill; his recovery is quite doubtful. He has lost his left eye by an ulcer which has been formed in it, and I fear it may affect sympathetically the other. He will certainly be unable to attend to any business this session."[18]

In 1860 the editor of the Cincinnati *Commercial* described Davis at fifty-one as "haggard looking," prematurely gray, with hands that were "thin, bloodless, bony, and nerveless."[19]

During the Pierce administration, while Davis was restrained from daily partisan politics by his role in the Cabinet, Judah Benjamin emerged as the most eloquent Southern spokesman in the Senate. He debated Senator William Seward of New York, the only man for whom he ever showed an intense dislike in public, and Senator Charles Sumner of Massachusetts, both leading Abolitionists, with barbed wit and ardent defenses of states rights, which the editors across the South relished in their newspapers.

The Constitution, he claimed, was a "compact" among equals. "Take away this league of love," he argued, his voice fervent with sincerity, "convert it into a bond of distrust; of suspicion, or of hate; and the entire fabric which is held together by that cement will crumble to the earth, and rest scattered in dishonest fragments upon the ground."

He used every orator's tactic to point out the inconsistency in the Abolitionist position. For example, he proposed that the Kansas–Nebraska question be submitted to the Supreme Court and argued that it was "strange, strange, sir," that the South, the section of the Union with a reputation of being "so excited, so passionate, so violent," was ready to submit the question to the court but that "the calm, cold, quiet, calculating North, always obeying the law, always subservient to the behest of the Constitution, whenever this question of slavery arises—and this alone—appeals to Sharpe's rifles instead of courts of justice."[20] Benjamin's position was not without a calculation of its own. The proslavery Dred Scott decision the next year, which held that Congress could not outlaw slavery in any territory under its jurisdiction, proved that the South had a majority on the Court, as Northerners had suspected.

Judah Benjamin's style in the Senate was to combine his official role with the use of social occasions for political purposes, especially to keep the lines of communication open to his opponents. In that way he functioned as a constructive senator, the kind who sought compromise and the common ground, who worked hard, even during his private hours in Washington, at maintaining the Senate's historic role as a deliberative body.

"Mr. Benjamin was exceedingly hospitable," Varina Davis wrote of him, "and had such perfect self-control that he felt able to bring the extreme men of each party together at his table; indeed he even hoped at one time to bridge the river of bitterness which flowed wide and brimming over between the North and South by bringing representative men of both sections together. If any man could have succeeded in doing this, his sweet disposition, rigid mastery of his temper, and thoroughbred manner would have eminently qualified him for success; but unfortunately the men of the North did not want to compromise any manner of dispute."[21]

Varina wrote admiringly about that quality of Benjamin because it was so much in contrast with the manner of her husband, who was stoical, distant, and so principled that even at dinner parties "there was an unspoken feeling of avoidance between the political men of both sections."[22] Jefferson Davis possibly saw Benjamin's efforts at compromise as a weakness or equivocation over what he regarded as rock-hard issues of principle.

Though she never revealed it toward Benjamin, Varina shared the stereotypical thinking about Jews that characterized Southerners of her era. When she described Major Alfred Mordecai as an "Israelite without guile,"[23] there is no reason to doubt that, following a prevailing view of the times, she considered Major Mordecai an exception to the general rule. Benjamin, the master of political negotiation and shrewd interplay with his opponents, may have conformed to the stereotype, but Varina was capable of appreciating his qualities.

A number of stories have been told that are illustrative of Benjamin's attitude toward Judaism in his Senate years. One of the most often-quoted is from Isaac Mayer Wise, the famous American rabbi, who wrote in his *Reminiscences* (1874) about a visit to Washington, which he dated as occurring in 1850, when he participated in a religious discussion with Daniel Webster, Lieutenant Matthew F. Maurer, later a well-known inventor and oceanographer, and Judah Benjamin. Wise writes that Webster turned to Benjamin and said, "Mr. Senator, my friend is of your race. I would have said coreligionist, but I do not know how much or how little you believe; and in truth, we four are all coreligionists, since we are all Unitarians. . . . Benjamin protested likewise, since in his opinion Judaism and Christianity were entirely different."

Wise continued that Benjamin was so intrigued with the discussion that he invited all three men to dinner for further conversation that night. Wise described the discussion of the others and closed by writing, "Benjamin alone was not satisfied. He had a confused notion of orthodox Portuguese Judaism; and although he rarely heard anything about it, and was never guided by it, he yet insisted that he had no coreligionists beside the Jews. The conversation was most interesting to me; only I felt very sorry that Benjamin could not cite one Jewish source, while Webster was thoroughly versed in the Bible, and had a full knowledge of history."[24]

Bertram Korn, a scholar of American Jewish history, challenged the story on the grounds that it could not have taken place in 1850, because Benjamin did not take office as a Senator until 1853, and Webster had died the year before. Wise might easily have been mistaken about the date and the participants other than Benjamin; it is doubtful, however, that he would have been mistaken in the substance of the conversation with America's first Jewish U.S. Senator. The story is important, because it is one of the few recorded instances of Benjamin's acknowledgment of his Jewishness, and it comes from the published memoir of one of the most distinguished rabbis of the day.

Historians cite another minor incident as evidence of a Jewish consciousness on Benjamin's part. Gershom Kursheedt, the leader of the New Orleans Jewish community, wrote on March 20, 1848, to his friend Isaac Leeser, publisher of the *Occident,* one of the most important Jewish publications of the times: "Before I forget it let me state on Friday last Mr. J. P. Benjamin handed me $5.50 for you." He enclosed the payment, which he suggested was for Benjamin's subscription to the *Occident.* Leeser had sent free copies five years earlier to a list of distinguished Jews in hopes they would later subscribe. While Korn dismisses the incident as a tardy payment of a one-time renewal, he pointed out that it did confirm that Leeser identified Benjamin as a Jew in 1843 and that Benjamin knew Kursheedt as a trusted agent of Leeser. It also is evidence that Benjamin received the *Occident,* possibly for a long period of time, and presumably read it and thought well enough of it to renew his subscription.[25]

In 1854, discrimination against Jews in an American treaty with Switzerland aroused Jewish public opinion across the country. Swiss cantons (the equivalent of counties in America) would not allow Jews to take up residence within their borders, and the Swiss government insisted in the treaty that each canton be permitted to determine whether non-Christian American citizens should be exempted from such restrictions. Benjamin has been criticized by Jewish scholars for not speaking immediately on the subject of the treaty, but Senator Lewis Cass (later Secretary of State) spoke eloquently against the treaty. In Benjamin's behalf, other scholars have suggested that perhaps Benjamin thought it better and more effective that the stage be left to supportive non-Jews. He was not silent on the subject of the rights of Jewish Americans abroad. According to the *Congressional Globe,* "Mr. Benjamin presented . . . a petition of citizens of the United States, professing the Jewish religion, praying that measures may be taken to secure to American citizens of every religious creed, residing or traveling abroad, their civil and religious rights; which was referred to the Committee on Foreign Relations."[26]

While a member of the Senate, Benjamin appeared in a number of cases before the U.S. Supreme Court. He was not alone in such activity; the Supreme Court was located in a room in the Capitol and customarily heard from senators. He would learn that even the lofty office of U.S. Senator did not protect him from religious prejudice. Once, after he had made a particularly brilliant pleading, a Supreme Court Justice said to the opposing lawyer as the lawyer passed on his way to the podium to counter Benjamin: "You had better look to your laurels, for that little Jew from New Orleans has stated your case out of court."[27]

Benjamin not only argued before the Supreme Court in behalf of clients while in the Senate but also made many business trips as a lawyer to California, Ecuador, the Galapagos Islands, and Mexico. The Mexican trip in 1857 was to revive once again the Tehuantepec railroad across the Isthmus by influencing the Mexican government through his friendship with President Buchanan and Secretary of State Cass. He went with several associates, and the *True Delta* reported: "We all know how . . . little Benjamin ran from one saloon to another in Mexico, pulling out from his breeches pocket in each, the well-thumbed autograph of the Sage of Wheatland [Buchanan] which, like Mahomet's signet, the little babbler fancied would be gazed upon and obeyed by his astounded acquaintance in the halls of Montezuma."[28]

Benjamin succeeded in securing from President Juarez a right of transit for sixty years plus an option for an additional twenty-five years, as well as 500,000 acres of right of way on the banks of rivers. In Washington, he even arranged for the Postmaster General to deliver California mail via the Tehuantepec route for one year and set up a trip to England to purchase the iron to begin laying tracks.

Benjamin must have counted on the project to be resurrected after the Civil War. In the National Archives in Washington are the contents of a black box belonging to Benjamin that had been confiscated by Union troops. The box contained twenty-nine bonds of the Tehuantepec Company at $1,000 each; certificates of company stock in his name for $94,100; and a record showing he was to receive $45,000 in bonds as a commission upon the issuance of $900,000 in bonds for the new company.[29] It was a project combining private gain and public good, and he would have profited greatly in both ways had it been built, but the Northern senators would never have supported, at that point in history, a project of such benefit to the South. The war and other events undermined the project permanently. For twenty years, Tehuantepec had remained his personal mirage that always seemed just beyond his grasp. Though he worked on it all through his public career, it would never be realized.

One of Benjamin's most important cases was *United States* v. *Castillero*, involving the title to the New Almaden silver mine in California, at that time one of the richest silver mines in the world. Castillero was a Mexican officer who had received his title from the Governor of Mexico in 1845, but once California became a state, the U.S. government sought to declare his claim invalid and, in a sense, confiscate his property. The case went to the U.S. Supreme Court eventually and was the most important of many mining cases involving valuable metals and mineral rights stemming from statehood.[30]

Castillero's case was different from those of other Mexican nationals who lost property because he had leased his mine to wealthy English mining interests, which were extracting millions of dollars of silver a year and therefore had sufficient money to battle the claim. The litigation went on for ten years, with Benjamin and four other lawyers representing Castillero and therefore the English company.

Benjamin spent four months in San Francisco in the fall of 1860, and his opening argument lasted four days. He charged the government with "spoliation and oppression" and with violation of its treaties. "There is no treaty of the Government of the United States pledging the faith of a great nation in favor of one single quartz-miner in the State of California; but there is a published treaty pledging in the faith of a great nation in favor of a Mexican mineowner, whose Government ceded this territory to the United States; ceding to us nought but what it held itself. We acquired from Mexico nothing but what Mexico owned, and she did not own this mine when she ceded this territory to the United States. It belonged to one of her citizens. She did not claim it—did not pretend it was hers. Whence then the right of the Government of the United States?"[31]

The case did not reach the U.S. Supreme Court until 1863, and even though he was then a high official in the Confederacy in the midst of a war, the counsels for the company filed his brief with the court. With three judges dissenting, Benjamin's clients lost their case. Benjamin reportedly received $25,000, one of the largest fees paid for legal services in this country up to that time.

Benjamin's visit to California became the source of another debate concerning his attitude toward his Jewishness. Herbert Ezekiel, the Richmond historian, reported in his book *The History of the Jews of Richmond from 1769 to 1917* that "there are those who seem to delight in claiming that Benjamin was not a Jew, because he took no part in communal affairs. . . . No less an authority than the late Dr. Isaac M. Wise told the writer that Benjamin delivered an address in the synagogue in San Francisco on Yom Kippur, 1860."[32]

Wise's oral recollection has been contested by Bertram Korn, who analyzed it in detail in a 1949 article for the American Jewish Historical Society publication.[33] Korn said that Wise had never been in San Francisco and relied on the only Jewish newspaper there, *The Gleaner,* for all of his information about San Francisco. *The Gleaner* did not report such a speech, Korn wrote, and most assuredly would have done so had it occurred. What *The Gleaner* did report, as Korn quoted it at length, was a speech by Benjamin at a local academy, and Korn suggests that Wise's memory was playing tricks on him. The paper reported that Benjamin "next referred in a very happy manner to the injustice in the distribution of offices and asked why the citizens of his religious tenets were not favored by those who have it in their power to bestow offices of emolument and trust. In a very pathetic manner he asked, 'Would the great Washington have excluded a citizen from holding a federal appointment because of his religion?' "

Korn claimed that the author of the article in *The Gleaner* confused that speech with one that Benjamin delivered in the Church of the Advent in San Francisco, where Benjamin and his co-counsel in the *Castillero* case did appear at a fundraising event to win the favor of the pastor, who was the son of the judge in *Castillero.* A letter in the National Archives, probably from one of the government lawyers in the case, reports with some sarcasm mixed with admiration that the lectures put "some two or three thousand dollars into the fingers of the Judge's son. When you consider that Benjamin is a Jew, his labors in behalf of a Christian church display a spirit of toleration pretty nearly unexampled."

Korn sums up by saying, "Isn't it ironic that the only instance in which Benjamin was supposed to have spoken in a synagogue turns out to be one of the many occasions when he spoke in, or for, the benefit of a church?"[34]

However, Korn's statements rest on assumptions about the sources of Wise's information that may or may not have been correct. What may be more indicative about the incident is that Wise, who was one of America's most celebrated rabbis and a contemporary of Benjamin, did not think such a report was as incredible as later historians considered it to be and was confident enough of its possible veracity to repeat it to one of the principal Southern Jewish historians of the time.

Benjamin also traveled for a client to Ecuador and the Galapagos

Islands to check on guano deposits, which would have provided cheaper fertilizer for Southern agriculture. Had it succeeded, newspapers wrote, he would have made $200,000, but the reports of large deposits turned out to be false.[35] Contacts in Europe were refreshed during his annual trips to Paris to visit Natalie and Ninette, and from time to time, European clients engaged Benjamin. It is estimated that he made $40,000 to $50,000 a year as a lawyer during the 1850s, an extraordinary sum for that time.[36]

After Buchanan's election, Benjamin sought through John Slidell the ambassadorship to France in order to be near his family, according to the *True Delta.* The paper also reported that Slidell was trying to obtain the ambassadorship to Spain for the husband of his niece, August Belmont, the New York lawyer who represented the Rothschild family. "Both gentlemen are of the Hebrew faith," the *True Delta* noted, "as is, I believe, Senator Slidell himself."[37] When Belmont turned down the offer to Spain, Slidell pushed Benjamin, who received a letter from Buchanan on August 31, 1858:

> I write for the purpose of tendering you the appointment of Minister of Spain and expressing a strong desire that you may accept it. I feel satisfied that the Country will unite with me in opinion that this is an appointment eminently fit to be made. Indeed I am not acquainted with any gentleman who possesses superior, if equal, qualifications to yourself for this important mission. Such being the case I think your Country has a right to benefit of your services.

Buchanan then added, "I told your friend Slidell yesterday that he might inform you I had determined to offer you the Spanish mission and his letter may probably reach you before this can arrive."[38] He then sought to reassure Benjamin that he was not being relegated to political oblivion: "Repeating my ardent wish that you may accept the mission and assuring you that I shall do all in my power to make it agreeable to yourself, useful to your Country and promotive to your own fame." The offer was made public and was applauded by the Jewish press, sensing the irony of his returning to the land from which his ancestors were expelled. But it was ultimately rejected by Benjamin, who had second thoughts and decided to remain in the Senate.

Benjamin's Jewishness was never far from the minds of his Senate opponents. Once, during the debate on the extension of slavery into Kansas, Senator Ben Wade of Ohio goaded Benjamin: "Why, sir, when old Moses, under the immediate inspiration of God Almighty, enticed a whole nation of slaves, and ran away, not to Canada, but to old Canaan, I suppose that Pharaoh and all the chivalry of old Egypt denounced him as a most furious abolitionist . . . there were not those who loved Egypt better than they loved liberty. . . . They were not exactly Northern men with Southern principles; but they were Israelites with Egyptian principles."

There is some debate as to Benjamin's answer, and historians differ as to whether the remarks attributable to Benjamin were actually uttered by him, but the legend of his answer exists and should be recorded. "It is true that I am a Jew," he is reported to have said, "and when my ancestors were receiving their Ten Commandments from the immediate hand of Diety, amidst the thunderings and lightnings of Mount Sinai, the ancestors of my opponent were herding swine in the forests of Great Britain."[39]

Historians provide at least four different versions of when, where, and to whom that retort was made. Disraeli is also said to have made a similar one. The quote cannot be verified, but the statement remains a part of the legend of Judah P. Benjamin, even though it indicates an uncharacteristic acknowledgement in public of his Jewishness.

There are a number of physical descriptions of Benjamin during this period. From the photographs and paintings, one can see that he had inherited a full Mediterranean face from his Portuguese father—the large Sephardic forehead, a wide fleshy nose, thin lips, and bright, dark eyes. As Varina pointed out, there was an olive cast to his complexion, and his dark, curly hair completed the stereotyped portrait of the Jew among the Gentiles. Benjamin's features and coloring reminded him every day of his life that in the race-conscious South, others saw only the face of the Jew when they spoke to him.

He wore no moustache, and his beard was closely cropped. His optimistic and ebullient manner made him easily approachable by strangers. His ample cheeks, almost cherubic in their plumpness, seemed to tug the corners of his mouth upward into a permanent half-smile, giving him the amiable aura of a man at peace with himself and content in his life's work. The smile, which contrasted with the angry mood of almost everyone else in the U.S. Senate, became even more noticeable as the somber reality of war divided friends and families. It infuriated his enemies and gave solace to his friends. No matter how tense the situation, brutal the debate, or dark the event, whether before juries or generals or kings, Judah P. Benjamin appeared serene and unflappable, his smile reflecting, to observers, almost a nonchalance over whatever issues confronted him.

Varina wrote of another side of him to Lawley that "notwithstanding Mr. Benjamin's sweet-tempered, considerate ways with mankind in general, he was a very high-spirited, sensitive man, and somewhat touchy in his intercourse with others. He fought at least one duel before he came into the Senate, and several times narrowly escaped repetition of the same catastrophe while serving there."[40]

What she neglected to mention was that her husband was possibly the near "catastrophe" to which she was referring. A dramatic moment in the personal histories of both men occurred in 1858 in the midst of a routine discussion over the purchase of breech-loading arms in an Army appropriation bill. Military supply and weapons was a subject about which Davis considered himself to be absolutely expert in the Senate, and he was rarely challenged. The *Congressional Globe* reported the discussion that was on the record, and other participants filled in the details:

BENJAMIN: I do not understand that the Secretary of War has asked for any part of this $100,000 here appropriated in the House bill, to purchase the breech-loading arms. If he has, I am very much mistaken.

DAVIS: Oh, I will state the very simple fact that he asks money to buy breech-loading guns. Whether it is in this $100,000 or out of the Treasury, I do not know.

BENJAMIN: It is easy for the Senator from Mississippi to give a sneering reply to what was certainly a very respectful inquiry.

DAVIS: I consider it is an attempt to misrepresent a very plain remark.

BENJAMIN: The Senator is mistaken and has no right to state any such things. His manner is not agreeable at all.

DAVIS: If the Senator finds it disagreeable, I hope he will keep it to himself.

BENJAMIN: When directed to me, I will not keep it to myself; I will repel it instanter.

DAVIS: You have got it, sir.

BENJAMIN: That is enough, sir.[41]

Benjamin then proceeded to complete his remarks on muskets while Davis's anger apparently subsided. Others reported that Davis then hissed in a low voice that he had "no idea that he was to be met with the arguments of a paid attorney in the Senate chamber." Benjamin inquired if he had heard correctly the words "paid attorney," at which Davis glared at him and replied, "Yes, those were the very words."

Tom Bayard, the son of the Senator from Delaware, took notes on what followed:

> Benjamin peremptorily challenged Jefferson Davis for rude language in debate and brought the note to my father in the session to be copied and delivered. My father handed the note to Davis in the cloakroom of the Senate. He read it and at once tore it up and said "I will make this all right at once. I have been wholly wrong." He walked back to his desk in the Senate, and at the first opportunity, rose and made the most distinct withdrawal of what he had said, and regretted any offense most amply. No one in the Senate but my father knew what had called forth from Davis this apology; for Benjamin had sat down in silence when Davis made the rude interruption. But writing instantly at his desk, Benjamin called him to account by the note, which contained a direct challenge, without asking for a withdrawal or an explanation.[42]

Davis apologized in the well of the Senate, on the record, saying "I have been wholly wrong. . . . I cannot gainsay that my manner implied more than my heart meant." His behavior, he said, was "sometimes unfortunate, and is sometimes, as my best friends have told me, of a character which would naturally impress that I intended to be dogmatic and dictatorial."

Benjamin replied that he had been hurt by the tone of the remarks from one whom he respected and admired and that he would forget all between them "except the pleasant passage of the morning."

What is extraordinary about the incident is that it reflects totally uncharacteristic qualities in both men. Varina was mistaken when she wrote that Benjamin had previously been involved in a duel. Even for one who lived as a young man in so raucous a city as New Orleans, there is absolutely no record, not even the suggestion, of dueling in his earlier life. His challenge was hurled at the spur of the moment from an experienced Jewish lawyer-senator who had kept his cool demeanor under far greater provocation in courtrooms, in political clashes in Louisiana, and on the Senate floor. He was always, in similar situations, the master of the counterthrust in debate, handling challenges deftly. In addition, the issue was so minor, even meaningless, that the exchange obviously represented something deeper than what was on the surface.

From Jefferson Davis, a contained and controlled military man, who had battled the most acid Yankee tongues in the Senate on far greater matters without a flicker of anger, the outburst was also unusual. And he was facing the inquiry not of an avowed enemy but of a colleague who shared his views on almost every matter of substance.

In her letter to Lawley, Varina described Benjamin in the incident in general terms, but the reader senses a defense of her husband between the lines:

> Each time he had an angry contest with any of his colleagues, someone was sure to say, "How can anyone get provoked with Mr. Benjamin; he is so gentle and courteous." In fact, the truth was that Mr. Benjamin's courtesy in argument was like the salute of the duelist to his antagonist whom he intends to kill if possible. He was master of the art of inductive reasoning, and when he had smilingly established his point, he dealt the coup de grace with a fierce joy which his antagonist fully appreciated and resented. I never knew him in those days to be very much in earnest without infuriating his antagonist beyond measure. Mr. Slidell, who loved him like a brother, once said to Mr. Davis, "When I do not agree with Benjamin I will not let him talk to me; he irritates me so by his debonair ways."[43]

Perhaps that irritation with Benjamin's manner pricked Davis's ordinary veneer of control so deeply that he could not contain himself. Davis had been called up short trying to finesse a budgetary item that was not listed in the War Department budget, and perhaps he was more angry at himself than at Benjamin. It is also possible that he could not fathom Benjamin's motive, and leaped upon the most unseemly prospect—that a possible client was involved—without any evidence except gossip. While it was unlike Davis ever to back down in an argument, he obviously realized his error and apologized immediately.

Benjamin, on the other hand, was stunned at the sneering response, all the more so since it came from a political friend. He had regularly raised questions of waste and economy in government. He probably considered the question to Davis to be a routine clarification, not an effort to embarrass a fellow-Southerner. Benjamin was deeply sensitive to the charge of dishonesty: Suspicion of his representing a client's interest would undermine his reputation as a Senator. He could not let so serious a charge stand without correction, especially from someone as respected by other Southerners in the Senate as Davis. Benjamin chose the clearest possible way to challenge Davis, one that word of mouth would carry all over the Senate. Knowing Davis to be a man of impeccable honor who would recognize the error, Benjamin probably counted on the return of Davis's customary coolness under fire, in which case an apology would be forthcoming. Benjamin guessed right, and the cavalry man from Buena Vista did not take up the gauntlet of his rotund opponent, who had never served a day in the army. In the long run, Davis would respect a man who would not allow anyone to stain his character, especially one who adhered to a Southern standard as high as his own. Davis was large enough in spirit to withdraw an unconsidered insult and to do it publicly.

Political enemies in rival factions in Louisiana plotted against Benjamin in his reelection campaign in 1858, searching his voting record for weaknesses. The *True Delta* referred to him as a "subservient creature" of John Slidell and said that "we do not want a Senator to say ditto" whenever an issue or a vote arose. If no other candidate than Benjamin could be found, the paper urged, "then, in God's name, let Slidell himself be chosen, for he may just as well have two votes in his own person as to be able, on every occasion, to command the service accompaniment of his facile coadjutor."[44]

The heart of the *True Delta*'s claim and the most publicized issue against Benjamin was a charge of scandal linking him to Slidell concerning title to a tract of 20,000 acres in an area of several hundred thousand acres 50 miles north of New Orleans that belonged originally to the Houmas Indians.[45] The title to the land was vague, but it had been purchased in good faith by Slidell and business associates in 1835. Because of the vagueness of title, a large number of squatters had settled on the land, believing it to be wilderness, and speculators, taking advantage of that belief, had also sold land to other unsuspecting settlers.

Benjamin presided over the Committee on Private Land Claims in the Senate and managed to slip a provision into a pending bill in 1859 confirming Slidell's claim to 8,000 acres unless claimants to the title instituted suit within two years and proved a better claim. The Washington correspondent for the St. Louis *Republican* charged that "this section legislated into the pocket of Mr. Slidell a half million dollars and turned out of their homes about five hundred families."[46] Settlers held a number of mass meetings, and rival politicians and newspapers began to refer to Slidell as "Houmas John." He defended himself with a speech on the Senate floor in which he said that he bought the land for $72,000 in 1835 and had offered it on the market at $40,000, and no buyers had bid on it. It had been assessed, he claimed, at $15,000, and his claim had been validated in 1848 by the Louisiana Supreme Court in earlier litigation in the case, in which Benjamin had been an attorney.[47]

The New York *Times* claimed that Benjamin received $10,000 for getting the provision through the Senate, but that was never verified. Settlers in Louisiana raised such public opposition through mass meetings and protests that the Senate suspended action on the bill pending an investigation, and the charges of scandal were projected into Benjamin's reelection campaign. Because of that, and because he was being opposed by an upstate member of Congress whose backers objected to having two Senators from New Orleans, it took Benjamin forty-two ballots to win reelection in the Louisiana legislature. The New Orleans *Picayune* called it "the most excited contest for Senator ever held in the state."

Butler and Meade both point out that there was room for differences of opinion in the Houmas case as to the validity of Slidell's claim. The issue was unfairly exaggerated for political motives, according to Butler; in fact, Benjamin's opponent, J. M. Sandidge, had done as much in the House of Representatives in behalf of the Houmas bill as Benjamin had done in the Senate.[48] Moreover, Benjamin had been one of the lawyers in the earlier cases surrounding the contested titles in the 1840s and knew the background of the claims well. The problem was the settlers, and a way had to be found to negotiate their interests in a fair way; Benjamin's solution put the burden of proof on the families to institute their claims against a valid title holder, Slidell, who had evidence of his payment. The fact that the title holder was John Slidell smacked of political self-interest and favoritism, though it was consistent with his earlier representation. Whatever the justice of the case, it was naive to think that such a Senate resolution would not be misunderstood and distorted so close to an election. So Benjamin's actions, however sincere and honest he claimed them to be, almost cost him his seat in the U.S. Senate.

The *Delta* congratulated the legislature on his reelection. "As a profound lawyer," it stated, "Mr. Benjamin has stood for years at the head of a bar that has no superior in the Union; as an orator, his reputation is as wide as the country itself, while as a man, his life has been singularly pure."[49]

Contemporaries in the Congress rated him one of history's most talented statesmen. Representative J. L. M. Curry wrote that there was no better debater in the Senate, that "Benjamin was collected and self-possessed in debate . . . did not use notes . . . and had a memory like Macaulay's."[50] A noted Maryland lawyer, Reverdy Johnson, who had argued cases with him before the U.S. Supreme Court, said, "Benjamin had a power of argument rarely, if ever, surpassed."[51] In 1903, Senator George Vest of Missouri wrote that he had once asked Dennis Murphy, the official reporter of the Senate for nearly forty years, who, in his opinion, "was the ablest and best equipped Senator he had known during his service as a reporter. Murphy replied without hesitation 'Judah P. Benjamin of Louisiana.' "[52]

All during his first six-year term, Benjamin had visited Natalie and Ninette annually in Paris. During the remainder of that time, they corresponded frequently, but only one sentence from a fragment of a letter from Natalie has survived his destructive hand. The sentence says simply, "Oh, talk not to me of economy, it is so fatiguing."

Enticing his wife back to Washington had been at the back of his mind from the beginning, and he must have painted pictures for her of the parties and balls at the White House and the diplomatic receptions. It was an emotional and social gamble on his part, but after his reelection to the Senate in 1858 she finally agreed to return. Benjamin went about preparing for her return with the fervor of a new bridegroom.

He spent tens of thousands of dollars decorating the Decatur house in Washington with the finest paintings, crystal, silver, and china in preparation for Natalie's homecoming. He notified the social hostesses and hired servants experienced in party-giving. Though Benjamin welcomed her with high anticipation, the gossip mill started grinding soon after she arrived. Her return to Washington turned into a nightmare. The Congressional ladies, after much clucking over the rumors about Natalie, decided to pay her a call on a reception day. The results are recorded in Virginia Clay-Clopton's gossip-laden memoir of the era entitled *A Belle of the Fifties*:

Here, too, was run the American career of another much-talked-of lady, which, for meteoric brilliancy and brevity, perhaps outshines any other episode in the chronicles of social life in Washington.

The lady's husband was a statesman of prominence, celebrated for his scholarly tastes and the fineness of his mental qualities. The arrival of the lady, after a marked absence abroad, during which some curious gossip had reached American ears, was attended by great eclat; and not a little conjecture was current as to how she would be received. For her home-coming, however, the Stockton Mansion was fitted up in hitherto undreamed-of magnificence, works of art and of vertu, which were the envy of social connoisseurs, being imported to grace it, regardless of cost. So far, so good!

The report of these domiciliary wonders left no doubt but that entertaining on a large scale was being projected. The world was slow in declaring its intentions in its own behalf; for, notwithstanding her rumoured delinquencies, the lady's husband was high in the councils of the nation, and as such was a figure of dignity. Shortly after her arrival our "mess" held a conclave, in which we discussed the propriety of calling upon the new-comer, but a conclusion seeming impossible (opinions being so widely divergent), it was decided to submit the important question to our husbands.

This was done duly, and Senator Clay's counsel to me was coincided in generally.

"By all means, call," said he. "You have nothing to do with the lady's private life, and, as a mark of esteem to a statesman of her husband's prominence, it will be better to call."

Upon a certain day, therefore, it was agreed that we should pay a "mess" call, going in a body. We drove accordingly, in dignity and in state, and, truth to tell, in soberness and ceremony, to the mansion aforenamed. It was the lady's reception day. We entered the drawingroom with great circumspection, tempering our usually cordial manner with a fine prudence; we paid our devoirs to the hostess and retired. But now a curious retribution overtook us, social faint-hearts that we were; for, though we heard much gossip of the regality and originality of one or more dinners given to the several diplomatic corps (the lady especially affected the French Legation), I never heard of a gathering of Washingtonians at her home, nor of invitations extended to them, nor, indeed, anything more of her until two months had flown. Then, Arab-like, the lady rose in the night, "silently folded her tent and stole away" (to meet a handsome German officer, it was said), leaving our calls unanswered, save by the sending of her card, and her silver and china and crystal, her paintings, and hangings, and furniture to be auctioned off to the highest bidder![53]

Varina wrote to Lawley: "His life in his family must have been gruesome, but he always spoke of himself as the happiest of men. His indulgence towards those connected with him was boundless. His wife was a Creole—not in your sense colored—but born and reared in the lower part of Louisiana—musical to her finger tips, with a divine voice—little education, and as my mother used to say, 'unassisted human nature.' "[54] Meade interviewed the daughter of Senator Yulee, who told him that "Mrs. Benjamin was very gay and very unhappy. My father and mother condemned her strongly because of the treatment of her husband. [Benjamin] idolized her and gave her everything she wanted. I do not think he knew what was going on. It came as a terrible shock to him."[55]

The rumors about Natalie's escapades were the talk at every concert, play, and party, and eventually the gossip reached her ears. She returned to Paris sometime in 1859, a few months after she arrived, never to set foot in America again. Defeated by his final effort to win her back, Benjamin decided to sell everything and move back to a more easily managed life.

He left the city during the auction of their fine furnishings and did not witness the crowds that came to the house.

Everyone in Washington now thronged to see the beautiful things, and many purchased specimens from among them, among others Mrs. Davis. By a curious turn of fate, the majority of these treasures were acquired by Mrs. Senator Yulee, who was so devoutly religious that her piety caused her friends to speak of her as "the Madonna of the Wickliffe sisters!" The superb furniture of the whilom hostess was carried to "Homosassa," the romantic home of the Yulees in Florida where in later years it was reduced to ashes."[56]

Such was the fate of his finest acquisitions—the candlesticks of Sheffield plate, the handmade candelabra of French bronze, the eggshell teacups.

Natalie had almost wrecked his life in Washington; his actions reveal his relief at her return to Paris. At least he could go about his work without emotional stress and personal humiliation. He knew, after that, they would continue to see each other only once a year, which meant prolonged separation from sixteen-year-old Ninette.

Oddly, with everything, he trusted Natalie to raise Ninette properly in Paris, with taste, intelligence, and good values. Natalie was able to manage her life without him around. The tensions between husband and wife arose only when they were together. Without her, he would be spared the humiliation of an unfaithful wife publicly affronting his friends and colleagues.

Election to the U.S. Senate had given Benjamin the chance to start over in a new and challenging environment and put the embarrassments of his early days in New Orleans behind him. In New Orleans, he had been a part of neither the Catholic nor the Jewish world, and Natalie's absence had left him noticeably alone in a city where her family was well known. In Washington, he would be on the top rung of the social ladder.

The public auction of his household goods was a very strange event for a member of the U.S. Senate. It was a public humiliation, saying to others that even with the finest of possessions, he could not keep her with him.

Yet, there was a positive aspect to the sale as well. It was a public way to renounce her, to cast her out of his life. It seemed indicative of a permanent separation, evidence for all to see that every trace of her would be removed and that his illusion of having a conventional marriage had been shattered. There was a finality to selling all of their prized possessions because they would not be needing them any more. It said to official Washington that she was gone and would not be back.

Of course, there was a financial dimension to it, but the auction also dissociated Benjamin in the eyes of officialdom from social frivolity, implying that the rugs, porcelain, and silver were Natalie's refinement, not an expression of his values. He, on the contrary, preferred a simpler life. More importantly, it signaled his acceptance that they would never again live together in America.

Leaving his Washington mansion was another form of starting over after a traumatic experience. It was Yale, Charleston, New Orleans, Bellechasse, and Washington all over again—recasting his life after a low point and changing his environment. He seemed to like radical change in his life.

Benjamin must not have had very high expectations of the intimate rewards of marriage. His, like his father's, had been a marriage of aspiration and of disappointment. His mother had been a strong, proud working woman, preoccupied much of the time with her shop and unavailable to his father or to him. In her eyes, his father was weak and disappointing, and Rebecca did not spare Philip her feelings just because the children were present. Perhaps Benjamin had come to expect that the woman in his life would be absent most of the time, would neglect him, would be too busy to spend time with him, would be selfish and self-centered.

Perhaps, in his thoughts, he followed Natalie to Europe, already harboring the fantasy of retirement abroad where he could live a better life, far from conflicts, hatreds, and the clouds of his past. Natalie in Paris might have represented the golden door of eventual escape, the assurance that he could never lose everything, that there was a future for him beyond the turmoil of public life and the terrible war that, by 1859, many foresaw.

In Ninette he imagined the beauteous child of his fantasy, blessed with a cultural polish her mother never attained. She would belong to Paris, not New Orleans; she would be steeped in a civilization many centuries old, not the poor imitation of French manners on the Confederate frontier. She would not suffer, as the child of a Catholic and a Jew, the pains of her father. Ninette and Natalie would be building a haven for his advancing years, and the germ of that idea would grow as war descended upon him.

Events would not await Benjamin's efforts to sort out his personal life. In October 1859, John Brown and a small group of fanatics seized the arsenal at Harpers Ferry, Virginia, and launched a slave insurrection. A garrison of Marines led by Robert E. Lee captured him, and Davis helped lead a Senate investigation committee, which stirred suspicions of Northern sympathy. In December Brown was tried and hanged. Tremors of fear and hysteria swept across the South, hardening the positions of its leadership against any compromise. Davis and Benjamin moved forcefully over the next few months to block the Democratic presidential nomination of Senator Stephen A. Douglas of Illinois, who had enunciated early in his Senate career and most forcefully during the Lincoln–Douglas debates the doctrine that the people of a territory could determine for themselves whether they would allow slavery or reject it. The South dubbed that "squatter sovereignty," and Benjamin delivered his most bitter speech in the Senate, complimenting Lincoln for adherence to principle while excoriating Douglas for breaking his word to the South: Under "the stress of local election," Benjamin exclaimed of Douglas, "his knees gave way; his whole person trembled. . . . He is a fallen star."[57] Douglas's doctrine so angered the Southern leadership that the Democratic convention in April 1860 split apart, opening the way for the election to the presidency of the man Douglas had defeated for his Illinois Senate seat in 1858, Abraham Lincoln.

A month after the convention, Benjamin was still capable of a modicum of moderation, even if his colleagues were not. On May 24, 1860, Benjamin opposed Jefferson Davis and other leading Southern Senators and supported a bill to maintain with food, clothing, and shelter a group of 1,200 slaves in Key West captured from illegal slave ships and to enter into contracts to pay for their return to Africa. The United States government was "bound by treaty stipulations to aid in the suppression of the slave trade," he successfully argued in the Senate. "If that treaty binds us, it is our duty to carry it out in good faith," which meant providing the supplies the slaves needed.[58]

But time was running out. Although others would blame the outbreak of the Civil War on the lack of statesmanship of the Southern leadership, Benjamin believed that larger forces were at work. "You know how absurd is the fiction put forward by our enemies in the Northern states," Benjamin told Lawley the year before he died, "that the great Civil War which raged between 1861 and 1865 would never have taken place but for Jefferson Davis and myself. Such mighty convulsions, which amount indeed to revolutions, are never the work of individuals, but of divided nations."[59]

Abraham Lincoln's election on a platform of containing slavery was interpreted across the Deep South as utter intransigence and a challenge to the future of slavery. Davis cautioned his colleagues to delay secession, and Benjamin, in California to try a land case, wrote a letter "to repel the absurd and self-contradictory charge that we seek to dissolve the Union." Speaking in a San Francisco church on the day after Lincoln's election, he praised the Constitution and looked with a "glowing heart . . . at the majestic march of our Union, which, like the great river upon whose banks I dwell, still pursued its resistless course into the unknown ocean which lies beyond, swelling it as it advances, receiving its tributaries each distinct yet each uniting in forming one common reservoir of wealth and power, and each, I trust, to remain, so united."[60] He hoped for a better understanding of the Constitution. "Then and only then will the horrid sectional disputes, which now stun our ears with their discordant din, be hushed forever." As late as December 11, 1860, the New Orleans *Picayune* reported that Benjamin "opposes secession, except in the last resort."[61]

A majority of Southerners, especially in the cities, opposed secession, but the tide was turning. On December 20, South Carolina
seceded. Davis wrote that "my associates considered me too slow
and it was probably true that they were right in their belief that I
was behind the opinion of the people of the state as to the propriety
of a prompt secession."[62]

In Louisiana, the secession movement gathered irresistible momentum. "We cannot get any compromise," Benjamin wired from Washington.

Historians consider Benjamin's farewell to the U.S. Senate on New
Year's Eve, 1860, one of the great speeches in American history.
The gallery was packed to hear the most eloquent voice of the
South. It was a moment both of tragedy and triumph as he pleaded
with his colleagues against the war of brothers to come:

> And now, Senators, within a few weeks we part to meet as Senators
> in one common council chamber of the nation no more forever.
> We desire, we beseech you, let this parting be in peace . . . indulge
> in no vain delusion that duty or conscience, interest or honor,
> imposes upon you the necessity of invading our States or shedding
> the blood of our people. You have not possible justification for
> it.[63]

Varina wrote that "his voice rose over the vast audience distinct
and clear . . . he held his audience spellbound for over an hour
and so still were they that a whisper could have been heard."[64]

And history would record that he had warned them:

> What may be the fate of this horrible contest, no man can tell
> . . . but this much, I will say: the fortunes of war may be adverse
> to our arms, you may carry desolation into our peaceful land,
> and with torch and fire you may set our cities in flame . . . you
> may, under the protection of your advancing armies, give shelter
> to the furious fanatics who desire, and profess to desire, nothing
> more than to add all the horrors of a servile insurrection to the
> calamities of civil war; you may do all this—and more too, if
> more there be—but you never can subjugate us; you never can
> convert the free sons of the soil into vassals, paying tribute to
> your power; and you never, never can degrade them to the level
> of an inferior and servile race. Never! Never!

Benjamin stood between two desks, intentionally, not in the well
of the Senate, but apart from the usual point of attention, to dramatize

his independence of the Senate rules and his farewell to its formalities. He was calm and controlled, one hand in his pocket, the other toying with a watchchain.

"You may set our cities in flame," he had stated. He quoted Thomas Jefferson, who had written the lines in the Declaration of Independence that Benjamin interpreted as defending the right of the people of the South "to alter or abolish and to institute a new government."

At the moment of his defiance, he let go of his watch chain as if to free the South of its bond to the North, turned to take his seat as if finished and then, rising again, turned directly to the audience and said again, "Never! Never!"

Not loudly, but simply; fist-pounding and rebel yells were not his style. An orator knows that an emotion-charged audience will add its own yeast to an eloquent statement of its principles.

There was an immediate rush of reaction to the speech from the Southern contingent and tumultuous applause from the galleries. Varina reported that "many ladies were in tears. The Vice President tried in vain to prevent the applause but could not control the multitude who were wild with enthusiasm."[65] There were even grudging compliments from the Northern press and a quote from a London correspondent that "it was better than our Benjamin could have done."[66]

Benjamin would meet Disraeli someday and be recognized by historians as his counterpart on the North American continent.

The enthusiasm in the South was matched by the venom in the North. The Boston *Transcript* of January 5, 1861, published an editorial under the heading "The Children of Israel" in which it attacked the support Benjamin and other Southern Jews gave to secession as indicative of the disloyalty of all American Jews.[67] Isaac Wise vehemently replied to the charge by pointing to support of the Republican party by thousands of Jews in the North. Senator Henry Wilson of Massachusetts, who would be elected Vice President of the United States in 1872, condemned Benjamin because "his bearing, his tone of voice, his words, all gave evidence . . . that his heart was in this foul and wicked plot to dismember the Union, to overthrow the government of his adopted country which gives equality of rights even to that race that stoned prophets and crucified the Redeemer of the world."[68]

Louisiana seceded from the Union on January 26, 1861, and on February 4 Benjamin and Slidell officially withdrew from their seats in the Senate.

He made another, this time short, farewell speech with his customary deft style and with the added theatrics of a pistol at his side. His peroration was quoted by schoolboys across the South for decades:

And now to you, Mr. President, and to my brother Senators, on all sides of this Chamber, I bid a respectful farewell; with many of those from whom I have been radically separated in political sentiment, my personal relations have been kindly and have inspired me with a respect and esteem that I shall not willingly forget; with those around me from the Southern states, I part as men part from brothers on the eve of a temporary absence, with a cordial pressure of the hand and smiling assurance of sweet intercourse around the family hearth. But to you, noble and generous friends, who, born beneath other skies, possess hearts that beat in sympathy with ours . . . to you, who, on our behalf have bared your breast to the fierce beatings of the storm . . . in your devotion to constitutional liberty; to you, who have made our cause your cause and from many of whom I part forever . . . one priceless treasure is yours—the assurance that an entire people honor your names, and hold them in grateful and affectionate memory. . . .

When, in after days, the story of the present shall be written; when history shall have passed her stern sentence on the erring men who have driven their unoffending brethren from the shelter of their common home . . . your children shall hear repeated the familiar tale . . . and they will glory in their lineage from men of spirit as generous and of patriotism as high hearted as ever illustrated or adorned the American Senate.[69]

"The Senate was hushed in stillness," wrote Senator Bragg of North Carolina, "so that every word in his soft but distinct utterance fell clearly upon the ears of his hearers." Bragg reported that both Benjamin and Slidell shed tears, and that he shook their hands, "too full to say a word."[70]

The admiration was not unanimous. Three weeks later, Senator Andrew Johnson told Charles Francis Adams of the distinguished Boston family, "There's another Jew—that miserable Benjamin! He looks on a country and a government as he would a suit of old clothes. He sold out the old one; and he would sell out the new if he could in so doing make two or three millions."[71]

Jefferson Davis did not resign from the Senate until January 21,

1861, after he received official notification that the State of Mississippi had seceded. He was so ill that he delayed his appearance and could hardly walk to the Senate chamber. It was a disappointing speech, uninspired and full of typical Davis legalisms. Only Varina thought his voice sounded like "a silver trumpet."[72] It was a phrase she would use again years later to describe Benjamin's voice the first time they met.

Judah P. Benjamin was part of the small band of moderates who had tried to hold the union together but were not able to compromise on slavery. They believed in a strong South in a decentralized Union, given the freedom to pursue its destiny all the way to the Pacific. Most had not wanted this war, and Benjamin must have wondered how history would view those, like himself, who were willing to play for time in hopes that compromise and statesmanship would find a way to settle the struggle without bloodshed.

2

�֍

"DARK PRINCE"
OF THE
CONFEDERACY

1861–1863

7

From Attorney General
to Secretary of War:
The Unprepared Warrior

❄❄

Jefferson Davis returned to Brierfield during the calm before the storm, determined to join the military as general-in-chief of the army and to lead the South on the battlefield. But the convention of Southern states meeting at Montgomery, Alabama, searching for consensus and divided between other candidates, in four days unanimously elected the hero of Buena Vista as the first President of the Confederacy. Varina and he were in their rose garden when a messenger came with the news.

"I thought his genius was military, but that as a party manager, he would not succeed," she wrote with insight in her memoirs. "He did not know the arts of the politician and would not practice them if understood, and he did know those of war."[1] Varina had recognized the main factor in his favor at the Montgomery convention. Others aspired to the presidency, but he was a U.S. Senator with West Point and military service in his background, as well as a term as U.S. Secretary of War under Pierce. He was a natural choice.

He made twenty-five speeches along the route to Montgomery, where he was greeted by cheering crowds and an oratorical flourish by the great fire-eater, William L. Yancey, who proclaimed, "The man and the hour have met."

At his inauguration a happy crowd, dressed in finery and innocent of the travail to come, cheered him lustily. The band played a new song entitled "Dixie," composed by a Northern minstrel, and Davis made a short and ordinary speech. The next day he settled down to consultations on the selection of his Cabinet.

For political reasons, he made certain that each state had at least one Cabinet member. He wrote later, "Not even a single member of the cabinet bore to me the relation of a close personal friendship."[2] That included the Senator from Louisiana: "Mr. Benjamin of Louisiana had a very high reputation as a lawyer, and my acquaintance with him in the Senate had impressed me with the lucidity of his intellect, his systematic habits and capacity for labor. He was therefore invited to the post of Attorney General."[3]

That rather formal observation is virtually the only mention of Judah P. Benjamin in the two-volume Jefferson Davis work on the war entitled *The Rise and Fall of the Confederate Government.* (An order signed by Benjamin is quoted in the second volume.) As the only Louisianian in the first Cabinet, Benjamin was summoned to Montgomery, Alabama, in February 1861 for the swearing in of the provisional government, which would run for election the following November. (Today, on the Capitol steps in Montgomery, a six-pointed Star of David marks the spot where the President took the oath of office on February 18, 1861. No one knows how it got there—some just call it the mark that Judah P. Benjamin left on the Confederacy.)

Since it was a civilian office, the leadership in Montgomery considered the Attorney General's job of little consequence, but Benjamin did not let its nonmilitary definition deter him. He immediately plunged into the policy debates on all aspects of preparedness.

At the first Cabinet meeting, according to Secretary of War Leroy Walker, describing it after the war, "there was only one man there who had any sense and that man was Benjamin. Mr. Benjamin proposed that the Government purchase as much cotton as it could hold, at least 100,000 bales and ship it at once to England. With the proceeds of a part of it, he advised the immediate purchase of at least 150,000 stand of small arms, and guns and ammunitions. . . . The residue of the cotton was to be held as a basis for credit."[4] Benjamin lost that argument, because everyone at the meeting ridiculed the idea of a long war. Walker himself confessed that he had gone about the State of Alabama promising to "wipe up with my pocket handkerchief all the blood that would be shed." Davis and the government met the challenge of the Northern blockade with a cotton embargo of their own, for they believed that "cotton was King" and that by imposing a "cotton famine" in Europe they would force Britain and France to recognize the Confederacy and come to its aid. Already aware of loyalty as the measure by which Davis would judge him, by April Benjamin also became a strong advocate of cotton diplomacy in his utterances to the foreign press.

Mrs. Clement Clay wrote of the talk of the interminable Cabinet meetings that "sometimes the Cabinet would depart surreptitiously, one at a time, and Mr. Davis while making things as plain as did the preacher the virtues of the baptismal, finds his demonstrations made to one weak, weary man, who has no vim to contend."[5]

If only one person stayed for the completion of a meeting, we can safely assume that it was Judah Benjamin. He loved details, complexity, and problem-solving. He made himself totally available as an administrator to the President, handling the hordes of office-seekers descending on the government and checking up on directives. He became the "greeter," seeing the people the President was too busy to meet and talking to the planters, Congressmen, newspaper reporters, and yeoman farmers who wanted to tell Mr. Davis their secret plan to win the war.

One visitor to Richmond, seeking a favor, described his role: "It appeared to be the custom of the attachés, when in doubt, to refer the stranger to Mr. Judah P. Benjamin, the 'Poo Bah' of the Confederate Government."[6]

As the spring proceeded, Davis and Lincoln both played for time in order to maneuver for support in the border states and in the slave states that were still wavering. North Carolina, Tennessee, Virginia, and Arkansas watched and waited; Missouri, Kentucky, Delaware, and Maryland defeated secession resolutions and remained in the Union.

The Confederate Congress authorized the creation of an army of 100,000 men, creating an immediate shortage of arms, ammunition, uniforms, and other supplies. It would take more than enthusiasm and chivalry to wage war. The South had less than 10 percent of the manufacturing output of the North, less than one-third the bank capital, and less than half the railroad mileage. It had no navy and no capacity to build one. But volunteers were signing up and were accepted only if they brought with them their own knapsacks and rifles.

Mary Chesnut's diary criticized the "stay-at-home men . . . ab-

sorbed as before in plantation affairs, cotton picking, negro squabbles
. . . like the old Jews while Noah was building the Ark."[7]

After several months of cat-and-mouse games with Lincoln culmi-
nated in the firing on Fort Sumter in mid-April, events seemed to
follow an inexorable course. As Lincoln called for 75,000 volunteers,
the wavering slave states came off the fence into the Confederacy,
opening the way by the first of June for the government to move
to Richmond, away from the mosquitoes and cramped quarters of
Montgomery. It would be a city more suited to Judah P. Benjamin's
urbane tastes and personality.

The case for Richmond as the capital overcame the misgivings
of Benjamin and others, who felt it was too close to Washington
and endangered the government. Virginia was rich, influential, and
historic, and Richmond had railroads, ports, warehouses, and the
Tredegar Iron Works, the only facility in the Confederacy capable
of manufacturing heavy arms. The most convincing argument rested
in the aspiration and self-image of the President. If Jefferson Davis
wanted to be an effective Commander-in-Chief, then he should be
close to the fighting, and Virginia would be the first battlefield.

"All we want is to be left alone," Davis had said after Sumter.
With scarcely enough men, money, materiel, manufacturing, and
railroads, the South adopted a defensive strategy. It could win the
war by not losing it. Its greatest asset was the enormous amount of
territory the North would have to conquer. Surely, if the South
were to win the early battles and endure, the North would tire
and quit in discouragement.

Richmond turned itself into a vast staging area for maneuvers, a
combination of marching regiments, constant parades, a picnic, and
a party for the officers, with politicians and enlisted men pouring
into the city. They arrived in all manner of dress, none more colorful
than the Louisiana Zouaves recruited from the jails of New Orleans,
dressed in red caps, bright blue coats, baggy red pants, white leggings,
and black boots.

Benjamin traveled to Richmond with his brother-in-law, Jules St.
Martin, now a young man in his late twenties and, though slight in
stature, attractive to women, with a shock of black hair and the
patrician Creole features of his sister Natalie. For Benjamin, Jules
St. Martin was a link to the roots of his missing family, born to
Natalie's parents soon after her marriage to Benjamin and raised
almost as their son. Varina said that Benjamin was protective and
spoke of his young brother-in-law as if he were a small boy. They

lived together at the Davenport house on Main Street throughout the war, and we can assume that Benjamin arranged for Jules's job as a clerk in the War Department. Varina wrote that

> . . . he had living with him a very well educated and elegant young brother-in-law, Jules St. Martin, whom he loved dearly. When he first spoke of Mr. St. Martin, whom we did not at the time know at all, I thought he must be a very charming boy of twelve or fifteen years old; and when the refined, accomplished young gentleman of perhaps thirty years old made his bow to me in Washington, I found difficulty in believing this was the "Jules, dear little fellow, who will be lonesome if I do not go home," with whose name all Mr. Benjamin's particular friends were intimate. When Mr. Benjamin came to Richmond, Mr. St. Martin came also, and the two set up a comfortable house, where they entertained their friends in as elegant a manner as blockaded bon vivants could do.[8]

Duncan Kenner, the Representative from Louisiana, also lived at the Davenport house, and he and Benjamin formed the nucleus at the gathering place and "mess" of the Louisiana delegation. Kenner was an influential and wealthy sugar planter from Ascension Parish who had run against Benjamin for the Whig nomination to the U.S. Senate in 1852. With John Slidell, Benjamin and Kenner had plotted and wrangled their way through the slippery shoals of Louisiana politics for more than twenty years and had become best of friends. They had a special intimacy that came with years of shared experience in legislative backrooms and at the card tables. Though Kenner was a large slaveowner, he had been educated in the Northeast and had traveled widely in the United States and Europe. He saw slavery as an economic necessity, not a moral or religious issue, and he had even found himself embarrassed by it on his frequent trips to England after slavery had been abolished there. Kenner was the only one in official Richmond with whom Benjamin could talk frankly about the war, knowing he would protect confidences. To Benjamin, trust was earned, and Louisianians were home-grown stalwarts who shared the struggles of his early career and had proved themselves steadfast in the fiercest storms. He also kept a guest room for visiting friends, like Colonel Richard Taylor, son of Zachary Taylor and Jefferson Davis's former brother-in-law, who had a plantation in Louisiana.

As late as April 16, 1861, Benjamin could write General Beauregard, the "Great Creole" from New Orleans, a congratulatory note about Fort Sumter, saying, "I am a Louisianian—heart and soul."

It was becoming clear that Secretary of War Walker, a Southern gentleman from Alabama, was ill-fitted for his post, bogged down, disorganized, and ineffectual. Benjamin began to spend more time at the War Department. J. B. Jones wrote in his *Rebel War Clerk's Diary at the Confederate States Capital* that "Mr. Benjamin is a frequent visitor at the department, and is very sociable; some intimations have been thrown out that he aspires to become, some day, Secretary of War. Mr. Benjamin, unquestionably, will have great influence with the President, for he has studied his character most carefully. He will be familiar not only with his 'likes' but especially with his 'dislikes.' "[9]

In mid-July, Union General McDowell moved 31,000 troops out of Washington toward Manassas in Virginia, and the South positioned an equal number on the banks of Bull Run to meet them. Richmond became electric with expectation.

On July 21, word came that the Battle of Bull Run had started, and a restless Jefferson Davis could not bear to sit in Richmond with the Confederate Congress. He boarded a train and went looking for the action; he commandeered horses after he had gone as far as he could by rail. Riding past the wounded toward the battlefield, he was convinced by their faces that they had lost. He comforted them with dramatic phrases about dying for the cause. Meanwhile he searched for the field headquarters of Generals Beauregard and Johnston.

Benjamin had been closeted with the Cabinet for hours in a small office in the War Department, impatient and pacing in the cigar smoke. It occurred to him that the Cabinet would surely hear first if the battle were a defeat, but if it were a victory, Varina would know before anyone else.

He left the room and hurried down the street to the Spotswood Hotel to get the exhilarating news from her. Benjamin returned to the Cabinet with as much speed as his dignity would allow, mounted a chair, and spread his arms to the crowd in the War Office.

He asked for their undivided attention and paused a moment to wring the drama out of the situation, "his eyes on fire," J. B. Jones said, "like Daniel Webster after taking a pint of brandy."[10] He spoke slowly, relishing the moment: "We have received the following wire from President Davis at Manassas." And then shifting to an official tone: "We have gained a glorious but dear-bought victory. Night closed upon the enemy in full flight and closely pursued."[11] There was a shriek of exultation from the assembled crowd as the men hugged and whirled the women who had followed Benjamin over for the announcement. The reporters, who had scribbled Benjamin's official words, scrambled off to their newspapers to write and file the story.

"Joy ruled the hour," the diarist J. B. Jones continued. "The city seemed lifted up and everyone appeared to walk on air."[12] The South had routed the Yankees in the first battle of the war.

In the aftermath of the battle, all of Richmond was asking the same question: Why had the Confederates not pursued the Yankees all the way back to Washington and captured the Northern capital? The answer was that they did not have enough rations, materiel, and organization for hot pursuit. The press descended on the Davis government. Its target was the inept leadership in the War Department. Jefferson Davis considered himself the most competent Secretary of War in the Confederacy by virtue of his service under Pierce. What he needed was a dependable administrator to carry out his every order down to the last detail, a trusted confidant who would be absolutely loyal and a figure the public knew to be highly talented. Benjamin became acting Secretary of War in September and was confirmed by the Senate a month or so later.

Benjamin, as a Jew, would have to be more loyal to the Cause than anyone else—more outspoken in the Cabinet, more courageous, and willing to wage war with all the energy that total war demanded. And if he understood Jefferson Davis, loyalty to the President as the symbol of the Cause was the measure of a man's worth to the Confederacy. It was common knowledge that Davis wanted to be a general when the war began, not a political leader, and astute Cabinet members like Benjamin knew he would not tolerate men who sat with the Cabinet presuming to know of drawn swords and cavalry charges when they had never served a day in the army.

Benjamin brought his unquestioning loyalty with him to his appointment as the second Secretary of War and entered the office with his accustomed energy and thoroughness. After all, his predecessor, Leroy Walker of Alabama ("a slow coach," he was called, and "a profuse spitter"), had been an administrative disaster, and the sheer magnitude of the task of unscrambling affairs required a mastery of bureaucratic detail. Benjamin had an almost obsessive commitment to systematic paperwork, along with an encyclopedic memory for detail. Besides, Benjamin was clearly trying to win the respect of the military and Davis with crisp answers, contrasting the new Secretary with the old. He sought to answer letters the day they arrived, to cut down on the length of replies, and generally to take administrative charge of the war.

"You certainly left me a bed of roses," Benjamin wrote in his farewell letter to Walker.[13] The scope of his responsibilities extended from Virginia to Texas and westward to Missouri and the Indian territory. He was in charge of coastal defense in states too afraid of invasion to lend troops to each other. He had to move supplies, scarce armaments, and information over sabotaged railroads, rutted dirt roads, and faulty telegraph wires. He had to mediate the demands of competing generals, handle outsized egos, and scrape together the means of war for the armies of Virginia as well as scattered garrisons across the South. Thousands of communiqués poured out of his office in six months, all of them written by hand, copied by clerks, and duly recorded in his letter book for history. He would turn prejudice to his favor and play on the Southerner's instinctive respect for the Jewish mind with a brilliant performance.

His strategy worked, and the press response was excellent, at first.

"No one comes from an interview with him," reported the New Orleans *Courier,* "who does not speak in terms of wonder and admiration at his quickness of perception and promptness of decision. He dispatches more business in one hour than most men could accomplish in a day."[14]

From the beginning, he saw the War Office's success as intimately related to foreign affairs:

"When it is considered that the government of the United States with all its accumulation of arms for half a century," Secretary Benjamin wrote the President, "and all its workshops and arsenals, public and private, and its untrammelled intercourse with foreign nations—has already been compelled to disband a number of cavalry regiments on account of the difficulty of arming them, and has been driven to the necessity of making purchases in Europe of very large quantities, and of saltpeter by thousands of tons, some faint idea may be formed of the difficulties against which this department has been and is now struggling in the effort to furnish arms and munitions for our troops. The difficulty is not in the want of legislation. Laws cannot suddenly convert farmers into gunsmiths. Our people are not artisans except to a very limited degree. In the very armory here at Richmond, the production would be greatly increased if skilled labor could be procured. In the absence of home manufacturers, no recourse remains but importation, and with our commerce substantially restrained with foreign nations, the means of importation are limited."[15]

All of those factors, known only to a few, were coloring Davis's military and political decisions. Delay meant waiting for a Union invasion, but the public debate on the "defensive" war was symptomatic of the need for Southerners to attack and sweep ahead in gallant conquest. Davis was growing to trust Benjamin as an administrator and wanted to test him as a warrior. Perhaps Davis was wary because Benjamin was intelligent, analytical, and verbal, but also because he came from a Judaic culture that Davis did not understand, and therefore automatically suspected. Thus, Benjamin had determined to be absolutely and intensely loyal to the President. Davis began to return that loyalty with an unbreakable bond of trust.

"It was to me a curious spectacle," Varina wrote, "the steady approximation to a thorough friendliness of the President and his War Minister. It was a very gradual rapprochement, but all the more solid for that reason."[16]

In less than a month after his appointment as Secretary of War, Benjamin was quareling with General Beauregard.

When Beauregard, fresh from his heroics at Bull Run, decided to send a lieutenant to Richmond to recruit volunteers for adding a rocket battery to his command, Benjamin wrote him that it was "without warrant in law," but because his motive was good and it represented merely "a defect of judgment" he would "go unpunished."[17]

Beauregard exploded with an angry letter to President Davis. "I feel assured," he wrote, "I need not attract your attention to the unusual and offensive style adopted by the Secretary of the War Department. . . . I am quite willing, indeed, that you decide whose judgment has been most at fault—that of your general, who has simply done what was *essential* to provide men to handle the rockets as soon as ready for use, and thus materially increase his means of defence . . . ; or that functionary at his desk, who deems it a fit time to weave technical pleas of obstruction, to debate about the prerogative of his office and of your Excellency's and to write lectures on law while the enemy is mustering on our front, with at least three times our force in infantry and four times as much artillery." He continued his attack on Benjamin's legal background: "Coming to see this, he will then, I am assured, understand that this is no time for the display of his capacity for irritation or his legal and Constitutional erudition. He will see such displays are now as much out of place as were a learned disquisition from an admiralty lawyer on the intricacies of the rules of flotsam and jetsam to the captain of a ship in distress."[18]

Davis defended Benjamin with a patronizing letter to Beauregard, making light of the matter. "Now, my dear sir," Davis replied, "let me entreat you to dismiss this small matter from your mind. In the hostile masses before you, you have a subject more worthy of your contemplation."[19]

But before the Davis letter could arrive, Benjamin, on October 17, 1861, fired off another message to Beauregard on an even more sensitive subject. Beauregard was the proponent of offensive war, and it was no secret, especially to the newspapers to which he openly complained, that he had wanted to attack Washington with full force after the victory at Bull Run. He also had argued to Davis and Benjamin in behalf of treating the armies of the Potomac (headed by Beauregard) and of the Shenandoah (headed by General Joseph Johnston) as two corps of one army, giving him the authority to select his own ordnance and other officers. If not, he wanted to be relieved from his "false position."

No West Point–trained Commander-in-Chief could allow such independence, and Benjamin, after consulting with Davis, wrote a strong letter in return, laced with sarcasm and what for Beauregard was even more irritating legal instruction:

> I have your letter . . . in which you state that if you are no longer in Command of an Army Corps, you request to be relieved forthwith from your present false position. . . . I beg to say in all kindness that it is not your position which is false but your idea of the organization of the Army as established by . . . Congress, and I feel confident you cannot have studied the legislation . . . you are *second* in command of the *whole* Army of the Potomac, and not *first* in command of *half* the army . . . if you will take the pains to read the sixth section of the "act to provide for the public defense" . . . you will see that the President has no authority to divide an army into two "corps d'armée," but only into brigades and divisions. Now your rank being superior to that of a Commander of a brigade or division, and there being no other component parts into which an army can be legally divided, you *necessar-*

ily command the *whole* army; but having present with you an officer of equal grade but older commission who also commands the *whole* army, you become second in command.

I have entered into these details because in conversation with the President since his return from your headquarters, he has informed me that he found the same error as to the organization of the army which you seem to entertain . . . generally prevalent. . . . I hope in a few days to communicate to you such general orders in relation to this whole subject, as will dissipate all possible conflict of authority, unite the army under one common head, and give to all its leaders appropriate and satisfactory positions.[20]

Beauregard was once again enraged and again dashed off a letter to Davis, pleading for the President, "as an educated soldier . . . to shield me from these ill-timed, unaccountable annoyances."[21]

But Davis understood that the issue of independence for each army general was a formula for chaos and that there were other forces at work as well. After Bull Run, the "Beauregard for President" movement had begun, and the man who fancied himself a Confederate Napoleon was ingratiating himself to the public with self-serving patriotic rhetoric at Davis's expense. This time, Davis was more direct, not even trying to placate his general.

"I do not feel competent," Davis wrote, "to instruct Mr. Benjamin in the matter of style; there are few whom the public would, probably, believe fit for the task . . . it cannot be peculiar to Mr. Benjamin to look at every exercise of official power in its legal aspect, and you surely did not intend to inform me that your army and yourself are outside the limits of the law. It is my duty to see that the laws are faithfully executed and I cannot recognize the pretension of anyone that their restraint is narrow for him."[22]

J. R. Jones reported in his diary on the political gossip in Richmond, which seemed always to find Benjamin in the middle, being criticized for carrying out the military policies of Jefferson Davis, for political reasons. "I understand," Jones wrote, "a dreadful quarrel is brewing between Mr. Benjamin and General Beauregard. . . . General B. being the only individual even hinted at as an opponent for Mr. Davis for President, the Secretary of War fights him on the vantage ground and likewise commends himself to the President."[23]

Looking back, Benjamin's troubles with Beauregard probably began with a naïvely obsequious note that Benjamin wrote as a Louisiana Senator after Fort Sumter. "My dear General," he had written, "In the midst of the eclat of your glorious triumph, you will no doubt value but little the tribute of a poor civilian who knows nothing of war." It was the kind of letter a future Secretary of War might have wished he had never written.[24]

Benjamin's political troubles began to pile up as events turned against the South. When Savannah was threatened in November 1861, Governor Joe Brown of Georgia demanded the withdrawal of Georgia troops from the Virginia battle front to protect their home state from invasion. Secretary Benjamin called the request "suicidal," pointing out that general safety would not permit the scattering of "armies into fragments at the request of each Governor who may be alarmed for the safety of his people."[25]

Brown replied that if the Secretary could not spare him Georgia troops, would he let Georgia have the five thousand Confederate rifles that had just arrived in Savannah. Secretary Benjamin answered that he would do what he could, but "I beg you to remember that the other Governors are making just such demands as yourself. . . ."[26]

Collision with the governors was an inevitable result of having to balance competing demands, and Benjamin was criticized no matter what choices he made. If he was assertive, he was charged by the military with interference and second-guessing a local situation from the comfort of Richmond. If he was lenient, it suggested that he did not understand the needs of warfare and was not tough enough or was too legalistic for the job.

In a congressional investigation of the fall of New Orleans, letters were put in the record with the following exchange:

From Louisiana Governor Thomas O. Moore in New Orleans wrote to Benjamin:

"I, notwithstanding your advice to the contrary, seized the pork in the city, and telegraphed you (but have had no reply), and shall hold it unless requested by you to act otherwise, as I see no way to feed our troops without it, but hope you do, as your advice was to that effect. Write me fully on that point."

Reply from Benjamin the next day:

"I can conceive of no possible reason for seizing pork, and cannot approve it. There is an abundance of food in our country, and private rights ought not to be invaded, except in cases of necessity for public defence."

He had not yet learned that war often causes inequities and that the army came first, even at the expense of the civilian population (and old friends and family) in his home city.[27]

Events were bringing Judah P. Benjamin and Jefferson Davis closer together, and the President began to rely on his Secretary as an originator of ideas, as a sounding board for new policy, and for follow-through on current decisions.

Benjamin and Davis were working together twelve to fourteen hours a day, and the pace and pressure was beginning to show on the President's face, adding gray to his hair and chin whiskers.[28]

Davis suffered from neuralgia, the doctors called it, a kind of total seizure of nerves resulting in migraine headaches, nausea, and failing eyesight, which sometimes left him bedridden for weeks at a time. But he held himself ramrod straight when he walked, concealing whatever pain he had. His angular face was now severely drawn, and his lips were tightly compressed. His one good eye gave him the visage of an angry Cyclops, a "cruel wizard look."[29] This was not a man to be trifled with. He resented criticism, with a swiftness so deep in its passion that he saw debates over policy as personal vendettas against his honor. Jefferson Davis *was* the Confederacy, and to disagree with him was to dishonor the Cause and to undermine its very symbol.

Davis's lifelong worship of a code of personal honor was so exaggerated that it passed for aloofness and made others in his presence feel that he looked down on them as lesser mortals. To the common man, he was still the hero of Buena Vista, the man who once led the most famous cavalry charge of the Mexican War. But to close observers, his controlled, self-contained manner created an air of mystery about him. It was no wonder that Senator Clement Clay called him the "Sphinx of the Confederacy." Many considered him in 1860 "too austere, moody and metaphysical" to lead the Confederacy. Yet with Varina and Benjamin he could still laugh and show some of the charm beneath his stoic surface.

Davis seemed to have almost two personalities—one for social and domestic life and the other for official life. Expressing the first, he would joke and mimic, sing Indian songs from his frontier days, and spin webs of conversation so charming that women were entranced by him. In his public life, he was the personification of duty. On a particular issue he would exhaust all sources of information, study, and ponder his choices, but once he reached a conclusion, he would allow no further discussion. Though his enemies called him stubborn, he expected loyalty and support without grumbling or a hint of opposition. In war, political and military power merged: Davis was the supreme commander, and his responsibility and authority were absolute.

Varina wrote later that "Mr. Benjamin was always ready for work; sometimes, with half an hour's recess, he remained with the executive from ten in the morning until nine at night and together they traversed all the difficulties which encompassed our beleaguered land . . . both the President and the Secretary . . . worked like galley slaves, early and late. Mr. Davis came home fasting, a mere mass of throbbing nerves, perfectly exhausted; but Mr. Benjamin was always fresh and buoyant."[30]

Varina contrasted Benjamin's temperament with her husband's dark moods. "There was one striking peculiarity about [Benjamin's] temperament. No matter what disaster befell our arms, after he had done all in his power to prevent or rectify it, he was never depressed. No reverses tortured him exceedingly, as it did Mr. Davis, who though he was too reticent and self-controlled to betray his anguish, suffered like one in torment. Mr. Benjamin was serenely cheerful, played games and talked wittily as usual."[31]

While Varina wrote that paragraph in a letter about Benjamin, what is also interesting about it is the perspective it offers on the President. Benjamin only *seemed* to be less bothered by the reverses in the war; his role in social situations, at mealtimes with the Davis family, or at receptions was to join with Varina to take the President's mind off his troubles, not to intensify them. Perhaps he shared only with Varina the truth that the President's soul was being tortured each day and that the strain was also taking a physical toll as conditions worsened and the burdens grew more crushing.

The evidence has mounted for years that Davis was not the unfeeling and solitary helmsman of the Confederacy that has been portrayed. In 1978, a packet of letters from Davis was uncovered. They had been written between 1864 and 1882 and hidden for almost a hundred years in the bank vault of the First Tennessee Bank in Memphis. The thirty-five letters were written or sent by the President to his son-in-law, Joel Addison Hayes, who had been a teller in the bank where the letters were stored.[32]

The letters, which deal with both business and personal matters, belie history's view of Davis as cold, aloof, austere, and arrogant. He emerges as a warm and caring man, sensitive and dependent on the affections of his loved ones, tender and expressive. Most of the letters were in Davis's own handwriting, though some were dictated to Varina, and they radiate intimacy. He poured out his emotion for his daughter and his granddaughters, expecting the letters to be read to them:

Your mother sends her love and wishes you and the other children were here to eat grapes that come in by the bushels and are very sweet. . . . Tell the baby that the sand is very clean on the beach and we have had a succession of high tides so that she might roll in the sand, or walk on the lawn, look at the lambs, hear the mockingbirds but feel never a mosquito. Her grandmother has some splendid red lilies that she might pull, too. With my tenderest love to my children and to you as one of them, and a message to the Baby from her grandmother, she must come soon."[33]

There are poignant moments in the letters, such as a request for a picture of Jeff, Jr., the last of his four sons, who died in the late 1870s. Only two of his six children outlived him.

"I recently received a letter from a brother member of Jefferson's in the Kappa Sigma fraternity. He writes very affectionately of my boy, and asks for the society, a picture of him. One of the last he had taken."[34]

Those losses echoed in other letters as well:

We shall be greatly disappointed if we do not have you and Maggie and the baby with us at Christmas. You are all we have left to us save our child who is far away. . . . You have the precious baby now. . . . May time render her less necessary to you than our daughter is to us, when in the chances and changes of life it shall be your fate to be parted from her.[35]

None of the letters expressed anger, bitterness, or animosity toward the Union for defeating him. His son-in-law once sent him a clipping from a Detroit newspaper repeating a rumor that the South had desecrated the body of Colonel Ulrich Dahlgren, who had led a group of Northern raiders to the outskirts of Richmond. Davis refused to enter publicly into such a "misshapen controversy" but was obviously stung enough by the false charges to deny them to his family. "He was killed," he wrote, "but we warred not upon the dead."[36]

He confessed that he was unable to forget the suffering of the Confederate soldiers during the war and the hardships they faced after it had ended. To the Mississippi State legislature, which was considering a pension and a home for wounded and indigent soldiers, he wrote:

The wish that something be done for Confederate soldiers has ever been nearest to my heart, but often, as the thought unbidden arose, it has met with the remembrance that arson, pillage and confiscation had impoverished our people, and that they had no other recourse than direct taxation to provide for their needy and disabled defenders. . . .

They left their homes to defend the rights they inherited, and if they survived the War, hoped to return to those from whom they parted. . . . Brave Mississippi . . . may peace and plenty ever be throughout her borders is the prayer of one whose boyhood aspiration was, and whose desire in age is, for her honor and prosperity.[37]

He expressed a certain acceptance of death which made him even more eager for the love and warmth of his family and friends. He opened up to a Mrs. Merriwether that "only one who has been broken by the storms of Fate and who finds himself a waif on the current of life and drifting near to the sea of eternity, can feel the full force of a friendship which follows him still."[38]

The letters displayed a mood and a coloration missing from all the Davis biographies. Historians portray the President from a distance, the warrior general and career army man, mistrusting and thin-skinned, erect and egotistical, ordering his minions into battle over the advice of his generals, coldly arrogant and untouched by the human cost. One wonders how the Jefferson Davis of these recently discovered letters, whose soul seems so exposed and vulnerable, whose heart was so sensitive, could have stood the suffering, the pain, the awful pressures of the defeats and dwindling supplies, the starvation and deaths of the young and the tears of widows and families over the four terrible years of the Civil War. Behind the mask, what was the truth? How great was the tension between what seemed to be and what was, and how great was the cost of such a charade?

For all his talent and loyalty, Judah P. Benjamin did not fare much better as Secretary of War than did his predecessor, and it would be another year before the Confederates would again taste a significant victory. Disasters seemed to mount all at once and on all sides. Union armies freed western Virginia; Ulysses Grant campaigned in the West, driving all Southern armies out of Kentucky and western Tennessee; Union troops captured Fort Hatteras at the entrance to Pamlico Sound in North Carolina, threatening Roanoke Island. The only optimistic event of the fall was the odd spectacle of the *Trent* affair, which raised the tensions between Lincoln and the British Government.

Senator John Slidell, the newly named Confederate Ambassador to France, and James Mason, the tobacco-spitting Virginian whom Davis had named Ambassador to England, had taken the same ship to run the Union blockade to Nassau, St. Thomas, and finally Havana. They had picked up a British mail steamer, *Trent,* bound for England, thinking the risky part of the voyage behind them. But the next day a Union sloop shot across the bow to stop the *Trent,* even though it was flying the Union Jack. The two diplomats were seized and taken for safekeeping to Fort Warren in Massachusetts. That was just the kind of foreign policy blunder Davis and Benjamin had been praying for. England was outraged over the removal of passengers sailing under the protection of its flag, and 8,000 British troops boarded transports for Canada as the British Foreign Office demanded an apology from the former colonies.

Lincoln was in a corner, since no American President could apologize or even give in to British threats. Davis protested vigorously about the "piracy." After much breast-beating, cooler heads would take over in London and in Washington. The two Ambassadors were released after two months in custody, but for several months it was high tide in Dixie hearts.

Benjamin could be tough and judgmental when confronted with injustice. When five guns from the Tredegar Iron Works exploded, killing the men who were manning them, Benjamin wrote the harshest letter of his term to the director, Joseph R. Anderson: "It is bad enough that our brave defenders should expose their lives to the fire of the enemy under such odds as exist against us, but to furnish them with arms more dangerous to themselves than to the enemy, is utterly inexcusable."[39]

Anderson had the bearing of a West Point man, though he had left the military as a young man because he was "one of those who are not born to fortunes." A civil engineer, he had built his fortune on his talent for organization and finance and on the use of slave labor, which enabled him to compete with Northern ironmakers. Anderson wore the uniform of a brigadier general, though the army had asked him to run his manufacturing company rather than serve on the battlefields. He was a stern and haughty man, a disciplinarian who saw whatever job had to be done and mobilized the resources to do it.

Anderson was outraged and claimed sabotage, but a subsequent investigation showed that the guns had been badly designed. As a result, the War Department set up a procedure to test all the Tredegar guns before allowing them into the field. Anderson retained his bitterness toward Benjamin throughout the war.

An internal threat could be as dangerous to the Confederacy as a direct attack of Union troops. There had been an insurrection in a remote mountain area of east Tennessee, Andrew Johnson's home, where opposition to the Confederacy took on the quality of a religious crusade. Bands of armed men had assembled to assist an unexpected Union advance through the Cumberland Gap, burning bridges and cutting off the strategic Virginia–Tennessee Railroad. Davis had ordered Benjamin to quash the insurrection with troops from Memphis and Pensacola, and now the Confederacy faced the issue of what to do with the captured loyalists, which included the "Fighting Parson" William G. Brownlow, a charismatic former Methodist minister who was editor of the Knoxville *Whig.*

Benjamin and Davis discussed the wire from the colonel in charge at Knoxville, who pointed out that to turn the collaborators over to the civilian courts would be a "mere farce," for they "really deserve the gallows . . . if consistent with the laws."

Davis and Benjamin argued the options. The laws of insurrection required that the perpetrators be tried by military court martial and hanged on the spot.

If the Confederacy took such a step, however, the President would be jeopardizing the lives of thousands of the Confederacy's sympathizers in the North, many of whom were imprisoned.

Yet those men, under arms, had blown up bridges. If the government were not harsh with them, the South could face insurrection throughout the region. Not only should they be hanged, but the President agreed that the general in charge should be ordered to dangle them from the burned bridges for a week.

Parson Brownlow had been away from home the night of the burnings, and his complicity was unclear. However, the parson had been arrested anyway with a few legislators because they were leaders and spokesmen. Since his guilt for the actual destruction was unproved, Benjamin worried that if Brownlow was jailed merely for being a troublemaker, he would become a martyr. Besides, Davis had been making complaints about "upright men . . . dragged to distant dungeons" in the North, so Benjamin and Davis decided on another course: to hold the parson for a few weeks and then release him to cross Union lines. Mercy on the Confederate side should be matched by leniency in the North for Confederate prisoners. They could issue a statement about allowing their most dangerous enemy to go free rather than sully the honor of the Confederate Government by jailing an "upright man" in Knoxville. That would be a clear message to Lincoln to send the South back its own captured soldiers rather than keep them in Yankee prisons.

Benjamin had never been so tested by the President, and he quickly wrote the dispatch. "The insurrectionists not proved to be bridge burners are to be held as prisoners of war," he wrote; so much for the parson. He continued, "while the others identified as burners are to be tried summarily by drumhead court martial, and, if found guilty, executed on the spot by hanging." He then added to the order: "It would be well to leave their bodies hanging in the vicinity of the burned bridges."[40] For Benjamin, it was unlike any prior act of his career, or any other act thereafter, and it brought him face to face with the ugly reality of war: Hang those who actually did the deed but be less severe with the others.

Before carrying out the sentence, General W. H. Carroll telegraphed Benjamin for the President's approval. Benjamin replied with a wire that was an order, but carefully constructed to protect himself: "Execute the sentence of your court-martial on the bridge burners. The law does not require any approval by the President, but he entirely approves my order to hang every bridge-burner you can catch and convict."[41]

On April 30, 1864, Senator Andrew Johnson attacked Benjamin bitterly for this order. The New York *Tribune* reported that "the blood of these men, like Abel, cried aloud from the ground against the author of their death, and for succor to their wives and little ones. He read the order of Judah P. Benjamin, the Rebel Secretary of State, directing their execution, with directions that their bodies be left hanging near the burned bridges. He ventilated the conduct of this doubly-dyed traitor as a member of Congress, on the Crittendon and other propositions of Compromise, and showed him up to detestation of every honorable-minded man."[42]

When Parson Brownlow crossed the Union lines a few weeks later, he exulted: "Glory to God in the highest and on earth peace, good will toward men, except a few hell-born and hell-bound rebels in Knoxville."[43]

Brownlow, who would serve briefly as Governor of Tennessee in the Reconstruction era, had a long history of public anti-Semitism and virtually made a career of his outlandish attacks on Jews. In

February 1860, when the Congress for the first time invited a rabbi to open a House session with a prayer, Parson Brownlow commented that when "they called into their aid one of the murderers of Christ, their heads and minds were prepared for anything."[44]

One of his favorite targets was Judah Benjamin. If Benjamin throught that the Confederacy's leniency would soften Brownlow's voice, he was badly mistaken. After Brownlow was expelled, the parson asserted that he expected "no more mercy from Benjamin than was shown by his illustrious predecessors towards Jesus Christ." He claimed that Benjamin "threatened to hang [me] with or without evidence. My only wonder was that he did not threaten to crucify me."[45]

The Baltimore *Clipper* criticized Brownlow, but not in a way to give any comfort to Benjamin. "Parson Brownlow is not generally very choice in his language . . . but it is in extreme bad taste, and obnoxious to the censure [sic] of every right-minded man, thus to identify a great religious and national people with such a consummate rogue and hangman as this Benjamin."[46]

It is ironic that whereas his strengths overcame some of the President's weaknesses, Benjamin's own weaknesses as Secretary of War accentuated the President's most serious shortcomings. Benjamin had no military background and therefore no experience in the special problems of the military at war. Moreover, he had never tried to run a large bureaucracy but had always in politics served in the legislative arena. Thus he brought none of his own preconceptions to the task of implementation, no way to sift and weigh the President's demands and balance their reasonableness against the inertia of the military and governmental bureaucracies. Perhaps that was one reason Davis chose him. Davis had fought in the field and also had run the nation's Department of War under President Pierce. He wanted an expediter around him, not an experienced military man. He wanted a complete master of detail at his side at all times, someone to argue with other centers of power on his own behalf. In Judah Benjamin, he developed the perfect alter ego and technician, one whose experience never tempted him to substitute his own judgment for the President's.

Thus, Benjamin's inexperience fed the President's stubbornness, strengthening the President's view of himself as the supreme commander who knew better what to do from Richmond than did the generals in the field. Judah P. Benjamin was New Orleans, not West

Point—operating almost as a technocrat, not an equal. If the President ordered something done, Benjamin was not equipped to protect Davis from himself.

For Benjamin, seeking power and position was an early theme in life. He might reasonably have supposed that influential positions would provide a shield against anti-Semitism. The more he could become assimilated into the Christian world, the less his career would be limited by his Jewishness, and the farther he could advance. He wooed and won a non-Jewish wife from one of the wealthy families in New Orleans; he cultivated John Slidell, a powerful political friend; he joined the slaveholding aristocracy as the owner of a large plantation; he pursued wealth for the independence and the protection and access it would bring. When secession came, he faced a turning point at which any of the options he chose could have been successful. He could have accepted the ambassadorship to Spain offered by Buchanan; he could have gone to England then instead of five years later, and been a Confederate sympathizer there; he could have, like so many others from New Orleans, chosen the expatriate's life in Paris with his wife and daughter. It is fascinating that of his many options, he chose the one with the greatest risk— the Confederacy, a war that he knew would be drawn out and painful, the choice that placed triumph and disaster side by side.

Perhaps it was the gambler in him, the high-stakes card player who sought out the difficult games because the easy ones were not worth playing. A gambling man in politics constantly plays for ever increasing rewards. Judah P. Benjamin joined the Confederacy, where the risks were greater, but so was the chance of reward.

Once having joined the Cabinet, staying in it was his only option. He could not go to war, as others in the Senate and House had, because he had no history of military service or qualifications. His reputation in Richmond and Montgomery was that of an excellent lawyer—a talented administrator and adviser with a need to serve his "client," to lose himself in Jefferson Davis's shadow. But the key to his response to power in the Confederacy was in his Jewishness. His were the actions of a man surrounded by Christian distrust, who knew he was always a possible target of opprobrium, who lived in a storm of racism and smoldering violence. His solution was to be as unobjectionable as possible, to work hard, to do a thorough and competent job, and, above all, to serve Jefferson Davis.

Once Louisiana fell to the North, Benjamin lost the political source of his power. Davis no longer needed to mollify or rally a wavering state. That Benjamin was a Louisianian did not matter as much politically later in the war as it had in the beginning. Now Benjamin, as a Jew in the Cabinet, was even more reliant on Davis as the source of his influence. His dependence, which Davis saw as loyalty, coupled with acknowledged brilliance, made Benjamin an ideal choice for an insecure Confederate President to place in positions of ever widening responsibilities.

8

The First Lady and the
Secretary of State:
A Strategic Friendship

❧❧❧

The Secretary of War was not just another Cabinet officer but an intimate of the Davis family who spent considerable time at the Confederate White House. In fact, the routine of the President was such that the White House almost became Benjamin's second home in Richmond.

The Confederate White House was a graceful three-story mansion designed in the Federal style by an architect who had studied with Thomas Jefferson. Built between 1816 and 1818, the pale gray stucco caused many a wag to call it the "Gray House," but the plantation character of it—high ceilings and full-length windows opening onto a garden with fruit trees and flowers—reminded Varina of her childhood.

The eight tall columns, lined two-by-two across the front veranda, protected the porch yet were spaced so that one could sit there and look out into the gardens. The veranda extended around to the side of the house, where, because of the slope of the property, it stood 12 to 15 feet above the ground, providing a magnificent view of the James River and the Virginia valley. Its red roof seemed to crown the structure with a special country charm, as did the small white steeple on the top.

"Queen Varina" was what the press called the First Lady in a derisive reference to her style of entertainment and dress. It seemed that she could do nothing right. If she entertained at all, the press criticized her for frivolity; if she did not entertain enough, she would be accused of neglecting her duty as First Lady. She tried to find a compromise by holding an open house twice a month and giving a modest number of parties, thereby reducing the President's isolation from people in Richmond and bolstering his morale. She came to see the political wisdom of keeping an open White House, as time and time again she watched the informal lines of communication work to bypass the formal chains of command when junior officers in the army and lesser officials in the government could just walk. up to the President or a Cabinet officer and talk. She felt it was good for them and for their wives to be involved with the leadership in an easy atmosphere of Southern hospitality, so that they could hear statements directly from the President rather than through the biased editorials of Edward A. Pollard and John M. Daniel at the Richmond *Examiner.*

Much has been written of the décor, furnishings, and customs of the Confederate White House; many have described in detail snatches of conversation, the many quotations, and letters of description. Even menus have been preserved for the historian. Judah Benjamin, particularly, stood out in the diaries of women, who wrote of his immense charm. A contemporary memoir said of him: "Hebrew in blood, English in tenacity of grasp and purpose, Mr. Benjamin was French in taste."[1] In war-torn Richmond, the moments of enjoyment and sporadic luxury glittered in the memories of those who mostly faced deprivation.

Varina reported that "intimate friends received verbal invitations" from Benjamin, who said, "Do come to dinner or tea; we succeeded in running the blockade this week."[2] Varina wrote that she and Benjamin always knew what "running the blockade" meant: preserved fruits, loaf sugar, some good tea, and real coffee, not the awful hot water strained through dried beans and peanuts that was ordinarily served as a substitute. Benjamin would often arrive at the White House with candies and small gifts for the Davis children, who played under the sycamores on Clay Street, collecting the pods off the ground from the honey shuck tree.

Today, the Confederate White House has been restored in loving detail with its worn marble stairs, silver doorknobs, mantelpieces, and some of the original furnishings.

The entry hall is a small room dominated on the left and right of the doorway by two life-size black statues of a female Comedy and Tragedy, draped in the Greek style and holding gas lanterns in their hands. They provide a paradoxical greeting for visitors. Comedy is the larger of the two, hulking and ominous but with a surprising dagger in her right hand almost hidden from view. Tragedy's left hand is outstretched, holding a tragic mask. Tragedy is made all the more eerie by the slight smile on her face, as if she were enjoying the painful expression on the face of the mask.

To the right of the entryway is a spiral staircase that leads upstairs to the President's office, the Davis's bedroom, and the children's nursery. One can imagine Varina making her way down the staircase to greet visitors.

Varina was tall and heavy-set, and she wore her black hair in a bun that emphasized her features; her ready smile added crinkles of approaching middle age to her dark, expressive eyes. Her moods and emotions were so symbiotic with those of her husband that she both hated his enemies and loved his friends with equal intensity, and her eyes did not allow her to disguise either emotion.

Varina Davis was no ordinary woman. She was brilliant, tart-tongued, well educated, and perceptive. Never mind that Southern purists questioned her loyalty because she was the granddaughter of Richard Howell, the Revolutionary Governor of New Jersey. It meant a life bred to politics, and Davis loyalists like Benjamin respected that breeding.

Although Varina had been raised a Southern woman whose principal role in life was to flatter the men around her, she had grown impatient with such demands at an early age. She understood Southern male vanity well enough and was not above using the cavalier tradition for her own purposes. But she had been raised with Yankee competence as well, almost as a son to her father, fired by ambition inappropriate for a Southern girl and a sense of destiny. She had made the transition from Southern belle to plantation manager with ease and relief, eagerly leaving behind the helplessness that other girls were instructed to display in order to catch a beau. Now her problem was a matter of masquerade. Men bristled when she argued with them and blustered into speechless fury when she turned their own arguments against them to win a point soundly. She delighted in those triumphs, although they generated barroom complaints that Jefferson Davis was being "totally dominated by that woman."[3]

Varina's tongue had gotten her in trouble many times, but she was too confident to change her ways. At parties she was often found standing among the clusters of men listening to military talk and absorbing the information. She was wise enough not to speak out in such situations, for that would cross the bounds of propriety for Southern womanhood, but sometimes she could not resist a tart remark when some pompous brigadier suggested an outlandish tactic. Other women did not take well to her invasion of the male preserve. They talked of the war, too, but their special perspective was the home front—caring for the wounded in the hospitals and rolling bandages from tablecloths, sheets, and napkins, and, as some women confessed, even cutting up their fine linen underwear into 2-inch wedges for surgical compresses. Varina did her share of that kind of thing herself, mostly to set an example to others, but she did not enjoy it. She preferred to play a more lofty and ceremonial role. So she visited many hospitals instead of settling on just one, delivering supplies, bringing cakes and candies in a large basket, or just paying a call to thank everyone for their hard work and devotion. She aspired to become the President's personal emissary in the city of Richmond. Once, when a patient broke out with smallpox that threatened the other patients and nurses, she rushed back home and got the President to issue an immediate order quarantining him.

She was deeply frustrated by the war. As a woman she was relegated to the sidelines; she could not speak, and yet she saw the reality more starkly than her husband. In a letter to Lawley at the end of her life, she wrote: "The dear but desperate days of my Richmond life were the more painful to me as silence was necessary on my part, but from the first day of secession I felt like some poor creature circulating about a whirlpool, helpless and drawing every moment nearer to the vortex. My dear husband's noble faith in the final triumph of the right, I never shared. The paper blockade quietly permitted by foreign nations and acknowledged as binding seemed to me to close all avenues to the repair of the war's waste—I felt the birthright of our people was well worth the war, but knew from the first we had lost it."[4]

When Benjamin visited her, he often sat with Varina on a horsehair sofa around a marble-topped center table with a tea kettle wrapped in a quilted cozy and cups ready for serving. To an objective eye, the furniture in the White House is ordinary, in contrast with the grand style of the architecture. Varina was criticized by the aristocracy of Richmond in the early days because the furnishings did not compare with Lincoln's White House, a sure sign, they pointed out, of her frontier upbringing and lack of taste. Mrs. Chesnut, the Confederate diarist, said Mrs. Wigfall described her as "a coarse western woman."[5] The criticism stung her. Varina had a "Natchez chin," her husband always said, which reflected an upper-class Whig background. The fact was that the house had been purchased by the city of Richmond from a wealthy merchant but had been furnished economically. Varina had not brought her furniture with her from Mississippi, though she did bring her engraved silver and fine china. The President had insisted that they keep the house modest and not redecorate during the war, while the rest of Richmond was suffering. They had been dropped into this world like visitors from another country.

Richmond wives constantly scoffed over the fact that Varina was not the President's first choice for a wife. Since his first wife had been the daughter of a future President of the United States, Varina had to suffer the suggestion that another woman might have been a more suitable First Lady.

Davis had been thirty-seven and she eighteen when they were married in 1845, and the difference grew more apparent as the war continued and he seemed to age so quickly. But when the Davises and Benjamin were together, he seemed younger, for he abandoned some of the somber rigidity of the public man and removed the stolid mask of office.

In the dining room, when Benjamin visited, the round rosewood dining table with the birdseye maple inlay was set for only three places. Varina liked to use her prize-winning Sèvres china, the rose-patterned coffee cups in blue and gold, and her demitasse spoons with the engraved "D" on them.

She recorded in a letter that Benjamin liked McHenry sherry, anchovy toast, and beefsteak pie. She recalled that Benjamin broke through the crust, breathed in the aroma deeply, then, with the care of one of the great chefs of Paris, forked the morsels into his mouth with his eyes closed, savoring every nuance of the spices, saying, "I have only eaten it in this perfection on the Cunard steamers and I shall enjoy the memory of the scream of the sea birds, the lashing of the sea, and the blue above and the blue below."[6]

After she offered him some hot bread with flour from a noted mill in Virginia and watched him spread a walnut paste on it derived from a huge tree on the White House grounds, Benjamin sighed, "Ah, with bread made of Crenshaw's flour, spread with paste made of English walnuts and a glass of McHenry's sherry, a man's patriotism becomes rampant."

When Varina asked the secret to his happy disposition, his reply was that "to every long Cabinet meeting, I carry a small cake which I eat when I feel fatigued." It was an early hint of Benjamin's lifelong bout with diabetes, which ultimately weakened his heart and took his life.

Varina wrote that Benjamin "was a gourmet after the most refined and absteminous model. He ate little but if that happened to be coarse and badly cooked, he really suffered. He loved 'lollipops' as he called candy, like a child; and he has often been heard to declare that absence of hors d'oeuvres depressed his vitality and mentality, though when he had them, he partook of them most sparingly."

Varina described Benjamin's feelings for Jules St. Martin, who often stayed at home to eat with the other members of the Louisiana delegation who boarded at the Main Street house:

> One day when there happened to be a prospect of our having some very good brains en papillotte and afterwards some mayonnaise, we invited Mr. Benjamin to dinner. He stopped midway in a criticism upon *Les Miserables* by Victor Hugo, which had just reached the Confederacy, and whispered to me, "I do not enjoy my dinner, but Jules would like these dishes—he is young and values such things." I begged him to let me send some of the dinner to his house—but he declined saying "The papillotes would fall flat, and the salad would fade; but if I might take him some cake and lollipops, I should feel very happy." He would not allow a servant to carry them, but took them in a parcel covered with a napkin and walked home, beaming with the hope of conferring pleasure upon his beloved Jules.

Varina invited Benjamin and Jules to dinner together and observed their interaction: "Jules, upon one occasion, feeling as many small men do, that his tiny proportion required more stateliness of address than if he had possessed height, protested upon Mr. Benjamin's testifying his tenderness to him by some caressing words by saying, 'You will make Mrs. Davis think that I am a child.' Mr. Benjamin looked apologetically at him, and said 'No man ever loved his child any better, but love like ours must be founded on respect, at least mine is for you;' and throughout their visit the gentle deference [he] manifested towards his wife's brother showed such a craving for affection, such unwillingness to offend that it almost brought tears to my eyes."[7]

There is a tragic undertone to this picture of Benjamin and Jules together. If he seemed excessive in his affection for Jules, it was because he was bereft and alone in Richmond, cut off from all other members of his family. He came from a large family and even as a young man loved performing for them by reading novels, telling ghost stories, and making up games for his nieces. All the frustration of his loneliness became focused on Jules, as if the young man were still an adolescent and Benjamin both of his parents. But his caring, his thoughtfulness, his nurturing drew upon Benjamin's best instincts in a city beset by pain, fear, and bereavement.

Jules St. Martin, really his brother-in-law, was in effect Benjamin's surrogate son. Raising the boy as his own, Benjamin's attachment was deep and paternal. Without a son of his own, in a marriage that Varina characterized as "gruesome," he seemed to have created a fantasy son in Jules to give him an outlet for the softer side of his nature. It would not have been surprising if Natalie had exhorted him to keep her brother safe.

He arranged for Jules to have a safe slot at the War Department and made sure that he remained there all during the war. Even as Richmond was stripped of all its able-bodied men, Jules worked as a clerk, probably because of Benjamin's intervention and insistence. One might take that fact as a measure of Benjamin's lack of patriotism when faced with a conflict between obligations to family and duty to country. When it came down to cases, he could encourage others to sacrifice their sons but could not do so himself. He was in this case, as in so many others to come, a realist, not a romantic.

There is a more sympathetic interpretation: that Benjamin bent the rules in order to have some remnant of emotional life in Richmond. It required a rationalization of his own importance to judge that the emotional and mental balance of a key Cabinet member was more important than one more body in battle. And thus, Benjamin was willing to court another possible embarrassment, to be mocked by colleagues and by friends, or be thought less than honorable by the President and Varina. By publicly treating Jules as much younger than he actually was, he made a psychological leap: Jules was a boy and too young for the armies in Virginia.

Frustrated generals who would not attack the President publicly had a convenient target in his new Secretary of War. As the Union forces struck back into every corner of the Confederacy, criticism of Benjamin mounted. He was not a military man, and his orders, though flowing from constant meetings with the President, were treated as originating from him and resented in the field as interference and amateurism.

On January 1, 1862, a restless General T. J. Jackson, already known as "Stonewall," celebrated the New Year by moving his troops in terrible weather into the western Virginia hills to challenge five thousand Federals assembled there. It took them two weeks to travel 35 miles in the sleet and snow. With news of their march preceding them, the Federals were gone when they arrived. He left General William W. Loring's division to hold the isolated little town of Romney and returned to his original position at Winchester, Virginia. Without food and proper clothing, Loring's men became desperate. Eleven officers and Loring himself petitioned the President and the Secretary of War to allow them to abandon their position on the grounds of hardship and strategic unimportance. Benjamin consulted Davis and General Joe Johnston, Jackson's commanding general, who feared that "Jackson had scattered his forces too far for safety." When intelligence arrived in Richmond of Union troop movements nearby, Benjamin telegraphed Jackson that "our news indicates that a movement is being made to cut off General Loring's command. Order him back to Winchester immediately."[8]

Jackson complied but shocked Benjamin with an additional paragraph in his letter. "With such interference in my command I cannot expect to be of much service in the field; and accordingly respectfully request to be ordered to report for duty to the superintendent of the Virginia Military Institute at Lexington. . . . Should this application not be granted, I respectfully request that the President will accept my resignation from the army."[9]

General Johnston wrote a conciliatory note; Governor Letcher of Virginia begged Jackson to withdraw his resignation as "a calamity to the country and the cause." State Comptroller Jonathan Bennett lashed out: "Mr. Benjamin, the Jew, is a most remarkable specimen of indiscretion, lack of judgment, and disregard of the courtesies." Jackson's name alone was "worth ten thousand men." A Richmond minister wrote that God would give Jackson victory above those who "put their trust in the strength of the flesh."[10]

Jackson reconsidered, but the generals could smell blood in the water. Johnston wrote that Benjamin was causing "great confusion and an approach to demoralization" by giving orders that should come "only from the commanding general."[11] Beauregard earlier had complained with contempt that Benjamin was a "functionary at his desk," who wrote him "lectures on law while the enemy is mustering in our front." Impressions of inexperienced decision-making were permeating the ranks through the newspaper reports of each flap. A Confederate soldier sensed the mood in the air and wrote in his diary that Judah Benjamin knew as much about war as "an Arab knows of the Sermon on the Mount."[12]

Benjamin's past seemed to shadow him, especially when feelings ran high and the anti-Davis faction in the Confederate Congress or in the army was looking for a target to blame for the bad news from the battlefield. Thomas R. R. Cobb of Georgia, one of the most relentless Davis critics and the brother of Howell Cobb, the former Governor of Georgia whom many had wanted to be President of the Confederacy, wrote his wife on January 15, 1862: "Speaking of Jews, this little contemptible persecutor of Howell's and mine, Benjamin, Secty. of War is an eunuch. The poor fool to try and hide it, married. The woman told of course, but unfortunately in the meantime had a baby. They have never been divorced. When she went to Washington the women had a 'pow-wow' on the question of visiting her but as they had no proof of his condition were obliged to receive her. She now lives in Paris with a paramour. This is the 'on-dit' of the City."[13]

Such a charge by an avowed enemy of Davis, suggesting that Benjamin was not a proper man, reeks of malice and is appropriately suspect. But it does provoke some questions about the nature of Benjamin's relationships with women. His only marriage was a disappointment, and so far as we know there were no other intimate relationships with other women, despite his clearly gentlemanly and charming manner with many women as reported by observers. Whether, in more intimate matters, he was merely reticent or suffered a deeper unhappiness is impossible to know on the evidence available. Cobb's letter might explain why the ladies of Washington were driven to such an extreme action as to convene a meeting to discuss whether they would receive Natalie: There may have been a rumor current, possibly started by Natalie herself, that Benjamin could not father a child and that, therefore, Ninette was someone else's child. It is also a sad possibility that, as long as three years after Natalie had left her husband, Benjamin's fidelity to his unhappy marriage lent credence to such ugly gossip, or "on-dit," in worldly Richmond.

Chastened by his previous conflict with General Jackson, Benjamin wrote an exceedingly flattering letter appointing Jackson to the Shenandoah command:

"The choice of the Government has fallen on you—This choice has been dictated not only by a just appreciation of your qualities as a Commander, but by other weighty considerations—Your intimate knowledge of the country, of its population and resources rendered you peculiarly fitted to assume this command—Nor is this all—The people of that District with one voice have made constant and urgent appeals to you, in whom they have confidence, should their defense be assigned."[14] But compliments would not shield him from events, especially when failures on the battlefield began to mount and the military needed a scapegoat.

The anger against Benjamin came to a head after the fall of Roanoke Island in early February 1862. Benjamin had been under intense pressure from General Henry Wise at Roanoke and Governor Clark of North Carolina to send many more men and arms to the garrison there. He had resisted for reasons that would not be known until twenty-five years after the war, and he accepted the public condemnation in silence to protect his country. Roanoke was sacrificed, because to have done otherwise would have revealed to the enemy just how desperate the South was.

In January 1862, Benjamin wrote a convincing letter of deception to General Wise in Norfolk:

> I have not yet seen your requisition for munitions, but think there can be no difficulty in sending you from here a moderate supply of fixed ammunition for field pieces; but our supply of cannon powder is *very* limited—at the first indication however of an attack on Roanoke Island a supply will be sent you—with the number of batteries now requiring supply we have a very small reserve that we can only part with to the point that may be actually attacked.[15]

Only the President, Varina, and Benjamin knew the truth—that he had sent no powder to General Wise at Roanoke because he had none to send; no cannon because the blockade was strangling the routes from Europe; no rifles or ammunition because the South did not have the skill or the iron to produce them fast enough. Rather than order an abandonment of the island, which could have revealed their dire situation, Davis ordered Benjamin to tell the 2,500 men garrisoned there to hold fast with the batteries they had, hoping that an island defense would be a sufficient equalizer. They never imagined that the Union could muster five-to-one odds: 13,000 assault troops put ashore in eighty gunboats at an undefended point down the 10-mile length of shoreline. The ensuing defeat introduced the Confederacy to a new "half-navy half-army" sea monster that could slither ashore breathing fire and devastation at any point on the Eastern Seaboard.[16]

At the dedication of the Robert E. Lee monument in Richmond twenty-five years after the war, Colonel Charles Marshall, an aide-de-camp on General Lee's staff, read part of a letter from Benjamin which revealed that President Davis had agreed to allow Benjamin to be publicly censured:

> I consulted the President whether it was best for the country that I should submit to unmerited censure or reveal to a Congressional Committee our poverty and my utter inability to supply the requisitions of General Wise, and thus run the risk that the fact should become known to some of the spies of the enemy, of whose activity we were well assured. It was thought best for the public service that I should suffer the blame in silence and a report of censure on me was accordingly made by the Committee of Congress.[17]

The criticism of Benjamin by the generals broke out in full cry among the Richmond population itself, since Roanoke was not a distant defeat in easily written off mountain terrain like eastern Kentucky and western Virginia; its loss threatened New Bern, North Carolina, and the train route directly to Richmond. General Henry Wise, the vituperative blusterer who knew politics better than warfare, had spent three days in Richmond arguing face-to-face with Benjamin, who could only listen with his irritating half-smile and tell his outpost commander that he would "part with" his small reserve of powder (of which there was none, in truth) at "the point of actual attack."

Wise lost his son, Captain Jennings Wise, in the battle, and his funeral at St. James Episcopal Church in Richmond brought thousands into the streets in the snow and slush to watch the cortège of one of the prize sons of Virginia, the captain of the elite Richmond Blues, killed at Roanoke, now being borne to the cemetery in a coffin draped with the flags of Virginia and the Confederacy, bearing the dead hero's cap and sword.[18] Benjamin could watch the procession from his window at the War Department, knowing that his presence could well have created an ugly incident to mar the ceremony. The Wise family never forgave Benjamin. One nephew, Jennings Wise, wrote that "my grandfather always charged Benjamin with his murder," and a grandson, John Wise, told Meade in an interview in 1936 that the "fat Jew sitting at his desk" was responsible.[19]

Captain Wise's brother, John Wise, wrote about Benjamin and Roanoke Island in a book entitled *The End of An Era*, published in

1899, which was so popular for its biting satire and blunt descriptions that it went through twenty-seven printings, selling 12,329 copies (a best seller of its time, with widespread readership in the South). He wrote that "Benjamin was an easy-spoken, cool, suave Jew, quiet and diplomatic in speech, never excited. It disturbed his nerves to have General Wise in his department." He described Benjamin as "oleaginous . . . his keg-like form and over-deferential manner suggestive of a shopkeeper. But his eye redeemed him and his speech was elegantly polished, even if his nose was hooked and his thick lips shone red amidst the curly black of his semitic beard." Benjamin, he continued, "had more brains and less heart than any other civic leader in the South. He was an English Jew and a lawyer of the first rank. He entered upon employment as attorney for a client. . . . If his client was in any case hanged . . . likely as not, he would be having a bottle of Madeira and a cigar at his club at the moment the hanging was taking place. . . . When a case was lost, he did not bemoan it; he found another. . . . The Confederacy and its collapse were no more to Judah P. Benjamin than last year's birds nest."[20]

A week later Benjamin met with the Congressional committee investigating the Roanoke Island disaster. Henry Foote had pressed the case brutally during several hours of questioning in which Benjamin time and again said, "I take personal responsibility for the decision at Roanoke."[21] By "personal," he was trying to protect Jefferson Davis from criticism for the loss.

Henry Foote, the archnemesis of the Davis administration, had been a journalist and a lawyer before the war, an orator of the fist-pounding and Bible-spouting variety who could hold a jury spell-bound for hours in the Mississippi heat. He was a small, wiry man with a bantam's combativeness, piercing black eyes, and, since his youth, a bald head, which exaggerated a brow permanently creased with anger. He had gone far in the extremist atmosphere of Southern politics, where fire-eating and threats substituted for reasoned argument. He carried a loaded revolver onto the floor of Congress, loved dueling pistols, and once fired a shot at a Tennessee colleague who hit him over the head with an umbrella. He was nicknamed "hangman" for having once threatened to hang an antislavery senator "from the tallest tree" in Mississippi. In 1851 he defeated Jefferson Davis for Governor of Mississippi by 999 votes out of 50,000 cast in a bitter campaign. As the two U.S. Senators from Mississippi, they had previously traveled together to Washington and had lived in the same rooming house; however, they broke with each other in a

Christmas morning fist fight over political and personal issues. They hated each other with the bad blood that politicians reserve for brothers from their own soil. That hatred gushed out of Foote at anyone in the Davis administration, although he reserved his most stinging lash for the man he called "Judas Iscariot Benjamin," the "Jewish puppeteer" behind the "Davis tyranny" and the cause of the South's hardship. A political opportunist who loved running for any office wherever he lived, Foote had moved to Nashville, Tennessee, and soon thereafter was elected to represent his district in the Confederate House of Representatives.

Soon after the hearing, Foote announced his intention to introduce a motion of censure in the Congress. "Mr. Benjamin is an able politician, a finished lawyer, and a man of silvery tongue," he stated "but he is not fit to be Secretary of War; he is utterly incompetent. [He] should not be allowed to be the destroyer of our country."[22] Foote also declared that he intended to propose to amend the Constitution so that "no Jew will be allowed within twelve miles of the capital."[23] That way he would dispose of two problems at once: the extortioners who speculated on the misfortune of others and the treasonous member of Mr. Davis's Cabinet.

In cold sheets of rain whipped by gusts of Northern wind, Judah P. Benjamin joined the procession of Cabinet members, governors, Congressmen, and generals that marched from the old Virginia House of Delegates to a platform just beneath the statue of George Washington to listen to the first inaugural address of Jefferson Davis. On lower pedestals around the base of the statue later sculptures of other heroes were placed: Patrick Henry with his arms outstretched in a pose bespeaking liberty or death and Thomas Jefferson, brooding on the inalienable right of the people to change their governments and throw off the yoke of tyranny. All those metaphors were translated into Southern rhetoric. The father of the country had come from Virginia, so it seemed fitting for Jefferson Davis of Mississippi to be inaugurated in his shadow.

The President wore a black suit for the ceremony instead of his usual gray, and Varina thought to herself that he looked like "a willing victim going to his funeral pyre."[24] Four Negro footmen, also in black with white cotton gloves, accompanied the carriage at such a slow pace that when Varina leaned forward to ask the coachman what was wrong, he answered, "This, ma'am, is the only way we always does in Richmond at funerals and suchlike."[25]

The crowd stood drenched in the rain, creating, in Varina's words, "a panorama of umbrellas,"[26] looking like an "immense mushroom bed,"[27] the rain splattering on them with such a drumbeat of sound that most people could not hear a word. Davis took the oath in dignity, and when he bowed to kiss the Book, a great cheer went up.

Benjamin sat with the Cabinet and listened to the President's somber speech, its tone underscored by the bad news from Roanoke Island and Tennessee.

"A million men," the President said to the crowd, straining to be heard over the rain, "are now standing in hostile array and waging war along a frontier of thousands of miles. Battles have been fought, sieges have been conducted, and although the contest is not ended and the tide for the moment is against us, the final result in our favor is not doubtful."[28]

His eyes were sunk deeper than ever in his sockets, and Varina wrote that he "stood pale and emaciated." His face was so drawn and gaunt that he took on the "mien of a fasting holy man" when he lifted his eyes and arms to heaven at the end of his speech.[29] "My hope," he said "is reverently fixed on Him whose favor is ever vouchsafed to the cause which is just. . . . To Thee, O God, I trustingly commit myself and prayerfully invoke Thy blessing on my country and its cause."[30]

The silence at the end of Davis's speech startled the audience. It was as if the city of Richmond were attending a church service with the people dispersing in an orderly fashion without applause, not in a spirit of rejoicing but in resolution and prayer. The President's speech was too sad and moralistic, but the President had insisted on such a somber tone. It revealed Davis's sanctimonious side, more the preacher at a graveside on inauguration day than the determined and fighting leader.

Varina had found him that morning on his knees praying and wanted to comfort him. But rather than rest up for the speech and the reception that evening, he had gone to the office before the ceremony to put in a couple of hours' work. Worried that he seemed unable to relax, she climbed into her carriage at the ceremony and returned home rather than see him struggle through the speech in the rain.

Benjamin might have felt that he and Varina were the only sane people in a world gone mad. They shared a dangerous knowledge that must never be revealed to anyone: that the President could go for days unable to function, brought down into deep depression by war news and bedridden with neuralgia, causing him throbbing headaches and stomach pains.

Diagnosis from this distance is hazardous, although the term "neuralgia" has had a long history. The 1801 dictionary defined it as "an affection of one or more nerves (esp. of the head or face), causing pain which is usually of an intermittent but frequently intense character." Medical histories in the nineteenth century used the term for a range of nervous disorders. It affected women differently from men. Men would suffer from the more debilitating forms of the malady that doctors today call "functional disorders." It usually had its onset after the age of forty and could be brought on by work pressures, tensions, and anxiety. In modern terms, according to the *Encyclopaedia Britannica*, "there is usually no evidence of change in the nerve tissue itself. The intense pain is usually described by patients as 'stabbing,' 'shooting,' or 'lightning-like.' . . . Areas around the nose and mouth become hypersensitive and, when touched, trigger an attack. Attacks are also touched off by talking, eating, drinking or exposure to cold." Its more serious and rarer form affected the pharynx, tonsils, back of the tongue, and middle ear, "often rendering the afflicted immobile and unable to speak." The cause was and is unknown, but "the pains may be excruciating beginning in the throat and radiating to the ears or down the side of the neck." Since there is no deterioration of the nerves or identifiable disease, the cause is characterized in the encyclopedia as "psychosomatic." Often the patient would just withdraw and remain quiet and bedridden until the symptoms subsided.[31]

Jefferson Davis also complained of "dyspepsia," a term for indigestion that nineteenth century sufferers used for all abdominal discomfort from chronic heartburn to more serious organic diseases. Early medical journals described dyspepsia as "various forms of disorder of the digestive organs, involving weakness, loss of appetite and depression of the spirits."[32] It could be associated with worry or fear (psychogenic indigestion) or with various types of food, such as coffee or spices. We now know that if it persists over a long period of time, it probably is an ulcer, and some doctors consider the term, in its historical usage when the condition is chronic, as synonymous with ulcers. Davis complained of stomach pains, and Varina reported instances of nausea and vomiting over the course of the war, all symptoms consistent with an ulcerative condition.

His physical problems were another theme in the letters uncovered in 1978 and in the personal bills for medical care that were also discovered in the Memphis bank vault.[33] The illnesses that plagued Davis during the war followed him the rest of his life. He complained in the letters of "suffering from rheumatism in my back and neuralgia in my head," fears of yellow fever and scarlet fever, swollen limbs, coughs, nausea, colds, and continuing headaches.

Jefferson Davis suffered intensely from various illnesses over the course of his life. He had almost died from the same yellow fever that had taken his first bride and suffered almost annually from fevers in the plantation years. Varina revealed that his nervous system had been so affected by the wounds at Buena Vista that he had taken ten years to recover fully. He himself described his physical condition just before the war as wasted by "protracted, violent disease."[34] Varina reported of the persistence of illness during the war in her memoir—of his nerves "throbbing," his need for rest to ease the headaches, and his decisions to "fast" at critical times to prevent abdominal pains.[35] His newly found letters reveal that after the war his maladies continued, but since he lived to the age of eighty-one, one clear possibility is that they were ulcers, not a more serious organic disease, and that his problems were psychosomatic in origin and yet debilitating nonetheless.

Judah P. Benjamin was the opposite. He was well known for his pleasant disposition, his humor at dark times, and his capacity for long hours and exacting work. His diabetes did not become serious until the end of his life. Moreover, he was not distracted by personal or family responsibilities in Richmond. He could throw himself body and soul into the war, making himself totally available to the President and Varina in emergencies and becoming such a frequent visitor to the White House that he was almost a member of the family.

In health, outlook, and availability, he became the strong rock for Davis to lean on, the instrumentality for policy and detailed administration while the President was incapacitated, the extension of the President's frail hand and body.

Severe and chronic illness psychologically deprives a person of control, and in the case of Jefferson Davis it caused a reaction that made him even more assertive in those areas of his life over which he could exercise power—his working life especially. For a man raised with a strict code of honor, overcoming pain was an element of his military breeding. Part of his personality was to collapse and recover, then pull himself together in spite of his pain. The continuing pain was like having a secret. Benjamin's administrative skills then were part of the disguise, an essential instrument for the President's need to exercise continuing control.

It was the President's sporadic bouts with illness and overall poor health that projected Benjamin so powerfully into Confederate history. The presidency operated as a collaboration, not in the person of a single man, and flowed smoothly regardless of the President's incapacities. For long periods, and on subjects of varying levels of importance, Judah P. Benjamin acted in Davis's name, wrote speeches and dispatches for him, and presided over an occasional Cabinet meeting. Generally, Benjamin served as his alter ego, his "right hand," as Varina described the role.[36] As an intimate listener and energetic second-in-command, Benjamin also served as keeper of his uncertainties, instrument of action, sharer of the burden. Unlike the President, he bore no responsibility to issue public statements or inspire the populace, no need for eloquence or vaulting rhetoric; he had no need to make appearances, deal with political pressures, stroke the generals, or put up with the pettiness of the bureaucracy and the Congress in quite the same way as the President. He was free to absorb everything, to become the encyclopedia and the true eye, to know the unbiased truth even if he hesitated to voice it.

In a private letter after the war to his friend James Mason, who had requested information, Benjamin wrote, "I have hardly anything to which I can refer to refresh my memory, but I have . . . a bound copy of the President's messages to Congress, which you (who were in on our secrets) know to have been written by me, as the President was too pressed with other duties to command sufficient time for preparing them himself."[37]

Except for the reference in this letter, Benjamin was silent on his role in history. In the 1860s the President, especially if he was a man as proud as Jefferson Davis, was expected to draft his own speeches. It would have been an open invitation to intense criticism by political enemies to reveal otherwise.

Mary Chesnut's diary describes a number of the anti-Semitic reactions to Benjamin's relationship to the President. For example, she quotes from a conversation with a leader in the Confederacy who complained to her, "They say Benjamin wrote the President's message. Never. Jeff Davis writes his own messages. Besides, the blame of all our disasters is laid on God the Father in this message. If Benjamin had written it, the Jew would have accused Jesus Christ instead."[38]

Mary Boykin Chesnut's *A Diary from Dixie*, published in 1905, is the chatty, intelligent and often witty account of a good listener at the top of the social ladder, complete with reports, conversations, gossip, and pithy comments on the times written on a daily basis over the course of the war. The book has been dissected and reworked by the historian C. Vann Woodward, who discovered that Chesnut sharpened and condensed her material until 1886. With the suppressed passages restored, it remains the most extraordinary firsthand record of the Civil War. The new version, entitled *Mary Chesnut's Civil War* and published in 1981, has fifteen references to "Jews," where the previous standard edition had none, and it is a great deal saltier than the edited version on the subject of Judah P. Benjamin.

"The mob calls him 'Mr. Davis's pet Jew'," she writes in the unexpurgated version, "a King Street Jew, cheap, very cheap, &c&c."[39] In another passage she reflects the ambiguity of Southern attitudes toward Jews: "Not one doubt is there in our bosoms that we are not the chosen people of God. And that He is fighting for us. Why not? We are no worse than Jews, past or present, nor Yankees."[40]

In many ways, Benjamin was not equipped for the role the President assigned him. His selection, as a nonmilitary man, to be Jefferson Davis's right hand reflected the President's insecurity. Davis wanted an implementer, someone who because of a lack of previous military training spoke only in the President's name and would be perceived as having no independent military point of view. Benjamin was a brilliant lawyer, to be sure, but inexperienced in military affairs; Jewish, and because of that doubly despised by the generals for what they felt were political rather than military decisions. Thus Benjamin was shackled by biblical antagonism and suffered the fate of the Sephardic court Jews from whom he was descended—they could serve but could not challenge. Being Jewish made him more vulnerable, but it also made him more loyal, more careful, eager for a less visible role. His only option was loyalty to the failing policies of the President. In that sense, he shares a greater responsibility for the tragic outcome than has previously been recognized.

Benjamin had watched Davis's growing impatience with Secretary of State Robert Hunter come to a climax after the inauguration. In an intense Cabinet discussion of military strategy, Hunter had ventured a lame opinion, and Davis had snapped at him: "Mr. Hunter, you are Secretary of State, and when information is wished of that department, it will be time for you to speak."[41] Hunter had been Virginia's favorite son candidate for President, and no one speaks to a Virginian that way. Hunter's resignation was on Davis's desk the next morning.

In the same period, the President received a note from the War

Department saying that, because of Roanoke Island, a lack-of-confidence resolution had been offered in Congress calling for Secretary Benjamin's dismissal. The President brushed it aside. He had the votes to block such a resolution in the Congressional committee, and in any case he had determined on a more novel way of solving his "Benjamin problem." He would appoint his loyal colleague Secretary of State.

Varina explained that "while many of their constituents objected to Mr. Benjamin's retaining the portfolio of War, because of reverses which no one could have averted, the President promoted him to the State Department with a personal and aggrieved sense of injustice done to the man who had now become his friend and right hand."[42]

Henry Foote had another explanation: Though Benjamin was a "fiendish character," he felt that "the Confederate Senate was persuaded to confirm him—mainly, as one may reasonably conjecture, because of its being known that Mr. Davis needed constantly the aid of a facile and polished writer in the preparation of his messages and other important political documents."[43]

Sallie Ann Brock Putnam, who in 1867 wrote a memoir about the war entitled *Richmond During The War,* described the deeper reactions to the new Secretary of State:

> Mr. Benjamin was not forgiven. His neglect seemed culpable, yet
> we had the mortification to behold his promotion to a position
> of higher grade, though at the time of less vital importance to
> us. This act on the part of the President, in defiance of public
> opinion, was considered as unwise, arbitrary, and a reckless risking
> of his reputation and popularity. . . . Although no complaints of
> want of efficiency as Secretary of State were made against Mr.
> Benjamin, he was ever afterwards unpopular in the Confederacy,
> and particularly in Virginia.[44]

Davis's reasons for promoting Benjamin were many. First of all, he needed Benjamin around him as an alter ego, speechwriter, and confidant. In addition, the time had come to move aggressively on the foreign affairs front with an appointee whom world leaders would know spoke for the President. The real question for the future was not strategy in the field but the materiel of war and the involvement of other countries in the struggle. They had to bring England and France into the war, open up a second front from the sea, break the blockade, and obtain some credit in Europe to buy arms. No one in the South had the ability to handle something that complicated as well as Judah Benjamin.

Benjamin was the only one in his Cabinet who was a true internationalist, who had traveled extensively and handled international commercial negotiations, who knew both England and France intimately and spoke fluent French and Spanish, and who could handle the press and diplomats with skill. He had spent more time in Paris and London than in Richmond. His enemies, and they were, in truth, the President's enemies, would bray at the Benjamin appointment, but reasonable people would feel that he was the right man for the job.

On March 17, 1862, Davis reached out for his third handshake welcoming Judah P. Benjamin to a post in his Cabinet. The Richmond *Examiner* greeted the appointment with an editorial from John M. Daniel that stated: "The representation of the synagogue is not diminished; it remains full."[45]

Benjamin and the President knew that they faced enormous obstacles, including the U.S. Government, which had been manipulating European politics for a long time.

They would try to exploit the suspicion of the Yankees on the part of Lord Russell and Prime Minister Palmerston and the wish of the British to see America divided into two nations. The problem with Palmerston was that he introduced the first petition against the British slave trade in the 1820s and led the fight to abolish it in their possessions. So he would use slavery as his excuse not to enter the war. But the truth was that the English were so suspicious of the French, the Russians, and the Germans that they thought if they once again sent troops over to North America, Louis Napoleon's France or another country might attack them in Europe. The upper classes in England favored the South, and the lower classes were for the Union, but the Government was worried more about being stabbed in the back in Europe than about the war in America.

Napoleon III, one of the most cunning and conspiratorial men in Europe, was dubbed "Napoleon the Little" by countrymen who admired the towering presence of his famous uncle. However, Benjamin and Davis did not derogate him just because he was physically unimposing. True, the Emperor was squat, had a hesitant way of speaking, and, according to John Hay, walked sideways, like a "gouty crab."[46] But he had big ambitions for France and an imperial tradition to live up to.

Napoleon and his court loved intrigue and would rather be involved in a conspiracy than dance at a royal ball. Empress Eugénie, Napoleon's wife, was more ambitious and cynical than the Emperor, for she wanted to see France control the throne in Mexico. She would be influenced by the Duke de Morny, the bastard son of Napoleon's mother, who was utterly corrupt and lived in outrageous extravagance. The duke was a gambler, an entrepreneur in sugar, and a leader in fashion and wit, but he needed money and he sold state secrets on the stock exchange to get it. Because gold from abroad slipped into his pockets, the Southern leaders knew enough not to put any there without promises of specific steps to enlist France on the South's behalf.

Intrigue was one reason why Jefferson Davis picked John Slidell as Ambassador to France. He must have assumed that if Slidell and Benjamin could master Louisiana politics together, the French court would be a familiar briar patch.

Napoleon wanted to help the South, because Confederate success would weaken the Monroe Doctrine, help him win Mexico, and reestablish the French in North America. On the other hand, Napoleon would not do anything militarily against the North unless the British joined in. Besides, some part of him wanted a strong, united America to keep England preoccupied. To him it was a standoff unless President Davis decided to lift the embargo on cotton to meet the needs of French manufacturing.

Davis knew that Benjamin had been right in the first Cabinet meeting and that his own judgment had been wrong. England had a year's supply of cotton to begin with and had opened up India as a new source, and Davis's embargo just played into the hands of Lincoln's blockade. The South had helped the North to cut the South off from Europe. Benjamin was instructed to use cotton in every way he could—promise it, dangle it, borrow on it, use bales like poker chips to separate France from England, do whatever he thought he could do to get the South credit to buy ships and powder and arms in Europe. He could even tell Napoleon that France and England could have it if they would come and get it.

The new Secretary of State only hoped that the blockade was not so strong now, since mere promises of cotton delivery to Europe would have no credibility. France could be bribed, but England would have to be won. Benjamin and Davis faced another antagonist in this chess game of international diplomacy: William H. Seward, Lincoln's brilliant Secretary of State, who had a smoldering hatred for Benjamin. Whatever Benjamin did, Seward would be trying to stop him—with gold, with threats of war, with Northern wheat (which England also desperately needed), with as shrewd a grasp of the international exercise of power as existed in the world.

Davis had a final job of making arrangements for Benjamin at the War Department. The Tredegar plant had forged the sheets of armor for the *Merrimac,* and she was ready to sail to Hampton Roads to see what she could do. He had decided to rename his "floating battery" the *Virginia* for the occasion, and Secretary of the Navy Mallory said she was ready for a test run. If things went well with the ironclad, instead of raising the blockade, the South would sink it.

Davis named George W. Randolph, an ex-midshipman, to the War Department the same day Benjamin was appointed Secretary of State. Politically, Randolph was a brilliant choice to succeed Benjamin as Secretary of War: grandson of Thomas Jefferson, born at Monticello, a Richmond lawyer who had been a ranking officer in the prewar Richmond militia and was now serving with Magruder as an artillery commander, soon to be a brigadier. How he would fare between Davis and the generals was another question, but Congress would rejoice in the idea of replacing a Jew from Louisiana with an aristocrat from one of the first families of Virginia. At the same time, Davis announced his intention to bring General Robert E. Lee into the government and put him in charge of military operations under Davis's direction. Two Virginians would make Congress do handstands while at the same time it grumbled at Benjamin's move to Secretary of State.

9

Richmond:
The Stage for Intrigue

❄❄❄

The steady pressure on Richmond by Union General George McClellan in the spring of 1862, nine months after the Southern victory at Bull Run, had been an almost unbearable torment for the people of the city. At Alexandria, the North had assembled the largest invasion fleet in history—113 steamers, 188 schooners, and 88 barges carrying enough food, ammunition, wagons, cannons, horses, and beef cattle to support McClellan's army of 146,000 men. Slowly, ever so slowly, for more than eight months, like a gigantic tortoise, McClellan's army moved up the peninsula between the James and the York rivers. "What Are You Waiting for, Tardy George?" became one of the most popular songs in the North. But George was coming, inexorably, step by step, day by day, ever tightening the noose of Federal assertion around Richmond. Soon, the arc of danger was so close that the people of Richmond could see glowing in the hills the bright campfires of Union troops with twice the manpower of the defenders. It had been a strange few months of cat-and-mouse between a methodical Yankee and a cautious Southerner, as General Joe Johnston, the dapper, balding little gamecock of Jefferson Davis's generation at West Point, slowly withdrew the Confederate Army of Northern Virginia up the peninsula in front of McClellan, feinting right, then left, saving his troops for the defense of Richmond.

From the high ground around the city, Richmond was cradled in the mist and gray clouds of the spring of 1862, suspended momentarily in the almost mystical landscape, as if unconnected from the suffering in its war-strained streets. The city rested on the north side of a graceful bend in the James River, but the eye immediately was drawn up the slopes from the black river water to the Grecian-white Capitol building of the State of Virginia, designed by Thomas Jefferson to be located on a grassy hilltop in the very center of the city. To the left, the tall spire of St. Paul's Episcopal Church extended skyward, as if a sentinel of God had been ordered to protect the heart of the Confederate government. The Capitol on the hill looked like the Acropolis, rising majestically from the James River, with its A-shaped roof pointing upward like hands praying, cupping an invisible dome 20 feet inside the roof in its architectural palms.

There was a rhythm to this war that added irony to every season. In the harsh winters, both armies dug in, for they could not move on the frozen roads. So the city relaxed in the howling winds of winter, secure in the safety of the snow while both armies recuperated.

But when the earth absorbed the final traces of the cold and the wild flowers and apple trees blossomed, lifting the spirits of poets in celebration of new life, death awakened in the long-quiescent battlefields as the armies blue and gray began to crawl out of their tents and make their fierce cannons ready for thunder and destruction again.

Every morning, Secretary of State Judah P. Benjamin walked the mile to his office from the Davenport House on West Main Street down to the imposing government building, where he would meet President Jefferson Davis for an early military briefing on the previous day's events. He walked past houses with black iron latticework, reminiscent of New Orleans. At the beginning of the war, his walk was a time for reflection in a civilized world of abundance—past stores and shops that sold antique clocks, pianos, rare books, and French wines. By 1862 darkness pervaded the shops, skeletons of prior activity, including the salon of the once much sought-after services of Ducquesne, the Paris hairdresser. The peeling paint, broken clapboards, and refugees sleeping in gardens or on porches invaded his subconscious with the realities of the war, the latest sad chapter in Richmond's proud history.

There was much history on Main Street. Thomas Jefferson had come over many times from Monticello to shop there; James Monroe's

Attorney General had lived in the colonial house with the three-story porch and an octagonal living room; and Jenny Lind, whom P. T. Barnum sent to Richmond, once bought a parasol on Main Street before a concert for which a scalper could sell a ticket for as much as $105.00. In Richmond's four-year struggle for survival, such memories were reassuring.

One can retrace Benjamin's steps in Richmond today. At Fifth Street, the walk descended sharply down a hill, from the calm residential heights of west Richmond to the tense world of warfare in the banking and government offices.

Richmond seemed the perfect setting for the South to greet spring with the ambivalent welcome the new season deserved. Wisps of clouds wafted across the metallic blue sky like whirls of gunsmoke, and the ground was damp with the melting chill of the early season.

In Confederate times a magnificent iron fence encircled the block around the Capitol—black spears based in granite, giving the grounds the impression of an inviolate sanctuary from whatever assaults were going on outside the magic ring. At the bottom of the hill sat the Bell Tower, which rang vigorously for fires and emergencies, as it did on Pawnee Sunday in the first months of the war, signaling a false alarm to warn of Federal gunboats on the river.

A hundred feet from the side entrance to the Capitol, on a broad expanse of flat ground on the crest of the hill, stood the high granite pedestal with the statue of George Washington on horseback. He was in full battle dress, his sword at his side, his arm raised and extended its full length, his fingers pointing ever southward to the future of the country. Southerners like Benjamin thought that General Washington, a Virginian and a slaveowner, was a proud symbol of the first American revolution, the predecessor to Jefferson Davis, not Abraham Lincoln. Thus the pointing statue of Washington was placed in the center of the seal of the Confederacy as a symbol of the South's defiant past.

In Benjamin's day, black freedmen and slaves crowded the streets, gathering in the center of town. Slaves and soldiers were in the hills, digging trenches, building embankments, and filling sandbags around the armaments, from sunup to sundown. The shovel brigades had earned Robert E. Lee the early nickname "King of Spades," but the swamplands east of the city would keep the first battle for Richmond a few miles from its gates.

In 1860 the city was 38 percent black, but by 1862, as the population grew, it would reach over 50 percent at its peak. A preponderance of the slave population was male. This fact created, in the minds of the white population, a threatening side to Richmond slavery, a fear deeper than in any other city in the South. In most Southern cities, there was a surplus of slave women serving as house slaves, because the men were sold for work on the plantations in the surrounding countryside. But Richmond industries demanded large numbers of young male slaves, and defense of the many points of possible invasion required the importation of even larger numbers of pick-and-shovel slaves. In addition, thousands more blacks fled to Richmond as the Confederate armies retreated from the Virginia peninsula. With such an excess of black men over black women, sustaining slave families became much more difficult. To maintain order, the city tolerated brothels and gambling halls in the black sections of "Screamersville" and "Penitentiary Bottom" near the prison on the river. In addition, more and more of the leading white families sent their daughters and wives away from the dangers of the impending battle. With the steady arrival of new white recruits every day to supply Lee's army, and the constant stream of furloughed veterans, the city at times seemed to seethe with an undercurrent of racial conflict and fratricidal pressures made more intense by the absence of the ameliorating influence of women.[1]

Benjamin was not an early riser, preferring to work late, but he sought to arrive every morning so that he would already be in his office when the chimes of St. Paul's Church tolled the hour of nine o'clock.

He kept a large map of the United States on his wall and daily consulted the morning dispatches to shift the colored pins, reflecting troop movement and strength. Though he was responsible for foreign affairs, he knew that the decisions in Europe would be more influenced by the battlefield than by the machinations of ambassadors in the royal court of Napoleon III or the Confederate partisans among the upper classes in the British Parliament. Besides, since he was interviewed often by foreign journalists, having the war displayed on his wall allowed him to pepper his comments with precise details and the latest information.[2]

From his office window, Benjamin could see the ships out on the bend of the James River and beyond them the straight edges of the Kanawha Canal. The James River historically linked Richmond to the port of Norfolk, but the waterways, once providing easy access to Yankee shipping had turned into dangerous coiled snakes poised to strike at the heartland. A superior United States Navy was strangling the South with Lincoln's "Anaconda"—a blockade of all Southern ports—and the fighting ships of Admiral Farragut were moving up the mouth of the Mississippi River, isolating New Orleans and then Natchez. Farragut's ships would ultimately join Ulysses S. Grant's army coming down from Tennessee to dominate the entire Mississippi Valley. The "Anaconda" was circling the Confederacy.

From the window he could also see the smoke billowing from the stacks of the Tredegar Iron Works, 5 acres of buildings that were the brute muscles of the Confederacy. Twelve hundred of the most broad-shouldered slaves sweated and groaned around the clock, many wasting away in the hellish heat of its molten rivers of glowing iron. It was a state within a state, with its own hospitals, administrative structure, rules, and slave quarters.

From the beginning, Richmond had been the focal point of Yankee strategy. It was the terminus of five railroads that arrived there from North and South. The city fathers had banned railroad tracks from the center of the city, filling the streets before the war with teamsters and slaves hauling tobacco to the sprawling warehouses, where it was placed in hogsheads and aged, and bringing in wheat, which was crushed and sifted into flour in the giant mills—as many as 400,000 barrels in 1860—and packed off to the North by way of the Potomac steamships in exchange for manufactured goods. Slaves were brought on those railroads from all over the South to work in the industries of Richmond, particularly in the open-hearth furnaces and the boilers in the bowels of the Tredegar Iron Works, which turned iron ore and coal from the mountain country of western Virginia into railroad tracks, engines, and, since secession, cannons and ammunition for the Confederate army. So the shiny bronze guns rumbled out of Tredegar bound for the conflict, while battered and scarred field pieces wobbled back on their way to the arsenal for refitting.[3] The most persuasive argument for moving the capital from the inland protection of Montgomery, Alabama to the exposed outer rim of Richmond had been the vital necessity of protecting the muscle and fiber of Tredegar, which employed more than 20 percent of the work force of Richmond. If Richmond fell, so would the Confederacy and that desperate fact permeated the city with a frantic quality all during the war.

Over the course of the war, war-worn horses drawing carriages loaded with wounded men plodded their sad way eastward through the city toward Chimborazo Hospital, a reminder of the declining numbers of Confederate soldiers capable of fighting. Chimborazo Hospital was developed on the plateaus of the hills, a 175-acre complex of 150 one-story buildings, more than a hundred huge tents to serve men in convalescence, five large icehouses, a Russian bathhouse, a bakery and a brewery of its own, and two hundred cows and five hundred goats. The grease from the five great soup kitchens was mixed with lye to produce soap. In four years, more than 76,000 men would pass through Chimborazo, and thousands more through the sixty other hospitals in the city.

Hundreds of other acres to the north and west were devoted to the expanding cemeteries, which obeyed a strict hierarchy based on the status of the dead. Schockoe Hill Burying Ground in the northern part of the city since 1821 had been reserved for the middle- and upper-class white Protestants; Jews bought land adjacent to the area, reflecting their high social status in the city; lower-class whites and enlisted men were buried in Oakwood Cemetery; and nearby was a potter's field for paupers, strangers, and Yankees. In the 1840s, a group of prominent Richmonders had visited Boston and were so impressed with a rural cemetery they saw there that they established Hollywood Cemetery on a rolling hillside just west of the city. When the remains of Presidents James Monroe and John Tyler were reinterred there just a few years before, and tens of thousands of the dead filled up the other burial grounds, Hollywood emerged as the home of heroes, the rich, and any others with a claim to esteem. But by now, because of the scarcity of foodstuffs and inflation, an equality of meagerness joined together the classes of the city, and the capacity of whites to maintain this war alone diminished with every funeral.

A city of 38,000 in 1860 had by 1862 more than tripled with refugees, the wounded, slaves, and new recruits. As housing grew scarcer and rents rose to outlandish heights, more and more families slept and lived in single rooms, subsisting in winter on a diet of potatoes and imagination.

In May 1862, the beleaguered city waited daily for McClellan to attack, but the Federal commander was meticulously going over all the details of what he believed would be the last great battle of the war. He wanted to leave nothing to chance: superiority in armaments, men, and cavalry; a flow of reinforcements; naval units; intelligence and contingency plans for lines of retreat and counterattack;

and secret plans of surprise. Resting and gathering themselves for the assault were 128,864 men with 300 big guns, but for McClellan, with memories of Manassas haunting him, that was still not enough. He asked Lincoln for insurance—McDowell's force of 40,000 left in Washington for protection—so he was waiting, waiting for Mc-Dowell, the man who had commanded the Union troops at Bull Run, now seeking his redemption, to join McClellan at history's turning point for the capture of the capital of the Confederacy.

"Richmond must not be given up; it shall not be given up," Robert E. Lee announced in tears to the Cabinet.[4] He was only a military adviser to Davis, newly arrived in Richmond, and he developed a plan in stages: The first objective was to stop the Union troops and McDowell from enlarging the already massive concentration of forces facing Richmond. Lee would do that not by direct attack, since the South had neither the men nor the arms to spare from Richmond's defense, but by attacking two lesser generals in the Shenandoah Valley, hurting them badly enough for them to call for reinforcements, thereby alarming Lincoln by playing on his worst fears that a Washington left undefended would be occupied before Richmond could be captured. It was psychological warfare of the shrewdest sort. Lincoln would order McDowell to return back across the Potomac, and McClellan would be left waiting at the gates of Richmond with the ghosts of Manassas in his head. The instrument for implementing step one in the rescue of Richmond was none other than the taciturn, intense, fanatic legend of the Shenandoah Valley, General Thomas J. "Stonewall" Jackson.

Already his eccentricities were renowned—his diet of raspberries and plain bread and milk, no pepper because it made his left leg ache, and the lemons, the ever-present lemons, saddlebags full of them, always sucking and chewing on them, dotting his black beard with yellow peelings. No dashing officer he, his coat was a threadbare, single-breasted relic of his service in the Mexican War; his cap was the same as those worn by the VMI cadets to whom he once taught mathematics, only with a broken visor; and his boots were a floppy size or so too big for him. At night he would stare for hours into the fire—brooding and lonely, like an ancient mystic. In battle, his lanky frame looked even more dramatic, because he rode a muscular, undersized mount the men derisively called "Fancy." Horse and rider made a curious sight in battle, but Jackson rode with intensity, and his eyes radiated in the charge and the gunsmoke with a glow so strong they called him Old Blue Light. Jackson's religious fervor stirred him to believe he was a Southern Joshua, molding his 17,000 Shenandoah Valley troops, as he wrote his wife, into "an army of the living God as well as of its country."[5]

For eight months, Jackson had roamed the valley, memorizing every inch of it, calculating its distances in miles as well as in the minutes it took to move his men. And move them he did, fifty minutes every hour, then lie prone to rest, then up again to step out in cadence for 200 or 300 yards, breaking into route march, miles to cover in prescribed intervals. If any man faltered or straggled, he was a coward, wanting in patriotism, deficient in manliness. His men worshiped him, they cheered him while they marched, they fought for him, and they won the name they would be known by: Stonewall's Foot Cavalry.

Union forces chased Jackson all over the valley, but he sidestepped and parried, and when they charged, he had disappeared into air. They never knew where he was. When they thought him in front, he attacked from the rear. He was in the hills above them, then in the valley alongside, lunging and retreating, playing havoc with supply lines, capturing the enemy's food for his troops. He was an apparition, teasing and taunting. Lincoln, sworn to bag this legend, called him "the game" and sent McDowell with 38,000 men and 11,000 animals to do it. But Stonewall ended up behind the hunters, threatening the capital. In the end, after Lincoln ordered McDowell back across the Potomac, Stonewall, his mission accomplished, skipped back to Richmond to join Lee for the climactic battle of the spring.

The morning Richmond *Examiner* blared the headline "New Orleans Falls," and the leaders in the Southern capital read with shock about the fate of Judah P. Benjamin's home city. General Ben Butler's 18,000 Yankee troops arrived in New Orleans with Farragut on April 26, 1862 to find a sullen mob greeting them at the docks. An American flag had been torn down from the staff over the Mint, and when Butler found a man with a scrap of bunting in his buttonhole, he brought him before a drumhead court and hanged him publicly from a window of the building where the flag had flown.

The sight struck fear into the city's men, but the women of New Orleans continued to harass the troops, snubbing them on the streets and spitting at them. In the French Quarter, a woman poured a bucket of slop from an upper window right on Farragut's head, sending Butler into a rage.

"Hereafter," his general order said, "when any female shall, by word, gesture or movement, insult or show contempt for any officer or soldier of the United States, she shall be regarded and held liable to be treated as a woman of the town plying her avocation."[6] When a Yankee insults Southern womanhood, he touches the quick of Southern chivalry. From all over the South, at every dinner table and fancy ball in Richmond, the reaction to the order brought swift condemnation and stirring calls to arms.

"Men of the South!" Beauregard's Creole tongue retorted (and every male in Richmond reverberated with the sentiment). "Shall our mothers, our wives, our daughters and our sisters be thus outraged by the ruffianly soldiers of the North, to whom is given the right to treat, at their pleasure, the ladies of the South as harlots? Arouse, friends, and drive back from our soil those infamous invaders of our homes and disturbers of our family ties."[7]

Jefferson Davis answered with an order of his own. If "Beast" Butler or his men be captured, they should be treated as animals and executed. History has forgiven Butler his excesses, attributing much of the surviving account to exaggeration. But rumor at the time knew no restraint.

Stories of greedy confiscation continued to reach Richmond. When Butler uncovered a cache of 418 bronze plantation bells, contributed in response to Confederate pleas for more metal to build ironclads, he had them sent to Boston, where souvenir collectors among the wealthy paid $30,000 each to hear them ring in Yankee steeples.

Benjamin had a personal concern about New Orleans. His sisters Harriet and Penny and her daughter, Leah, were there among the marauders and plunderers loosed on the city.

His fears were not unfounded. Butler had a special penchant for attacking Jews. "The most active agents," he was quoted as saying, "and most effective supporters [of the Confederacy] have been the same quasi-foreign houses, mostly Jews . . . who all deserve at the hands of the Government what is due to the Jew Benjamin, Slidell, Mallory and Floyd."[8] He called Benjamin's brother-in-law in New Orleans "a Jew famed for a bargain" and wrote that those who traded in paper money "were principally Jews, and as Benjamin, the Confederate Secretary of State, was a Jew, and his brother-in-law was a broker, I suppose there were some of the Jew brokers who would get true intelligence from Richmond."[9] He later referred in a report to the capture of "150 rebels, 90 mules, 60 contrabands [Negro slaves] and 5 Jews."[10] In Butler's value system, Jews were rated lower than rebels, mules, and slaves; Lincoln thought the report was a joke when he read it. In another connection, Butler made reference to the "progenitor of the tribe of Benjamin, the Jewish Secretary of State."[11]

Butler set the tone for New Orleans, but even the sympathetic Northern press recoiled when an Associated Press writer in New Orleans urged that Jews in the South be "exterminated." Both the *Commercial* and *Daily Times* of Cincinnati denounced the story and called for an end to "Jew-baiting."[12]

An English visitor wrote: "Mr. Benjamin told me that his property had lately been confiscated in New Orleans, and that his two sisters had been turned, neck and crop, into the streets there with only one trunk, which they had been forced to carry themselves. Everyone was afraid to give them shelter, except an Englishwoman, who protected them until they got out of the city."[13]

We know something of Benjamin's outrage at Butler from a letter he wrote to Slidell in Paris:

> The press of the civilized world has already informed you of the nature of the tyranny exercised over that unfortunate city by the brutal commander who temporarily rules over it. The order inviting his beastly soldiery to treat the ladies of New Orleans as "women of the town pursuing their avocation" is not only authentic but has been tacitly approved by his government. . . . His thousand similar acts of atrocities . . . all combine in stamping upon him and upon the Government which sustains and supports him indelible infamy.[14]

The loss of New Orleans, the danger to his family, and the threat to Richmond raised many personal issues for Benjamin. As the battle of Richmond drew closer, he had to have asked himself a profound question: Should anything happen to him, where did he want to be buried? He could die in the battle; he could be assassinated by a Yankee sympathizer; he could be captured, tried for treason, and hanged.

New Orleans was gone. Richmond was not home. No Jewish congregation would accept an unconverted wife, thus ruling out the Hebrew cemetery. It is reasonable to assume that one of his nightmares had to be that if Richmond fell, the Yankees would leave him dangling from a rope as had been done to the bridge-burners at the Cumberland Gap.

Jules St. Martin, who had inherited from his father substantial business interests in New Orleans, accepted the news of the fall of New Orleans with Creole aplomb: " 'This must hit you hard,' someone said. 'I am ruined, voilà tout,' Jules replied (with a characteristic gesture of throwing care to the winds)."[15]

The horse-drawn funeral trains of Richmond daily wound along the rutted mud roads from Schockoe Hill, where the Hebrew cemetery stood, toward Hollywood cemetery. No stone had marked the grave of Henry Adler, the young Jewish private who was a member of the Richmond Blues at Roanoke Island, since Jewish custom required a one-year wait. The Hebrew cemetery stood on a slight rise, commonplace but adequate for its somber purpose.

Once through the gates of Hollywood, one entered the high ground and descended into the valley of the shadow of death. It was soundless, except for the bird songs in the distant trees.

The hills enveloped any mourner in an embrace of unsurpassed beauty. Tall pines reached to the sky, and the spreading shade of water oaks, giant magnolias, and weeping willows shielded the sculptured hillsides rich with the graves of the dead.

To accommodate the steep terrain, tombs were scooped out of the sides of the hills and mausoleums were constructed as though to inter the bodies in natural caves. Carved on the mausoleums were the names of the Virginia families buried there: Madison, Tyler, Wise, Brockenbrough. Today, one's eyes are drawn to the winged angels, crosses, and tall obelisks, and the constantly shifting perspective from the road make the markers seem as if they are moving in a giant, silent minuet. Behind the black elm is a large Madonna with head bowed.

Judah P. Benjamin was an outsider not only here but also at the Hebrew cemetery. His Southern Jewish soul had left him suspended, floating and unwelcomed in both worlds. He could not choose; he could not postpone choosing.

The military graves dotted a meadow like a regiment of tablets in formation. A small mounted cannon pointed toward a cluster of graves in silent salute. Batteries had erected memorials to their fallen comrades—"faithful soldier" and "humble Christian" with crossed swords carved in stone. Every gravestone was an echo: "he rode with Stonewall" or "sacrificed at Bull Run" or "the first Confederate soldier killed at Bethel, Virginia." And those were the lucky ones who were brought home to rest. Visitors could hear the cannons and the sound of the charge in their imaginations. In the haunting silence they absorbed the screams, the wounds, the instant and lingering death. The dates of birth added to the tragedy, almost everyone of them born in the 1840s.[16]

Benjamin's best friend, Gustavus Myers, the leading Jewish lawyer in Richmond, who married the Gentile daughter of a former Governor of Virginia, was buried in a plot in Hollywood. The records have since been burned, so we do not know of Benjamin's intent should anything happen to him, nor do we know if he had plans to prevent the use of his body as an example. If he were to have turned to anyone to carry out his wishes, it would have been to Myers. Gustavus Myers had influence and would have understood that the Talmud stated that a man's life was enough payment for a crime, that burial should be prompt. Gustavus Myers would have made certain that the Jewish laws of burial were obeyed.

My Fellow-Citizens
To Arms

I have just received a message direct from the highest authority of the Confederacy, to call upon the Militia Organizations to come forth, and upon all other Citizens to organize Companies for the defense of this City against immediate attack of the enemy. They are approaching and you may have to meet them before Monday morning. I can do no more than give you this warning of their new approach.

Remember New Orleans!

Richmond is now in your hands. Let it not fall under the rule of another BUTLER. Rally, then, to your Officers tomorrow morning at 10 o'clock, on BROAD STREET, in front of the CITY HALL.

Joseph Mayo
Mayor of Richmond

May 28, 1862[17]

Though McClellan still had a two-to-one advantage in men, he had been forced by topography to divide his troops around Richmond on either side of the winding Chickahominy River, swollen by days of "Confederate weather." The separation enabled General Joseph Johnston to throw twenty-seven Southern brigades against a single Northern corps. At the battle of Seven Pines, however, the confusion, chaos, and mismanagement of the South in its first campaign in months enabled McClellan to withdraw and regroup, and Johnston lay wounded with a piece of shrapnel in his chest. On June 8, 1862, a historic day in the short history of the Confederacy, on the ride back from Johnston's tent just four miles from the frightened city, Jefferson Davis offered Robert E. Lee the command of the Army of Northern Virginia.

Lee seemed destined for legend from the beginning. His name was synonymous with Virginia's proud history.

Three days after the greatest torchlight parade in the history of Richmond to celebrate the night Virginia voted for secession, when thousands sang the new anthem "Dixie" as Roman candles and rockets blazed across the sky lighting up the city like daylight, Virginia's Governor Letcher had offered Colonel Robert E. Lee the post of Major General commanding the Virginia forces. Fifty-four years old, erect and handsome, with a strong black mustache, Lee had turned down a formal offer from President Lincoln to command the Northern armies. Leaving his stately home in Arlington, where he owned not a single slave, yet the hero of the white South for putting down John Brown's raid at Harpers Ferry, Lee gave a brief acceptance speech to a cheering convention, underscoring his loyalty to birth and land.

After all, Robert E. Lee had traces of George Washington's blood in him and had married the daughter of the adopted son of the first American President, thereby representing for Davis and the Confederacy a link to the first revolution. Also, in the early days of the war, some newspapers had compared Lee's decision to reject Lincoln's temptation to "the agony and bloody sweat of Gethsemane." (His old general from the Mexican War, Winfield Scott, had told Lee, "You have made the greatest mistake of your life but I feared it would be so.")[18]

But Lee had not lived up to that early promise. In fact, his record in western Virginia had been so undistinguished in the early years of the war that when Jefferson Davis had appointed him as military adviser to the President, it was not widely cheered by either political or military leaders and was hardly noticed at all by the newspapers. He was thought to be too plodding, too adept at engineering rather than fighting, without demonstrated achievements in the field. They called him "Granny Lee" because of his record of bumbling in western Virginia. He was seen as a caretaker general "too tender of blood," who had a "pious horror of guerrillas," without talents other than digging trenches, designing fortifications, and defending fixed embattlements.[19]

Robert E. Lee was a jumble of contradictions. He was raised in the heroic tradition, outsiders thought, but his father had deserted the family when the boy was six, leaving his mother in financial ruin. His unusual marriage to his distant cousin, the dominating and spoiled Mary Custis, had drained his personality of much of its joy, but he sought the admiration of women, often writing long, intimate letters to young girls he had met only once. He even held unorthodox views on slavery, having written to his wife in 1856 that "in this enlightened age, there are few I believe, but will acknowledge that slavery as an institution is a moral and political evil in any country."[20]

Lee was handsome, and his bearing was thoroughly military. Benjamin had almost nothing in common with him—not politics, ambition, family, or history. On both sides of the war, the generals and leaders had come out of a common military past at West Point, but Sherman had left the army for almost a decade to pursue careers in education and administration; McClellan left to become a railroad executive; and Jefferson Davis to make a fortune as a planter. Lee, however, had spent thirty years in the army, rising only to the rank of lieutenant colonel with a salary of $1,200 a year, bitter toward the officers who sought advancement with their charm and good manners rather than their swords. Benjamin and he shared a penchant for hard work, but Lee worked out of an exaggerated sense of duty and the obligations of his Virginia birthright, whereas Benjamin came from Jewish roots with modest beginnings that drove him to seek recognition, status, and the respect of his peers.

Judah P. Benjamin's new duties as Secretary of State placed him in an office that was not only on the same floor as the President's but less than 100 feet away. Each morning they would visit to bring each other up to date on army news, then meet for several hours during the day. Often the President would ride out around the city to show himself to the populace and bolster morale while Benjamin took care of the paperwork.

Benjamin's own office was a plain room in the center of which was a black walnut table with a green cloth covered with a multitude of state papers. One corner contained bookshelves. None of his favorite classics were there, unless they were of professional use: Headley's

History, The Parliamentary Debates, and a dozen separate copies and bound volumes of the *Atlantic Monthly.*[21]

The bonds between Varina and Benjamin were maturing also, made more intense by a common commitment to the President. She was not just an onlooker but a participant who could take advantage of her position as First Lady to help the State Department smuggle messages abroad.

"Many of Mr. Benjamin's inimitable state papers," she wrote, "were an account of the dangers of the blockading squadron, transmitted to Miss Rosine Slidell through me under an assumed name, and the answers were returned to her in the form of friendly letters in which the 'high contending parties' were spoken of under assumed names also."[22]

Benjamin treated her as an equal and never censored himself in her presence. He wanted her to read what she was transmitting and talked with her about his strategy. She returned his trust, independent of her husband, as an emerging third dynamic at the top of the Confederacy.

"They were most interesting reading for me," she wrote of the secret papers she transmitted to Paris and received in turn, "and Mr. Benjamin's clear explanation of the antagonistic policy of the Duke de Morny and the Emperor made them very plain—his tact was exhibited too in a pleasant way about the letters—he never put on a manner of reserve towards me nor did he caution me to 'observe the utmost secrecy towards every one about their contents' as another man who knew less of secret affairs did. Of what he knew I must be cognizant, he spoke freely when alone with me, but no more reticent man ever lived where it was possible to be silent."[23]

But Mason and Slidell, the ambassadors to London and Paris, were doing their jobs with less success. Diplomacy followed the logic of the battlefield, and the string of Southern defeats had caused the diplomats of Europe to watch and wait for the outcome of the battle of Richmond.

"I need not say," Slidell wrote from France, "how unfavorable an influence these defeats"—Roanoke and Forts Henry and Donaldson in Tennessee—"following in such quick succession, have produced in public sentiment. If not soon counterbalanced by some decisive success in our arms, we may . . . bid adieu to all hopes of seasonable recognition."[24]

Success or not, Benjamin and the President felt that Napoleon's ambitions for a Hapsburg throne in Mexico and the well-known corruption of the court made France the most likely recipient of a Confederate offer, with "white gold"—cotton—as the bait. Benjamin carefully drafted his first and most brilliant state paper after only a few weeks in office, "conceding to the French Emperor the right of introducing French products into this country, free of duty, for a certain defined period if it were possible to induce his abandonment of the policy hitherto pursued." Then he instructed Slidell to offer the Emperor "a certain number of bales of cotton to be received by the merchant vessels of France at certain designated points. In this manner, one hundred thousand bales of cotton . . . costing this government but $4,500,000 would represent a grant to France of not less than $12,500,000." And to link that with the duty-free offer, "such a sum would maintain afloat a considerable fleet for a length of time quite sufficient to open the Atlantic and Gulf ports to the commerce of France."

The Secretary of State declared that the government was wide open to a bargain of even greater profit: "I do not state this as the limit to which you would be authorized to go in making a negotiation on the subject but to place clearly before you the advantage which would result in stipulating for the payment of cotton."[25]

Dispatches from Richmond could take as long as four months to get through the blockade, whether Benjamin used Varina or not. If the papers were captured, they could end up on the front page of the New York *Tribune.* But Benjamin had made special arrangements for this one on a French steamer by special courier.

When his old friend Count Henri Mercier, the French Minister to Washington, came to Richmond, Benjamin considered it opportune. The blockade was playing havoc with his dispatches, and he would not hear from Slidell again until mid-July. Mercier had come to test the resolve of the Confederacy and would return to Paris immediately to report his personal impressions to Napoleon III.

Benjamin knew that his exact words would be transmitted back to the Emperor, and he chose them carefully so as to leave no doubt that might undercut Slidell.

"I know your good feeling for us, and we require no proof of it," Mercier reported that Benjamin said. "But you know that we are a hot-blooded people and we would not like to talk with anybody who entertained the idea of the possibility of our dishonoring ourselves by reuniting with a people for whom we feel unmitigated contempt as well as abhorrence."[26]

Mercier was convinced of the determination of the Southern leaders to gain independence no matter what the cost. France could proceed with negotiations in good faith.

The fall of New Orleans had left Southern sympathizers in Paris in a state of shock. So many people had business links, relatives, loved ones, and friends there. The Creoles in Paris were outraged over the terrible stories of looting and molestation of women in New Orleans. "Beast" Butler sounded to them like a savage.

All war news was exaggerated and magnified by distance. Paris thought Richmond was doomed and the war would be over in a few weeks. Slidell was already beginning to consider schemes for his permanent residence in Paris.

At the age of forty-two, Slidell had married twenty-year-old Mathilde Douglas, daughter of one of the leading Creole families in New Orleans. She spoke only French until she was fifteen, and Slidell's French was perfect. Through Creole contacts in Paris, where many had fled before the fall of New Orleans, the Slidells would be in constant touch with Natalie and Ninette.

The Slidells were keeping up the spirits of the Southern community. Everyone was charmed by them, and Empress Eugénie invited Mathilde and her daughters to every event. The Slidells' oldest daughter had become engaged to Baron Erlanger, the head of a Jewish banking house, said to be one of the most influential men with Napoleon. Because of Benjamin, the Erlangers pursued Natalie socially. Oddly, in this instance, she was more socially desirable *because* of Benjamin's religion, which was usually a basis for exclusion, than she would have been otherwise. Mercier returned to Paris with messages of affection for Natalie and Ninette, a direct report for the Emperor, and personal regards for the Slidells.

The streets of Richmond were bustling with the activity of defense preparations. Thousands of slaves and soldiers were at work digging trenches, building fortifications, driving pilings into the James River to prevent a naval attack, and lifting batteries of artillery up to Drewry's Bluff overlooking the river. With the surrender of Norfolk and the Gosport Navy Yard, the Confederate dreams of a navy had ended; even the proud *Merrimac* had to be scuttled to keep it from falling into the hands of the enemy. Richmond would have to defend its river approach from the batteries on the shore.

The morale of the city was sagging, although it had not yet experienced the sting of actual attack. Citizens still had faith in their proud fighting men. Just a few weeks before, Longstreet's division had marched through the streets of Richmond, mud-stained but high-spirited, as the city turned out to cheer them, the women carrying armloads of spring flowers, which they tossed to the passing soldiers or stuck in the muzzles of their guns. The troops were showered with spring violets, yellow jonquils, and hyacinths as they marched past the handkerchief-waving crowds to the tune of "Dixie" and "Bonnie Blue Flag."

A craggy veteran spotted a young man and a woman in a window and yelled out to the lad, "Come right along, sonny! Here's a muskit for ye!"

"All right, boys," he answered, "Have you got a leg for me, too?" The boy stuck the stump of his leg on the window sill, and with one impulse, the battalion halted, faced the window, and spontaneously came to "present arms" as the ringing rebel yell rattled the windows of the block.[27]

A sense of dread crept over Richmond as it waited in the nine straight days of rain that followed Lee's assumption of command. There was tension in the President's deep-set eyes and, for the first time, traces of desperation. Richmond was swarming with spies. Even the most secret details in Cabinet meetings would be gossip in the lobby of the Spotswood Hotel by nightfall. Word traveled so fast that General Johnston's troops had heard about his military strategy before he could get back to the encampment to write up the orders.

Varina and the children, with other wives and families, had been sent to the safety of Raleigh, North Carolina, and Davis prowled the White House like a nervous lion. Varina was not around to steady him and make him rest.

Davis and Lee delighted in the rains, because it made the roads behind McClellan as impassable as those in front, undermining "Little Mac's" confidence. In that mud, the President asserted, McDowell could not get here to save McClellan, no matter what Lincoln decided.

The courage and daring that Richmond needed to survive were embodied in Jeb Stuart. He was the scout who preceded the army, and he was called "Lee's eyes." Loving glory, he had been restless under the retreat-and-wait game all spring, having had no chance for personal distinction since he had cut up the Yankees at Manassas. Here was the kind of flamboyant hero who creates cavalry legends—

high boots up to his thighs, a yellow sash and gauntlets that dangled halfway down his arms, a theatrical red-lined gray cape, a big-brimmed soft hat with one side pinned up with a gold star, and a foot-long ostrich plume. Stuart's features were unattractive, yet his cinnamon beard and light blue eyes lent color to a cavalier horseman in gray. His West Point classmates recognized he was dashing from a distance though homely up close, and they nicknamed him "Beauty" Stuart.

At 2:00 A.M. one night in June 1862, he assembled 1,200 troopers for his expedition (not a "scouting party," he insisted) with orders carefully drafted by Lee, who knew his man. "You must bear constantly in mind" Lee wrote, "not to hazard unnecessarily your command . . . but be content to accomplish all the good you can, without feeling it necessary to obtain all that might be desired."[28]

Stuart rode out at the head of his column as if headed for Shenandoah, but only he knew the real destination. For three days he was not heard from, and the weather was turning "Union"—dry enough for McClellan to think about reinforcements and his turn to punch first. Even with the head of the Union cavalry (Jeb's father-in-law) chasing him with particular fury, he completely circled McClellan's army and jangled into headquarters after two days in the saddle with 170 prisoners, 300 horses and mules, and precisely the information Lee had sent him for. He reported that the roads were worse than in Richmond, so big guns could not be moved on them; what was more, the flanks were open to an attack by Jackson. The Southern and Northern newspapers hailed Stuart as if he had twisted McClellan's moustache. He had done it all with only one casualty!

The time had come, but the date would be dictated by Stonewall's rate of march. Lee sent Jackson a directive to start moving his men to Richmond, disguising the movement as a pursuit of the enemy. "I should like to have the advantage of your views and to be able to confer with you. Will meet you at some point on your approach to the Chickahominy."[29]

A few days later, a slumping, dusty horseman with one aide alongside came riding into army headquarters near Richmond. Stonewall Jackson had ridden fourteen hours in the saddle on relays of commandeered horses to have that talk with his commander. After several hours of discussion, Jackson mounted and rode back out again to rejoin the "Foot Cavalry," which was already on its way to meet him.

"The prayers of the Confederacy will have more effect if Benjamin was dismissed," the Richmond *Examiner* complained.[30] It seemed that John M. Daniel, editor of the *Examiner,* took special pleasure in linking Benjamin and Jewishness to Confederate failure, speculators, gamblers, and all manner of ills.

Daniel had a small head with large features. One biographer described him, with the bias of the times, as having "a decidedly Jewish face." His mouth was wide, unpleasing, and overhung by a thick, black moustache. His cheeks were thin, and his weak chin was covered by a dense, coarse, jet-black beard. Even his friends said that he had a cold, self-contained, and gloomy disposition and a body racked with the pain of a rising and receding tuberculosis. He carried a derringer pistol, had a history of dueling, and kept at his home a barber's chair in the parlor, elevated above the ordinary chairs in the room. To visitors, he seemed like an editorial pontiff, looking down from his throne. He lived alone with his two dogs, which he liked to goad into fighting. He cackled as they mauled each other, after which he would drive them off with a flick of his horsewhip. The author of a pro-slavery tract called "The Nigger Question," he was unyielding in his extremism, publishing a paper that was well known all over the Confederacy and the favorite of the army. Criticism of the Davis government always received coverage, especially the anti-Semitic comments of Congressman Foote. If the Jews of Richmond had feared that Benjamin's high offices would mean that all the Confederacy's troubles would be blamed on the Jews, Daniel was doing his best to make their fears come true.

If Benjamin wanted another identity, neither his Richmond critics nor his friends would allow him to have it. Regardless of Benjamin's beliefs, even fellow members of the Cabinet could not leave aside the question of his religious background. Postmaster General John Reagan wrote in his *Memoirs:*

> I will mention another incident in which I was relieved from a dilemma. I had invited members of the Cabinet to dine with me. Among the dishes on the table was one of fried ham and eggs. Knowing that Mr. Benjamin, Secretary of State, was a Jew, I was perplexed to know whether I should offer them to him. But to my relief, he told me that the night before a burglar had broken into his smokehouse and stolen all of his fine hams.[31]

In late June 1862, President Davis paced his office restlessly as the pressures mounted toward the battle of Richmond. Hearing the guns booming in the distant light, he could stand it no longer. He ordered Benjamin and other Cabinet members to join him on the bluffs, which Benjamin relished, having never been in battle.

From Drewry's Bluffs in the east and the hills beyond, thousands of fires in Yankee camps could be seen flickering in the summer night.

Benjamin's horse bolted back from the roar of cannons, and he glimpsed flashes of lights at the start of the Seven Days battle. The roads were oddly crowded for such an early hour as people flocked out to the bluffs to get a better view. McClellan's troops were now only 8 miles from the city, and Lee made the daring decision to count on McClellan's caution, strip the defenses of Richmond of fighting men, and wage an all-out assault on the flanks of the Union army.

As Lee rode his horse, Traveller, out to his headquarters, the sun came out through the fine, misty rain, and a beautiful rainbow was formed across the city. The Southern generals considered it an omen. All waited for Stonewall to assault the rear and unhinge McClellan, causing him to push his troops back to cover. But Jackson, for the first time in his life, was three hours late.

Stonewall had driven his men relentlessly for four days with only ten hours of sleep. They had met resistance and were delayed in the steaming heat, and he had gone into bivouac to rest them before the battle, satisfied he was in position.

The others attacked without him, and since he arrived late in the afternoon, with only a few hours of daylight remaining, he waited for Lee to drive the enemy back into his guns rather than assault them himself.

The plains were splashed with gunfire and cavalry. Without Jackson, the crucial element of pressure and alarm was missing, and the balance turned against Lee's army.

Just at the moment of peril, Lee spotted among the shellbursts Davis and Benjamin, now joined by Secretary of War Randolph and a number of Congressmen, watching the battle below. The general was furious—a single shell might kill them all—and rode over to them quickly.

With a steely salute, Lee asked, "Mr. President, who is all this and what is it doing here?"

Davis blushed with embarrassment, like a small boy who had been caught at the keyhole. "It is not my army, General," he said.[32]

Lee replied with an icy tone in his voice, "It is certainly not *my* army, Mr. President, and this is no place for it."

Davis motioned with his wide-brimmed hat to his invited guests to fall in behind him as he wheeled his horse about, saying, "Well, General, if I withdraw, perhaps they will follow." Benjamin tugged at his reins, ending his first and only brush with "the taste of battle."

Lee conferred personally with Stonewall the next day, and the junior general returned to his old self. The sound of rebel yells on the flank shook the confidence of the Union troops, which had withdrawn to a powerful position in the weeds to await an all-out charge. Bayonets flashing, the Confederates lost a thousand men in one charge against the embankment, but the sacrifice paid off as the Federals turned and scampered up the hill, stumbling across a second line of riflemen, which joined them in flight. But this was not Bull Run again. McClellan orchestrated a well-organized retreat with a cool head and the foresight of a month of planning against all eventualities. It was, as one of his generals said, "a big skedaddle."

But the important fact remained: Richmond had been rescued from the threat of destruction, and the momentum of the war had shifted. The cost was terrifying: Now the East had a battle to exceed bloody Shiloh in the West by more than half; 20,614 Confederate casualties and 15,849 Federals for a total of 36,463 (as against 23,741 at Shiloh). Those were not mere statistics. McClellan described an unforgettable scene of carnage as he looked across a field of five thousand dead and dying Confederates, "enough of them alive and moving to give the field a singular crawling effect."

On the Fourth of July, blackberry-picking time in Virginia, a strange truce came over the contending armies. As one private described it in his diaries later, "Our boys and the Yanks made a bargain not to fire at each other, and went out in the field . . . and gathered berries together and talked over the fight, traded tobacco and coffee and exchanged newspapers as peacefully and as kindly as if they had not been engaged for the last seven days in butchering one another."[33]

Richmond was turned into one vast hospital. Ambulances, litters, carts, and wagons rolled into the streets, stacked with bodies of the dead mixed with the wounded with missing limbs who could not walk. Those who could move at all or who had friends to help them hobbled back into the city—thousands of bloodied and bandaged men, some blinded in both eyes, so many that the back porches, the hallways, the parlors and drawing rooms of the Richmond mansions were crowded with the wounded and the half-dead. The doors of the houses were opened to as many as could get in, and women stood in the streets with basins of water and baskets of food, looking for their loved ones and then helping any man who came by. Church pew cushions were sewn together to create mattresses for the badly wounded. Others less critically injured just slept on bare boards or on the floor with their knapsacks as pillows.

Chimborazo Hospital gave off odors like the "vapors of the charnel house." The amputation room was a Stygian nightmare. Arms and legs were piled outside the door, covered with flies, waiting to be carted away; inside was a scene of such gory horror that it was all the volunteers could do to stop themselves from vomiting. The building was 30 by 100 feet, and men were packed solidly on tables along the whole length of it. The morbid stench of gangrene and burned skin pervaded the air as the men groaned with pain and delirium, a constant low refrain of suffering interspersed with screams of agony and violation, as the surgeon hacked and sawed away at their limbs, then cauterized the wounds with a hot poker. Phoebe Yates Pember, the legendary Jewish matron of the hospital, stood guard over a barrel of whisky with a pistol strapped to her hip, protecting it for only those who needed it most. Without supplies, the hospital survived on improvisation: persimmon juice as a styptic, hemlock for opium, and wild cherry for digitalis.

At Hollywood, the gravediggers worked feverishly in the rain to bury the hundreds of coffins stacked in the mud awaiting the shovel and the packed, wet earth. The rain washed away all the dirt from some of the shallow graves, leaving the coffins partially exposed. The upper classes undertook a more dignified burial of their officer-rank dead as the women, with pale, sad faces, wept over an unending parade of funerals. Each had its sword, cap, and riderless horse with reversed, empty boots. Each had its dirge. For days the sad music and the muffled drums engulfed the city in the heavy sounds of death and mourning.

Richmond struggled through the aftermath of the battle as Lee's army began to push McClellan back across Virginia, back "to the country he came from." The news from further South, however, was not good. "Beast" Butler's men had pushed into Mississippi and sacked Brierfield, the family home of Jefferson Davis. Benjamin still had heard no news from New Orleans of his sisters Harriet and Penny and her daughter, Leah. The anxiety filled him with melancholy.

Benjamin asked the War Department to make inquiries through spies in New Orleans. Finally he received some news. According to reports from the War Department, one night about 9 P.M. a Union lieutenant arrived and told Penny and Leah that the house was needed for a military hospital and they would have to be out in the morning. The lieutenant said he would send some soldiers over immediately to protect them—but they knew what that meant: "Beast" Butler did not get his other nickname, "Spoons," for nothing. He was going to make sure he had some men there to watch them pack.

They began packing immediately. In a while, the soldiers came. The women had held some whiskey in reserve and, plying the soldiers with some of Benjamin's best cognac and bourbon, they were able to humor them into helping to move all their furniture into an adjoining empty house. All through the night they worked, packing and moving. They even bribed a next-door neighbor into forgetting a debt they owed by giving him their cow. In the morning a squad of Butler's best showed up to relieve the easygoing guards of the night before. "Madam?" one of the soldiers said. "Are you the sister of the arch rebel, Benjamin?" Penny said yes, though timidly. "Then you are not to remove anything from this house. It is a military necessity."[34]

But nothing happened. The unit was relieved in the afternoon, and the women bluffed their way out by telling the new officer in charge that they had permission to move. Since half their things were already moved, he assumed that they were telling the truth. Penny and her daughter and sister were then smuggled into a two-room apartment in the French Quarter to wait to hear from Benjamin.

Secret agents inquired quietly and arranged for the women to go to La Grange, Georgia, where they would be safer, in a small town away from the fighting. Benjamin sent $900 by secret courier, thankful that his family had survived the battle of New Orleans with Benjamin ingenuity.

All of Richmond turned out for the Excelsior Minstrels to celebrate the victory. The show featured the banjo-picking of Old Joe Sweeney, who traveled all over the Confederacy to entertain the boys in the army camps, and "Brudder Bones" and the "jig dancer," complete with an acrobat and tightwire walker.

Crowds welcomed Varina home outside the Metropolitan Hall as the carriages arrived for the evening's performance. To all present, her return from North Carolina was a sign of victory, reassuring and hopeful, and set spirits rising in Richmond again. The carriage doors opened for the elite of the government and the military. The

President was relaxed as well, and as Benjamin and the Cabinet lined up behind the President to enter the hall triumphantly, the band struck up "Dixie." Written on the program was the theme of one of the acts:

The Celebrated Burlesque

RECRUITING UNBLEACHED CITIZENS OF VIRGINIA

FOR THE CONFEDERATE STATES ARMY

A trained bear chased a Yankee soldier up a tree, the dancing chorus did a Virginia reel, and a soprano sang "The Moments Were Sad When My Love and I Parted," followed by a duet of "The Soldier's Return."

The whites in blackface assumed their positions, with their outlandish costumes of spangled ties and tails and glittering orange bowlers. The end man and interlocutor began their routines:

INTERLOCUTOR: Whut's de first duty of de Suthrin' people?

END MAN: To keep out of de army. (*The hall burst into laughter.*)

INTERLOCUTOR: And whut's de second duty?

END MAN: To make all de money they can out of the government since wars come so seldom.[35]

The audience laughed, but hatred was growing for the speculators and the profiteers pouring into Richmond.

10

Lee Invades the North: *Enticing France and Britain*

After the Battle of Richmond, Robert E. Lee's army chased McClellan right out of his command, as Lincoln replaced "Little Mac" with a crafty but not very imaginative pair from the Western successes: Major General John Pope and General Henry "Old Brains" Halleck. Pope, who was to head the new Army of Virginia, immediately issued a ringing statement entitled "Headquarters in the Saddle." It announced: "I come to you from the West where we have always seen the backs of our enemies."[1] That was the trouble with the Yankees, one of Jeb Stuart's old cavalry veterans responded, "they got their headquarters where their hindquarters ought to be."

Lee's infinite patience and tact, and still more his serenity of purpose and spirituality, won another crucial battle in Virginia, the battle for the trust and confidence of Stonewall Jackson. At last, Jackson was learning how to fight in coordination with others, no longer as the lone commander, the elusive ghost of the Shenandoah, where he had to shimmy, sting, and strut off in the night to hide and fight again. He was learning how to show his moves intentionally and draw a charge, and thereby weaken another flank for Lee's fresh assault. He was learning how to probe and sally, to count on help, to believe in a strategy that depended on others. Lee, for his part, was learning how to use his general creatively: to ask the impossible, because Jackson's men loved the challenge; to use the legend of his ubiquity and the rebel yells to frighten the enemy into overcompensating for him and covering every possible position; to build on Stonewall's reputation for the unexpected, to let him lead left while another command slashed right. Lee was molding a team of commanders who believed enough in each other to move instinctively even before he gave the order to do so.

The Second Battle of Manassas in late August drove the Union forces back into Washington, and Lee paused to consider his options: whether to sit tight, attack Washington, or move north into Maryland.

Lee had wired back his misgivings to the capital: "The army is not properly equipped for an invasion of an enemy's territory. It lacks much of the material of war, is feeble in transportation, the animals being much reduced, and the men are poorly provided with clothes, and in thousands of instances, are destitute of shoes . . . what occasions me the most concern is the fear of getting out of ammunition."[2]

Benjamin and Davis argued the pros and cons of the next step. Lee could not sit still for lack of supplies, and he could not attack Washington, where the enlistments were arriving to the tune of Stephen Foster's song, "We are coming Father Abraham, three hundred thousand more." Maryland was the choice—it was a divided state where thousands were already serving in Lee's army and where thousands more could be expected to join. If Lee could win a victory there, Benjamin argued, then England and France would have to take the South seriously and give it the recognition it deserved.

On September 7, 1862, Lee crossed the Potomac, and the army soon arrived at the little village of Sharpsburg and the Battle of Antietam Creek. For the first time in the war, the Confederates had invaded the North.

Benjamin was obsessed with enticing France and Britain into the war. The maneuverings over the previous three years were taking on a pattern of their own so that he could almost predict the rhythm of events. When the Confederacy did well on the battlefield, interest in financial inducements bubbled in Europe; but if the war was going badly, the French and British became an audience for the drama, awaiting the outcome to decide what steps would be to their advantage.

For example, news of the Southern victory at Richmond in 1862 reached Napoleon while he was soaking himself in the waters at Vichy, where Slidell went as soon as he received Benjamin's dispatch to offer 100,000 bales of cotton. The dispatch did not arrive until July 6, more than three months after it was written, but with McClellan in retreat and a firm offer in hand, it could not have been more timely. Napoleon agreed to spend an hour or so talking, a conversation partly in French for Slidell's pleasure and partly in English to show off the Emperor's pride in his own mastery of the language.

Slidell and Benjamin knew that bales of cotton were not as appealing to France as to Britain, for even in normal times England bought 5 million bales a year from the South, as against France's 500,000. Indeed, the scarcity of cotton even brought some benefits to the competing linen, silk, and woolen industries on which the French had to place greater reliance. The problem with winning Southern sympathy in France was slavery: The upper classes were blasé, but the French masses were vehemently against it, and some of Napoleon's advisers were afraid that overt entry into the war without Britain could unseat him from his shaky throne.

Slidell, taking advantage of his previous ambassadorship to Mexico in 1845, shifted his conversation with Napoleon to ways in which the South could aid France in Mexico. Benito Juarez had overthrown a conservative Mexican regime in a people's revolution, had undertaken stern measures against the Catholic Church, and had repudiated the international debts of his predecessors. The canceled debts were just the excuse Napoleon needed to intervene. Encouraged by Duke de Morny, who had been secretly promised a share of whatever debt was restored by the bankers involved if France would act, Napoleon persuaded Great Britain and Spain to join him in sending troops to Mexico as a show of force to recover their debts. Slidell did not know that when the other countries were compelled to withdraw under United States pressure, Napoleon would leave his troops there to execute an even more grandiose plan—to march to Mexico City, unseat Juarez, and install Maximilian as emperor on a Hapsburg throne in Mexico. All that was in Napoleon's mind to do when Slidell stated flatly (though Benjamin's memorandum did not say it) that since Lincoln's government was a Juarez ally, the Confederacy "could have no objection to make common cause with France against a common enemy."[3]

Slidell suggested a range of steps short of French entry into the Civil War—mediation, recognition, a six months' armistice—but Seward in Washington had threatened war with France in Europe if there were any alliance with the Confederacy from Mexico, and Slidell reported to Benjamin the Emperor's response in a precise transcription:

"Your Majesty," Slidell pleaded, "has now an opportunity of securing a faithful ally, bound to you not only by ties of gratitude, but by those more reliable—common interest and congenial habit."

"Yes," the Emperor replied, "you have many families of French descent in Louisiana who yet preserve their habits and language." The Emperor continued, "But the policy of nations is controlled by their interests and not by their sentiments. I committed a great error and I now deeply regret it. France should never have respected the blockade. And she should have recognized the Confederacy. . . . But what can now be done? To open the ports forcibly would be an act of war."[4] He held steady to the view that France could not act without Britain.

Slidell realized that Napoleon needed time to consider these new questions and left the Emperor a crucial piece of information to appeal to an experienced conspirator. "This proposition," Slidell concluded to Napoleon, "is made exclusively to France. My colleague in London knows nothing about it."[5]

The English attitude toward the Confederacy had not changed since the Confederacy was formed, but Robert E. Lee gave Benjamin a chance to test the water again. The London *Times* had summed up the attitude of the British government about the South in an editorial after the *Trent* affair: "But we may as well observe," the *Times* said, "[that] the Messrs. Mason and Slidell are about the most worthless booty it would be possible to extract from the jaws of the American lion. They have long been known as the blind haters and revilers of this country. . . . So we sincerely hope that our countrymen will not give these two fellows anything in the shape of an ovation. . . . The only reason for their presence in London is to draw us into their own quarrel. The British public has no prejudice in favor of slavery, which these gentlemen represent. . . . They must not suppose, because we have gone to the verge of a great war to rescue them, that they are precious in our eyes."[6]

James Murray Mason oozed Virginia aristocracy from every pore and looked the part of the Southern diplomat—tall, big-framed, dignified, with graying temples and a large, impressive head. "A fine old English gentleman," correspondent Russell of the London *Times* wrote, "but for the tobacco."[7] James Mason chewed tobacco and spat its juices, which did not charm the English as a quaint American frontier custom. Except for the fact that he was the quintessence of Southern manhood, Mason in every other respect was the worst possible representative for Davis to have sent to England. He was

one of slavery's most ardent defenders, a fierce advocate of its extension into new territories, author of the hated Fugitive Slave Law,
and a fire-eating proponent of secession in 1850. He even had written
a public letter praising South Carolina's Preston "Bully" Brooks for
bludgeoning Senator Charles Sumner with his cane on the floor of
the U.S. Senate. To the North, Mason symbolized the South's inhumanity and, to make matters worse, a traitor to his heritage of democratic
principles, since his grandfather was George Mason, who refused
to sign the U.S. Constitution unless it included the Bill of Rights.

It is understandable that the British virtually ignored Mason. Other
than being polite, officials would have almost nothing to do with
him, refusing even to grant him appointments. One cannot treat a
Virginia aristocrat like a bootblack for long, however, and eventually
Benjamin received a dispatch from Mason saying that he intended
to press his next proposal for recognition "as a demand of right;
and if refused—as I have little doubt it will be—to follow the refusal
by a note that I did not consider it compatible with the dignity of
my government, and perhaps with my own self-respect, to remain
longer in England."[8]

While Southern strategy abroad was stymied, at home all social
customs were being uprooted; both races were caught in the uncertainties of the turmoil. The war was working a strange transition
on the relationships between slaves and masters. Having been told
they were free if the North won the war, what should be the attitude
of slaves who had worked all their lives for the same household?
How were they to live, facing the fears of an unknown called "freedom," cast out alone into the cruelties of a world more terrifying
than the certainties of the plantation life they were leading? Whites
were asking themselves what was going on behind the eyes of the
family servants.

Slavery had been an immutable fact of Southern life, a condition
unto eternity of subjugation. But now, with the white man gone
from the plantations and deprivation gnawing away at the order of
things, whites could sense rumblings of dissatisfaction among the
slaves as the walls holding back the tides of change began to crumble.

Nowhere was the disquiet deeper than in Richmond. Thousands
of male slaves gave the city its sinew, and the Yankee spies and
sympathizers played on the white fears. They spread rumors of sabotage and whispered secret plans of mass uprisings that never came.
Enticed by bribery or promises of freedom, trusted household servants now stole jewelry for the speculators.

But the prospects of invasion also stirred the slaves with misgivings. On the plantations, as the enemy approached, slaves fled to the hills in terror of being kidnapped for Lincoln's black legions, the two hundred Negro regiments the U.S. Congress had authorized.

There was no predictability any longer; that was the hell of it. When Dahlgren's Raiders arrived at the Seddon plantation just outside of Richmond, it was a black maidservant who buried the family silver; on the other hand, Colonel Chesnut received the news from Camden, South Carolina, that his slaves had stolen all of his corn crop. Loyal house slaves went door to door to perform the humiliating task of selling the dresses of their mistresses and candelabras of the family on consignment. Some Negroes were so obvious a part of the Yankee spy network that they dressed like dandies and walked the streets sporting canes and fat cigars.

Lee's message from the field was unusual in that it commented briskly on political matters but in a most natural way, as if Lee had not been consumed by three months of battle but had been sitting right in Richmond all along debating government policy. The message urged the President, in view of the military situation, to make some kind of public peace proposal to the North, based on permanent separation and recognition of the Davis government.

"Such a proposition, coming from us at this time," Lee wrote, "could in no way be regarded as suing for peace, but, being made when it is in our power to inflict injury upon our adversary, would show conclusively to the world that our sole object is the establishment of our independence and the attainment of an honorable peace. The rejection of this offer would prove to the country that the responsibility of the continuance of the war does not rest upon us, but that the party in power in the United States elect to prosecute it for reasons of their own." Lee foresaw the move as having a positive impact on the fall elections in the North, strengthening the Northern peace parties by enabling the voters to decide "whether they will support those who favor a prolongation of the war, or those who wish to bring it to a termination, which can be productive of good to both parties without affecting the honor of either."[9]

Benjamin and Davis were not sure. They thought that Lee was heading into Maryland for one of the turning-point battles of the war. If they asked for peace now, that battle was still going to take place. They thought that nothing but the outcome of the battle would influence Lincoln or his Cabinet.

Britain and France would surely await the results of the battle before acting. If Lee won it as decisively as he had been winning recently, then the Confederate leadership knew the diplomatic situation could break wide open. If the South lost or the battle was a draw, Europe might still provide arms, loans, and informal assistance, although the European leaders would probably hold back recognition.

In addition, the Congressional elections in the North were six weeks off. Once again, the battle would be the decisive factor, not what the government in Richmond did or said.

A crucial question was the impact that a peace statement might have on the battle itself.

That worried President Davis and the Secretary of State. The Confederates had been fighting to save their homes and their capital. Now a whole new dynamic would be entering the equation: engagement on terrain the South did not know well against an enemy who would be fighting for *his* survival. The South would be the invader. And the peace proposal now might change the chemistry. It would sound weak and apologetic at a time when the troops should be getting their battle blood up. It could have a detrimental effect not only on the morale of Lee's men but also on the troops in the West, where things were not going well either. Besides, suing for peace would give President Davis political troubles with the Congress. Tough, courageous talk was the kind of rhetoric needed for the press right now, not a lively debate over whether or not a peace treaty was timely.

There were some disquietingly bad signs out in Maryland. More than one-fourth of the soldiers were without shoes; "Confederate disease," as dysentery was called, was rampant from the green corn and unripe berries the soldiers had been eating; and the desertion rate was way up—the quartermaster had Lee listed with 66,000 men, but the actual count was about 50,000. That meant there were more than 15,000 soldiers absent without leave, most of them deserters.

The dispatch revealed more about Lee's state of mind than about the realistic strategic options of the South. His morale was down; he was concerned about stretching the supply lines too far. Plainly, he would like to avoid this next step if he could. Benjamin and Davis agreed that Davis should do all he could to respond to Lee's military concerns while delaying a peace feeler. Davis tried to get the news out that volunteers were pouring into Richmond from the other states to fight in Maryland and beyond. That would shake Lincoln and the British more than peace talk.

Varina was struck by Benjamin's good humor and optimism through discussions of the gravest consequence. She wrote:

His demeanor puzzled us so much that at last I asked him what comfort came to him. Was he hopeful of a fortunate termination? Then from his answer I discovered he was a fatalist. He said he believed there was a fate in the destiny of nations, and it was wrong and useless to distress one's self and thus weaken one's energy to bear what was fore-ordained to happen.[10]

With Lee threatening in Maryland by moving toward Baltimore and Washington, McClellan, who had been put in charge solely of the Washington fortifications, moved out on his own to join others in the battle to save his capital. Again faced with the super-cautious McClellan, Lee audaciously divided his army into four parts. His General Order 191 described the intricate convergence he wanted to execute as the armies approached Antietam. But three Union enlisted men came across an abandoned Confederate encampment and, while foraging around for some food or booty, found three cigars wrapped in a very important-looking document. They gave the paper to their company commander, who showed it to the colonel, who took it to his general, who rushed it to McClellan. There it all was before his eyes: the General Order with names, places, plans, Lee's army divided in front of him so that the full force of his army could split them and knock them down like tenpins, a segment at a time.

"I have all the plans of the rebels," he wired Lincoln, "and will catch them in their own trap if my men are equal to the emergency."[11]

McClellan started to move, elated and on the offensive, more confident than he had been since he had moved toward Richmond in May. Even Stonewall was startled by his change of spirits.

"I thought I knew McClellan," Jackson wondered, "but this movement of his puzzles me."[12]

A Maryland sympathizer who was in McClellan's headquarters galloped with the news to Jeb Stuart, and Lee discovered the reason for McClellan's enthusiasm. With his quadrant of 19,000 men facing 90,000, the only answer was retreat—hurried and complete, try to save as many men as possible and not worry about the supply wagons; break out of the trap; join the quadrants together; pull back.

McClellan waited overnight, and then another day, careful, always careful, so that Lee was able to rush his men through Turner's

Gap, to consolidate with one other command, and to repair some of the damage.

Because of the divided Confederate army, the battle of Antietam was really three separate battles. The contending armies slugged it out in bloody fighting on September 17, 1862, from dawn till dusk, in every direction. In the end, each side lost about one-fourth of its men in the bloodiest single day of the war—11,000 Confederates and 12,000 Union. Lee could not afford such losses at this point, and he retired from Maryland with his bloodied, exhausted troops, back to the safety of the Shenandoah, Stonewall Jackson's old briar patch. Not a rout by any means, more of a desperate standoff, but it gave Lincoln the confidence he needed. Five days later, on September 22, 1862, Abraham Lincoln issued his Emancipation Proclamation.

Lincoln's Emancipation Proclamation unnerved white Richmond and stirred its deepest fears. For one thing, there were now thousands of blacks in the city digging trenches and building fortifications, working at the Tredegar Iron Works and for the railroads. Whites in the city talked to each other quietly in a state of deep concern. It was the middle sentence of the Proclamation that frightened them: "The Executive Government of the United States, including the military and naval authority thereof . . . will do no act or acts to repress such persons, or any of them in any efforts they may make for their actual freedom."[13] As the South saw it, Lincoln had issued a call for black insurrection; his proclamation was an invitation to violence. The Richmond *Examiner* spoke for the city when it charged that it was "an act of malice towards the master, rather than one of mercy to the slave."[14]

President Davis declared the proclamation illegal. In his January 12, 1863, message to Congress he said: "We may well leave it to the instincts of common humanity to pass judgment on a measure by which millions of human beings of an inferior race, peaceful and contented laborers in the sphere . . . are encouraged to a general assassination of their masters by the insidious recommendation."[15]

Some Abolitionists claimed it was a clever but meaningless document that freed only those slaves now firmly under Confederate control, in states where Lincoln had no power to do so. "A poor document but a mighty act," the Governor of Massachusetts said to a friend.[16]

It did not matter in its details. Lincoln would be known to history as "the man who freed the slaves," and the Proclamation had the impact he wanted in the two places it was aimed—in the North and in Europe. In one stroke, Lincoln had transformed this war of brothers into a bold crusade to end slavery.

In the fall of 1862, Secretary of State Benjamin summoned Belle Boyd to Richmond for a public ceremony. She was already an internationally renowned Confederate spy at the age of nineteen, and Benjamin conceived the idea of sending her to France and England on a public relations mission.

She was fresh out of a Yankee prison, where she had tacked up a picture of Jefferson Davis in her cell, had sung Confederate songs to the prisoners, and had frustrated the prison guards, who would find her in her cell reading *Harper's Weekly* and eating peaches with one leg propped up on her bunk. To the prison superintendent who had offered to exchange her freedom for an oath of allegiance to the North, she declared, "If I ever sign one line to show allegiance, I hope my arms fall paralyzed to my side." "Bravo, bravo," the other prisoners shouted from their cells, and the whole incident ended up the next day in the papers, North and South. The Union army was so exasperated that it offered to exchange her to get rid of her, and she arrived as the toast of Richmond.

Belle's figure was so splendid that Northern officers would become infatuated and spill out their deepest secrets to her. Never mind that she had a homely face—what was below her neck made up for that. She was tall and athletic, with "wild, raging blue eyes." The new Confederate goodwill ambassador wore a closely cut gray riding costume of an "honorary captain."

The newspapers said she had "an utter abandonment of manner" and a "dash about her," and they were right. The "Cleopatra of Secession," as the British press called her, was a deliciously curvaceous creature with too long a face and a prominent chin, in truth, part Cleopatra, part clown. She was indeed a publicity prize who would charm the foreign press and generate columns of praise in London and Paris, to give the sympathizers in the foreign capitals a personality to celebrate and rally round. But she was also an effective Confederate agent. Belle, born in the Shenandoah Valley, had moved so effortlessly behind the enemy lines that she had become a crucial spy for Stonewall Jackson's 1862 Valley campaign.[17]

The most celebrated incident of Belle's career, recounted in newspapers all over the world, exemplified her extraordinary panache. In a long, low-cut dress, with a revolver in her sash and Yankee shells bursting all around, she ran through an open field to bring her hero Stonewall word that Fort Royal was vulnerable, then waved the Confederates to victory with her bonnet. The French papers, which called her "La Belle Rebelle," carried a drawing of her brandishing a saber and leading a charge.

She carried a letter from Stonewall Jackson with her at all times, composed at Fort Royal: "I thank you for myself and for the Army, for the immense service you rendered your country today. Hastily, I am your friend, T. J. Jackson, CSA."

Now Belle Boyd had come to see the Secretary of State in his office. On behalf of President Jefferson Davis and the entire Confederacy, Benjamin presented her with $2,500 in gold. He instructed her to leave soon for Canada, England, and France and to carry the message of the Confederate cause proudly as his public relations envoy. Benjamin, sensing a rare opportunity, would instruct his diplomats to use her wisely.

"I have been quite surprised," Slidell wrote Mason and Benjamin, "at an uninvited suggestion on the part of a respectable banking house of a disposition to open a credit to our government of a considerable amount—the basis to be cotton delivered to the parties making the advance at certain parts of the interior."[18]

The offer regarding Southern cotton came from Erlanger & Cie., the Jewish bankers who headed the most distinguished banking house in France. As intimate advisers of Napoleon, the Erlangers were trusted intermediaries. Moreover John Slidell's daughter had recently become engaged to marry the Baron Erlanger. The term "uninvited suggestion" must have amused Benjamin, who remembered Slidell's expression of surprise at the "uninvited" victories of the Democratic Party in Louisiana.

The deal Erlanger was offering had a decidedly "Slidellian" flavor to it. The details revealed that it was not really a loan at all but a complex scheme to speculate in cotton for European purchasers. The firm would obtain 8 percent bonds at 70 points to be sold at 100; the bonds would be backed by a promise to exchange each one at face value *after* the war for cotton at 12 cents a pound, which was exactly half of what cotton was selling for already. The total involved was about $25 million.[19]

The Erlanger house saw in events an opportunity to make a great deal of money for itself by handling the bonds while at the same time doing a profitable favor for everyone involved. The market would be the thousands of rich Southern sympathizers among the upper classes in England and France, along with speculators in Europe who were watching the Confederate successes on the battlefield and Napoleon's diplomatic maneuvering in England and Russia. The Confederacy would reap desperately needed funds from the deal, but also a form of recognition in the European financial community that would carry political weight in the North and the South.

Benjamin balked. He felt Slidell wanted the Confederacy to give cotton away in exchange for an enormous debt in Europe. He feared the proposal was such a giveaway that banking circles would think the Confederacy had no confidence or money sense. Erlanger wanted to come to Richmond to discuss it, and Benjamin agreed.

Slidell was right that the South would be doing Napoleon and the French a favor; in fact, Benjamin would not have been surprised if half the money ended up in the Duke de Morny's pocket. But Erlanger was close to Napoleon, and it might be worth it to be linked to France economically. Benjamin would have to improve the deal to make it palatable to the South.

The fact that Emile Erlanger himself was coming meant that two Jews would be sitting down to hammer out a financial deal for the Confederacy. The Cabinet looked to Benjamin alone, not the Secretary of the Treasury or the President, to handle the negotiation, probably because of Benjamin's presumed connections with the Rothschilds and the Erlangers. After all, famous Jews were supposed to know each other, to speak a special language to one another and be involved in international intrigue. Even Erlanger and Benjamin could not escape the shadow of Gentile suspicion. *Harpers Weekly,* the Cincinnati *Gazette,* and other papers criticized Jews because of Erlanger's assistance to the Confederacy, and Isaac Wise was so concerned that he wrote in his paper "Baron Erlanger is not one of those common Jews and usurers . . . he was baptized many years ago!"[20]

The Southern newspapers trumpeted a quotation from England's Chancellor of the Exchequer, William Gladstone: "There is no doubt that Jefferson Davis and other leaders of the South have made an army," Gladstone said at a banquet in Newcastle. "They are making, it appears, a navy, and they have made what is more than either— they have made a nation." When the cheering and the cries of "Hear, Hear!" subsided, Gladstone added, "We may anticipate with certainty the success of the Southern states so far as regards their separation from the North."[21]

Davis smiled for the first time in months, because both he and Benjamin knew what those words might mean. The third-ranking

British official had spoken; England must be wavering, and recognition and intervention could not be far away.

A few weeks later Napoleon summoned Slidell for an audience, in which he announced that he felt the time was ripe for a joint mediation by France, England, and Russia to end the war. "My own preference is for a proposition of an armistice in six months," Slidell reported that Napoleon said. "This would put a stop to the effusion of blood, and hostilities would probably never be resumed. We can urge it on the high grounds of humanity and the interest of the civilized world. If it be refused by the North, it will afford good reason for recognition, and perhaps for more active intervention."[22] A week later, with Benjamin's cotton working its quiet magic, Napoleon notified his ministers in Europe to "exert their influence at Washington as well as with the Confederates to obtain an armistice."

But Lincoln's Secretary of State, William Seward ("Old Billy Bowlegs," his enemies called him), was watching events carefully and was not about to let Benjamin score that kind of triumph. His bushy eyebrows wiggling and an ever-present cigar bouncing as he talked, Seward dispatched Ambassador Charles Adams, breathing fire and hinting of war, to see Foreign Minister Russell in London. Russell assured Adams that England intended to remain neutral. Benjamin knew what that meant: The British government wanted to wait longer, to see if the South had staying power, before jeopardizing its supply of Northern wheat. It was time to launch a propaganda campaign with the British public.

Slidell may have seen through the simple anti-Americanism of Britain's policy from the beginning, in which Britain favored neither side, only an extended conflict. "I am satisfied," Slidell wrote Benjamin in August, "that [England] desires an indefinite prolongation of the war, until the North shall be entirely exhausted and broken down. Nothing can exceed the selfishness of British statesmen except wretched hypocrisy."[23]

Benjamin was deeply frustrated by the prize dangling in front of him. His letters indicated that he thought he was close, enticingly close, to winning the war for the South, if only France would intervene; but the British were holding firm, which was causing the French to hesitate. Still, the news from Paris was not bad. Slidell was making progress with Erlanger, and for the moment the negotiations in Europe were leaning the South's way.

Emile Erlanger was dressed so elegantly when he arrived in Richmond that by comparison Benjamin must have looked as drab as a poor relative. Maybe it would help negotiations if Erlanger were to see that the South needed the money more than he did. For the entire day, they would speak in French. The baron was a tall, quiet man, with long, slender fingers and a sensitive face. This was not the bloated figure of the overfed banker, but a cosmopolitan who loved the arts, collected sculpture, and moved with ease in rarified social and professional circles all over the world. They had many hours to speak of the Champs Elysées and of the Emperor and Empress; of the Tuilleries and of Notre Dame and of the recent wedding of Erlanger to the Slidell's daughter; of Natalie and Ninette.

They moved from the sitting area over to Benjamin's black walnut table covered with green cloth, where Erlanger spread his papers and laid out the plan carefully. Their discussions lasted into the evening. Benjamin had done his homework and had mastered the numbers on both sides of the table. He knew the impact on the bargain of every possible change in percentage point, size of loan, and length of time for payment. He had studied the firm's brokerage activity and evaluated its risk. He made it clear that the Confederacy was interested, but not at Erlanger's proposed terms. After hours of wrangling, the amount of the credit involved was lowered to $15 million, the interest rate to 7 percent, and the starting price of the bond to Erlanger raised to 77 points.

It was now a better bargain for the Confederacy, but still quite lucrative for both Erlanger and the French. In the end, even with a questionable agreement, Benjamin felt that the loan was worth the price if it encouraged Napoleon to be more interested in the outcome of the war. Benjamin's chips were more political than financial.

A week later, in Congress, when Davis announced the results of the negotiations, including the improvement in terms, Congressman Henry Foote sarcastically described Benjamin's meeting: "On the occasion of the recent visit of Mr. Erlanger," Foote said, "Minister Plenipotentiary, Envoy Extraordinaire from His Highness, the Emperor of France, to his Highness the would-be Emperor of the Confederate States, Judas Iscariot Benjamin had spoke for two hours in French."[24]

News of an agreement with France lifted spirits momentarily, and the gossip in Richmond about Benjamin over the next year reflected that. "Everything Mr. Benjamin said we listened to," Mary Chesnut wrote in her diary, "bore it in mind, gave heed to it diligently. He is a Delphic oracle. He is one of the innermost shrine, supposed to enjoy Mr. Davis' unreserved confidence."[25]

11

Anti-Semitism
and the Jews of Richmond

❈

The Richmond Jewish community, comprising 3 percent of the population, had historic ties to Virginia, and the attitudes of the Jewish "first families" somewhat mirrored the condescension of other Virginians. The early wave of immigrants had risen to high station. They fought alongside the patriots in the American Revolution and successfully allied themselves with the Founding Fathers such as Jefferson and Madison to enact in 1786 the statutes of religious freedom assuring the rights of Jews to vote and hold office. Isaiah Isaacs was elected to the Richmond Common Hall two years after the statutes were passed; Jacob Cohen, who once hired Daniel Boone to survey his land, was also elected to the Common Hall, to replace a nephew of George Washington. Isaacs and Cohen cofounded Beth Shalome, the Sephardic congregation in Richmond.[1]

Richmond's most distinguished Jewish leader in 1860 was Gustavus Myers, an outstanding attorney and a civic and religious leader from one of Richmond's oldest and wealthiest families. Myers was Judah Benjamin's closest friend in Richmond: As young lawyers they had worked together on cases of national and international importance. Tall and lean, Myers had clear, dark blue eyes, light, curly hair and a prominent, straight nose. His face reflected an artistic temperament—an expression of extraordinary kindness and sensitivity reminiscent of Rembrandt's paintings of the Jews of Amsterdam.

198

His eyes had a melancholy look, as if he had inherited the wisdom of the ancient prophets, with a commitment to a far distant past and the prescience of an uncertain future.

However, Myers also had a pragmatic side to his personality. He had been a member of the Richmond City Council for thirty years and its president from 1843 to 1855, so he understood the special pressures on Jews in public life. Unlike Benjamin, however, he was a pillar in the Jewish community. He was head of Beth Shalome and contributed at the same time to the more recently organized German congregation at Beth Ahabah. He must have fascinated Benjamin, because he was so at ease with his Jewishness. Benjamin could relax with him as with perhaps no other person in Richmond, sharing interests in nonreligious matters such as the law and politics.

Myers and Benjamin were, then, contrasting in their Jewishness, yet similar in background. Descendants of early waves of Jewish immigration, both were successful lawyers, holders of political office, and cultivated men. Both had married into the upper reaches of the non-Jewish world, Myers to Anne Giles, daughter of the Governor of Virginia and a member of the Episcopal congregation in Richmond. Both men had a strong sense of their own personal destiny. As it was the custom among some early Dutch Jews of Richmond to name their sons after an admirable figure in history, Gustavus Adolphus Myers carried the name of the King of Sweden and the symbol of Swedish independence. Such a heritage led him early to public life.

Benjamin's roots were not in public service, but he grew into politics naturally through the law. He and Myers shared connections with the Jewish banking house of August Belmont in New York and the international contacts implicit in such friendships. Myers, too, had traveled widely. He once presided at a meeting to protest the treatment of the Jews of Damascus, since he felt himself at one with the suffering of Jews everywhere.

"Saw a lovely Jew," Mary Chesnut wrote in her diary. "Elsewhere Jews may be tolerated. Here they are *haute volée.* Everybody everywhere has their own Jew exceptions."[2]

J. B. Jones was a Northern journalist with Southern sympathies who settled in Richmond at the age of fifty-one and wrote a diary of the war. A job in the War Department gave him an inside view of the action, and his two-volume *A Rebel War Clerk's Diary at the Confederate States Capitol* offers invaluable observations of the day-by-day events. Jones disliked Jews. In his original (unedited) diaries he mentions the word "Jew" in a derogatory way forty times, with special hatred for Benjamin and other Jews of prominence. His anti-Semitism gives insights into the thinking of the times.

The atmosphere in Richmond against all Jews, even the "exceptions," grew worse as the impact of the war unsettled the economy. Jones wrote that A. C. Myers, the "Jew Quartermaster General," met the plea of soldiers for blankets with the answer, "Let them suffer." He called the distinguished Gustavus Myers "the little old lawyer for Jew clients." "Illicit trade," he wrote, "has depleted the country of gold and placed us at the feet of Jew extortioners." He reported laughter in the streets of Richmond "when a Jew is asked what will be the price of shoes, etc., tomorrow." Finally, he concluded, "These Jews . . . have injured the cause more than the armies of Lincoln."[3]

Southern Punch magazine also vented its rage against the Jews to its Richmond readers: "Who are our capitalists at the present time? . . . The dirty greasy Jew peddlar [sic], who might be seen, with a pack on his back, a year or two since, bowing and cringing even to Negro servants, now struts by with the air of a millionaire."[4] The German Jews were subjected to special scorn: They were considered foreigners, charged with avoiding conscription, and suspected of antislavery sentiments. The Richmond *Examiner* hammered home this theme, to the consternation of the Jews of Richmond:

> While many of our people have been dragged from their homes and frequently from sick and needy families by the inexorable demands of conscription, thousands of Jews . . . have gone scot-free simply for the virtue of denying their allegiance to the country in which some of them were born and which many of them by the plainest acts have pretended to adopt.

The editorial grew in vituperation as it enlarged its attack:

> They have flocked here as vultures and birds of passage. One has but to walk through the streets and stores of Richmond to get an impression of the vast number of unkempt Israelites in our marts. . . . Every auction room is packed with greasy Jews. . . . Let one observe the number of wheezing Jewish matrons . . . elbowing out of their way soldiers' families and the most respectable people in the community.[5]

The German Jewish community reacted to the harangues with an outburst of patriotism, sending its sons to war and raising funds for supplies and food when they lacked such essentials themselves.

Rabbi Maximilian Michelbacher at Beth Ahabah prayed that "a way may be opened whereby we, the people of the South, may pass with dry feet in safety to the position of peace and plenty, attended with the protection which Thou gavest to thy chosen people of old."[6]

Phoebe Yates Pember of South Carolina, a fiery Jewish woman who moved to Richmond to be with her wounded husband and stayed on to preside over a section of Chimborazo Hospital, wrote defiantly in *A Southern Woman's Story:* "At last I lifted my voice and congratulated myself at being born of a nation and religion that did not enjoin forgiveness of its enemies, that enjoyed the privilege of praying for an eye for an eye."[7] Her Old Testament militance reassured her non-Jewish friends of her patriotism.

Congressman Foote delivered another attack on "foreign Jews, spirited here by extraordinary and mysterious means." Foote alluded to Benjamin as the culprit, the high official granting passage to Jews from outside the South, almost inviting them. He claimed that "it was by official permission that this swarm of Jews from all parts of the world had come to this country invited to trade with us, and permitted in many cases to conduct illicit traffic with the enemy without much official examination into this part of their transaction."[8] With the phrase "official permission," Foote thus blamed the economic troubles of the Confederacy on the Jews and then tied their presence to Judah Benjamin for allowing them to travel freely. "If the present state of things were to continue," Foote said a friend had told him, "the end of the war would probably find nearly all of our property in the hands of Jewish Shylocks."[9]

Foote ranted on the floor of the Confederate Congress that "foreign Jews were scattered all over the country, under official protection, engaged in trade to the exclusion of our own citizens, undermining our currency." Senators Chilton of Alabama and Hilton of Florida agreed. Hilton said Jews "had swarmed here as the locusts of Egypt. They eat up the substance of the country, they exhausted its supplies, they monopolize its gains . . . they flocked as vultures to every point of gain. . . . They should be dragged into the army."[10]

The attacks persisted all over the Confederacy, with Judah Benjamin as the special target of the Richmond *Examiner*'s fulmination and the Jewish "extortionists" as the enemies in the local newspapers. In Richmond, the *Examiner* quoted Foote as saying he would never "consent to the establishment of a Supreme Court of the Confederate States so long as Judah P. Benjamin shall continue to pollute the ears of majesty Davis with his insidious counsels."[11] In Alabama a candidate for office referred to "that infamous Jew . . . Judas P. Benjamin."[12]

Even an effort at praise seemed to have a certain bite to it. A contemporary observer said Benjamin was a "Hebrew of Hebrews, for the map of the Holy City was traced all over his small, refined face . . . [He] was of the highest type of his race."[13]

For years Benjamin had faced the anti-Semitic slanders of Jefferson Davis's political enemies, who found it easier to blame the Jews for their troubles than to face the somber realities of the war. It did not matter that some of the first families in Richmond were Jews, for their fancy carriages only seemed to confirm the darkest suspicions of profiteering from the war. Speculators were called Jews, rising prices and money troubles were blamed on Jews, a suffering army had the Jews to thank. *Southern Punch* referred to Richmond as "Jew-rue-sell-'em" and Jews as "Richmond Yankees."[14] The convenience of having a Jew at the President's right hand made the juicy parlor gossip an easy pastime. Perhaps Benjamin's own ambivalence about his Jewishness encouraged those who hated him; they knew their remarks were a way to prod him and raise his temperature. The political writers in the North as well as the European writers who covered the war invariably chose to describe his "decidedly Jewish features" after an interview.

Finally, Richmond's Rabbi Michelbacher delivered a sermon in defense of the Jews, which was printed in newspapers in both the South and the North. According to Bertram Korn in *American Jewry and the Civil War,* the nation was experiencing the greatest outpouring of "Judaeophobia" in its history, and Rabbi Michelbacher's unusual remarks touched a responsive chord.

Rabbi Michelbacher was thin, wore steel-rimmed glasses, and had a long face. His black hair stuck out from under his German yarmulke, which looked like a flattened chef's hat. He was beloved by his congregation. He fathered three children by his first wife and ten by his second, which won a certain admiration for him from his wartime congregation. Michelbacher said that if the Jews were guilty of the charge against them, they would find no defender in him, because he prided himself in the fact that "I always speak of your faults without fear, favor or affection." He had investigated the conduct of Jewish merchants personally and was convinced that "the Israelites are not speculators or extortioners." He buttressed his argument with details, pointing out that the Jewish merchant specialized in "rapid turnover sales," while the speculator made his fortune by "hoarding." Besides, he pointed out, Jews did not even deal in the basic commodities in which speculation was most common: flour, meal, wheat, corn, bacon, beef, coal, and wood. And if Jews were extortionists, how could they stay in business? Wouldn't the trade go to non-Jews, who by implication were "free of all taint of profiteering?" He concluded that the condemnation of the Jews was "instigated" so that those who were "actually guilty could escape punishment."[15]

In Richmond, the *Examiner* had kept Benjamin's Jewishness in the spotlight where it could operate on everyone's subconscious, especially that of the new German immigrants, who must have shuddered every time it published the slurs of Henry Foote or printed the editorials of John M. Daniel. Daniel was the pen of anti-Semitism, and Foote was its voice.

A Jewish reader wrote a letter of complaint to another Richmond paper, the *Sentinel,* complaining about Congressional coverage by the *Examiner* and other papers in the city:

That a man like Foote should habitually denounce the Jew is to be expected; he denounces everybody and everything; his mouth is a "well-spring" of slander and I should doubt the beauty of virtue, itself, should he chance to praise it. But, that the whole press of your city (your paper excepted) should add fuel to these fires of persecution, and should seek to direct public opinion in such foul channels, surpasses my comprehension.[16]

When Lazarus Straus of Talbotton, Georgia, whose son Oscar later was to create his own legend after the war when he purchased Macy's in New York City, heard that a Talbotton grand jury had condemned Jewish merchants, he packed the family up to move to Columbus, a few miles away. Every member of the grand jury called on him to stay; every minister in the town asked him to change his mind; every leading citizen explained that there had been no intention to reflect on *his* ethics or *his* faith, just on the Jews in general. The incident is an example of how a climate of prejudice had gotten out of hand across the South.

There is no written verification that Judah P. Benjamin ever attended or contributed to a synagogue in Richmond or in any other community where he lived. However, *The History of the Jews of Richmond from 1769 to 1917* by Ezekiel and Lichtenstein reports on an interview with an old Richmond citizen who said that he had seen Benjamin "called up to the reading of the Law at Beth Ahabah synagogue."[17] The truth of that statement has been contested by historians, because it does not seem to square with their own impressions of Benjamin as a nonbeliever. It is unlikely that such a noteworthy event would have left behind no corroborating testimony, they argue. They point out also that Beth Ahabah, the German Jewish synagogue of the new immigrants, was the congregation of the family that had lost Private Henry Adler at Roanoke Island, the battle for which Benjamin had been publicly blamed. Beth Ahabah still stands, and in fact there are no records substantiating the visit.

The eyewitness account becomes more credible, however, if one assumes that the congregation in question was actually Beth Shalome, the older Sephardic synagogue. Unfortunately, the building and records of Beth Shalome were destroyed in the evacuation fires of 1865, so the truth of the matter will probably never be known.

Benjamin might well have visited Beth Shalome at least once in his four years in Richmond, because its president was Gustavus Myers. Myers's close friendship with Benjamin gives some credence to the eyewitness account since it would have made it natural for Myers to have invited him to the synagogue, and courteous as well as respectful for Benjamin to have accepted.

Because of Myers, the common view among the older Jewish families in Richmond was that Jews of high station reflected well in the eyes of both the Gentiles and other Jews by serving in visible office. For the Gentiles, they would be patriots. For the Jews, they would serve as signals to the new immigrants that Jews were an integral part of the Confederacy, that they could aspire to any position and could become as accepted and influential as their talents allowed.

It was true that regardless of his thirty years on the City Council, Gustavus Myers was still essentially an outsider to the Gentile community, still not accepted in its inner social circles. Both he and Judah Benjamin were court Jews, whom those in power had anointed to help organize the realm. It had been ever so. But Gustavus Myers did not depend on the Gentiles' acceptance for his self-worth. He lived his life as an open and proud Jew, a Southerner, a citizen of Virginia and of Richmond. Myers thought Jews had to set an example, and the only kind of Jew the Gentiles did not understand was one who was ashamed of being Jewish.

Myers could argue with his friend that, looking to his own example, it would be wiser for Benjamin to declare himself as one with the Jewish community of Richmond. The Gentiles would identify him with them no matter what. Would non-Jews not respect him all the more? Benjamin, who had learned at Yale to read Hebrew, Latin, and Greek, would feel at home at Beth Shalome. It was, after all, a Sephardic synagogue like his father's house of worship in Charleston, with a service he would recall and find comforting. As a friend of Gustavus Myers, the congregation would welcome him. Besides, as the war went badly, the President had ordered a "day of prayer" for the entire city. It would have been appropriate for a loyal member of the Cabinet to honor the proclamation.

The President frequently sought to involve the churches in the war, especially when news grieved the city and he sensed that the people needed an uplifting experience that would be good for morale. As required on such days, Benjamin's staff participated, so he must have faced a dilemma. To work would only point up his lack of affiliation and make him appear insensitive to the religious backbone of the city.

Gustavus Myers by example showed the Jews of Richmond that, as a city council member, he was neither above them nor distant from his religion. Myers's positive approach could not have been lost on Benjamin. Jews in Richmond had been concerned about Benjamin's visibility, the animosity it was sure to raise, the blame and denunciation that might descend on them should anything go badly. And indeed, events were confirming the fear that if he failed, all the Jews would be blamed for it; his Senate career had proved to him that anti-Semitism was real. He could do nothing about that; all he could do was let the Jewish community meet him and hope that they would be more accepting than afraid.

Jewish issues had come to Benjamin's desk more than once during the war. Rabbi Michelbacher at Beth Ahabah in Richmond sent him a letter to pass on to Robert E. Lee, requesting High Holy Day furloughs to "soldiers of the Jewish persuasion in the Confederate States Army." Benjamin must have thought that an unwise request, but he understood the fervor of the new German Jewish community, even if he did not share it. We do not know the private advice he offered to Lee, but with as many as ten thousand Jews in the Confederate Army, Lee handled the request in a careful and politically astute manner. Lee addressed his response to Rabbi Michelbacher as "Preacher, Hebrew Congregation, House of Love" that "I feel assured that neither you nor any other member of the Jewish congregation would wish to jeopardize a cause you have so much at heart by the withdrawal even for a season of a portion of its defenders."[18]

With his background in the Charleston Jewish community, Benjamin would have been at home with the Sephardic character of the beautifully decorated Beth Shalome synagogue with its stained-glass windows and its altar in the center. He would have approved of the English prayerbooks, the hymns, the English sermon from the rabbi. All in all, it had a service that even a nonbeliever could understand and appreciate.

The German Jews who had flooded into the South in the 1850s had worried the old, settled Jewish families. They were highly visible, peddling all over the South; they spoke English with an accent and actually went to the cabins of free Negroes to sell their trinkets. True, their religious services were in German, not Hebrew or English, and Benjamin's father Philip would have approved, but their cultural ties to Bavaria, their observance of dietary laws, and their belief in resting on the Sabbath only confirmed to the Gentiles the foreign and exotic nature of the Jews. Men who acted like strangers would be treated that way.

Jewish leaders were concerned about the image of Jews in the Southern mind. Regardless of his own beliefs, Benjamin's position as a Cabinet member helped to increase the acceptability of Jews in the South, especially among the poor whites. Rabbi Einhorn preached fire and abolition from Baltimore, pretending to be a prophet speaking for the Jews. The Southern rabbis were more circumspect. Many Jews in the Deep South welcomed the sermons of Rabbi Morris J. Raphall in New York City, who claimed slavery was sanctioned in the Bible because the ten commandments mentioned slaves and the Hebrew patriarchs Abraham, Isaac, and Jacob were all slaveholders. Jews in the South feared that they would be physically attacked if tarred with the antislavery views of the Abolitionists. In that sense Judah Benjamin's identification with the Southern cause and Judaism could help insulate the Southern Jews from calamity. Southern whites might respect all Jews if they had confidence in the few they knew best.

The Confederacy heralded David Lopez, the talented builder who was working to create the South's first torpedo boat; M. C. Mordecai, who outfitted his steamer as a blockade runner; Benjamin Mordecai, organizer of the "Free Market of Charleston," which was supporting more than six hundred families during the war at a cost of $8,000 a month. But those men were not well enough known to influence the opinion of the Gentiles. Only Benjamin symbolized the Jew who was also a Southerner—one who was loyal to the Confederacy, who could provide an antidote to the suspicion among Southern Gentiles that Jews at heart were Abolitionists.

It is well known that Benjamin was not an observant Jew, to say the least. He did consider himself an intellectual Jew, however, steeped in his people's literature and culture, in their philosophy and language. He could debate issues in the Old Testament. He was a Jew of the head, not the heart.

An invitation from Myers to attend Beth Shalome, if nothing else, would have served a governmental purpose for Benjamin in that it would provide him a place to join the rest of the Cabinet and the Congress at worship on an official day of prayer and fasting.

If Benjamin did attend, he would have been a celebrated visitor and guest of the congregation president. As was customary with distinguished visitors, he most certainly would have been "called up to the reading of the law."

Benjamin would not have been a stranger to the reading of the Torah. He would have studied it for his confirmation before going off to Yale, even though the protests and eventual expulsion of his father from the Charleston congregation may have been a distraction. He was familiar with the Five Books of Moses as literature, as law, as moral parables, and was known to quote them in discussions.

The ancient parchment of the Torah with the Hebrew letters had been at the center of Jewish life for two thousand years. Even when times were good, the Jews were singled out as if they had leprosy and expelled from every country in Europe, their property seized or unequally taxed. They were ghettoized by special laws and barred from entering the professions, owning land, getting an education, practicing a trade, or worshiping their God. When times were bad, as they now were in Richmond, they had always been blamed and were banished into the wilderness or even massacred—as witness the terrible episodes of the Inquisition and the Crusades.

Why did Christians mistrust them so? It was ingrained from childhood. Here in the South, even though Jews wanted to assimilate, to be the Christians' friends and equals, they would never let Jews grow up as part of them. Southerners made the Jews different from them, apart, both a devil and a prophet figure. They admired the Jews, but they feared them too. Jews were of the same faith as Jesus, and yet they were the people who crucified Him. They loved the Jews, they hated the Jews, and neither emotion was ever far from the surface. They blessed the Jews, they blamed the Jews, and the choice was unpredictable. They must convert the Jews or suspect them, because Jews were responsible for His suffering on the cross and must pay the price for the crucifixion. Whichever the Christians chose, admiration or condemnation, the Jews could not be ignored and just left alone.

Benjamin surely was outraged when the courier brought the Union message to him from Memphis. "General Order No. 11, December 17, 1862: Jews as a class violating every regulation of trade established by the Treasury Department and also department orders, are hereby expelled from the department [of Tennessee] within 24 hours from the receipt of this order. Signed, U.S. Grant, General, United States Army."[19] That was the most celebrated event of the war concerning Jews.

General William Sherman had earlier complained of "swarms of Jews and speculators" flocking into Memphis on the Mississippi and had falsely accused the Jews of buying up or stealing thousands of bales of cotton with the intention of selling them for huge profits in the North to the reopening textile mills.[20] Confederate spies had conclusive proof that the army itself was involved in speculating in cotton, yet Grant nonetheless had issued this order.

Southern Jews who had lived in the Tennessee district for decades, even former Jewish Union soldiers, were forced to pack up their families hurriedly and leave. Parson Brownlow was one of the few to applaud the order. "It is useless to disguise the fact that nineteen out of every twenty cases brought to light of all this smuggling, turns out to be the work of certain circumcised Hebrews."[21]

Had the order been issued in Louisiana when Benjamin was still in New Orleans, he himself could have been loading a carriage again like his ancestors in Spain. Penny and Leah, had they not fled to Georgia but to the Tennessee district, could have been among the banished Jews. For Jews in the South (and many in the North), Grant's order was deeply disturbing; it raised the ancient question of security. Could Jews ever be assured of a home in the war-torn South? Must they always have secret plans to flee, always keep an escape route in mind and an emergency trunk packed in the attic?

It was seemingly easier for the Union generals to believe that the Jews were bogeymen than to accept the facts about speculation in the midst of an economy in ruin. Grant and Sherman had to know the truth behind the stories—that a gold rush over cotton speculation had broken out, spreading a get-rich-quick mania around Union lines of such magnitude that cotton fever had even gripped the military. The temptations were so great that even Grant's own intimate circle of advisers was involved. Records show that $12,000 could buy 1,500 pounds of cotton in Mississippi, which could be resold for $500,000 in Kentucky. Charles Dana of the New York *Tribune* wrote: "Every colonel, captain or quartermaster is in secret partnership with some operator in cotton; every soldier dreams of adding a bale of cotton to his monthly pay."[22] A close friend of Grant's strongest Congressional supporter, who had traveled with the general, confessed to making $25,000 during the trip, his only regret being that he "could have made an eternal, hell-roaring fortune."[23] There is evidence that cotton deals were offered to Grant himself, but never a hint that he accepted the bribes.

Grant sent a detailed explanation with his order to the War Department. It stated: "The Israelites especially should be kept out. . . . The Jews seem to be a privileged class that can travel anywhere. . . . If not permitted to buy cotton themselves they will act as agents for someone else, who will be at a military post with a Treasury agent to receive cotton and pay for it in Treasury notes which the Jew will buy up at an agreed rate, paying gold."[24]

There was the smell of corruption to the order and some evidence that influential cotton buyers and their officer cronies in the Union army persuaded the gullible general to issue the order to make way for larger profits. Rabbi Isaac Wise pointed out later in his journals from Cincinnati that the price of cotton in Tennessee dropped from 40 cents a pound to 25 cents after the expulsions, but the price in the North remained high. "The Jews must leave," Wise said, "because they interfere with a branch of military business."[25]

The General Order projected anti-Semitic feelings all over the North. Citizens had to decide whether their most celebrated general had acted correctly. In some, it unleashed deep feelings that spilled over onto other issues.

Senator Henry Wilson of Massachusetts stated in a Senatorial debate on fiscal measures that "you will have every curbstone Jew broker . . . and the class of men who fatten upon public calamity . . . using all their influence to depreciate the credit of the government." He described the issue of the nation's financial structure as "a contest between those curbstone brokers, the Jew brokers, the money changers, and the men who speculate in stocks, and the productive, toiling men of the country."[26]

Jews in the North organized themselves to petition Lincoln in behalf of their Southern brethren. A delegation of Jews, summoned by Rabbi Wise and Cesar Kaskel of Paducah, Kentucky, visited Lincoln with affidavits from leading Republicans and military authorities. According to the record, the following conversation took place in the White House:

LINCOLN: And so the Children of Israel were driven from the happy land of Canaan.

KASKEL: Yes, and that is why we have come unto Father Abraham's bosom to ask for protection.

LINCOLN: And this protection they shall have at once.[27]

Lincoln rescinded an order of his most popular general in the middle of the war. He was moved not only by the plight of the Southern Jews; some of those deported had been Union soldiers, and Wise cleverly organized the Jewish relatives of Northern Jewish soldiers to complain. Still, it would have been easier for Lincoln to keep his blinders on and not risk a collision with Ulysses S. Grant.

General-in-Chief Halleck interpreted the order for Grant in a letter that Grant could understand: "The President has no objection to your expelling traitors and Jew Peddlers, which I suppose, was the object of your order; but as it is in terms proscribed an entire religious class, some of whom are fighting in our ranks, the President deemed it necessary to revoke it."[28]

12

Christmas in the White House:
Growing Bonds of Trust

❄❄❄

The winter of 1862 was especially cold and unyielding in a city without blankets or fuel, with the wounded crowding the hospitals and prisoners crammed into the Libby Prison. The weather quieted the battlefields and gave the troops much needed respite from constant marching and fighting, but the cold was so undeserved, the snow so cruel, that it seemed God was punishing the Southern warriors as He had Job: Starvation, fire, and death were not sufficient. Let them feel ice.

As the war raged on, the South chafed under the ever-increasing demand for more soldiers to march into the maw of battle. The calls on the civilian population to support the Confederate war machine became increasingly overbearing and impossible to meet.

In a strange way, the Yankees were holding the South together. The pressure of active invasion was the only thing that was keeping the fabric of political life from unraveling. But the Davis government in Richmond called for still more sacrifice, still more supplies, still younger and older men.

Impressment, the hated law by which arrogant Confederate officials seized crops, wagons, horses, and mules, left not enough to feed the families and slaves who had worked the land to produce the food seized. Without the implements and animals to farm, civilians were left helpless for the next season. Worse, the government agents impressed supplies fiercely around camps, railroads, and in cities but left more remote areas alone. So farmers refused to bring their produce to markets where it would be seized. Thus Richmond and other cities were deprived of food even when it was available.

Conscription—administered in Richmond by what most people sarcastically called the "Bureau of Exemptions"—undermined morale in the army, because it turned "a rich man's war into a poor man's fight." Exempted from the draft were railroad men and industrial workers, telegraph operators and state officeholders, professors and mail carriers, schoolteachers with twenty pupils, Quakers, apothecaries, and one editor from each paper. The exemption of overseers with twenty slaves—the so-called "twenty nigger law"—caused a storm of protest, because young planters used it for themselves; no one dared abolish it, however, because the specter of hundreds of thousands of uncontrolled slaves was too frightening.

The rich could either buy an officer's commission or pay a farm boy to serve as a substitute. The price of substitutes had reached $6,000. One distinguished son of the South argued that since his substitute had been killed, he himself was dead as far as the draft was concerned.

The demands from Richmond brought violent reaction from the states, many of whose leaders thought they had seceded to begin with to escape the despotism of a central government. Vice President Alexander H. Stephens, "a little, slim, pale-faced consumptive man," almost dwarflike in appearance, had returned to his native Georgia to tell the Georgia legislature that conscription was unconstitutional. Governors Joseph Brown in Georgia and Zebulon B. Vance in North Carolina threatened to use state troops, if necessary, to prevent impressment on their farms and conscription of the state militia. Their argument was grounded so deeply in constitutional principle that Joseph Browne could assert states rights even as the war moved to Georgia soil, knowing that if other states agreed, Georgia would have to fight alone. It was no wonder that Jefferson Davis could remark that if the South succumbed to the North, they could write on its tombstone "Died of a Theory."

To reassure the armies of the West that the government in Richmond was not concerned solely with the defense of Virginia, the President embarked on a 2,500-mile trip on December 11, 1862, down to Mississippi, looping up to Montgomery, Atlanta, and the Carolinas, speaking to crowds on each of the twenty-five days he was gone. During his triumphant return to Mississippi, where he said, "This was the land of my affections, here were situated the little of worldly goods I possessed." But Benjamin had been interested in another passage, which he imagined being read in Britain and in France:

> In the course of this war our eyes have often been turned abroad. We have expected sometimes recognition, and sometimes inter-vention, at the hands of foreign nations; and we had a right to expect it. Never before in the history of the world have people so long a time maintained their ground, and shown themselves capable of maintaining their national existence, without securing the recognition of commercial nations. I know not why this has been so, but this I say: "Put not your trust in princes" and rest not your hopes on foreign nations. Their war is ours; we must fight it ourselves. And I feel some pride in knowing that, so far, we have done it without the good will of anybody.[1]

At the White House on Christmas morning in 1862, the Davis children gathered around the tree, sparsely decorated (with candy at $8 a pound), playing with the wooden soldiers and other toys that Varina and the absent President had given them. Like other families, Varina, the older children, and the slaves were all involved in repairing old toys for an orphanage, and one slave had even built a dollhouse replica of the White House for a little girl who would be selected for the prize. Cabinet wives had contributed little Confed-erate uniforms made from the torn clothes of the wounded and the dead.

For almost a month, Benjamin and Varina saw each other at the end of every day, two people alone in the capital. She would give him news of the President's trip, and he would keep her up to date on the war.

The war news from Mississippi was depressing. Brierfield itself was invaded and sacked. Old Joseph Davis had reported to his brother that after the overseers had fled, the slaves had begun breaking down doors and robbing the house, carting off all of the family's finest possessions. He also reported that the slaves would not remain to cultivate the new cotton crop, and Confederate troops had burned all the bales currently in storage to prevent them from falling into the hands of the enemy.

Otherwise, the President's journey continued to go well. In Chatta-nooga crowds serenaded him at the hotel, and he presented a promotion to Brigadier John Morgan, the hard-riding son of a saddle-spur who had ridden out with two thousand men, taken on four times that number near Nashville, and had come away with 1,700 prisoners and a wagon train, then had ridden hard for Murfreesboro to fight somebody else.

On December 26, 1862, Davis told the Mississippi legislature that he looked on the Mississippi soldiers with a pride and emotion such as no other sight inspired. There was weeping in the hall as he continued: "You have been involved in a war waged for the gratification of the lust of power and aggrandizement, for your conquest and subjugation, with a malignant ferocity and a contempt of the usages of civilization entirely unequaled in history." The President was getting wound up. He told them what he had heard—that the enemy said they had handled the other states with gloves, but Mississippi was to be handled without gloves; that the Yankees were a ruthless foe, and to Mississippi they had devoted the direct vengeance of all. "But vengeance is the Lord's," he said, "and beneath His banner you will meet and hurl back these worse than vandal hordes."[2] The response was electric. He thought the legislators were going to storm out of the State Capitol and whip the whole Union army.

General Johnston's wound from Seven Pines had healed completely, and Davis persuaded him to stay on in Mississippi to confront Grant and Sherman. Johnston still despised the assignment and thought Davis had banished him to the boondocks. Davis thought Johnston craved Virginia because there was more glory to be had there, and he liked to see his name in print. The South was undermanned in Mississippi and split badly, with one army up in Tennessee and the other in Mississippi. Johnston said that he would rather have fifty men of his own than a split command. But the Confederates drove back Sherman from Vicksburg, thanks to Nathan Bedford Forrest, another heroic cavalryman, who cut Sherman's supply lines and stopped the Yankee advance. Davis's brother Joseph had moved with as many of his belongings as he could take to a friend's plantation near Jackson, where the President had spent several several days visiting him.

"Beast" Butler's troops stripped the Brierfield plantation bare of anything left, but the house was still standing. A big sign on it said "The House that Jeff Built." As long as they did not burn it down, Varina felt she could spruce it up again after the war. But Joseph's fortune had disappeared. It was difficult to get a cotton crop in with shells going off all around and his slaves gone. Still, he told

Davis, he had plans in the spring for another planting. The President had some cause to share his brother's optimism.

There was a new song in Washington that went: "Abraham Lincoln, what yer 'bout, stop this war. It's all played out." Such things raised spirits in Mississippi. The women were wearing homespun as a badge of honor, and President Davis thought they looked fine in it.

The formal garden behind the Richmond White House invited strolling on mild days. Its winding paths were designed to make flowering elliptical designs of double hearts and half-moons filled with flowers in spring, but now they wore the gray of winter to match the somber news of the Yankee sacking of Brierfield. Varina must have worried about the impact of such a personal loss on the President—the double pain of the fall of Mississippi and the destruction of his home.

But it was Christmas, a time for celebration and a moment's respite from bad news. Varina had baked a mince pie as a surprise, using substitute ingredients. After a noon luncheon, she took her family by carriage to St. Paul's and they were met by the director of the orphanage, who ushered them downstairs to the room where the children were gathered and waiting.

The orphan children cried for joy over their Christmas gifts: eyeless dolls, three-legged horses, tops with the upper pegs broken off, and stuffed monkeys with the squeak gone silent. Richmond ladies had painted fresh faces on rag dolls gone lifeless without their cotton stuffing, which was needed for the hospitals. Varina presented the model White House with the doll furnishings to an "honor girl," who was too small to handle it. As the other children crowded around to see it, the little girl dropped it, and it shattered into pieces.[3]

Benjamin and Varina had been tossed together constantly and shared secrets that they both considered necessary for their respective roles in the President's life. Benjamin needed to know the day-to-day state of the President's health in order to respond to him in his office, and she needed to know in timely detail the pressures of his office in order to deal with him at home. Together and by turns, they could help him over the most difficult days.

They had a special relationship. The First Lady could not talk about her husband to anyone but Benjamin. He was a safe and intimate sounding board, a man of absolute discretion, and, of course, an appointee without ambition for higher office who owed everything to her husband. Benjamin was an intelligent and informed listener as well as her instructor; he provided her with a way to feel competent, insightful, and powerful.

Varina attributed to him almost mystical powers: "No shade of emotion in another escaped Mr. Benjamin's penetration—he seemed to have a kind of electric sympathy with every mind with which he came into contact, and very often surprised his friends by alluding to something they had not expressed or desired him to interpret."[4]

When she was a girl, Judge Winchester nurtured in her a sense of power and a feeling for politics. Davis may have resembled the great judge physically, but Judah P. Benjamin was more like him intellectually. One cannot imagine a Jefferson Davis listening to her as seriously as Benjamin did. Conversations with Benjamin allowed her to participate in public affairs, gave her the sense that she understood politics and could be a factor if only given a chance. At the end of her life, she wrote to Lawley that Benjamin's "greatness . . . was hard to measure; his humanities were so many and sincere—I loved him dearly."[5]

For Benjamin, Varina was the ideal woman for his purpose. She offered him a bridge to the powerful as Natalie had in New Orleans, only this time it was not to the Creole establishment but to the President of the Confederacy. Varina, like Natalie, was unavailable to him, but in fundamental ways she was the very antithesis of Natalie. Natalie was beautiful, frivolous, and faithless; Varina was plain-featured, serious, and loyal. Natalie had abandoned him; Varina was a devoted wife who would do anything for her sometimes indifferent and preoccupied husband. Varina offered Benjamin the model of a partner he had never had. Seeing her often and knowing her well introduced him vicariously to a loyal and loving woman who would tolerate a man totally absorbed in his work and his mission in life. She was undemanding and ever available. She would remain his friend, and he would be her intimate adviser for the rest of his life.

When the President returned in January 1863 to Richmond, Varina was appalled at his state of exhaustion. As they went inside the White House, they heard drums and bugles outside, bringing a crowd of several hundred to the mansion to welcome him home. He could not disappoint them. Surely he could not deprive them of at least a sampling from the speech he had been giving around the South. Though near collapse, he seemed to warm to his denunciation of the North as the crowd warmed to him and grew more demonstrative.

You fight against the off-scourging of the earth. (*Applause*) Every crime which could characterize the course of demons has marked the course of the invader . . . from the burning of defenseless towns to the stealing of forks and spoons. (*Hisses*) For what are they waging war? They say to preserve the Union. Can they preserve the Union by destroying the South? (*No, no*) Do they hope to reconstruct the Union by striking at everything which is dear to man?—by showing themselves so utterly disgraced that if the question was proposed to you whether you would rather combine with hyenas or Yankees, I trust every Virginian would say: "Give me the hyenas!" (*Shouting, whistling, laughter and cheering*)[6]

Varina invited Benjamin to breakfast the next morning, knowing he would be as eager as she to hear about the trip. Though the fatigue was still etched in his face, the President was in considerably better spirits than when he had left in December. The people of Mississippi had faith in Lee and Jackson, he said, and hoped they would go North again in the spring and end it all.

Benjamin's personal life did not revolve solely around Varina, official functions, and his work. He relaxed around the card tables of Richmond with friends and strangers and seemed to enjoy high-stakes encounters.

Benjamin was an inveterate gambler who had become addicted to cards at an early age. His skills had been sharpened by the city where he had earned his reputation and wealth. New Orleans was a sinner's town. Benjamin often had met the elite of the city and its wealthy visitors in its gambling halls, where he had been known as a man who rarely lost. In Richmond, he frequented the various dens of iniquity, which attracted a mixture of Confederate officials and lowlife, using the poker and faro tables to relax from the rigors of the day.

The source of the stories about Benjamin's gambling was William Howard Russell, a correspondent of the London *Times*, who toured the country at the beginning of the war and wrote a series of articles that became a book entitled *My Diary North and South*. In the book he wrote that Benjamin was "the most brilliant perhaps of the whole of the famous Southern orators . . . but his love of the card-table rendered him a prey to older and cooler hands, who waited till the sponge was full at the end of the session, and then squeezed it to the last drop."[7]

Benjamin was so concerned that such a report would appear in the most important English newspapers that he made reference to it in a humorous way to Lieutenant Colonel Arthur Fremantle, an English visitor who came to interview him in 1863:

> Mr. Benjamin complained of Mr. Russell of the *Times* for holding him up to fame as a "gambler"—a story which he understood Mr. Russell had learnt from Mr. Charles Sumner at Washington. But even supposing that this was really the case, Mr. Benjamin was of [the] opinion that such a revelation of his private life was in extremely bad taste, after Mr. Russell had partaken of his [Mr. Benjamin's] hospitality at Montgomery.[8]

Benjamin was offended that Russell had taken the word of Sumner, the fierce Abolitionist Senator from Massachusetts, and had portrayed him as unskilled at cards when his reputation was just the opposite. Because it was such a small point, and awkward, he chose to handle it with a bit of cultivated humor.

The Richmond *Examiner* once reported that at a gambling saloon the previous night, "it is said that a cabinet minister, who was in one of the inner chambers reserved for distinguished guests, effected his escape by jumping from a window."[9] The "minister" referred to clearly was Benjamin.

A Confederate Treasury official noted Benjamin's visits to a low place called Johnny Worsham's on the wrong side of town. Henry Foote, too, complained that "this man Benjamin was notoriously occupied every night during his stay in Richmond in betting at faro, and on several occasions while thus disreputably engaged is reported to have owed his escape from the vigilance of the officers of the law alone to his dexterity in leaping from the back-doors of the gambling halls."[10]

His reputation was part of the undercurrent of Richmond gossip. Mary Chesnut recorded a brief bit of conversation involving Jules St. Martin:

> "People call names so differently. Now, Mrs. Grundy says 'Saint Martin.' So do I. I like straight English. The little sinner calls himself *Samartan.*
> "Why sinner?"
> "Ain't he Benjamin's brother-in-law?" &c&c&c[11]

There are many accounts of the dark side of Richmond during the war. The streets were crowded with drunken soldiers, prostitutes, barkers, black marketeers, and hustlers of all kinds as night enveloped Richmond. If Benjamin walked along Martin Street away from the west side, he would have been walking away from the "best people," who would never, this late at night, be caught in the streets of Richmond without their carriages. If so, the scene must have reminded him so much of the New Orleans French Quarter that he felt at home. It might have afforded him some relief to escape for a while from the staid first families of Virginia, who used their tenuous cousinships with the Founding Fathers to lord it over the Confederate officials, whom they treated as coarse outlanders. The British papers described Richmond as a new city "modeled after Sodom and New York."

Johnny Worsham's gambling den was not the best emporium in the city. It attracted a mixed clientele of lowlife and gentlemen who enjoyed a bawdy and salacious atmosphere for their games. It has been described in a number of histories of Richmond as a huge, barnlike place with a stage for dancing girls. By the door, like twin statues, stood two giant black bouncers in bowler hats and identical suits. The gamblers could take a drinking break at a bar two steps up all around the walls, under a balcony of upstairs rooms for more private pursuits. The house was filled with cigar smoke and piano music, absorbed customers and powdered women, who strolled about to lubricate the action at the tables. Gamblers eager to try their luck had their pick: roulette, dice, or cards.

Card games demanded total concentration. They lifted the player above the ordinary experience of the day and washed away his troubles in a sea of cards, numbers, and suits, which his mind had to reorganize quickly into a coherent strategy. Pure chance, like roulette or dice, never appealed to Benjamin: Not enough of his brain was involved. He liked poker and faro, the game in which players bet on a special board as the dealer draws two cards from his box. It is a game that rewards the ability to recall and chart the frequency of numbers and colors. Poker, on the other hand, was a game where he could hone his skill at bluffing and assert his will over his opponent, rewarding a controlled temperament.

In poker, as well as faro, he was the selector; he chose the course, and determined the risks. The outcome was instant, the results immediate. By contrast, in wartime his brilliance would always be overshadowed by the Beauregards, the Lees, the Jacksons. The most careful planning in the President's office could be totally wrecked by a blunder in the field, for which he would always be blamed. But if there was victory, the soldiers and the generals received the accolade, not the mere politician back in Richmond.

Benjamin's mind could work through the cautions that were necessary to deal with the unfamiliar chemistry of a new game. If his foe was a political enemy, it required a special kind of control. A successful poker player never let his emotion prevail over his cards; he used the antagonism of his opponents as a weakness to be exploited. Poker was a game of cunning. Benjamin could spread confusion among his opponents while keeping a clear head. Poker was also a game of probability and intelligent risk; the object to any player, especially one as brilliant as Benjamin, was to reduce that risk by absolute concentration. It was a skilled ambivalence, reducing risks and taking risks simultaneously.

There is some evidence at just how good Benjamin was at poker. In 1870 Benjamin met General Robert Schenk, the American Minister to England, at a party where poker was being played. Schenk had also once been an Ohio legislator and was an expert on draw poker, having even written a book on it:

"I recollect very well, General Schenk," said Benjamin, "when we last met over a game of poker."

"So do I," Schenk replied, "for I remember well what you won from me."

"Well, sir, if I did, you have had your revenge, for since then I have lost and you have won a bigger stake than that."[12]

To win consistently at poker was to dismiss enmity and fear of humiliation, to know when to withdraw, not to reveal weakness, to wait to fight another day when the odds were better—to be consistently inconsistent. If a player is looking for the big kill, the objective is to increase the range of options at the crucial moment, to reduce the need for the stunning hand at the showdown and win with ordinary cards.

Players of poker relish that one hand when the stars are humming in the heavens and both players think they have the strength for the test. Sometimes even the most skilled players would withdraw, but eventually one had to gamble, to choose the precise moment for engagement or else lose the edge. A player felt a confrontation approaching when his opponent dramatically upped the stakes. Diaries of the time report that the crowd in Johnny's would sense blood and begin to gather around the table. Other players folded adroitly and left the two adversaries to face each other in the bearpit. Then no matter what the cards, the skilled player would play out his hand until the end. If bluff was the name of the game, then bluff he would.

We can imagine Benjamin's disappointment when Johnny Worsham interrupted the game with news they were about to be raided. He must have been led to a street-level window, smiling calmly at the matter-of-factness of the situation, and foiling once again the sporadic forays of the temperance ladies and the hellfire preachers.

Benjamin was willing to take risks in life as well as in games, and as in cards, he sometimes lost, and lost heavily. His list of disappointments was considerable: Yale, marriage, being a son to his father, being a father to his daughter, his tenure as Confederate Secretary of War, and his growing frustrations as Secretary of State. He had been successful as a lawyer and as a U.S. Senator, and, presumably, as a friend and a provider. He excelled at being a survivor, triumphing over defeats, accepting his failures and facing forward.

One could almost discern something in Benjamin that compelled him to take progressively greater chances, seemingly to court failure. For example, to know nothing of the military yet accept an appointment as Secretary of War had all the elements of a gamble destined for failure. So also did pushing ahead with the Erlanger loan, unwisely confident in a foreign policy linked to cotton when the South was trapped in a blockade. But when a gambler loses he has to gamble again, and if his losses are too great he must increase the stakes in order to recover. Benjamin was not a man who liked to stop and think about his life. From boyhood onward, he was always pushing forward. As the fortunes of the Confederacy began to fade, the question about the gambler who was Secretary of State was whether this lifelong pattern would catch up to him, and the risks become so dangerous that the laws of probability finally would get the upper hand and consume him.

Benjamin's success as a gambler in Richmond was not matched by success in his financial gamble overseas. The first issue of the Erlanger bonds was oversubscribed as the price went to 95½, and it seemed as though Benjamin's plan would work. But Seward's agents went to work in Paris and London, quoting from a statement by Jefferson Davis (issued just before the war) that the State of Mississippi should repudiate its debts to the Federal government. They passed the rumor strongly, in financial back rooms that thrived on whisper: that if the South won the war, Davis would again repudiate the bonds. They said the entire effort was a Confederate stunt to milk money from Europe. When the price of the bonds fell precipitously, Benjamin, in order to counter the rumors and reassure the French bankers of the South's good intentions, ordered Mason to reinvest the first $6 million in the bonds to shore up the market for them. For a moment that worked. But in the next few weeks, it did not. The bonds dropped to 36, and all the investors were hurt except Erlanger. He had insisted on a 5 percent commission on every bond sold.[13]

Though a financial disaster in the end, along the way the bonds did stir Napoleon to greater interest in intervening in the war. But at every turn, the answer was the same: Prime Minister Palmerston in London was taking seriously Seward's threats to cut off wheat shipments and his hints that British intervention might cause the United States to extend Seward's own "Manifest Destiny" policy to the seizure of Canada. Palmerston quoted a nursery rhyme to a friend: "Those who in quarrels interpose, are apt to get a bloody nose."[14]

Benjamin was furious at the shilly-shallying in Paris, the duplicity in London, and the manipulation by Seward. "This war may not last beyond the present year," he wrote to Slidell in anger, "perhaps not beyond the sickly season of a Southern summer, and yet he suffers himself to be restrained from decisive action by alternative menaces and assurances uttered with notorious mendacity by leaders of the frantic mob which now controls the government of the United States."[15]

On January 1, 1863, Lincoln signed his Emancipation Proclamation, ninety-nine stormy days after he announced it. It was a curious compromise document, in that it exempted all the divided states (Maryland, Kentucky, Missouri, and Tennessee) as well as the areas of Louisiana and Virginia under Federal control. Many supporters in the U.S. Congress thought it a tragic error that would have no effect whatsoever except "to unite and exasperate the South"—which it certainly did—without freeing a single slave within Lincoln's domain. But to the 3.5 million black souls involved, the Abolitionists in the North, and the Union soldiers in the field, the proclamation did say, loud and clear, that the future of slavery would be decided on the battlefield, and that wherever the Union army marched, freedom for the slaves would march with it.

Though individual battles had gone badly for the North for months, the brutal arithmetic of war was still with the North: 918,000 men under arms, as against 446,000 for the South. Put simply, the North could afford to lose men, the South could not. Too, the country above the Mason–Dixon line was growing stronger. Howe's invention, the sewing machine, had created 180 new factories in just two years in Philadelphia—and already the name "the garment industry" had achieved coinage. The new McKay boot-stitching machine could finish a hundred pairs of boots in the time it used to take to sew one pair. A drought in Europe caused England in 1862 to import from the United States 5 million quarters of wheat and flour, as compared to 100,000 three years before. Seward again had a knife at England's throat—even as Lee was scavenging the battlefield for boots, blankets, and arms.

13

Fateful Defeats:
Stonewall's Funeral and the Battle of Gettysburg

❊❊❊

They called it "Degradation Proclamation." When it was signed, fear gripped the streets of Richmond. Street robberies were common, and Richmond blamed the lack of safety on the rising number of slaves in the city and the inevitable attraction to a military center of every swindler, pickpocket, and thief within a hundred miles. Davis accused Lincoln of issuing an "invitation to a slave uprising."[1] The Confederate government responded by turning over Richmond's streets, jails, and civil liberties to a gang of secret police wielding billy clubs and chains, known to the citizenry as "Winder's detectives." General John H. Winder was a stout old man who had demanded a commission based on an old association with Jefferson Davis as an instructor in tactics at West Point. Once appointed, he moved with brutal dispatch, arresting and jailing without trial anyone on the street who got in the way of his men. His prison was called "Castle Thunder." Rumors of whippings and beatings there circulated through Richmond. Law and order came to the streets in the form of a hip-pocket justice more corrupt than the criminals it was called upon to stop. Richmond saw the hardened enforcers as "plug-uglies," common lowlife from big cities like Baltimore and Philadelphia, illiterate petty thieves set loose on the streets of Richmond to do whatever they wished.

When the War Department decided to require passports to root out the Yankee spy system, Winder's men were soon selling them for a hundred dollars apiece. Many a soldier on furlough spent the night in jail after one of Winder's roundups, then had to pay his way out to report back to his unit. Once Jeb Stuart and his men, thirty strong and without proper credentials, challenged Winder's men to lay a hand on them. Like all bullies, the "plug-uglies" stepped aside.

To try and win back public favor, Winder decreed a ceiling on food prices. Farmers stopped bringing their food into town, and speculators, some of them in league with Winder's detectives, bought what there was to hold for the future. The city experienced shortages in the midst of overflowing warehouses of food. Finally, when Winder removed the controls, prices of staples doubled overnight. Everyone criticized the Jews for creating such havoc and profiteering on food. The Richmond *Examiner* joined in, of course, and the editor's finger of blame seldom strayed from the direction of Judah P. Benjamin.

When the President called for another "day of fasting," people in Richmond derisively renamed his order "a day of fasting in a famine."

Richmond was growing tense from the scarcity of food and seemed to need only a single spark to start a riot. Benjamin could not have missed an incident outside his window: A giant of a woman with a pistol in one hand and a Bowie knife in the other, wearing an incongruous picture hat with a long white feather, harangued a crowd of about three hundred women and children in the area where the wives usually gathered to buy bread. Her name was Minerva Meredith and she worked as a butcher's assistant. With Minerva taking dramatic giant strides at the head, the mob marched off shouting, "Bread! Bread!" making for the shops on Main Street. They were halted by the mayor, who read the Richmond Riot Act to them, but they were not to be denied. They hooted and surged past him, breaking windows and stealing meal, flour, shoes, clothing—anything. The armed militia gathered to charge when suddenly, as if sent by some divinity, a tall, gaunt man appeared on horseback. His presence seemed to halt the women from their mischief. Jefferson Davis addressed the crowd: "You say you are hungry and have no money. Here"—and he emptied his pockets of change and bills—"is all I have. It is not much but take it." And with that, Davis tossed the money into the crowd. He pulled out his watch and looked at the militia:

"We do not wish to hurt anyone but this lawlessness must stop.

I will give you five minutes to disperse. Otherwise you will be fired on." He gazed directly at the women with forceful intensity.

It was over. In five minutes, the streets were empty of people. The militia returned to its station.[2]

"When the Southwestern army fights a battle," the Richmond *Examiner* grumbled, "we first hear that it has gained one of the most stupendous victories on record; that regiments from Mississippi, Texas, Louisiana, Arkansas . . . have exhibited an irresistible and superhuman valour unknown in history this side of Sparta and Rome. As for the Generals, they usually get all their clothes shot off, and replace them with a suit of glory. The enemy is, of course, simply annihilated. Next day more dispatches come, still very good, but not quite so good as the first. The telegrams of the third day invariably such as make a mist, a muddle, and a fog of the whole affair."[3]

If the Union could lose all those men at Fredericksburg and still be strong and fighting hard; if still another Southern victory had turned out not to be "a turning point in the war," what would it take to subdue the Yankees?

In the West, Grant had made seven attempts at either taking or bypassing Vicksburg. In the East, Lincoln had placed "Fighting Joe" Hooker in command of the army. Hooker moved out in mid-April toward Chancellorsville with 133,450 men supported by seven batteries with 412 guns.

Facing him on the other side of the Rappahannock River was Lee's army, less than sixty thousand strong, its general, newly nicknamed "Audacity," pondering his next strike.

Benjamin had another critic inside the government, Robert G. H. Kean, the head of the Bureau of the War, who kept a diary throughout the war. His entry for May 3, 1863, says: "Mr. Benjamin circulated a story last night of a telegram from Colonel R. H. Chilton [Lee's chief of staff] to Jackson that the Yankees were fighting badly, that we had driven them five miles and held the fords by which they had crossed the [Rappanannock] river. . . . Mr. Benjamin is the most unreliable of news reporters, believes anything, and is as sanguine as he is credulous."[4] On August 13, 1863, he added that Benjamin "is a poor adviser. He is a smart lawyer, a ready, useful, drawer-up of papers but perhaps the least wise of our public men."[5] A year later, he summed up: "The fickle manner in which the President has dealt with the *honorable* men he has had in the War office—

Walker, Randolph, and Seddon—and the acceptableness of Benjamin to him there and elsewhere, is the strongest fact against his sense and capacity as a President I know."[6]

Jefferson Davis lay ill with what he called diurnal fever, almost a daily occurrence that left him burning and exhausted by the end of the day. This was followed by a difficult case of bronchitis, which left him unable to speak or to meet Varina, who would be returning home soon from her father's funeral in Natchez.

When the train arrived, Varina was still dressed in black. She seemed inordinately subdued and unrecovered from the shock. She was surprised not to find the President at the station but relieved in one way, because she never liked burdening him with her troubles. Her mother had survived the funeral well, the way old people do, accepting bereavement because it was no stranger in the war. The funeral had been difficult, but Varina told Benjamin she now felt a unity with the thousands of women mourning losses from the war.

For each battle, whether victory or defeat, the numbers of dead and wounded mattered more than the outcome. Nowhere was that more true than at Chancellorsville, where Jackson and Lee crouched together over a fire studying the maps of the terrain.

With two hours of daylight left, Old Blue Light looked down on the enemy positions and felt his battle blood rising. The rear line of Hooker's army lay resting with thousands of men playing cards, smoking, butchering rumps of beef, and clustered in front of fires and tents, relaxed and unsuspecting. Jackson ordered sabers drawn, then Jackson's horse, Fancy, reared at his command, and the rebel cavalry attacked hell-bent for slaughter, slashing at heads and bodies as the enemy fled in a jumble of pots and pans, long underwear, and blue coats.

Confederate foot soldiers followed the cavalry, bayonets flashing, and charged into the tents. They merged into the crowds of fleeing Union soldiers. Then some resistance was offered, causing a slight hesitation by the Confederates in front. To the Confederate soldiers in the rear, their comrades ahead loomed as indistinct silhouettes. "Cease fire! Cease fire! You're firing at our own men." A Confederate bullet slammed into Stonewall's arm, another through his raised palm. His horse bolted and turned its rider into a new volley, whirling out of control in fear until an officer could catch the bridle. Another officer helped Jackson down to lie on the grass under a tree. "My own men," he muttered, and closed his eyes in pain.

Word of Stonewall's wounds spread over the countryside as the horse-drawn ambulance passed among the lines of the people of Virginia, offering from their empty kitchens such as they had: fresh buttermilk, hot biscuits, and fried chicken. The general, his wife at his side, lay for several days, babbling battle orders in his delirium. "Order A. P. Hill to prepare for action! Pass the infantry to the front. . . . Tell Major Hawks—" and then he put the two years of battle weariness behind him as he uttered his last words, "Let us cross the river and rest under the shade of the trees."[7]

While the battle raged on at Chancellorsville, Richmond was in an uproar over the imagined hoofbeats of Northern General George Stoneman's raid. Word spread that the Union cavalry had broken through to the Confederate rear to tear up railroad tracks between Richmond and the front. The city was edgy over its vulnerability, stripped of all soldiers to build up Lee's army, and rumor escalated quickly into panic.

"Everyone in the building, out into the streets!" someone screamed to the office workers in the Customs House where the state treasury and the executive offices were housed. "Man the barricades!" people shouted as they saw clerks running for their weapons toward the arsenal. The aged, the city employees, and the women who could shoot all gathered at Capitol Square to defend the city against the marauders.

Jefferson Davis, who had lain speechless for several weeks before Chancellorsville, suddenly awoke to find the upstairs of the White House almost deserted because Varina had been spending the evening at the Chesnuts. Sentries guarded the door, but inside, the servants were running around frightened. Some were on their knees praying. Soldiers yelled at them that the Yankees were not that close, when suddenly a slim, drawn figure appeared at the top of the stairs. Jefferson Davis was propping himself up against the banisters, with his head hanging and arms dangling with loaded pearl-handled pistols in each hand.

Rumors aside, Stoneman was still 40 miles from Richmond, bogged down in mud and blocked by a swollen river. By morning, troops arrived from Petersburg to thwart his mission, which ended up accomplishing the burning of two barges on the James River and the destruction of a couple of hen houses.

In the meantime Jeb Stuart had assumed command of Jackson's brigades. With the call "Charge for Jackson," he continued to rout the Yankees in his dying leader's name. Chancellorsville was Jackson's last battle, and a masterpiece it was—some say the greatest that Lee and his general had ever fought. Outgunned and outmanned two-to-one, they managed to take more than 4,000 prisoners and inflict losses of 17,287 on the Union.

Jackson's death left Benjamin with some mixed emotions. Stonewall, after all, had been one of the generals demanding his resignation during his difficult tenure as Secretary of War. An English visitor recalled:

> Talking of the just admiration which the English newspapers accorded to "Stonewall" Jackson, [Benjamin] expressed, however, his astonishment that they should have praised so highly his strategic skill in outmaneuvering Pope at Manassas, and Hooker at Chancellorsville, totally ignoring that in both cases the movements were planned and ordered by General Lee, for whom (Mr. Benjamin said) Jackson had the most "childlike reverence."[8]

Stonewall Jackson's body arrived in Richmond at five o'clock in the afternoon of May 11, 1863. The city was transformed into a vast house of mourning. Every flag stood at half-mast, candles burned in the windows of the houses, every business and home was draped with black crepe. As the caisson bearing the body passed through the streets, thousands lined the way, heads bare and weeping. Behind the cortege followed an almost spontaneous procession of the wounded and invalid veterans of the Foot Cavalry, on crutches and limping, marching with rifles reversed and downcast faces, marching one last time for their fallen commander.[9]

At high noon the next day at St. Paul's Church, the President and the Cabinet attended a memorial service in honor of the dead hero. The sanctuary and the galleries around it were packed with official Richmond, the military contingent in full dress grays with yellow sashes and medals. Benjamin sat next to Varina in the Davis family pew, which was in the center of the sanctuary, directly beneath the eye of the great dome of the church.

The President, who had been bedridden for a month, sat on the aisle, erect but lifeless, chalk-pale and creased as a corpse. Varina was dressed in black with veil, her eyes downcast in the repose of the mourner. Before them, over the columns behind the altar, were the words, "The Lord is in his holy temple. Let all the Earth keep Silence Before Him."

"Stonewall" had been the least suitable name for him, many thought, for he was ever in motion, swooping down like an eagle on his prey. His way was to mystify, mislead, and surprise—a phantom ever mobile and adroit—but the name stuck.

The walnut pews and stone floors contrasted with the rich velvet cushions the color of blood. Below the mourners on the floor were the small knee cushions. At the closing prayer everyone, including Benjamin, slipped out of their seats and knelt as the minister waited for the congregation to quiet down so that he could begin.

Even today, in the sanctuary of St. Paul's, the receding sun darkens the stained-glass windows, casting the church into a dim kind of twilight. High above the congregation, one can observe a triangular shape with hundreds of golden spokes extending outward from the center of the dome. The letters in the center of the triangle are barely visible in the cool gray dimness of the church. Had Benjamin looked up, he would have noticed that they were Hebrew letters— the ancient unspoken name of God—JHVH. The letters grow darker and more precise in the failing light, like lettering looming in the clouds, hovering over the kneeling congregation, just as they must have done at Stonewall's funeral when all faiths gathered to mourn his passing.

The defeat at Chancellorsville so alarmed Lincoln that he ordered Grant and Sherman immediately to set out still again to assault Vicksburg, the Southern Gibraltar on its powerful bluffs over the Mississippi River. They were determined to succeed this time, and after losses of 4,000 men on the steep rocks, they vowed to do it with the most difficult but passive tactic of all, the siege. For more than forty days they would seal off the city, driving the inhabitants into caves to eat dogs and dead mules to stave off starvation.

In the East, Longstreet, Lee's best general with Stonewall gone, had been doing some calculations and was disturbed by what he discovered. The South could not afford any more spectacular "victories" like Chancellorsville: Four more battles in which the South was outnumbered two-to-one and inflicted casualties at a rate of three Union soldiers to four Confederates, and Lee's army would be destroyed.

The Cabinet debated whether to send Lee south to the defense of Mississippi and to try to lift the siege of Vicksburg. But Lee approached them with an even bolder plan: move north again, far north into Pennsylvania, toward Gettysburg, and await the enemy's response. By so doing, he would force Lincoln to pull Grant away from Vicksburg, free the Virginia countryside for harvest, defend Richmond by threatening Washington, encourage the peace parties of the North, win a battle, and thereby attract European recognition. Davis's heart ached for his home state of Mississippi, but Lee would not hear of moving his troops so far from his own Virginia. At least, not so far south.

Lee had won four battles, each against a different commander; now he would get a fifth. In early June, Lincoln replaced "Fighting Joe" Hooker with General George Meade.

Meade was called a "snapping turtle," because he was small and testy; he was devoid of flair, and his balding head and frazzled beard made him look more like a professor than a soldier.[10] But he was decisive. The very next morning he called early reveille, and the 94,000 men of the Army of the Potomac moved north themselves, paralleling Lee in case he should turn toward Baltimore, all the while heading for the rendezvous at Gettysburg.

Neither army had planned to meet at the little college town, but the Southerners had been drawn there by reports of a large storehouse of shoes in the town. "I'm going to get those shoes," one of Lee's generals said, and so two armies almost blundered into each other. But once the battle began, it was fought with fury. For three days they fought, the South battling to take Cemetery Ridge and Devil's Den. Without Stonewall, Lee did not have his nimble left hook to draw enemy strength away from the main clash. On the climactic third day, over the objection of Longstreet, Lee ordered Major General Pickett to lead 15,000 men in a four-fifths-mile charge at Meade's center across open, flat ground. "Pickett's Charge" became synonymous with bravery, but to the men in the long gray line mowed down at Cemetery Ridge like waving wheat before the scythe, the charge meant certain death.

The Union losses at Gettysburg were 23,000, as against the Confederacy's 20,000, but that was almost one-third of Lee's army. Longstreet had been right: With continued costly battles, whether victory or defeat, Lee's army could not survive the grim arithmetic of the war. The South's defeat at Gettysburg devastated the Army of Northern Virginia and left its leadership ranks grievously shattered. This time the pundits did not have to exaggerate: Gettysburg was indeed "the turning point battle of the war."

For the leaders back in Richmond, too, July 4, 1863, was the most decisive day of the war. The depressing news of Lee's defeat at Gettysburg was joined by the simultaneous fall of Vicksburg on the Mississippi.

For weeks, Benjamin had watched the President sinking into what Varina called "the acutest anxiety." General Joe Johnston, always preferring to give up territory rather than men, was yielding Davis's home state to the invaders, and the President had even considered leaving his desk to go out into the field and fight. "If I could take one wing and Lee the other," he confided to Varina, "I think we could between us wrest a victory from those people."[11] It was not just a fanciful exaggeration; he meant it.

Even at so dark a moment, Benjamin was the South's best propagandist.

Lieutenant Colonel Fremantle of the British Coldstream Guards spent three months in the Confederacy in the early half of 1863, traveling with the armies, talking with leaders, and noting his observations and experiences in a diary. He reported that Judah P. Benjamin had told him, the South's peace terms: "On a blank sheet of paper [he wrote] the words 'self government.' Let the Yankees accord that, and they might fill up the paper in any manner they chose. All we are struggling for is to be let alone."[12]

He also reported on the state of mind of Jefferson Davis: "Walking home with Mr. Benjamin, he told me that Mr. Davis' military instincts still predominate and that his eager wish was to have joined the army instead of being elected President."[13]

The generals were arguing among themselves in recrimination, and newspapers were battering away at the ineptitude of the Richmond government. Still, almost as a ritual, Davis rode out daily among the people of Richmond, stiff and regal. Varina had pleaded with him not to do it, but he wanted to show the people that he was not afraid.

One evening, a bullet whistled past his ear. Instead of fleeing, Davis boldly turned his horse right toward the source of the shot and galloped into the shanties, where a crank was found shivering. Davis did not prosecute the man but sent him to a more useful fate: to General Lee as a soldier.

The war was now reaching into the Southern heartland of Alabama, and the need for more soldiers was becoming desperate.

Where were new recruits to come from? How could Lee's army

be replenished? One suggestion would come from Lincoln himself, who had urged General Grant to recruit and train slaves in the Mississippi area. "I am not abolitionist nor even what could be called antislavery," Grant admitted, but he had carried out the order. Could the Confederacy, which so far had used blacks militarily only for digging trenches and building fortifications, risk issuing their own Confederate Emancipation by arming slaves to fight against the North and freeing them in exchange? How would the slaves behave under fire? Would the Southern slaves treat the war as a battle for their homeland and their families, like the men who fell at Fredericksburg and Gettysburg?

Several months after Gettysburg, Benjamin received an apologetic letter from the brother-in-law of his old law partner in New Orleans, now a cotton mill owner in Alabama. The letter was apologetic because it dared to suggest arming the slaves, but Benjamin took it seriously, for he himself was beginning to ponder it and was turning over in his mind the practical problems of such a momentous step. He drafted a careful reply with a detailed analysis of the issues the government would face:

1st. Slaves are property. If taken for public service, they must be paid for. At present rates each regiment of 1000 slaves would cost $200,000 at the very least, besides their outfit, and the Government would become a vast slave holder, and must either sell the slaves after the war, which would be a most odious proceeding after they had aided in gaining our liberties, or must free them to the great detriment of the country.

2nd. If instead of buying, the Government hire them, it would stand as insurer for their return to their owners; it would be forced to pay hire for them the outfit and rations; and it would have to pay hire according to the value of their services on a fair estimate. Now negro men command readily $30 a month all through Virginia. How could we possibly afford such a price, and what would be the effect on the poorer classes of whites in the army, if informed the negroes were paid $30 a month, while the white man receives only $11.

3rd. The collection and banding together of Negro men in bodies in the immediate neighborhood of the enemy's forces, is an experiment of which the results are far from certain. The facility which would be thus afforded for their desertion in mass might prove too severe a test for their fidelity when exposed to the arts of designing emissaries of the enemy who would be sure to find means of communicating with them.

Finally, Benjamin argued, the male slave population was performing an important service already, more perhaps than the South could expect from them in uniform.

A nation cannot exist without labor in the field, in the workshop, in the railroad, the canal, the highways, and the manufactory. In coal and iron mines, in foundries and in fortifications we could employ the total male slave population that could possibly be spared from the production of supplies for subsistence. This is the appropriate field for negro labor to which they are habituated, and which appears at first sight to be altogether less liable to objection, than to imitate our enemies by using them in military organizations.[14]

Benjamin selected carefully the phrase "less liable to objection"; he knew the fire-eaters in the Congress would be driven to frenzy over the use of slaves for any other purpose than labor, and some would even be nervous at placing slaves anywhere in the vicinity of ammunition and armament. But his objections were practical, not a matter of principle. The Confederacy, he said, simply could not afford at this point to purchase or rent slaves. He mentioned freeing the slaves after the war, so he understood that there were other forms of compensation for slaves. Indeed, the subject had been before him earlier in the war.

A month after Lincoln's Emancipation, in October 1862, Benjamin heard that James Spence, a Confederate financial agent in England, was publicly opposing slavery and suggesting that emancipation would bring about a speedy British recognition of the Confederacy. Spence was no ordinary Liverpool merchant but the well-known author of *The American Union,* a popular two-volume defense of the Confederacy that had gone through four large editions in less than a year, and the man who had organized two London associations to help the South. Spence had become convinced that the popularity of his books had given him the independent moral stature to influence the South. The Richmond *Enquirer* demanded his dismissal, complaining that "here we are paying a man for abusing us as a nation of criminals steeped in moral evil! The operation of our State Department seems to be against us, not for us."[15]

Benjamin as the Confederate statesman, in Stephen Vincent Benet's words, "the dark prince . . . with the slight perpetual smile." A contemporary observer described him as a "Hebrew of Hebrews for the map of the Holy City was traced all over his . . . refined face." As the war took its toll, he was bitterly attacked. "The mob calls him 'Mr. Davis' pet Jew,' " wrote Mary Chesnut in her diary. Others used him as a scapegoat for all the South's failures. One congressman consistently referred to him as "Judas Iscariot Benjamin." Benjamin never reacted publicly to the taunts and managed to achieve a career, in the words of a British newspaper, that "is not likely to be repeated [with] all the fascinations of a brilliantly narrated romance."

Judah P. Benjamin's wife, Natalie St. Martin *(top left)*, whom he married in 1833, was the daughter of a leading Catholic and Creole family in New Orleans. Their only child, Ninette *(top right)*, was born in 1843. Benjamin built the grand house at the Bellechasse plantation in Louisiana *(bottom)* in the early 1840s and furnished it lavishly as a showcase for balls and parties for Natalie. Natalie left Benjamin and fled to Paris in 1845, taking Ninette with her. Thereafter he saw them only once a year. She preferred to call him by his French name "Philippe." Only one revealing sentence survives from her letters to him: "Oh, talk not to me of economy, it is so fatiguing." Her notorious reputation was a constant source of embarrassment to him. A diarist of the time wrote that she had "rumored delinquencies" which "affected the French legation" and once "stole away (to meet a handsome German officer . . .)." A Confederate Congressman wrote she "lives in Paris with a paramour." Although she stayed in a different country from her husband for almost forty years of their marriage, Benjamin never wholly abandoned her.

Varina Howell Davis *(top)* and Jefferson Davis *(bottom)*, circa 1849, when she was twenty-two and he was forty-one. By this time, they had been married for four years, and he had already been elected to Congress; had fought in the Mexican War and returned to Mississippi as a wounded war hero; and had been appointed to his first term in the U.S. Senate. She wrote her mother when they first met that "he is the kind of person I should expect to rescue me from a mad dog at any risk, but to insist upon stoical indifference to the fright afterward." Varina, an unusually intelligent and sensitive woman, was to play a critical role in bringing Judah P. Benjamin and Davis together, acting as Benjamin's confidante throughout the Civil War and for the rest of his life.

HON. J. P. BENJAMIN.

Senator Judah P. Benjamin of Louisiana *(top left)*, circa 1853, and Senator Jefferson Davis of Mississippi *(top right)*, circa 1858. Varina wrote of them: "Sometime, when they did not agree on a measure, hot words in glacial, polite phrases passed between them." Because of a suspected insult on the floor of the Senate, Benjamin challenged Davis to a duel. Davis quickly and publicly apologized, and the incident of honor defended and satisfied drew them together in a relationship of mutual respect. The formal portrait *(top left)* was painted in 1853, shortly after Benjamin was elected to the U.S. Senate, where he was considered one of the greatest orators in Senate history. The drawing *(bottom)* has printed on it the words "from Daguerrotype by Brady, 1856."

Jefferson Davis *(top left)* and Varina Davis *(top right)* as President and First Lady of the Confederacy. He was the rigid, West Point–trained President they called the "Sphinx of the Confederacy," and she was referred to as "Queen Varina." Varina wrote of Davis's relationship with Benjamin that "it was to me a curious spectacle, the steady approximation of a thorough friendship of the President and his War Minister . . . a gradual rapprochement, all the more solid for that reason." The White House of the Confederacy in Richmond *(bottom)*, where the President and the First Lady of the Confederacy lived and entertained, was called the "Gray House" by wags. Benjamin visited there often for intimate meals, meetings, and receptions. It looked somewhat like a Northern townhouse, in contrast to the Union White House, which, if anything, reminded visitors of a Southern mansion.

JEFFERSON DAVIS AND HIS CABINET.

With General Lee in the Council Chamber at Richmond.

Jefferson Davis and the first Confederate Cabinet *(top)* in council with General Lee. This idealized lithograph, copyright 1866, was produced to sell to the public. Benjamin, second from left, is sitting closest to Jefferson Davis. "There was only one man there who had any sense," said Secretary of War Walker, just behind Benjamin in the picture, "and that man was Benjamin." Benjamin *(right)*, in 1860, served first as Attorney General, then as Secretary of War, and finally as Secretary of State. He was even honored, dubiously it turned out, on the Confederate two-dollar bill, issued in 1862 *(bottom left)*.

Secretary of State Benjamin *(top left)*, circa 1863, showing the strains of the war, in a recently discovered photo by Rees, a popular photographer in Richmond. John Slidell *(top right)* was the senior Senator from Louisiana and the state's political boss. More than anyone else, Slidell was responsible for Benjamin's election to the Senate, the first acknowledged Jew to sit in the U.S. Senate. Slidell's political enemies accused him of being a Jew himself, their only explanation of so strange a political action. Benjamin later persuaded Jefferson Davis to support his political mentor as the Confederate Commissioner to Paris. Gustavus Myers *(bottom)*, Benjamin's best friend in Richmond, was a leading lawyer; member of the Richmond City Council for thirty years and its president from 1843 to 1855; and president of the Sephardic synagogue in Richmond. Myers was married to the daughter of the Governor of Virginia. Because of him, Mary Chesnut could write in her diary: "Elsewhere Jews may be tolerated. Here they are haute volee." His position did not spare him from ugly criticism, however; J. B. Jones called him in his diary "the little old lawyer for Jew clients."

As Secretary of War, Benjamin had highly publicized quarrels with General P. G. T. Beauregard *(top left)* and General T. J. "Stonewall" Jackson *(top right).* Beauregard called Benjamin in a letter to Davis "that functionary at his desk, who deems it a fit time to write lectures on law while the enemy is mustering at our front." Jackson threatened to resign, writing Davis that "with such interference in my command, I cannot expect to be of much service in the field." Davis defended his "right hand," as Varina described Benjamin, who was working twelve and fourteen hours a day with Davis and was being blamed by the military for carrying out the President's orders.

Union Generals Benjamin Butler *(bottom left)* and Ulysses S. Grant *(bottom right).* Butler was in command of the Union forces that conquered New Orleans. He said that "the most effective supporters [of the Confederacy] have been . . . mostly Jews . . . who all deserve at the hands of the government what is due the Jew Benjamin." Grant issued the infamous General Order 11 on December 17, 1862: "Jews as a class," it said, were to be expelled from Tennessee in twenty-four hours. "The Israelites should be kept out," he wrote, and though Lincoln rescinded the order, it was the most controversial event of the war affecting Jews.

The Confederate Cabinet flees south over the Georgia Ridge in April 1865; Benjamin can be seen just behind Davis in the silk hat. This sketch was made by an *Illustrated London News* artist, Frank Vizetelly, who traveled with the Cabinet during the flight.

IN MEMORY OF ABRAHAM LINCOLN.

As the Lincoln funeral train *(bottom)* made its way back to Illinois in a three-week trip through unimaginable grief, millions of Americans lined up at stops along the way to file past the casket. Lincoln's last photograph *(top left)* was taken on April 10, 1865; tens of thousands of Americans displayed this photograph and others of him in their homes for years after his death. Killed on Good Friday of what was later to be called "Black Easter," Lincoln was deified in two thousand sermons, and his apotheosis was dramatized in drawings, paintings, and newspaper cartoons *(top right)*. Ministers saw in Lincoln the martyred Christ figure, whose assassination was compared to the crucifixion, his life taken for his country by John Wilkes Booth, whom some called the "American Judas."

THE LAST DITCH OF THE CHIVALRY, OR A PRESIDENT IN PETTICOATS.

A Currier & Ives cartoon depicts the capture of the Confederate President *(top)*, forever ridiculing him for having picked up Varina's cloak in the dawn light. Davis was jailed and accused of treason, though he was released after two years without ever facing a trial. Earlier, Benjamin had taken leave of the President to travel alone in a broken-down wagon, disguised first as "Monsieur Bonfals," a Frenchman who spoke no English. The name itself showed bravado—probably translated from the Cajun French "a good disguise." Later, he changed to the ragged clothes of a farmer. His escape to England over several harrowing months, barely avoiding capture and death at sea, became a Southern legend, as depicted in these 1938 drawings *(bottom left and right)* from the book *Flight into Oblivion,* by A. J. Hanna, illustrations by John Rae.

The dictatorial Edwin Stanton *(top left)*, the Union Secretary of War, blamed the assassination on the Confederate leadership and took steps to prove it with high-handed legal tactics, bribery, and false testimony. William H. Seward *(top right)*, the Secretary of State in Lincoln's Cabinet, had a smoldering hatred for Benjamin, his Confederate counterpart, and once said in a Cabinet meeting that he believed "Booth and Surratt had conferred with Benjamin [who] had encouraged and subsidized them." Seward even sent a detective to London to try and find a connection between Benjamin and Surratt, but the detective reported his lack of success to Congress.

Andrew Johnson *(left)*, the new President, who muttered "they will pay for this" when he heard the news, had once attacked Judah P. Benjamin on the floor of the Senate as "Another Jew . . . that miserable Benjamin." President Johnson, in a meeting with a number of senators, suggested that Davis, Benjamin, and others be hanged. In the maze of assassination conspiracy charges that eventually followed, however, all three men were themselves accused.

FINALE of the "JEFF DAVIS DIE-NASTY."
"Last Scene of all, that ends this strange eventful History."

The mood of the country was vindictive. A cartoon *(top)* depicted Jefferson Davis hanging over an open grave, as other Confederate leaders, including Robert E. Lee, awaited their turns with John Wilkes Booth, nooses dangling over their heads. Benjamin is third from the left. John Surratt *(bottom)*, the messenger whom Judah Benjamin sent with dispatches to the Confederate spies in Canada, was wanted as an accomplice to John Wilkes Booth. Surratt was discovered eighteen months later in the Vatican, where he was serving in the Papal guard (photo shows him in his uniform). He escaped to Alexandria, Egypt, where he was eventually captured and brought back to the United States for trial but not convicted.

As the voice of her imprisoned husband, who was shackled in irons in a prison cell, Varina Davis *(top)* fought for his release in letters, public statements, and visits to influential newspaper editors and Republican businessmen. This portrait, taken by Brady probably during a highly publicized trip to Washington to plea personally for her husband *(bottom)* in the White House office of President Andrew Johnson, reflects those desperate and forlorn years. Benjamin met Jefferson and Varina Davis a number of times in England, when the President, once released from prison, sought business opportunities abroad. Though they had worked together for interminable hours each day throughout the war and shared its few triumphs and many desperate chapters, Davis wrote only one sentence about Benjamin in his two-volume, 1,500-page treatise on the war.

Despite lingering suspicions and investigations by his enemies in the United States, Benjamin had an extraordinary second career in England, rising to the position of Queen's Counsel, which qualified him to practice before the House of Lords. He wrote a brilliant legal treatise still studied by law students today, known as *Benjamin on Sales*, and as one of the leading international commercial lawyers in England contributed to British financial and commercial hegemony in the nineteenth century.

Benjamin was buried in 1884 in Père Lachaise cemetery in Paris under the name of "Philippe Benjamin" in the family plot of the Boursignac family, the in-laws of his daughter. In 1938, the Paris chapter of the United Daughters of the Confederacy provided an inscription that finally identified the man in the almost anonymous grave.

Benjamin did not write, as one might have expected, an angry letter demanding Spence's resignation, a retraction, or even an explanation. For more than a year, he allowed Spence to speak out in favor of emancipation. In the meantime, to scotch rumors in Europe that if peace came the South intended to reopen the African slave trade, Benjamin circulated through his diplomats copies of the Confederate Constitution, calling attention to the provisions that specifically denied the power. Benjamin also noted in other documents in June 1863 that Negro troops had performed bravely for the North in the battle of Port Hudson.

Finally, in October 1863, Spence wrote Benjamin a letter explaining his views on emancipation, and the government was obliged to release him from his post.

But in his reply to Spence, written several months later, Benjamin apologized for the "intemperate attacks" of the Richmond newspapers, which he said were regarded "with pain and mortification by all men." Benjamin explained that the attacks on Spence were really aimed at himself, not Spence, "by unscrupulous partisans." As to Spence's views of emancipation, Benjamin admitted to "some embarrassment in replying to them." As a private citizen Spence would not "with self-respect conceal or color his views," Benjamin said, because they were a "matter of principle." Benjamin even said that Spence's opinions on slavery made his advocacy more effective with people who agreed with him, but it would be impossible to keep him in the service of the State Department. Benjamin did not express anger at public airing of such controversial views or personal disagreement with those views; on the contrary, he said "as a man of the world" he would meet Spence "on the most cordial terms without the slightest reference" to his views on slavery.[16] Benjamin seemed to be saying that continued agitation on this subject would neither destroy his own personal regard for Spence nor impair Spence's future access to the Secretary of State. It sounded as if he wanted Spence to continue to advocate a more radical step and to maintain lines of communication to report on the English response to his advocacy. If Spence was correct and emancipation would influence Parliament sufficiently to guarantee British entry into the war, then the Confederacy would have to consider such an action seriously, with survival and even victory in the balance.

The atmosphere of desperation intensified as losses mounted. The Alabama Legislature in 1863 recommended to the government the enlistment of slave soldiers but, of course, made no mention of emancipation. Adoption of that kind of sweeping proposal would require the strong support of the military. With such a profound issue at stake, a fierce, bare-knuckle debate could be expected both inside and outside the army.

The defeats at Gettysburg and Vicksburg had their expected impact in Britain and France as well. Benjamin had already become exasperated with Napoleon. When the Emperor had placed Maximilian on the Mexican throne, he hatched a surreptitious plan for enticing Texas to leave the Confederacy and become a buffer state and a source of cotton for the French mills. Not only had Confederate relations with the French soured, but the hardening of opposition in the British Parliament and despair among the sympathizers in the British Government caused Benjamin at last to accede to the request of Commissioner Mason in London that he be allowed to withdraw.

"Perusal of the recent debates in the British Parliament," Benjamin wrote to Mason, "satisfies the President that the government of Her Majesty has determined to decline the overtures made through you for the establishing by treaty, friendly relations between the two governments, and entertains no intention of receiving you as the accredited minister of this government and the President therefore requests that you consider your mission at an end, and that you withdraw, with your secretary from London."[17]

After months of being snubbed, Mason was happy to walk away from the mission. He went to Paris to await developments with Slidell, who himself had become disgusted with the machinations of the French court. Slidell had written to Mason in sympathy: "The time has now arrived when it is of comparatively little importance what Queen or Emperor may say or think about us. A plague, I say, on both your houses."[18]

To Benjamin, dealing with the British Government in London had been almost impossible. Britain was governed by a small clique, and whatever his point of entry into their circle—whether through friends, millionaire shippers, or the press—once inside, he was stopped.

A few months after Mason's withdrawal, Davis and Benjamin decided to go even further and expel the remaining British consular agents in the South. Plans were completed after Davis left for a short trip to settle a dispute that had broken out among the generals in Tennessee. The more virulent anti-Davis Confederate press excoriated Benjamin for taking a step "no other man in the Confederacy would have dared to take." Benjamin called a Cabinet meeting on his own and received "unhesitating and unanimous" approval to expel the representatives. Only the most confident second-in-command would convene, preside over, and seek approval of a policy change in the absence of the President.[19] The South was in such desperate straits that almost any proposition, no matter how preposterous, seemed to have merit. After the war Benjamin revealed how he took advantage of the English rumor mills and discussed the gullibility of the English upper classes when a forged letter surfaced alleging that he had offered to make the son of Queen Victoria the King or Emperor of the Southern States of America:

"The letter," he said to the correspondent of the New York *Daily Tribune* after the war, "is a fiction but to some extent it is founded on fact." He elaborated:

> I have always gone on the principle of speaking to fools according to their folly. There was, some twenty years ago, among the upper classes in England a general desire to believe that the republican form of government was an impossible one . . . it was imagined that all the British colonies were future kingdoms for the children of the Queen, and I was constantly asked by letter and verbally by Englishmen not only of high position but more than average intellect whether it would not be better for the South to have a monarch than a president. I humored this idea or fancy and said on many occasions to persons who I thought would advantageously echo my words that the best thing that could happen to the Southerners would be for Queen Victoria to make them a present of her second son and place her third son over Canada. This produced the effect in certain clubs as I had intended. The Duke of Argyll was strongly of the opinion that there would be monarchial governments all over America before the end of the century.[20]

Benjamin, it seemed, would toss any rumor into the English social scene to win sympathy for the South, even an idea as preposterous as the restoration of the monarchy in America.

It was a strange war. The North had offered a $500 bounty in Ireland for men to emigrate and fight for the Union, and 75,000 had decided that soldiering was preferable to starving. It was a cynical way to recruit, and Benjamin thought the North vulnerable to certain countermeasures. He dispatched emissaries to Dublin with pamphlets describing the hatred and violence in Boston and New York against

Irish immigrants; he sent another emissary to Rome to see Pope Pius IX, who offered little solace but did say that gradual emancipation of the slaves would be looked upon with favor by the Church.

Dangling attractive promises to gain foreign intervention was exhausted as a policy. "Look not to princes," Davis had said; Benjamin was turning his mind to more devious ways to lure the Europeans into the war.

For Benjamin, Sunday mornings were a time of deep loneliness.

With so many churches on Grace Street, the clatter of carriages took over the mid-morning, leaving Judah Benjamin alone in his garden to think and dream. It was his own choice neither to acknowledge his Judaism to the Gentiles nor to partake in the social wellsprings of Christianity. He would have been welcomed at St. Paul's Episcopal Church if only he pretended to be a searching Jew who wanted to sample its service. The word "conversion" need not be spoken, since Christians in the South always consider conversion to have occurred when they meet a Jew two Sundays in a row in church. So the minister and the old congregation would have welcomed him with their eyes, and it would be a sincere welcome, because his presence would be seen as an acting out of the New Testament prophecies concerning the conversion of the Jews.

Today one can sense his feeling of isolation when walking on the Capitol grounds on Sundays, in the utter tranquility and solitude of the day. Benjamin could have sat alone in the shadows of Thomas Jefferson's building and Washington's statue, secure in the knowledge that the President and all the members of the Cabinet, the generals and Congressmen, were absorbed in the Bibles and hymnals at their pews. They were all preoccupied, so he could rest his mind for a few minutes—not losing ground, not alert in his nerve endings, not defensive to the point of paranoia, not outthinking adversaries or critics.

Alone.

On the hill of the Capitol grounds overlooking St. Paul's Church, for the moment, Benjamin could have floated in inner space unchallenged, the nonbeliever in a Christian world, a detached rather than an involved heart.

At noon the bells of St. Paul's signaled the end of the Sunday service, and the good Christians of Richmond would be leaving the churches, returning to their homes for Sunday dinners, Sunday teas, and conversations about the war.

Why did they hate him so? Why did Christianity sometimes wear a smoky cloak of cruelty?

White Southerners seemed to project on him the dark qualities of Iago: of stealth and cunning, manipulation and distrust. Was it their own sense of guilt? That they were blessed and touched by destiny on this continent, but had defiled this Eden by bringing a primitive evil to these shores? Slavery. They knew God would curse it, that slaves would rise up here against them as the Hebrews had against Pharaoh. The whites were steeped in the Bible, and it told them that the Jews were once slaves. And the white Southerner would never trust an ex-slave, for deep down the whites knew that a man who had known slavery and tasted freedom could not be trusted, though he be white like them, Southern like them, even a member of the Cabinet guiding this war in their behalf.

Historians of Confederate times have written that, on Sundays around Capitol Square, one could hear the gabble of the Negroes who had left the African Church a block away and were coming for a walk around the square. It was a grand, mixed crowd of all classes, since the African Church boasted of having the largest Negro congregation in the world. Some congregants strutted in fancy duds, with bowler hats and canes, and a few were in calico dresses with hoops and bustles, like the white ladies they served. But mainly there were poor men in clean work clothes and a few women in simple dresses. A few couples were out to sashay around Screamersville, but the preponderance of the crowd, men alone without women or families, seemed aimless and without destination.

In Richmond, the war was taking its greatest toll on the poor.

The White House was only a few blocks away. The Sunday church hour was over, and Benjamin was often invited for Sunday dinner with Varina and the President. It was time to resume the air of vigilance and climb back into the stream and the pulse of Richmond's political life.

Lee's offer to resign after Gettysburg filled Jefferson Davis with apprehension and dismay. Davis knew he could not go on without Lee, as he confessed to Benjamin in a rare show of humility. Benjamin advised him to write Lee and tell him that he had not lost the confidence of either the soldiers or his Commander-in-Chief.

Davis knew Lee well, and Benjamin would help draft a reply that would play upon Lee's pride and honor. It was a difficult letter to compose because it required Davis to adopt a deferential tone that was not usual for him and to give Lee the chance to resign without giving the appearance that the President was begging him to stay. The letter read:

> "Expressions of discontent in the public journals furnish but little evidence of the sentiment of the army. . . . But, my dear friend . . . where am I to find that new commander who is to possess the greater ability which you believe to be required? . . . Our country could not bear to lose you. To ask me to substitute you by someone in my judgment more fit to command, or who could possess more of the confidence of the army or of the reflecting men in the country, is to demand of me an impossibility."[21]

For the rest of the war, there would be no more talk of Lee's resignation.

While Davis might have been slightly cheered in the autumn of 1863 at the news of a victory of sorts at Chickamauga Creek in Tennessee, the casualty list was again so long—18,000 Confederates—that the attrition far outweighed the objectives won or lost. Whatever comfort might be drawn from a costly victory was quickly overcome with Grant's capture of Lookout Mountain and the fall of Chattanooga. Now Johnston's army was the only barrier separating Grant and Sherman from the prize of Atlanta.

Harsh criticism of General Braxton Bragg by his generals in Tennessee required a trip by the President for an on-the-scene assessment of Bragg's capacity for command. Soon after Davis left Richmond, Benjamin received news that members of the British consulate in Savannah had forbidden British subjects who had enlisted in the Confederate army to "be brought into conflict with the forces of the United States." The Confederate newspapers were outraged over this "breach of sovereignty," and Congress demanded instant action. Benjamin convened a Cabinet meeting at his own initiative and, after a unanimous vote, expelled the British consulate in a swift action that would receive worldwide attention. Benjamin then wrote to the President on October 8, 1863:

> You had scarcely left Richmond when an exigency occurred which seemed to me to call for immediate action, but at which I could not assume the responsibility of acting in your name during your absence without the clearest responsibility. I accordingly requested my colleagues to meet me yesterday and found them

unhesitating and unanimous in the conclusion that the British consular agents should be at once expelled from the Confederacy. . . . The letter to Mr. Fullerton will put you fully in possession of the facts on which the decision of the Cabinet was based, and we were all of the opinion that as soon as an offensive encroachment on the sovereignty of the Confederacy had been made public, it would be very unfortunate to delay action till you could be heard from . . . the telegraph would be insufficient to put you in possession of the whole case. . . .

I am very sensible how grave is the step taken without your sanction but trust you will not consider me as having overstepped the bounds imposed by necessity under the circumstances."[22]

The letter is extraordinary on several counts. First, there is the clear implication that Benjamin was empowered to act in the President's name during Davis's absence and, if he thought it urgent enough, without even notifying the President first. Second, Benjamin was the individual in charge who did not simply convene a Cabinet meeting but could "ask my colleagues to meet with me." Thus they were advising him on an agenda that he determined and, with their vote, they gave him the constitutional authority to act. Third, Benjamin was confident enough of Davis's trust to announce the action and seek presidential approval after the fact. In a sense, in this episode, Judah P. Benjamin was actually "Acting President" of the Confederacy, issuing orders in the name of the government with authority possessed by no other person in the government. But even Benjamin knew that there were limits to his power. In a postscript to the letter, he wrote that "it would be gratifying to me to hear by telegraph that our action meets your approval."[23]

It was a chill November night in Richmond when the Davises walked from the river fortifications and the wharves back to the mansion. Their route took them past Libby Prison, which Varina hated because it reminded her of the difficulties that the government had in providing food and care even for its own army, let alone for the thousands of prisoners packed into the old converted warehouse.

"Halt! Who goes there?" A sharp voice abruptly stopped them near the prison gate.

"I am Jefferson Davis," the President answered in a loud, clear voice from the darkness. The sentry challenged him and lifted his rifle to hold them fast. Davis suddenly pulled his sword cane, and the sentry cocked his rifle. Varina screamed and jumped in front of her husband, urgently assuring the young soldier that it really was Jefferson Davis and asking him to lower his rifle. Hearing a woman's voice startled the sentry, and he peered more intently at the approaching two figures now becoming more visible in the light of a lamp. He recognized the President, apologized profusely, and let them pass.[24]

3

THE STRUGGLE AGAINST DEFEAT

1864–1865

14

Tragedy at Home

❈

Richmond in 1864 lay almost still, grieving for the dead of Gettysburg the previous summer and for the shattered illusion that a single Southerner could whip a dozen Yankees in a fight. Women stole mosquito netting out of Chimborazo Hospital to use for party dresses; the wounds of soldiers made for bizarre scenes at social events—a handsome face scarred by sabers; a small lead ball lodged permanently in the throat of a lieutenant so that he wheezed to the belles at the parties around the city; an eye lost at Antietam; a jaw shattered at Shiloh.

Stories of mass defections, epidemics, and imminent surrender circulated widely by means of the Yankee spy network. A report that President Davis had committed suicide rushed like wildfire all over Richmond and across the enemy lines. The rumor was telegraphed to the Yankee press, which whipped it into fact. Richmond ladies whispered the news that "Beast" Butler had been transferred from his salacious conquest of New Orleans to fight against Lee in northern Virginia. Henry Foote criticized "the Israelitish Secretary of State," and the Richmond *Examiner* whined: "One could almost earnestly wish . . . that the first tentatives towards a foreign policy . . . were entrusted to an uncircumcized Christian man."[1]

Carriages cost $25 an hour and a new dress of the plainest material more than $500. A half-dozen cups and saucers brought $160 at an auction, and one could easily spend $1,500 in two hours of shopping. The price of everything was going up as gold supplies dwindled and the Davis government in Richmond, the states, and the individual cities printed money to meet their needs. Tredegar paid for slaves with iron bars and rails, products more valuable than money to the plantation owners. Prices of everyday essentials, too, were already outrageous: A pair of shoes cost $60; boots were $100; a cord of wood $40; a pound of butter $4; chickens $12 a pair; a pound of sugar $20; a whole ham $350; a barrel of flour $300. Food speculators stored staples in warehouses, knowing that the price would rise. Farmers kept their goods off the market for the same reason. But the needs were enormous, just to maintain the human beings involved in the war, not to mention finding money for weapons for the army. To feed the work force at the Tredegar Iron Works alone, itself almost a separate state of black slaves and white overseers, the government needed yearly 300,000 pounds of bacon, 600,000 pounds of beef, and 40,000 bushels of corn. Such amounts were out of the question.

In those days, Benjamin wrote to an admirer who had sent him a substantial amount of brandy: "I made no scruple of receiving the presents you sent me previously, because they were of small pecuniary value and were regarded by me as testimonials of friendship which were cordially accepted; but a demijohn of brandy at present prices represents quite a sum of money, and in my public position it makes me feel somewhat uncomfortable to accept presents of any value."

But he did not, in Richmond's time of scarcity, want to return the brandy. "I trust you will fully appreciate my motives and will not think that requesting your permission to reimburse the cost of the brandy I am actuated by any but the kindest feelings towards yourself."[2]

The city seemed to one observer to be "crazed on the subject of gaiety," almost like Paris during the French Revolution.[3] Belles and young men on their way to the war referred to the starvation parties as "dancing on the edge of the grave." Women coming home from tending the sick and dying at the hospitals could catch the sounds of music and dancing wafting out into the street. Lovers promenaded on the hillside behind Third Street in the evening to catch the breezes from the waterfalls on the James and watch the intermittent glow of the belches from the Tredegar blast furnaces.

The apricot and cherry trees that bloomed in Richmond in April 1864 signaled, as at no time previously, both the hope and the despair of the Confederacy. For the city had learned by bitter experience that the blossoms that had been tossed on the soldiers marching off to war could also be cut into sprigs for a funeral cortege.

The more sensitive souls of the social elite gathered at "waffle worries" or "muffin matches," in which they served a simple pastry enriched with poetry reading and discussions of essays they had composed or the latest literary news. They played charades at Mrs. Semmes's or went to plays at the Iveses', where Mrs. Clement Clay starred as Mrs. Malaprop in *The Rivals* and Constance Cary as the romantic lead. And there was music. The Rittenhouse orchestra played at intermissions of plays, and there were band concerts at the old Fair Grounds.

Varina wanted to hold a lavish affair as in the early days to show the wives of the Cabinet and the Congress and foreign representatives that there was still some grace left in the South. She arranged a "luncheon for ladies," at which she served gumbo, duck, chicken in jelly, oysters, chocolate cream, jelly cake, claret cup, and champagne. The guests drank from ruby-red tinted glasses, and the servants were dressed in frilled maid and butler outfits, special for the occasion.

Richmond seemed to be caught in a drama within a drama, acting out its old patterns to try to forget the acts of the present. Often at social events, the hostess would select a spirited play and assign the guests parts; they would go at their roles with great vigor, as an escape from the storm. But it was spring, and the actors in uniform were restless to send the curtain up on still another act in the passionate drama on the battlefields.

To show the South that the North knew where its advantage lay, Lincoln issued a call for 500,000 men in early 1864 to replace the men who had enlisted after Fort Sumter and whose two-year tours were coming to an end. With Congress eager to be assertive because it was facing an election year, Lincoln allowed it to pass a previously rejected bill creating a new rank in the army. The bill would require the President to appoint a senior officer to take military command in Washington and reduce his own powers as Commander-in-Chief.

There was no question whom the public or Congress wanted for the job: General Ulysses S. Grant, whose initials after Vicksburg had come to stand for "Unconditional Surrender." Once Lincoln was assured that Grant had no interest in running against him in the fall, the general had the job. To replace Grant in Chattanooga for the final drive through Georgia, Lincoln appointed the red-bearded nemesis who had already cut "a swath of desolation" across Mississippi: Grant's second-in-command, William Tecumseh Sherman.

It was the fourth spring of the war. Having given up on foreign intervention, the Confederates now rested their hopes on the outcome of the 1864 elections in the North and on the emergence of a peace candidate to challenge Lincoln. That meant eight months of solid fighting with no spectacular, all-or-nothing battles to lift the morale of the North, but a season of standoffs to convince the Northern voters of the South's irreconcilability to rejoining the Union. But to play for time, the South needed "cannon fodder"—thousands of men to match Lincoln's numbers. To get them, Davis proposed and Congress passed a new law extending the age of conscription down to seventeen and up to fifty. Benjamin saw Davis grieve over the measure: "We're about to grind the seed corn of the nation," the President said.

Others were considering a more radical solution. At a meeting on January 2, 1864, of the general officers of the Army of Tennessee, General Patrick Cleburne, a division officer whose admirers called him the "Stonewall Jackson of the West," had read aloud a paper he had written advocating "that we immediately commence training a large reserve of the most courageous of our slaves and further that we guarantee freedom within a reasonable time to every slave in the South who shall remain true to the Confederacy."[4]

He recommended that the South emancipate its slaves and "change the race from a dreaded weakness to a strength. . . . We can do this more effectually than the North can now do, for we can give the negro not only his own freedom, but that of his wife and child, and can secure it to him in his own home." He also thought that emancipation "would remove forever all selfish taint from our cause and place independence above every question of property. The very magnitude of the sacrifice itself, such as no nation has ever voluntarily made before, would appall our enemies . . . and fill our hearts with a pride and singleness of purpose which would clothe us with new strength in battle."[5]

General Johnston had held the "Cleburne Memorial" for a month, but finally General Walker of Georgia, a Cleburne critic, sent a copy to the President expressing outrage at the "incendiary document." Davis ordered the debate promptly closed before it became public and through Secretary of War Seddon ordered "suppression not only of the memorial itself but likewise of discussion and controversy growing out of it."[6]

But Judah Benjamin had been thinking in similar terms for much longer, and perhaps the recommendation of so respected an officer was just the impetus he needed. Ever since Lincoln's proclamation, the idea had been in the air. Why not issue a Confederate Emancipation Proclamation to free the slaves who would agree to fight for the South? It was the kind of stroke the South needed, a bold action that would at once electrify the watching world and solve many of the South's problems: manpower, military, and, more crucial, diplomacy, for it would remove the one barrier that was preventing England and France from entering the war. But the explosion among senators from slaveholding states would be horrendous, bitter beyond imagination, perhaps even causing outright rebellion. To them, what was the Cause if not slavery? Benjamin knew the arguments well. He had heard the rationale from the pulpit that God was saving the heathens and the South was His instrument. He had heard the debate in the legislative halls that each state was sanctified and independent and its people had the right to choose their own destiny. He understood the profound change implied in his forbidden thoughts. The whole Southern "way of life" rested upon slavery. To abandon it precipitously might create social chaos that would plunge the nation into anarchy.

But was not the nation already on the precipice? Each new Union victory created thousands of black freedmen, though many more were fleeing the Yankees from fear of the unknown and rumors of a new kind of slavery under the boot of the Union army. Richmond was brimming with frightened blacks. Whatever the pains of slavery, at least it represented certitude. Dare the government give the slaves arms in exchange for a promise of freedom when they then could seize that freedom for themselves?

For all the risks, there was no doubt in Benjamin's mind that emancipation could be the one grand stroke to save the South from defeat. He had been able to convince Davis that slaves should be allowed to serve as drivers and carriers for the army, paying their masters for their services. But that proposal accepted the premises of slavery and was just another form of hiring out property or taking property under the law of eminent domain. Emancipation, with all the drama and moral and political weight of a Presidential proclamation, would require the most careful preparation, even as to the right approach to the President. Varina's help was crucial. Benjamin could not make a start without her, because the President would instantly turn to her for advice. Support by the military would be vital to winning political support in the Congress. Tennessee and Joe Johnston had no leverage with the President. It would require Virginia and the army in defense of Richmond itself, and that meant Robert E. Lee. Benjamin would have to ponder the most adroit way to approach Lee.

He had not really considered the personal risks to himself. It was Benjamin's pattern to be more cerebral about issues, to break them down into component parts and overlook any personal factors in the equation. But could he, as a Jew, dare risk masterminding such a step? Emancipation was no ordinary issue. If the Richmond *Examiner* were to discover that the President's closest adviser was involved, it would raise the cry of treason, and many would zero in on the phantom Jewish manipulator in the bosom of the Confederacy as the target for all the South's ills.

Benjamin could consider the reaction to the Cleburne paper as a possible dress rehearsal for his own ideas. What he heard was shock, condemnation, and denunciation as the generals called it "a monstrous proposition," "revolting," and "incendiary," and predicted that if it were even *proposed,* "the total disintegration of the army will follow in a fortnight."[7] And that was from the military—what would be the reaction of the politicians?

In contrast to Lincoln, who had to wait until the war was going well to proclaim emancipation, if Benjamin intended to advise Davis to do the same, he would be wise to wait until the South was even more desperate.

Varina was seven months pregnant with a sixth child, as if she were struggling to make a commitment of faith in the future before the sunshine of spring brought war back to Virginia. The embittered population was setting fire to some of the finer homes in Richmond out of resentment over its own deprivation. A few days earlier, Varina had accompanied with her friends, the Lyons, to survey the smoke and ruins of their home. When they found some tea cups, a scorched kettle, and a surviving ounce of tea in the burnt-out kitchen, they just decided on an impulse to have tea under the same clump of trees where they had gathered in better times, to remember how pleasant life had once been.

Davis had encouraged Varina to join him during the day at lunch, so she often came to the President's office carrying a picnic basket. The President had lost sleep over Sherman's victories in Mississippi and had lost all appetite, which had given him the wasted look of his soldiers. Just as she had done in Washington when he was too sick or anxious to keep food down, Varina would prepare a tempting lunch and bring it over to his office where she would stay and make sure he ate it.

Sherman had struck Davis's home state with a special fury and had issued orders to his men that had chilled the capital: "Vigorous war . . . means universal destruction," and just north of Jackson, his soldiers had burned 10,000 bales of cotton and 2 million bushels of grain, and had stolen 8,000 slaves and thousands of horses and mules needed not only for war but for the spring planting. Sherman was living by his credo that "war is cruelty. There is no use trying to reform it. The crueler it is, the sooner it will be over."[8]

The South was disillusioned. Two governors—Zebulon Vance in North Carolina and Joseph Brown in Georgia—cared not where the war was, but wanted to fight it only when the Yankees came to their own front yards.

They gave Davis no choice. He had to suspend the right of habeas corpus to save the country; he had to seize food in Georgia to feed the army in Virginia; he had to seize wagons in Georgia to help the war in Tennessee; he had to conscript Georgia boys so Alabama boys would not die in vain in Mississippi.

Davis had wanted to serve his people nobly, but they called him "despot"; he wanted to lead as a patriot, but they called him a "scoundrel"; he tried to provide strength for the army, but they said he was "power mad," a "Caesar." Senator Robert Toombs in Georgia had even spoken of "leaving a glorious name like Brutus."

The saddest day that spring was the day that five-year-old Joe Davis fell from the first floor portico to the brick pavement below.

"Oh, no . . . no," Varina muttered as she kneeled over the broken body of her son. Davis bent down beside her, and together they straightened the boy's legs and gently slipped the President's coat under his broken skull to make a pillow. Dr. Garnett came running up with his bag, and the boy's eyes opened ever so slightly, his chest heaved and then collapsed with a child's sigh. He was dead.

They were all paralyzed for a moment. Then the President lifted his hands to the heavens and cried out, "Not mine, oh, Lord, but Thine." He stood and walked over to the columns of the house, repeating those same phrases over and over. A courier came riding up urgently with a message. The President looked at it for more than a minute, not even reading it, and handed it to Benjamin saying, "I must have this day with my little child."[9]

That night, a small open coffin surrounded by flowers sat in the center of the huge living room. At its foot the family knelt in prayer. As they knelt, the wide-open windows of the mansion let the soft spring night waft through the curtains. Jeff, Jr., the seven-year-old, whispered in his mother's ear, "I have said all the prayers I know how, but God will not wake Joe."[10] When the silent prayers ended, the President shut himself in his room and paced the floor all night.

A large crowd turned out for little Joe's funeral and watched the President, "straight as an arrow, clear against the sky," standing by the tiny grave of his son. Varina's dark eyes were swollen and empty, scarcely noticing the hundreds of school children marching up the hillside to the cemetery, each carrying a bouquet or a green wreath, which they placed carefully among the white flowers massed around the grave. Varina, a pregnant mother mourning a lost child, was grieving death and nurturing life simultaneously.

Even worse times were coming to Richmond.

Red auction flags dotted the buildings along Main Street as people sold the last of whatever they had. The dragnet of the conscription agents had herded sullen young men from the city offices and auction rooms into compounds, where Winder's detectives kept them under bayonet until the old uniforms of the dead could be issued to them and they could be sent out to the field in locked wagons.

Out on the battlefields, short of medical supplies and racked with scurvy, soldiers had dug for sassafras roots in the woods while their horses turned into bony skeletons for lack of forage during the winter.

Not all the women at home on the plantations were heroines, but many were. Some plowed with old saw ponies, brought in a tobacco crop, and, if there were slaves, worked alongside them, while little girls did the hoeing and the spinning. Others were so helpless that they begged their men to desert and come home. They were all vulnerable to the marauding Yankee soldiers, the fierce Confederate impressment agents, and the Southern riffraff and scalawags careening over the countryside to steal whatever they could.

Some Southern ladies destroyed choice wine and whole libraries lest the Yankees enjoy them. But in one town while the militiamen poured liquor bottles in the streets the locals sopped it up with their shirts so they could wring it out in their boots.

It seemed odd, in an atmosphere of deprivation, that Richmond society would engage in a night of revelry, but the Cary sisters often gave "starvation parties," and in the city with a tradition of conviviality one took advantage of every opportunity for enjoyment. The women prepared for those parties with a strong sense of duty. Robert E. Lee himself had encouraged them—"Go and look your prettiest"—so his men would have the charm of the women of Richmond to look forward to.

It was all make believe. The parties served no food and only water in wine glasses. They pretended that everything was just the way it used to be, like children at play, and perhaps for a few fleeting moments things would be the same as they were.

Judah Benjamin and Jules St. Martin attended those parties even in the darkest times. Jules always dressed "Parisian style" for social events—hand-tooled boots and a dark suit trimmed in velvet—just to remind the Richmond belles that the St. Martins were Creoles from New Orleans who knew how to live with flair and dress with distinction.

The scenes are recorded in novels and diaries from the times: As the elite walked the few blocks to a party, they might pass a group of scarecrow soldiers in a semicircle around a little black boy dancing the jig, a hat at his feet with several coins in it. The streets were filled with dusty gray uniforms of seasoned soldiers, wounded or furloughed, alongside the fresh grays of the raw recruits. The veterans shuffled along in broken shoes or with feet wrapped in burlap, visual lessons to the innocent eyes of the draftees. Drums continued to roll all day, measuring the death marches of the officers to Hollywood Cemetery. Bugles blared and bells tolled for the new brigades arriving at the Virginia Central Depot. Lines of prisoners in blue shuffled silently and aimlessly toward Libby Prison; deserters in gray shamefully slinked into Castle Thunder. And in the parks, very young boys and old men drilled for civil defense under the watchful eye of a one-armed ex-artilleryman.

Wallowing in lawlessness and decadence while near exhaustion, Richmond was still a city of passion, with a raw edge to its mood that reminded Benjamin of New Orleans. In Locust Alley, the painted whores languished in the doorways to help the bruised young men forget the terrors of their first battles and give the wily veterans some soft memories to take back to the tents at the front.

Richmond was alive in other ways than the direct, licentious barter on the streets. After the city had driven back the invaders in the first battle of Richmond, the women had begun to return to the city—wives, daughters, bereft brides, eager spinsters, young widows—of all ages, alone in the city while the thousands of Congressmen, generals, diplomats, captains, Senators, aides-de-camp, colonels, ironworkers, cavalrymen, journalists, profiteers, spies, and commanders went about their work. Every moment of life, every minute of warmth was dear. As defeat followed defeat, everyone's bravado had been shattered. It would be a long war and they knew it; one had to squeeze the kernels of possibility out of every day.

Constance Cary and her Baltimore cousins, the sisters Hetty and Jenny, were known as the Cary Invincibles—three high-spirited thoroughbreds with a kind of spunky distinction.[11] Constance had a breezy column in the *Southern Illustrated News,* and Jenny had set to music the poem *Maryland, My Maryland* and had sung it at patriotic meetings, but Hetty was the beauty of the three. She had crossed the Potomac one night in a small boat, sitting on her trunk, after waving her Confederate flag from her window in Baltimore while the Union troops marched by. Hetty had a thick mane of auburn hair. She had brought along sumptuous Northern dresses of deep velvet and dramatic colors, which impressed the clothes-starved belles of Richmond. Every lieutenant in the army dreamed of her. Jeb Stuart once dashed up on his horse, his plume waving from his hat, flung aside his scarlet-lined coat, and held a ladder for Hetty to climb up on and perch while he sang her a ballad.

This was the world Judah P. Benjamin and Varina Davis knew as the war moved into 1864. The mood at the parties has been recorded carefully in various diaries and histories. The young girls seemed like dusty butterflies, chattering in their faded hoop skirts with threadbare sashes and flower-shaped cutouts sewn at irregular places on dresses to cover moth holes. They were fishing for beaux even in the slim pickings of the wounded officers. Quick wartime romances and marriages afforded them special excitement and poignance.

Some of the officers' uniforms were cleaned for the party, but most were frayed and stained. Their boots were shined with gun grease but scuffed beyond repair and worn down to irregular heels. A young captain sat in the corner talking to a belle, whose dress billowed out to cover the stump of his leg, where his trouser leg was sewn neatly for a crisp appearance. Another couple danced clumsily because the lieutenant's left arm was missing; he could only hold his partner's waist for the turns of the waltz. She tried to cover his obvious embarrassment by holding her free arm at her side, but it occasionally swung out as they whirled.

Guests accepted the water in wine glasses graciously, even though later in the war the water works of Richmond were in such a sorry state that the water invariably had a muddy brown hue to it. Hostesses had to boil and strain it to an acceptable clarity.

Varina wrote about Benjamin's solicitude toward a young woman at a ball in Richmond:

> A very modest quiet girl, by no means pretty, and quite uninterest-ing, having suddenly discovered that her frock was too decolleté, had gone into a corner, unwilling to dance under the circumstances. Mr. Benjamin passed, and though he had rarely spoken to her, saw her embarrassment, and sat down by her. After a little desultory ballroom talk he said, "How very well you are dressed . . . I could not suggest any improvement in your costume." He told me afterwards how the poor little creature brightened up, and how he took some "grist to her mill" in the shape of partners. "Thus," he said, "I made two green blades grow where only one had been before."[12]

Another woman recalled that Benjamin provided the parties with "his charming stories, his dramatic recitation of scraps of verse, and clever comments on men, women and books."[13]

One observer looked about the room at the number of cripples in it—young men with arms and legs missing, surrounded by fluttering belles—and wrote bitterly in her diary, "Cupid has crutches."[14]

The older women, wives of generals and high officials, gathered at parties of this sort and seemed to imitate the attitudes of their husbands. Some of them acted like faded belles who had not easily made the adjustment to new responsibilities.

"I hear she buys from the black market," Mrs. Lydia Johnston, the wife of General Joseph Johnston, wrote about Varina in a letter to a friend. "She lives like Queen Varina in her palace," Mrs. Johnston continued, "while the rest of us suffer."[15]

Mrs. Henry Foote echoed criticism of Varina with home state vigor: "She is not even pretty, dresses badly and in no taste. She takes little notice of her children because she had public affairs to attend and they go about with their clothes tossed on in any and every style."[16]

The wife of the Adjutant General was heard to remark, "Well, if you ask me, she's just a squaw."[17]

Everybody in Richmond talked about "Crazy Bet," the old hag who wore a young belle's clothes like a rag doll—a torn bonnet, a dirty dress. It was rumored she was a spy who harbored escaping Northern prisoners in a secret attic in her house. Once she even came to the White House to ask for protection from the threats the rumors brought to her house. But Varina liked her and even had taken her advice on hiring a free slave woman for the White House.

One night, during a typical party at the White House, someone smelled a trace of smoke. When the door to the cellar was opened, a thick cloud of white smoke poured into the room. Guests helped with the bucket brigade—men in dress uniform and formal clothes and women in long dresses—with the President barking instructions to the group. There was evidence of arson in the basement: wood shavings that only because of dampness produced smoke but little flame.

That night, Mary Elizabeth Bowser, the free black servant recommended to Varina by "Crazy Bet," ran off to the North with the Davis's most loyal male house-servant.

In late February 1864, Union Colonel Ulric Dahlgren's daring cavalry raid into Richmond to free the prisoners in Libby Prison dramatized an issue that had been raging throughout the war. The raid was a total failure, and Dahlgren himself was killed. What had occasioned the raid was the condition of prisoners exchanged during the previous three years of the war.

In Fitzhugh Lee's account, President Davis did not take the raid or its implications seriously and even used it to tease his Secretary of State:

Upon one of Kilpatrick's officers—Colonel Ulric Dahlgren, who was killed—some remarkable papers were found, including a sort of an address to the soldiers to burn Richmond, kill Jeff Davis and Cabinet, and do many other horrible things. The United States Government promptly disclaimed any knowledge of such orders, and so did Meade. Dahlgren was a daring, dashing young fellow, but was too enthusiastic. It is certain the papers published at the time were taken from his person. The Southern President laughed as he read over the originals in his office, and turning to Mr.

Benjamin, his Secretary of State, who was with him, said, when he reached the word Cabinet, "That is intended for you, Mr. Benjamin."[18]

For Benjamin, the lesson of Dahlgren's raid was clear enough: If the Union was capable of launching a behind-the-lines attack to free prisoners in the South, why shouldn't the Confederates try the same thing in the North? But the plan Benjamin discussed with Davis was much more grandiose: a well-funded secret service mission would be set up in Canada to (1) conduct raids across the Great Lakes into the prison camps and free Confederate prisoners; (2) make contact and common purpose with the thousands of Confederate sympathizers or copperheads along the Canadian border who either belonged to or gave comfort to the Knights of the Golden circle and the Sons of Liberty; and (3) seize U.S. arsenals to arm this fantasy army of freed prisoners, copperheads, and antiwar fanatics and build them into such a significant force that they might foment a revolution or march South. At a minimum they could disrupt the elections of 1864 and help the Democrats oust Lincoln. Perhaps, also, they might sabotage the bridges and supply lines in the North; stir up more riots against Lincoln's conscription laws in the cities; and perhaps even create such concern in Washington about Canada that the Union might do something foolish and move troops onto Canadian soil, thus forcing Britain to enter the war to protect Canada from American conquest.

Davis flinched at the wild whimsy of such a scheme, and his answer indicated the roots of his doubts: "Find me a West Point man," he said to Benjamin. But a respected military man would not take the job. Instead, after a number of others turned it down, Jacob Thompson, former Governor of Mississippi and former Secretary of the Interior under Buchanan, was persuaded to try the Canadian mission. Thompson, the man Davis had defeated by one vote in his reelection to the Senate in 1858, was approved by the President, though with reservations since he was not a West Point graduate. Benjamin arranged the funding, $900,000 in a combination of gold and English pounds through the sale of 25,000 bales of cotton abroad and a drawing account on Canadian banks (and no accountability except his honor). Thompson was given the broadest possible charge in a letter from Davis on April 27:

> Confiding special trust in your zeal, discretion, and patriotism, I
> hereby direct you to proceed at once to Canada, there to
> carry out such instructions as you have received from me verbally,

in such manner as shall seem most likely to conduce the further-ance of interests of the Confederate States of America which have been instructed to you.[19]

In order to alert Slidell to his latest moves, Benjamin notified him of part of the plan in the "hope of aiding the disruption between the Eastern and Western states in the approaching election in the North. It is supposed that much good can be done by the purchase of some of the principal presses, especially in the Northwest."[20]

15

The Confederate Emancipation Proclamation

❦

The "mud truce" of the winter 1863–64 was over, and Grant began to implement his plan, which Sherman later was able to put into very few words: "He was to go for Lee and I was to go for Joe Johnston. That was his plan."

Grant moved out into the field, where he concentrated 120,000 troops to develop maximum fighting strength and firepower against his Virginia opponent. He brought "Beast" Butler up from New Orleans to join Meade. Their instructions indicated that this was not to be just another "On to Richmond" campaign. "Lee's army will be your objective point," his orders said to his generals. "Wherever Lee goes, you will go also."[1]

In the West, Sherman's orders were to "move against Johnston's army, to break it up, and to go into the interior of the enemy's country as far as he could, inflicting all the damage he could upon their war resources." Atlanta would be Sherman's objective, Richmond would be Grant's and whoever conquered first would turn to help the other toward "speedy termination."[2]

Grant's plan was to attack Lee from three sides. Lincoln characterized it as "those not skinning can hold a leg."[3]

Because of Grant's tenacity and determination to gain position, the Union army marched extensively at night, and the sky lit up with night fighting in the tangled undergrowth of the Wilderness area of Virginia. For twelve days the armies battled at Spotsylvania, until Grant decided on an all-out assault.

Six thousand Union soldiers were killed or wounded in one hour, but within weeks Grant had fresh men to replace them.

In the meantime, Grant decided to send "Little Phil" Sheridan on a cavalry raid behind the lines to Richmond, which Lee countered with the prize of the Confederate cavalry, Jeb Stuart. Stuart now rode with a banjo player at his side, because the strumming of the music and the singing stirred him to do battle. The purpose now was not to engage, however, but to avoid a confrontation. Sheridan, outnumbering Stuart by better than three to one, kept trying to draw the Confederates into a head-to-head battle, but Stuart refused to oblige him.

Eventually Stuart had to meet Sheridan in heavy hand-to-hand combat with pistols, sabers, bayonets, and fists. Jeb Stuart, in his red-lined cape and plumed hat, kept urging his men on, riding to the heat of battle, motioning with one hand and firing his silver-plated pistol in the other. "Go back, General, go back," one of his men screamed, but it was too late. Almost a year to the day after Stonewall's death, Lee lost his "eyes" and the South lost the dashing Jeb Stuart to a single gunshot fired from 30 feet away.[4]

Grant took advantage of the blindness. In eight hours, 101 pontoons were laid across a supposedly uncrossable 2,100-foot-wide point of the James River, and Grant marched his army to Petersburg, 23 miles south of Richmond, to destroy Lee's supply source.

Lee intercepted him just outside Petersburg. Through June the armies battled in the extensive trenches surrounding the city. On June 25, 1864, a division of Union miners spent one month digging a long tunnel under the Confederates lines, which they blew up on July 30 with four tons of powder, making a crater 170 feet long, 60 feet wide, and 25 feet deep. The Union soldiers, apparently as stunned by the blast as the Confederates, did not follow up vigorously. Bungling their greatest opportunity, Grant's army again and again tried various assaults, until Grant finally settled for the same strategy that eventually won him Vicksburg. The ten-month seige of Petersburg began.

When Andrew Johnson, the Governor of Tennessee, received the nomination for Vice President to run on the Lincoln ticket in 1864, it stimulated the memory of Rabbi Isaac Wise, the founder of Hebrew Union College and the leading Reform Jewish leader in the country. Wise, who was also editor of the *Israelite,* asked his literary editor,

H. M. Moos, whose former service as a guide for Federal troops in Tennessee gave him proven Union party credentials, to write a letter to Johnson about a remark Johnson had made in 1860. Johnson had been lashing out at a number of Southern senators for dividing the Union. "Mr. Benjamin, of Louisiana," he had said, "—one that understands something about the idea of dividing garments; who belongs to that tribe that parted the garments of our Savior, and for this venture cast lots—went out of this body [U.S. Senate] and was made attorney general, to show his patriotism and disinterestness."[5]

Moos wrote Johnson, "I cannot believe that you . . . could have said that Benjamin was of that cursed race which stoned the prophets and crucified the redeemer of the world &c &c, leaving an impression upon the ignorant mass, calculated to have a baleful influence on those who are already too much prejudiced against my people." Moos also complained about the remark of Governor John Brough of Ohio, who declared in a 1864 campaign speech that Benjamin was not very trustworthy because "he is a Jew by birth and a politician by trade." Moos complained that "loose and uncalled for remarks against my race . . . will deprive us in the coming election of ten thousands of votes. . . ."[6]

It was significant that Benjamin was being defended by one of the most noted Jewish journals of the day and that its editors considered anti-Semitic slurs against him to be aimed at all Jews in America, North and South. They even suggested to a probable Vice President of the United States that such remarks might cost the Lincoln ticket a substantial number of votes.

The campaign caused feelings about Jews to run high. The Hudson, New York, *Gazette* claimed that Jews were prepared to "crucify Abraham Lincoln as they had crucified the Savior."[7]

While Grant was moving on Lee at Petersburg, the red-bearded General Sherman began his pursuit of Joe Johnston and the prize of Atlanta.

Outnumbered by Sherman by 110,000 to 45,000, Johnston was true to his history, this time more than ever out of necessity. He kept retreating, hoping to catch his opponent in a mistake, postponing the battle for Atlanta as long as he could in the expectation that the longer the war went on, the stronger would grow the opposition to Lincoln in this fourth spring of fighting. Sherman stalked him, carefully forgoing the prize of Atlanta for the moment. The destruction of Johnston's army was his immediate purpose. For two months they shadow-boxed, Sherman flanking, Johnston retreating, a Union feint to the left, a Confederate step back. The Confederate army fell back as if in a giant waltz with Sherman, all the way from Tennessee, just as it had in that second year of the war when McClellan stalked Johnston back toward Richmond. During the retreat, the temper of the population of Georgia rose to a boiling point, because each place that Johnston abandoned would end up in ashes a few days later.

Johnston crossed the Chatahoochee River in front of Atlanta, destroyed the bridges, and paused to take stock. The two armies, like giant crabs measuring each other, had come three-fourths of the way to Atlanta and had still not fought a major battle. Years later, Judah Benjamin sized up Johnston crisply to Jefferson Davis: "From a close observation of his career," Benjamin wrote in 1879, "I became persuaded that his nervous dread of *losing a battle* would prevent at all times his ability to cope with an enemy of nearly equal strength, and that opportunities would thus constantly be lost."[8]

Varina's birth screams shook the White House. The President sat in the downstairs parlor waiting the delivery of the child.

The President had reason to worry deeply about her. Varina was now thirty-seven, her black hair showing traces of gray. Mourning the death of one child had sapped her energy just when she needed the strength to bear another. Davis began to pace nervously, the cries upstairs of Varina alerting him to the closeness of birth.

Suddenly the sound of a baby wailing came from the room, and a voice called for him. Varina lay in the bed, drawn and white, holding a girl in her arms as it cried softly. Davis smiled at the bundle, all red-faced and healthy, and bent down to kiss Varina.

They called the baby Varina Ann and nicknamed her "Winnie," Davis's pet name for Varina herself. Winnie would always be known as the daughter of the Confederacy. The sounds of another baby crying must have added a tragic reminder to the White House of the two sons who had died as children.

The bad news from every corner emboldened Representative Duncan Kenner of Louisiana to consider moving politically against slavery on a public front. He had been exploring with friends and with contacts in England and France ways in which the South could entice either country into the war. He felt that foreign intervention was the South's only chance now and that England was disposed to help. England, after all, had lost two wars to the United States government and wanted to see two governments on the North American continent. But England would never come into the war on the side of slavery. Since the fall of New Orleans in 1862, Kenner had concluded that emancipation was the only hope of staving off defeat.

Kenner planned to move in Congress that a special commission be sent to Europe with a proposal for the English and French governments: If they would acknowledge the Southern Confederacy, the South would abolish slavery. If the commission received a positive sign, he believed, Jefferson Davis should issue an Emancipation Proclamation, freeing the slaves at some future date. That would be followed immediately by formal recognition from Britain and France and a call by them for a sixty-day truce, and insistence on the lifting of the blockade.

Kenner agreed with Benjamin that if the Union won the war, the slaves would be free anyway, and that everything the South had been fighting for—freedom, nationhood, slavery—would be lost under the boot of Federal authorities. He wanted Davis to move immediately, to shift the moral burden of the war away from the South and onto the North, to show the world that this was not a war against slavery but a war to preserve Union wealth and dominance over the South. The bold stroke would do it, he felt. The North would be hypocritical to fight on after such a step by Davis, and if it did, England and France would not stand for it. In one instant, he said, the South could pull the rug out from under Lincoln and shift the burden of explaining the war to the North. Kenner asked for Benjamin's help. He asked Benjamin to convince the President that slavery was over anyway now—not only had England abolished it in 1833, but slavery was in retreat as an outmoded institution all over the world and could not survive no matter what the South did.

Benjamin saw that Kenner had arrived at a conclusion similar to his own and could be useful. He would be an excellent schemer in the Congress, but Benjamin had to play his cards with care. The impetus must come from the military and must not surprise the President. That would be a complicated hand to play.

Benjamin knew that neither Jefferson Davis nor the Congress would even consider emancipation unless it looked like the only way to avoid defeat. Even then, Benjamin wasn't sure that they would not rather lose the war.

It was ironic that Benjamin, who had once owned slaves, and Duncan Kenner, who had owned even more slaves until Grant conquered Louisiana, would be planning to discuss emancipation with a slaveowning President of the Confederacy. Benjamin knew that Davis would be shocked at the suggestion and worried about the desperation Kenner's introduction of such a resolution might reveal, as well as concerned with the morale of the troops should such a debate occur in the middle of the war. He also knew that Davis would dismiss Kenner as a former slaveowner with nothing more to lose. But Benjamin thought it good for the President to hear the proposal as groundwork for his own plans.

While Sherman marched on Atlanta, the Thompson mission to Canada turned into a comic opera. By August 29, 1864, Thompson had spent tens of thousands of dollars on a plan to bring thousands of copperheads to Chicago for demonstrations during the Democratic Convention. The theory propounded by Tom Hines, who had been one of Joe Morgan's Raiders, was that at least a hundred thousand peace party sympathizers would be in Chicago. They would join five hundred armed men calling for a revolution and would storm the prison, Camp Douglas, then the federal arsenal, and "by dawn" the Northern cities would be aflame. An informer notified authorities, who called for three thousand troops; Federal agents confiscated, in boxes marked "Sunday School Books," more than four thousand revolvers and 135,000 rounds of ammunition. Only twenty-five volunteers had answered the call for five hundred. Three of the Confederate planners were arrested, and Thompson had to foot the bill for round-trip tickets for several hundred "demonstrators."

In September, a Confederate soldier of fortune named John Yates Beall persuaded Thompson to try a scheme that had been rejected for at least eighteen months by Secretary of the Navy Mallory. The idea was to capture the *USS Michigan,* the only Federal gunboat patrolling the Great Lakes and—"by dawn" again—to "raze the lake shore cities," "storm the Johnson Island prison," and "capture the federal arsenal at Sandusky and start the revolution." A former Confederate cavalryman named Cole would give a dinner in honor of the captain and mates aboard the *Michigan,* serve them drugged champagne, and send up flares to signal the waiting marauders after the crew had passed out.

Beall and twenty others first seized a steamer ferrying passengers between Detroit and Sandusky. They then pulled up alongside another ferry, threw grappling hooks onto its deck, and boarded. Beall kicked open the wheelhouse and dramatically announced, "This ship is a prize of the Confederate States of America. I warn you not to resist."

The captain did not even stand up or stop smoking his pipe. Almost casually he replied, "The ship is yours." Beall put the passengers and crew ashore, towed the ferry to the middle of the lake, and scuttled it. He then awaited the flare that never came. Cole had been arrested on a tip by an informer from Beall's own ranks. The men of the raiding party, having learned that they had been found out, demanded to be put ashore on the Canadian side of the lake (Beall forced them to sign a statement saying it was their decision, not his). Once ashore, they turned the captured steamship back with no one aboard and watched it burn in the gray dawn.

Beall was later arrested for trying to wreck a passenger train and rob an express office to finance further operations. He was convicted of "guerrilla warfare against the United States Government" and hanged.[9]

Thompson and his entourage in Canada decided on more daring measures after the fizzles in Chicago and on the lakes. Under the leadership of a Bible-quoting Confederate lieutenant named Bennett Young, a handful of men (fewer than twenty) were dispatched to the sleepy town of St. Albans, Vermont, just on the other side of the Canadian border. They arrived in pairs over successive days, during which time Young spent his time discussing theology with a pretty girl he met in the town's hotel. On the agreed-upon day, they walked into the town square wearing heavy overcoats, which, once in position, they all flung off, revealing Confederate uniforms. Young announced from the steps of the hotel, "This city is now in the possession of the Confederate States of America!"

Local farmers, dozing in their wagons, thought they had not heard right. Then four horsemen, also in uniform, pranced their horses at the head of the main street and, with a wild rebel yell, dashed down the street brandishing revolvers as other horses in town reared in fright and the townsfolk scattered. The invaders robbed three banks and made off with $175,000, but not without considerable ceremony and delay. First an oath of allegiance to the Confederacy and Jefferson Davis was administered to the bank presidents and the tellers. Then the stolen bags of gold were found to be too heavy to drag out of the banks, so the booty was divided into smaller sacks. The robbers sat down with a Mr. Armington, who regularly visited the town to buy gold, and calmly negotiated a deal for their loot based on the prices quoted in the financial columns of the St. Albans *Messenger.* When the invaders' horses still could not stand up under the load across their saddles, they emptied out the less valuable silver in the street and rode to the livery stables to steal more horses.

By then the townspeople had gotten guns and had started to open fire. The stable owner aimed at Lieutenant Young and pulled the trigger three times, but each time all he got was a "click." He threw down his pistol and went back to the stable.

The Confederates tore up and down the main street tossing forty bottles of Greek fire, a phosphorus-based hand grenade, into the doorways of the hotel and the stores, and with a whoosh the street was in flames. The townspeople turned their attention to forming a bucket brigade. Then the raiders galloped out of town, split up, and eluded the St. Albans posse, which had trouble rounding up horses for the pursuit.

The headlines on a special issue of the local paper, the *Messenger,* said, "St. Albans Has Been Surprised and Excited Today." The Governor called out the militia, which crossed the border and captured Young and seven of his men. But the British garrison refused to let the prisoners be taken back to the United States. It held them for two weeks despite demands from Seward for their extradition. The Confederates were tried in Montreal in a festive, pro-Confederate atmosphere. Their lawyer sent them chilled wine and sliced chicken every day in jail in the hands of pretty sympathizers.[10]

Back in Richmond, Benjamin and the President met to discuss the Thompson mission. The President complained that because Thompson was no military man, he was merely playing spy games in Canada. St. Albans was not exactly Benjamin's idea of a "secret" service mission either, with uniforms, speeches, daylight bank robberies, and rebel yells. However, the court in Montreal was calling for signed orders from Richmond, without which Young and the others would be charged with a felony, extradited, and probably hanged.

Benjamin wrote out an indignant complaint to Thompson and entrusted it, with the required military orders, to the most reliable courier to Canada, John Surratt, "Little Johnny," so called because he was six-foot-three but could slip in and out of any place in a variety of disguises. Johnny enjoyed the secrecy and the excitement of the life of a high-level secret courier; he was familiar with all the backwaters and knew the men with rowboats, rafts, or oyster boats who for a few dollars would help. He could smuggle himself into Washington and then travel by train to Canada. He knew the Union capital and its countryside well, because he and his mother lived there in a boardinghouse that catered to Confederate sympathizers.

Little Johnny would get through. He always did.

The judge in the St. Albans trial, thanks to the evidence offered by the defense in the form of orders from the Confederate Secretary of State, ruled that the raid had been "a hostile expedition by the Confederate States against the United States" and not a felony, hence not extraditable. The raiders were rearrested for violating Canadian neutrality; in three weeks they were found not guilty and freed.

Young wrote a letter to the manager of the hotel in St. Albans asking that his regards be given to the president and teller of one of the banks. "We have heard nothing from the old gent. . . . I presume he is still faithful to the pledge and is fixed in that old armchair. If so, tell the old 'boozer' his term of sentence is now expired. . . . Please remember me to the lady next door whose good opinion I had the good fortune to win, on account of our theological proclivities. Make to her your best bow."[11]

"Let us destroy Atlanta," Sherman said, "and make it a desolation."[12]

Davis had replaced Johnston with General John B. Hood, a hard-driving bulldog who had lost an arm and a leg in battle and had to be strapped into the saddle.

But Hood could not hold off Sherman. On the night of September 2, after Hood's withdrawal toward Tennessee, enormous explosions shook the city of Atlanta as the rebels burned and exploded eighty-one carloads of ammunition and five locomotives. Fire and looting struck the abandoned city, and refugees crowded the roads leading out.

The South wanted to deny the invaders their spoils and leave Atlanta in ashes, but what was left standing, Sherman finished. Black smoke arose over the ruined city. "All the verbal descriptions of hell I have ever seen," a Union major wrote, "never gave me half so vivid an idea of it as this flame-wrapped city tonight."[13]

With Hood fleeing northward, the entire south Georgia countryside lay before Sherman's eyes, defenseless and ripe, sloping down to Savannah and the coast.

"I propose that we break up the railroad," he had written to Grant when he began, "from Chattanooga forward. . . . Until we can repopulate Georgia, it is useless for us to occupy it; but the utter destruction of its roads, houses, and people will cripple their military resources. . . . I can make Georgia howl."[14]

On November 12, William Tecumseh Sherman began his infamous March to the Sea.

The fall of Atlanta assured Lincoln's reelection and stirred Benjamin to make his move at last. Regardless of Davis's exhortations to victory, only Lee's starving army, trapped in the siege of Petersburg, stood between the misery of the present and the inevitable fall of Richmond. The oncoming winter of 1864 would bring terrible suffering to the army, more than half its men without shoes, but it was a gift of time. Benjamin calculated that the South had five months to win the war with a last-minute grand gesture.

The news was growing worse. Sherman was massing overwhelming superiority to assault Georgia all the way to Savannah. Lincoln had moved Grant to Virginia to confront Lee. It would be a painful autumn, but it was time for Benjamin to implement his plan.

Varina must have been stunned the first time she heard of it. For more than two years, the South had kept in reserve the one step that could turn the whole war upside down overnight. It would be shocking to many and stunning to the enemy, but Benjamin had come to the conclusion that this step was their only chance. He wanted the President to agree to issue a Confederate Emancipation Proclamation.

His plan consisted of two steps: First, the Confederacy would send Duncan Kenner to London with an offer to exchange emancipation for British entry. Only if the South received firm and absolute guarantees would the President issue the edict. The Senate would scream at first, but if the British came in and broke the blockade, and if Grant was forced to pull back to protect Washington from a foreign invasion, ultimately the South would come to see the President as a far-seeing leader who had saved them.

There were few things Davis and Benjamin, as leaders, could now do. The truths were no longer in their principles but on the battlefield, where it would all end if they did not act. Benjamin wanted Varina to talk to the President, to help persuade him to send Kenner to Europe in the name of the Confederacy. If the British and the French showed enthusiasm, Confederate leaders could decide their next step, based on the President's judgment of the situation.

Desertion and sickness rates were depleting Lee's army to the point where his men had to fight twice their numbers. Benjamin wanted Davis to permit slaves to fight for the South in exchange for their freedom. The key to success was getting Lee to request it.

Lee had already supported the impressment of slaves as haulers, cooks, teamsters, and blacksmiths. Fighting as soldiers was the natural next step. If Lee agreed to write a letter of support, then Varina and Benjamin would have to convince the President to back it. The President would only be doing what was right, that is, complying with the request of his best general in the field.

Without Lee, the politicians who already hated Davis would all turn on Benjamin and Davis with fresh vehemence. But if Lee agreed, the fire-eaters would find themselves outflanked, opposing a request of their best general. All Davis would have to say was, "If Lee wants it, so be it."

Varina must have seen the problem most clearly from Davis's point of view. Would the President have to make a speech in favor of emancipation? It was a shrewd question. Perhaps if it were too humiliating for Davis to speak out, that would be a problem. What is more, he was probably incapable of making the kind of speech that would carry the day. Benjamin suggested an answer.

He agreed that he, as Secretary of State, would make the presentation at an open meeting of the Congress and other interested people.

He wanted to move forward right away, sending Kenner to London. It would take at least a month for Kenner to get there, for an audience to be requested and granted, and for the British to answer—a month, if they were lucky. The blockade could make it longer, and British timidity, still longer. While the South waited for that answer, the government would proceed immediately with the debate on enlistment and emancipation.

The card player in Benjamin had learned to assess risks. If the Confederacy did nothing, the slaves would be freed anyway. The Yankees were using Negro troops against them, many of them born in the South and recently dressed in blue uniforms. They called it "liberation." The Yankees burned plantations, then took the liberated slaves and outfitted them as soldiers to burn more.

"If the enemy burn and forage corn in our route," Sherman said at the beginning of his march to the sea, "houses, barns, and cotton gins must also be burned to keep them company."[15]

Sixty-two thousand men began the march from Atlanta, singing "Glory, Glory Hallelujah" and "We'll hang Jeff Davis from a sour apple tree," with orders from Sherman to "forage liberally" among the squealing pigs, fatted hens, and stuffed corncribs in the rich Georgia countryside, so far untouched by the war because the Governor had been saving its provisions for Georgia soldiers.

It was crazy. Lee was starving because the Virginia farms were trampled, and Georgia believed in a version of states rights that kept the cornucopia to itself and demanded that Georgia boys be taken from Lee's army to defend their homes. After all, Governor Brown asked, "Isn't this a war to defend states' rights?"

Sherman's intention was clear: to visit a "devastation more or less relentless." Though the written orders asked for restraint and respect of private property, the troops were not disciplined against violations of honor. They pillaged, robbed, and burned plantations, gleefully brushing aside the mothers and daughters whose men were off fighting. When officers were not with them, parties of foragers would do worse. The only resistance to the blue marauders lay in squads of old men and young boys, roughly assembled in the hundreds as militia and easily slaughtered in the skirmishes that passed for battles in the eyes of the locals.

Twenty-five thousand slaves joined the march behind Sherman, but the general suggested to their ministers that they be sent home, not wanting to be "loaded down with useless mouths." When the army crossed a river, it burned the bridge. Hundreds of blacks drowned in the crunch of eager paraders. In Milledgeville, the state capital, the army ransacked the state house, tossing books out the window. Soldiers held a mock session "in the spirit of mischief" in the Hall of Representatives, repealing the articles of secession. Two hundred miles of railway were transformed into "Sherman's neckties"—twisted steel tracks standing in the air like bows.

Finally the Union forces reached Savannah. A soldier looked back at what they had done. "The destruction could hardly have been worse," he wrote in his diary, "if Atlanta had been a volcano in eruption and the molten lava had flowed in a stream 60 miles wide and five times as long."[16]

THE NEW YORK HERALD TRIBUNE
NOVEMBER 27, 1864

Attempt to Burn City
Discovery of Vast Rebel Conspiracy
Twelve Hotels Fired by Torpedoes and Phosphorus
Prompt Frustration of the Scheme
Arrest of Four of the Principals

The Perpetrators to be Tried by Court Martial
and Hanged Immediately
Full Development of the Plot

It was a twenty-eight-column story in the New York *Herald Tribune* that revealed the full details of the "rebel conspiracy": A small group of men had arrived in New York with suitcases containing 140 firebombs. They had rendezvoused and had set a specific time for the simultaneous burnings that they hoped would engulf the whole city. The details, the paper said, were revealed by an informer who sat in on the meetings in Toronto with Confederate Commissioner Jacob Thompson and the men involved. The paper also noted that the informer had been paid $70,000 in gold for the information.

Most of the story told of the reactions in the hotels and the dramatic events at P. T. Barnum's Museum, where elephants trumpeted, tigers roared, and a giant 7-foot woman went berserk, requiring twelve men to subdue her. When the fugitives who were not yet caught read about the plot in the paper, complete with details about themselves right down to the color of their eyes and clothes, they immediately took a train to Albany and crossed over into Canada, past dozens of police searching for them. They were eager to report the details to Thompson. The truth was that the attack was another fizzle—smoke in some hotels, less than a thousand dollars' damage in others, one big fire—just enough to make New Yorkers furious, but not enough to hurt anything.

The incident aroused nationwide speculation as to whether such widespread destruction of civilian property was now official Confederate policy, in retribution for Sherman's march.

L. Q. Washington, the private secretary to Benjamin during the war, wrote to Lawley:

I was present at the time when Mr. Thompson received his instructions from Mr. Benjamin. They were oral and largely suggestive and informal. Much was left to his discretion and wisely; for he was an experienced and conservative man. But there was not a word or a thought that looked to any violations of the rules of war, as they exist, among civilized nations. As a matter of fact, Mr. Davis, Mr. Benjamin, General Lee and the other leaders of the Confederacy believed to the last that it was not merely right, but the wisest and best policy to maintain and respect every one of the humane restrictions in the conduct of war which are upheld by the publicists.[17]

Benjamin was embarrassed and furious about the mission. The damage done, or lack of it, did not matter—after all, look what Sherman was doing in Georgia. But once more it was hideously bungled: full stories in the newspaper, lack of discretion in choosing the parties to the plot, and the selection of targets, as if hotels were military installations. The most the raid could accomplish was to create excitement, stirring up vast numbers of people against the South without destroying crucial supply depots, military trains, or arsenals to make the mission worthwhile. It made the papers without making any difference.

The President had lost his patience. He felt that Thompson was just throwing away money in Canada; there were rumors that any deserter could get a couple of thousand dollars by just saying he wanted to organize a Sons of Liberty operation somewhere.

Benjamin agreed. Thompson had asked to come home, but he was in the middle of a campaign to induce thousands of Yankees to exchange their paper for gold and to hoard it as protection against the collapse of the North. Benjamin would instruct him to see that episode through, to wrap up other activities, and to shut down as soon as he felt it was possible.

Thompson's gold plan was also meaningless and ill-conceived. He handed $100,000 out of his Confederate accounts to a Nashville banker to spend in New York in an attempt at creating a run on the gold market. Not only did the propaganda campaign fail to create panic, but it was naive to suppose such a small purchase of gold would have any impact on the market at all.

The truth was that at this stage of the war, the financial crisis lay in the empty shell of the Confederate dollar, not in the stability of Yankee greenbacks.

The Confederate spies, facing ridicule for their cavalcade of bungled operations, began to try more bizarre capers to recoup their reputations. In late December they tried to derail a train with the aim of freeing a group of high-ranking Confederate prisoners and taking them to Canada. Apparently it never occurred to them that all the captive generals and colonels could be killed in a successful derailment. Because it was snowing, the rescue group traveled in sleighs. When they reached the site chosen for the derailing, they discovered they had forgotten to bring a crowbar. Unable to pull up the tracks, they simply laid a small iron rail across them and waited in the shadows to pounce on the guards when the train jumped the tracks.

They watched the one-eyed colossus come barreling through the night. As it passed the ambush point, it merely brushed the rail aside like a toothpick and continued down the tracks. The disgusted Confederates climbed into their sleighs and returned home.

The spies, still more panicked after yet another failure, began to freelance more, with less and less control by Thompson. Two Confederates came up with the idea of kidnapping Vice President Andrew Johnson and demanding as ransom the release of all Confederate prisoners "by dawn." The Vice President was visiting Louisville, Kentucky, and the would-be kidnappers mulled over their elaborate plan: One would engage Johnson in conversation in his room about a possible job. The other would burst in through the door, left unlocked by the first man, and would get the drop on the Vice President with a pistol. The two would tie him up and gag him, place his coat over his head and shoulders, and pretend they were taking a sick friend to the hospital.

The plotters hired a closed carriage for the job but had to postpone the abduction the first night because no driver showed up. On the second night, all signs were positive. The pair stealthily crept down the hall to the Vice President's door. They knocked. Everything was perfectly planned, except that the Vice President had left for Cincinnati after lunch that day.

Lee meanwhile agreed to the "Negro enlistment" plan, but he felt that whatever had to be done should be done at once; it would take time to "organize and discipline the Negroes."[18]

Lee did not specifically mention the nature of immediate reward for the Negroes in his letter, but he did say that he could see no way of attracting the large numbers the South needed without some promise of postwar emancipation. He suggested that the government initially use 40,000 Negroes in the army as workers and not consider arming them except in dire necessity. That would give him the discretion to issue arms. If Benjamin and the President ended up advocating emancipation as a reward for service, he agreed to support them publicly during the debates.

Lee was motivated by the condition of his army. His soldiers were shivering like children in the snow—no overcoats, no shoes, living on a pint of cornmeal a day, so many weevils in it, they could barely stomach it, and an ounce of rancid bacon. The riflemen were limited to eighteen caps a day, while the Federals were getting bruised shoulders from squeezing off a hundred rounds a day. So the men scavenged for shells and metal scraps after dark, risking death, because Lee would reward them with furloughs if they were successful.

The Yankees were so close that Lee's men sometimes could smell their food cooking. Some of the boys deserted for food, a blanket, and some boots.

Lee's hair and moustache were totally gray now. Although he had aged, his face was ruddy and his eyes clear. His own diet was no more than some boiled cabbage. Each day he rode out among his troops, always an inspiration to them. They would end up fighting with sticks and stones if something were not done soon.

In November 1864, the President's annual message to the Congress contained words written by Benjamin that paved the way for the Secretary of State's proposal by advocating "a radical modification in the theory of law" that treated slaves "merely as property," subject to impressment like a horse or a wagon. The new theory, stated to the Congress, was that "the slave bears another relationship to the state—that of a person" and that "emancipation should be held out to him as a reward for faithful service."[19] That was an extraordinary change in principle, but the speech portrayed such a step as a mere extension of the law already in existence, which enabled the short-term impressment of slaves to serve as cooks, as teamsters, or for work on fortifications and in hospitals. Benjamin's "modification" would enable the government to use slaves for longer periods in more responsible positions, working as engineer laborers, constructing camps, driving and parking supply wagons—without compensating the masters.

Davis would not endorse Benjamin's entire proposition. He was adamant against "immediate manumission" or "arming the slaves for the duty of soldiers." He asserted that "until our white population prove insufficient for the armies we require and can afford to keep in the field, to employ as a soldier, the negro, who has merely been trained to labor, and as a laborer [to] the white man, accustomed from his youth to the use of firearms, would scarcely be wise or advantageous." The long-term goal, he said, was the "fulfillment of the tasks so happily begun—that of Christianizing and improving the conditions of the Africans, who have, by the will of Providence, been placed in our charge."[20]

No record exists of the crucial meeting that occurred between

Benjamin and Davis in which Benjamin laid out the details of his plan to emancipate the slaves in exchange for European intervention in the war. Kenner had expressed willingness to undertake the mission for the Confederacy. He would work through Mason and Slidell in Paris and would go to London and Paris in person for direct talks.

Davis balked. He would not agree to free them all at once, just like that, as Lincoln had. He wanted to ensure a fair and reasonable adjustment on both sides. If the British and French wanted to hear more, Benjamin could tell Kenner to say that Davis would go to Congress with a bill to let the slaves go free if they would fight for the South.

At least Kenner would have a chance.

Benjamin hurried over to Kenner's office in the Capitol with the word from the President. Kenner was to sound them out as to what effect emancipation would have—"not suddenly and all at once, but so far as to insure abolition in a fair and reasonable time."

It was, at least, a final gamble at saving the South.

16

The Speech to Free the Slaves

❀❀

In the dark days, the social set in Richmond looked forward to weddings, which provided the only genuine excuse for parties and celebration. The churches stayed open and lighted through the night to accommodate the young couples. Whatever the tomorrows would bring, no one admitted the risks or spoke of them aloud, and the weddings took on the gay colors and sounds of happier times. Parents scrimped before and after each ceremony to provide a bountiful table of fresh bread, butter, apple toddies, and wild turkeys and venison. Only for the most special occasions would a family use extra ammunition for hunting.

To newcomers to Richmond, the costumes for weddings might have appeared somewhat bizarre: At one wedding the bridesmaids wore black and the bride a gray homespun she had worn all winter long.

No wedding of the season created greater anticipation than that of the beautiful Hetty Cary to young General John Pegram. Many a beau had sought her hand, but she had finally yielded to the son of one of Richmond's finest families. Friends recalled the string of unsettling omens on her wedding day: A mirror was accidentally broken on the bride's dressing table; horses balked and refused to draw the wedding carriage; and the bride stepped on her ivory-white wedding veil and tore it as she entered Saint Paul's Church.

Hetty rode as far as Petersburg on the train for the honeymoon. Three weeks later she accompanied her husband's body back to

Saint Paul's for his funeral. This time she wore a widow's veil at the altar, standing on just the spot where she had been married.

"Old Man" Francis Blair had known every U.S. President since Andrew Jackson. Because he was one of the few common friends of Abraham Lincoln and Jefferson Davis, his letter to Davis in early January of 1865, asking for an audience "to unbosom my heart frankly and without reserve [as to] the state of affairs of our country," had to be taken seriously.[1]

The timing was bad, however. There was a solid bloc in Congress demanding some settlement, and the leaders in Georgia were virtually conducting their own negotiations. Blair's visit from Washington was a chance to regain the initiative, to tell the turntails in the Confederate Congress that Davis had talked to him and that the Yankees were still pressing unconditional surrender.

Blair was an old friend of Davis's Washington days, and Varina resolved to greet him warmly and with spirits high. Still, the Richmond *Examiner* could complain "it is impossible to conceive of any two Yankees in all the North more unlikely to have an honest errand in coming to Richmond at this day: any given couple of Hebrew blockade-runners would be much more welcome visitors."[2]

Blair's plan or, as he called it, his "suggestions," were fanciful, involving a cessation of hostilities for as long as it would take to drive Emperor Maximillian and the French out of Mexico, with an expeditionary force led by none other than Jefferson Davis: "After the Monroe Doctrine is restored to the continent, the two governments could sit down in common victory to work out a peace."[3]

Davis and Benjamin conferred alone and agreed to send Blair back to Washington with a letter saying they would send a commission to a peace conference if one were arranged. In four days, Lincoln agreed by return letter. For the first time in four years, Benjamin and the President conferred with their Vice President, who was to lead the Hampton Roads commission, Alexander Stephens of Georgia.

The prickly, dwarflike Vice President arrived in Richmond for a no-frills, down-to-earth meeting, with no mention of his troublemaking in Georgia with Governor Joseph Brown. Stephens, deeply chagrined over Sherman's march, was in no mood to object to anything that might stop the destruction at home. Davis appointed Stephens and two others known as "submissionists" to see Lincoln on a ship docked at Hampton Roads, Virginia.

After Stephens retired for the night, Benjamin and Davis conferred. Benjamin carefully drafted the instructions: "In conformity with the letter of Mr. Lincoln . . . you are requested to proceed to Washington City for a conference with him upon the subject to which the letter relates."

He slid the paper across the table for Davis to read. It was difficult to know how to instruct the commission, so Benjamin had left the wording as general as possible. Davis scribbled on the paper with his head bowed in concentration.

He handed the document back to Benjamin, who scanned it quickly: ". . . you are requested to proceed to Washington City for an informal conference with him upon the issues involved in the existing war, and for the purpose of securing peace to the *two countries.*"[4]

Benjamin surely understood what those last two words would mean to the mission, for Lincoln's letter had used the phrase, "with the view of securing peace to the people of our one common country."

Davis had scuttled the peace mission before the emissaries had even left Richmond.

Benjamin worked behind the scenes to rally support in the slave states for the idea of emancipation. To a former classmate in Charleston, he wrote in December 1864 that "for a year past I have seen that the period was fast approaching when we should be compelled to use every resource at our command for the defense of our liberties . . . it appears to me enough to say that the negrocs will certainly be made to fight against us if not armed for our defense. . . . I further agree with you that if they are to fight for our freedom, they are entitled to their own."

He was writing with uncustomary bluntness to an old and trusted friend, laying out steps to "modify and ameliorate the existing condition of that inferior race by providing for it certain rights of property, a certain degree of personal liberty, and legal protection for the marital and parental relations, as to relieve our institutions from much that is not only unjust and impolitic in itself, but calculated to draw upon us the odium and reprobation of civilized man."

He suggested a specific strategy, almost dictating a statement for his friend to place as "articles in your papers, always urging this point as the true issue, viz, is it better for the negro to fight for us or against us? The action of our people on this point will be of more value to us abroad than any diplomacy or treaty-making."[5]

Duncan Kenner made his way under an assumed name and in disguise to New York, where he was smuggled through the blockade to Paris. Mason and Slidell were waiting for him, the latter with a warm greeting for his old Louisiana friend. "I am directed to show my instructions to both of you and no one else,"[6] Kenner said formally to underscore the absolute confidentiality of his mission. Reassured of loyalty in the office, he gave his instructions to Slidell's clerk, who translated them by using the key to the Confederate code.

Mason and Slidell were both astonished at the text as Kenner unfolded the details. Mason huffed a plantation sneer, but Slidell knew from Kenner's quick reply that Benjamin meant for the instructions to be carried out to the letter. Benjamin had expected Mason to balk, and Kenner answered him matter-of-factly that if he refused to help, Mason would be immediately suspended.

The reactions from Napoleon III were predictable. The Emperor said slyly that slavery was never the issue for France anyway, but he would recognize the Confederacy if England did so.

Kenner and a grumbling Mason then returned to London and sounded out the Prime Minister. He did not waver: Under no circumstances, including Confederate emancipation, would Her Majesty's Government recognize the Confederacy. When the envoys asked a Tory leader friendly to the South to take soundings in the Parliament, he returned in a few days with the results. "The time," he said, "has gone by."[7]

Now the only question for Benjamin was what uses could be made of slaves in the trenches at Petersburg. Armed with a second letter from Lee, which went further than the first, Benjamin made a careful proposition to Davis.

"We must decide," Lee had written, "whether slavery shall be extinguished by our enemies and the slaves used against us, or use them ourselves at the risk of the effects which may be produced upon our social institutions. My own opinion is that we should employ them without delay. I believe that with proper regulation they can be made efficient soldiers."[8]

Benjamin predicted as divisive and stormy a public debate as the government had ever witnessed. For that reason, he suggested that Davis allow him to make the speech advocating the emancipation measure. That way, the President's capacity to lead would not be impaired.

Benjamin stressed the urgency of an immediate decision so that the slaves could be trained and organized. His plan was to go all out—to offer the slaves freedom in exchange for military service. The President asked for Benjamin's timetable.

According to Pierce Butler, Varina, out of sight but nearby, listened in on the crucial Cabinet meeting. "Mrs. Davis writes me (October 12, 1904) that she was an auditor in an adjoining room, when the Cabinet met . . . and that it was Benjamin who suggested and insisted on a public meeting 'to feel the pulse of the people.' "[9]

Benjamin proposed holding a mass rally at the African Church on February 9 to ask the people to sacrifice and redouble their efforts. The word would be passed ahead of time that important new government initiatives would be introduced and that the President and others would speak. In the meantime, Benjamin would leak the news of the specific proposal with the rest of General Lee's letter, so that Lee's feelings would be known before reaction set in.

His eventual performance at the African Church gives ample evidence to support the view that Benjamin must have ached for a return to the limelight. Having been cooped up in his office too long, he was itching to climb onto the center stage and hurl some lightning bolts. By God, he would give them a speech they would never forget. When it was over they would know for certain that Judah P. Benjamin was back in the thick of the public arena.

The farcical attack at St. Albans and the pursuit of the Confederates by American troops back into Canada focused unwanted attention on the Confederate spy mission in Toronto. From Benjamin's point of view, the expedition had been a diplomatic disaster, leaving aside its military inconsequence and the public ridicule it inspired.

In self-defense, the Canadian Parliament passed an Alien Act, requiring that foreigners suspected of warlike acts be heavily fined, expelled, and all arms and ships bound for them be seized. Now the Confederate spies were almost outlaws; their main achievement had been to turn a friendly government north of the Union into an anxious enemy, worried about Yankee reprisals if it harbored the Confederates beyond the reach of Union action.

Benjamin quickly took the steps on March 2, 1865, that he knew he should have taken months before. He shut down the mission and ordered Thompson to return to Virginia after making sure that all agents had the funds to escape back to the South or to other assignments that the secret service might conceive for them.

Benjamin must have sighed with relief. At least he would not be embarrassed in front of the President any more.

Benjamin would also be spared the barbs of his most caustic critic. Henry Foote had objected to the measure to compensate captors of soldiers who were absent without leave because "the Jew extortioners, the greatest nuisance on earth, would take advantage of it to make money."[10] In January Foote was arrested with his wife trying to cross the Potomac. He denied that he was merely trying to save his own hide and announced that he was on his way to Washington to sue for peace. When he was sent back, a vote to expel him from the House failed to gain two-thirds, so he promptly left again, this time for Canada, where no authorities would take him seriously. He sailed for London and drafted a thirty-page pamphlet asking his constituents to secede from the Confederacy and rejoin the Union.

The African Church, just off Capitol Square, had the largest auditorium in the city, but even it could not accommodate the more than 10,000 people who turned out for the mass meeting on February 9, 1865. The overflow crowded inside and outside the building; they sat in windows and poked their heads through the doors; two-thirds could not see or hear anything, but those peeking through windows reported to those behind them what was happening on the platform. A small posse of police, now more respectful since the government had sent Winder's "plug-uglies" to Georgia to act as prison guards, cleared a small aisle so that the speakers could reach the platform.

The meeting was scheduled for high noon, but hundreds of ladies had arrived early in the morning to get good seats. The crowd buzzed with anticipation as the bells of St. Paul's tolled the appointed hour and the procession from the Governor's mansion proceeded to the church. The Armory band occupied the choir gallery. As the speakers and dignitaries entered the hall and edged their way to the speaker's stand, the band struck up the Marseillaise Hymn.

Richmond and the "submissionists" like Vice President Stephens were shocked by the results of the Hampton Roads conference—Lincoln would not negotiate an honorable peace but would consider terms only after an unconditional surrender, when there was a restored union without slavery, meaning total submission to Federal law. He had stung Southern pride and stirred chivalrous Southern blood. Mass meetings like this one were being held all over the South, with the spirit and intensity of revival meetings.

The Reverend Moses Drury Hoge of the local Presbyterian Church opened the meeting with a prayer. Just after the "amens," a thin figure in worn gray homespun appeared in the back of the hall, walked through the doorway, and made his way down the aisle.

Jefferson Davis received a ten-minute thundering ovation with hats sailing in the air, whistles, and rebel yells. He stood quietly at the lectern acknowledging the cheering throng, the lights shifting on his feeble, stricken face.

The President, almost a specter of pain, gathered himself to make a speech of "surpassing eloquence," the best of his career, some said, drawing strength from the warm response of the crowd. He talked for more than an hour. "Old man eloquent," one reporter called him. When his health warned him he might be attempting too much and he paused, the crowd cried "go on, go on!" and he continued, in an even voice, spare of gestures.

He condemned Lincoln, "who wanted us back as a conquered people, submitting to all legislation including the abolition clause." He would have "no common country with the Yankees," for his life was "bound up with the Confederacy" and he would "live and die with it." He asked for the absentees to return to Lee's army "to teach Grant a lesson" and said that Sherman's march through Georgia "will be his last." He railed at one of Lincoln's Cabinet members for gloating over a Yankee cartoon that showed "a long procession of public men of the Confederacy moving toward the gallows to expiate the crime of 'rebellion.' " He called out to the people: "Let us unite our hands and our hearts; lock our shields together, and . . . before another summer solstice falls upon us, it will be the enemy who will be asking *us* for conferences . . . to make known *our* demands."[11]

There was a thunder of applause and cheering, again and again.

Benjamin clapped vigorously and began to revise his notes. There was a certain irony to his addressing the subject of emancipation to an almost all-white audience in a black church. In view of the speech he was about to give, he must have cringed when he heard Senator Robert Hunter of Virginia, one of the three peace commissioners, report on the Hampton Roads conference: "[I]f we go back to the bonds of the Union, we go back [with] three million slaves loosed in the midst of Southern society; we ourselves slaves, and our slaves freedmen."[12] It was not the speech he would have selected to precede his own.

Benjamin rose firmly to assume the lectern. He would mince no words today.

"The number of persons composing this meeting," he began, "and the cheers with which I hear you greet every expression of patriotic sentiment, shows the defiance with which your breasts are swelling,

and the hot flush which all feel, at the thought of the ignominy
which an arrogant government has proposed to you."[13]

He lashed out at the real meaning of Lincoln's demands, "that
you should bend the knee, bow the neck, and meekly submit to
the conqueror's yoke; and all give assurance that the fire of freedom
burns unquenchably in your souls."

He looked back at the mood of the Confederacy before the Hampton Roads conference and contrasted it with the spirit of revival
he said was sweeping the South, which now understood there was
no negotiable resolution:

> How different from one week ago! It seems an age, so magic has
> been the change. Then, despondency and hope deferred oppressed
> and weighed upon; men were querulous, and asking if it were
> true that no honorable peace were attainable except by continued
> warfare. Then, it was said it was our perverse indisposition to
> negotiate that led to the arrogance of the invader. . . .
>
> Now, cheerful voices are heard all around, and hope beams
> on every countenance. Now, the resolute and war-worn soldier
> is nerved anew. . . .
>
> What then is the cause of this change? It is the knowledge
> that has come home to the understanding and the hearts of the
> people. We now know, in the core of our hearts, that this people
> must conquer its freedom or die.

The crowd burst into cheering, and Benjamin could feel the people
moving with him.

"The people know, as one man, the path which they must tread
or perish. . . .

"What is our present duty?

"We want means. Are they in this country? If so they belong to
the country, and not to the man who chances to hold them now.
They belong either to the Yankees or to the Confederate States."

Benjamin was edging closer to the subject, but first he needed
to stoke the fires of sacrifice: "I would take every bale of cotton in
the land. I have a few bales left in my distant Southern home, which
is a free gift to my country. . . . I now ask, has any man the right
to hold a bale of cotton from his country?"

The crowd responded to the sound of his voice with a resounding
"No!"

"I say the same thing in regard to tobacco. Take all the cotton and tobacco and make it the basis of means, without which we cannot go on."

A burst of applause interrupted him again, and he became more sweeping in his demands.

"I want more. I want all the bacon—everything which can feed the soldiers—and I want it as a free gift to the country. Talk of rights! What rights do the arrogant invaders leave you!"

"Nothing," someone shouted, and the crowd bubbled with anger at the mention of the Yankees.

"I want one other thing. War is a game that cannot be played without men."

The crowd cheered wildly at the mention of the soldiers. With their minds focused on them, Benjamin expanded on that theme:

"Where are the men? I am going to open my whole heart to you. Look to the trenches below Richmond. Is it not a shame that men who have sacrificed all in our defense should not be reinforced by all the means in our power? Is it any time now for antiquated patriotism to argue a refusal to send them aid, be it white or black?"

Someone caught his meaning and shouted from the audience, "Put in the niggers." The crowd cheered him hoarsely. Benjamin painted in the picture with the facts, to show the odds against them.

"I will now call your attention to some figures, which I wish you to seriously ponder. In 1860 the South had 1,664,000 arms-bearing men. How many men have the Yankees sent against us? In 1861, 654,000; in 1862, 740,000; in 1863, 700,000; in 1864 they called out 1,500,000. Here you have figures that they brought out 3,000,000 men against 1,644,000 Confederates, who lived at the beginning of the war to draw sword in their country's service."

His voice was rising, and he wanted to point the figures in the direction of the slaves.

"Our resources of white population have greatly diminished; but you had 680,000 black men of the same ages; and could Divine prophecy have told us of the fierceness of the enemy's death grapple at our throats—could we have known what we now know, that Lincoln has confessed, that without 200,000 Negroes which he stole from us, he would be compelled to give up the contest, should we have entertained any doubts upon the subject?"

"We will make him give it up yet," another voice shouted from the audience at the mention of Lincoln's name.

Benjamin seized the issue by the throat and asserted flatly that the slaves should be emancipated and armed to fight.

"Let us say to every Negro who wishes to go into the ranks on condition of being made free—'Go and fight; you are free.' If we impress them, they will go against us. We know that everyone who could fight for his freedom has had no chance. The only side that has had the advantage of this element is the Yankee—a people that can beat us to the end of the year in making bargains. Let us imitate them in this. I would imitate them in nothing else."

Some of the crowd suddenly shifted on him, and he was caught in a cacophony of conflicting sounds: "No! Never!" one man shouted, and others took up the cry of fury, like a giant growling beast.

Benjamin charged on to override the hatred in the hall, to play to the applause and the support he was getting from the rest of the audience. Being attacked personally, he reacted personally.

"My own negroes have been to me and said: 'Master, set us free, and we will fight for you; we had rather fight for you than for the Yankees.' But suppose it should not be so—there is no harm in trying."

Someone shouted again, "Send in the slaves." Benjamin sensed the crowd shifting back to him and against those yelling epithets at him. He continued to emphasize his own support of slavery, his ownership of slaves and his respect for state sovereignty on the issue.

"With all my early attachments and prejudices, I would give it all up. It can only be done by the States separately."

Feeling the need to involve the audience with him, he took up a sequence of rhetorical questions to bring them to his position.

"What states will lead off in this thing?"

A voice cried out, "Virginia," and the crowd cheered in answer.

Benjamin picked up on the reply: "South Carolina, I know, will follow Virginia, as well as every other Southern state, if she but gives the lead.

"When shall it be done?" he asked.

Voices filled the hall with the response, "Now," and Benjamin could feel himself carrying the day. He needed to show them the way to action.

"Now," he echoed. "Let your legislature pass the necessary laws, and we will soon have twenty thousand men down in those trenches fighting for the country. You must make up your minds to try that, or see your army withdrawn from before your town. I came here to say disagreeable things. I tell you, you are in danger unless some radical measures are taken."[14]

Varina wrote, "Never was he more eloquent or inspiring than when . . . Mr. Benjamin made a speech to the people in the African Church which was thronged with officers and men who had ridden in from the front to hear what had happened. He sent those who had come discouraged and desperate knowing as they did the overwhelming forces which confronted them back to camp full of hope and ardour, and I think made the most successful effort of his life."[15]

J. B. Jones recorded in his diary: "There is much excitement among the slaveowners, caused by Mr. B.'s speech. They must either fight themselves or let the slaves fight." A series of resolutions were introduced in the Confederate Congress that "the views of Secretary Benjamin [were] derogatory to his position as a high public functionary of the Confederate Government . . . and an insult to public opinion." But the resolutions were tabled.[16]

Benjamin had achieved his purpose. He had advocated a radical position in front of Virginia's Governor "Extra Billy" Smith and dozens of members of the Virginia Legislature and the Confederate Congress. If they could see this large a crowd accepting the message that Benjamin had laid out without being tarred and feathered or booed off the stage, perhaps they would have the courage to respond to Lee's needs and give him the black troops he required. Nothing less could save Petersburg. And Richmond.

Buoyed by the reaction to his speech, Benjamin wrote two days later directly to Robert E. Lee that "you may perhaps have seen at the public meeting Thursday I spoke of the necessity of instant reinforcement for your army. In order to disarm opposition as far as possible and to produce prompt action, I proposed that those slaves only who might volunteer to fight for their freedom should be at once sent to the trenches . . . some of the opponents of the measure are producing a strong impression against it by asserting it would disband the army by reason of the violent aversion of troops to have Negroes in the field with them. . . . If we could get from the army an expression of its desire to be reinforced by such Negroes as for the boon of freedom will volunteer to go to the front, the measure will pass without further delay. . . . If this suggestion meets your approval, the different divisions ought at once to make themselves heard, and there will be no further effective opposition in any of our legislative bodies, State or Confederate."[17]

Davis was making use of Benjamin for another of his most unpleasant tasks. It had been evident for some years that Benjamin was not so committed on slavery that he could not abandon it in favor of what he considered to be the higher purpose of winning the war.

Davis must have thought that men like Benjamin, who always searched for the common ground, essentially favored expediency over principle. When the issue was whether to seek a negotiated surrender or fight to the end, the President was always more focused on honor than result. And it was not the honor of rationality based on reality, which would lead to saving lives or stopping needless bloodshed when the end was near; it was the honor of the proud soldier, ready to sacrifice all, make the last stand, and keep faith with those who had fought and died for the cause.

But Benjamin was ever the pragmatist, as lawyers have to be, and when a lawyer cannot win in the courtroom he looks for a settlement in order to obtain the best result for his client. He was the only person around Davis trying to sort out the options for a dying dream.

The President's four-year muzzle on the talented voice of Judah Benjamin was not a policy applied to other members of the Cabinet. They defended policy publicly; Benjamin rarely did so. Benjamin seemed to be aware of Davis's jealousy of any around him who received public acclaim. For him, the President's trust was more important than anything else. Policy statements by Benjamin, as a public personage known to be close to the President and speaking in the President's name, would have risked stirring up bitterness without winning adherents to his point of view.

But at that point Davis suddenly needed Benjamin as a public figure, a man to float the trial balloon of a controversial proposal in order to reassure General Lee's supporters that the President was behind him and yet allow him to keep his distance himself from the proposal just enough to be protected from the diehard wing of the Senate. Benjamin had been involved in the question of Confederate emancipation for several years, playing a dangerous game of manipulation of the President and of the political forces in the country. He had counseled outsiders, recruited adherents, and planted stories as he had never done on any other issue, especially one with so much domestic volatility. He came to believe that Confederate emancipation was the single action that could win the war. He was therefore willing to risk his safety by becoming its most persuasive advocate, knowing that it was up to him to make the proposal if the idea was to have any chance at all.

The Confederate sympathizers who gathered at Mary Surratt's boarding house in Washington found a warm camaraderie with each other, and agents from Canada, such as Lewis Powell and David Herold, met there often. Little Johnny Surratt often met with them, carrying the gold pieces he had picked up from Secretary of State Benjamin's office for delivering messages from Canada.

But tonight two other men were joining them: George Atzerodt, a friend of Surratt who ran a ferry boat service down on the Maryland peninsula over to Virginia, which Surratt and other couriers often used, and an out-of-work actor named John Wilkes Booth, who had recently returned from Canada, where he had performed in a number of plays. The conversation turned to guerrillas like Quantrell and Mosby in the Virginia valley and John Morgan's raiders in Ohio, men who hid and struck and then retreated only to strike again. Booth, inspired by the Kentucky kidnapping plot that had failed earlier, had dreamed up a lunatic scheme of his own. He knew that Lincoln often went to the Soldier's Home to rest and at those times was rarely guarded. Booth thought it would be a good idea to kidnap the President.

The group agreed, and for several weeks they tested disguises. Booth seemed to have the whole operation figured out: kidnap Lincoln, take him on George Atzerodt's boat across into Virginia, follow Johnny's route back to Richmond, where Lincoln would be held hostage for all the Confederate prisoners in the North—all the veterans held in prison from Jackson's Foot Cavalry, Lee's rout at Fredericksburg, and the Tennessee campaigns. Booth envisioned that he and his comrades would be heroes, all of them heralded by history for winning the war with one bold, singular stroke.

Weeks later, the conspirators hid by a road for hours waiting for the gold-inlaid carriage drawn by a single horse. When they saw it, curtains drawn across the windows, they couldn't believe their luck— no guards! How easy could it be?

They pulled their pistols, spurred their horses, bounded out into the road, to surround the carriage. One of them opened its door in breathless anticipation and saw—Chief Justice Salmon Chase, out for a ride in the President's carriage. They slammed the door, jumped on their horses, dashed away cursing, and returned in anger to the boarding house. It was as if any plans hatched among anyone who had been in Canada were doomed to a comic outcome.

"If we are right in passing this measure," Robert M. T. Hunter of Virginia argued to the Senate a few days after Benjamin's speech, "we were wrong in denying the old government the right to interfere with the institution of slavery and to emancipate slaves."[18]

Howell Cobb, the former Governor of Georgia, wrote from Georgia: "Use all the Negroes you can get, for the purpose for which you need—but don't arm them. The day you make soldiers out of them is the beginning of the end of the revolution. If slaves will make good soldiers our whole theory of slavery is wrong."[19]

Robert Toombs also wrote from his Georgia plantation, even in the face of Sherman, that "the worst calamity that could befall us would be to gain our independence by the valor of our slaves. . . . The day that the army of Virginia allows a Negro regiment to enter their lines as soldiers they will be degraded, ruined and disgraced."[20]

On the streets of Richmond, the people said, "If the Negro was fit to be a soldier, he was not fit to be a slave."

In just four days, the Senate gave Davis and Benjamin their answers. The Senators were divided on a resolution that stated: "Judah P. Benjamin is not a wise and prudent Secretary of State and lacks the confidence of the country."[21] A week later, Benjamin sat down to compose a letter offering his resignation to the President. He held it for a few days and then, after watching the furor grow in intensity, sent it to the President's office.

Department of State
Richmond 21 February 1865

Confidential

My Dear Sir

I have been recently disturbed in mind on a subject which I can no longer refrain from placing frankly before you.

It is unnecessary to remind you that I accepted office with reluctance and have retained it solely from a sense of duty. Separated from my family for nearly five years past, my eager desire to see them has been repressed by the belief that my services were not without value to you. . . .

For some months past, however, I have doubted whether my withdrawal from office would not rather promote the success of your administration than deprive you of useful assistance. It has been apparent that I have been the object of concerted and incessant assault by those who are inimical to me personally, as well as by all in Congress and the press that are hostile to you. . . . If our affairs were in a more prosperous condition, I should tender my resignation unconditionally. But in the present juncture I shrink from giving Color for an instant to the suspicion of a desire to shield myself from danger or responsibility by abandonment of duty.

I must therefore beg you to let me know your own conclusion with entire unreserve. Will your administration be strengthened or any opposition to it disarmed by substituting another in my place in the Cabinet? If so, I will at once seek to return to your assistance in the Legislative Department of the Government, in which I know I can be serviceable in sustaining you in this great struggle. If not, I shall cheerfully continue the sacrifice of private inclination and family affection to the call of duty, at all hazards, and under all responsibilities—

I am with entire regard and respect

Your friend and obedient servant,
Judah P. Benjamin[22]

There was every reason for Davis to accept his resignation. Foreign affairs, after all, Benjamin's main responsibility in the Cabinet, had ceased to be relevant. Davis needed the cooperation of elements inside the Congress who hated Benjamin and would be relieved if the President were to dismiss his controversial Secretary. Lastly, Davis knew that Benjamin would stay anyway as an adviser if the President asked him to, even without the title. Benjamin had written the letter because of the resolution; the Senate had given him no other option. The truth was that he could see no real reason for the President to keep him except that they had come so far together, like two soldiers in the same foxhole. Besides, lately he could never really predict what the President might do on a given day—he could be meek one minute, explosive the next, and vacant a minute after that. Benjamin was reconciled to whatever the decision might be, based on the President's mood of the moment.

Davis quickly turned aside the letter and the Senate resolution. He would stand by his friends and loyal colleagues, and he needed Benjamin to get him through this wilderness. They shook hands to renew their bond. Then Davis launched into the business at hand.

Davis did not like losing on something Lee wanted. It would be disloyal to rebuff his greatest general, so they would fight for the enlistment bill and give Lee the black soldiers he needed to hold on in Petersburg. If he could not beat the Georgia trio of Stephens, Cobb, and Toombs, when the state was already out of the fighting while Virginia was facing life and death, then he just did not know politics any more. If the Union could use Negro troops for subjugation, then the South could use them for self-defense.

For two more weeks the Congress wrangled over the Negro enlistment bill. Finally, in early March, the Congress passed it. It fell far short of Benjamin's hopes: The slaves had to be volunteers "patriotically rendered by their masters"; the President could receive only one-fourth of the male slaves between eighteen and forty-five years old from a single state; and though they were to get equal pay and rations, there was no mention of emancipation in the final bill.[23]

Only a handful of blacks straggled into Capitol Square a few weeks later. Benjamin watched from the window as they marched in a drill ceremony. Some were in new uniforms—a strange sight even for whites these days—and small boys jeered and splashed mud and threw rocks at them as they paraded. Like so many steps Benjamin had tried, this idea had collapsed, too.

17

Escape

✖✖✖

G rant had been poking at Lee's lines outside Petersburg for weeks. The news from there was growing more ominous. The railroad stations in Richmond were crowded again with the wealthy and the powerful, as even members of Congress were beginning to abandon the city.

The President ordered Varina to take the children south with as little public stir as possible. He might be moving his headquarters to the field, he said, and his family's presence would "embarrass and grieve me instead of giving comfort." Varina begged him to let her stay, but he would not hear of it. "You can do this but one way," he said, "by going yourself and taking the children to a place of safety. If I live, you can come to me when the struggle is ended."[1]

Varina acquiesced, then began to worry about their silver and other valuables. The President refused to let her burden their friends with the silver for fear that Yankees might discover and harm whoever was hiding it. Instead, they sent it out to auction. When she asked the servants to take two barrels of flour with them to help withstand a possible siege, the President told her that "you can't take anything in the shape of food from here." With flour at $1,500 a barrel, he would not have his own family "acting like hoarders."[2]

To her shock, he then handed her a small Colt pistol, gave her cartridges, and showed her how to load and fire it. "You can at least," he said, "if reduced to the last extremity, force your assailants to kill you."[3]

"Grant has the bear by the hind legs while Sherman takes off the hide,"[4] Lincoln said as Sherman's avenging demons turned from Georgia and headed north to South Carolina.

Sherman's army relished this moment, because South Carolina had been the first state to secede. "Having sown the wind, she shall reap the whirlwind,"[5] one infantryman wrote home. Wisconsin soldiers ran past blazing buildings yelling, "This is the nest where the first secession egg was hatched—let her burn!"[6]

The Sherman legend had spread all over the South, for he had achieved his purpose: Darken the day with black smoke, show no mercy, and there will be panic in your path. The Southern "bummers" would often loot some little hamlet, beating him to the booty before he arrived. Anarchy had broken out to do his bidding for him. In Sherman's words, casual and jocular, "Make a smoke like Indians do on the plains. . . . I hope you will burn all cotton and save us the trouble."[7] So the veterans sang as they marched right through the inpenetrable swamps to the state capital:

> Hail, Columbia, happy land
> If I don't burn you, I'll be damned.[8]

And burn they did, 84 of the state capital's 124 blocks, some of them with the help of Southern loyalists, who were burning just ahead of the soldiers to keep supplies out of Sherman's hands. It was as mighty a conflagration as the South had seen, as Sherman's troops, drunk from an afternoon of consuming confiscated liquor, joined with the local population to make good on their pledge to the frightened people who had surrendered under a white flag: "You'll catch hell tonight."

After Columbia, Sherman ordered his army north, heading for Richmond to join his army of 60,000 men with Grant's 110,000 for the final conquest. Lee, having been confirmed as general-in-chief by the Congress, called General Joe Johnston out of retirement to lead the scattered Confederate army in the North Carolina Piedmont area. There was no more fantasy in Richmond: The South was now staring into the burning fires of hell.

"I mean to end this business here," Grant wrote in late March as he spread his men along a 53-mile front so that Lee's line protecting Petersburg, in Lee's own words, would be "stretched until it has broken."[9] Assaults on both ends of the line left the middle vulnerable, and Grant stormed it along a 12-mile front, 60,000 Federals against fewer than 15,000 Confederates. The ten-month seige at Petersburg ended. On a Sunday morning, after dawn, as shells were bursting all around him tearing the guts out of horses and men, Lee could see the blueclads several hundred yards away. He ordered a quick retreat toward Appomattox and hurried off wires to Richmond telling the President and the Secretary of War that the capital city was now endangered and should be evacuated by nightfall. Petersburg gone and Richmond abandoned—Lee's only worry now was the survival of his army.

At 10:40 A.M. on Sunday, April 2, Secretary of War Seddon received the wire from General Lee advising the evacuation of Richmond. A messenger rushed to St. Paul's Church, where the President was occupying his usual pew, and gave him a sealed envelope. Davis rose and unsteadily made his way up the aisle as uneasy whispers rippled through the congregation.

As word spread through the city, groups gathered at street corners, children ran about with the news, and then, like animals before a brush fire, the evacuation of Richmond began.

Judah P. Benjamin rushed to his office to destroy all secret corre-spondence. With his clerks, he packed documents all day, making ready to leave in the early evening with the rest of the Cabinet on the train that was taking the government to Danville, Virginia.

The French Consul, Alfred Paul, was summoned to Secretary of State Benjamin's office at 2:00 P.M. on April 2 for a handshake of farewell, since he had helped Benjamin to stay in touch with Natalie during the war.

"I found him extremely agitated," Paul later reported to the Foreign Ministry in Paris, "his hands shaking, wanting and trying to do and say everything at once. He was preparing to leave at five o'clock with the President and his other colleagues. . . .

"Mr. Benjamin said to me in a trembling voice, 'I have nothing in particular to say to you, but I wanted to be sure to shake your hand before my departure. We are going to Danville. I hope that the railroad will not have been captured at the Burkeville Junction and that we will be able to pass through. General Lee insists on the immediate evacuation of the city by the government. It is simply a measure of prudence. I hope that we will return in a few weeks.'

" 'Really?' I cried, carefully watching Mr. Benjamin to try to discern if he was motivated by a persisting illusion or by a lack of sincerity, two things which characterize this statesman. 'Do you think you will be able to return?' "

Benjamin, keeping up pretenses, told Paul he was not "sure" the army would evacuate that night. But Paul wrote that "all well-informed people had been sure for an hour. . . . Mr. Benjamin is a very reticent man."[10]

Benjamin had already been preparing for this emergency by sending his clerk southward to Charlotte, North Carolina, several days earlier with trunks, other baggage, and six boxes of State Department papers. He was not alone in such preparation; for several weeks, others in the government, forseeing an evacuation, had been packing to move south. On April 1, Benjamin and other officials were issued treasury warrants; Benjamin's funds were issued from the Secret Service account for $1,500 in gold.

Judah P. Benjamin was thus being far-sighted, looking beyond the immediate departure from Richmond. He was making sure that he had options no matter what dark events lay beyond the horizon, and one of those options would surely be the possibility of having to flee alone.

The excited crowds passed, the men carrying what baggage they could; the women and children also loaded with such goods as they could snatch from the burning factories and stores being looted by the frenzied mob.

Elizabeth Van Lew, her disguise as "Crazy Bet" now made unnecessary by her invitation to General Grant to have tea (an invitation he would accept), wrote: "The constant explosion of shells, the blowing up of gunboats, and of the powder magazine, seemed to jar, to shake the earth and lend a mighty language to the scene. All nature trembled at the work of arbitrary powers, the consummation of the wrong of years . . . the burning bridges, the roaring flames added to the wild grandeur of the scene."[11]

Sallie Ann Brock Putnam, a friend of Varina, described in her diary that day on which "thousands of citizens determined to evacuate the city with the government. Vehicles commanded any price in any currency possessed by the individual desiring to escape from the doomed capital. The streets were filled with excited crowds hurrying to the different avenues for transportation, inter-mingled with the porters carrying huge loads, and wagons piled up with incongruous heaps of baggage, of all sorts and descriptions. The banks were all open and depositors were busily and anxiously collecting their specie deposits, and directors were busily engaged in getting off their bullion. Millions of dollars in paper money, both State and Confederate, were carried to the Capitol Square and burned."[12]

John M. Daniel, who had predicted the collapse of the Confederacy, died three days before it occurred. His brother wrote later: "The *Examiner* shared the fate of the Confederacy . . . it was destroyed in the conflagration of Richmond . . . and the last number of the *Examiner* printed on the day preceding the evacuation of Richmond, contained the announcement of his death."[13]

The President ordered the mansion spotlessly cleaned, cleared his desk neatly of its remaining items, then rode with dignity, head high and eyes forward, on his horse, Kentucky, through this scene of chaos, panic, and random fires and looting. "Night came on . . . confusion worse confounded reigned, and grim terror spread in wild contagion."[14]

Davis had given special instructions to the Treasury Department to box up all the gold and silver on hand—coins, bricks, ingots, even Mexican silver, about $528,000 worth—and place it aboard a special train to be guarded by sixty midshipmen from the academy training vessel, which had been scuttled with all other vessels on the James River.

The two trains, one with the gold and the other bearing the President and the Cabinet, pulled out at midnight. Diaries described hearing the train blow its whistle with a mournful sound of sorrow that some would remember the rest of their lives. When it had passed the bridge over the James River, the people watching saw the bridge burst into flames as the Confederate army tried to seal off the train from hot pursuit. Then the arsenal exploded with an earthshaking blast, and suddenly it was calm.

It was a clear April night in Virginia, and the stars were so close that the black waters of the river sparkled with their light. But few slept or could sleep. Families guarded their own worldly goods from looters, and the wagons continued to roll out of the city. Torturously, the night passed, as Richmond awaited the arrival of the Union army.

A trip ordinarily a few hours long took more than sixteen, with crowds standing along the tracks through the night hoping for the President to pause and address them.

Navy Secretary Mallory, depressed by the frantic turn of events, commented that Benjamin's "dark complexion had become a shade darker within the last twenty-four hours." He described Benjamin's confident spirit, writing that his "Epicurean philosophy was ever at command . . . with a 'never-give-up-the-ship' sort of air, he referred to other great national causes which had been redeemed from far gloomier reverses than ours."[15] He had brought Jules with him for the trip to an unknown destiny, and assuring his safety was one more problem to deal with.

But no amount of brave talk among the officials on the train could hide the truth from the people gathered at each stop. The Confederate government was now in flight. Tonight its capital was Danville. Soon, it would be on the tracks heading south.

Once in Danville, Benjamin was offered a room at the house of a friend of Dr. Moses Drury Hoge, the minister of Richmond's Presbyterian Church, who personally had shepherded more than 300,000 Bibles from England through the blockade. There is no report of Jules's presence, so presumably other arrangements were made.

Hoge reported that he and Benjamin had had a friendly argument about the place Tennyson would occupy in history. Benjamin was a "passionate admirer of Tennyson," Hoge said, and ranked him above all English poets, "Shakespeare, of course, excepted." When Hoge suggested that Tennyson "had never written anything comparable to *Comus,* or *Il Penseroso,* or *L'Allegro* or to Dryden"—Benjamin was always ready with a reference to some passage of Tennyson to refute Hoge's assertions. Hoge was amazed that Benjamin seemed to be "as familiar with literature as with law." Among public men he could not recall one who was a "more accomplished belles lettres scholar."[16]

While Benjamin awoke the next morning to a good breakfast and a proud reception at Danville, Richmond trembled at the arrival of the Union troops.

A woman who wished to remain anonymous wrote to a friend the story of the morning after the government's departure from Richmond:

"All was commotion in the street and agitation in the hotel. The city government had dragged hogsheads of liquor from the shops, knocked in their heads, and poured the spirits in the gutters. They ran with brandy, whiskey and rum and men, women, and boys rushed out with buckets, pails, pitchers and in the lower streets, hats and boots to be filled. Before eight o'clock, many public buildings were in flames, and a great conflagration was evidently imminent. The flames swept up Main Street where the stores quickly burned, and then roared down the side streets almost to Franklin.

"The doors of all the government bakeries were thrown open and food was given to all who asked it. Women and children walked in and helped themselves."[17]

Nellie Grey did not flee. She wrote about the next morning: "Exactly at eight o'clock the Confederate Flag that fluttered above the Capitol came down and the Stars and Stripes were run up. We knew what that meant! The song 'On to Richmond!' was ended—Richmond was in the hands of the Federals. We covered our faces and cried aloud. All through the house was the sound of sobbing. It was the house of mourning, the house of death.

"Soon the streets were full of Federal troops, marching quietly along. The beautiful sunlight flashed back everywhere from Yankee bayonets. I saw Negroes run out into the street and falling on their knees before the invaders to hail them as their deliverers, embracing the knees of the horses, and almost preventing the troops from moving ahead."[18]

Another eyewitness took up the story: "Through throngs of sullen spectators; along the line of fire; in the midst of the horrors of a conflagration, increased by the explosion of shells left by the retreating army; through the curtains of smoke; through the vast aerial auditorium convulsed with the commotion of frightful sounds, moved the garish procession of the Grand Army, with brave music, and bright banners and wild cheers. A regiment of Negro cavalry swept by the hotel. As they turned the street corner they drew their sabers with savage shouts, and the blood mounted even in my woman's heart with quick throbs of defiance."[19]

The story continued: "Drunken men shouted and reeled through the streets, a black cloud from the burning city hung like a pall over us, a black sea of faces . . . from the ten thousand Negro troops . . . cheered by the Negroes on the streets."

Against the warnings of Seward and the misgivings of Admiral Porter, who accompanied him, Abraham Lincoln himself arrived by ship in Richmond.[20] When he stepped on the wharf, a dozen joyous Negroes flung themselves at his feet, one white-haired old man exclaiming, "Bless the Lord, the great Messiah!" Lincoln, embarrassed but controlled, replied "Don't kneel to me. That is not right. You must kneel to God only, and thank Him for the liberty you will enjoy hereafter."[21] They rose and answered with the hymn, "All Ye People, Clap Yo' Hands." Lincoln waited before proceeding on the 2-mile walk to the Davis mansion.

Blacks and whites draped over the limbs of trees and lined the streets to watch this tall stringbean of a man, taller in his stovepipe, stride through Richmond. He swept without pause into the mansion and across Varina's beautiful blue rug to the presidential desk and slipped wearily into his rival's chair. "I wonder if I could get a glass of water?" he asked.[22]

After lunch, he climbed into a carriage and with a squad of two dozen soldiers toured the city.

"About four in the afternoon," a Southern woman wrote to her daughter, "a salute of thirty-four guns was fired. A company of mounted dragoons advanced up the street, escorting an open carriage drawn by four horses in which Mr. Lincoln sat and a naval officer, followed by an escort of cavalry. They drove straight to Mr. Davis's house, cheered all the way by Negroes, and returned the way they came. I had a good look at Mr. Lincoln. He seemed tired and old— and I must say, with due respect to the President of the United States, I thought him to be the ugliest man I had ever seen."[23]

A general turned to Lincoln and asked how he should treat the people of the city. "If I were in your place," he answered, "I'd let 'em up easy; let 'em up easy."[24]

In Danville for a few days, Benjamin turned himself into an ideal house guest. He was never late for morning prayers and arranged his retiring for the night and rising to cause the least inconvenience to his hosts. He even attended Sunday church services with the family instead of staying at home or choosing to accompany Jefferson Davis and the Cabinet to religious services.

On April 5 he climbed the rickety stairs of the Danville *Register* and personally delivered to its editor a proclamation written in the President's name after a long Cabinet meeting. The editor reported that Benjamin showed no anxiety and that the proclamation was written by Benjamin on very poor quality paper. However eloquently phrased, its ideas were pure Jefferson Davis:

We have now entered a new phase of a struggle the memory of which is to endure for all ages. . . . Relieved from the necessity of guarding cities and particular points, important but not vital to your defense, with an army free to move from point to point and strike in detail detachments and garrisons of the enemy, operating on the interior of our own country, where supplies are more accessible, and where the foe will be far removed from his own base and cut off from all succor in case of reverses, nothing is now needed to render our triumph certain but the exhibition of our own unquenchable resolve. Let us but will it, and we are free.[25]

Lee's retreat from Petersburg west toward the Appomattox Court-house turned into a race between Grant and starvation. The siege had stripped the countryside surrounding Petersburg of all foodstuffs, and the provisions Lee had ordered from Richmond never came, for his message requesting them had arrived after the last trains had departed going South and the storehouses had been sacked.

For three days, without food, his scarecrow army of 20,000 men dwindling daily through exhaustion, collapse, and desertion, Lee maneuvered against the inevitable. When a bedraggled North Carolina straggler was accosted by a Federal soldier and ordered to throw down his rifle, he cursed and said, "You've got me and a helluva git you got."

On April 9, Palm Sunday, Lee asked Grant for an "interview" to discuss "the surrender of this army." Before dawn he rose and slipped into a clean new gray uniform, a pressed white shirt, and freshly shined boots and tied a red sash around his waist to which he buckled an ornate sword and scabbard. With his glittering gold buttons and silver beard, he looked so splendid that an aide expressed astonishment. He answered, "I have probably to be General Grant's prisoner, and I thought I must make my best appearance."[26]

Grant arrived in muddied boots, splattered trousers, and rumpled uniform. On seeing his foe, he immediately apologized for his dress and explained that his baggage had been misplaced. Lee excused him: "I am very glad you did it that way."

Grant's terms, considering his reputation, were generous: the laying down of their arms, paroles based on pledges not to take up arms against the Government, and, at Lee's request, permission for those who owned horses and mules to return to their farms with them. In addition, Grant sent rations for 25,000 to the Confederates.

Lee rode back through his men, who were lined up to receive him with cheers and sporadic rebel yells despite their weariness and hunger, hands reaching out to touch him and touch Traveller, muttering, "I love you just as well as ever, General Lee." The news spread, and the roads were packed with troops, some with caps off and heads bowed, hands reaching and passing gently over Traveller's flanks, some too choked to speak, others saying "Goodbye" and "God bless you, General," while Lee rode with tears trickling into his beard, his hat off and his body erect, looking neither left nor right.

On April 12, the day set for formal surrender, the Confederate Army of Northern Virginia marched onto the field in front of the Appomattox Courthouse and "by divisions and parts of divisions deployed into line, stacked their arms, folded their colors, and walked empty handed to find their distant, blighted homes."

The news of Lee's surrender struck the Cabinet and especially Judah P. Benjamin with devastating impact. Benjamin returned to the home of his hosts in Danville and after a cheerful greeting, because ladies were present, he summoned Dr. Hoge to a room upstairs.

Hoge wrote Lawley about that moment, when Benjamin said to him, "I did not have the heart to tell those good ladies what I have just learned. General Lee has surrendered and I fear the Confederate cause is lost."[27]

Hoge asked him what he would do, and he replied that he would accompany the Cabinet to Greensboro. How would he escape capture, traveling with a group of top Confederate officials?

"I will never forget the expression of his countenance or the pitiless smile which accompanied his words when he said, 'I'll never be taken alive.' "[28]

Butler in his Benjamin biography felt it necessary to add: "Since various stories of theatrical effect, hinting at suicide by pistol (this more in keeping with the Mephistophelian or Borgian character ascribed to him at the North) [or] the concealed poison of a ring, have been circulated, it may be well to add that Dr. Hoge distinctly states there was no such puerility in his calm statement of his determination."[29]

With Lee's surrender, Davis ordered the Government and its treasure train to move southward to Greensboro, where he convened a council of war of the Cabinet with Generals Beauregard and Johnston. The generals had been summoned from the field, where they were outnumbered 350,000 to 25,000, to discuss what they thought was termination, but the President babbled as if in a mad dream about raising a large army of deserters and conscripting men who had previously escaped the draft. The generals pointed out that men who desert when times are difficult do not return when times are critical. The meeting broke up for a day until a complete report could be obtained of the details of Lee's surrender.

The next morning, knowing the details of Lee's laying down of arms, Johnston pressed his case: "My views are, sir, that our people are tired of war, feel themselves whipped and will not fight. . . . My men are daily deserting in large numbers. Since Lee's defeat they regard the war as at an end."[30] He declared there was no choice but total surrender.

Benjamin was the only Cabinet member to support the President in his foolhardy determination to continue the fighting. General Joe Johnston reported that Benjamin "made a speech for war much like that of Sempronius in Addison's play."[31] The speech Johnston referred to reads:

> *My voice is still for war*
> *Gods! can a Roman senate long debate*
> *Which of the two to choose, slavery or death!*
> *No, let us arise at once, gird our swords,*
> *And, at the head of our remaining troops,*
> *Attack the foe, break through the thick array*
> *Of his thronged legions and charge home upon him.*

It must have seemed an astounding performance to the Cabinet; to make such a speech in front of Beauregard and Johnston, especially when they would have to do the fighting, must have struck them as the height of grandiosity and self-delusion. What is more, it did not, as we know from his earlier conversation with Hoge, represent Benjamin's own view of the situation. It can be explained only in terms of loyalty to the President. Perhaps he feared the effect of isolation on Davis at that moment or felt that the time was not yet right to urge a dignified surrender and that Davis needed Varina around him to bring him to his senses. In a few days Benjamin would side with the rest of the Cabinet in recommending the terms of surrender. But not now.

Davis pushed the Cabinet on to Charlotte, where he was to meet Varina. He was belligerent and determined to press on with his escape, ultimately to lead a resurrected South from bases in Texas and Mexico.

On April 14, 1865, just after the Confederate Cabinet arrived in Charlotte, Lincoln was assassinated in Ford's Theater by a man well known to the audience, the actor John Wilkes Booth. The assassin was traced to the house of a Mrs. Mary Surratt in Washington, the mother of the Confederate courier John Surratt, and then pursued into the Virginia countryside.

The papers reported a simultaneous attack on Secretary of State Seward in his own bedroom by a man who slashed the Secretary's cheek with a bowie knife. Seward survived, but the simultaneity of the attacks suggested a coordinated assault, a conspiracy with political, not personal, motives.

It was much more politically useful for Union Secretary of War Edwin Stanton and the rest of the Federal leadership to imagine a high-level Confederate conspiracy than to think that the men involved had acted on their own. On April 20, 1865, General George S. Boutwell, later to be a radical Republican Representative and U.S. Senator from Massachusetts, wrote to General Benjamin Butler: "If there be evidence connecting any of the rebel leaders with the plot to assassinate the President, indictments should be found that we may follow them to other countries. It is not unlikely that Davis, Breckinridge and Benjamin had a hand in the business."[32]

Stanton moved ruthlessly, "like a dictator," an associate said, determined to lay the blame for the assassination at the feet of the leaders of the Confederacy.

At 4:44 A.M., while Lincoln was sinking toward death, Stanton wired Major General Dix, commander of the Union army in Maryland: "It appears from a letter found in Booth's trunk that the murder was planned before the fourth of March, but fell through then because the accomplices backed out until 'Richmond could be heard from.' "[33]

The trunk he referred to was in Booth's room at the National Hotel. At the bottom was a cipher code identical to the official Confederate ciphers found by U.S. Assistant War Secretary Dana at Richmond on April 6 in the offices of Judah P. Benjamin.

Lincoln died at 7:22 A.M. Within a few hours, Stanton wired Charles Francis Adams, the U.S. Minister to England: "The murderer of the President has been discovered, and evidence obtained that these horrible crimes were committed in execution of a conspiracy deliberately planned and set foot by rebels, under pretense of avenging the South and aiding the rebel cause."[34]

The day Lincoln died, a U.S. War Department official was told that "the President is dead and Mr. Stanton directs you to arrest Jacob Thompson," the leader of the Canadian spy ring.[35] Ten days after Lincoln's death, an indictment in the form of a Presidential proclamation was issued "for combining, confederating, and conspiring with one John H. Surratt, John Wilkes Booth, Jefferson Davis," and seven Canadian spies, including Jacob Thompson, "to kill and murder . . . Abraham Lincoln, late, and William H. Seward, Secretary of State."[36] Benjamin was not mentioned but the names of Surratt and Thompson were clear signals to him that he was a possible suspect.

The assassination occurred on Good Friday. On the following Sunday, memorable in American history as "Black Easter," thousands of ministers and other speakers all over the nation delivered sermons on the event. Almost every one of them drew parallels between the assassination and the crucifixion. One declaimed: "Jesus Christ died for the world; Abraham Lincoln died for his country."[37]

The timing and circumstances of his death were elevating Lincoln into American sainthood, a martyr to his struggling country, who sacrificed his life for its victory. Edward Everett Hale in Boston said that Lee's surrender at Appomattox and the assassination were like "the divine contrast between the triumph of Palm Sunday and the wretchedness and glory of the crucifixion."[38]

"Now he belongs to the ages," Stanton is supposed to have said as Lincoln breathed his last. He had been the first President whose photograph had been circulated nationwide, and people tacked it to the walls of their homes. They felt attached in a deeply personal way to his somber visage. The sacrifice of thousands of families would now be embodied in Lincoln's death, his blood mingled with their own, his death like a story in a New Testament of America's struggle for nationhood.

Even Southerners understood the impact. Mary Chesnut wrote: "That mad man who killed him. Now he will be Saint Abe for all time, saint and martyr."[39]

The New York *Times* on May 1, 1865, denounced the New York *Tribune's* pleas for amnesty and stated that Davis, Benjamin, and Confederate Secretary of War Breckinridge "should die . . . the most disgraceful death on the gallows."[40] Andrew Johnson was reported to be pacing in his room when he heard the news, wringing his hands and saying, "They shall suffer for this, they shall suffer for this."[41] General Grant recalled that Johnson "seemed to be anxious to get at the leaders to punish them. He would say that the leaders of the rebellion must be punished, and that treason must be made odious."[42] Even before the assassination, Johnson was vengeful. When he had spoken a few weeks earlier at a huge rally in Washington, he had mentioned Jefferson Davis's name and the crowd had shouted, "Hang him! Hang him!" Others, like Davis, he continued, were "infamous in character, diabolical in motive . . . and when you ask me what I would do, my reply is—I would arrest them, I would try them, I would convict them, and I would hang them."[43] This speech was reprinted widely after the assassination, including in one of Benjamin's hometown newspapers, the New Orleans *Tribune,* on April 21, 1865. The paper reported that the speech had a "double interest and meaning . . . since the terms laid down in it will undoubtedly be the policy of the new president."[44]

The mixed references to Christianity, patriotism, and judgment were a fundamental part of Johnson's rhetoric. The new President had previously spoken in the U.S. Senate and had said: "I trust in God that the time will come, and that before long, when these traitors can be overtaken in the aggregate and we may mete out to them condign punishment, such as their offense deserves." He then caught the flavor of another aspect of the holy war: "Let us look forward to the time when we can take the flag, the glorious flag of our country, and nail it below the cross, and there let it wave as waved in olden time, and let us gather round it, and inscribe as our motto, 'Liberty and Union, one and inseparable, now and forever.' Let us gather round it, and while it hangs floating beneath the cross, let us exclaim, 'Christ first, our country next.' "[45]

And he had several times spoken of Jews in the same view: "I might take you to Jerusalem, and tell of the persecution by the Jews of Christ, and his crucifixion upon the cross, and now their dispersion to all parts of the globe. I will not assume that it was the interposition of Divine Providence, or the result of a general law, but it is a great fact, and the Jews have been dispersed and rebuked."[46]

General George Custer, too, expressed the universally bitter reaction of the Union Army when he wrote, "Extermination is the only true policy we can adopt toward the political leaders of the rebellion, and at the same time do justice to ourselves and posterity."[47]

There is some testimony that Jefferson Davis was determined to face his accusers. Edward Pollard reported Davis's reaction to the news of the assassination of President Lincoln: The "event, [Davis] declared, confirmed his resolution not to leave the country. He inferred from the newspapers that he was accused as an accomplice in the crime, and he remarked to one of his staff officers that he 'would prefer death to the dishonor of leaving the country under such an imputation.' "[48]

On the other hand, the proclamation filled Benjamin with alarm, as revealed in a letter he wrote to his sister from Nassau several months later during his escape: "I heard . . . of the proclamation in which a large reward was offered for the capture of the President, who was most outrageously accused of having connived at the assassination of President Lincoln. Everything satisfied me of the savage cruelty with which the hostile government would treat any Confederate leader who might happen to fall into their hands, and I preferred death in attempting to escape, to such captivity as awaited me, if I became their prisoner."[49]

Benjamin was not overdramatizing. According to former Speaker of the House James G. Blaine, Senator Ben Wade of Ohio met with Andrew Johnson to discuss the treatment of Confederate leaders, when and if caught. It would never do, he said, to hang a large number. "I think if you could give me time, I could name thirteen that stand at the head in the work of the rebellion. I think we would all agree on Jeff Davis, Toombs, Benjamin, Slidell, Mason and Howell Cobb."[50] Blaine reflected the mood of the times, calling Benjamin the "Mephistopheles of the Rebellion, the brilliant, learned, sinister Secretary of State."[51]

Benjamin was being realistic. A year later in England, when asked "what the Northerners would have done to him if they had caught him," Benjamin said that they would have "probably put him to death."[52]

Benjamin must surely have remembered the time in the U.S. Senate when Andrew Johnson called Florida's Senator David Yulee "that contemptible Jew"[53] and added "there's another Jew—that miserable Benjamin!" He had to sense that Andrew Johnson would personally relish the hanging of Judah P. Benjamin. But there was another explanation for Johnson's extreme reaction, stemming from one of the oddest of John Wilkes Booth's actions on the day of the assassination. Before going to Ford's Theater that night, Booth dropped by the Kirkwood Hotel and sent a signed card up to the secretary of the then Vice President Andrew Johnson. It said simply, "Don't wish to disturb you. Are you at home?" Booth had planted a time bomb of suspicion at the door of the new President.[54]

When the newspaper stories blaming the Confederate leadership reached Benjamin, he had to have been deeply shaken: Lincoln dead, Johnson now President, and Jacob Thompson and John Surratt accused! Now Benjamin was no longer just another member of a fleeing Cabinet. His escape was now mandatory, for if Thompson and Surratt could be linked to Booth, they could certainly be linked to him. Benjamin would be blamed and hanged with them if caught. The Yankees could link him to the Canadian spies easily by his own messenger. In this hysteria, a fair trial? Never. The ancient blood ritual hung heavily in the air. If he went on trial, Lincoln would become Christ crucified, and he would be transformed into the guilty Christ-killer. No Jew would have a chance in such a spectacle of revenge and hatred. The search for an American Judas had an element of fundamentalist instinct; the assassin was Booth, but how much more thrilling for the mob if it could blame Benjamin, the Jew in the Confederate Cabinet.

Lincoln had been the South's only hope for mercy, amnesty, and reconciliation. Now, thousands of brave Confederate soldiers would suffer for this wild act of insanity. Vengeance would surely rule.

England would be Benjamin's refuge. He was a British subject by birth, and there were Confederate sympathizers there. He had to get to England.

To relieve his saddle sores, Benjamin rode in an ambulance at the rear of the Cabinet in flight. Heavy April showers caused the ambulance to get stuck in the oozing red clay as nightfall crept in, and he made camp with a former presidential assistant, Burton Harrison, who set down his memories of the Secretary of State in this moment of despair: "I could see from afar the occasional glow of Benjamin's cigar. While the others of the party were perfectly silent, Benjamin's silvery voice was presently heard as he rhythmically intoned, for their comfort, verse after verse of Tennyson's 'Ode on the Death of the Duke of Wellington.' "[55]

While on the road, Benjamin concentrated his whole physical being on his escape, but his mind was able to transport him to other worlds:

> *Lead out the pageant; sad and slow*
> *As fits an universal woe.*
> *Let the long, long procession go . . .*
> *All is over and done.*
> *Let the bell be toll'd*
> *And a deeper knell in the heart be knoll'd*
> *. . . We are a people yet.*
> *Tho' all men else their nobler dreams forgot.*

Those lines of Tennyson had given him much consolation through his life; never had he needed them as desperately as he did now.

By the time the train reached Charlotte, Varina had fled ahead of it, fearful of marauders and leaving a note for the President. "Why not cut loose from your escort?" it said. "Go swiftly and alone with the exception of two or three. . . . May God keep you, my old and only love."[56]

Fearful of reprisals, few in Charlotte would give the Cabinet homes to rest in; finally Benjamin and Jules were provided a place in the home of Abram Weill, a prominent Jew and an admirer who earlier had given a place to Varina. Only one man would house the President, a bachelor who ran "a sort of open house" with lots of liquor; locals called him "a graceless scamp." In gratitude for the Weill family's courage and hospitality, Benjamin presented them with a beautiful gold-headed cane, which, he said, had been on one side of him with his pistol on the other when he made his final speech to the U.S. Senate. The cane may have been an invented souvenir—since no one ever reported such an accoutrement during his speech—but Benjamin was in the mood for dramatics and wanted the Weill family to remember the gift.

Between April 13 and 18, General Johnston met with Sherman to discuss surrender terms. Sherman, the South's most hated adversary, who inflicted pitiless desolation on entire states and cities, unpredictably offered exceedingly generous terms for surrender. Out of touch with the turmoil of Washington, Sherman thought that Lincoln's policies were still in place and that the war should end on a note of reconciliation.

President Davis requested that each Cabinet member respond in writing, and on April 22, Benjamin wrote his last official document, a long and under the circumstances quite blunt memorandum, declaring that the terms offered to General Johnston were "the best and most favorable that we could hope to obtain by a continuance of the struggle." He defined it "as an agreement that if the Confederate states will cease to wage war for the purpose of establishing a separate government, the United States will receive the several states back into the Union with their state governments unimpaired, with all their Constitutional rights recognized, with protection for the persons and property of the people and with a general amnesty." As always, he analyzed the facts, pointing out that Johnston's army had dwindled from 70,000 to 20,000 and added: "We could not at the present moment gather together an army of 30,000 men, by concentration of all our forces east of the Mississippi. . . . We have lost possession in Virginia and North Carolina of our chief resources for the supply of powder and lead. We can obtain no aid from the Trans-Mississippi Department, from which we are cut off by the fleet of gunboats that patrol the river. We have not a supply of arms sufficient for into the field even 10,000 additional men if the men themselves were forthcoming." Guerrilla warfare, he wrote, "would entail far more suffering on our own people than it would cause damage to the enemy."

Benjamin then, with no equivocation, urged acceptance and recommended a series of steps: "The President should by proclamation inform the states and the people of the Confederacy of the
facts above recited; should ratify the convention so far as he
has the authority to act as commander-in-chief, and . . . should declare his inability with the means remaining at his disposal to
defend the Confederacy or maintain its independence, and should
resign."[57]

Davis never had a chance to respond. Stanton and the Union Cabinet
sternly overruled Sherman, insisting that any surrender be accepted
only on the same terms as Lee. Johnston promptly surrendered at
Bennett Place near Durham Station, North Carolina on April 26,
1865, the same day that John Wilkes Booth died in Virginia.

On April 23, a week after "Black Easter," Davis attended church
in Charlotte with other members of the Cabinet. Benjamin had attended church in Danville and may have done so again. The congregation heard the Episcopal minister deliver an angry condemnation
of the assassination of Lincoln as "a blot on civilization . . . topping
off a fountain of blood, which, unchecked, will burst forth and flow
onward through the South as well as the North, and bear on its
gory bosom a reign of terror." He urged "every Christian to set his
face against it."

As Davis left the church, he turned to Burton Harrison and said
smiling, "I think the preacher directed his remarks at me; and he
really seems to fancy I had something to do with the assassination."[58]

At Abbeville, South Carolina, the President and Benjamin met alone
for a private talk. Davis intended to convene the Cabinet the next
day for a formal discussion to lay out a future course for the Confederacy in view of Johnston's surrender, but Benjamin had conceived a
special mission for himself.

It was Benjamin's suggestion that he should separate himself from
the presidential party, using a logic that appeared to maintain his
support for Davis's fanciful strategy. He wrote later:

Early in May . . . I proposed to the President that, as we could
not communicate with our agents abroad in any other way, I
should leave him to pursue his journey across the country to
the Trans-Mississippi and proceed myself to the Florida Coast,
cross to the Islands, give the necessary orders and instructions
to all our foreign agents, and rejoin him in Texas, *via* Matamoras.
The plan was highly approved . . . with no one in on the secret

of my purpose except the President and Cabinet. To this prudent precaution I owe my safety.[59]

Davis pursued with new determination his vision of a new Confederacy rising from the ashes. He predicted that thousands would see the reborn Confederacy dart and strike against the foe, and thousands more would hear of their exploits and come to join him. Benjamin had constructed a plan that met the President's need for contact with Confederate agents in Europe to purchase arms, gunpowder, and cannons. But Benjamin inwardly must have realized that a reinvigorated cause was still another of the President's delusions. Benjamin volunteered to be Davis's European contact only because he knew full well that such a promise was futile. He would be loyal to the last and leave it to events to deliver the final blow.

The next morning, the President called together the Cabinet and, in the parlor of the large house where he had spent the night, addressed them, his jaunty spirits contrasting with the somber faces of the group. "Even if the troops now with me be all that I can for the present rely on," he declared, "3,000 brave men are enough for a nucleus around which the whole people will rally when the panic which now afflicts them has passed away."

An awkward silence fell over the room. Then each member of the Cabinet spoke in turn, except Benjamin, expressing unanimous disagreement with the President.

What the country was now undergoing, they said, was not panic but exhaustion. They all agreed that the Confederacy no longer had the means to prolong the war. To do so would be a cruel injustice to the people of the South and to the remaining soldiers with them, since if the troops persisted in a conflict so hopeless, they would be treated as brigands and would forfeit all chance of returning to their homes.

Another silence descended. The President looked at each of them as if searching for a way out of checkmate. He protested: "Then why, if all hope is exhausted, are they still in the field? Answer me that."[60]

The response was calm and matter of fact:

The troops were here to assist the President and the rest of the Cabinet in an escape. They would risk their lives in battle for that purpose. But the generals and officers had told the Cabinet privately that though they would follow President Davis until his safety was assured, they would not fire another shot in an effort to continue hostilities.

A number of eyewitness accounts tell of Davis's reaction. It was as if they had slapped the President with the back of their hands. His cheeks were flushed, and he sat in stunned silence.

Davis waited for a response, for pledges of fresh support and renewed commitment. But no one spoke. The silence drained him white with the realization that the end had come. The lines around his eyes and mouth dropped with dismay. "Then all is indeed lost," he muttered.[61]

He rose to leave the room, his legs so unsteady that a general had to help him to the door.

The Cabinet approved the division of the gold remaining in the treasury—$39,000 to Johnston's troops ($1.15 each); $108,000 to pay the soldiers accompanying them ($26.25 each); $35,000 reserved for the President and the members of the Cabinet; the remainder stored in secrecy for safekeeping, either in trunks to finance the rest of the flight or in the false bottom of a carriage to be sent to Charleston and then smuggled to England for future guerrilla action from the West. About $230,000 in worthless securities would be returned to the Richmond banks that owned them.

Hard riding lay ahead for the Presidential party, and Benjamin was neither an accomplished rider nor an old soldier. He wanted to go alone, and his saddle sores would be a convenient excuse. In any event, the party did not want to be encumbered by a plump rider unused to long hours on horseback.

It was time for Benjamin and the President to part. Three other Cabinet members had already left to be with their families. The President had said so many goodbyes that even this one was without special character. He said only that they would meet again some day west of the Mississippi. Benjamin confessed to John Reagan, now Secretary of the Treasury, that he was going "to the farthest place from the United States . . . if it takes me to the middle of China."[62] The remark suggested not just escape but the anonymity of a faraway land, far from the reach of the U.S. Government. Reagan was the first member of the Cabinet to hear of Benjamin's plan to disguise himself for an escape. "He had a trunk in the carriage with his initials, J. P. B., plainly marked on it. I imagined whether that might betray him. 'No,' he replied, 'there is a Frenchman traveling in the Southern states who has the same initials, and I can speak broken English like a Frenchman.' "

Years later, Varina wrote of the details of Benjamin and Davis's parting, which she presumably heard from her husband:

Mr. Davis then decided to make his way on horseback to Texas followed by a few officers. This involved great risk and still greater fatigue and Mr. Benjamin came to him and said, "I could not bear the fatigue of riding as you do, and as I can serve our people no more just now, will you consent to my making an effort to escape through Florida? If you should be in a condition to require me again I will answer your call at once." This was his considerate manner of saying all was lost in his opinion; like Samson's lion after his strength was spent, he sent "forth sweetness."[63]

She summarized the nature of their relationship as they bade each other farewell: "Thus these two master minds which seemed to be the complement of each other parted with mutual respect and affectionate esteem as well as a hearty appreciation of the virtues and gifts his friend possessed, after breasting as one man the heavy storm which beat upon them for five bitter years."[64]

They separated, Davis on horseback with about twenty men, and Benjamin into an ambulance pulled by a pair of broken-down old grays. He assumed a calculated disguise, which Colonel John Taylor Wood, an aide to Davis (and incidentally the nephew of Sarah Knox Taylor), noted in his diary: "With goggles on, his beard grown, a hat well over his face, and a large cloak hiding his figure, no one would have recognized him as the late secretary of state of the Confederacy."[65] Benjamin traveled under false documents as a Frenchman named M. M. Bonfals, who spoke no English to strangers. The name itself showed a kind of bravado—probably a play on the Cajun French for "a good falsification" or "a good disguise." It must have given him a certain pleasure to tease his pursuers with a Cajun word-game.[66]

In Charlotte, the group had been joined by a Colonel Henry Leovy of New Orleans, who offered to accompany Benjamin southward and translate for "M. M. Bonfals." With regard to Jules, Benjamin decided that it would be safer for him to travel alone than to risk capture with a fugitive. He mentioned Jules in a subsequent letter to Varina, writing that "he was made prisoner at Montgomery and paroled, and then went to N.O. where he spent some weeks with my sister, in joint solicitude about me, both believing from my long disappearance that I must have perished." He wrote his sister that "in passing through Georgia, I left with a friend nine hundred dollars in gold" to be sent to his younger sisters at La Grange, Georgia, for passage back to New Orleans. Through money and good fortune, he managed to reunite his family.[67]

The portrayal of Benjamin by others during the escape from Richmond has an element of the grotesque about it. His demeanor was like no one else's around him, so different that every aide and Cabinet member who wrote about the trip remarked upon it. At a time of deepening desperation and hopelessness, he was reciting poetry, discussing literature, and smoking a cigar calmly by the campfire. It was as if, in his heart, he had already assumed a psychological disguise, distancing himself from the tragedy about him.

Perhaps he was responding to Davis's despair, as he had throughout the war, worried that the President was on the edge of collapse and needed counterbalancing personal and emotional support at the darkest hour. His attitude was showy, public, openly calm, almost as if he were aware he was being watched and would be written about. In that dire circumstance, one can assume, the self-confidence and nonchalance described in the accounts was the way he wanted to be perceived, not the way he was. That was further evidence of a man who could control his personality and, as time passed, the considered persona of a man who was calculating his chances and had already decided that he was going to flee.

Judah P. Benjamin, dressed in rags, rattled his wagon onto the roads where thousands of men, wounded and exhausted, were straggling home in dazed defeat. The war was over, his country lay in ruins, and he was fleeing for his life. Jefferson Davis, Robert E. Lee, Robert Toombs, and Judah P. Benjamin—all outlaws, when just a short time ago they were recognized the world over as leaders of the Confederate nation.

Benjamin had always been able to see himself from a distance. How ironic for him to be in disguise, sitting in the Georgia mud and trying to avoid the name Judah P. Benjamin, when he had spent a lifetime building it.

His life was in a strange period of suspension, having neither past nor future. Stripped of office and identity, his status resembled that of a runaway slave. It was his body they sought. It was so physical, so elemental, so base, like the relationship of terrain to a pursued animal. He had to be conscious of rivers and inlets, of forests and pathways, of sounds and signs, of weather and time of day. He had to cross his devastated land dressed in another man's rags, like a prince in the guise of a pauper. Before, if he had wanted to reach out to common people and tell them personally of their bravery, he was separated from them by his own notoriety and heritage. Now he was part of their bone and their blood, but separated by his anonymity. Although he stood in the ranks of the defeated, the straggling Confederates along the road viewed him as a wandering Frenchman untouched by their tragedy. In some way, there was no difference: By whatever name—Judah P. Benjamin or M. M. Bonfals—he was an observer of this painful aftermath.

Benjamin traveled ever southward, using Captain Leovy to pretend to interpret for a French-speaking refugee. Once in Florida, he changed his disguise to that of a destitute farmer, in search of land on which to settle with some friends who wanted to move from South Carolina. A Southern farmer's wife made him some homespun clothes just like her husband's. He bought for his horse the commonest and roughest tack he could find, and he journeyed as far as possible on backroads, always passing around towns and keeping in the least inhabited districts.

His progress was necessarily slow, about 30 miles a day, until he reached central Florida. Everywhere were posters offering a large reward for Jefferson Davis and Jacob Thompson for the assassination of President Lincoln. In one author's words, it was a "time of rage, horror, dread and wild rumor."[68]

He was not the only refugee on the roads heading South. The roads were swollen with returning veterans and burned-out families searching for husbands and fathers. The women stopped every hobbling cripple along the way with questions. Released Yankee prisoners on the road looked as bedraggled and hungry as the Southerners. Bands of marauders stole everything in sight. The freed slaves rushed in exhilaration and panic toward who knew what fate. Freedom to many of them meant no more work, and they were flocking to the cities, to the new paradise. It was a Southern nightmare come true.

After two weeks on the road, Benjamin was alarmed by the sound of a galloping horse overtaking him. He recognized Colonel John Taylor Wood from the President's entourage. "Mr. Secretary," the Colonel gasped as he reined in his lathered horse beside the wagon, "the President has been captured."[69]

The President had heard that Varina and the children were in danger of being attacked by disbanded Union soldiers, Wood explained, and Davis had ridden night and day on his exhausted mounts to reach her. Two regiments of Union cavalry closed in on their camp at sunrise on May 2. Davis grabbed for a raincoat and inadvertently picked up Varina's shawl in the dawn light. When Varina saw a soldier draw a point-blank bead on her husband, she ran toward him with a cry and flung her arms about his neck. Soon they were surrounded by dozens of cavalrymen in a circle around them, all with carbines pointed at the two figures clinging to each other in the center. Only Wood had escaped by bribing one of the soldiers he found rifling through the President's personal trunks looking for gold. Varina recorded Davis's words when he realized it had ended: "God's will be done."[70]

A newspaper showed a cartoon of the President fleeing through the woods in a hooped calico dress, brandishing a bowie knife. The caption contained the quote from the officer who captured the President: "Jefferson Davis, surprised by the dawn attack, hastily put on one of Mrs. Davis's dresses and started for the woods, closely pursued by our men, who at first thought him a woman, but seeing his boots while running, suspected his sex at once. The race was a short one and the rebel President was soon brought to bay."[71]

It was a lie that would follow Davis through history in cartoon and legend. P. T. Barnum offered the government $500 for the dress and, though he could not obtain what did not exist, had Davis portrayed in a hoop skirt in his shows.

Wood galloped off toward the southern horizon. Colonel Leovy and Benjamin were left alone again in their meandering wagon. A letter he wrote to Varina several months later (which will be examined in another context), suggests that Benjamin's mind dwelled on the final scene of capture, on the ridicule and humiliation heaped on the proud figure of the President, of Varina alone after he was taken.

Benjamin needed to hasten his escape. It was time to part from Colonel Leovy, who would return to New Orleans. Leovy subsequently wrote that Benjamin never appeared "so great as during the time of adversity. Traveling in disguise, sleeping at night in log huts, living on the plainest fare, subjected to all the discomforts of such a journey, with all his plans shattered and without definite hope for the future, his superb confidence and courage raised him above all, and he was the great, confident, cheerful leader that he had been in the days of highest prosperity."[72]

The imprisonment of Davis at that moment could not have offered a greater contrast. A newspaper reported that Davis was in a "living tomb" and "buried alive" in Fort Monroe.[73] He was in chains and under watch twenty-four hours a day.

Now events would test Varina's capacity to improvise in hours of danger. Jefferson Davis's humiliation was her disgrace as well.

She and the President must pass through this fire as symbols for the rest of the South. If only Lincoln had lived; Lincoln spoke for a goodness in the spirit of both countries that was now buried with him, his policy of reconciliation a victim of the false allegation of a Confederate plot.

Though outwardly cheerful, subsequent letters reveal that Benjamin's heart was heavy at the prospect that Jefferson Davis should spend his days languishing in prison. If events had gone differently at Gettysburg or Antietam and if the assassination had not intervened, would Lincoln and Seward be fleeing now in fear of being hanged? Davis was no criminal. He was a leader of a proud people, but the new leaders would not be kind to a prisoner accused of treason and assassination. The President was much more frail than they knew. Only Varina could keep him alive through his despair.

Twelve days after the assassination, John Wilkes Booth was shot to death by pursuing Union soldiers on a farm in Virginia.

On July 6, 1865, after a trial that many said was too hasty, four people, including Mrs. Mary Surratt, the mother of John Surratt, were hanged for the conspiracy to murder President Lincoln. Mrs. Surratt was the first woman hanged in American history. A storm of controversy broke out after her death over the scanty evidence used to convict her. It was widely assumed that she was being held as bait to lure her son back from his escape in order to trace a link to the Confederacy. Years later, in 1873, former President Andrew Johnson charged that Judge Joseph Holt, who presided over the military commission that tried the conspirators, withheld and suppressed the recommendation of mercy for Mrs. Surratt, which had been signed by five members of the nine-member military commission that convicted her. Holt claimed that President Johnson had examined and read the recommendation in his presence before deciding not to grant clemency. As Lewis Powell, one of the convicted co-conspirators, walked to the gallows, he insisted that Mrs. Surratt had not known of the plot to which he had confessed. Mrs. Surratt's last words to her priest were, "Father, I wish to say something . . . that I am innocent."[74]

As Lincoln's funeral train wound its way north and then west for more than two weeks, at the same time as the Confederate entourage made its way south, the myth of Lincoln gathered strength. Millions of people saw the body, ordinary people lining the railroad tracks or, when it stopped for orations and prayers, filing past as Lincoln lay in state in Washington, Philadelphia, New York, Cleveland, and Chicago. The canonization of Lincoln was beginning. The people were acting out an ancient myth: mourning the figure of the "dying god," more humane and understanding than mere mortals, suffering through his travail for mankind's sake, and taken from his people just as he completed his mission.[75] Lincoln had sacrificed his life so that the country could live in peace; he was its just king and its patriarch. "We are coming, Father Abraham," the song went and the nation was seized by one of mankind's most powerful urges— revenge for the murder of the father. Blood lust was in the air, and someone had to pay for the "Black Easter" murder of Lincoln.

While Benjamin was fleeing southward, a nation of Christ-haunted people searched instinctively for the Jewish scapegoat who would make the myth complete. The Easter sermons mourning Lincoln would define Benjamin in the legend, should he be captured. The phrase "Christ-killer" had to be lodged in Benjamin's soul as a latent childhood memory. As the Jew in the South who had risen the highest, he now was in danger of falling the farthest. In a world filled with vengeance and hatred, he was facing the nightmare of his darkest dream: the trial of Judah P. Benjamin, the Jew. Lincoln's transformation into a crucified Christ figure was almost complete, his resurrection into sainthood only a matter of time and history. The people still clung to his lifeless body in an act of deification. Shot on April 14, he would not be buried in Springfield, Illinois, until May 4.

The dilemma for Judah Benjamin was painful and impossible. He had placed himself completely in the service of the Confederacy and its President; they had been his life and his purpose. He had held back nothing and had earned the deepest trust of his Com-mander-in-Chief. But there was no way Jefferson Davis could under-stand the Jew in Judah Benjamin, and Benjamin barely recognized it in himself. His lifelong habits of response took over: He was experi-encing all over again the disgrace of Yale and the humiliation of Charleston. The patterns of guilt and reaction were repeating them-selves: the urge to flee to somewhere new, to start over and seek out another enormous challenge, to replay the triumph of New Or-leans and Louisiana in a new country.

The President, who preferred "death to the dishonor of leaving the country" under the cloud of the assassination, could well have seen Benjamin's decision to leave him after four years as evidence of a lack of courage. Davis could not help but feel abandoned—by his people, by his Cabinet, by his military escort, and now by his closest associate. Unwillingness to face the final accounting represented in Jefferson Davis's scheme of values a fundamental flaw, an absence of honor. Still more disappointing, that flaw was appearing in the man he trusted most, Judah P. Benjamin.

Benjamin knew the Union soldiers would be combing the countryside for him. He hid during the day and traveled by night. His escape was almost fictional, as miracles seemed to light his way.

Early one morning he became confused as to which of two roads to take. Since daytime was upon him, he decided to tether his mule and rest for a while in some brambles just off the road.

During his sleep he heard a shrill, high-pitched voice say, "Hi, for Jeff." He thought he was dreaming and dozed off again, until he heard it again: "Hi, for Jeff." He looked up and saw a parrot talking away among some other birds. He knew the parrot had to belong to a Southern sympathizer, for who else would to teach such a greeting to a bird? He threw a stone at the bird and followed his colorful flying guide to a farmhouse. There he found Confederate friends, who allowed him to stay for several days to rest and plan his next steps. They were raided once by a Yankee search party, but Benjamin ran out the back door and hid in a thicket. While hiding he had to clutch the muzzle of the family's yelping dog, which had followed him out the back door. He asked the farmer's wife to sew pleats in the back of his vest and waistband to carry gold. Now he was plump with gold pieces and the overweight target of every swindler, turncoat, and thief from North Carolina to the Florida keys.[76]

Since a substantial reward was being offered for him, he hesitated to tell anyone his true identity. But he confessed it to his new friends. One of them was an ex-Confederate officer named Captain Tresca, who offered to take him by boat, since there were too many Federals on the land routes.

He subsisted on turtle eggs, fish, and coconut milk. When a Federal gunboat was sighted, Captain Tresca ordered Benjamin to don a cook's apron and a skull cap, to go down to the galley and smear himself with soot and grease, and to pose as the boat's Jewish cook. It was the impulse of a rural Southerner to disguise the Jewish Secretary of State in such a demeaning, but successful, way. One of the Yankees searching the boat remarked he had never before remembered a Jew performing common labor.[77]

About July 7, the day Mrs. Surratt and the other conspirators, none of whom had been named in the original accusation, were hanged in Washington, Benjamin reached Knight's Key at the southern end of the Florida coast. He set sail for Bimini in a small boat, with a plan to catch larger ships for Nassau, Havana, and finally Southampton in England.

In a letter to his sister, he described the dramatic story of his hazardous escape, caught between the pursuit of the Federals and the dangers of the sea.

He had set sail in a "little boat at sea" with two guides to try to reach Bimini: "I had never seen a water-spout, and often expressed a desire to be witness of so striking a phenomenon. I got, however, more than I bargained for." Suddenly, while riding out several squalls, "a very heavy, lurid cloud in the west dipped down toward the sea, and in a single minute two large water-spouts were formed, and the wind began blowing furiously directly toward us, bringing the water spouts in a straight line for our boat." The two spouts created "long waving column[s] that swayed about in the breeze and extended from the ocean up into a cloud. . . . We would have been swamped in a second, but before they reached us the main squall was upon us with such a tremendous blast of wind and rain combined that it was impossible to face the drops of water which were driven into our eyes with such violence as to compel us instantly to turn our backs to it." The account continued:

> On turning our backs to this tremendous squall, judge of our dismay on seeing another water-spout formed in another squall in the east, also traveling directly towards us . . . we had scarcely caught sight of this new danger, when the two spouts first seen passed our boat at a distance of about one hundred yards . . . tearing up the whole surface of the sea as they passed, and whirling furiously into the clouds, with a roar such as is heard at the foot of Niagara Falls. The western blast soon reached the spout that had been coming toward us from the east. . . . It wavered and broke and the two other spouts continued their awful race across the ocean until we lost sight of them in the blackness of the horizon. A quarter of an hour after, all was calm and still, and

our boat was lazily heaving and setting on the long swell of the Bahama Sea. It was a scene and picture that has become photographed into my brain and that I can never forget.[78]

H. A. McLeod, one of Benjamin's companions, interviewed some years later, reported that after the "squalls and the water spouts and the tropical storms came near finishing us," the boat was filled with water. In the calm of the sea just after the storm, Benjamin, who was bailing desperately with his hat while his companions used tin pans, said with a smile, "McLeod, this is sure not like being Secretary of State." McLeod described him as "an awfully nervy man."[79]

At Bimini Benjamin boarded a small sloop stuffed with a cargo of tightly pressed wet sponges. When the sponges started to dry and harden, the boat burst apart at its seams and sank so quickly that Benjamin barely had time to jump into a skiff with three Negroes. The craft was so crowded that only 5 inches of it were out of the water. Though 35 miles at sea with only a pot of rice and a single oar, the four managed to scull a course toward land for eight hours. After avoiding "rescue" by two Yankee steamers, they were finally picked up by a local yacht. Benjamin chartered a second boat for Nassau, which ran into storms and headwinds and took six days to make the trip. From Nassau, he boarded a schooner for Havana, then a steamer bound for Southampton, England, but "after being nine hours at sea, a fire broke out . . . at about ten o'clock at night. . . . By almost superhuman effort, the flames were kept under control till we reached St. Thomas with seven feet of water in the forehold that had been pumped by hand . . . without however extinguishing the fire." Several crews in the harbor helped put out the fire. After three more days the steamer was in "ship-shape," and he set sail again for England.[80]

He was penniless for the moment. Safe passage, bribery, and gratitude had cost him $1,500, almost all of his remaining gold, but somehow he liked the drama of his destitution. A man was not his possessions or his office but his brains, talent, energy, and his capacity for improvisation and adaptation. To lose all could be oddly exhilarating, if one had risked all.

He could stand as a metaphor for the South itself: broke and bent but determined, by sheer will and faith, to overcome the odds and start all over again.

We know something of what was on his mind because of a chance meeting on the ship to England. William Preston, another fleeing Confederate, talked with him during the voyage and wrote Varina of their conversation: "I met Mr. Benjamin," he wrote, "who had made a wonderful escape. . . . Mr. Benjamin told me he feared you were destitute, and could not give me any satisfactory answer till we reached Europe, but manifested the most friendly interest and purpose in your behalf. . . . I left Mr. Benjamin in Europe. He does not intend to return to America."[81]

Benjamin felt an enormous surge of relief not only at surviving a harrowing trip but at having cheated the Yankees of a prize. He wrote to Senator Bayard of Delaware, an old friend from his Senate days, that he arrived in Southampton "on the 30th of August, nearly four months after my separation from the President, during which time I had spent twenty-three days seated in the thwart of an open boat, exposed to the tropical sun in June and July, utterly without shelter or change of clothes. I never, however, had one minute's indisposition nor despondency but was rather pleased by the feeling of triumph in disappointing the malice of my enemies."[82] The escape seemed to reinforce his belief that he was being reserved for a special destiny.

He would try vainly to put events behind him. With John Surratt still at large and the most wanted man in the world, the tragedy of the last days of the Confederacy was on the front page of every newspaper. Reminders were everywhere during his escape: a glimpse of newspapers that announced the progress of Lincoln's funeral train back to Illinois; the swearing in of Andrew Johnson; the photographs of the four hooded bodies dangling from the gallows, one of them in a long black dress. All of history would be changed by Booth's rash act. Brutus, after all, was a colleague in Caesar's Roman Senate; Booth was just a random fanatic. No future leader would be safe from an assassin's bullet, perhaps neither were the Confederate leaders, like Jefferson Davis and himself, accused in the plot. The rules of civilized warfare had been violated; the assassins would turn the Yankees into jackals bent on vengeance and dictatorial victors seeking utter domination of the South.

The spies in Canada had been Benjamin's idea, but he had never envisioned the kind of desperation that would drive them to those evil outrages. Were the spies guilty? If so, what part of the fault indirectly could be his? Those men were sustained by Confederate dollars for too long a period, and he had approved the master plan for the borders, then had been too self-confident to weigh the irrational, to sense that their failures would drive them to more reckless measures like attempting to kidnap the President or burn down New York. He should have foreseen that they would ultimately go too far and should have ended it much earlier. Thompson was honorable, he knew, but what of the others? Even if the Canadian spies were innocent, he had to be appalled that fate had chosen a young messenger whose mother would be accused of plotting with Booth and hanged. The death of Lincoln would cast a shadow over his whole previous life. It would leave a deep scar across his own memories of the war, his earnest but largely hopeless efforts and now this bitter, disgusting aftermath.

"Your country is desolate," saith Isaiah. "Your cities are burned with fire: your land, strangers devour it in your presence . . . the whole head is sick, and the whole heart faint."

He had never meant to unleash such havoc on his South or such brutality on Lincoln and Seward. Surely, in the last accounting, intent would matter.

The war had been a giant chess game for him, an intellectual exercise, a personal achievement even in defeat. Now he was caught up in its final horror. There was no escape except to go far from the source of the memory. He wanted to find solace in a quiet old age, away from power and public controversy.

If God would just grant him the grace to put behind the suffering landscape that was now the South, he would burn all shreds of it from his memory and never speak of it again.

4

❄❄❄

REFUGEE
FROM THE
LOST CAUSE

1865–1884

18

England:
From Law Student to Queen's Counsel

❀❀❀

The England that awaited Judah P. Benjamin in 1865 had only recently abolished the shackles of restrictions against Jews. It had been a liberating century. By the end of the Napoleonic Wars in 1815, Jews had begun to win acceptance at all levels of English society: They could settle freely, own businesses, purchase land, and vote in parliamentary elections. But as late as the 1850s political representation was still barred to Jews. No Jew could sit in Parliament or in a municipal council. No Jew could hold any office under the crown. The oath of office entailed swearing loyalty "on the true faith of a Christian." Even in the early part of the century, when two acts of Parliament granted Catholics and "Nonconformists" the right to sit in Parliament, Jews were pointedly excluded.[1]

Then, in 1847, just as Judah P. Benjamin was emerging in the politics of Louisiana, the city of London elected the distinguished banker Lionel Rothschild on the Whig ticket as its member of the House of Commons. When he refused to pronounce the oath, there was a bruising debate over the Jewish Disabilities Bill. One member of Parliament described the underlying issue: "This Jew Question is a terrible annoyance. I never saw anything like the prejudice which exists against them."[2] During the days of debate, the focus of attention was Benjamin Disraeli, a Jew by birth and a Christian by religion, who broke with the leaders of the party he aspired to lead in one of his most memorable speeches.

"Where is your Christianity if you do not believe in their Judaism?" he asked. "They are, humanly speaking, the authors of your religion. . . . On every sacred day, you read to the people the exploits of Jewish heroes, the proofs of Jewish devotion, the brilliant annals of past Jewish magnificence." He warned the majority that "you are influenced by the darkest superstitions of the darkest ages that ever existed in this country. . . . Whatever may be the consequences on the seat I hold . . . it is as a Christian that I will not take upon me the awful responsibility of excluding from the legislature those who are of the religion in the bosom of which my Lord and Saviour was born."[3]

Parliament rejected Disraeli's plea, voted to retain the oath, and refused to seat Rothschild. However, for the next ten years the middle-class voters in London proceeded to reelect Rothschild to the same seat. Each term, he would reenact a pantomime designed to embarrass the conservatives—approach his seat, sigh audibly, turn, and walk out. The Tories persisted in upholding the oath, reflecting the attitudes of the aristocrats, the squires, and the Anglican bishops, who feared the rise of the middle class. "The rabble of London," a puzzled Henry Drummond asserted after Rothschild's reelection in 1857, "partly out of love of mischief, partly out of contempt for the House of Commons, and partly from a desire to give a slap in the face to Christianity, elected a Jew."[4] In 1858, after the Tory leadership became convinced that Jewish restrictions were becoming an embarrassment, an act was finally passed that allowed each house of Parliament to establish its own rules of oath-taking, and Lionel Rothschild was seated. That was the year Judah P. Benjamin was elected to his second term in the United States Senate. Even with the victory in Parliament, it was not until 1871 that Parliament authorized Oxford and Cambridge to award degrees to Jews, thereby lifting the last remaining legal restrictions on Jews in the country, a full six years after Benjamin landed in England from his perilous voyage of escape from the American Civil War.

From Southampton, where he landed on August 30, 1865, Benjamin went immediately to London for a week to assist Mason in winding up the affairs of the consulate. Then he hurried to Paris to see his wife and daughter for the first time in five years. He wrote to his sister not of Natalie but of his joy at seeing Ninette, who looked "as blooming as a rose."[5] He was also happy to hear that Jules St. Martin had safely made his way back from the war. "I also found letters from Jules giving an account of his visit to New Orleans and of his seeing you all, and he even committed the gross flattery of writing to my wife that 'Ben's sister is charming.' "[6]

Old friends begged him to stay in Paris. John Slidell arranged for him to meet a number of French bankers, who told him that "it would be easy to obtain an honorable and lucrative position in financial circles." An old New Orleans friend, Madame de Pontalba, was "imperious in her urgency" and promised aid should he remain in Paris. But Benjamin had different plans: "Nothing is more independent, nor offers a more promising future, than admission as a barrister to the bar of London."[7]

On the surface, Paris would have been a safer short-term choice. The emancipation of the Jews that had swept Europe decades earlier had begun in France, the home of the celebrated Revolution and of fraternity and equality. Jews had sat in the French Chamber of Deputies since 1834, and Benjamin's New Orleans and Confederate connections would have given him access to influential clients. But France was also the home of Napoleon III and of a strong Catholic Church that had resisted Jewish advance. Anti-Semitic feelings smoldered just beneath the surface of fine manners at the royal court. To join a banking firm would have placed limits on his opportunities. More importantly, as he pointed out, it would have forced him to give up the independence of a law practice. With the enmity of the U.S. Government facing him in the person of Secretary of State Seward, any banking firm could be influenced to control him, not welcome him in international negotiations, or perhaps drop him altogether as a price in some international arrangement. He would be vulnerable. On the other hand, as a barrister in England he would have many clients and sources of income and not be dominated by the views and demands of a single institution. He wrote to his former law partner in New Orleans that "when called to the bar I shall take the Northern Circuit which includes Liverpool where I hope to get my first start with the aid of some of our old clients there."[8] Liverpool was home to the largest number of Confederate sympathizers—shipping firms and mercantile institutions whose owners had supported the South during the war and, having known Benjamin from his days as the South's reigning international lawyer, would welcome his services once again. They would be the core clients of a profitable practice.

England was an island nation of traders with aspirations for an even more expansive colonial empire. Perhaps he was already framing for himself a role in such a grandiose future. He spoke its language elegantly and was welcomed in its highest councils; he carried English citizenship and was always at home psychologically in English culture. He had risen fast in one port city in America, and he would start over in a second port city in England. Liverpool and then London would reward his experience both in law and in politics; a nation that exchanged goods for raw materials and exotic luxuries all over the world required just the kind of legal practice he relished. He spoke French and Spanish and knew the laws and cultures of other countries. He also knew that if he could regain his reputation— through clients, books, articles, and successful cases—as a master of international law, his future in the nation of traders was assured.

There were, of course, personal considerations in choosing England over France. Seeing Natalie again in Paris—her Paris—must have confirmed Benjamin's decision. They had largely lived apart for twenty-one years, except for the short disaster in Washington during his time in the Senate. Her infidelities had humiliated him then, and Richmond whispered of the other men in her life during the time she was without her husband in Paris. The court of Napoleon III was not known for its high moral fiber, and she possessed an intriguing combination of beauty and access to the powerful. He would not build another castle of respectability only to have it end again in ruins, leaving him a second time to retreat in shame. He had learned his lesson in Washington. England, separated from her waywardness but close enough to visit on his own timetable, would be his choice.

Natalie's life was comfortable, while his would be a struggle. He was once asked by the daughter of an old friend why he was living apart from his family. She reported his answer "that he can't have them with him in London because he cannot afford to keep them in the style they should be."[9] Natalie now had roots in Paris and knew his prodigious work habits. If given the choice, she would surely remain in Paris living in the "style" to which she had become accustomed even if he was living a student's life in London.

But as a fugitive, how would he be treated in his adopted England? Many Southern expatriates lived abroad, but he was the most notorious expatriate of them all. In his letters to his sisters, however, he seemed genuinely surprised at his reception and reassured them that he was being treated with "great kindness and distinction" and "would be called on by a large number of public men." He wrote that "Mr. D'Israeli [sic] also wrote a friend of mine expressing the desire of being useful to me when he would arrive in town, and I have been promised a dinner at which I am to be introduced to Gladstone and Tennyson as soon as the season opens."[10]

When James Bayard, a Senator from Delaware and an old friend with whom he corresponded for decades, offered financial aid, Benjamin declined and reassured Bayard that he was not penniless. He wrote that he had arrived in England with little more than a few months' support for himself and his family but had soon received a hundred bales of cotton that had "escaped Yankee vigilance." That was all that had gotten through of the six hundred bales he had purchased before he fled. He reported to Bayard that "the price here is so high that it has given me $20,000." He was able to add $10,000 more by using "information furnished by a kind friend in relation to the affairs of a financial institution, in which I invested my little fortune" from the cotton. "So you see I am not quite a beggar," he wrote. Aware that he was in far better circumstances than his compatriots in the South, among them Jefferson Davis, he wrote that he was "as cheerful and as happy as possible for me to be while my unfortunate friends are in such cruel confinement and my unhappy country in so deplorable a condition."[11]

Initially, Lincoln's Inn, which controlled the practice of law, would not relax its three-year requirement for admission to the bar. As Benjamin studied English law, he kept up with events in the South and was depressed by what he heard. "The news from the other side fills me with alarm and concern," he wrote to his sisters, "and I cannot penetrate into the dark future that seems to await my unhappy country. The unholy passions of the wretched Northern fanatics seem to require no fresh fuel in order to burn with fiercer intensity: and until the mass of people hurl them from power, God knows what excesses they will commit."[12]

He was beginning to circulate among the powerful of England, and he wrote to his sisters in New Orleans proudly that "I have made some valuable acquaintances here and shall have many more as soon as Parliament assembles. I have dined with Mr. Gladstone and was greatly pleased with him."

On a three-day outing "in the midst of the proverbial splendor and comfort of an English gentleman's country seat, and with a crowd of titled and fashionable guests, I found their tone, manners, and customs just what I would have expected—quiet, easy, courteous, and agreeable. The style, of course, exceeds anything seen on our side of the water. I was very hospitably received and warmly pressed to prolong my visit but I have no time to yield to pleasures, till I have secured some lucrative business."[13]

He had heard terrible rumors of the South, paralyzed without its freed slaves, and tales of woe associated with Reconstruction. "I confess that I have always looked with the utmost dread and distrust on the experiment of emancipation so suddenly enforced on the South by the event of the war. God knows how it will all end!"[14]

Eight months after he arrived in London, an English banking firm failed, sweeping away with its demise much of Benjamin's accumulated capital. He was concerned about money again, but even so wanted to share whatever he had with his family in New Orleans. He assured his sister of his ability to help his other sisters "Sis and Hatty" if they were "the least in want." He had sent them $900 in gold before he fled "as they must have suffered if they had none but confederate notes," and he assured them that he could always spare a few hundred dollars and had no fear of his ability "to make a handsome competence at the bar."[15]

His letters to E. A. Bradford, his old law partner in New Orleans, described in minute detail his struggle to make a new life. His portrayal of his situation to his former law partner was certainly more realistic than the brave face he put forward for the members of his family.

"I am now entered as a student at Lincoln's Inn," he wrote soon after he began his studies on January 13, 1866, "and do not expect to be called to the bar until next fall." His plan was to study for a year before asking for special admission to the bar rather than ask immediately for a waiver or wait the customary three years. He would thereby comply partially with the requirement and at the same time brush away the intellectual cobwebs regarding the intricacies of English law, familiarizing himself with the courts and various institutions in the legal system. "In the meantime, I am making enough to pay my personal expenses by an engagement to contribute one leading article a week to one of the daily papers, for which I am paid 5 pounds a week and am thus enabled to devote the small sum that I was able to save from the wreck to the maintenance of my family till I can obtain some practice at the bar." One cannot know precisely to what money he was referring, but it is reasonable to assume that "the small sum . . . from the wreck" at sea was the small amount of gold that he had sewn into the lining of his clothes for his escape. With the loss of a large amount of his money, he was living simply. "I have enough with close economy to get through three years and by that time may be able to secure a decent practice," he wrote. He was sending Bradford his power of attorney for handling his affairs in New Orleans regarding his family, and he wanted Bradford to know that he was not desperate. "I could make 600 to 800 pounds a year by consenting to become sub-editor of the daily paper . . . but that would take up nearly all my time and prevent my preparation for the bar."[16] He then listed for Bradford all his expenses associated with Lincoln's Inn and admission to the bar:

> Stamps 25 pounds - 2 - 6. Lectures 5 pounds - 5 - 0. Admission fee 5 pounds - 12 - 6. Printed form 11 pounds - 1 - 0, making a total of 37 pounds - 1 - 0. I had then to deposit 100 pounds as security that I would pay for my dinners. The next step was to enter a barrister's chambers with view to learn the course of practice, and for this the fee was 105 pounds - 0 - 0. I am now in the chambers of Mr. Charles Pollock, son of the Chief Baron of the Exchequer Sir Frederic Pollock.[17]

The Bradfords visited London during this period, and he confessed to them his struggling circumstances, belying the somewhat rosier descriptions in his letters to family and friends in America. He slept in bachelor's quarters at the least expense and dined furtively on occasion, sometimes on bread and cheese, at cheap restaurants "where a barrister would not want to be seen."[18] He took to walking, because again it would have been considered beneath his dignity as a barrister to be seen riding a penny bus. Somehow, he seemed so sure of his ultimate success that he was relishing this moment at the bottom of the ladder and expected to enjoy the climb back to the top that much more.

From his perspective, the social order at Lincoln's Inn for a man of his age and experience was touched with humor. His situation must have unsettled the barristers and judges as well. He described the scene to Bradford, giving a unique insight into his daily life:

> You would be greatly amused to see our dinner at Lincoln's Inn. There are tables at the head of the room for the Benchers, who are the old leaders of the bar. . . . Next come the tables for the barristers, of whom some forty or fifty always are found at dinner. Next, the students to the number of about 150 including your humble servant, all seated at long tables and dressed in stuff gowns, which the waiters throw over us in the ante-chamber before we enter the dining hall.[19]

One can only imagine the lesser tables filled with the young students fresh from Oxford and Cambridge, and sitting among them a portly, fifty-five-year-old man, the former Secretary of State of the fallen Confederacy. He described with detail the social protocols of these dinners and the food:

> To each four persons, who constitute a mess, the waiter serves a dinner composed of soup, one joint, and vegetables, one sweet dish and cheese; a bottle of sherry or port at choice is allowed to each mess (fiery stuff it is) and bitter beer *ad libitum.* The charge for the dinner is two shillings. No one at the mess helps another, but the etiquette is each in turn helps himself, one being the first for soup, the next first for the joint and so on. One dines almost every day with some stranger, but the rule is that all are presumed to be gentlemen and conversation is at once established with entire abandon, as if the parties were old acquaintances.[20]

Benjamin was fortunate, but probably in his case adroit and far-seeing, in having arranged to be apprenticed with Charles Pollock. Pollock had developed a large practice in mercantile law, which was to be Benjamin's specialty. It was eighty-three-year-old Baron Pollock who persuaded his son to take on Benjamin, even though the office already had two students, because the old man argued that Benjamin "had no need to learn law, only to see something of the practice of the English courts and to meet members of the bar."

Charles Pollock later wrote of one of the first cases assigned to Benjamin, dealing with the rights of the police to search suspects in custody before trial or conviction. "Alluding to the *Trent* affair," Pollock said, "here is a case made for you on the right of search." Benjamin quickly researched the case in a single morning and wrote a memorandum, of which Pollock later said: "The only fault to be found was that the learning was too great for the occasion going back to first principles on each point. Many years after, I was told that the opinion was held in high respect and often referred to by the police and at the Home office."[21]

Benjamin's well-known charm worked its magic on the Pollock family, and he was invited for luncheons and weekends at the Baron's estate. Pollock wrote that "he always put forward the amusing side of things" and spoke "with anything like bitterness" of only two injuries inflicted upon him by the Yankees—"they had burnt his law library and drank his cellar of old Madeira, a wine much cherished in New Orleans."[22]

The Benjamin public persona in this new period in his life followed the same formula as it had in Richmond: the constant half-smile, the good humor, the facile turns of phrase, the anecdotal response to trauma, always surprising the listener with his seemingly cavalier reaction to great events. Perhaps he was aware that he was always on stage, that mental notes were being made by whoever was talking to him, and they would be writing about him later. He did not want to appear morose, regretful, sorrowful, or depressed about his past; perhaps he overcompensated by being too cheerful, excessively genial, obviously casual.

But he was capable of lapses; at times the curtains would part slightly to reveal his true feelings. One of Baron Pollock's daughters described a moment of unintended candor on a weekend visit to the Baron's estate: "I had not met Benjamin and had pictured to myself an American of the Jefferson Davis type. To my surprise, when he entered the room I saw a short, stout, genial man, of decidedly Jewish descent with bright, dark eyes, and all the politeness and *bonhomie* of a Frenchman, looking as if he had never had a care in his life."

That was the vintage Benjamin style. If anything, his status as an ex-Confederate leader on the run increased the air of mystery and adventure that surrounded him.

The next morning, Miss Pollock and Benjamin both arrived early for breakfast. He told her "most interesting and thrilling details of his perilous escape." She wrote that "I was most struck by his candor" and "I asked what the Northerners would have done to him if they had caught him." Whether he replied for shock value or in a moment of utter openness with a young woman, she inadvertently became the only person to whom there is any record of a confession of his inner feelings. "He said they probably would have put him to death. When I exclaimed in horror at such an atrocity, he said, apologetically, that as party feeling ran high just then his side might have done the same thing had the circumstances been reversed."[23]

Through the influence of new friends in high places, Benjamin was able to dispense with the usual three-year apprenticeship requirement and was called to the bar on June 6, 1866, just six months after he entered as a student. His petition for admission stated he was a "political exile"; that his parents were both natural-born British subjects of British ancestry and that he, consequently, was a "natural-born subject of Her Majesty." It stated that he had been taken to the United States during his infancy, where during his minority his father was naturalized and he "thus became entitled to all the rights of a citizen of the United States without abjuring native allegiance."[24]

His estimation of the probable results of his capture was not exaggerated. Four people had been hanged already for the plot to assassinate Lincoln; Jefferson Davis was in prison, and John Surratt was still at large. Though Judah P. Benjamin was facing forward, all his energy and intellect channeled into a new career in a new land, he could not altogether avoid the lengthening shadow of events in the United States.

At a Cabinet meeting in Washington on October 16, 1866, Secretary of State Seward, himself a target of the assassins the night Lincoln was killed, read some papers from the American ambassador in Rome, including a statement from a man named Henri B. Ste. Marie, a private in the Papal Zouaves. Ste. Marie had gone to the American legation in Rome and informed the minister in residence that John Surratt, a member of his regiment, had "admitted his connection with the assassination of the President" and that he had also implicated Jefferson Davis, Judah P. Benjamin, and the rest of the Confederate Cabinet "as being privy to it."[25]

The reactions of President Andrew Johnson's Cabinet to this sensational disclosure were described in the diaries of Orville H. Browning, a former Senator from Illinois and the Secretary of the Interior under Johnson. According to Browning's diary, the report from Rome stated Ste. Marie had testified that "the plot had been discussed at Richmond—that [Surratt] and Booth used to visit Richmond every week and that they had laid the scheme before Mr. Benjamin, that he had presented it to the cabinet, and it had undergone discussion there, and that money had been advanced to further the enterprise."[26] Browning also recorded Seward's response to the letter: "Mr. Seward expressed his belief that Booth and Surratt had conferred with Benjamin upon the subject, and that Benjamin had encouraged and subsidized them; but he did not believe that the matter had ever been under discussion before the Richmond Cabinet or received the countenance of other members of the Cabinet than Benjamin."[27]

The Cabinet responded immediately upon hearing of Ste. Marie's testimony: "Our minister was directed to pay him $250 in gold, and to ascertain from Cardinal Antonelly whether Surratt would be given up on the demand of this government." Later, Ste. Marie received an additional $10,000 reward for the information he had given, even though Secretary Stanton had revoked the reward for John Surratt a year earlier.[28]

A certain note of hysteria crept in as Ste. Marie's statement contin-ued. Because Mary Surratt was a Catholic and her son had been hidden initially by Catholic clergy in Canada and had found his way to the Vatican, the testimony would lead later to conspiracy theories involving the Catholic Church. "I believe," Ste. Marie wrote, "he [Surratt] is protected by the clergy, and that the murder is the result of a deep-laid plot, not only against the life of President Lincoln, but against the republic, as we are aware that priesthood and royalty are and always have been opposed to liberty."[29]

Although the testimony by Ste. Marie was later proved to be false, and another witness who corroborated Surratt's confession of involve-ment was found guilty of perjury, Secretary of State Seward began to negotiate with the Vatican to arrest Surratt, a complicated problem because there was no extradition treaty with the Vatican. While discussions were under way, the Papal government took action on its own account. Surratt was arrested by Papal guards but he suddenly broke free, leapt over a precipice, and fled to Naples, where he boarded a ship in the harbor. A month later, on November 27, 1866, he was recaptured in Alexandria, Egypt, more than twenty months after the assassination. Now he could be easily extradited.[30]

Historians have noted that after the uproar over the hanging of Mary Surratt, Stanton and the U.S. Government simply did not want to apprehend John Surratt, even when they had the chance to do so.

As early as September 1865, Stanton and Seward were fully aware of Surratt's whereabouts in Liverpool and of Surratt's intention to go to Rome. Yet they refused to have him arrested. Henry Wilding, the Vice Consul in the United States Consulate in Liverpool wired the State Department in Washington on September 30, 1865, one month after Benjamin also landed at Liverpool, that "the supposed Surratt has arrived in Liverpool and is now staying at the oratory of the Roman Catholic Church of the Holy Cross. . . . I can, of course, do nothing further in the matter without Mr. Adams's [U.S. Minister to England] instructions and a warrant. If it be Surratt, such a wretch ought not to escape."[31]

The Vice Consul must have been shocked at the reply from William Hunter, the acting Secretary, on October 13, 1865; "Your dispatches . . . have been received. In reply . . . I have to inform you that, upon a consultation with the Secretary of War and the Judge Advocate General, it is thought advisable that no action be taken in regard to the arrest of the supposed John Surratt at present."[32]

Wilding's informant, the ship's surgeon on the ship that carried

Surratt to Liverpool, was so eager to pick up the $25,000 reward that he took his case to the U.S. Consul in Montreal. That consul wired the State Department on October 25, 1865: "It is Surratt's intention to go to Rome. . . . If an officer could go to England, I have no doubt that Surratt's arrest might be effected, and thus the last of the conspirators against the lives of the President and Secretary of State be brought to justice."[33]

The ship's surgeon, seeing the reward slip away, tried to arouse the government to action by testifying, "Surratt remarked repeatedly that he only wished to live two years longer, in which time he would serve President Johnson as Booth did Mr. Lincoln."[34]

Stanton did make a move, but it was the opposite of what the surgeon expected. On November 24, 1865, he issued an order that "the reward offered for the arrest of John Surratt is hereby revoked."[35] He later explained that since it was known that Surratt was abroad, government officials would be involved in his capture, and they should not be rewarded for performing their duty.

It was clear from the actions of the government that there was no longer any taste for another assassination trial, especially one that would open up the wounds of Mary Surratt's hanging and cause a new look at the evidence that convicted her. The delays continued. Even the gunboat returning John Surratt to the United States from Alexandria took an unusual forty-five days to reach its destination, arriving in late February 1867.

A fictional account of the plot behind the assassination appeared in a dime novel in 1866 with the cumbersome title of *The Great Conspiracy: A Book of Absorbing Interest! Startling Developments, Eminent Persons Implicated, Full Secrets of the Assassination Plot, John H. Surratt and His Mother, with Biographical Sketches of J. B. Booth and John Wilkes Booth, and the Life and Extraordinary Adventures of John H. Surratt, the Conspirator.*

A chapter entitled "Interview with the Rebel Officers" purported to report a conversation between Booth and a Lieutenant Carter Braxton. Booth speaks first:

"Would it not be possible to provide a messenger to bear the glorious news to Richmond?"

"We could hardly do that, it will however be known in Richmond, soon enough."

"How so?"

"About six weeks ago," replied Braxton, "I went to see Benjamin, to transact a little business, and he desired me to call in the evening. I . . . was at his office at eight o'clock; we were alone, and after I had done my errand, I rose to go, but he asked me to sit and chat awhile and opened the conversation, by observing that the Fall Campaign had terminated disastrously . . . and that an impeachment was sure to follow; but there was one way to cut this gordian knot."

"And what was that?"

"He would not answer, I repeated the question, and after a short pause, he replied LINCOLN'S DEATH. I was prepared for this, but did not expect such a frank avowal."

"He is right," interrupted Booth, "I expected that he would say so, nothing else, but Lincoln's death will settle this matter. . . ."

"Benjamin then said," resumed the speaker, "that he had hoped someone would spontaneously have undertaken this task and that the Confederacy, secretly, but effectually, would do all that was necessary."

"Did he tell you Davis knew any thing of this?"

"I think that he did."[36]

The sensational dime novels in the 1860s made quick money and took advantage of the biases and preconceptions that already existed in the mind of the public. Though dismissed by historians, they were widely read and are significant not as a source of information—they were often sheer invention—but for what they tell about the dark side of public opinion during that period. For Judah Benjamin, the publication and widespread distribution of *The Great Conspiracy* was an uncomfortable addition to the forces shaping public opinion in America.

As Surratt's gunboat, the *Swatara*, made its way back from Egypt, Washington was awash in new rumors. One of them involved Frederick Seward, the assistant Secretary of State and son of the Secretary of State, and the fear of what Surratt's testimony might be. The Springfield *Daily Republican* stated: "Those who have a taste for the horrible will find satisfaction in a new Washington rumor to the effect that the secret mission of Fred Seward on the steamer 'Gettysburg' is for the purpose of intercepting the 'Swatara' and offering to John Surratt the promise of a pardon from President Johnson if he will not implicate the President in the assassination of Mr. Lincoln. Young Seward is supposed to have a filial motive for wishing to induce Surratt to keep silence, as it is part of the horrible theory that Secretary Seward was in the assassination plot, and consented to be almost killed in order to disarm suspicion!"[37]

In February 1867, while Surratt awaited a trial that was to begin the following June, former General George H. Sharpe, an investigator from the State Department, arrived in London. The intent of his mission is known from the diaries of Benjamin Moran, the secretary to the American Embassy in London, who had served in various posts in the embassy since the early 1850s. His voluminous journal, kept with scrupulous care from 1857 to 1874, revealed a person with "a grossly exaggerated sense of his own importance" but at the same time gives the reader a sense of the day-to-day happenings in the American Embassy during that period.[38]

On February 11, 1867, Moran reported that "Mr. George H. Sharpe, the detective, has been sent here to hunt up evidence against the persons implicated in the assassination of President Lincoln. He is a bullet-headed person and is determined to catch Benjamin if possible."[39]

A week later, the diary continued on the same subject, reporting that "General George H. Sharpe also called. He thinks he will be able to prove that Judah P. Benjamin was implicated in the assassination of Mr. Lincoln. I hope so."[40] Again on March 14, he wrote that "General Sharpe came up. He is on the track of George McHenry and Benjamin and thinks he will be successful."[41] McHenry had worked as an assistant to Edwin DeLeon, a journalist and propagandist for the Confederacy in Paris from 1862 through 1864.

Moran's diary has a number of other derogatory references to Benjamin, referring to him as "the little Jew,"[42] "the Jew Benjamin,"[43] and "a great scamp who deserves hanging."[44] He even began to get into the chase himself two days later, writing that General Sharpe and he met to visit a hotel "to ascertain if J. P. Benjamin and George McHenry saw John Surratt and supplied him with money after Mr. Lincoln's assassination in London."[45]

The investigation continued for several more days, and Moran reported: "In the afternoon, I went to Fenton's for General Sharpe about Benjamin and Surratt, but could get no reliable information."[46]

The search yielded nothing. Nine months later, in December 1867, after the trial of John Surratt, General Sharpe's report to Secretary of State Seward was made public in a special report to Congress. It was a document so vague in language that one had to know its background to understand its import.

"In the month of January last," Sharpe wrote, "I left for Europe pursuant to instructions from the State Department in which I was told there might be reason to apprehend . . . 'citizens of the United States in Europe other than those who have heretofore been suspected or charged with the offence, were instigators of or concerned in, the assassination of the late President Lincoln, and the attempted assassination of the Secretary of State.' It was deemed proper, in connection with the anticipated trial of John H. Surratt, to make an effort to identify those persons, and it was made my duty to examine any evidence existing abroad, so that the government might judge whether or not it ought to demand the surrender of any persons in Europe."[47]

The report never mentioned names, but Benjamin's reputation in London made it obvious to Seward and the Congress that he was at least one of the targets of Sharpe's investigation.

"A patient investigation," the report continued, "was given to all circumstances tending to throw light on Surratt's connection with rebels known to be in London at that time." He thanked the American consuls in Europe, especially Moran, for "every assistance" and stated that "every fact was inquired into which had any significance under my instruction."

His conclusion was: "This examination failing to disclose any state of facts deemed sufficiently well established or of sufficient importance to bring to the knowledge of the department, attention was turned to the manner in which Surratt entered the Papal States." He left no room for doubt in the final lines of his report:

"Conscious that earnestness was brought to the attempt at identifying the loathsome instigators of the great crime, and that every possible assistance was received, I have to report that, in my opinion, no such legal or reasonable proof exists in Europe of the participation of any persons there, formerly citizens of the United States, as to call for the action of the government."[48]

John Surratt's trial began on June 10, 1867, and was a sensational national event that lasted sixty-two days, involving the questioning of more than two hundred witnesses. Surratt, then twenty-four years old, did not take the stand during the trial but rested his case on his proof that he could not have been in Washington on the day of the assassination. A jury could not reach a verdict, and a judge later reported that eight of the twelve were ready to vote for acquittal.[49]

Three years later, on December 6, 1870, in Rockville, Maryland, Surratt gave a long public lecture to a packed courthouse, telling for the first time his side of the story. He said that he had been a courier in the Confederate Secret Service Bureau since 1861; he confessed that he had met Booth and plotted with him, but only for the abduction of the President, "rash, perhaps foolish, but honorable." In his role as courier, Surratt said that he had received $200 from Secretary of State Judah P. Benjamin on the Friday before the evacuation of Richmond to carry some dispatches from Richmond to Canada. "That was," he said "the only money I ever received from the Confederate government in any shape or form. Booth and I often consulted together as to whether it would not be well to acquaint the authorities in Richmond with our plan, as we were sadly in want of money, our expenses being very heavy. In fact, the question arose among us as to whether, after getting Mr. Lincoln, if we succeeded in our plan, the Confederate authorities would not surrender us to the United States again, because of doing this thing without their knowledge or consent. But we never acquainted them with the plan, and they never had anything in the wide world to do with it. In fact, we were jealous of our undertaking and wanted no outside help. I have not made this statement to defend the officers of the Confederate government. They are perfectly willing to defend themselves. What I have done myself I am not ashamed to let the world know."[50]

He continued describing the dispatches, which he delivered to Montreal, to Confederate General Edwin G. Lee, whom Secretary of State Benjamin had appointed to succeed Jacob Thompson, "to whom the dispatches were directed, and delivered to him. These dispatches we tried to introduce as evidence in my trial, but his Honor Judge Fisher ruled them out, despite the fact that the government had tried to prove that they had relation to the conspiracy to kill Mr. Lincoln. They were only accounts of some money transactions—nothing more or less."[51] Lee, a relative of Robert E. Lee, confirmed the legitimacy of the Surratt mission in testimony at the trial.

Until the trial in June 1867 and the lecture in late 1870, there was no way for Judah P. Benjamin to have known what Surratt's testimony would be. If the U.S. Government had been willing to hang Mary Surratt, in what many considered a cruel miscarriage of justice, to force John Surratt to return to trial, how far could he have assumed Stanton and others would be expected to go to link Judah P. Benjamin and Jefferson Davis to the crime? In the end, Surratt fortunately could prove his whereabouts in New York State on the day of the assassination. But Benjamin could not have known of Surratt's alibi for twenty months after the deed, nor could he have known the details of Surratt's story until the lecture more than five years after the assassination. Secretary of State Benjamin had used Surratt as a courier and had given him $200 and a mission three weeks before the assassination. Benjamin knew the dispatches to General Edwin Lee in Montreal were of minor consequence, but he also knew that the government would try to link the dispatches to the plot. Even if Benjamin was confident of his own innocence, he could not vouch for Surratt's. Perhaps the young man had been involved. If so, he could choose to implicate high officials to save his neck from a noose. With evidence of funds and papers having passed between them, Benjamin might have thought it wiser to destroy all of his papers and not speak of it again than to risk the distortion of the financial records, and the suggestion of a deeper connection should the papers fall into the hands of men of such "savage cruelty," in his words, as the unscrupulous and ruthlessly South-hating Secretary of War Edwin Stanton. After five years of public attacks on his Jewishness, what chance would he have had before a military tribunal that ordered Mary Surratt hanged and in the hands of a President who allowed the sentence to be executed and had a history of anti-Semitic remarks aimed directly at Benjamin?

The link to the Canadian spies had been tenuous to begin with. Booth had visited Montreal six months before the assassination and had deposited $455 in the Ontario Bank, the same bank in which Thompson kept Confederate funds. That was all the evidence there was in Canada; without a case, Stanton and the government simply held Davis in prison for two years without a trial. Varina wrote that after the President was captured, "he leaned over me in bidding goodbye on the ship, and whispered 'No matter what proof is adduced by the North, remember that my dying testimony was to you that I had nothing to do with the assassination, or causing any other deed unworthy of a soldier, or of our cause.' With this assurance," she wrote, "he bade farewell."[52]

A few hours later, when General James Wilson, the commanding officer of the Union garrison that captured Davis, showed him the proclamation by Andrew Johnson charging the Confederate President in the assassination conspiracy, Davis immediately asserted, "There is one man at least who knows the charge to be false, the man who signed the proclamation, for he well knew that I greatly preferred Lincoln to himself."[53]

Benjamin's rise in the British bar was not instantaneous. It required the cultivation of clients, attention to reputation, and a great deal of hard work. The very fact that the requirements for Lincoln's Inn were waived caused eyebrows to be raised on both sides of the Atlantic—in the South especially, where it was realized that a former high-ranking Confederate official had claimed British citizenship since birth, and in England, where exceptions were rarely made for admission to the bar.

Pollock reported on one of Benjamin's first cases, a complicated challenge permitting only a few days of preparation, requiring him to revise totally the very lengthy rules for an old and established ship insurance company. Two other lawyers had turned the case down because the meeting to approve the new rules was to occur in just forty-eight hours.

"The very next morning," Pollock wrote "commencing after an early breakfast, and never pausing for a midday meal, he worked on steadily, and shortly before eight, the hour at which he usually dined, the rules were complete, written out in his own neat hand . . . with scarce an alteration or correction from beginning to end, as if he had been composing a poem. I doubt if any draughtsmen within the two Temples could have done them so efficiently within the same time."[54]

He was working hard but enjoying it and would prove himself by performance, not prior high office. "I am as much interested in my profession as when I first commenced it as a boy," he wrote Mason, "and am rapidly recovering all that I had partially forgotten in the turmoil of public affairs."[55]

As his record of successful appearances in cases grew, so also did his reputation. Even the *American Law Review* reported in October 1866 that he had won "golden opinions for his text and ability." The *Review* continued: "No one ever questioned Mr. Benjamin's ability. If his moral qualities had been equal to his intellectual, there was no position in his native country beyond his reach. He seems properly to have joined in the Northern circuit and the secessionist sympathizers at Liverpool ought to give him good business."[56]

Legends also began to grow up around him, just as they had in America, giving him a larger-than-life quality. Once, a well-known firm sent him a packet of papers to examine with a request for an opinion, attaching a paltry fee of five guineas. After a few days, when a clerk from the firm appeared asking for them, the papers were still sitting on his desk untouched. The clerk asked if there had been a mistake.

"Not at all," Benjamin replied, "the fee proffered covered taking in the papers, but not examining them."

The clerk reported that exchange to his superiors. Benjamin would not let the legal establishment take advantage of his new practice and devalue his efforts. Twenty-five guineas were dispatched. When the solicitor some years later confessed that his client had insisted on a Benjamin opinion, Benjamin replied, "If you had told me at the time, I should not have looked at the papers for twice the fee."[57]

He attributed part of his struggle to win a significant place at the bar to the favoritism and interrelationships of families and connections among the upper-class jurists practicing with him:

> The growth of business here is so very slow and the competition so severe that the attorneys give their briefs, whenever they possibly can, to barristers who are connected or related with them or their families; and in an old country like England, these family ties are so ramified that there is hardly an attorney who has not in some way a barrister whom it is in his interest to engage. I therefore have but little chance for a brief whenever it *can* be given elsewhere, and this accounts for the difficulty under which anyone in the world must labor, if not connected in some way with the attorneys and their families.[58]

He did not stay idle. He landed on the very same idea that had propelled him to the top of his profession in New Orleans thirty years earlier. Then, with Tom Slidell, he had written a comprehensive guide to Louisiana law. Once again he noticed a gap in the legal literature. What was needed was another comprehensive guide, this time to the law of sales on two continents, encompassing American, French, and English law. It was an enormous task, but on April 17, 1867, he wrote his sisters that "as I have so little to do at the bar compared with former professional life, I am turning author and have in preparation a law work which will be ready for publication I hope in November or December next and will bring me into more prominence with the profession and perhaps secure a more rapid advance in getting me business."[59]

The old warhorse in him, apparently, could not settle down to the easy pace of a gentleman at the bar. His mind was working, his curiosity was ever engaged, and his understanding far outpaced the capacity of a class-bound legal system influenced by blood lines to use his extraordinary talents.

He wrote his sister: "My book is nearly finished, but the nearer I get to the end, the more fastidious I become about correcting, amending and improving it . . . but who told you it had a jaw-breaking name? It is a simple Treatise on Sale under the English law, which is very different from the law of Louisiana, and the subject quite a difficult and troublesome branch of professional learning here."[60]

The rumors his sisters had heard were not altogether incorrect. His now famous *Treatise on the Law of Sale of Personal Property, with Reference to the American Decisions, to the French Code and Civil Law* was published in August 1868 and became an instant success in Britain, the United States, and the British possessions. Known simply by its shorthand title, *Benjamin on Sales*, it was almost immediately recognized as a legal classic that met a long-felt need of the British bar. It went through three printings over the course of Benjamin's life and became a standard for decades.[61]

One morning soon after publication, when Baron Samuel Martin took his seat on the Bench, he asked a clerk for a copy of the new volume.

"Never heard of it," the young clerk replied.

"Never heard of it!" the Baron bellowed. "Mind that I never take my seat here again without that book at my side."[62]

Benjamin was proud of it and wanted his family at least to see it, even though they would have little understanding of it. "As poor Kitt's article gave you the face-ache," he wrote his sister, "I shall not upset you entirely with my law book; but I suppose some copies of it will reach New Orleans, and you can read the title-page and look at the outside without much risk of serious injury."[63]

The book marked a turning point in Benjamin's career and won him both admirers and clients, just as he had planned.

"If I had not written my book," he remarked in a letter to his sister in New Orleans, "I should be 'nowhere' in the race, but that has done me an immensity of good, and will give me further fruits of business and reputation."[64]

Even as late as February 8, 1870, money worries were still bothering him greatly, and he confessed that "I cannot get along with less than 1,400 pounds, say about $7,000 a year, including my professional expenses at the Temple for rent, clerk-hire, bar-mess, robing room, wigs and gowns, etc, etc, which are endless. I had hoped strongly that by this year at furthest I should be able to make both ends meet, but I have not reached that point."[65]

His reputation was outstripping his income, leading to exaggerated reports of his success in the American press. He was very straightfor-ward and candid with his sisters in New Orleans: "[A]lthough my success at the bar is absurdly exaggerated in some accounts that I have seen in the newspapers, I have really 'turned the corner' at last, and . . . my receipts for the last twelve months have exceeded ten thousand dollars. . . . I think my reputation at the bar is increasing and I can see my circle of clients is daily widening."[66]

Pollock observed that Benjamin had certain advantages coming from America that enabled him to succeed in England:

One great and early advantage for Benjamin was . . . that . . . he was educated in the State of Louisiana . . . the law taught and administered within it was that which took its origins in the code of Justinian, and was afterward adopted by the nations of Europe and continued to be the law of France until the code Napoleon. . . . This . . . gave him a distinct position superior to his brother advocates when arguing appeals from the English colonies of French origin.[67]

Moreover, Pollock continued, his experience as an American lawyer gave him a broader perspective, because "the professions and duties of barrister and solicitor, which in England are separate, are discharged by one and the same person. . . . His clients [in New Orleans] were numerous, their business being principally of a mercantile character, and few men had a sounder or wider range of knowledge and experience of the law-merchant, including shipping, insurance, and foreign trading than Benjamin."[68]

Finally, the pinnacle of the English bar came within reach. A letter from Benjamin in August 1872 gave his family in America the exciting news of his elevation to the inner circle of influence through a new appointment.

"I have had high professional promotion lately," he wrote his sisters. "A number of judges united in recommending to the Lord Chancellor that I should have a 'patent of precedence' above all future Queen's Counsel." For a lawyer trained in America, the promotion was unprecedented, just seven years after his arrival, but it also had a theatrical dimension unheard of in his own country. "I have now to wear a full-bottomed wig, with wings falling down my shoulders and knee breeches and black silk stockings and shoes with buckles and in this ridiculous array, in my silk gown, to present myself at the next levee to Her Majesty to return thanks for her gracious kindness. . . . As it is usual to have photographs made of one's self on these occasions I will send some to enable you all to laugh at 'how like a monkey brother looks in that hideous wig.' "[69]

Benjamin was able to write intimate and revealing letters while aware how his explanations of the pomp of the English bar, details of his income, and descriptions of his colleagues might sound like conceit to unsympathetic ears. Sensitive to his enemies in America, he lectured his sisters about showing his letters to others.

"Before I forget it," he wrote, "I must just mention that I don't want anything of this sort that I write for the family to get into the papers, for if it were repeated here, it would be known that such details must have originated with me and I should be suspected, to my great mortification, of writing puffs of myself, than which nothing is deservedly regarded with more contempt."[70]

He did, however, want the New Orleans community and then a wider public to know of his rise to prominence, and he instructed his sisters carefully. "Of course, the *fact* of my promotion being announced could do no harm, but none of the details which can come *only* from *me* must get into the papers."[71]

The photograph was to him such a symbol of his good fortune that he sent it also to his friend James Mason, the former Confederate diplomat now living in Canada, saying "it may be very long, if ever, before I can hope to press your hand." Already he seemed certain he would never return to America. When he informed Mason of the departure from London of Colin McRae, an ex-Confederate friend of both Mason and Benjamin, he called McRae the "last of the Romans" and lamented, "I shall be left alone."[72]

While Benjamin was absorbed in building his law practice, he watched with growing alarm what was happening in America and criticized the extremism of the Northern radicals: "[I]f the Southern states are allowed without interference to regulate the transition of the negro from his former state to that of a freed man," he wrote to Bayard, "they will eventually work out the problem successfully, though with great difficulty and trouble, and I doubt not that the recuperative energy of the people will restore a large share of their former material prosperity much sooner than is generally believed."

He warned of the results of the current policy: "But if they are obstructed and thwarted by the fanatics, and if external influences are brought to bear on the negro and influence his ignorant fancy with wild dreams of social and political equality, I shudder for the bitter future which is in store for my unhappy country."[73]

In October 1866, after Davis had been imprisoned for more than a year, Benjamin wrote Mason that he feared "an additional rigorous season, passed in confinement should prove fatal." He criticized those who had the power to act but refused out of a misguided sense of retribution: "It is the most shameful outrage that such a thing should be even possible, but I have ceased to hope anything but justice or humanity demands from men who seem now to have uncontrolled power over public affairs in the United States. I believe Johnson would willingly release Mr. Davis, but he is apparently cowed by the overbearing violence of the Radicals and dare not act in accordance with his judgment."[74]

Benjamin's rise to prominence and success abroad created intense jealousies in the South on the part of those suffering at the hands of carpetbaggers and scalawags. So grossly exaggerated were reports of his income that some Americans thought he was living the life of the English gentry. In defense, even to his own family, he began to disclose many details about his actual income. Former Senator Wigfall of Texas, who had been a bitter enemy toward the end of the war, accused him of stealing that part of the Confederate treasury remaining abroad:

"As to Benjamin, he turned out to be an Englishman," Wigfall wrote to Clement Clay from London in 1866, "and he has plenty of money and can attend the clubs, entertain friends, and extend his acquaintance, he found no difficulty in being admitted after six months at the Inns. I have not seen him but saw his name in the list of stock holders of Overand, Gurney and Co. after their bankruptcy for a good round sum of pounds sterling." The cotton money was, in Wigfall's view, possible evidence of Benjamin's speculation while escaping. Benjamin, his letter continued, "had managed somehow or other to accumulate about two hundred bales of cotton at Liverpool and drew his salary after getting here. He also drew from the Confederate agent on the Islands between 3 and 4 hundred pounds on his way here. On his arrival here he reported himself authorized by the President to take charge of financial matters and my own belief is that he and the agents have divided among themselves all that was left of Confederate funds. But enough of this disgusting subject."[75]

Meade heard other stories in his interviews about Benjamin, part of the legend of Judah P. Benjamin repeated through the years, to the effect that somehow he stole the Confederate gold in those final days. The same public charge was made against Davis by none other than former Confederate General Joseph E. Johnston, who suggested in a newspaper interview that Davis stole more than $2 million in gold from the Confederate treasury in the closing days of the war. But in Davis's case, others rose to his defense. Davis himself was the personification of honor and stoicism; he remained silent, not dignifying the charge with an answer. His accuser was proved wrong by the outraged but careful testimony accounting for the gold by other officials in letters, articles, and speeches, all provided in detail in Varina's memoirs.

The mystery of what happened to some of the Confederate gold may never be known. It has inspired a legend and a literature all its own.[76] Most of the treasure of cash, bonds, bank notes, gold and silver coins, and bullion was accounted for, but in the chaos of the closing days of the war, wagons were looted and many were eager to grab what they could and bury it for later. It is unlikely that any substantial amounts ended up in the hands of the fleeing Judah P. Benjamin, traveling alone, needing to move quickly to avoid capture. And if he managed to hide it somewhere, why did he never return to reclaim it?

But no one ever seemed to rise in defense of Judah Benjamin. The fact that such a charge would stick to Benjamin over the years testifies to the complicated view his contemporaries had of him. Benjamin was the Jewish Confederate, the manipulator, the internationalist. For the Southern psyche, the image of the rapacious stereotype of the Jews gave the charges resonance. Davis braved such insults to character in proud silence; Benjamin remained silent too, perhaps letting the defense of Davis speak for his own innocence as well. When Wigfall visited London, Benjamin wrote to Mason that "he called on everybody but me when he arrived, and it was very agreeable to me not to meet him. I do not know how he continues to exist, but I suppose he must receive remittance from the other side."[77]

19

The Lincoln Assassination: *Lingering Suspicion*

✹

When Judah P. Benjamin arrived in England on August 30, 1865, four months after he had left President Davis, he wrote to Varina within one day of his arrival a particularly heartfelt letter.

"I only arrived here night before last, and my first care yesterday was to relieve as far as possible the anxiety which had been increasing during my whole trip relative to the practicability of aiding myself and your husband in any possible manner." He wanted her to know that Colin McRae, the Confederate business agent in London, at his suggestion had placed the equivalent of $12,500 to her credit, which "I considered . . . was the first and most sacred claim" on the remaining Confederate funds, "being the President's salary up to 30th June last." The letter continues:

> The money now placed at your disposal, my dear Mrs. Davis, is your husband's: it is the money of the government paid to you in his behalf: you are indebted for it to no individual and are under no obligations to any one for it. You can therefore use [it] without any scruple of delicacy. I beg however that you will not apply any of it toward the personal use of Mr. Davis or any expenses of his trial of defence; for I know, I am absolutely certain, that a very large sum, five times as much as will probably be wanted, is already placed in perfectly safe hands, to be used solely for his service, and for the expenses of his defence and that of the other prisoners, until his release from captivity.[1]

The letter is filled with more personal references than any other surviving exchange between them, as well as expressions of Benjamin's loyalty and concern for the President.

Having thus disposed of pressing business matters, I refer to others which it is impossible to touch upon without the deepest emotion. God knows what I have suffered since my first reception of the horrible news that my beloved and honored friend was in the hands of the enemy. It was in May that I first learned the fact from John Taylor Wood, whom I met in Florida and who had just escaped from the scene of the calamity. I toiled on, night and day, with the vague hope that I could do something to aid him, if I were once beyond the limits of the U.S. I was very unlucky in my efforts.

He wanted her to know that it had been dangerous for him as well, and he was obviously eager to have her understand that he had not simply fled for his life but was serving the President's long-term military plan. Perhaps he was being disingenuous in this regard, but he wanted to assure her he had survived without injury and that he was aware of her plight:

I will not recount to you the details of my journey nor the scenes through which I have passed. After weeks spent in solitary travel on horseback through the forests and marshes of Florida in constant peril of capture: after passing twenty-three days in an open boat at sea, and crossing the Gulf Stream in a yawl: after being forced to put back to St. Thomas in the Steamer on which I had taken passage for England in consequence of the ship's taking fire at night at sea: after every imaginable contretemps and danger, I reached London on the night of the 30th instant nearly four months after I parted from the President, charged by him to perform certain public duties in Nassau and Havana, and then to rejoin him in Texas. During this whole time, I have been incessantly harassed by the most poignant anxiety both on your account and his. Knowing your devoted love for your husband, I cannot imagine how you have survived the terrible distress which must have overwhelmed you when the extent of the calamity became apparent as revealed by his barbarous treatment, and aggravated by the inhuman refusal to allow you access to him.

He was still ready to serve and wanted her to feel that he was available to perform any request that might help them:

However, I am here at last, without means, but with unimpaired health and undiminished energies. Can I, my dear friend, do any thing, in any way, by any sacrifice, to aid you or Mr. Davis in this dreadful crisis? If so, command me without scruple. Suggest any idea that occurs to you as opening any chance of benefit to him or yourself and I will leave no effort unemployed to accomplish something. You know me too well to harbor a moment's suspicion that I am making mere profession: you know that I mean all that I say.

There was a foreboding in his words, as if he expected the worst:

Good bye, my dear Mrs. Davis. God bless you and your little ones. I dare not trust myself with the expression of my feelings for your noble husband, for my unhappy friend.

Ever yours devotedly
J. P. Benjamin[2]

The news of Jefferson Davis's cruel treatment as a prisoner at Fort Monroe turned him, in the mind of the public in the North, from the leader of the rebellion into a Southern martyr. He was kept in absolute isolation. Not even letters were allowed between him and Varina for three months. He was manacled unnecessarily with leg irons on his second day in prison after a terrific physical struggle with four soldiers in which "the prisoner showed unnatural strength"; being watched every moment in a cell that was lit by a lamp around the clock, thus torturing the sight in his remaining eye. The press reported that Davis suffered terribly from this intentional humiliation. The lack of exercise, the dampness, and the stressful circumstances began to cause a serious deterioration in his health. Varina sent a frantic wire to President Johnson: "Is it possible you will keep me from my dying husband? Can I come to see him?"[3] She received visitation rights but was shocked to see him "patiently, uncomplainingly fading away and [I] cannot help him."[4]

When news of Davis's further decline in health reached England, Benjamin wrote his sister: "We are all in intense anxiety on the subject of our honored and noble chief, Jefferson Davis. By the last accounts there was every probability that those in power at Washington would succeed in getting rid of him by the tortures inflicted on him in prison, and the delay in trying him was intended to give time for this moral assassination. No nobler gentleman, no purer man, no more exalted patriot ever drew breath; and eternal infamy

will blacken the base and savage wretches who are now taking advantage of their brief grasp of power to wreak a cowardly vengeance
on his honored head."[5] In the context of the times, it was unusual
to find the word "assassination" used to describe the Northern treatment of Jefferson Davis.

Benjamin also wrote a public letter of protest to the London *Times*
on September 11, 1865, which was reprinted two weeks later on
the front page of the New York *Times*. Because it was one of his
two public statements on the war in the nineteen years following
it and came at a time when Benjamin had freshly arrived in England
while Jefferson Davis was imprisoned, the letter deserves close scru-
tiny.

Given the fact that he was under suspicion himself, the letter is
interesting as much for its omissions as for its stated defense of the
imprisoned President. Benjamin chose to defend Davis against "the
accusation made by the Federal authorities that prisoners of war
were cruelly treated by the Confederates—not merely in exceptional
cases by subordinate officials, but systematically, and in conformity
with a policy deliberately adopted by President Davis, General Lee
and Secretary of War Mr. Seddon." The letter does not mention
the other principal charge under which Davis was being held, complicity in the assassination, a subject on which Benjamin presumably
could have contributed direct counter-testimony, since the Canadian
spy ring, which was his responsibility, was central to the accusation.
He chose instead to argue on the narrow question of prisoner treatment and exchanges, but the language he used seems to show he
had the larger question in mind:

> As a member of the Cabinet of President Davis from the date of
> his first inauguration under the Provisional Constitution to the
> final overthrow of the Confederate Government by force of arms,
> as a personal friend whose relations with Jefferson Davis have
> been of the most intimate and confidential nature, I feel it impera-
> tively to be my duty to request your insertion of this letter in
> vindication of honorable men, who, less fortunate than myself,
> are now held in close confinement by their enemies, and are
> unable to utter an indignant word in self-defence.[6]

Looking at the problem from Benjamin's perspective, he could
not remain silent in the face of Davis's imprisonment, if for no other
reason than that every other Cabinet member and general was protesting the cruelty of the confinement and the unreasonableness of hold-

ing the ex-President without a trial. But to have defended Davis against the charge of complicity in the Lincoln assassination would have looked self-serving, because Benjamin would have had to defend himself as well. In the aftermath, he would surely have called up a chorus of counterattacks upon himself when, as a matter of legal propriety, he had not been officially charged in Andrew Johnson's sweeping proclamation to begin with. Thus, he could only argue by indirection and defend Davis—and himself—obliquely, not by obvious, blunt defense. The letter must be read in that spirit. Moreover, he was writing at the time of the trial of Captain Henry Wirz, the onetime commander of the prison at Andersonville, Georgia. Wirz was brought to trial by Holt's Bureau of Military Justice on August 21, 1865. He was found guilty of mistreating prisoners and hanged on November 10, 1865.

Benjamin complained that the Federals sent back only "sick and disabled prisoners as were incapable of performing military service . . . in a condition so prostrate as to render death certain." He said that "efforts were made in vain to correct this evil."

He denied that the Confederate Government stood in the way of the humanitarian exchange of prisoners. It was in the South's interest to facilitate such exchanges, he pointed out, "in order to recover soldiers whom we could replace from no other source. On the other hand, interest and humanity were at war in their influence on the Federal officials. Others must judge of the humanity and justice of the policy which consigned hundreds of thousands of wretched men to captivity apparently hopeless. . . . I write not to make complaint of it but simply to protest against the attempt of the Federals so to divide the consequences of their own conduct as to throw on us the odium attached to a cruelty plainly injurious to us, obviously beneficial to themselves."

Benjamin then moved to the central question of Davis's character and morality in war, which lay at the center of the assassination charge:

The sense of duty which prompts this letter would be imperfectly satisfied were I to withhold at this juncture the testimony which none so well as myself can offer in relation to the charge of inhumanity made against President Davis. For the four years during which I have been one of his most trusted advisers, the recipient of his confidence, the sharer to the best of my abilities in his labors and responsibilities, I have learned to know him better, perhaps than he is known by any other living man. Neither in private conversation nor in Cabinet council have I ever heard him utter one unworthy thought, one ungenerous sentiment. On repeated occasions, when the savage atrocities of such men as Butler . . . and others were the subject of anxious consideration, and when it was urged upon Jefferson Davis, not only by friends in private letters, but by members of his Cabinet in council, that it was his duty to the people and to the army to endeavor to repress such outrages by retaliation, he was immovable in his resistance to such counsels, insisting that it was repugnant to every sentiment of justice and humanity that the innocent should be made victims for the crimes of such monsters.

He then called on what the Confederate leadership considered the chief example of Northern cruelty—Dahlgren's raid in 1864, an effort late in the war to free Northern prisoners at Libby Prison in Richmond and, according to Southern newspapers, attack the officials of the Confederacy. It was a controversial subject, because Northern military officials claimed that Dahlgren's body had been mutilated and displayed in Richmond. In addition, the Union leadership in Washington had suggested that the Lincoln assassination had been in retaliation for Dahlgren's raid. However, Benjamin used the incident skillfully in his defense of Davis:

Without betraying the confidence of official intercourse . . . when the notorious expedition of Dahlgren against the City of Richmond had been defeated, and the leader killed in his flight, the papers found upon his body showed that he had been engaged in an attempt to assassinate the President and the heads of the Cabinet, to release the Federal prisoners confined in Richmond, to set fire to the city, and to loose his men and the released prisoners, with full licence to gratify their passions on the helpless inhabitants.

The instructions to his men had been elaborately prepared, and his designs communicated to them in an address; the incendiary materials for firing the town formed part of his equipment. The proof was complete and undeniable. [In] the action in which Dahlgren fell, some of his men were taken prisoners. They were brought to Richmond, and public opinion was unanimous that they were not entitled to be considered as prisoners of war; that they ought to be put on trial as brigands and assassins, and executed if found guilty. In Cabinet Council, the conviction was expressed that these men had acquired no immunity from punishment for their crimes,

if guilty. . . . A discussion ensued which became so heated as
almost to create unfriendly feeling, by reason of the unshaken
firmness of Mr. Davis in maintaining that although these men mer-
ited a refusal to grant them quarter in the heat of battle, they
had been received to mercy by their captors as prisoners of war,
and as such were sacred; and that we should be dishonored if
harm should overtake them after their surrender, the acceptance
of which constituted, in his judgment, a pledge that they should
receive the treatment of prisoners of war. To Jefferson Davis alone,
and to his constancy of purpose, did these men owe their safety,
in spite of hostile public opinion, and in opposition to two-thirds
of the Cabinet.

Benjamin ended the letter by calling on "all who are desirous of
seeing justice done to the illustrious man of whose present condition
I will not trust myself to speak."[7]

His message was plain: Although the North had plotted to assassinate Davis and had sent a secret mission to accomplish it, when
the soldiers were captured, Davis protected them and treated them
as ordinary prisoners of war. Benjamin pointed out that Davis was
not vengeful or brutal; he did not order trials and immediate hangings.
Thus, arguing between the lines, it is unwarranted and impossible
to believe that the President would then participate in a plot to
assassinate Lincoln when he stood so firmly against popular opinion
and the Confederate Cabinet in opposing capital punishment for
those who were guilty of attempting to assassinate the Confederate
president.

When the New York *Times* reprinted the letter two weeks later,
it included a rebuttal from a "Commander H. A. Wise, U.S. Navy,"
who contested Benjamin's view of Dahlgren's motive in the raid
and accused the South of planting the assassination plans on his
dead body. It must have been a rude awakening for Benjamin to
realize that his every interaction with American public opinion on
the war would stir up controversy; it may have contributed to his
subsequent reticence on the subject.

The intent of his letter and his reaction to the New York *Times*
treatment of it were made plain in a subsequent letter to Varina
written from Paris on November 16, 1865:

In relation to your suggestion about my writing something in
refutation of the slanders and calumnies relative to the disposal
of the public moneys that were on the wagon train, and to the

alleged cause of the failure of negotiations at Hampton Roads, I have consulted with one or two valued and tried friends, and they all concur with me in opinion that this is not the time to discuss such issues; that it would do more harm than good. You have however seen perhaps the letter I published in the *Times* on the subject of the infamous accusation that Mr. Davis was using cruel treatment towards prisoners of war as matter of public policy. This letter was intended to vindicate him before the public opinion of Europe, and I think had a very good effect that way, but nothing can *at present* be written by *me,* that would do him any good in the U.S. You will comprehend why I have underscored some words. The time will come when even in the U.S. my written Statements will be read and believed in spite of all.[8]

Appeals by Davis's lawyers to obtain a trial were rebuffed. After dozens of letters and appeals to high officials and influential citizens, Varina received permission in May 1866 to see President Andrew Johnson at the White House. The meeting, which received extensive press coverage, was granted because Johnson was clearly on the defensive publicly over the treatment of Davis. Varina described the conversation with him in detail:

The President was civil, even friendly, and said, "We must wait, our hope is to mollify the public toward him." I told him that the public would not have to be mollified but for his proclamation that Mr. Davis was accessory to the assassination, and added, "I am sure that whatever others believed, *you* did not credit it." He said he did not, but was in the hands of wildly excited people, and must take such measures as would show he was willing to sift the facts. I then responded that there was never the least intercourse between Mr. Davis and Booth, or an effort to establish it . . . , and remarked that "if Booth had left a card for Mr. Davis as he did for you, Mr. President, before the assassination, I fear my husband's life would have paid the forfeit. . . ." I remarked that, having made a proclamation predicated upon the perjury of base men suborned for that purpose, I thought he owed Mr. Davis a retraction as public as his mistake. To my astonishment, he said that he was laboring under the enmity of many in both houses of Congress, and if they could find anything upon which to hinge an impeachment they would degrade him; and with apparent feeling he reiterated, "I would if I could, but I cannot."[9]

Information about efforts on his behalf, whether private or in newspapers, was smuggled regularly into Davis's cell in prison, but it is not known whether he read Judah P. Benjamin's defense of him in the New York *Times.* Davis's prison doctor, Dr. John Craven, spent hours in discussion with the ex-President, giving him news of the outside world and listening to Davis talk on many subjects. In fact, he became so friendly that he was removed from his post. In his book entitled *The Prison Life of Jefferson Davis,* he reported that Davis told him "Benjamin was the ablest and most faithful member of his advisory council; a man who realized that industry is the mistress of success, and who had no personal aspirations, no wishes that were not subordinate to the prosperity of the cause."[10]

In the immediate aftermath of the assassination, the responsibility for the investigation and the collection of evidence fell upon Joseph Holt, Judge Advocate General of the U.S. Army and head of the Bureau of Military Justice. Holt had been born in 1807 into one of Kentucky's leading families and had made his fortune early in the practice of law in Kentucky and Mississippi. He bought a home in Washington and as a Southern Democrat began to rise in social and political circles. President Buchanan named him Postmaster General in 1859. In the final months of Buchanan's administration, when the secessionist members were leaving his Cabinet, Buchanan appointed Holt U.S. Secretary of War and named Edwin Stanton U.S. Attorney General. He thus became close to Stanton, who later appointed him as Judge Advocate of the Union Army in the Lincoln war years and trusted him to carry out Stanton's wishes at the Bureau of Military Justice—nicknamed by the Southern press the "Bureau of (In)justice."

Holt was a cultured Southerner, gracious and polite, solicitous of ladies, distinguished in manner. Although he was a Southerner, he supported the preservation of the Union at all costs and embraced the Union cause with the zeal of the religious convert. Southerners hated him with the special passion reserved for turncoats, and he returned their animosity with what one writer called "the fury of the scorned."[11] He once charged in a public letter that anyone in Kentucky who did not support the Union was either a "maniac or a monster," a charge that included his mother and brother and many other members of his family.[12]

Like Stanton, he was convinced from the night of the assassination on that the murder of Lincoln was part of a plan orchestrated by the Confederate leadership. He would stop at nothing to prove that, no matter how false or highhanded the allegations. After just a week and a half of wholesale arrests, imprisonments, threatened witnesses, loose application of reward money to buy testimony, mysteriously discovered letters, hearsay, and a wide range of questionable tactics and procedures, Holt got what he wanted. Stanton announced on April 24, 1865, just ten days after the assassination: "This Department has information that the President's murder was organized in Canada and approved in Richmond."[13] Holt supplied the names of the conspirators for the sensational proclamation under which Jefferson Davis and the Canadian spy ring were charged, and Davis was jailed for having "incited, concerted, and procured . . . the atrocious murder of the late President, Abraham Lincoln."[14]

The most incriminating witness was Sanford Conover, who had quit the Confederate War Department in 1863 and made a career as a part-time journalist and spy. He testified that he was intimate with all the Canadian spies mentioned in the proclamation and that Jacob Thompson told him about the assassination plan and even asked him to join in the plot. He also testified that he was in Thompson's office between April 6 and April 9 when John Surratt arrived from Richmond with letters from Davis and Confederate Secretary of State Judah P. Benjamin. After reading the letters, Conover said, Thompson tapped them with his hand and said, "This makes the thing all right."[15]

His testimony under oath was supported by other witnesses, supposedly independent. The New York *Tribune* stated: "It is either overwhelmingly conclusive of the complicity of the Confederate leaders in the assassination conspiracy or it is an unmitigated lie from beginning to end."[16]

Almost immediately, it began to look like the latter. A letter turned up from Conover, using his alias, to Thompson, dated March 20, 1865, which began, "Although I have not had the pleasure of your acquaintance. . . ." His long-term "friendship" and intimacy were a fraud.[17]

Still, Conover became Holt's personal agent, combing the country for witnesses. He produced eight of them with sworn depositions, who testified to meetings, dates, and details. One of them broke down under questioning and confessed that Conover had written his testimony word for word and rehearsed him in its delivery in a Washington hotel before escorting him to the courtroom to recite his lines under oath. Holt informed Stanton that "Conover has been guilty of a most atrocious crime."[18] Conover promptly disappeared.

Not until the fall of 1866 was Conover arrested. He stood trial under his real name, Charles A. Dunham, for perjury and suborning of perjury and was sentenced to ten years in prison. He confessed that he had coached the lying witnesses out of a hatred for Davis, who had sentenced him in 1863 to six months in a Richmond prison.[19]

Stanton had already begun to back off the grand conspiracy theory. In November 1865 he withdrew the offer of rewards for John Surratt, Jacob Thompson, and the others named in the original proclamation on the grounds that they were abroad and as fugitives would be arrested by government agents who had no right to a reward. By so doing, however, he was removing an incentive for their arrest.

Anything seemed to be grist for Holt's campaign to convict Davis and Benjamin. In his papers in the Library of Congress is a bogus letter to Jefferson Davis, received on June 9, 1865, by the Charleston *Courier.* Dated May 1, 1865, it reads:

> *His Excellency Jeff Davis*
> *President of the Confederacy*

My Dear Sir—

I received the twenty thousand in gold you sent to me by the hands of our friend the Hon. Judah Benjamin. I think I have done the job exactly according to your instructions. Bob Toombs promised to be on the spot, but I have not seen him. I received my commission signed by the Secretary of War, John C. Breckinridge. Much obliged to you. . . . I am afraid I will soon be a dead dog, and you too.

> *Yours truly*
> *J. Wilkes Booth*
> *Lieut. Col. C.S.A.*[20]

It was a clumsy letter on many counts and an obvious fraud, since Booth died on April 26.[21] The *Courier* never published it, nor is there any account of Holt's ever using it, but it remained in his papers as an example of the mood of the times, the kind of hysteria that had infected the minds of many people in the aftermath of the assassination.

After the collapse of Conover's testimony, Stanton and Holt began to grasp at straws to defend the continued incarceration of Jefferson Davis and pressed the House Judiciary Committee, which they controlled, to exaggerate some insignificant correspondence from the captured Confederate archives and declare: "These documents are conclusive upon the point that Davis, Benjamin, and Walker, in the years 1861, '62, '63, '64, and '65, received, entertained and considered propositions for the assassination of the chief members of the government of the United States, and thereupon a probability arises that they took steps to accomplish the purpose."[22]

Why had Judah P. Benjamin not been listed in the original proclamation? It was clear that Stanton and Holt initially considered Surratt and the messages from Benjamin as a critical centerpiece of the conspiracy. It was also clear that the U.S. Government would continue to investigate Benjamin in order to establish some connection to Surratt.

The proclamation was not a carefully considered document but was hurriedly thrown together for political impact in the confusion of the times. In all likelihood, Stanton and Holt felt that their primary purpose was to convict Jefferson Davis, and they did not want to complicate the complex task of proving a grand conspiracy by putting anyone in the indictment between Davis and the operational conspiracy. Besides, the audience for the proclamation was in the North, where Benjamin was not well known. They decided to concentrate on the major target rather than a minor one. After all, Benjamin was in England, free and active, while Davis was in prison under their control.

The cipher found in the bottom of Booth's trunk the night of the assassination turned out to be incidental, since evidence was offered that Booth was taught the code by a Confederate agent and a boarder at Mrs. Surratt's house who was close to John Surratt and had access to it. It seemed a more important link at the time than it turned out to be.

In the middle of 1866, according to Chief Justice Shea of the Marine Court, Thaddeus Stevens, one of the leaders of the Radical Republicans in Congress who hated Jefferson Davis and attacked him with vehemence, insisted that Holt allow him to examine the evidence in support of the proclamation. Stevens pronounced it "insufficient in itself and incredible." He continued: "Those men are no friends of mine. They are public enemies and I would treat the South as a conquered country and settle it politically upon the policy best suited for ourselves. But I know these men, sir. They are gentlemen and incapable of being assassins."[23]

However, Davis continued to languish in prison, a prisoner now of the inaction of the government. A year after his capture, in May

1866, because the government could not present convincing evidence of complicity in the Lincoln assassination, new indictments were issued naming Davis, Robert E. Lee, John C. Breckinridge, Judah P. Benjamin, and others on a "lesser" charge of treason, thus shifting the venue to a civil court. The indictment meant that Benjamin was under risk of arrest should he choose to return and that his fate would be bound up with the political effort to free Davis. Meanwhile, for the ex-President there was still no trial. As the year stretched to eighteen months and others were released, Davis became the only "Confederate state prisoner," as high officials were designated, still behind bars.

Varina and the children were living in Savannah, having been officially assigned by Stanton and Holt to a hotel there, where she could be watched and her letters monitored. She was advised to seek the help of prominent Republicans. In desperation she drafted her most defiant and passionate letter to Horace Greeley, the powerful and influential editor of the New York *Tribune*:

> How can honest men and gentlemen of your country stand idly by to see a gentleman maligned, insulted, tortured and denied the right of trial by the usual forms of law? Is his cause so strong that he must be done to death by starvation, confined air, and manacles?
>
> With all the archives of our government in the hands of your government, do they despair of proving him a rogue, falsifier, assassin, and traitor—then they must in addition guard him like a wild beast, and chain him for fear his unarmed hands still in a casemated cell subvert the government? Shame, shame. . . . Is no one among you bold enough to defend him?[24]

When four-year old Billy came home one day singing, "We'll hang Jeff Davis from a sour apple tree," having been taught it by a former Union soldier, Varina, by now free to go where she wished, decided to leave Savannah and move to Canada to be with a community of Confederate sympathizers. It was not the first such incident with the children, and she was worried for their safety.

On the way to Montreal to set up a home, she visited Greeley. Afterward she peppered him with fervent appeals, writing him in one letter, "I am utterly helpless and well-nigh broken hearted. If a nation's tears could wash out venom, then mine ought to have cleansed many a heart filled with the lust for vengeance—and for blood."[25]

Varina was coming into her own as a public figure, as the strong, outspoken, self-confident wife of a silent husband. She became the voice of outrage at injustice and the shaper of public opinion, North and South.

"It used to be said," Dr. John Burgess wrote, "that she and Benjamin ran the machine at Richmond. However that may be, I can testify that she was capable of running that or any other machine, with or without Benjamin or anyone else. She was a personality with the instincts of a sensitive woman and the judgment of the strongest man. She was also endowed with tender feeling and indomitable will. Her powers of conversation and description were superior to those of any other woman I have ever known."[26]

The injustice of the prolonged imprisonment, coupled with what Greeley called the "complete muddle on the subject" by the Congress, President, and Chief Justice, touched Greeley's sense of fairness. Greeley wrote a blistering editorial demanding that President Johnson publicly retract the charge against Davis of complicity in the assassination and that Davis be released. He saw Davis's release in both legal and historical terms: "How and when did Davis become a prisoner of war? He was not arrested as a public enemy, but as a felon officially charged, in the face of the civilized world, with the foulest, most execrable guilt—that of having suborned assassins to murder President Lincoln, a crime the basest and most cowardly known to mankind." He questioned the delay. After all, he pointed out, the President had said in his proclamation that the government had the evidence of "complicity with Wilkes Booth and Co. . . . so there was no need of time to hunt it up."

"It is neither just nor wise to send forth a prisoner of state with the brand of murder on his brow; a naked failure to prosecute is but equivalent to the Scotch verdict, 'Not proven' . . . a great government may deal sternly with offenders, but not meanly; it cannot afford to seem unwilling to repair an obvious wrong. . . . We feel confident that magnanimity toward Davis . . . will powerfully contribute to that juster appreciation of the North at the South which is the first step toward a beneficial and perfect reconciliation."[27]

Greeley's editorial stirred Republican circles. A prominent New York lawyer, Charles O'Conor, volunteered his legal help. Varina, now an object of sympathy pleading for her very ill, unjustly incarcerated husband, visited John W. Garrett, president of the Baltimore & Ohio Railroad and a close friend of Stanton from the days when the War Secretary had served as counsel for the railroad before

joining Lincoln's Cabinet. Garrett sensed that the continued imprisonment of Davis would undermine the credibility and public trust of
the Johnson administration and personally visited Stanton to plead
Varina's case. Stanton finally relented and gave his permission to
work out the details of Davis's release.

In early May, O'Conor secured a writ of habeas corpus, and Davis
was taken from his cell by his former aide Burton Harrison and
brought to Richmond, where he would soon appear before a Federal
court. As he was driven in an open carriage through the streets of
Richmond, crowds watched from windows and rooftops as well as
along the street. Varina observed that men "simply and silently uncovered in token of his presence" and women waved white handkerchiefs
and cried. He and Varina were taken to the Spotswood Hotel and
shown to the same suite they had lived in when they first arrived
in Richmond. Varina wrote that her husband said to her, "I feel
like an unhappy ghost visiting this much beloved city."[28]

On May 13, 1867, more than two years after his capture, Davis
was brought before the Federal court, which was located in a room
that had once served as the President's old office. He was accompanied
by Harrison and the Reverend Charles Minnegerode, the rector at
St. Paul's, who had visited him many times in prison and once had
pleaded his case personally before Stanton. After a cut-and-dried,
prearranged proceeding, Davis was released on $100,000 bail, which
was promptly signed by a number of men, among them Horace
Greeley and a representative of Cornelius Vanderbilt.

All present shook Davis's hand, and someone rushed to the window
and yelled at the top of his voice, "The President is bailed!" Others
relayed the cry from street to street and up and across the hills of
Richmond. When Davis came out of the building, he was greeted
with triumphant rebel yells. Burton Harrison wrote that "the carriage
was beset with a crowd perfectly frantic with enthusiasm, cheering,
calling down God's blessing, rushing to catch him by the hand. . . .
I shall never see such boisterous profound joy in a crowd again."[29]

A throng of well-wishers awaited Davis at the Spotswood Hotel.
When he stepped down from the carriage, a strange silence fell
over the crowd. A voice commanded "Hats off, Virginians!" and, in
Harrison's words: "Five thousand uncovered men did homage to
him who had suffered for them."

Once inside his suite, Davis turned to Varina, Harrison, the Reverend Minnegerode, and others and said, "In my sufferings you have
comforted and strengthened me with your prayers. Should we not

now kneel together and return thanks?" Around a center table, all went to their knees and prayed silently, shedding "tears of emotion." Minnegerode later wrote: "There, in deep-felt prayer and thanksgiving, closed the story of Jefferson Davis' prison life."[30]

To preserve his health, the Davises and their friends decided to take a steamer to New York that night. Davis rested for a few days at O'Conor's home in Washington Heights. "He is looking very thin and haggard," Harrison wrote, "and has very little muscular strength. But his spirits are good."[31] From New York they made their way to Montreal to be united with the children. It had been two years of constant fear and worry for Varina and of enormous physical and mental strain for Davis. They were ready to begin the next chapter in their lives.

"We have all been in great jubilee here," Judah P. Benjamin wrote his sister "at the news of our poor President's release from his shameful capture. I have not yet had a letter from him but am expecting one every day, as I am eager to learn how he is, whether his health is improving, and whether his constitution has been undermined by his suffering."[32]

In Canada, Varina referred to their status as "threadbare great folks," since Davis had no employment and could not bring himself even to seek a position. Distressed about his poor health and depression, she reported to friends that "the motion and life about us drove my husband wild with nervousness; he said the voices of people sounded like trumpets in his ears."[33] They moved to a small village to seek a quieter life, and also because "we found housekeeping too expensive and have gone to boarding."[34] They began to visit old friends like James Mason, also living in exile in Canada.

From England, Benjamin wrote to Mason requesting that he forward a letter to "our dear friend whose release from captivity is a source of so much joy among us here." With Davis's release, the U.S. Congress began debating amnesty bills. Many former Confederates living abroad began thinking of returning to their homes. Almost forlornly, as if he were inquiring more for himself than out of friendly interest, Benjamin asked if Mason would find it "consistent with self-respect" to return to Virginia. Benjamin wrote: "There cannot be the least risk of persecution now, and of course no one could expect you to ask for a 'pardon'! God save the mark!"[35]

For the ex-President in Canada, the pressure to find respectable employment was increasing. He had to support not only his wife and four children but also Varina's younger sister, her two brothers who had fled to Canada also and were jobless in Montreal, and her mother living in Vermont.

Varina suggested that he write his history of the war to bring in some income and relieve the emptiness of his days. They sent for his message books, which had been smuggled into Canada in his daughter's trunks and placed in the Bank of Montreal for safekeeping. For a few days, he just read aimlessly among the messages, but when he came upon the final days of the war, he began to pace the floor nervously. Varina wrote that "all the anguish of that last great struggle came over us as we saw our gaunt, half-clothed and half-starved men . . . mowed down by a countless host of enemies, overcome, broken in health and fortune, moving along the highways of their desolated home." He declared to Varina, "Let us put them by for awhile. I cannot speak of my dead so soon." The war was personal, and he considered the losses "my dead."[36]

Jefferson Davis was notified that he would have to go to Richmond in November 1867 for his long-awaited trial under the "treason" indictment. In planning a trip back to the Southern capital, the Davises decided that they would also return to Mississippi to see his family and to determine if any income could be derived from the Brierfield plantation. They went by boat to avoid the harsh Canadian winter, stopping off in Havana and New Orleans. Judah Benjamin had reported to Varina some two years earlier that funds had been deposited in a Cuban bank for the education of their children.

When Davis arrived in Richmond, Chief Justice Chase did not put in an appearance, and the trial was postponed for six more months to May 1868. The Johnson government, it seemed, was afraid it would be disgraced by the failure of its case against Davis. It was facing a growing storm of controversy, and it seemed possible, for a number of larger political issues in Congress, that President Andrew Johnson would face impeachment. The government had clearly trapped itself: It could not try Davis under the indictment, because under the Constitution secession was not treason. The case would collapse, and Stanton and Johnson would be humiliated.

Varina and Davis set sail for Havana, where they stayed in a hotel owned by a Southern woman. Their hostess entertained them lavishly in her parlors with a steady stream of Southern sympathizers from among the Spanish population. Davis withdrew the modest sums left for him in the bank and proceeded to New Orleans for another round of receptions with old friends. Then he went back to his plantation home in Mississippi, where he came upon a dispiriting scene. "We found our property all destroyed,"[37] Varina recalled, "our friends impoverished, and our old brother [Joe] very feeble." They returned to Canada without mustering a dollar of income from the Mississippi trip; indeed, they had even left money for the support of the former Davis slaves who had stayed on the plantation. Having confronted postwar misery and devastation, Davis realized that he would have to look beyond the South for a livelihood.

Life was not easy in other respects as well. When he visited other cities, Davis's public reception was by no means filled with accolades and ovations. Once, as he was getting into a carriage, a man rushed up to him, handed him a note, and disappeared. When Davis opened it, he saw one scribbled word: "Andersonville." Two plots to assassinate him were reported, and he wrote Varina's brother that "there exists a conspiracy in the States to murder me, and many persons are engaged in it. . . . There is a proverb that threatened men live long. I hope I can be an example of it."[38] For former Confederates linked in any way to Lincoln's assassination, the possibility of vengeance was a constant terror.

Public opinion in Washington had taken a strange turn in the previous year, as the Republican Radicals stepped up the intensity of their animosity toward Andrew Johnson. The original proclamation itself was reinterpreted by the Radicals as a cover for his own guilt in the assassination of Lincoln.

From exile in England, Jacob Thompson struck back at the proclamation in a public letter to the New York *Tribune* on May 22, 1865, stating that "I know there is not half the ground to suspect me as there is to suspect President Johnson himself.

"First. There was an absence of motive on my part. . . .

"Second. A paper is found in President Johnson's room . . . signed by the assassin himself. . . . It is certain that if it had been sent by any other man at any other time . . . it would have implied previous intimacy . . . and a wish to have an interview without witness. . . .

"Third. President Johnson goes to bed on the night of the assassination . . . and is asleep . . . when an anxious gentleman leaves . . . to inform the new incumbent of his great good fortune."[39]

Beverley Tucker, another of the Confederate agents in Canada named in the proclamation, wrote a public letter to the Montreal *Gazette* on May 23, 1865, pointing out "the fact that Andrew Johnson is the only solitary individual of the thirty-five million souls comprised in that land who could possibly realize any interest or benefit" from the assassination. He continued: "He . . . must expect to be dealt with as a man, not as a potentate. . . . If God spares my life, Andrew Johnson, and not I, shall go down to a dishonored grave."[40]

The effort by President Johnson to carry out Lincoln's policy of reconciliation brought him inexorably into collision with Stanton and the Radicals. Finally he fired Stanton, who challenged the action by refusing to leave his post until expelled from his office by force. The House of Representatives then introduced impeachment proceedings against the President in the U.S. Senate and the subsequent trial lasted three months. The charges against Johnson were for "high crimes and misdemeanors," but nine out of the ten charges dealt with Stanton's removal from office.

In mid-1868, three years after Jefferson Davis's capture, Washington politics and the impeachment trial of President Johnson dictated another postponement of Davis's treason trial until the fall. In the aftermath of the one-vote victory for Andrew Johnson on May 26, 1868, which defeated his impeachment and brought about the resignation of Stanton the same day, Davis was advised by his lawyers that it would be useful if he went to England for a few months. With a presidential election due in the fall, the lawyers were hopeful of some resolution in his favor during political debates ahead. Davis dictated a letter to Varina for Howell Cobb, former Governor of Georgia: "I have decided to go to Liverpool to see what may be done in establishing a commission house, especially for cotton and tobacco. An Englishman of very high character and social position who has been extensively engaged in the India Trade as a commission merchant has proposed to me a partnership."[41]

Varina added a postscript of her own to the letter: "I trust that at last we see our way clear to be raised above the sense of idle dependence which has so galled us. . . . I am sorry to say that Mr. Davis looks wretchedly. I think much of his indisposition is induced by his despair of getting some employment."

They left for Liverpool on July 26, 1868, and as the troubles of the South receded below the horizon behind him, Davis seemed to recover from his melancholy. He even walked the deck without his walking stick.

A crowd of more than one hundred met the ship at Liverpool; Benjamin could not be there because of a case in London but sent his regrets. To one woman, Davis appeared "placid and calm and gentle, like the soft waves of the sea after a mighty storm."[42]

Benjamin and the Davises arranged to meet in London.

"We saw Mr. Benjamin quite often, and always with increasing pleasure," Varina wrote. "He had now become Queen's Counsellor, and was very successful. He appeared happier than I had hitherto seen him." She seemed surprised by his attitude toward the war, adding that "though he gave Mr. Davis one long talk about Confederate matters, after that he seemed averse to speaking of them. He was too busy to spend much time anywhere, but was sincerely cordial and always entertaining and cheerful. His success at the English bar was exceptional, but did not astonish us. In speaking of his grief over our defeat, he said that his power of dismissing any painful memory had served him well after the fall of the Confederacy."[43]

Davis and Varina were infuriated at the accounts of the war published that autumn by Edward Pollard, the former editor of the Richmond *Examiner.* Pollard attacked Davis in a 400-page diatribe that referred to Varina as "a woman who was excessively coarse and physical in her person, and in whom the defects of nature had been repaired neither by the grace of manners nor the charms of conversation. Mrs. Davis," he continued, "was a brawny, able-bodied woman who had much more of masculine mettle than feminine grace. Her complexion was tawny, even to the point of mullatoism; a woman loud and coarse in her manners; full of social self-assertion."[44] He referred to Davis as a "distinguished loafer" who had "descended into the counting house."[45]

Pollard had not overlooked, in his hatred for Davis, the role of the Confederate Secretary of State in the plots of the Canadian spy ring: "The author recollects a remarkable article," he wrote, ". . . to which rumor assigned Mr. Benjamin, Secretary of State . . . warning the North that but a few secret hands might suffice to commit her finest cities to the flames, and to inflict an injury as great as that which Sherman's army had done to Atlanta. It was a new mode of warfare thus suggested; it was, of course, not large enough to affect, to any considerable degree, the fate of the contest; it was not useful, and scarcely considered as such; it was *revengeful.*"[46]

He accused Davis of having "luxurious conceit," a "temper . . . almost as one of insanity," and wrote that he "folded his arms idly in the face of the war—'waiting for Europe' as Mr. Benjamin expressed it with the perpetual smile that basked on his Jewish lips."[47]

But even Pollard defended Jefferson Davis against the assassination charge: "There have been those who have believed—few believe it now—that the strange warfare which the South proposed to conduct by secret agents and emissaries in the North, and in which we have seen Mr. Davis might have borne an indirect share, might possibly have extended to a conspiracy against the life of the Northern President. It is an absurd and foul imagination, without a particle of evidence to support it. . . . Mr. Davis never could have carried it to the point of cold-blooded assassination, and that as against a President whose death could not possibly benefit the South, and who, at the time, was more tolerable to it than the man who would succeed him."[48]

Davis asked Benjamin's advice on answering the charges in the book, and Benjamin responded from his knowledge of the British press and "on the close observations of men and things" in England: "If you publish the statement you will find it impossible to remain silent under the replies, and your existence here will be empoisoned by the necessity of engaging in a newspaper warfare at every disadvantage against hosts of unscrupulous enemies. The book you notice, I never heard mentioned, and it will drop still-born into oblivion, unless you advertise by your notice of it."[49]

It was advice that Benjamin applied to himself on all matters dealing with the war.

Davis and Varina also visited Paris. There they met the Confederate expatriate community that included Benjamin's old friends from New Orleans, the Slidells. Rosine Slidell had become Baroness Erlanger, having married Emile Erlanger of the Jewish banking family, and the Slidells were well situated.[50] Benjamin joined the Davises in Paris. He and Natalie attended the rounds of receptions and dinner parties. The elegance was touched with irony: All the former Confederates were prospering except the guests of honor, who were without position or steady income.

In 1874 Benjamin's old nemesis, Henry Foote, published his book on the war entitled *Casket of Reminiscences.* In it he linked the reunion of Davis and Benjamin in England after the war to insinuations of wrongdoing involving the Confederate treasury:

I have been frequently asked whether Mr. Davis made any money by the war in which he and his associates had succeeded in involving the cotton states and to this question I have never been able to respond satisfactorily. I know that I always expected him and Mr. Benjamin to get rich by the war, and I often ventured to predict that they would be found whenever the Confederate cause

caved in to have provided largely for in Liverpool, whither the
Confederate Government had sent considerable amounts of
cotton.[51]

For Foote, the fact that Davis and Benjamin had met in England
was all the evidence he needed. "Mr. Benjamin's sudden flight to
England immediately on his decamping from Richmond was to my
mind always quite a suspicious circumstance," he wrote, "knowing
well as I did that devoted fondness for money which he had evinced
even from his earliest boyhood. Mr. Davis' subsequent movement
in the direction was a strong confirmatory fact. The public is at
least entitled to a fuller explanation on this subject than it has yet
received."

He charged that Jacob Thompson had taken some $200,000 in
gold to England. "Did he and Mr. Davis divide the money? Did the
immortal Benjamin get his share . . . ?"[52]

The charge would reverberate and grow until Benjamin would
have to answer it. For the time being, he much preferred silence
to the visibility that self-defense would have brought to him.

The election of General Ulysses S. Grant as President in the fall
of 1868 improved Davis's political and legal situation. Even in his
absence, his lawyers advised that he press for the trial to proceed
in Richmond in late November. The court could not reach a decision,
and Chief Justice Chase instructed a reporter to record him as voting
to quash the indictment for treason and to bar all future proceedings,
citing the Fourteenth Amendment. He wanted his opinion to be in
the public record. On Christmas Day, 1868, outgoing President Johnson issued a general amnesty proclamation. Davis could consider
himself free, though his case was left dangling, and the charges of
complicity in the Lincoln assassination were never examined, presented to a jury, or withdrawn. He was excluded from the official
amnesties of 1872 and 1876, and his right to citizenship was never
restored.

After a year in Europe, without success in any of his business
ventures, Davis returned to America to examine an offer from an
insurance company in Memphis. Although he and Benjamin would
correspond on a number of official questions over the next fifteen
years and would see each other on five other Davis trips to England,
they never developed a postwar intimacy. Benjamin's impatience
at Davis's obsession with correcting the public record manifested
itself when he replied to an invitation from the ex-President to discuss

various issues regarding the war in March 1874: "I too am very desirous of a long talk with you, but rather I must confess, about our old friends, than about the misrepresentations of Confederate affairs which I have ceased to hope it possible to rectify, at least for the present."[53]

Davis was facing backward to defend his personal defeat; Benjamin was facing forward to a new life and career.

20

The British Barrister
from America

❀❀❀

Benjamin's reputation at the bar grew enormously, and he once again began to behave as if on a stage acting out his own legend. In April 1869 he argued in behalf of his friend Colin McRae, the Confederate agent in London, who had handled the funds from the Erlanger loan. In *United States* v. *McRae* he defended McRae against a bill filed in England by the U.S. Government to obtain an accounting of all the money and goods in McRae's hands as belonging to "the pretended Confederate government during the late insurrection."[1]

In addition to a number of procedural matters, the case revolved around the question of whether the relief sought should be limited to money and goods originally the public property of the United States or could be extended to include funds raised by loan from foreigners in England and France. Just as it appeared that the Vice Chancellor was going to order an inquiry into the foreign funds, Benjamin suddenly rose from his seat and "to the astonishment of everyone present, began to speak in a stentorian voice." He said: "Not withstanding the somewhat off hand and supercilious manner with which this case has been dealt . . . if you will only listen to me—if you will only listen to me (repeating the same words in a crescendo)—I pledge you will dismiss this suit with costs."

The court sat in amazement as Benjamin calmly laid out the background to the case "for an hour or two." Word of his performance was whispered out of the courtroom to the hallways of the Inn, and crowds gathered to hear him. He was the great Senator from Louisiana again, returning with his heralded persuasive powers of oratory to defend the South and its actions against the unjust inquiry of the Federal government. His audience listened in rapt fascination to the elegant phrasing, to his deep grasp of the history of the loan in question, to the origins of the law and its application to this case. When he was finished and sat down, the judges discussed the case briefly and promptly dismissed it in favor of his client.[2]

Benjamin excelled at arguing directly to judges as well as at trials involving witnesses and juries. Most of his energies were devoted to appeals courts, but when involved in a jury trial he enjoyed the interplay with witnesses and the sheer theater of the trial. Baron Pollock called him "an effective cross-examiner" and described his legal style at handling a witness in one particular case.

An expert testified for a store owner whose walls had collapsed, damaging the cotton belonging to Benjamin's client.

"I think, sir," Benjamin asked "you said you had great experience in building of warehouses?"

"Yes."

"And you have carefully considered the causes which lead to their weakness?"

"Certainly."

"And you have applied those considerations to the present case?"

"I have done so."

"Then will you kindly answer me one more question? Why did that warehouse fall?"[3]

Pollock reported that, caught off guard, "the witness paused and Benjamin with a pleasant twinkle in his eye sat down with almost a bump on his seat. The pause continued, and the effect was so striking that jurymen, bystanders, all could not resist a hearty laugh, which terribly diminished the effect of a long and reasoned reply which the expert gave as accounting for his conclusion. . . . The result was irresistible." Benjamin won his verdict. It was a stunt that turned an expected and predictable course of questioning to his advantage. Pollock pointed out that he "thoroughly knew the rules of the game [and] presented his client's case with great force to a jury."[4]

Butler reported on one episode later in his career, revealed in the Lawley papers, "that made a deep impression in England . . . and [was] echoed in nearly every one of the English reminiscences" about him. In a very difficult case, with puzzling facts, Benjamin proceeded with his arguments even though the members of the House of Lords were showing impatience. As was his usual technique, he stated a bold proposition he intended to defend, but this time he overheard the Lord Chancellor mutter to himself "Nonsense!" "Changing color slightly . . . Mr. Benjamin proceeded to tie up his papers. This accomplished, he bowed gravely to the members of the House and saying 'That is my case, my Lords' he turned and left the House." The next day, when a junior counsel appeared, the Lord Chancellor apologized publicly "for the unfortunate remark. . . . I certainly was not justified in applying such a term to anything that fell from Mr. Benjamin." To stalk out of the House of Lords was a daring maneuver calculated to increase the respect of the bar; it placed Benjamin's dignity and honor above all other considerations, including the outcome of a case. It also contributed one more story in the Benjamin legend. But perhaps, just as had happened when Benjamin as a young U.S. Senator challenged Jefferson Davis to a duel over a callous remark, the experienced American barrister knew his man. "I wish you to convey to him my regret," the Lord Chancellor said, and Benjamin replied with a note accepting the apology.[5]

In December 1870, Benjamin proudly wrote his former law partner Bradford that he had argued his first case in the House of Lords. At last, he wrote Mason soon after, he was earning enough money to put something aside to support his family "when I am no longer able to work, in the place of what our Northern friends confiscated [from] me."[6]

Benjamin was so much in demand that he had to cut short a Christmas vacation when a client offered him one hundred guineas for three days' work, "and I could not afford the luxury of a holiday at that rate."[7] In another instance, he had to leave London for Liverpool on a Thursday night for a case the next day, then return on the train to London the following night for a special hearing on Saturday.[8] He once wrote that he spent eleven hours on a Sunday to master a brief in order to make an argument the next day "and was at my desk till two hours past midnight with only an interval of half an hour for taking some light food as one cannot dine when so deeply absorbed."[9] In another letter, he was "straining every nerve to get through the work this coming week" when he would leave on another trip and sometimes had to "avoid as much as possible using my eyes by gaslight. . . . I have so much writing to do, that they get fatigued before I finish my day's work."[10] He complained about the English legal system as the cause of his backbreaking schedule: "The attorneys are terrible in this respect, giving us no time to get up heavy cases, but thrusting them on us at the last moment."[11] It was not a convincing complaint; Benjamin had been working the same fierce hours all of his life.

When a visitor came to call, the busy barrister was the very essence of order and quietly intense organization. "If you called on him in his chambers," wrote John George Witt, his friend and executor, "you were perfectly sure to find him seated at his table, writing a letter with a gold pen, in the best of style, with nothing on the table except the note paper and a tidy blotting pad." Those were habits of a lifetime carried over from his war years. They presented a picture unforgettable to those who witnessed it, part of the Judah P. Benjamin mystique. "No papers littered about—no untied briefs," Witt continued. "He welcomed you with the air of a man who had nothing just then to do except to enjoy a chat. If he wanted to find a paper for you, he unlocked the proper drawer in his table, and at once handed you the document. . . . Mr. Benjamin was never in a hurry, never important with this big thing or that big thing— never pretentious, always the same calm, equable, diligent, affable man, getting through an enormous mass of work day by day without ostentation and without friction."[12]

Hard work was paying off. He had reached a stage where, except under special retainer of one hundred guineas, he refused to appear anywhere but the House of Lords or in his favorite forum, the Judicial Committee of the Privy Council, where judges heard cases from all over the British Empire. His past experience in diplomacy, his facility in French and Spanish, and his knowledge of the laws and legal customs of other countries enabled him to argue his cases with an intimate knowledge of the facts and superior expertise rare for his time. Between 1872 and 1882, he appeared in no fewer than 136 reported cases before those tribunals in cases of great legal significance or involving important financial interests.

The most significant case he ever argued was *Queen* v. *Keyn* in 1876, which is known in international law as the *Franconia* case.[13] Benjamin defended Keyn, captain of a German vessel that ran down and sank an English steamer, causing the death of an English passenger. Keyn was tried and convicted for manslaughter. Appealing on Keyn's behalf and arguing that the court lacked jurisdiction, Benjamin faced the greatest battery of lawyers in England. The case received high-level representation and widespread publicity, because the Government felt that the lives of English subjects and the security of the English coast were at stake. The case was front-page news in the London *Times,* and for months the English newspapers reported the brilliant repartee and sparring of the lawyers and judges. Benjamin wrote his sister that "I have been acquiring a good deal of reputation lately in a great cause that I had to argue before fourteen judges, presided over by the Lord Chief Justice of England, in behalf of the captain of a German ship, the *Franconia.* As it involved a question of international law, the papers were full of it, and I received many compliments."[14] Benjamin seemed to enjoy the publicity again, having been intentionally absent from the press for more than a decade.

During his summation, which laid out the facts, history, and commentary from books, articles, and cases all over the world, Benjamin took several days to complete his argument because of interruptions and questions from the bench. When a judge asked him how much longer he would take, Benjamin replied that it depended upon the discussion from the bench. In tribute to his superior knowledge of the law and the international implications involved, which he had explained carefully to them over several days, the Lord Chief Baron answered, to the laughter of the other judges, "You might pertinently ask us the questions."

Three months later, the judges voted 7 to 6 in Benjamin's favor on the grounds of lack of jurisdiction, and freed Keyns. Parliament soon afterward passed the Territorial Waters Act to remedy the jurisdictional gap in the law.

His victory in the *Franconia* case elicited comment in the American press. A London correspondent wrote to the Cincinnati *Commercial* that Benjamin "must be regarded as the most famous advocate at the English bar at the present moment." The correspondent had once heard him speak in the U.S. Senate. He said Benjamin had improved "in manner as well as power" and was "eagerly sought for in all great cases." He noted what a hopeless case the *Franconia* captain seemed to have at the beginning and commended the choice of Benjamin as "the best defender of forlorn hopes." He suggested Benjamin's Confederate experience as the reason he "had been appearing in some desperate cases." Benjamin certainly did not win all of his cases. The American correspondent pointed to "three severe falls" that he suggested might be attributable to a reaction setting in to his great reputation.[15]

According to the Lawley biography, one member of the House

of Lords commented that "Mr. Benjamin's mode and method of argument [was] peculiar and strange" to the English judges in the early years. "His habit was to commence his arguments with an abstract lecture upon the law affecting the case before the court. Most elementary principles would be very minutely explained. If the court differed from or doubted any of his propositions, members of the tribunal were informed that they certainly were wrong, and that it was desirable they should have the state of law more fully explained to them."[16] Sir Henry James, the Attorney General, cautioned him about his didactic manner and later recalled: "Right well he accepted all I had to say, and agreed that he had not yet fallen into our ways."[17]

Benjamin's speaking style was often commented upon. The London *Times,* looking back on his life, observed: "His great faculty was that of argumentative statement. He would so put his case, without in the least departing from candor, that it seemed impossible to give judgment except in one way."[18] Baron Pollock, on the other hand, reflecting a cultural bias, commented that he was "not eloquent as a speaker." Others noted his American accent and what they termed the unpleasant tone of his voice.[19]

But in the nineteenth century, Benjamin was unique—an American at the top of his profession in England who had received all of his training and prior legal experience in American courts. Many of the English legal observers were hearing their first brilliant American in a daily interaction on the highest levels of the law, and one could expect a condescending and critical reaction to the style of his oratory. But among his colleagues he was almost universally admired. A fellow barrister said that "he makes you see the very bale of cotton that he is describing as it lies upon the wharf in New Orleans."[20]

Old enemies back in the United States reacted with grudging admiration to his growing reputation and prominence. James G. Blaine wrote, "His ability and learning were everywhere recognized, but it was at the same time admitted that he owed much of his success to the sympathy and support of that preponderant class among British merchants who cordially wished and worked for our destruction." Blaine complained that the "manner in which he was lauded into notoriety in London, the effort constantly made to lionize and to aggrandize him, were conspicuous demonstrations of hatred to our government, and were significant expressions of regret that Mr. Benjamin's treason had not been successful."[21]

Because of the charges made against him by Wigfall and by some of the newspapers in the North, suspicious of his rapid rise at the English bar, both Butler and Meade examined Benjamin's fee books with care.[22] The records showed that his income began to grow dramatically after 1870, when he was promoted to Queen's Counsel and had special access to the highest courts.

In 1867 his fees totaled 495 pounds, or less than $2,500. By 1871 his fees had risen to 2,100 pounds, or $10,500; by 1873 his fees were 8,934 pounds, or more than $44,000. That represented a four-fold increase in four years! The pace of this extraordinary advance eased a bit in 1874 to 9,874 pounds, or more than $49,000. But by 1876 he had reached an income of 13,812 pounds, or more than $69,000; by 1878, a total of 15,742 pounds, or more than $78,000; in 1880, a maximum of 15,792 pounds, or almost $80,000. In 1881 and 1882, as he began to organize his retirement, his income dropped to 14,632 and 12,789 pounds respectively, or more than $73,000 in 1881 and $63,000 in 1882. The total for the sixteen years from 1867 through 1882 was 143,900 pounds, more than $700,000.[23] A New York *Times* correspondent who interviewed him in 1879 judged his income to be $150,000 a year, including his investments and the income from his book on *Sales,* which by then had sold enough copies to have reached a third printing.[24]

Butler pointed out that "popular fancy dazzled by the rapidity of Mr. Benjamin's success, had placed his earnings at a much higher figure; they are surely sufficiently amazing, however without fantastic increments."[25] Benjamin, from his perspective, wrote to his family that "although my success at the bar is absurdly exaggerated in some accounts I have seen in the newspapers," he felt confident that "in the event of my death a comfortable subsistence will be secure for my family."[26] This comment was made in the early 1870s in response to the charges by Wigfall and others that he was so rapidly successful that he must have illegally taken funds that belonged to the Confederacy.

In 1873, when he was sixty-two years old, he wrote a friend at Cambridge University that he was looking forward to retirement and even daydreamed about a university career:

> I quite envy your pleasant life. I am sure that at my age I could dream away the remnants of life there quite content, but my battle with the world is not quite ended, though I hope in two or three years at most to feel satisfied that I can withdraw from active work without disquietude as to the means of living in the modest way that suits my tastes.[27]

He began to ease up on his work habits, explaining that "I make it a rule that I will not work after dinner, that after wine in the evening I do as I please."[28]

His executor, John George Witt, wrote that "he had a good appetite for his dinner, drank his wine, smoked his cigar, and took life like a philosopher. His conversation was very bright, full of humor, and not too full of anecdote, and for years he managed to end his day of toil before the dining hour."[29]

The loneliness of his existence in England during his struggle to rebuild his life is revealed most poignantly in his letters to his family in New Orleans. His notes to his sisters and his nephews and nieces have a desolate quality, as if he longed for a connection to small children that would never be: "I suppose that Ernest and Julius and my saucy little coquette, Becky, have long since lost all memory of me. Your other little one I have never seen, but it seems you might send" some photographs "with the portraits of all of you."[30] He asked a second time for photographs "of all the family, for those I received in Richmond are in my trunk which is concealed on the other side, and I perhaps will never recover it."[31] When the photographs came, he wrote that he had "fallen desperately in love with your little blossom Alma, whom I have never seen, but I can imagine from the photograph what a darling cherub she must be."[32] When he discovered that the children were saving stamps from his letters, "I searched in vain for some time" and finally found a shop "which I believe is the only place in this great world of a city where they could be found. So now they will get Chinese, and Egyptian and Turkish!!!"[33] Sending exotic stamps to children was a delight he clung to for twelve years, even though they were later too old to appreciate them yet too considerate of their "Uncle Ben," as he referred to himself, to tell him so.

He gave advice to his nephews who "must be made to take an education, not be allowed to fancy a profession or business yet, for boys are really incapable of forming judgments of such things, and only long to get into business to seem grown up; let it be a good education first; if you will, let them come to me; after they are fitly educated, then business or profession, what you will."[34]

He longed to be with them, "looking forward to the day when restored peace to our unhappy South will enable me to devote a long vacation to a full month's visit to you all, and when I shall have nothing to do but be petted and stuffed, and get no scoldings unless my appetite fails."[35]

In his first year in England, he wrote his Louisiana family that "I long beyond measure to see you all once more, but I am plainly to be disappointed this year. The simple truth is that I cannot afford the visit."[36] But as his law practice gained momentum, another rationale kept him from them—the suggestion of concern for his safety. In 1872 he wrote: "Pen says that she will celebrate her silver wedding . . . next year, and if I dared look forward so far, it would rejoice me beyond measure to be [part] of the party. But while the political excitement lasts, and while the Senate rejects amnesty bills, and the South is kept crushed under negro rule, it sickens me to think of the condition of things. After the Presidential election, it may be that a general amnesty bill will pass; but it is a wonder to me that so much bitterness against the conquered can endure the lapse of seven or eight years."[37]

Then, in 1874, he was more definite: "You say, my dearest, that I never now speak of visiting you all. I never can consent to go to New Orleans and break my heart witnessing the rule of negroes and carpetbaggers. I have hoped year by year that some change would be effected which would place decent and respectable men at the head of the administration of affairs, and it seems to me that the time is now fast approaching. I long and yearn to press you all to my heart once more, and for some of us at least age is creeping on and not much time is to be lost."[38] The next spring, a Negro named Pinchback was registered by the U.S. Senate as the Republican Senator-elect from Louisiana to occupy the seat of Judah P. Benjamin.

Benjamin looked forward in September 1874 to the marriage of Ninette, then just past thirty years old, to Henri de Bousignac, a captain in the French army.

"Of course," he wrote to his sister, "I cannot but feel anxious at thus giving up my only child, but, as far as human foresight can predict, I have assurance that the match will prove happy."

He was pleased at the "match" because of the captain's professional potential. "Captain de Bousignac, her intended, is represented on all sides as one of the most promising officers in the French army. At the age of thirty-two, he has acquired a distinguished position on the general staff from his merits both as an artillery and engineer officer." Benjamin was also impressed with his social standing and personal qualities. "He is of excellent family, irreproachable habits, beloved by all around him for his frank, gay and amiable character and I know no better test of a man than his possession of the affection of those most intimate with him."[39]

They were married in a Catholic ceremony in the church of St.

Pierre de Chaillot in Paris. The ceremony was performed by the bridegroom's uncle. Natalie's brother, Jules St. Martin, who came from New Orleans to attend the wedding, is listed as witness on the marriage certificate. He stayed on with the Benjamin household for many months because of an illness.

Benjamin was concerned about Ninette's financial security as a military wife. "By giving up all my savings," he wrote, "I have been able to settle on Ninette three thousand dollars a year, so that her future is now secure against want."[40] The decision was not without consequences for him. "I must now begin to lay up a provision for the old age of my wife and self. I undertake this new task with courage because we shall not require a great deal, and the practice of my profession is now so much more lucrative than it ever was before, that I hope in two or three years to see the end of necessary labor and be able to work as little or as much as I please."[41] The next spring, he wrote that his new son-in-law was "all that I could desire."[42]

His success now enabled him to make grand gestures, such as sending a thousand dollars as a wedding present to one of his nieces. He gave to Southern causes and sent money to impoverished friends, such as the widow of a former judge in New Orleans "whom I knew in old times and who wrote me a most pitiful story of her distress."[43] But having diminished his savings mainly with gifts to his family, he again went to work in earnest. "In after years," because his schedule changed again under the pressure to earn more income, J. G. Witt, his executor, wrote, "he was compelled to work late in the evening, and that was a necessity against which his whole soul revolted. But his determination to make money not for himself . . . but for those he loved conquered his aversion."[44]

There were more severe losses driving him as well. His brother Joseph lost $25,000 that Benjamin had sent him for a business venture, but Benjamin mentioned it only casually to his sisters. And he continually sent them money at regular intervals and special gifts at holidays and birthdays.

Benjamin was close to his younger brother Joseph, who had served in the Confederate army and after the war had fled to Mexico and then to Spanish Honduras. When asked once why he left America, Joseph answered, "I wouldn't take the oath of allegiance to the United States." According to Meade, who interviewed a friend of Joseph, Joseph once read the friend a letter from Judah Benjamin who invited Joseph to England to live with him and, in case Joseph did not have the money, would send him all that he needed. But in the end Joseph did not wish to leave his family or his property in Honduras.[45]

One other sad event left him even lonelier. "I am depressed in spirits on account of the condition of poor Jules," he wrote to his sister. "In the meantime, I am using every means in my power to get Capt. deBousignac stationed at Paris so as not to break up the household, for my poor brother-in-law Jules St. Martin is in a very precarious state of health and will remain in the South of France during the coming winter (if he lives so long)."[46] Jules's death in 1875 greatly affected Benjamin and Natalie, who had raised him from early childhood. Natalie now felt doubly alone with Ninette away.

In preparation for his retirement, Benjamin built a large mansion at 41 Avenue d'Iena in Paris. It was in the grand style—three stories joined by an ornate and impressive marble staircase. He reported that Natalie and Ninette "are busy as bees deciding on shades of color for the decorations, patterns of paper for every room . . . the two . . . are finishing the furnishing and ornamentation of the 'grand salon' and threatening to give several soirees during the winter on the pretext that they want to establish intimate relations with certain grand personages who can aid in the more rapid promotion of the captain."[47] He concluded that "we shall be housed like princes, but the cost will be greater than I supposed, and including additional furniture, etc., etc., I don't get off for less than $80,000. However all is now paid off."[48] He was repeating the pattern of his New Orleans years, when the young and successful lawyer built the Belle-chasse plantation, symbolic of his newly achieved station in life. His purpose was revealed in a letter to his sister in 1867, when a struggling Benjamin faced an uncertain future and was ready to settle for far less. "I am getting too old," he wrote, "to care now for anything except ease and tranquility, with means sufficient to live in comfort, but without any desire for splendor, for show, or what are called pleasures."[49] Now he would have all three, as befitting a successful retired barrister. The house in Paris ultimately became the residence of one of the members of the Rothschild family.

The Avenue D'Iena is one of six avenues extending out from the Place de l'Etoile, where the Arc de Triomphe stands. The arch, started in 1806 and finished in 1836, could possibly have been seen from the upper floors of his house and certainly was then, as it is today, an imposing presence just a half-mile away. Today his address is a modern apartment building, and the mansion is gone.

The houses next door at 42 and across the street at 63 are similar grand mansions of Benjamin's era, extraordinary residences with heavy doors, high windows, and sculpted casements on the front of the buildings, proud relics among the modern structures on the street.

The avenue is wide and tree-lined, in Benjamin's day able to accommodate six carriages across, perhaps more. It rises majestically from the Arc de Triomphe to a crest, from which one looks down a slight decline to his house and a view of the Eiffel Tower, begun the year after his death and completed four years later. Benjamin would live out the rest of his life in the splendor of this fashionable Paris neighborhood, in velvet isolation, away from his friends and his own history.[50]

Jefferson Davis in 1869 had accepted a position as president of the Carolina Insurance Company in Memphis, but his two-year tenure in the job ended in disaster when the company collapsed, taking with it most of his savings and leaving him once again in financial ruin. The death of his brother Joseph in 1870 opened up old wounds for Varina. Joseph left no written deed to the Brierfield plantation, others testified, because of his dislike for Varina, who he feared would gain control of it at the death of his brother Jefferson. Both Davis and the grandchildren of Joseph claimed the inheritance, and the ensuing bitter and embarrassing family struggle lasted until 1877, when Davis finally won his claim.[51]

In the meantime, Davis was rescued from his impoverished state by an ardent Confederate admirer, a wealthy widow named Sarah Anne Dorsey. She was a dark, vivacious woman who was descended from two wealthy cotton families. Her literary tastes and talents had produced four books under the pen name "Filia." She knew Louisiana politics well: One of her books, *Recollections of Henry Watkins Allen,* was about a Confederate brigadier general and a former Governor of Louisiana. Mrs. Dorsey had spent time in England, where she liked to collect celebrities, and had met Judah P. Benjamin there. Knowing of her literary interests and earlier collaborations concerning his home state, Benjamin may have suggested that she help Jefferson Davis write his history of the war.

After her husband died in 1876, Mrs. Dorsey moved to Beauvoir, a beautiful 600-acre plantation on the Gulf coast of Mississippi with running streams, thick forests, and beach front views that were, in all directions, "beautiful to see." She invited Davis to occupy a separate cottage, where he could write in peace. She offered to serve as his amanuensis, taking dictation each day and arranged to employ a former Confederate major as a collaborator to help with research and the collection of documents and information. Varina was in England visiting her daughter when Davis moved his furnishings and belongings down from Memphis. When she heard he had moved to the plantation of a wealthy widow, Varina was furious with jealousy, especially after Mrs. Dorsey gave an interview to a newspaper, and her assistance to Davis became public knowledge. After Varina returned to Memphis and Davis suggested that Mrs. Dorsey visit her, Varina's jealousy shone through in a blunt letter:

"There is only one thing, my dear Husband," she wrote from Memphis, "that I have to beg of you. Do not—please do not let Mrs. Dorsey come to see me. I cannot see her and do not desire ever to do so again. . . . Let us agree to disagree about her, and I will bear my separation from you as I have the last six months—as but I can and hope for the better times the history being once over."[52]

When he needed Varina's memory of events, he was reduced to writing her letters. For more than a year and a half, Varina persisted before giving in to the inevitable and moving to Beauvoir. It was a wise step: Mrs. Dorsey sold Davis part of the estate for a nominal sum, and then died of cancer in 1879 after naming Jefferson Davis the sole heir to all her properties. The Davises at last had an appropriate estate for their old age.[53]

In completing the book, Davis also sought information from Judah Benjamin in England. For Benjamin, unlike his chief, the shadows of the war had begun to lengthen behind him, and the letters from Davis were an unhappy echo from his past. Davis wrote several letters asking his recollections on the controversy over the removal of General Joseph E. Johnston from his command during the battle of Atlanta. Only one of the letters survives, written in 1874, in which Davis wrote: "I feel as you do that it is hopeless to correct the false impressions which have been created, but it seems to me both proper and due that the truth should be stated by those who alone know it." It was the President's special compliment to him that he counted Benjamin as one of those who "alone" knew the truth. Davis was sensitive to Benjamin's eagerness to avoid public attention and assured him that "I do not wish to involve you in controversy but only to have the benefit of your memory."[54]

In 1879, while Davis was working on his two-volume history, he wrote Benjamin again about Johnston. Benjamin replied with generous opinions, and concluded the letter:

I have thus given you my dear friend the recollections which you asked for. So far as the use of my name is concerned, I freely confess that it is not agreeable to mix in any way in the controversies of the past which for me are buried forever. If at any time your character or motives should be assailed and my testimony is needed, I should be indeed an arrant coward to permit this feeling to interfere with my prompt advance to your side to repel the calumny. But in any other case, I long for repose. I seek rest and quiet after the exhausting labours of 68 years of a somewhat turbulent or rather adventurous life.[55]

For the first time in his life, Benjamin began to relax and to enjoy the fruits of a lifetime of arduous effort. "I am beginning to go into society," he wrote his sister, "which I had relinquished for years, and to accept invitations to dinner which I habitually declined. I am all the better for it."[56] He could ease up on his work schedule, leave his "dull lodging," stroll in the park. He "loved to bask in the sun like a lizard" and enjoy a spring day "with a sky as blue as my memory paints the California sky to have been some fifteen years ago."[57]

Then, in 1880, when the Paris mansion was almost completed and he was still in England but beginning to shift to living in the first home of his own since the Bellechasse plantation, Benjamin was growing impatient with English weather and wrote: "I have felt work more this winter than ever before, and in addition to advancing age, which of course must tell on me, I attribute much to the dreadful weather which we had early in the season and which carried off very many persons advanced in life."[58]

He received a letter from Varina detailing the problems of publishing her husband's history, and Benjamin wrote back in April 1881 to give her his British perspective on the lack of public interest in the war:

I have been expecting for some time to hear of the publication of "the book" but from your letter I begin to think that the prospect of its appearance is still remote. Public interest in our struggle has now quite died out in England though of course military men will read with great interest any account of the Campaigns—But here political questions have grown up so numerous and important that in the present feverish action of men in all spheres of life, what happened 15 years ago is regarded as "ancient history."[59]

Jefferson Davis's two-volume *The Rise and the Fall of the Confederacy* was published in June 1881 and was a complete failure as a publishing venture. Like Davis himself, the books were excessively legalistic, filled with pages of constitutional argument, almost as if he were writing the brief to defend himself in the treason trial that never occurred. Benjamin wrote his biographer Lawley asking when the book would be available in England. When he read it, he must have had mixed feelings. In all the 1,500 pages, there is only a single comment on Benjamin and one other passing reference. Describing the selection of his first Cabinet, Davis wrote that "Mr. Benjamin of Louisiana had a very high reputation as a lawyer, and my acquaintance with him in the Senate had impressed me with the lucidity of his systematic habits and capacity for labor. He was therefore invited to the post of Attorney General."[60]

Why did Davis give such short shrift to Benjamin's role in and contribution to the war? There were so many ways in a book of personal history for the former President to have indicated their intimacy and show his appreciation without violating Benjamin's wish not to be embroiled in the controversies of the past. He did not even address issues one would have expected—why Davis appointed Benjamin Secretary of War; the truth about Roanoke Island and Benjamin's willingness to accept the blame for the nondelivery of arms and munitions the South did not have; why he appointed Benjamin Secretary of State; Benjamin's international role. Yet, on all those matters and more, beyond that single comment, he was coldly silent, almost as if he had intentionally drained away the intimacy for reasons of pique or reproach.

It represented an odd neglect, at the least ungenerous, but what is more curious, inaccurate, given the tone of the book with its ponderous details and mountainous facts. There are a number of possible theories to explain the omission, each of which throws light on their relationship.

First, there is the known request from Benjamin that he not "mix in any controversies of the past which for me are buried forever." Responding, Davis might simply have been honoring the request of a friend, but doing so with a scrupulous, almost perverse thoroughness bordering on spite.

There are more subtle possibilities. Benjamin's role during the war was so intimately involved in the President's day-to-day activities that Davis may have considered him entirely an instrument of the President's will, with no independent capacity for action. Thus he was not separate but an alter ego, an extension of Davis's personal and official direction, and whatever he did was done in the President's name and office. Judah P. Benjamin was so much his loyal servant in the Cause that no case was to be made for a separate analysis of his activities and role. Speeches, letters, orders, messages, all emanated under Davis's name, and from Davis's point of view authorship was irrelevant. He signed them or read them, and they were his and his alone. Benjamin's comment in a letter to Mason confirms that view: He reported to Mason, in apologizing for his inability to supply information on an inquiry about the war, that "I have hardly anything to which I can refer to refresh my memory but I have . . . a bound copy of the President's messages to Congress which you (who were in on our secrets) know to have been written by me, as the President was too pressed with other duties to command sufficient time for preparing them himself."

The phrase "you (who were in our secrets)" reveals a great deal of Benjamin's attitude on the subject as well as Davis's. Whatever Benjamin did for the President, he did so in private, as the loyal aide, quiet and deferential; his was a total bending of his independence, identity, and performance to the President's purposes.

Besides, at the time Davis wrote his autobiography, his purpose was essentially political in nature: to defend himself from those who were blaming him for losing the war and to tell the story of the Confederacy from his own perspective. In those circumstances, to give excessive credit to Benjamin was to diminish himself. By the time he wrote the book, Davis was in poor health and wanted to be a symbol for the remnant of the Confederacy; he wanted to leave a legacy that would show that he had done his best for the Cause. It would have been uncharacteristic for a man as self-centered as Davis to confess to any intellectual help from his brilliant adviser.

For decades, Judah Benjamin had been conditioned to a lawyer–client relationship. Both men must have considered their roles in that context. Benjamin could differ with the President privately but never publicly; he could assess options and advise on decisions, but in the end the final responsibility was the President's. And once policy was set, until it was changed, the lawyer in him prepared the paperwork and followed through with the details.

He was the master of detail: He knew the amount of powder left in a regiment, the closest available supplies, the number of days' travel for so many men over that terrain based on previous experience, the morale of the troops, and the desertion rates, so that he could estimate actual men rather than reported men. He had a larger vision and understood the impact of Pyrrhic victories when loss of men made the outcome meaningless. He had international experience and a grasp of the French court, the English press, and the world price of cotton. Above all, Davis trusted him and was willing to assign him all manner of responsibility, including writing in the President's name. But he was never willing to acknowledge that trust publicly.

Perhaps the explanation is clearer when it is placed next to Benjamin's refusal to reveal anything about his own role. It is almost as if there were a common agreement between them pledging mutual silence; to do otherwise would violate a bond of intimacy between two men who probably understood at the time that Benjamin could best serve by agreeing always to keep his real role secret. It was as if Benjamin were too privy to Davis's internal doubts and too close a participant in Davis's decisions to second-guess history and make critical judgments about them. Benjamin played a key role for Davis, who came to expect him to be totally informed, steeped in reality, not romance. Moreover, he had presented options and alternative scenarios, calculated risks, and advised in the total confidence that Davis would always accept the responsibility as his own.

Anonymity was inherent in the job, except when visibility served a purpose, such as accepting blame for Roanoke or the speech at the African Church that floated the idea of emancipation. Benjamin therefore probably did not expect recognition, and the book was too formal and official a presentation of the war to allow such expanded references.

Davis may have felt some resentment over their postwar relationship. Davis suffered in prison for two years, while Benjamin prospered as no other high-ranking official of the war. A few hundred Southerners went abroad after the war, and some of them had built up bank accounts in Europe during the war. Slidell, Toombs, Breckinridge, and Benjamin (after a few years of struggle) all lived in relative luxury. With his pious sense of honor, Davis might have felt their actions to be vaguely dishonorable. He even refused to allow Varina to save the family silver or take anything of value with them when they fled Richmond. He seemed to want to sink into ruin, as his nation did, out of exaggerated idealism. It would be difficult to imagine Jefferson Davis, fleeing in disguise with gold strapped around his waist, purchasing six hundred bales of cotton during the final days of the war and sending them ahead to England to cover future living expenses. Davis, ever the military man, believed in the soldier's code: fight until the end, then have courage to face the enemy when captured. He was the elected leader who must not, at all costs, abandon his people.

After all, Davis may also have felt justified in thinking that at least part of the notoriety and fame that helped launch Benjamin's career in England was Davis's gift to him and therefore entitled Davis to much more assistance after the war than Benjamin gave him. Davis was searching desperately for business contacts in England up until 1877 and may well have concluded that Benjamin could have done more for him, perhaps even invested in one of his ventures.

There certainly was resentment on the part of Davis over the reluctance of Benjamin and others to provide him with information, impressions, and memories for his book. He even complained to Lucius B. Northrop, the former Commissary General, of the "impossibility of getting men to state in a manner to be used the truth as known to them orally." They had told him things in person that, "in that miserable spirit of harmonizing now endemic," he complained, "they cannot be induced to put into writing." He even apologized publicly in the foreword of his book for the reluctance of those who participated to answer his inquiries. Benjamin was not alone in his wish for privacy, but Davis must have been especially disappointed in him as one of "those who alone know" the truth.

Finally, there is a more haunting possibility of more deep-seated disappointment by Davis in Benjamin's peripheral and blameless, but nonetheless damaging, association with John Surratt and Jacob Thompson, who were charged with complicity in the Lincoln assassination. As Secretary of State, Benjamin was responsible for the Canadian spy ring, and in point of fact it was Benjamin's messages to Canada delivered by Surratt that lay at the center of the accusation against Davis. In that sense, the cloud that remained over Davis's career and reputation was a Benjamin-created cloud. Although no court of law, no reliable document, no unperjured testimony, no responsible investigation, no respectable witness ever proved any link, in Davis's strict sense of the military code Benjamin was responsible for the link that lent an impression of validity to the charges against him. John Surratt's role, of which evidence was insufficient and inconclusive, even happenstance as it turned out to be, lay there for Stanton, Holt, and others to grasp and use to attack the reputation and honor of Jefferson Davis. That Davis was even accused was a deep shock to the President; it had to have been unsettling that his most trusted adviser and closest confidant would be the bridge to the unfounded charges against him through the unfortunate choice of a messenger whose mother owned the boarding house where John Wilkes Booth stayed. That Benjamin would select as his most trusted courier a young man who knew Booth personally and even plotted with Booth to abduct Lincoln and other hare-brained schemes must have been seen by Davis as a failure of judgment of profound proportion by his Secretary of State and, even more serious, a professional failure of the intelligence staff developed by Benjamin for investigating the background of people before trusting them with vital responsibilities. For two years in prison, Davis had long hours to ponder the quirk of history, as it were, that linked him in any way whatsoever to Booth. Like Benjamin, for five years he would not know what John Surratt's testimony would be. But he had no doubt, especially after Wirz was tried and hanged, that men who would threaten and then hang the first woman in history in order to force her son to surrender would stop at nothing to implicate the President should her son be captured. What would this young messenger say if faced with the same gallows that had taken his mother and given the chance for immunity if he would but name Benjamin and Davis? For five years, until Surratt's 1870 lecture, Davis's career, his personal honor, and his role in history would be in the hands of the most wanted man in the world, the young messenger to his closest adviser. He had a right to feel that John Surratt was Judah Benjamin's blunder, a fateful lapse of judgment that had provided their unscrupulous enemies with the baseless thread of evidence to weave into a tapestry of accusation.

21

Paris:
Hidden from History

❧

Benjamin in 1878 wrote his old law partner in New Orleans that, looking back on his career in England, he felt it was "almost a miracle," and "I sometimes feel ashamed of my own success, when I see others quite as deserving still forced to continue the battle against fortune."[1]

He was interviewed by a New York *Times* correspondent on New Year's day in 1879. As usual whenever he met the press, Benjamin the actor was very much on stage. "Rarely have I met a smile so genial," the correspondent wrote, "as that which welcomed me from the little gentleman whom Abraham Lincoln considered the 'smartest' of all the Richmond Revolutionary Junta." He reported that Benjamin's "physique is imminently Southern, of that jolly, well-fed Southern type which so nearly resembles John Bull."

"Nobody will call you a Yankee, anyway," the correspondent remarked. He reported that "Benjamin laughed and said he was born what he now was—an Englishman." When asked whether the English held his American or Southern roots against him, Benjamin replied in the negative, "except that I should have been a Queen's Counsel several years earlier if some of the powers that be had not imagined that to honor me might not be regarded as friendly by the Washington government."

The correspondent was struck by Benjamin's appearance. "Very seldom indeed," he wrote, "does one meet a man who, having almost attained the scriptural three score years and ten, looks and acts like a man of forty. Mr. Benjamin is the best preserved man I have ever seen."[2]

Benjamin was beginning to enjoy himself more. On a trip to Toulouse, he wrote his sister, there were dinner parties "followed by extempore music and dancing in the evening and this 'old man' was made to dance by invitations from the young ladies who refused to dance at all if he would not. What do you say to that?"[3]

He viewed the British elections of 1880 from his comfortable perch atop the bar, writing, "It amuses me to look on, as I do not take the slightest part in politics and shall never again be induced to emerge from the quietude of private life . . . great efforts have been made to induce me to become a candidate but I laugh them off." He was surprised at Disraeli's defeat, because "nothing is so abhorrent to me as Radicalism which seeks to elevate the populace into the governing class."[4] It was more of a comment on reconstruction in America than on affairs in Britain.

At the end of his life, looking back on this time, he wrote to Mrs. Bradford, the wife of his former law partner: "You say I look on things through the *couleur de rose* of success. Not so, but through the *couleur de rose* of a temperament, blessed birth gift, that under all circumstances and every trial, took to the bright side and absolutely rebels against distrust of the future. I was complimented on my 'pluck' . . . it was simply elasticity of natural temperament: a total absence of . . . despondence and brooding over adverse circumstances."[5]

Almost nothing Benjamin left hints at any feeling of regret over his marriage to Natalie, except for two lines in a long letter to his niece Eugenia, who had turned to her uncle for advice because of family objections to a suitor she wanted to marry. "Don't imagine I am going to read you a moral lesson," he wrote, "for I hate them whether as giver or receiver." He thought back over the course of his life and his marriage. "I *don't* forget this, and I feel for you just as I felt for myself over fifty years ago. . . . What I want to warn you against is the impatience and rashness which are so natural at your age and which may prove fatal to your happiness."[6]

Then, in May 1880, he was "thrown to the ground with great violence in a foolish attempt to jump off a tram-car in rapid motion."[7] He broke his shoulder blade and his right arm and received a forehead fracture. His doctors said he would never fully recover but required him, in order to reduce the pain, "to take a liqueur glass of cognac pure three times a day . . . and altogether accustom myself to getting a little 'tight' each day. I shall soon be an accomplished 'tippler,' " he joked, "and then my 'cure' will be complete."[8]

The rumors of the disposition of Confederate funds in Europe continued to pursue him, even as he was reaching the final chapter in his life.

Under the headline "NO CONFEDERATE FUNDS IN EUROPE," the New York *Tribune* of January 20, 1882, printed a letter of November 28, 1881, from Benjamin to S. L. M. Barlow, a successful corporate lawyer in New York who had written Benjamin "concerning the rumors that vast sums of money had been deposited by the Confederate Government in the Bank of England and elsewhere in Europe."[9] The Confederate bonds had been subject to speculation on the stock exchange, and the New York *Times* of November 6, 1881, had editorially commented: "It is said that there is on deposit in the Bank of England some seventeen-odd millions of Confederate gold which will be surrendered to the bondholders. If there is any such deposit it belongs to the United States. . . . Would not Mr. Benjamin, for instance, find in these facts some grounds for the recovery of a commission of 500,000 pounds, that being in excess of any fair fee for any bona fide financial operation? He might be somewhat puzzled as to whom to make plaintiff in the case, but that would be a minor objection to any one who proposed to get Confederate assets out of the Bank of England."[10]

Benjamin wrote a very careful letter in reply to Barlow, almost as if he were drafting a brief, pointing out that the "Confederate Government never had but two means of raising money in Europe— one was by the export of cotton, all of which was consigned to the house of Fraser, Trenholm & Co. of Liverpool; the other was by loan effected through Messrs. Erlanger & Co. and Schroeder & Co., the proceeds of which were all received by Colin J. McRae, the financial agent of the Government."[11]

He wrote with confidence of the case he once argued and won:

At the close of the war the United States Government, claiming the right to receive the entire assets of the Confederate Government, instituted suits against Fraser, Trenholm & Co. and against McRae. After a determined and protracted litigation, Fraser, Trenholm & Co. were driven into bankruptcy, as their whole business was destroyed and their credit broken by the apprehensions created in the mercantile world of the result of the enormous claims hanging over them, when they really owed little or nothing; and I think the United States ultimately recovered a few thousand dollars as a compromise.

McRae proved in his case that he had rendered a full and faithful account to the Confederate Government of the entire proceeds of the loan in payment of supplies and munitions of war to the various commissarial and quartermaster officers in this country and of the coupons on the bonds.

He felt as if he had to defend McRae's honor and pointed out that "he was ready to render his accounts over again if the United States would agree to reimburse him any balance found due in his favor. This was declined. (The case is reported in Law Rep 8 Eg 69). Poor McRae! In shattered health and with a few hundred pounds, the wreck of his fortunes, he emigrated to Spanish Honduras, where he sought to earn a support on a small stock farm, but he died in extremely reduced circumstances."

He described the desperate state of affairs over the course of the war and asserted, as if impatient with the constant questions and charges regarding his own integrity: "The last payment of coupons on the Confederate loan was only affected after great effort by means of cotton sold through Fraser, Trenholm & Co. as all the proceeds of the loan had long since been exhausted. The United States Government also recovered some supplies, machinery and several vessels. In fact, everything that remained from the wreck; and I do not believe that one penny is to be found anywhere in Europe of the assets of the defunct Confederacy. If anything can ever be recovered by the bondholders, it can only be by government action in the United States, and you can judge better than I can if there is the remotest hope of any action."[12] It was unusual for Benjamin to use a phrase of such bluntness and finality as "defunct Confederacy," but at the end of his life he was surely tired of the rumors of Confederate funds in Europe and aimed the letter at a public audience partly in defense of his own reputation and honorable actions at the end of the war.

That sudden concern in his later years for history's judgment of his postwar success caused him to be more public about his financial affairs in a number of ways. He made his fee books available to Lawley, the London *Times* correspondent planning his biography, and the details of his earnings and his financial history were

published.[13] And he was even more specific in an interview with
the last American known to have called upon him, a legal scholar
from Cincinnati named Gustavus Wald. Wald, a graduate of Harvard
Law School, for several years was dean of the Cincinnati Law School
and the American editor of Frederic Pollock's book on contracts.
Pollock was the nephew of Baron Pollock, Benjamin's mentor and
early sponsor. Because of Wald's friendship with Pollock, Benjamin
showed him openness and courtesy that Wald found unusual. From
the details Wald later reported, it was clear Wald was taking notes,
and Benjamin must have sensed he was speaking for the record
and for publication to a legal audience in America.

"I suppose that the lawyers in America think we make much less
money here than they do," he confessed to Wald, "because you
don't hear often of large single fees in cases here as you do on the
other side, but I have done quite well. Now I practice only in three
courts, the Court of Appeals, the Privy Council, and the House of
Lords; I take no brief accompanied by less than fifty guineas, and
generally none marked less than one hundred guineas. As I try no
cases at *nisi prius,* and so, of course, get my cases on a record
made up, I have simply to prepare the law applicable to a fixed
state of facts, and that I can do in most cases overnight. From the
time each case of mine is called until the argument in it is concluded,
I receive in it a refresher of ten guineas a day. As I can be in only
one court at a time, while I am engaged in a case in one of the
courts my refreshers in a case or cases in one or both of the other
courts are running on. And what is the most delightful thing about
the practice here is that I never have to talk to, or even see, a
client. My terms here are known, and solicitors either choose to
employ me on them or they don't; of course, there is no such thing
as bargaining about fees."[14]

It was time to slow down the pace of law practice. "I still keep
up my old jog-trot, but my work is less absorbing now. I have cut
off a good deal of my practice preparatory to withdrawing but my
withdrawal now depends entirely on our success in getting Ninette
and her husband back to live with us, as I should hardly know
what to do in the 'big house' all alone with my poor wife, who is
constantly fretting for her daughter."[15]

He railed at the British weather in the years after the mansion
was finished, but his work and his clients prevented his moving
fully to Paris.

"I am tired of work and need repose—I suppose that this feeling overcomes me by reason of the shock given to my whole system in May 1880, for which it seems impossible for me to recover radically—I am always ailing in some way, and I 'give up'—. . . . Such weather as we have here! fog, fog, fog! I am most impatient to [go] somewhere where I can breathe."[16]

A severe heart attack brought on by diabetes on Christmas 1882 sent him to bed and forced his retirement. It was reported that he returned to clients briefs and retainers worth $100,000. He was genuinely surprised by the reaction to the announcement from the press and from his colleagues, and he wrote his sister, "Every leading London newspaper, with the *Times* at the head, has made my retirement a matter of national concern and regret and my table is covered with piles of letters (some sixty or seventy at least) from my brethren of the bar, expressing the warmest sympathy and regret. . . . For the last few days, I have hardly kept my eyes free from tears on reading these testimonials to rectitude and honor of my professional conduct, such as no member of the bar has ever received."[17]

The *Times* noted that in mercantile law, Benjamin had "equal authority with a standard textbook"[18] and that he had seemed "more like an assessor of the Supreme Courts of Appeal than a simple practitioner." The *Morning Telegraph* of London, for which he wrote in his early days in England, sought to sum up the life of "the gifted stranger" somewhat later:

> Such a career as that of Judah Philip Benjamin is not likely to be repeated. The man and the circumstances were both unique. As a parliamentary and forensic record his life has all the fascinations of a brilliantly narrated romance. He conquered fame and fortune by the exercise of a robust, and at the same time subtle, intellect, and by rare gifts of expression and persuasion. His industry was immense. It was his custom to master every intricacy of the most lengthy brief—to leave no detail, however slight, unnoticed. Of him it may be truly said that he touched no legal subject which he did not adorn with the clear light of a luminous intellect and with the force and grace of an exquisite eloquence. He knew when to wait, and when to strike, both as a statesman and as an advocate. Men of his stamp are born to success. . . . Beginning life afresh in a new country, and at an age when most professional men contemplate retirement from the active pursuit of their vocation, he took up the same line of action which had served him

so well in the past, before the defeat of the Confederate cause drove him to seek a safe asylum upon our shores. That such an able and eloquent advocate should have found a warm welcome and a generous appreciation at the hands of the English Bar is, indeed, a high testimony to that great institution, and to the gifted stranger, possessed of strength of will and force of intellect to engage the unstinted admiration of kindred spirits, raised far above mean and petty jealousy.[19]

He thought that he would disappear quietly to Paris, but once again the English bar surprised him. He wrote his sister: "A letter from the Attorney General informs me that he has received a requisition signed by more than eighty Queen's Counsel, and by all the leading members of the bar of England, desiring him to offer me a public dinner in order to take a 'collective farewell' of me and to testify their high sense of honor and integrity of my professional career, and of their desire that our relations of personal friendship should not be severed. The correspondence will be made public. This is the first time that such an honor has been extended to a barrister on leaving the profession."[20]

The dinner took place in the ornate halls of the Inner Temple amid dark wood-paneled walls decorated with royal coats of arms, large somber paintings, and marble statues. In the chair sat Sir Henry James, the Attorney General; on his right sat Benjamin and on his left the Lord Chancellor. The noteworthy came to honor him: the Lord Chief Justice, the Solicitor General, the Lord Advocate for Scotland, the Attorney General for Ireland, and more than two hundred judges, Queen's Counsel, and other lawyers. The Attorney General spoke for the assembled audience: "You know how Mr. Benjamin came among us and how we received him. . . . We found a place for him in our foremost rank; we grudged him not the leadership he so easily gained—we were proud of his success, for we knew the strength of the stranger among us and the bar is ever generous even in its rivalry toward success that is based on merit. And the merit must have been there, for who is the man save this one of whom it can be said he held conspicuous leadership at the bar of two countries? To him, the change of citizenship and transition in his profession seemed easy enough. From the first days of coming he was one of us. . . . The years are few since Mr. Benjamin was a stranger to us all, and in those few years he has accomplished more than most men can ever hope in a lifetime to achieve."[21]

Benjamin replied with appreciation, made his farewells, and then added: "From the bar of England I never, so far as I am aware, received anything but warm and kindly welcome. I never had occasion to feel that any one regarded me as an intruder. I never felt a touch of professional jealousy. I never received an unkindness. On the contrary, from all quarters I received a warm and cordial welcome to which, as a stranger, I had no title, except that I was a political exile, seeking by honorable labor to retrieve shattered fortunes, wrecked in the ruin of a lost cause."[22]

He returned to Paris to face his last winter.

Lawley visited and pleaded with him one last time for his help in a possible biography.

"I would much prefer that no 'Life,' not even a magazine article should ever be written about me," Lawley reported that Benjamin told him. "But even if I had the health, and desired ever so much to help you in your work, I have no materials available for the purpose. I have never kept a diary, or retained a copy of a letter written by me. No letters addressed to me by others will be found among my papers when I die."[23]

Benjamin paid special tribute to Varina, with whom he continued to correspond regularly even after he was out of touch with Jefferson Davis: "With perhaps the exception of Mrs. Jefferson Davis, no one has many letters of mine, for I have read so many American biographies which reflected only the passions and prejudices of their writers that I do not want to leave behind me letters and documents to be used in such a work about myself."[24]

He advised John George Witt, the executor of his estate, "Never keep any letter or other document if you can help it. You will only give yourself infinite trouble, and if you die, you bequeath a legacy of mischief." According to Witt, "when he died, he did not leave behind him half a dozen pieces of paper."[25]

"We always talk French in our family circle," he wrote Lawley in 1882 of his life in Paris. "Indeed my wife and daughter have lived so long in Paris that they have almost forgotten their English." As for his longed-for grandchild, he wrote: "We have decided it is to be a boy and that he is to become Marshal of France." But he would be deeply disappointed, as "thus far each of her children has died shortly after it was born and thus the cherished hope of my life that I might have a grandchild to play with in my old age has not been granted to me. But I still live on hopes."[26]

He looked back on his life with wistfulness, having come full circle back to the Europe from which his Sephardic ancestors had fled: "I have been hard at work ever since I was ten years old and now I am 72, and have fairly earned some repose. The last ten or twelve years of my practice in London have been the most laborious in my life, not even excepting those which you doubtless remember when I toiled so hard at the State Department in Richmond."[27]

Even after eighteen years in England and in Paris, he was beginning to feel more attachment to the Southern soil of his early years. To a visitor from New Orleans he said, as if addressing his history, "Louisiana . . . remember me there."[28]

His poor health was taking its toll. He wrote a last letter to Varina as if to say good-bye. "I fancy I shall not recover. I would not have you hear of my misfortune from another than your friend, who is always affectionately yours."[29]

Judah P. Benjamin died on May 6, 1884, at the age of seventy-three, in his mansion in Paris. Varina wrote, "Thus passed from earth one of the greatest minds of this century."[30] Natalie had summoned a priest to administer the last rites, providing her husband with a contact with the Catholic Church at a final moment when he could not resist. Funeral services were held at the same church in which Ninette had been married, and Natalie had him buried in a crypt in Père Lachaise cemetery marked only for the families of St. Martin and Bousignac. Today the records in Père Lachaise cemetery still identify him only as "Philippe Benjamin," the name only Natalie called him, as if he had agreed with her intent to conceal his identity.[31]

Epilogue

❦

Père Lachaise today is an immense, aging, urban cemetery of somber confusion and mystery, built on the high ground of Paris to withstand the rising waters of the Seine. It contrasts with most Southern cemeteries in the United States, which are green and wooded on rolling hills, with flowers and plantings. New Orleans, however, with its fear of the frequently flooding Mississippi, has cemeteries like Père Lachaise; thus Judah P. Benjamin does not rest in altogether unfamiliar surroundings.[1]

More than one hundred years after Benjamin's death, Père Lachaise is as overcrowded as Paris itself, with thousands of tombs spreading over several square miles of hills in the midst of the city. High walls around the cemetery shield it from view of the street, adding to its forbidding character. Benjamin is not listed among the famous personages buried there, to whose graves all the tourists who enter are guided by maps: Colette, Rossini, Chopin, Bernini, Molière, Modigliani, Oscar Wilde, Sarah Bernhardt, Balzac, Bizet. The concierge at the entrance had not heard of him, and one has to know the burial date to find the location, in the southwestern corner a half-mile from the entrance.

Winding through the cemetery are cobblestone roads, cut around and through the hills so that the cluttered stones of the gravesites rise and fall against the eye like the rolling waves of a marble sea. It is so desolate that as one searches for the Benjamin grave, the scene recalls the psalmist's vision of "a walk through the valley of the shadow of death." In the stillness, any movement or noise catches attention—a wild-eyed cat darting out of a crypt or a bird fluttering—and one tries to imagine in the eerie silence what Judah P. Benjamin's funeral train must have been like. The clatter of horses' hooves and the creaking wheels must have echoed off the hard marble casements throughout the graveyard as the mourners maneuvered the coffin-laden carriage through the jumble of stones to a grave on the crest of a hill where the road divides.

Benjamin rests in a modest gravesite. The grand burial structures surrounding the site render his grave all the more humble to the visitor. An oak tree nearby provides shade; the sun casts angular shadows from the other tombs, and there are extreme differences of temperature between the shade, where one is surrounded by cool marble, and the sunlight, where the heat radiates off the marble slabs.

Mounds of dead flowers lie at intervals along the cobblestone roads, gathered by caretakers from the graves, reminding one that though this is a cold and barren place, it is linked to human memory.

Standing at the foot of Judah Benjamin's grave, one is struck by an irony. It is as if he tried to escape notice even in Paris, this Confederate statesman who is misplaced here, buried not in his city of New Orleans, where he lived the longest, or in the State of Louisiana, which he served in the U.S. Senate, but here, far away from his roots in the South. One can think of no other major American political leader buried so far from his origins.

But he is safe in Paris, hidden in the serpentine roads and the crannies of a historic burial ground, safe from the vengeful, the unfriendly, the defacers, and the anti-Semites; safe from the angry mob or the spiteful; safe from the false accusers who would dishonor his name. Almost anonymous in Père Lachaise, Benjamin has no mourners to wash his gravestone or to place flowers on his grave, but he never counted on such sentiments during his life. His task always seemed to be to erase the past, not to retain it. To him, surely, the fear of desecration and humiliation far outweighed the tears of Confederate sympathizers in determining his own preference for a final resting place.

He seems all alone in Père Lachaise. He came to Paris only in the last year of his life and, aside from his family, was without friends or admirers there. For a man born of the Jewish faith, the rare Jewish graves at Père Lachaise only add to the loneliness of his place there. The cemetery is overwhelmingly Catholic, with its crosses and crucifixes, images of Jesus, and Latin phrases etched in stone. It is so Catholic in its mood that a simple Kaddish—the Jewish prayer of remembrance—would seem foreign, a distant language, inappropriate. Natalie, surely with his acquiescence, arranged for a quiet, anonymous site, where he would never be disturbed, where he would be assimilated into his surroundings, far away from his South, and by all means protected from those seeking revenge for the crime he did not commit. A Jew by birth, he would be buried in secret among the Christians—alone, disguised, but safe.

When Jefferson Davis died in December 1889, E. B. Kruttschnitt, Judah P. Benjamin's nephew, served at the New Orleans funeral as one of the pallbearers, so chosen, the newspapers reported, because he was a descendant of the President's closest colleague. Three years later, after several states vied for the President's remains, Varina agreed that he should be moved to Hollywood Cemetery in Richmond with the thousands of other Confederate dead "as the proper place for the grave of him who loved them all and labored for their glory."[2] A life-sized statue of Jefferson Davis standing tall was placed on the gravesite.

In 1938 the Paris chapter of the Daughters of the Confederacy finally provided an inscription to identify the man in the almost anonymous grave in the Père Lachaise cemetery:

JUDAH PHILIP BENJAMIN
BORN ST. THOMAS WEST INDIES AUGUST 6, 1811
DIED IN PARIS MAY 6, 1884
UNITED STATES SENATOR FROM LOUISIANA
ATTORNEY GENERAL, SECRETARY OF WAR AND
SECRETARY OF STATE OF THE CONFEDERATE STATES
OF AMERICA, QUEEN'S COUNSEL, LONDON

In life, as in death, he was elusive, vanishing behind his agreeableness, his cordiality, his perpetual smile. To blend into the culture—whether Southern or English—was innate, bred into him, a matter of the Jewish Southerner's instinct for survival. But, the "dark prince" could not elude the Christian bias, released with unbearable intensity by the Civil War. He withdrew even more deeply—into hard work, loneliness, isolation, and a life without intimacy. The public man celebrated on two continents sought a kind of invisibility, not unlike the private man nobody knew. Shunning his past, choosing an almost secret grave, with calculated concealment, he nearly succeeded in remaining hidden from history.

Notes

❈

Full information can be found in the selected bibliography. Otherwise, the work will be cited in full in the notes.

CHAPTER 1
Charleston: Boyhood in the Reformed Society

1. *Encyclopedia Judaica* (New York and Jerusalem, 1971), 9: 477–78 (see verse 20, Obadiah).

2. *Ibid.,* 8: 431–59.

3. "The Inquisition," *Universal Jewish Encyclopedia* (New York, 1941), 5: 566–70. See also H. Ben Sasson (ed.), *A History of the Jewish People* (Cambridge: Harvard University Press, 1976), Part V, "The Middle Ages: Popular Pressure Against the Jews," pp. 574–93, esp. "Developments in Christian Spain (1391–1492)," pp. 583–84.

   For more details on the Spanish Jews, their flourishing history, the Inquisition, and the expulsion, see A. Ashtor (Strauss), *The History of the Jews of Moslem Spain,* Vols. I–II (Jerusalem, 1966) (in Hebrew); Y. Baer, *A History of the Jews of Christian Spain,* Vols. I–II (Philadelphia, 1961–66); L. Finkelstein, (ed.), *The Jews: Their History, Culture, and Religion,* 4 vols. (New York, 1960), Vol. I, pp. 216–49, 287–320; H. Graetz, *History of the Jews,* Vol. 4 (1927); J. R. Marcus, *The Jews in the Medieval World* (Cincinnati, 1938); C. Roth, *World History of the Jewish People,* 2d Series Medieval Period, Vol. II, *The Dark Ages* (Tel Aviv, 1966); and Abram Sachar, *A History of the Jews,* 5th Ed. Rev. (New York, 1967).

4. Also known as Mendez, de Mendes. See Robert D. Meade, *Judah P. Benjamin, Confederate Statesman,* pp. 3–5, 381–82.

5. "Judah" and "Tribe of Judah," *The Jewish Encyclopedia,* 7: 327–30.

6. Meade reported that Judah was the second son and Solomon the first. Malcolm Stern, author of *First American Jewish Families,* interview, June 1981, pointed out that Benjamin's paternal grandfather lived in St. Eustatius before moving to the Virgin Islands, where he was a *mohel* (a religious official trained to perform the ritual of circumcision). His record of circumcisions mentions an older Judah, who died in infancy, to be replaced, in Sephardic tradition, by the second Judah. The old man circumcised both grandsons and passed on the name Judah, as was the custom among Sephardics even if the grandfather was alive. Stern says he believes Meade was simply mistaken that Solomon was the oldest of the sons. Stern points out that Solomon was named after the maternal grandfather, Solomon De Mendes of Portugal, which, under Sephardic custom, would make him the second son.

7. Meade, *Benjamin,* p. 6.

8. Barnett A. Elzas, *Jews of South Carolina,* p. 184. For background and history of the Jews of Charleston, see Charles Reznikoff and Uriah Engelman, *The Jews of Charleston.*

9. Elzas, *Jews of South Carolina,* p. 185.

10. Elzas, *Leaves from Scrapbook,* Second Series, No. 6.

11. Pierce Butler, *Benjamin,* p. 24.

12. Recordbook Q, p. 183, August 16, 1817, and p. 20, March 28, 1817, Wilmington, N.C., courthouse.

13. For background, see *An Account of the Late Intended Insurrection,* (pamphlet, 1822), and contemporary issues of Charleston *Courier,* June, July, and August 1822.

14. Meade, *Benjamin,* p. 14.

15. Article VI of "The Constitution of the Reformed Society," published in L. C. Moise, *Biography of Isaac Harby with an Account of the Reformed Society of Israelites of Charleston, S.C.* (Central Conference of American Rabbis, 1931), p. 62.

16. Reznikoff and Engelman, *The Jews of Charleston,* p. 106.

17. *Ibid.,* pp. 125–28.

18. Article III of "The Constitution of the Reformed Society" is published in Moise, *Isaac Harby,* p. 62. Judah P. Benjamin turned thirteen on August 11, 1824, and the first meeting of the Society was on November 21, 1824; its petitions were in December.

19. *Ibid.,* pp. 82–83, excerpt from prayerbook of the Reformed Society. The first prayerbook, in Harby's own handwriting, was issued on November 24, 1824.

20. Solomon Breibart, *The Rev. Mr. Gustavus Poznanski* (Charleston, 1979); For an interesting discussion of the psychology of Southern Jews in this period, see Abraham J. Peck, "That Other 'Peculiar Institu-

tion': Jews and Judaism in the Nineteenth Century South," *Modern Judaism* 7, No. 1 (February 7, 1987), 99–114.

21. Elzas, *Jews of South Carolina,* pp. 185–87.

CHAPTER 2
Yale: A Mysterious Departure

1. Matriculation book in Yale records; for further background, see Dan A. Oren, *Joining The Club: A History of Jews and Yale.*

2. Reports on the Course of Instruction at Yale College, 1830; also, Kingsley, *Yale College* (New York, 1879), p. 277.

3. Elzas, *Jews of South Carolina,* pp. 163, 185.

4. W. W. Hoppin in an interview after Benjamin's death in May 1884. Undated clipping from collection of John O'Brien, New Haven, Conn.

5. Letter from Simeon North to Brayton, January 30, 1827, in Library of Congress; see also "Judah P. Benjamin's Guardian," New York *Times,* February 26, 1883, quoting from an interview with North in Utica *Observer,* February 24, 1883.

6. Calliopean Society Records, Yale University, from Anson Phelps Stokes, *Memorials of Eminent Yale Men,* pp. 196–97.

7. New York *Independent,* January 31, 1861.

8. For additional analysis, see Dan A. Oren, "Why Did Judah P. Benjamin Leave Yale?" *A Jewish Journal at Yale,* Fall 1984, pp. 13–17.

9. New Orleans *Delta,* March 2, 1861.

10. Letters to James A. Bayard and T. F. Bayard, March 19, 1861, and April 5, 1861. Callery Collection, Historical Society of Delaware, and Pierce Butler Collection, Tulane University.

11. Letter from Reverend Porter, Lawley Mss., Pierce Butler Collection, Tulane University; Chapter 1, located in Folder 10, Box 61, Day Family Papers, Ms. Group 175, YMAL.

12. Letter to President Jeremiah Day, Yale University Archives, noted in Meade, *Benjamin,* p. 29.

13. Letter from Simeon North to Brayton, January 30, 1827.

14. "Judah P. Benjamin's Guardian," New York *Times,* February 26, 1883, quoting from reminiscences by North in Utica *Observer,* February 24, 1883.

15. Stokes, *Memorials of Eminent Yale Men,* p. 263.

16. Oren, "Why Did Judah P. Benjamin Leave Yale?" *A Jewish Journal at Yale,* Fall 1984, p. 15.

17. Stokes, *Memorials of Eminent Yale Men.*

CHAPTER 3
New Orleans to Bellechasse: The Climb to U.S. Senator

1. For descriptions of New Orleans during this period, see Kendall, *History of New Orleans,* 3 vols. (Chicago, 1922); King, *New Orleans* (New

York, 1895); Rightor, *Standard History of New Orleans* (Chicago, 1900). For the Jewish Community, see Bertram Korn, *The Early Jews of New Orleans.* See also Butler, *Benjamin,* p. 32.

2. Meade, *Benjamin,* pp. 42–44.

3. Elzas, *Jews of South Carolina.* The entry in the Charleston directory for 1831 is as follows: "Philip Benjamin, fruiterer, 16 St. Philip St." In the directory for 1840–41, "Philip Benjamin, fruits, 29 Beaufuinand," and in 1849, "Philip Benjamin, 9 Princess." Thus, he did not move to Beaufort with his wife. Elzas wrote in *Leaves of My Historical Scrapbook,* which appeared in the Charleston *Sunday News,* March 8, 1908, "Philip Benjamin appears, like his distinguished son, to have been unfortunate in his domestic relations—apparently living apart from his wife." For more on Judah's trips to visit his family, see Lawley Mss., Pierce Butler Collection, Tulane University.

4. Lawley Mss., Pierce Butler Collection, Tulane University.

5. Butler, *Benjamin,* p. 34, quoting "an anecdote from the late Dr. Davidson."

6. For the impact of yellow fever on various families and the New Orleans Jewish community generally, see Korn, *Early Jews of New Orleans,* pp. 53, 162, 172, 174, 176–77, 231, 239, 243, 319.

7. *Ibid.,* p. 188. Benjamin was married on February 12, 1833, after being admitted to the bar on December 16, 1832. St. Louis Cathedral, New Orleans, Marriage registers 5, act 286.

8. Records of St. Martin's houses, Civil District Courthouse. Sale of Lot on Bourbon Street to St. Martin recorded July 28, 1835.

9. Judah P. Benjamin and Thomas Slidell, *Digest of the Reported Decisions of the Superior Court of the Late Territory of New Orleans and the Supreme Court of the State of Louisiana* (New Orleans, 1834).

10. Burton Hendrick, *Statesmen of the Lost Cause,* pp. 283–85, and Louis M. Sears, *John Slidell,* pp. 140–65. "Wire puller" phrase is by W. H. Russell in the London *Times,* December 10, 1861.

11. Meade, *Benjamin,* p. 39.

12. Letter to Robert Meade, April 8, 1931, in Robert D. Meade Papers, Manuscripts Department, University of Virginia Library.

13. Meade interview with Mrs. G. G. Myrover, Robert D. Meade Papers, Manuscript Department, University of Virginia Library.

14. Salomon de Rothchild, quoted in Jacob Marcus, *Memoirs of American Jews,* III: 104.

15. Dr. M. Wiener, writing in *Allgemeine Zeitung des Judentums* (Berlin), VI (1842): 294–95. About his trip to the United States, see Korn, *Early Jews of New Orleans,* p. 244.

16. Korn, *Early Jews of New Orleans,* pp. 240–43.

17. For details of Benjamin's life as a sugar planter, see Butler, *Benjamin,* pp. 48–60.

18. Butler, *Benjamin,* pp. 57–58.

19. Published first as articles in *DeBow's Review,* II (January 1848): 322–45, and V (April 1848): 357–64.

20. Butler, *Benjamin,* p. 62.

21. Meade, *Benjamin,* pp. 57–59, and William P. Spratling, *Old Plantation Houses in Louisiana* (New York, 1927), pp. 157–58.

22. Cemetery record for the Hebrew Cemetery, Canal and N. Anthony Streets, New Orleans.

23. Whitaker, *Sketches of Life in Louisiana* (New Orleans, 1847), pp. 27–30.

24. *McCargo* v. *New Orleans Insurance Company,* 10 Robinson's Louisiana Reports, pp. 202–39, 279. There were six suits in all and three briefs. See *Louisiana Annual Reports,* Vol. X. For full text of Benjamin's "What is a slave?" brief, see *Lockett* v. *The Merchants Insurance Co.,* brief for defendants, p. 18, in Howard Memorial Library, New Orleans. Also, see Louis Gruss, "Judah P. Benjamin," *Louisiana Historical Quarterly,* October 1936, pp. 1023–26.

25. *Congressional Globe,* 1st Sess., 34th Cong., pp. 1092–98. See also Benjamin to Bayard, May 3, 1858, in Bayard Papers, Callery Collection, Historical Society of Delaware; Louisiana *Courier,* May 11, 1856; and Meade, *Benjamin,* pp. 102–5.

26. Proceedings and debates of the Convention of Louisiana, New Orleans, 1845, pp. 89, 131–34, 142, 156–57, 187–89, 220–25, 382, 906–11. See also Butler, *Benjamin,* p. 52–56, and newspaper accounts: Louisiana *Courier,* November 19, 20, 23, 1845, and *Picayune,* January 14, 1845.

27. Benjamin Perley Poore, *Reminiscences,* p. 409.

28. For the background of the trial, see Butler, *Benjamin,* pp. 179–84, and *Delta,* January 3, 10, 11, 14, 18, and 23, 1851.

29. *Delta,* January 24, 1851.

30. *Delta,* May 23, 1851.

31. *McDonogh* v. *Murdock,* 15 Howard, pp. 367–415; Meade, *Benjamin,* gives an especially detailed account, pp. 68–71. Account from Washington *Union* quoted in the *Picayune,* February 2, 1854. See also Butler, *Benjamin,* pp. 139–40.

32. *Picayune,* January 7, 1852. For background, see James Luetze, *Judah P. Benjamin and the Tehuantepec Canal,* 1961, masters thesis, University of North Carolina.

33. The *Delta* covered Benjamin's railroad activities extensively: January 7 and 8, April 10 and 17, and June 8, 1852. For a detailed account, see Butler, *Benjamin,* pp. 119–36.

34. The *True Delta* remained opposed to him editorially, September 1851.

35. *Delta,* February 7, 1852.

36. Louis M. Sears, *John Slidell,* pp. 6–8. See also Willson, Beccles, *John Slidell and the Confederates in Paris;* Butler, *Benjamin,* p. 165; and Hendrick, *Statesmen of the Lost Cause,* p. 87.

37. *Delta,* February 7, 1852.

38. Mortality records and city directories, Charleston, Lawley Mss., Chapter 3; Ernest Kruttschnitt to Lawley, September 27, 1898, Pierce Butler Collection, Tulane University.

CHAPTER 4

Jefferson Davis: The Education of a Lonely Protestant

1. Jefferson Davis, "Autobiographical Sketch," in H. M. Monroe, Jr., and J. T. McIntosh (eds.), *The Papers of Jefferson Davis* (Baton Rouge, 1971), 1: 1xviii.

2. Varina H. Davis, *Jefferson Davis: A Memoir by His Wife,* I: 3–8, offers Davis's own account of his early childhood.

3. *Ibid.,* I: 4, 17.

4. For Davis's trip to Kentucky, his meeting with Andrew Jackson, and his years at St. Thomas, see *ibid.,* pp. 1–16.

5. For Davis's account of his trip home and his reactions to Mississippi as an adolescent, see *ibid,* pp. 16–21.

6. The five other members of the U.S. Senate were David Bishop of Missouri, Edward Hannegan of Louisiana, George Jones of Iowa, S. W. Jones of Louisiana, and Joseph R. Underwood of Kentucky. *Ibid,* pp. 22–31. See also, John D. Wright, Jr., *Transylvania: Tutor to the West* (Lexington, 1975), and M. N. Wagers, *The Education of a Gentleman: Jefferson Davis at Transylvania 1821–1824* (Lexington, 1943).

7. Personal papers, Samuel E. Davis, Accession no. 26130, Virginia State Library. Reported in Monroe and McIntosh (eds.), *Papers of Jefferson Davis,* 1: 4–5.

8. Varina H. Davis, *Memoir* I: 32.

9. Jefferson Davis Papers, Frances Carrick Thomas Library, Transylvania University, Lexington, Kentucky, reported in Monroe and McIntosh, *Papers of Jefferson Davis,* 1: 11.

CHAPTER 5

Melancholy War Hero

1. Varina H. Davis, *Memoir,* I: 34, reported in Monroe and McIntosh, *Papers of Jefferson Davis,* 1: 1xxviii.

2. Varina H. Davis, *Memoir,* I: 35, and Monroe and McIntosh, *Papers of Jefferson Davis,* 1: 1xxvix.

3. Monroe and McIntosh, *Papers of Jefferson Davis,* 1: 14–15.

4. *Ibid.,* p. 105.

5. L. Lasswell, "Jefferson Davis Ponders His Future, 1829," *Journal of Southern History,* XLI (November 1975): 516–22. See also, Clement Eaton, *Jefferson Davis,* p. 15.

6. Varina H. Davis, *Memoir* I: 475, and Eaton, *Jefferson Davis,* p. 37.

7. Varina H. Davis, *Memoir,* I: 191–92.

8. Hudson Strode, *Jefferson Davis: Private Letters 1823–1889,* pp. 19–38. Six of Davis's letters of courtship were saved by Varina.

9. Varina H. Davis, *Memoir,* I: 206.

10. *Ibid.,* I: 352.

11. *Ibid.,* I: 358.

12. *Ibid.,* I: 359.

13. *Ibid.,* I: 288.

14. Eaton, *Jefferson Davis,* pp. 33–46.

15. Janet S. Hermann, *The Pursuit of the Dream,* pp. 3–15. For a description of the life of slaves on the Davis plantations in the antebellum period, see pp. 3–37.

16. *Ibid.,* p. 12.

17. Varina H. Davis, *Memoir,* I: 179.

18. *Ibid.,* I: 178.

19. *Ibid.,* I: 479–80.

CHAPTER 6
Washington: A Senate Duel

1. Dunbar Rowland (ed.), *Jefferson Davis, Constitutionalist,* pp. 177–79.

2. Varina H. Davis, letter to Lawley, June 8, 1898, Lawley Mss., Pierce Butler Collection, Tulane University.

3. Charles Warren, *The Supreme Court in United States History* (Boston, 1924), 2: 516–19, and New York *Times,* February 14–15, 1853. For background, see Carl Swisher, *History of the Supreme Court of the United States: The Taney Period 1836–64* (New York, 1974), pp. 240–44. See also London *Times,* May 9, 1884.

4. Varina H. Davis, *Memoir,* I: 535.

5. John W. Daniel (ed.), *Life and Reminiscences of Jefferson Davis by Distinguished Men of His Time* (Baltimore, 1890), p. 32.

6. Stanley L. Falk, "Solder-Technologist: Major Alfred Mordecai and the Beginnings of Science in the United States Army," Ph.D. dissertation, Georgetown University, 1959, pp. 426–82.

7. *Ibid.,* pp. 546–93.

8. Varina H. Davis, *Memoir,* II: 535.

9. Hudson Strode, *Jefferson Davis,* I: 274.

10. Butler, *Benjamin,* pp. 149–50, and Meade, *Benjamin,* pp. 103–4.

11. Quoted in the Charleston *Courier,* May 11, 1856.

12. From a speech to the Senate, July 12, 1848, *Congressional Globe,* 30th Cong., 1st sess., Appendix, p. 907–14. Eaton calls this speech his first important speech in the Senate. Eaton, *Jefferson Davis,* pp. 68–69.

13. Varina H. Davis, *Memoir,* I: 361.

14. Strode, *Jefferson Davis: Private Letters, 1832–1889* (New York, 1906), p. 79.

15. Eaton, *Jefferson Davis,* p. 78. As a Congressman in 1847, Eaton noted he was "handicapped by bad health. He had severe earaches and inflamed, red eyes." *Ibid.,* p. 52.

16. Rowland, *Jefferson Davis, Constitutionalist,* III: 339–60, speech to Mississippi Legislature, November 16, 1858.

17. Eaton, *Jefferson Davis,* p. 104.

18. *Ibid.,* p. 102, and Benjamin letter to James Robb, March 18, 1858, James Robb Papers, The Historic New Orleans Collection.

19. W. B. Hesseltine (ed.), *Three Against Lincoln: Murat Halstead Reports the Caucuses of 1860,* pp. 119–21. Murat Halstead, editor of the Cincinnati *Commercial,* attended the Baltimore convention of the Democratic Party of 1860 and described Davis in detail.

20. For a full text of this noted speech by Benjamin, see *Congressional Globe,* 34th Cong., 1st and 2d sess., pp. 1092–98. Excerpts in Meade, *Benjamin,* p. 100–105.

21. Varina H. Davis, letter to Lawley, June 8, 1898.

22. *Ibid.*

23. Varina H. Davis, *Memoir,* I: 535.

24. Isaac M. Wise, *Reminiscences,* pp. 184–87. For an article analyzing Wise's statements and on Benjamin's Jewishness in general, see Bertram Korn, "Judah P. Benjamin as a Jew," *Publications of the American Jewish Historical Society,* No. XXXVIII, Pt. 3 (March 1949), pp. 153–71. Reprinted in Bertram Korn, *Eventful Years and Experiences: Studies in Nineteenth Century American Jewish History,* pp. 79–97.

25. *Occident,* I, no. 4 (July 1843): 216.

26. *Congressional Globe,* 33d Cong., 1st sess., XXVIII, part 2: 1144. See also Korn, "Judah P. Benjamin as a Jew," pp. 91–93.

27. George G. Vest, "A Senator from Two Republics: Judah P. Benjamin," *Saturday Evening Post,* October 3, 1903.

28. *True Delta,* May 2, 1959.

29. Meade, *Benjamin,* p. 120. Meade personally investigated the documents in the box.

30. *United States* v. *Castillero,* U.S. District Court, Northern District of California, no. 420.

31. *Ibid.,* New Almaden transcript of the record, 4 vols., San Francisco 1859–61, and Meade, *Benjamin,* pp. 131–32.

32. Herbert T. Ezekiel and Gaston Lichtenstein, *The History of the Jews of Richmond from 1769–1917,* p. 169.

33. Korn, "Judah P. Benjamin as a Jew."

34. *Ibid.*

35. See Butler, *Benjamin,* pp. 143–44, and *True Delta,* January 6 and 7 and November 15, 1855.

36. Meade, *Benjamin,* p. 91. See also *True Delta,* March 20, 1853, and William H. Russell, *My Diary, North and South,* p. 252.

37. *True Delta,* February 2, 1859.

38. Pickett Papers, Library of Congress (Meade suggests the letter may have been left in Benjamin's trunks when he escaped in 1865); mentioned in *Allgemeine Zeitung des Judentums* (Berlin), XXII: 553.

39. Gruss, *Judah P. Benjamin,* p. 937. See Max J. Kohler, *Judah P. Benjamin: Statesman,* pp. 83–84, citing *Senate Debates,* and Korn, "Judah P. Benjamin as a Jew," p. 97. Butler, *Benjamin,* p. 434, doubts the authenticity of the exchange. Senator George Vest of Missouri vouched for the story though attributing the taunt to someone else. *Saturday Evening Post,* October 3, 1903.

40. Varina H. Davis, letter to Lawley, June 8, 1898.

41. *Congressional Globe,* 35th Cong., 1st sess., June 8, 1858, p. 2775–82; Butler, *Benjamin,* pp. 177–79; and Meade, *Benjamin,* pp. 115–17.

42. Notes of Tom Bayard in Pierce Butler Collection, Tulane University. See also Bayard Papers, Callery Collection, Historical Society of Delaware.

43. Varina H. Davis, letter to Lawley, June 8, 1898.

44. *True Delta,* January 15 and 26, 1859.

45. For details of the Houmas affair, see Butler, *Benjamin,* pp. 166–70; Meade, *Benjamin,* pp. 117–19; and Sears, *John Slidell,* pp. 164–67.

46. *True Delta,* March 15, 1859, quoting from the St. Louis *Republican.*

47. *Congressional Globe,* 36th Cong., 1st sess., May 29, 1860, p. 2433.

48. Butler, *Benjamin,* pp. 166–67, and Meade, *Benjamin,* pp. 118–19.

49. *Delta,* January 26, 1859.

50. Edwin A. Alderman and Armistead Gordon, *J. L. M. Curry* (New York and London, 1911), pp. 402–3.

51. Reverdy Johnson during argument of *U.S.* v. *Castillero* in the U.S. District Court for the Northern District of California, No. 4220. See *Transcript of the Record,* 4 vols., San Francisco, 1859–61.

52. Vest, *Saturday Evening Post,* October 3, 1903.

53. Mrs. Virginia Clay-Clopton (Mrs. Clement Clay), *A Belle of the Fifties,* pp. 51–52.

54. Varina H. Davis, letter to Lawley, June 8, 1898.

55. Meade interview with the daughter of Senator Yulee, in Robert D. Meade Papers, Manuscripts Department, University of Virginia Library. Meade examined some of the objects bought at auction, which were still in the possession of the Yulee family.

56. *Ibid.*

57. *Congressional Globe,* 36th Cong., 1st sess., pp. 2239–41. Benjamin's speech made such an eloquent case against Douglas that it was reprinted by the Democratic National Committee and used as a campaign document for Breckinridge, the presidential candidate of Southern Democrats. A copy of the pamphlet is in the Library of Congress.

58. *Congressional Globe,* 36th Cong., 1st sess., p. 2309.

59. Lawley Mss., in Pierce Butler Collection, Tulane University Library.

60. Pamphlet copy of speech in New York Public Library. See also California News in New York *Times,* November 28, 1860.

61. *Picayune,* December 16, 1860.

62. *Personal Reminiscences of Jefferson Davis,* ms. in Confederate Memorial Hall, New Orleans.

63. *Congressional Globe,* 36th Cong., 2d sess., pp. 212–17.

64. Varina H. Davis, letter to Lawley, June 8, 1898.

65. *Ibid.*

66. Sir George Cornewall Lewis to Lord Sherbrooke, in Butler, *Benjamin,* p. 211. See also Alderman and Gordon, *J. L. M. Curry,* p. 401.

67. Quoted in *The Israelite,* VII, no. 30 (January 25, 1861): 238.

68. Quoted in *The Israelite,* VII, no. 38 (March 22, 1861): 301.

69. *Congressional Globe,* 36th Cong., 2d sess., p. 727 *et seq.*

70. Bragg diary, February 4, 1861.

71. C. F. Adams, *Charles Francis Adams 1835–1915: An Autobiography,* pp. 94–95.

72. Varina H. Davis, *Memoir,* I: 696–98.

CHAPTER 7

From Attorney General to Secretary of War: The Unprepared Warrior

1. Varina H. Davis, *Memoir,* II: 12.

2. *Ibid.,* II: 37–38.

3. Jefferson Davis, *The Rise and Fall of the Confederate Government,* I: 242.

4. Leroy Walker, personal conversation with Pierce Butler, reported in Butler, *Benjamin,* p. 234.

5. Clay-Clopton, *A Belle of the Fifties,* p. 158.

6. J. M. Morgan, *Recollections of a Rebel Reefer* (Boston, 1917), p. 36.

7. C. Vann Woodward (ed.), *Mary Boykin Chesnut's Civil War,* p. 217.

8. Varina H. Davis, letter to Lawley, June 8, 1898.

9. J. B. Jones, *A Rebel War Clerk's Diary at the Confederate States Capital,* I: 71.

10. *Ibid.,* I: 65.

11. Official Records, Series I, II: 986.

12. Jones, *Diary,* I: 65.

13. Benjamin to Walker, November 9, 1861, Confederate War Department *Letterbook,* National Archives.

14. New Orleans *Courier,* October 5, 1861.

15. Official records, Series IV, I: 760.

16. Varina H. Davis, letter to Lawley, June 8, 1898.

17. Benjamin to Beauregard, October 17, 1861, Official Records, Series I, V: 919.

18. Beauregard to Davis, October 20, 1861, Official Records, Series I, V: 920.

19. Davis to Beauregard, October 25, 1861, Official Records, Series I, V: 920.

20. Benjamin to Beauregard, October 17, 1861, Official Records, Series I, V: 904.

21. Beauregard to Davis, November 5, 1861, Official Records, Series I, V: 945.

22. Davis to Beauregard, November 10, 1861, Official Records, Series I, V: 945.

23. Jones, *Diary,* I: 88.

24. Benjamin to Beauregard, April 16, 1861, Wisdom Collection, Tulane University.

25. Brown to Benjamin, November 11, 1861, and Benjamin to Brown, November 12, 1861, Confederate Records, II: 142–43.

26. Brown to Benjamin, November 13, 1861, and Benjamin to Brown, November 13, 1861. *Ibid.,* II: 143–44.

27. Moore to Benjamin, September 29, 1861, and Benjamin to Moore, September 30, 1861, Official Records, Series II, I, pt. 4: 706–7.

28. Varina H. Davis, letter to Lawley, June 8, 1898.

29. Biographers have all described, at various points in his life, the gaunt look of Davis and the oddness of his gaze from his blind left eye. See William E. Dodd, *Jefferson Davis;* Strode, *Jefferson Davis,* 3 vols.; Eaton, *Jefferson Davis;* Shelby Foote, *The Civil War: A Narrative,* 3 vols.

30. Varina H. Davis, letter to Lawley, June 8, 1898.

31. *Ibid.*

32. Letters to Joel Addison Hayes, discovered in 1978, Memphis State University Library, Mississippi Valley Collection, gift of the Davis Family Association.

33. Jefferson Davis to Addison Hayes, Jr., March 28, 1880, *ibid.*

34. Davis to Addison Hayes, Jr., November 26, 1880, *ibid.*

35. *Ibid.*

36. Davis to Minor Merriwether, December 17, 1882, *ibid.*

37. Davis to Senators and Representatives of Mississippi State legislature, February 15, 1886, *ibid.*

38. Davis to Mrs. Merriwether, January 5, 1876, *ibid.*

39. Benjamin to Anderson & Co., March 12, 1862, Letters Sent, Secretary of War, Record Group 109, NA. See Charles B. Dew, *Ironmaker to the Confederacy: Joseph R. Anderson and the Tredegar Iron Works,* p. 181.

40. Official Records, Series 1, VII: 701.

41. *Ibid.,* I: 848.

42. New York *Tribune* April 30, 1864. See *The Papers of Andrew Johnson,* 6 (1862–64): 678–79.

43. W. G. Brownlow, *Sketches of the Rise, Progress, and Decline of Secession,* p. 386.

44. Quoted in *The Israelite,* VI, no. 36 (March 9, 1860): 283. See Bertram Korn, *American Jewry and the Civil War,* p. 167.

45. Quoted in *The Israelite,* IX, no. 22 (December 5, 1862): 172, and (December 12, 1862): 180. See Korn, *American Jewry and the Civil War,* p. 167.

46. Quoted in *Messenger,* XI, no. 14, (April 11, 1862): 111; see Korn, *American Jewry and the Civil War,* p. 171.

CHAPTER **8**

The First Lady and the Secretary of State: A Strategic Friendship

1. T. C. De Leon, *Belles, Beaux, and Brains of the 60's,* pp. 91–92.

2. Varina H. Davis, letter to Lawley, June 8, 1898.

3. A number of books contain or have collected anecdotes, stories, and quotations about or descriptions of the life of Varina Howell Davis. Her own book, *Jefferson Davis: A Memoir by His Wife,* 2 vols., provides many insights into her role as First Lady. One of her best friends was Mary Boykin Chesnut, whose diary contains many references to conversations, parties, and receptions with Varina. See Woodward (ed.), *Mary Boykin Chesnut's Civil War,* and a biography by Ishbel Ross, *First Lady of the South: The Life of Mrs. Jefferson Davis.*

4. Varina H. Davis, letter to Lawley, April 8, 1898.

5. Woodward (ed.), *Mary Boykin Chesnut's Civil War,* p. 136.

6. Varina H. Davis, letter to Lawley, June 8, 1898.

7. *Ibid.*

8. Official Records, Series 1, V: 1040–59. See also Frederick Morton, *The Story of Winchester* (Strasburg, Va., 1925); Lenoir Chambers, *Stonewall Jackson,* 2 vols. (New York, 1959); Burke Davis, *They Called Him Stonewall: A Life of Lt. General T. J. Jackson, C.S.A.* (New York, 1954); G. F. Henderson, *Stonewall Jackson and the American Civil War,* 2 vols. (New York, 1898); Frank Vandiver, *Mighty Stonewall;* and Meade, *Benjamin,* pp. 213–18.

9. Official Records, Series 1, V: 1051–53.

10. Letters from Johnston, Letcher, and Bennett in the personal papers of Jackson's grandson, General T. J. J. Christian, examined by Meade. See Meade, *Benjamin,* p. 218, and Robert D. Meade Papers, Manuscripts Department, University of Virginia Library.

11. Official Records Series 1, V: 1057–58.

12. Alexander Hunter, *Johnny Reb and Billy Yank* (New York, 1905), p. 566.

13. T. R. R. Cobb letter to his wife, January 15, 1862, T. R. R. Cobb Collection, Hargrett Rare Book and Manuscript Library, University of Georgia Libraries.

14. Benjamin letter to Jackson, October 21, 1861, T. J. Jackson Papers, Virginia Historical Society; for background see Vandiver, *Mighty Stonewall,* pp. 174–75.

15. Official Records, Series 1, IX: 132, 135–36. Original letter in author's personal collection.

16. For a description of the battle and the concern of Wise, see Foote, *Civil War,* I: 225–32.

17. Notes in Robert D. Meade Papers, Manuscripts Department, University of Virginia Library. Meade reported that Herbert Ezekiel, the Richmond historian, took notes at the occasion. For full text of the letter, see Frederic Maurice (ed.), *An Aide-de-Camp of Lee: Papers of Charles Marshall* (Boston, 1927), pp. 14–18; reprinted in Henry S. Commager, *The Blue and the Gray,* pp. 97–99.

18. For description of the funeral, see Richmond *Dispatch* February 15 and 17, 1862, and *Examiner,* February 17, 1862.

19. Notes from Meade's personal interview, Robert D. Meade Papers, Manuscripts Department, University of Virginia.

20. John S. Wise, *The End of An Era,* pp. 176–78, 401–2.

21. For the hearings, see Official Records, Series 1, IX: 183–90.

22. For more from Foote on Benjamin's fitness for office and Foote's campaign to remove him, see Henry S. Foote, *Casket of Reminiscences,* pp. 232–37, and *idem, War of the Rebellion,* pp. 356–57.

23. Quoted in Ezekiel and Lichtenstein, *The Jews of Richmond,* p. 167.

24. Varina H. Davis, *Memoir,* II: 183.

25. Constance Cary Harrison, "A Virginia Girl in the First Year of the War," *Century Illustrated Monthly Magazine,* XXX (August 1865): p. 610. See also her book, a compilation of articles, *Recollections Grave and Gray.*

26. Harrison, "A Virginia Girl," p. 182.

27. *Ibid.*

28. J. B. Richardson (ed.), *Messages and Papers of the Confederacy,* I: 183–88.

29. Varina H. Davis, *Memoir,* II: 183. See also Foote, *Civil War,* I: 217–19.

30. Dunbar Rowland (ed.), *Jefferson Davis, Constitutionalist: His Letters, Papers, and Speeches,* III: 198–203.

31. *Encyclopaedia Britannica,* VII: 276.

32. For a brief history of the term, see *Butterworth's Medical Dictionary,* 2d ed. (1978), p. 554.

33. Letters to Joel Addison Hayes discovered in 1978, Memphis State University Library, Mississippi Valley Collection, gift of the Davis Family Association.

34. Speech to Mississippi Legislature, November 16, 1858, and Rowland, *Davis,* III: 339–60.

35. Varina H. Davis, letter to Lawley, June 8, 1898.

36. *Ibid.*

37. Benjamin to Mason, February 8, 1871, James Mason Papers, Manuscripts Division, Library of Congress. See Butler, *Benjamin,* p. 395.

38. Woodward, *Mary Boykin Chesnut's Civil War,* p. 498.

39. *Ibid.,* p. 288.

40. *Ibid.,* p. 233.

41. Edward A. Pollard, *Life of Jefferson Davis with a Secret History of the Southern Confederacy* (Philadelphia, 1869), p. 151.

42. Varina H. Davis, letter to Lawley, June 8, 1898.

43. Foote, *Casket of Reminiscences,* pp. 233–34.

44. Sallie Ann Brock Putnam, *Richmond During the War: Four Years of Personal Observation,* p. 99.

45. Richmond *Examiner,* March 20, 1862.

46. R. T. Thayer, *The Life of John Hay* (Boston and New York, 1915), I: 235–36.

CHAPTER 9

Richmond: The Stage for Intrigue

1. For various descriptions, both primary and secondary, of Richmond over the course of the war, see Emory Thomas, *The Confederate State of Richmond: A Biography of the Capital;* Samuel Mordecai, *Richmond in Bygone Days* (Richmond, 1946); W. A. Christian, *Richmond: Her Past and Present* (Richmond, 1912); Mary N. Standard, *Richmond: Its People and Its Story* (Philadelphia, 1923); Louis H. Manarin (ed.), *Richmond at War: The Minutes of the City Council 1861–1865;* and Alfred Hoyt Bill, *The Beleaguered City.*

2. Edmund Kirke, "Our Visit to Richmond," *Atlantic Monthly,* September 1864; see also Meade, *Benjamin,* p. 245.

3. For a description of Tredegar and its inner workings, see Frank Vandiver, *Ploughshares into Swords: Josiah Gorgas and Conferate Ordnance* (Austin, 1952), and Charles B. Dew, *Ironmaker to the Conferacy: Joseph R. Anderson and the Tredegar Iron Works.*

4. Douglas S. Freeman, *R. E. Lee: A Biography,* II: 22.

5. T. J. Jackson to Mary Ann Jackson, April 7, 1862, in *Life and Letters of General Thomas J. Jackson* (New York, 1891), p. 248.

6. Butler's Order No. 28, text in *Rebellion Record,* Vol. V, Doc. 136; see also Hamilton Basso, *Beauregard: The Great Creole,* p. 235.

7. See Foote, *Civil War,* I: 534.

8. James Parton, *History of the Administration of the Department of the Gulf in the Year 1862* (New York, 1864), pp. 317–19. For a recounting of Butler's anti-Semitism, see Korn, *American Jewry and the Civil War* (New York, 1970), pp. 164–65.

9. Benjamin F. Butler, *Autobiography and Personal Reminiscences of Major General Benjamin F. Butler,* p. 510.

10. Quoted in *Messenger,* XV, no. 8 (February 26, 1864): 60. For Lincoln's response, see Simon Wolf, *The Presidents I Have Known from 1860 to 1918* (Washington, 1918), pp. 8–9.

11. Butler, *Autobiography,* p. 514.

12. Quoted in *Israelite,* IX, no. 33 (February 20, 1863): 258. See also Korn, *American Jewry,* p. 170.

13. A. J. L. Fremantle, *Three Months in the Southern States* p. 166.

14. Benjamin to Slidell, July 19, 1862, Official Records, Series 2, III: 462–63.

15. Harrison, *Recollections Grave and Gray,* pp. 79–80.

16. Author's visit, June 1982.

17. Richmond *Examiner,* May 29, 1862.

18. Winfield Scott to Lee, April 18, 1861. For Lee's interview with Scott and the background of Lee's decision, see Freeman, *R. E. Lee,* I: 432–43, 636.

19. For insights into Lee's early career and reputation, see Freeman, *R. E. Lee.*

20. Lee to his wife, December 27, 1856. Full letter quoting Lee's views on slavery in A. L. Long and M. J. Wright (eds.), *Memoirs of Robert E. Lee* (New York, 1887), pp. 82–84.

21. Edmund Kirke, "Our Visit to Richmond," *Atlantic Monthly,* September 1864.

22. Varina H. Davis, letter to Lawley, June 8, 1898.

23. *Ibid.*

24. Slidell to Secretary of State Hunter, March 10, 1862. Official Record Series 2, III: 356. For background, see Beccles, Willson, *John Slidell and the Confederates in Paris: 1862–1865.*

25. Official Records, Series 2, III: 387.

26. Mercier to Thouvenal, Washington, April 28, 1862 (received May 14, 1862), AMAE, CP, E-U, 127: 50–79, no. 97, and May 6, 1862 (received May 19, 1862), *Ibid.,* 85–105, no. 98.

27. T. C. De Leon, *Four Years in Rebel Capitals,* p. 192.

28. Lee to Stuart, June 11, 1862, Official Records, Series 2, III, pt. 3: 590–91. See Douglas S. Freeman, *Lee's Lieutenants,* I: 278. For eyewitness reports, see "Stuart's Ride Around McClellan," *Battles and Leaders of the Civil War,* II: 275.

29. Lee to Jackson, June 11, 1862, Official Records, Series I, VII, pt. 3: 914.

30. From the editor of the New York *Tribune,* reprinting a comment from the Richmond *Examiner,* quoted in Korn, *American Jewry and the Civil War,* p. 177.

31. John H. Reagan, *Memoirs,* p. 163.

32. Foote, *Civil War,* I: 482.

33. *Ibid.,* I: 519.

34. Butler, *Benjamin,* pp. 336–38. Butler heard this story from Benjamin's niece, Leah Popham.

35. Richmond *Dispatch,* April 1, 1861. See Albert Stoutamire, *Music of the Old South* (Rutherford, N.J.: Fairleigh Dickinson University Press, 1972), p. 197.

CHAPTER 10

Lee Invades the North: Enticing France and Britain

1. Official Records, Series 1, XII, pt. 3: 473–74.

2. Lee to Davis, September 3, 1862, Official Records, Series 19, II: 591. See Foote, *The Civil War,* I: 662.

3. Slidell to Benjamin, July 25, 1862, Official Records, Navy, Series 2, III: 484–86.

4. *Ibid.* See also Hendrick, *Statesmen of the Lost Cause,* pp. 316–18, and Frank L. Owsley, *King Cotton Diplomacy,* pp. 310–13.

5. Official Records, Navy, Series 2, III: 484–86.

6. London *Times,* January 11, 1862.

7. W. H. Russell in London *Times,* December 10, 1861. See Hendrick, *Statesmen of the Lost Cause,* pp. 234–35.

8. Mason to Benjamin, June 23, 1862, James Mason Papers, Library of Congress, Manuscripts Division; Official Records, Navy, Series 2, III: 446, 503–4.

9. Lee to Davis, Official Records, Series 19, II: 600. For background and details of Lee's thinking, see Freeman, *R. E. Lee,* II: 358.

10. Varina H. Davis, letter to Lawley, June 8, 1898.

11. McClellan to Lincoln, August 4, 1863, Official Records, series 19, I: 26; order quoted, p. 36. See Foote, *The Civil War,* I: 673. For detailed accounts, see Foote, *The Civil War,* I: 681–702, and Freeman, *R. E. Lee,* II: 367–414.

12. *Battles and Leaders,* II: 611.

13. For the full text of the Emancipation Proclamation, which Lincoln published on September 22, 1862, see Official Records, XXIV, pt. 3: 567, and New York *Times,* September 23, 1862.

14. Richmond *Examiner,* September 25, 1862. The *Examiner* published the full text on September 29, 1862; on January 7, 1863, it called the proclamation "the most startling political crime in American history."

15. Davis message to the Confederate Congress, January 12, 1863, in Richardson (ed.), *Messages and Papers of the Confederacy,* I: 291.

16. Governor John A. Andrew, letter to Albert Gallatin Brown, September 22, 1862. See A. G. Brown, *Sketch of the Official Life of John A. Andrew* (New York, 1868) pp. 74–75.

17. For the story of Belle Boyd, see her own story written in 1905, *Belle Boyd: In Camp and Prison,* reissued under the editorship of Curtis Davis (South Brunswick, N.J., 1968), and Louise A. Sigaud, *Belle Boyd, Confederate Spy* (Richmond, 1943).

18. Slidell to Benjamin, September 5, 1862, James Mason Papers, Manuscripts Division, Library of Congress; Official Records, Series 2, III: 568–72.

19. For detailed analysis of the Erlanger loan, see Judith F. Gentry, "A Confederate Success in Europe: The Erlanger Loan, 1862," *Journal of Southern History,* XXXVI (1970): 157–88, and Meade, *Benjamin,* pp. 269–70.

20. *Israelite,* X, No. 44 (April 29, 1864): 248. See also Korn, *American Jewry and the Civil War,* p. 160.

21. London *Times* October 8, 1862, citing William E. Gladstone, Chancellor of the Exchequer, in banquet speech at Newcastle, England, October 7, 1862. Also quoted in Crook, *North Carolina and the Powers* (New York, 1974), pp. 227–28.

22. Memorandum of an interview of Slidell with the Emperor at St. Cloud on Tuesday, October 28, 1862; enclosure B in letter from Slidell to Benjamin, October 28, 1862, Official Records, Navy, Series 2, III: 574–78. See also L. M. Case, and W. F. Spencer, *The United States and France: Civil War Diplomacy,* pp. 347–403.

23. Slidell to Benjamin, August 24, 1862, Official Records, Navy, Series 2, III: 520–21.

24. Richmond *Examiner,* 1863, and Foote, *Casket of Reminiscences,* p. 237.

25. Woodward (ed.), *Mary Boykin Chesnut's Civil War,* p. 542.

CHAPTER 11
Anti-Semitism and the Jews of Richmond

1. For histories of the Richmond Jewish community, see Ezekiel and Lichtenstein, *History of the Jews in Richmond from 1789–1917,* and Myron Berman, *Richmond's Jewry 1769–1976.* The Common Hall was the forerunner of the city council.

2. Woodward, *Mary Boykin Chesnut's Civil War,* p. 547.

3. Jones, *Diary,* I: 213.

4. *Southern Punch,* October 17, 1863.

5. Richmond *Examiner,* December 20, 1862.

6. The *Occident,* 18 (1861): 260.

7. Phoebe Yates Pember, *A Southern Woman's Story,* p. 168.

8. Foote in debate in Confederate House of Representatives, January 14, 1863, *Southern Historical Society Papers,* n.s. (Richmond, 1930), IX: 122; reported in Richmond *Examiner,* January 15, 1863.

9. *Ibid.*

10. *Ibid.*

11. Richmond *Examiner,* December 17, 1863.

12. Nicholas Davis of Alabama, quoted in *Israelite,* IX, no. 20 (November 16, 1860): 159, quoting from the Florence, Alabama, *Gazette;* see Korn, *American Jewry and the Civil War,* p. 158.

13. De Leon, *Belles, Beaux and Brains of the 60's,* pp. 91–93.

14. *Southern Punch,* October 10, 1863. See also Thomas, *The Confederate State of Richmond,* p. 151.

15. Sermon by Rabbi Michelbacher, delivered on May 27, 1863, reprinted in *Jewish Record,* II, no. 13 (June 5, 1863): 1.

16. Richmond *Sentinel,* reprinted in *ibid.* See also Korn, *American Jewry and the Civil War,* pp. 180–81.

17. Ezekiel and Lichtenstein, *The History of the Jews of Richmond from 1769–1917,* p. 170.

18. Lee to Michelbacher, August 29, 1861, Virginia State Library, Richmond; photograph of letter in Berman, *Richmond Jewry,* p. 192.

19. General Order No. 11, December 17, 1862, Official Records, Series 1, XVII, pt. 2: 424.

20. Major General W. T. Sherman to Colonel John A. Rawlins, July 30, 1862, Official Records, Series 1, XVII, pt. 2: 140–41.

21. Cincinnati *Daily Times,* January 17, 1863.

22. Dana to Stanton, Official Records, Series 1, LII, pt. 1: 331.

23. Letters from J. Russell Jones, United States Marshal at Chicago, to Congressman Elihu B. Washburne, January 28 and February 15, 1863, in Elihu B. Washburne Papers, Library of Congress.

24. U. S. Grant to H. P. Walcott, Assistant Secretary of War, Washington, December 17, 1862, Official Records, Series 1, XVII, pt. 2: 421–22.

25. *Israelite,* XV, no. 22 (December 4, 1868): 4.

26. Quoted in *Israelite,* VIII, no. 35 (February 28, 1862): 278.

27. The details of the meeting were described in *Israelite,* IX, no. 28 (January 16, 1863): 218.

28. Halleck to Grant, January 21, 1863, Official Records, Series 1, XXIV, pt. 1: 9.

CHAPTER 12

Christmas in the White House: Growing Bonds of Trust

1. Davis to Mississippi State Legislature, December 26, 1862, Mississippi State Archives, Jackson.

2. *Ibid.*

3. Varina H. Davis, "Last Christmas in the White House of the Confederacy," New York *Sunday World,* December 13, 1896.

4. Varina H. Davis, letter to Lawley, June 8, 1898.

5. Varina H. Davis, letter to Lawley, April 4, 1897.

6. Quoted in Richmond *Enquirer,* January 7, 1863.

7. Russell, *My Diary North and South,* p. 252.

8. Fremantle, *Three Months in the Southern States,* p. 210.

9. Richmond *Enquirer,* January 3, 1863.

10. Foote, *Casket of Reminiscences,* p. 236.

11. Woodward, *Mary Boykin Chesnut's Civil War,* p. 548.

12. Memorandum by Lord James of Hereford in Lawley papers, Pierce Butler Collection, Tulane University. See also Meade, *Benjamin,* p. 365.

13. For background on the Erlanger loan, see Judith Fenner Gentry, "A Confederate Success in Europe: The Erlanger Loan," *Journal of Southern History,* XXXVI (1970): 157–188, and Hendrick, *Statesmen of the Lost Cause,* pp. 216–32.

14. Quoted in Hendrick, *Statesmen of the Lost Cause,* p. 256.

15. Benjamin to Slidell, March 24, 1863, Official Records, Series 2, II: 724.

CHAPTER 13
Fateful Defeats: Stonewall's Funeral and the Battle of Gettysburg

1. Message to the Confederate Congress; details reported in Richmond *Examiner* January 15, 1863. For text, see Rowland (ed.), *Davis,* V: 493; for background, including reactions in the South, see Foote, *Civil War,* I: 704–10.

2. Varina H. Davis, *Memoir,* II: 375–76; see also Mrs. Roger Pryor, *Reminiscences of Peace and War,* pp. 251–59, and Emory Thomas, "The Richmond Bread Riot of 1863," *Virginia Cavalcade,* XVIII (Summer 1868): 41–47.

3. Richmond *Examiner,* January 6, 1862.

4. Edward Younger (ed.), *Inside the Confederate Government: The Diary of Robert Garlick Hill Kean,* p. 55.

5. *Ibid.,* p. 93.

6. *Ibid.,* p. 161.

7. For background on the battle of Chancellorsville and Jackson's death, see R. U. Jackson and C. C. Buel (eds.), *Battles and Leaders,* III: 172–223, and Vandiver, *Mighty Stonewall,* pp. 455–94.

8. Fremantle, *Three Months in the Southern States,* pp. 166–67.

9. For descriptions of Jackson's last hours and his funeral, see Mrs. Mary Jackson, *Memoirs of Stonewall Jackson* (Louisville, 1895), pp. 450–57; *Whig,* May 12, 13, and 14, 1863; Thomas, *The Confederate State of Richmond,* pp. 123–25; De Leon, *Four Years in Rebel Capitals,* pp. 251–52; and Harrison, *Recollections Grave and Gray,* p. 138. For the battle and its aftermath, see Vandiver, *Mighty Stonewall,* pp. 455–94.

10. Foote, *Civil War,* II: 453–54.

11. Varina H. Davis, *Memoir,* II: 392.

12. Fremantle, *Three Months in the Southern States* (New York: 1864), p. 167.

13. *Ibid.,* p. 169.

14. Benjamin to Benjamin H. Micou, Tallassee, Alabama, August 18, 1863, in Pickett Papers. See Meade, *Benjamin,* pp. 289–90, and notes about Micou from personal conversations with Micou's relatives, Robert D. Meade Papers, Manuscripts Department, University of Virginia Library.

15. Richmond *Enquirer,* May 7, 1863.

16. Benjamin to James Spence, January 11, 1864, in Pickett Papers. See Meade, *Benjamin,* p. 291.

17. Benjamin to Mason, August 24, 1863, Official Records, Series 2, III: 852.

18. Slidell to Mason, July 17, 1864, James Mason Papers, Manuscripts Division, Library of Congress.

19. Official Records, Series 2, III: 853–54.

20. New York *Daily Tribune,* May 25, 1884.

21. Davis to Lee, August 12 or 13, 1863, and Rowland (ed.), *Jefferson Davis, Constitutionalist: His Letters, Papers and Speeches,* V: 586–89.

22. Benjamin to Davis, October 8, 1863, Official Records, Series 2, III: 928–36.

23. *Ibid.*

24. Foote, *Casket of Reminiscences,* pp. 148–50.

CHAPTER 14
Tragedy at Home

1. Foote in Confederate Congress, January 6, 1864, Southern Historical Society Papers, V. 50, December 1953, p. 209.

2. Pickett Papers, Library of Congress. See Meade, *Benjamin,* p. 281.

3. Judith B. McGuire, *Diary of a Southern Refugee During the War,* p. 326.

4. Text of Cleburne Memorial in Official Records, Series 1, LII, pt. 2: 586–92.

5. *Ibid.* See also Robert F. Durden, *The Gray and the Black: The Confederate Debate on Emancipation,* pp. 53–63.

6. Seddon to Johnston, January 29, 1864, Official Records, Series 1, Vol. LII, pt. 2.

7. Brigadier General Patton Anderson to Lieutenant General Leonidas Polk, January 14, 1864, Official Records, Series 1, LII, pt. 2: 598–99.

8. Sherman letter to the Mayor and City Council of Atlanta, September 12, 1864. See William T. Sherman, *Memoirs,* II: 126.

9. Varina H. Davis, *Memoir,* II: 496.

10. Woodward, *Mary Boykin Chesnut's Civil War,* pp. 600–601.

11. Harrison, *Recollections Grave and Gray,* p. 67.

12. Varina H. Davis, letter to Lawley, June 8, 1898.

13. Harrison, *Recollections Grave and Gray,* p. 129.

14. See Bill, *The Beleaguered City,* p. 189.

15. For background on Lydia Johnston's enmity for Mrs. Davis, see Ross, *First Lady of the South,* p. 94.

16. Washington *Daily Morning Chronicle,* April 10, 1863.

17. See Ross, *First Lady of the Confederacy,* p. 130.

18. Fitzhugh Lee, *General Lee,* p. 324.

19. Official Records, Series 2, III: 174.

20. Benjamin to Slidell, *ibid.,* III: 1105–6.

CHAPTER 15
The Confederate Emancipation Proclamation

1. Grant to Meade, Spring 1864, in Foote, *The Civil War,* III: 491.

2. *Ibid.,* p. 318.

3. John Hay, *Lincoln and the Civil War in the Diaries and Letters of John Hay,* selected by Tyler Dennet (New York, 1972, reprint of 1939 ed.), p. 179.

4. John W. Thomason, *Jeb Stuart* (New York, 1930), pp. 498–501. See also Emory Thomas, *Bold Dragoon: The Life of J. E. B. Stuart.*

5. *Congressional Globe,* 37th Cong. 1st sess., p. 295. See also speech in support of Presidential War Program, July 27, 1861, *Papers of Andrew Johnson,* IV: 634.

6. Herman Moos to Governor Andrew Johnson, September 16, 1864, *Papers of Andrew Johnson,* VII (1864–65): 168–69.

7. Hudson *Gazette,* quoted in *The Jewish Record,* V, no. 7 (November 11, 1864): 2.

8. Benjamin to Davis, February 15, 1879, original letter in collection of Stephen B. Lemann, New Orleans.

9. See James D. Horan, *Confederate Agent,* pp. 151–62, 255–59, and John Bakeless, *Spies of the Confederacy* (Philadelphia, 1970).

10. See Foote, *Civil War,* III: 586–87.

11. For detailed description of the St. Albans raid and the trials, see Horan, *Confederate Agent,* pp. 166–80.

12. Sherman to Oliver O. Howard, August 10, 1864. For details of the battle of Atlanta, see Foote, *Civil War,* 3: 472–92 and 520–30.

13. See Samuel Carter III, *Siege of Atlanta 1864* (New York, 1973).

14. Sherman message to Grant, October 9, 1864, quoted in Sherman, *Memoirs,* II: 153.

15. For text of Field Order no. 120, November 9, 1864, see Sherman, *Memoirs,* II: 175.

16. Foote, *Civil War,* III: 651.

17. L. Q. Washington to Lawley, Lawley Mss., Pierce Butler Collection, Tulane University. See Butler, *Benjamin,* pp. 347–48.

18. Lee to Andrew Hunter, January 11, 1865, Official Records, Series 4, III: 1012–13.

19. Davis speech to Congress November 7, 1864, in Richardson (ed.), *A Compilation of Messages and Papers of the Confederacy,* I: 482–86.

20. *Ibid.*

CHAPTER 16
The Speech to Free the Slaves

1. Eaton, *Jefferson Davis,* p. 259.

2. Richmond *Examiner,* January 6, 1865.

3. Francis Blair Papers, Library of Congress.

4. Lincoln letter to Blair, January 18, 1865, and Davis reply in letter to Hunter *et al.,* January 28, 1865, Official Records, Series 2, III: 190–91. For details of Hampton Roads, see E. C. Kirkland, *The Peacemakers of 1864* (New York, 1927), pp. 222–58.

5. Benjamin to Frederick Porcher, December 21, 1864, Official Records, Series 4, III: 959–60.

6. Memorandum by W. W. Henry of a conversation with Kenner, sent March 24, 1899, in *William and Mary College Quarterly,* Series I, vol. XXV (July 1916).

7. Mason, quoting Lord Donoughmore, to Benjamin, March 26, 1865. See Eaton, *Davis,* p. 172.

8. Robert E. Lee to Virginia State Senator Andrew Hunter, January 11, 1865, Official Records, Series 4, III: 1012–13.

9. Butler, *Benjamin,* p. 351.

10. Richmond *Examiner,* February 24, 1863.

11. Richmond *Enquirer,* February 9, 1865. See Durden, *The Gray and the Black,* p. 188.

12. Richmond *Examiner,* February 10, 1865.

13. Richmond *Dispatch,* February 10, 1865. See also Durden, *The Gray and the Black,* pp. 192–94.

14. The fullest account of the speech and reactions appeared in Richmond *Dispatch,* February 10, 1865.

15. Varina H. Davis, letter to Lawley, June 8, 1898.

16. Jones, *Diary,* II: 416, and J. T. Leach of North Carolina on floor of Confederate Congress, Feb. 15, 1865, *Southern Historical Society Papers,* 53 (July 1959): 355.

17. Benjamin to Robert E. Lee, February 11, 1865, Official Records, Series 1, XLVI, pt. 2: 1229.

18. *Journal of the Senate of the Confederate States of America,* IV: 788.

19. Howell Cobb to James A. Seddon, January 8, 1865, Official Records, Series 4, III: 959–60. See also, Durden, *The Gray and the Black,* pp. 183–85.

20. Letter from Robert Toombs quoted in Foote, *Civil War,* III: 860.

21. *Journal of Confederate Senate,* IV: 550, 522, 553.

22. See Meade, Benjamin, p. 309.

23. See Durden, *The Gray and the Black,* p. 202, 289.

CHAPTER 17
Escape

1. Varina H. Davis, *Memoir,* II: 575–78.

2. *Ibid.*

3. *Ibid.*

4. Quoted in Foote, *The Civil War,* III: 864.

5. "History of the 104th Regiment Illinois Volunteer Infantry," pp. 309–10, and "Reminiscences of the Civil War," p. 176, in *Diaries of Members of the 103rd Illinois Volunteer Infantry,* quoted in Bruce Catton, *This Hallowed Ground,* p. 374.

6. "Story of the Service of Company E and the 12th Wisconsin Regiment," p. 104. See Catton, *This Hallowed Ground,* p. 376.

7. Sherman to Brigadier Judson Kilpatrick. See Foote, *The Civil War,* III: 788, and John Bennett Walters, *Merchant of Terror: General Sherman and Total War* (Indianapolis and New York, 1973).

8. George W. Pepper, *Personal Recollections of Sherman's Campaigns in Georgia and the Carolinas* (Zanesville, Ohio, 1866). For an eyewitness account, see Emma Florence LeConte, *Journal of Emma Florence LeConte* December 31, 1864, to August 6, 1865, Southern Historical Collection, Library of the University of North Carolina at Chapel Hill. For an overview of Sherman in South Carolina, see John G. Barrett, *Sherman's March Through the Carolinas.*

9. Grant told this to Sheridan when they met on March 26, 1865; see Foote, *The Civil War,* III: 853, 881.

10. Letter of French Consul Alfred Paul to Drougn le Llys, Minister of Foreign Affairs, April 11, 1865, Archives des Affaires Etrangères, Etats Unis; see Warren Spencer, "A French View of the Fall of Richmond," *Virginia Magazine of History and Biography,* April 1965, p. 181.

11. Journal of Elizabeth Van Lew, Archives Division, Virginia State Library, Richmond, p. 379. A number of diaries and papers exist, many published, describing the fall of Richmond and the flight of the President and Cabinet: F. Harrison (ed.), *The Harrisons of Skimino* (Burton Harrison's account first appeared in *Century Magazine,* November 1883; the Harrison Family Papers are in the Library of Congress); Katharine Jones, *Ladies of Richmond: Confederate Capital;* Frank R. Lubbock, *Six Decades in Texas;* Stephen Mallory, "The Last Days of the Confederate Government," *McClure's Magazine,* new edition by Bell Wiley (ed.) (Jackson, Tenn: 1959); Putnam, *Richmond During the War;* Raphael Semmes, *Memoirs of Service Afloat* (Baltimore, 1869); John T. Wood, *Diary,* Southern Historical Collection, Library of the University of North Carolina at Chapel Hill; and Younger, *Inside the Confederate Government: The Diary of Robert Garlick Hill Kean.* Secondary sources include Bill, *The Beleaguered City;* Burke Davis, *The Long Surrender;* A. J. Hanna, *Flight into Oblivion;* and Thomas, *The Confederate State of Richmond.*

12. Putnam, *Richmond During the War,* pp. 366–69.

13. Frederick S. Daniel (ed.), *The Richmond Examiner During the War, or The Writings of John H. Daniel with a Memoir of His Life.*

14. Jones, *Ladies of Richmond: Confederate Capital,* p. 275.

15. *McClure's Magazine,* December 1900. See Meade, *Benjamin,* p. 312, and Stephen Mallory, recollections in Southern Historical Collection, Library of the University of North Carolina at Chapel Hill.

16. Hoge to Lawley, August 14, 1897, Lawley Mss., Pierce Butler Collection, Tulane University.

17. From a collection of eyewitness accounts of the fall of Richmond. See Jones, *Ladies of Richmond: Confederate Capital,* and "The Evacuation of Richmond," *Southern Historical Society Papers,* IX: 542–56 (December 1881).

18. Nellie Grey was a pseudonym for a woman of Richmond invented by Myrta Lockett Avary, who wrote *A Virginia Girl in the Civil War.*

19. "Natalie" (anonymous), first published in the Norfolk, *Virginian.* Reprinted in Edward A. Pollard, *The Lost Cause: A New Southern History of the War of the Confederates* (New York, 1866). See Jones, *Ladies of Richmond,* pp. 280–81.

20. Lincoln's arrival in Richmond was described by U.S. Admiral David Porter. See Robert McElroy, *Jefferson Davis: The Unreal and the Real,* II: 460–61. See also Davis, *The Long Surrender,* p. 55, and Foote, *The Civil War,* III: 897.

21. Foote, *The Civil War,* III: 897.

22. *Ibid.,* p. 898.

23. "Agnes" to Mrs. Roger Pryor, April 5, 1865, in Sara Pryor, *My Day: Reminiscences of Peace and War.* See Jones, *Ladies of Richmond* pp. 284–87.

24. Lincoln's answer to Major General Godfrey Weitzel, who had received the surrender of the city, was recorded by Weitzel's aide, Major E. E. Graves. See Weitzel *Letter Press Books,* Cincinatti Historical Society, and Major Godfrey Weitzel, *Richmond Occupied: Entry of the United States Forces into Richmond, Virginia April 3, 1865,* Louis Manarin (ed.) (Richmond Civil War Centennial Committee 1965).

25. Jefferson Davis, *Rise and Fall,* II: 677–78. See Meade's interview with Joseph B. Anderson, Meade, *Benjamin,* p. 313.

26. Lee's surrender was described by Joshua L. Chamberlain, *The Passing of the Armies* (New York, 1915), pp. 230–42; Sir Frederick Maurice (ed.), *An Aide-de-Camp of Lee: Being the Papers of Colonel Charles Marshal* (Boston, 1927); *The Personal Memoirs of U. S. Grant,* 2 vols. (New York, 1885–1886), II: 489; and Colonel Horace Porter, *Battles and Leaders,* I: 729–46.

27. Hoge to Lawley, Lawley manuscript, Pierce Butler Collection, Tulane University.

28. *Ibid.*

29. Butler, *Benjamin,* p. 361.

30. Joseph Johnston, *Narrative of Military Operations Directed During the Late War Between the States* (New York, 1874, and new edition, 1959), pp. 396–400. See also Burton Harrison, "The Capture of Jefferson Davis," *Century Magazine,* XXVII (November 1883): 130–145.

31. Johnston, *Narrative.* See also Meade, *Benjamin,* p. 315.

32. Boutwell to Butler, April 30, 1865, *Letters to Benjamin Butler,* V: 598.

33. Stanton to General Dix, Official Records, Series 1, XLVI, pt. 3: 781.

34. Stanton to Charles F. Adams, *ibid.,* pp. 43, 784–85.

35. Charles Dana to U.S. Marshal, Portland, Maine, Official Records, Series 2, VIII: 493.

36. New York *Herald,* May 4, 1865, p. 1.

37. Reverend C. B. Crane at the South Baptist Church of Hartford, Conn., Sunday, April 16, 1865, quoted in Carl Sandburg, *Abraham Lincoln: The War Years 1861–1865,* p. 876.

38. Edward Everett Hale at his Unitarian Church in Boston on Sunday, April 16, 1865; more of the sermon quoted in *ibid.,* p. 877. For other sermons, see Thomas Turner, *Beware the People Weeping,* pp. 77–89, ch. 6, "Voices from the Pulpit."

39. Woodward (ed.), *Mrs. Chesnut's Civil War,* p. 795.

40. New York *Times,* May 1, 1865.

41. Testimony of Captain Williams, Johnson's guard, in J. E. Buckingham, *Reminiscences and Souvenirs of the Assassination of Abraham Lincoln* (Washington, 1894), p. 63. See also Turner, *Beware the People Weeping* pp. 45–46.

42. U.S. Congress, House, Committee on the Judiciary Impeachment Investigation, testimony taken before the Judiciary Committee of the House of Representatives in the investigation of the charges against Andrew Johnson, 39th Cong., 2d sess., 1867, and 40th Cong., 1st sess., 1867. Johnson used the phrase often. See his speech at Knoxville, April 12, 1864, in *Papers of Andrew Johnson* (Knoxville, 1983), VI: 670.

43. "Remarks on the Fall of Richmond," April 3, 1865, *Papers of Andrew Johnson, 1864–1865* (Knoxville, 1986), VII: 544.

44. *Ibid.,* VII: 546, note 5.

45. Andrew Johnson in the Senate, speech on the expulsion of Senator Bright, January 31, 1862, *ibid.,* V: 585.

46. Andrew Johnson's speech to the House of Representatives, January 21, 1864. See James Jones, *The Life of Andrew Johnson* (Greenville, Tenn., 1901), p. 111.

47. George Custer, New York *Times,* May 7, 1865. For other reactions, see Turner, *Beware the People Weeping,* p. 54.

48. Pollard, *Life of Jefferson Davis,* p. 521.

49. Benjamin to Mrs. Kruttschnitt, July 22, 1865. See Butler, *Benjamin,* p. 364.

50. James G. Blaine, *Twenty Years of Congress,* II: 14.

51. *Ibid.,* p. 22.

52. Charles Pollock, "Reminiscences of Judah Philip Benjamin," *Fortnightly Review,* LXIX (March 1898): 354–61, and *The Green Bag,* Vol. I, no. 9, September 1889.

53. Adams, *Charles Francis Adams 1835–1915: An Autobiography,* pp. 94–95.

54. The card was put into the box of Johnson's secretary, William A. Browning. L. I. Farwell, the ex-Governor of Wisconsin, who was present at Ford's Theater that night, hurried over to Andrew Johnson's room, adjoining his own, at Kirkwood House to tell him of the assassination. It was the first Johnson heard of it. Farwell's detailed statement in writing to Senator J. R. Doolittle of Wisconsin, March 12, 1866. In Manuscript Division, Library of Congress.

55. Burton Harrison, "The Capture of Jefferson Davis," *Century Magazine,* XXVII (November 1883): 130–45. See also Harrison, *Recollections Grave and Gray,* p. 223.

56. Varina H. Davis, to Jefferson Davis, April 1865, Confederate Museum, Richmond.

57. Benjamin to Davis, April 22, 1865. Copy in Edward M. Stanton Papers, Manuscript Division, Library of Congress. For background see McElroy, *Jefferson Davis: The Unreal and the Real,* pp. 492–93.

58. Harrison, *The Harrisons of Skimino,* p. 243. See also Davis, *The Long Surrender,* pp. 87–88.

59. Benjamin to Bayard, October 20, 1865, Bayard Papers, Callery Collection, Historical Society of Delaware.

60. Stephen Mallory, "The Last Days of the Confederate Government," *McClure's Magazine,* XVI (December 1900): 99–107, and (January 1901): 239–48.

61. *Ibid.*

62. Reagan, *Memoirs,* p. 211.

63. Varina H. Davis, letter to Lawley, June 8, 1898.

64. *Ibid.*

65. Wood, *Diary,* Southern Historical Collection, University of North Carolina at Chapel Hill. See also Hanna, *Flight into Oblivion,* pp. 195–96, and J. T. Wood, "Escape of the Confederate Secretary of War," *Century Magazine,* XLVII: 115.

66. See *A Dictionary of the Cajun Language,* by Reverend Monsignor Jules O. Daigle (Ann Arbor, Mich., 1984), pp. 68–69. The author is grateful to Diana Autin for pointing out that the "l" is silent in Cajun and therefore "Bonfals" would have been pronounced "fausse," meaning "to falsify, alter" or "untrue, fictitious."

67. Benjamin to Mrs. Kruttschnitt, July 22, 1865. See Butler, *Benjamin,* p. 365. See also Benjamin to Varina H. Davis, November 16, 1865, in Jefferson Davis Collection, Transylvania University.

68. J. G. Randall and David Donald, *The Civil War and Reconstruction,* p. 528.

69. John Taylor Wood, *Famous Adventures and Prison Escapes of the Civil War* (New York, 1893), p. 298.

70. Varina H. Davis to Francis Blair, June 6, 1865, in Crist-Blair Papers, Library of Congress. See also Varina H. Davis, *Memoir,* II: 641.

71. Cartoon collection, Library of Congress. Davis's own account of his capture denies the legend in *The Rise and Fall,* II: 701–2. Varina's account is in her letter to Francis Blair, June 6, 1865.

72. New Orleans *Times-Democrat,* May 13, 1900.

73. New York *Herald,* May 23, 1865.

74. Mrs. Surratt to her priest, Father J. A. Walter, in Rev. J. A. Walter, *Church News,* August 16, 1891. Paper read before the U.S. Catholic Historical Society, May 25, 1891.

75. Lloyd Lewis, *Myths After Lincoln* (New York, 1929), p. 106.

76. William H. Gregory, former governor of Ceylon, to Lawley, October 18, 1889; letter in Lawley Mss., Pierce Butler Collection, Tulane University. Benjamin told the story after a dinner party in London.

77. Rev. W. B. Tresca, son of Captain Tresca, in Lillie B. McDuffe, *The Lures of Manatee* (Nashville, 1933), p. 158.

78. Benjamin to Mrs. Kruttschnitt, August 1, 1865, copy in Pierce Butler Collection, Tulane University.

79. McLeod quoted in Galveston *Daily News,* May 27, 1894.

80. Benjamin to Mrs. Kruttschnitt, September 29, 1865, copy in Pierce Butler Collection, Tulane University.

81. William Preston to Varina Davis, November 1, 1865. Preston was appointed as the Minister "extraordinaire" to the court of Maximillian in Mexico. Original in Davis Papers, Transylvania University.

82. Benjamin to Bayard, August 30, 1865, in Bayard Papers, Callery Collection, Historical Society of Delaware.

CHAPTER 18
England: From Law Student to Queen's Counsel

1. Howard Sachar, *The Course of Modern Jewish History,* p. 114. See also "England," *Encyclopedia Judaica,* V: 161–74; Finkelstein (ed.), *The Jews: Their History, Culture and Religion,* Vol. I, Book 3; and Cecil Roth, *A History of the Jews of England* (Oxford, 1941).

2. George Bentinck to John Manners, in C. Whibley, *Lord Manners and His Friends,* 2 vols. (1925) II: 283. For the story behind the Jewish

Disabilities Bill, see also Sarah Bradford, *Disraeli,* pp. 177–88, and Constance Rothschild, *Reminiscences* (1922), p. 232.

3. Hansard, 3d series, XCV: 1323–31, and Sarah Bradford, *Disraeli.* For thorough early biography of Benjamin Disraeli, see W. F. Moneypenney and G. E. Buckle, *The Life of Benjamin Disraeli,* 2 vols. (New York, 1910–20).

4. See Sachar, *Course of Modern Jewish History.*

5. Benjamin to Mrs. Kruttschnitt, September 29, 1865; see Butler, *Benjamin,* pp. 370–72.

6. *Ibid.*

7. *Ibid.*

8. Benjamin to Bradford, February 21, 1866; see Butler, *Benjamin,* pp. 379–81.

9. Meade, *Benjamin,* p. 344, from diary of Mrs. Mary White Beckwith, Petersburg, Va., daughter of the Confederate blockade-runner John White.

10. Benjamin to Mrs. Kruttschnitt, September 29, 1865. Disraeli had been D'Israeli but had dropped the apostrophe as a young man. Benjamin was using the original spelling.

11. Benjamin to Bayard, October 20, 1865, Bayard Papers, Callery Collection, Historical Society of Delaware.

12. Benjamin to Mrs. Kruttschnitt, December 20, 1865; Pierce Butler Collection, Tulane University.

13. *Ibid.*

14. *Ibid.*

15. *Ibid.* For an earlier letter, see Meade, *Benjamin,* p. 328.

16. Benjamin to Bradford, February 21, 1866; see Butler, *Benjamin,* p. 379.

17. *Ibid.*

18. Butler, *Benjamin,* p. 378.

19. Benjamin to Bradford, February 21, 1866; see Butler, *Benjamin,* p. 379.

20. *Ibid.*

21. Pollock, "Reminiscences of Judah Philip Benjamin," *Fortnightly Review,* LXIX (March 1898): 354–61, and *The Green Bag,* Vol. I, no. 9, September 1889.

22. *Ibid.*

23. *Ibid.*

24. See Meade, *Benjamin,* p. 333, and *The Law Journal,* November 1932. For a full text, see *The Black Books of Lincoln's Inn,* V, *1845–1914,* pp. 133–41.

25. U.S. Court of Claims, *Henry B. Ste. Marie* v. *the United States,* amended petition No. 6415, May 6, 1873, and Leo F. Stock (ed.), *United States Ministers to the Papal States: Instructions and Dispatches 1848–1868,* 2 vols. (Washington, D.C.: Catholic University Press, 1933), I: 359, 360, 367, 377–78, 381–82, 388, 401. See also Thomas Reed Turner, *Beware the People Weeping: Public Opinion and the Assassination of Abraham Lincoln,* p. 227.

26. James G. Randall and Theodore C. Pease (eds.), *Diary of Orville Hickmar Browning,* 2 vols. (Springfield, Ill.: Jefferson's Printing and Stationery Company by the Trustees of the Illinois State Historical Library, 1933), II: 100.

27. *Ibid.*

28. U.S. Congress, House, Executive Document No. 9, 39th Cong., 2d sess., 1866, pp. 9–10; Letters from the Secretary of War *Ad Interim Relative to a Claim of Sainte Marie for Compensation Furnished in the Surratt Case,* 40th Cong., 2d sess., 1867, p. 24. See Turner, *Beware the People Weeping,* p. 228.

29. Henri Ste. Marie, statement in *Diplomatic Correspondence, 1867–1868,* Archives of the Department of State, quoted in G. S. Bryan, *The Great American Myth,* p. 387.

30. For the story of Surratt's escape and capture, see United States Government, *Trial of John Surratt in the Criminal Court for the District of Columbia, Honorable George F. Fishes, Presiding,* 2 vols. (Washington: Government Printing Office, 1867).

31. House of Representatives, 39th Cong., 2d sess., Executive Document No. 9, Consular Message No. 538.

32. *Ibid.,* Consular Message No. 476.

33. *Ibid.,* Consular Message No. 236.

34. *Ibid.*

35. *Ibid.,* Executive Document No. 17.

36. *The Great Conspiracy, a Book of Absorbing Interest! Startling Developments, Eminent Persons Implicated, Full Secrets of the Assassination Plot, John H. Surratt and His Mother, with Biographical Sketches of J. B. Booth and John Wilkes Booth, and Life and Extraordinary Adventures of John H. Surratt, the Conspirator,* pp. 36–37, 70, 111–13.

37. Springfield *Daily Republican,* January 28, 1867.

38. "Moran," *Civil War Dictionary,* pp. 151–52. His diary is in forty-three volumes (1851, 1857–1875), Manuscripts Division, Library of Congress.

39. Papers of Benjamin Moran, Manuscripts Division, Library of Congress, Vol. 18, February 11, 1867. The edited and published diaries of Moran do not contain these quotes.

40. *Ibid.,* Vol. 18, February 18, 1867.

41. *Ibid.,* Vol. XVIII, March 14, 1867. George McHenry assisted Edwin De Leon in Paris. De Leon was a Confederate journalist and propagandist in Paris from 1862 through 1864.

42. *Ibid.,* Vol. VII, July 22, 1859.

43. *Ibid.,* Vol. XX, April 17, 1868.

44. *Ibid.,* Vol. XV, July 27, 1865.

45. *Ibid.,* Vol. XVIII, March 16, 1867.

46. *Ibid.,* Vol. XVIII, March 21, 1867.

47. House, 40th Cong., 2d sess., Executive Document 68, Serial 1332, submitted to Mr. Seward, July 1867; transmitted by the Secretary of State, William Seward, to the President of the United States, Andrew Johnson, December 17, 1867; transmitted by message from the President to the House of Representatives, December 17, 1867.

48. *Ibid.*

49. United States Government, *Trial of John Surratt.*

50. John H. Surratt, "Lecture on the Lincoln Conspiracy," *Lincoln Herald,* Vol. LI, December 1949. For full text of the lecture, see also the appendix to Clara Laughlin, *The Death of Lincoln* (New York, 1909).

51. *Ibid.*

52. Varina H. Davis, *Memoir,* II: 704n.

53. See A. W. Thomson, "How Jefferson Davis Received the News of Lincoln's Death," *The Independent,* February 15, 1900, p. 436.

54. Pollock, "Reminiscences of Judah Philip Benjamin," *Fortnightly Review,* LXIX (March 1898): 354–61, and *The Green Bag,* Vol. I, no. 9, September 1889.

55. Benjamin to Mason, October 25, 1866, James Mason Papers, Manuscripts Division, Library of Congress.

56. *American Law Review,* I (1866–67): 220.

57. London *Times,* July 2, 1882. See also Meade, *Benjamin,* pp. 335–36, and Butler, *Benjamin,* p. 393.

58. Benjamin to Mrs. Levy, February 8, 1870. See Butler, *Benjamin,* p. 394.

59. Benjamin to Mrs. Kruttschnitt, April 11, 1867; see Butler, *Benjamin,* pp. 388–89.

60. Benjamin to his sisters, February 22, 1868; see Butler, *Benjamin,* p. 391.

61. *A Treatise on the Law of Sale of Personal Property, with Reference to the American Decisions, to the French Code and Civil Law* (1868).

62. London *Daily Telegraph,* February 10, 1883; see Meade, *Benjamin,* p. 337.

63. Benjamin to Mrs. Kruttschnitt, April 11, 1867; see Butler, *Benjamin,* pp. 388–89.

64. Benjamin to Mrs. Levy, February 8, 1870; see Butler, *Benjamin*, p. 394.

65. *Ibid.*

66. Benjamin to his sisters, October 15, 1871; see Butler, *Benjamin*, p. 397.

67. Pollock, "Reminiscences of Judah Philip Benjamin," *Fortnightly Review*, LXIX (March 1898): 354–61, and *The Green Bag*, Vol. I, no. 9, September 1889.

68. *Ibid.*

69. Benjamin to his sisters, August 10, 1872; see Butler, *Benjamin*, pp. 398–99.

70. *Ibid.*

71. *Ibid.*

72. Benjamin to Mason, May 29, 1867, James Mason Papers, Manuscripts Division, Library of Congress.

73. Benjamin to Bayard, November 11, 1865, copy in Pierce Butler Papers; see Butler, *Benjamin*, p. 427.

74. Benjamin to Mason, October 25, 1866, James Mason Papers, Manuscripts Division, Library of Congress.

75. L. T. Wigfall to Clement Clay, October 7, 1866, Manuscripts Division, Duke University. See Mead, *Benjamin*, pp. 342–43. For background on Wigfall, see Alvin L. King, *Louis T. Wigfall: Southern Fire Eater* (Baton Rouge, 1970).

76. For background on the gold, see Hanna, *Flight into Oblivion*, pp. 25–54 and 92, and Davis, *The Long Surrender*, pp. 121–31 and note 1, Chapter 8; the most reliable and detailed account is by Otis Ashmore, *Georgia Historical Quarterly*, 2: 119–33. Micajah H. Clark, a Confederate captain, has given an authoritative account in *Southern Historical Society Papers*, 9: 542–56. Paymaster John F. Wheless also wrote on the subject, *Southern Historical Society Papers*, 10: 138–41.

77. Benjamin to Mason, May 29, 1867, James Mason Papers, Manuscripts Division, Library of Congress.

CHAPTER 19
The Lincoln Assassination: Lingering Suspicion

1. Benjamin to Mrs. Davis, September 1, 1865, London, *Georgia Review*, XX (1966): 251–60. Original in Jefferson Davis Collection, Transylvania University.

2. *Ibid.*

3. Varina Davis to President Andrew Johnson, May 5, 1866, Johnson Papers, Library of Congress; see also Varina H. Davis, *Memoir*, II: 757.

4. For background, see Varina H. Davis, *Memoir*, II: 767–68.

5. Benjamin to Mrs. Kruttschnitt, Havana, August 1, 1865; see Butler, *Benjamin,* p. 367.

6. London *Times,* September 11, 1865, p. 1. and New York *Times,* September 25, 1865, p. 1.

7. *Ibid.*

8. Benjamin to Mrs. Davis, November 16, 1865, *Georgia Review,* XX (1966): 251–60. Original in Jefferson Davis Collection, Transylvania University.

9. Varina H. Davis, *Memoir,* II: 769–70.

10. John Craven, *The Prison Life of Jefferson Davis,* pp. 155–56.

11. Mary Bernard Allen, *Joseph Holt, Judge Advocate General 1862–1875: A Study in the Treatment of Political Prisoners* (Chicago, 1927), pp. 66–67.

12. *Letters from the Hon. Joseph Holt, Upon the Policy of the Government,* 2d ed. (Washington, 1861), p. 16; New York *Times,* August 20, 1894, p. 1, col. 2.

13. Official Records, Series 1, XLVII, pt. 3: 301.

14. Official Records, Series 2, VIII: 899, and *Messages and Papers of the Presidents,* 6: 307–8.

15. Ben Pitman, *Assassination of President Lincoln,* pp. 24–37; trial of the Alleged Assassins, pp. 132–42. See also Judge W. W. Cleary, "The Attempt to Fasten the Assassination of President Lincoln on President Davis and Other Innocent Parties," *Southern Historical Society Papers,* Vol. IX, July–August 1881.

16. New York *Tribune,* June 6, 1865, p. 4, col. 2.

17. Letter from Conover to Thompson, March 20, 1865, printed in the Chicago *Tribune,* July 1, 1865, p. 2. See Turner, *Beware the People Weeping,* p. 213.

18. Holt to Stanton, June 1865. For background and additional details, see Seymour Frank, "The Conspiracy to Implicate the Confederate Leaders in Lincoln's Assassination," *Mississippi Valley Historical Review,* XL (March 1954): 629–56.

19. For an informative account of the Conover chapter in the assassination, see Turner, *Beware the People Weeping,* pp. 216, 212–19, 221–23.

20. Papers of Joseph Holt, Vol. XLVII, Manuscript Division, Library of Congress.

21. The author compared handwriting in the fraudulent letter with validated letters by Booth in the Library of Congress. There were *no* similarities.

22. House of Representatives Report No. 104, p. 25.

23. Letter from Chief Justice George Shea to the New York *Times,* January 24, 1876. See George Bryan, *The Great American Myth,* p. 388.

24. Varina H. Davis to Horace Greeley, June 22, 1865, Confederate Museum, Richmond.

25. Varina H. Davis to Horace Greeley, September 2, 1866, Manuscript Division, New York Public Library.

26. John W. Burgess, *Reminiscences of an American Scholar* (New York, 1934), p. 292.

27. Horace Greeley, editorial in the New York *Tribune,* November 9, 1866.

28. Varina H. Davis, *Memoir,* II: 794.

29. Burton Harrison, "The Capture of Jefferson Davis," *Century Magazine,* November 1883. Harrison's verbatim account is in Harrison (ed.), *The Harrisons of Skimino* (1910). See also Burton Harrison to his fiancée, Constance Cary, May 13, 1867, B. N. Harrison Papers, Library of Congress.

30. Rev. C. Minnegerode, *Memoirs,* quoted in Strode, *Jefferson Davis, Tragic Hero* III, *1864–1869:* 310.

31. Burton Harrison to Constance Cary, May 13, 1867, Harrison Papers, Library of Congress.

32. Benjamin to Harriet Benjamin, June 5, 1867; see Butler, *Benjamin,* p. 390.

33. Varina H. Davis, *Memoir,* II: 797.

34. Varina H. Davis, to Mrs. Howell Cobb, September 6, 1867, New-York Historical Society.

35. Benjamin to Mason, May 29, 1867, James Mason Papers, Manuscripts Division, Library of Congress.

36. Varina H. Davis, *Memoir,* II: 799.

37. *Ibid.,* II: 624.

38. Jefferson Davis to William Howell, November 6, 1867. For further background of the plots to assassinate Davis, see Strode, *Jefferson Davis,* III: 323.

39. Letter from Jacob Thompson to New York *Tribune,* May 22, 1865, p. 4. Thompson fled to Paris, then to Naples, then to Egypt and to "Palestine to tread the ground our Savior trod . . . and escape the grossest slanders and foulest falsehoods." For his own descriptions of his travels and his plea for fairness, see letter from Thompson to William Delay, August 11, 1866, *Journal of Southern History,* Vol. VI, February 1940.

40. Letter from Beverley Tucker to Montreal *Gazette,* May 23, 1865.

41. Jefferson Davis to Howell Cobb, July 25, 1868; see Strode, *Jefferson Davis,* III: p. 323.

42. Mrs. Norman Walker, Journal, August 4, 1868.

43. Varina H. Davis to Lawley, April 4, 1897, Lawley Mss., Pierce Butler Collection, Tulane University.

44. Pollard, *The Life of Jefferson Davis,* pp. 154–55.

45. *Ibid.,* p. 445.

46. *Ibid.,* p. 407.

47. *Ibid.,* p. 151.

48. *Ibid.,* p. 413.

49. Meade, *Benjamin,* p. 345; see also Rowland, *Jefferson Davis, Constitutionalist,* 10 vols. VII: 246–51, and McElroy, *Jefferson Davis,* II: 612–13.

50. See Richard Lester, *Confederate Finance and Purchasing in Great Britain,* p. 23, note 99. It is generally thought that Slidell's daughter Mathilde married Erlanger's son, but she married Emile Erlanger himself, and the couple had a very happy life together. They were married October 4, 1864.

51. Foote, *Casket of Reminiscences,* pp. 150–51.

52. *Ibid.*

53. Benjamin to Davis, March 18, 1874, Shakespeare Birthplace Trust, Shakespeare Center, Stratford-upon-Avon, England.

CHAPTER 20
The British Barrister from America

1. *Law Time,* June 10, 1939, p. 391. See Meade, *Benjamin,* p. 337–38.

2. *Ibid.*

3. Pollock, *Fortnightly Review,* LXIX (March 1898): 354–61, and *The Green Bag,* vol. 1, no. 9, September 1889.

4. *Ibid.*

5. Memoranda by E. Russell Roberts and Richard Horton Smith in Lawley Mss., Pierce Butler Collection, Tulane University. See also *Law Reports Appeal Cases,* VI: 722–39, and Butler, *Benjamin,* p. 404–5.

6. Benjamin to Bradford, December 24, 1870, and Benjamin to Mason, February 8, 1871, James Mason Papers, Manuscripts Division, Library of Congress.

7. Benjamin to Miss Harriet Benjamin, February 21, 1872, in Pierce Butler Collection, Tulane University; text in Butler, *Benjamin,* pp. 397–98.

8. Benjamin to Bradford, June 13, 1872; see Meade, *Benjamin,* p. 351.

9. Benjamin to his sisters, March 17, 1875; see Butler, *Benjamin,* p. 407.

10. Benjamin to Miss Harriet Benjamin, February 21, 1872; see Butler, *Benjamin,* p. 397.

11. Benjamin to Bradford, April 22, 1873; see Meade, *Benjamin,* p. 352.

12. J. G. Witt memorandum to Lawley, undated, Lawley Mss., Pierce Butler Collection, Tulane University. See Butler, *Benjamin,* p. 423–24.

13. Meade, *Benjamin,* p. 358–60; London *Times,* June 16, 1876; and Earl of Oxford and Asquith, *Memories and Reflections,* vi: 72–79.

14. Benjamin to his sisters, July 16, 1876; see Butler, *Benjamin,* p. 408.

15. Cincinnati *Commercial,* June 18, 1876.

16. Lawley Mss., Pierce Butler Collection, Tulane University; see Butler, *Benjamin*, pp. 403–4.

17. *Ibid.*

18. London *Times*, May 9, 1884, and Butler, *Benjamin*, pp. 401–2.

19. Pollock, *Fortnightly Review*, LXIX (March 1898): 354–61 and *The Green Bag*, Vol. 9, no. 1, September 1889.

20. *Ibid.*

21. James G. Blaine, *Twenty Years of Congress*, II: 22–23.

22. Butler, *Benjamin*, p. 441, and Meade, *Benjamin*, pp. 354, 355, 364.

23. Lawley Mss., Pierce Butler Collection, Tulane University.

24. New York *Times*, January 2, 1879.

25. Butler, *Benjamin*, pp. 419–10, 441 (appendix), and Lawley Mss., Pierce Butler Collection, Tulane University.

26. Benjamin to his sisters, October 15, 1871; see Butler, *Benjamin*, p. 397.

27. Bradford papers, letter of February 25, 1871; see Meade, *Benjamin*, p. 354–55.

28. Benjamin to Bradford, April 22, 1873; see Meade, *Benjamin*, p. 354.

29. Witt memorandum to Lawley, Lawley Mss., Pierce Butler Collection, Tulane University.

30. Benjamin to Mrs. Kruttschnitt, August 1, 1865; see Butler, *Benjamin*, p. 367.

31. Benjamin to Mrs. Kruttschnitt, September 29, 1865; see Butler, *Benjamin*, pp. 370–72.

32. Benjamin to Mrs. Kruttschnitt, April 11, 1867; see Butler, *Benjamin*, pp. 388–89.

33. Benjamin to his sisters, February 22, 1868; see Butler, *Benjamin*, p. 391.

34. Benjamin to Mrs. Levy, February 22, 1868; see Butler, *Benjamin*, pp. 390–92; and Meade, *Benjamin*, p. 339.

35. *Ibid.*

36. Benjamin to Mrs. Levy, February 8, 1870; see Butler, *Benjamin*, p. 394.

37. Benjamin to Harriet Benjamin, February 21, 1872; see Butler, *Benjamin*, p. 398.

38. Benjamin to his sisters, March 17, 1875; see Butler, *Benjamin*, p. 394.

39. Benjamin to Mrs. Kruttschnitt, August 9, 1874; see Butler, *Benjamin*, pp. 405–6.

40. *Ibid.*

41. *Ibid.*

42. Benjamin to his sisters, March 17, 1875; see Butler, *Benjamin*, p. 407.

43. Benjamin to Mrs. Kruttschnitt, March 23, 1880; see Butler, *Benjamin,* p. 425.

44. Witt memorandum, Lawley Mss., Pierce Butler Collection, Tulane University.

45. Interviews by Meade, *Benjamin,* pp. 362, 413; Notes in Robert D. Meade Papers, Manuscripts Department, University of Virginia Library.

46. Benjamin to Harriet Benjamin, June 6, 1876, and Benjamin to Mrs. Bradford, September 6, 1875, in Robert D. Meade Papers, Manuscripts Department, University of Virginia Library.

47. Benjamin to his sisters (undated); see Butler, *Benjamin,* pp. 430–31.

48. Benjamin to Mrs. Kruttschnitt, November 6, 1879; see Butler, *Benjamin,* p. 409.

49. Benjamin to Harriet Benjamin, June 5, 1867; see Butler, *Benjamin,* p. 390.

50. Author's visit to Paris, June 1983.

51. For background of the lawsuit, see Eaton, *Jefferson Davis,* p. 264, and Ross, *First Lady of the South,* p. 344.

52. Varina H. Davis to Jefferson Davis, April 18, 1878, Confederate Memorial Hall, New Orleans.

53. For background to the story of Mrs. Dorsey, see Eaton, *Jefferson Davis,* pp. 264–65; Ross, *First Lady of the South,* pp. 328, 330, 405; and Strode, *Jefferson Davis, Tragic Hero,* pp. 421–43.

54. Lawley Mss., Pierce Butler Collection, Tulane University. Because this letter survives in the Lawley papers, one can assume it is one of the few letters written *to* Benjamin that he did not destroy.

55. Benjamin to Davis, February 15, 1879; see Meade, *Benjamin,* p. 369, and Rowland, *Jefferson Davis, Constitutionalist,* VIII: 350–57.

56. Benjamin to his sisters, March 18, 1877; see Butler, *Benjamin,* p. 408.

57. Benjamin to Bradford, May 16, 1875; see Butler, *Benjamin,* p. 390.

58. Benjamin to Mrs. Kruttschnitt, April 5, 1880; see Butler, *Benjamin,* p. 409.

59. Benjamin to Varina H. Davis, April 25, 1881, and Hudson Strode, "Judah P. Benjamin's Loyalty to Jefferson Davis," *Georgia Review, XX* (1966): 260.

60. Davis, *The Rise and Fall of the Confederacy,* I: 242.

CHAPTER 21
Paris: Hidden from History

1. Benjamin to Finney, March 12, 1878; see Meade, *Benjamin,* p. 367.

2. New York *Times,* January 2, 1879, quoted in Lynchburg, Virginia, January 30, 1879; see Meade, *Benjamin,* p. 366.

3. Benjamin to Harriet Benjamin, November 4, 1881; see Butler, *Benjamin,* p. 411.

4. Benjamin to his sisters, April 1880; see Butler, *Benjamin,* p. 410.

5. Benjamin to Bradford, January 25, 1880, copy in Robert D. Meade Papers, Manuscripts Department, University of Virginia Library; see Meade, *Benjamin,* p. 329.

6. Benjamin to Eugenia Kruttschnitt, May 8, 1880, copy in Robert D. Meade Papers, Manuscripts Department, University of Virginia Library; see Meade, *Benjamin,* p. 369.

7. Benjamin to Bayard, August 2, 1883; see Butler, *Benjamin,* p. 410.

8. Benjamin to Bayard, October 24, 1880; see Butler, *Benjamin,* p. 411.

9. New York *Tribune,* January 20, 1882.

10. New York *Times,* November 6, 1881.

11. New York *Times,* January 20, 1982.

12. *Ibid.*

13. Undated clipping, probably 1883, Bayard Papers, Callery Collection, Historical Society of Delaware.

14. Gustavus H. Wald, *Miscellany* (pamphlet, Cincinnati, 1906) pp. 35–44, reprinted in *Harvard Graduate Magazine,* XXXVI (June 1928): 538–42.

15. Benjamin to Harriet Benjamin, November 4, 1881; see Butler, *Benjamin,* pp. 410–11.

16. Benjamin to Bradford, December 15, 1882; see Meade, *Benjamin,* p. 376.

17. Benjamin to Mrs. Kruttschnitt, February 12, 1883; see Butler, *Benjamin,* p. 413.

18. London *Times,* February 9 and 10, 1883.

19. *Morning Telegraph,* May 7, 1884.

20. Benjamin to Mrs. Kruttschnitt, March 1, 1883; see Butler, *Benjamin,* p. 413.

21. The banquet occurred on June 30, 1883. Reported in the London *Times,* July 2, 1883; see Butler, *Benjamin,* p. 414–16.

22. *Ibid.*

23. Witt memorandum to Lawley, Lawley Mss., Pierce Butler Collection, Tulane University; see Butler, *Benjamin,* p. 424.

24. *Ibid.*

25. Witt memorandum to Lawley, Lawley Mss., Pierce Butler Collection, Tulane University; see Butler, *Benjamin,* p. 435.

26. Benjamin to Lawley, September 12, 1882, Lawley Mss., Pierce Butler Collection, Tulane University.

27. Benjamin to Lawley, September 2, 1882, Lawley Mss., Pierce Butler Collection, Tulane University.

28. Reported by Judge Henry C. Miller, member of New Orleans bar; see Louis Gruss, "Judah Philip Benjamin," *Louisiana Historical Society Quarterly,* October 1936, p. 1068.

29. Benjamin to Varina Davis, as reported by Varina Davis in letter to Lawley, June 8, 1898, Lawley Mss., Pierce Butler Collection, Tulane University.

30. Varina H. Davis to Lawley, June 8, 1898, Lawley Mss., Pierce Butler Collection, Tulane University.

31. Benjamin's will, written by hand and dated April 30, 1883, is preserved at Somerset House, London. It shows an estate of more than 60,000 English pounds ($300,000) in personalty and the mansion in Paris. The will left 10,000 pounds in various amounts to his three sisters, to his brother Joseph, and to his niece and nephews, and the residue "to my dear wife Natalie and to our only child, Ninette." The wills of Natalie, Ninette, and Henri de Bousignac are on file in the Archives de Paris. The mansion was passed to Ninette on Natalie's death in 1891; to Henri de Bousignac on Ninette's death in 1898 (her will stated: "I pray to God to reward my dear Henri for all his kindness, and for the good care and abnegation he showed by leaving the army at my earnest request.") Bousignac died in 1901, and his will contained an order to sell the mansion.

EPILOGUE

1. Author's visit to Père Lachaise cemetery, June 1983.

2. Varina H. Davis, letter to "The Veterans and Public of the Southern States," July 11, 1891, Fleming Papers, New York Public Library.

Selected Bibliography

❄

Newspapers

Charleston *Courier*
Cincinnati *Commercial*
Galveston *Daily News*
London *Daily Telegraph*
London *Times*
London *Morning Telegraph*
New Orleans *Crescent*
New Orleans *Delta*
New Orleans *Picayune*
New Orleans *True Delta*

New York *Herald*
New York *Times*
New York *Tribune*
New York *World*
Richmond *Dispatch*
Richmond *Enquirer*
Richmond *Examiner*
Richmond *Sentinel*
Richmond *Whig*

Periodicals

Atlantic Monthly
De Bow's Review
Fortnightly Review
The Green Bag
The Independent

The Israelite, Cincinnati
The Jewish Messenger, New York
The Occident, Philadelphia
Southern Punch

Articles

BENJAMIN, JUDAH P. "Louisiana Sugar," *De Bow's Review,* II (November 1846): 322–45.

———. "Agriculture," *De Bow's Review,* V, (January 1848): 44–57.

———. "Soleil's Saccharometer," *De Bow's Review,* V (April 1848): 357–64.

CLEARY, W. W. "The Attempt to Fasten the Assassination of President Lincoln on President Davis and Other Innocent Parties," *Southern Historical Society Papers,* IX (July–August 1881): 313–25.

DAVIS, VARINA H. "Last Christmas in the White House," New York *Sunday World,* 1905.

FRANK, SEYMOUR J. "The Conspiracy to Implicate the Confederate Leaders in Lincoln's Assassination," *Mississippi Valley Historical Review,* XL (March 1954): 629–56.

GENTRY, JUDITH. "A Confederate Success in Europe: The Erlanger Loan," *Journal of Southern History,* XXXVI (1970): 157–88.

GRUSS, LOUIS. "Judah P. Benjamin," *Louisiana Historical Quarterly,* October 1936, 964–1068.

HARRISON, BURTON. "The Capture of Jefferson Davis," *Century Magazine,* XXVII (November 1883): 130–45.

HENRY, W. W. "Memorandum of a Conversation with Duncan Kenner, Sent March 24, 1893," *William and Mary College Quarterly,* Series I, Vol. XXV, July 1916.

HUNE, MAJOR EDGAR ERSKINE. "The Days Gone By: Chimborazo Hospital, Confederate States Army—America's Largest Military Hospital," *The Military Surgeon: Journal of the Association of Military Surgeons of the United States,* LXXV (September 1934): 156–66.

KAPLAN, BENJAMIN. "Judah Philip Benjamin," essay in L. Dinnerstein and M. D. Palsson, *Jews in the South* (Baton Rouge, 1973), pp. 75–88.

KIRKE, EDWARD. "Our Visit to Richmond," *Atlantic Monthly,* September 1864.

KOHLER, MAX J. "Judah P. Benjamin: Statesman and Jurist," *Publications of the American Jewish Historical Society,* no. 12 (1904), pp. 63–85.

KORN, BERTRAM W. "Judah P. Benjamin as a Jew," *Publications of the American Jewish Historical Society,* no. XXXVIII, pt. 3 (March 1949), pp. 153–71.

KROUSE, ALLEN. "The Enigmatic Judah Benjamin," *Midstream,* October 1978, pp. 17–20.

LASSWELL, L. (ed.). "Jefferson Davis Ponders His Future, 1829," *Journal of Southern History,* XLI (November 1975): 516–22.

MALLORY, STEPHEN. "The Last Days of the Confederate Government," *McClure's Magazine,* XVI (December 1900): 99–107.

MEADE, ROBERT D. "The Relations Between Judah P. Benjamin and Jefferson Davis," *Journal of Southern History,* V (1939): 468–78.

OREN, DAN A. "Why Did Judah P. Benjamin Leave Yale?" *A Jewish Journal at Yale,* Fall 1984.

PADGETT, JAMES A. (ed.). "The Letters of Judah Philip Benjamin . . . ," *Louisiana Historical Quarterly,* XX (1937): 738–93.

PECK, ABRAHAM J. "That Other 'Peculiar Institution': Jews and Judaism in the Nineteenth Century South." *Modern Judaism,* Vol. 7, no. 1 (February 1987): pp. 99–114.

POLLOCK, BARON CHARLES. "Reminiscences of Judah Philip Benjamin," *The Fortnightly Review,* LXIX (March 1898) and *The Green Bag,* Vol. I, no. 9 (September 1889).

STRODE, HUDSON. "Judah P. Benjamin's Loyalty to Jefferson Davis," *Georgia Review,* XX (1966): 251–60.

SURRATT, JOHN H. "Lecture on the Lincoln Conspiracy," *Lincoln Herald,* LI, December 1949.

THOMSON, A. W. "How Jefferson Davis Received the News of Lincoln's Death," The *Independence,* February 15, 1900.

VEST, GEORGE G. "A Senator from Two Republics: Judah P. Benjamin," *Saturday Evening Post,* October 3, 1903.

WARREN, SPENCER. "A French View of the Fall of Richmond," *Virginia Magazine of History and Biography,* April 1965.

WOOD, JOHN T. "Escape of the Confederate Secretary of War," *Century Magazine,* XLVII (November 1893): 110–23.

Manuscripts

BAYARD, JAMES A., and THOMAS F. BAYARD, Papers, Callery Collection, Historical Society of Delaware, Wilmington, Delaware.

BENJAMIN, JUDAH P., collections:
• American Jewish Historical Society Collections, Waltham, Mass.
• American Jewish Archives, Cincinnati Campus, Hebrew Union College, Jewish Institute of Religion, Cincinnati, Ohio.
• Yale University Library, New Haven, Conn.

BUTLER, PIERCE, Papers and Collection, Howard-Tilton Memorial Library, Tulane University, New Orleans, La.

BROWNING, ORVILLE H. Papers, Illinois State Historical Society, Springfield, Ill.

DAVIS, JEFFERSON, papers of:
• Mississippi Department of Archives and History, Jackson, Miss.
• Rice University, Houston, Texas
• The Confederate Museum, The Virginia Historical Society, Richmond, Va.

DAVIS, JEFFERSON, Collection, Transylvania University, Lexington, Ky.

HAYES, JOEL ADDISON, Letters, Memphis State University Library, Mississippi Valley Collection, Memphis, Tenn.

Louisiana State University, Baton Rouge, La.:
• Gayaree, Charles E. A., papers
• Caffery, Donelson and family, Papers
• Liddell, Moses, St. John R, Moses, and family, Papers
• Farrar, Alexander K., Papers

- Photograph of Birth Record, Sherath Israel Synagogue, Charlotte Amalie, St. Thomas, Virgin Islands

MEADE, ROBERT DOUTHAT, Papers, University of Virginia, Manuscripts Department, Alderman Library, Charlottesville, Va.

Southern Historical Collection, University of North Carolina at Chapel Hill, N.C.:
- Perkins, John, Papers
- Alexander, E. J., Papers
- Davis, Jefferson, Papers
- Bragg, Thomas, Diary

WISDOM, JOHN MINOR, Collection, Howard-Tilton Memorial Library, Tulane University, New Orleans, La.

Library of Congress
The author is grateful to Gary J. Kohn, who compiled the references to Judah P. Benjamin for his book: *The Jewish Experience: A Guide to the Manuscript Sources of the Library of Congress* (American Jewish Archives, Cincinnati, 1986). Papers consulted were:

Banks, Nathaniel P.
Barton–Jenifer Families
Batchelder, John
Beauregard, P. G. T.
Benjamin, Judah P.
Blair, Francis P.
Burwell, William M.
Butler, Benjamin B.
Cameron, Simon
Causten-Pickett
Chesnut, James
Clay, Thomas J.
Colfax, Schuyler
Confederate States—State
    Department Papers
    (John A. Pickett Papers)
Corcoran, William W.
Crittenden, John J.
Curry, Jabez, L. M.
Cushing, Caleb
Dahlgren, John A. B.
Delano, Columbus
Early, Jubal A.
Easby-Smith Family
Eustis, George
Fillmore, Millard
Fish, Hamilton

Forney, John W.
Garfield, James A.
Goodwin, James H.
Gwinn, William N.
Hammond, James H.
Harris, Isham G.
Harrison, Burton
Holmes, George F.
Holt, Joseph
Hotchkiss, Jedediah
Hotze, Henry
Johnson, Reverdy
Johnston, Albert S.
Johnston, William P.
Lee, Samuel P.
London Exhibition of 1851
Lovell, Mansfield
Mangum, Willie P.
Marcy, William L.
Martin, Letitia B.
Mason, James M.
Maury, Matthew F.
McCook Family
McPherson, Edward
Milton, George F.
Moran, Benjamin
Myer, Albert J.

North, Simeon N. D.
Pecquet, de Bellet Paul
Phillips, Philip
Pickens-Bonham
Pickett, John T.
Pierce, Franklin
Reynolds, Thomas C.
Rives, William C.
Roman, Alfred
Sanders, George N.
Schoolcraft, Henry R.
Selfridge, Thomas O.
Sherman, John
Stanton, Edwin M.
Stephens, Alexander H.

Thompson, Jacob
Trenholm, George A.
Tucker, Nathaniel B.
Tyler, John
U.S. Library of Congress Archives
U.S. Works Progress Administra-
tion—Mallory, Stephen R.
Van Dorn, Earl
Wadsworth Family
Walker, Robert J.
Washburne, Elihu B.
Welles, Gideon
Wheeler, John H.
Willis, Edward

Books

Judah P. Benjamin

BENJAMIN, JUDAH P. *Treatise on the Law of Sale of Personal Property, With References to the American Decisions, to the French Code and Civil Code.* 1868.

BUTLER, PIERCE. *Judah P. Benjamin.* Philadelphia 1907, reprinted: New York and London, 1980.

MEADE, ROBERT DOUTHAT. *Judah P. Benjamin, Confederate Statesman.* New York, 1943, reprinted: New York, 1975.

NEIMAN, SIMON L. *Judah Benjamin.* Indianapolis, 1963.

OSTERWEIS, ROLLIN. *Judah P. Benjamin: Statesman of the Lost Cause.* New York, 1933.

RYWELL, MARTIN. *Judah P. Benjamin: Unsung Rebel Prince.* Asheville, N.C., 1948.

Jefferson Davis

ALFRIEND, FRANK H. *Life of Jefferson Davis.* Cincinnati and Philadelphia, 1868.

CRAVEN, JOHN J. *Prison Life of Jefferson Davis.* New York, 1866.

CUTTING, ELISABETH. *Jefferson Davis: Political Soldier.* New York, 1930.

DAVIS, JEFFERSON. *The Rise and Fall of the Confederate States.* 2 vols. New York, 1881.

DAVIS, VARINA HOWELL. *Jefferson Davis, Ex-President of the Confederate States of America: A Memoir by His Wife.* 2 vols. New York, 1890.

DODD, WILLIAM E. *Jefferson Davis.* Philadelphia, 1907.

EATON, CLEMENT. *Jefferson Davis.* New York, 1977.

ECKENRODE, H. J. *Jefferson Davis, President of the South.* New York, 1923.

MCELROY, ROBERT. *Jefferson Davis: The Real and Unreal.* 2 vols. New York, 1937.

MONROE, H. M., and J. T. MCINTOSH (eds.). *The Papers of Jefferson Davis.* 5 vols. Baton Rouge, La., 1971–85.

POLLARD, EDWARD A. *Life of Jefferson Davis, With a Secret History of the Southern Confederacy.* Philadelphia, 1869.

ROWLAND, DUNBAR (ed.). *Jefferson Davis, Constitutionalist: His Letters, Papers and Speeches.* 10 vols. Jackson, Miss., 1923.

STRODE, HUDSON. *Jefferson Davis.* 3 vols. New York, 1955–64.

WAGE, M. N. *The Education of a Gentleman: Jefferson Davis at Transylvania 1821–1824.* Lexington, 1943.

Primary and Secondary Sources

ADAMS, C. F. *Charles Francis Adams 1835–1915: An Autobiography.* Boston and New York, 1916.

AVARY, MYRTA LOCKETT. *A Virginia Girl in the Civil War 1861–1865.* New York, 1903.

BARRETT, JOHN G. *Sherman's March Through the Carolinas.* Chapel Hill, N.C., 1956.

BASSO, HAMILTON. *Beauregard.* New York, 1933.

BERMAN, MYRON. *Richmond's Jewry, 1769–1976: Shabbat in Shockhoe.* Charlottesville, 1979.

BILL, ALFRED HOYT. *The Beleaguered City.* New York, 1946.

BIRMINGHAM, STEPHEN. *The Grandees.* New York, 1971.

BISHOP, JIM. *The Day Lincoln Was Shot.* New York, 1955.

BLAINE, JAMES G. *Twenty Years of Congress: From Lincoln to Garfield.* 2 vols. New York, 1884–1886.

BRADFORD, SARAH. *Disraeli.* New York, 1983.

BROWNLOW, W. G. *Sketches of the Rise, Progress and Decline of Seccession.* Philadelphia, 1862.

BRYAN, GEORGE S. *The Great American Myth.* New York, 1940.

BUTLER, BENJAMIN. *Autobiography and Personal Reminiscence of Major General Benjamin F. Butler.* Boston, 1892.

CARROLL, DANIEL B. *Henry Mercier and The American Civil War.* Princeton, N.J., 1971.

CASE, L. M., and W. F. SPENCER. *The United States and France: Civil War Diplomacy.* Philadelphia, 1970.

CATTON, BRUCE. *This Hallowed Ground.* New York, 1956.

CHESNUT, MARY BOYKIN. *A Diary From Dixie.* New York, 1905.

CLAY-CLOPTON, VIRGINIA. *A Belle of the Fifties.* New York, 1905.

COMMAGER, HENRY STEELE. *The Blue and The Gray: The Story of the Civil War as Told by Participants.* 2 vols. Indianapolis and New York, 1950.

COTTRELL, JOHN. *Anatomy of an Assassination: The Murder of Abraham Lincoln.* New York, 1966.

COULTER, E. MERTON. *William G. Brownlow: Fighting Parson of the Southern Highlands.* Chapel Hill, N.C., 1937.

DANIEL, FREDERICK. *The Richmond Examiner During the War, or The Writings of John M. Daniel with a Memoir of His Life.* Richmond, 1868.

DAVIS, BURKE. *The Long Surrender.* New York, 1985.

DAVIS, CURTIS. *Belle Boyd: In Camp and Prison.* New York, 1905.

DE LEON, T. C. *Belles, Beaux and Brains of the 60's.* New York, 1907.

———. *Four Years in Rebel Capitals.* Mobile, Ala., 1890.

DEW, CHARLES B. *Ironmaker to the Confederacy: Joseph R. Anderson and the Tredegar Iron Works.* New Haven, Conn. 1969.

DONALD, DAVID (ed.). *Why the North Won the Civil War.* Baton Rouge, 1960.

DURDEN, ROBERT F. *The Gray and the Black: The Confederate Debate on Emancipation.* Baton Rouge, 1972.

EISENSCHIML, OTTO. *Why Was Lincoln Murdered?* Boston, 1937.

ELZAS, BARNETT A. *The Jews of South Carolina.* Philadelphia, 1905.

———. *Leaves of My Historical Scrapbook.* Charleston, 1907.

EVANS, ELI N. *The Provincials: A Personal History of Jews in the South.* New York, 1973.

EZEKIEL, HERBERT T., and GASTON LICHTENSTEIN. *The History of the Jews in Richmond From 1769 to 1917.* Richmond, 1917.

FOOTE, HENRY STUART. *A Casket of Reminiscences.* Washington, 1874.

———. *War of the Rebellion.* New York, 1866.

FOOTE, SHELBY. *The Civil War: A Narrative.* 3 vols. New York, 1958–74.

FREEMAN, DOUGLAS SOUTHALL. *Lee's Lieutenants.* New York, 1942.

———. *R. E. Lee: A Biography.* 4 Vols. New York, 1934–35.

———. *The South to Posterity: An Introduction to the Writings of Confederate History.* New York, 1939.

FREMANTLE, SIR ARTHUR JAMES LYON. *Three Months in the Southern States: April–June, 1863.* New York, 1864.

GRAETZ, H. *History of the Jews.* 4 vols. New York, 1927.

GRAF, L. P. and R. HASKINS (eds.). *Papers of Andrew Johnson,* Vol. 6: *1862–1864,* Vol. 7: *1864–1865.* Knoxville, Tenn., 1983, 1986.

The Great Conspiracy. A Book of Absorbing Interest! Startling Developments. Eminent Persons Implicated. Full Secret of the Assassination Plot. John H. Surratt and His Mother. With Biographical Sketches of J. B. Booth and John Wilkes Booth, and the Life and Extraordinary

Adventures of John H. Surratt, the Conspirator. Philadelphia, 1866. On file in Rare Books, Library of Congress.

HANCHETT, WILLIAM. *The Lincoln Murder Conspiracies.* Urbana and Chicago, 1983.

HANNA, ALFRED J. *Flight into Oblivion.* Richmond, 1938.

HARRISON, CONSTANCE CARY. *Recollections Grave and Gray.* New York, 1911.

HARRISON, F. (ed.). *The Harrisons of Skimino.* New York, 1910.

HENDRICK, BURTON J. *Statesmen of the Lost Cause.* Boston, 1939.

HORAN, JAMES D. *Confederate Agent.* New York, 1954.

HERMANN, JANET S. *The Pursuit of a Dream.* New York and Oxford, 1981.

JACKSON, MRS. MARY. *Memoirs of Stonewall Jackson.* Louisville, 1895.

JONES, J. B., *A Rebel War Clerk's Diary at the Confederate States Capital.* 2 vols. Philadelphia, 1866. New Edition with Introduction by Howard Swiggett. New York, 1935.

JONES, KATHARINE. *Heroines of Dixie.* New York, 1955.

———. *Ladies of Richmond: Confederate Capital.* New York, 1962.

KORN, BERTRAM. *American Jewry and the Civil War.* New York, 1970.

———. *The Early Jews of New Orleans.* Waltham, Mass., 1969.

LEE, FITZHUGH. *General Lee.* New York, 1894.

LESTER, RICHARD. *Confederate Finance and Purchasing in Great Britain.* Charlottesville, Va., 1975.

MANARIN, LOUIS H. (ed.). *Richmond at War: Minutes of the City Council 1861–1865.* Chapel Hill, N.C. 1966.

MARCUS, JACOB RADER. *Memoirs of American Jews, 1775–1865.* 3 vols. Philadelphia, 1955.

———. *The Jew in the Medieval World: A Source Book: 315–1791.* New York, 1969.

MCFEELEY, WILLIAMS. *Grant: A Biography.* New York, 1982.

MCGUIRE, JUDY. *Diary of a Southern Refugee.* New York, 1867.

MILTON, GEORGE. *The Age of Hate: Andrew Johnson and the Radicals.* New York, 1930.

MOISE, L. C. *Biography of Isaac Harby: With an Account of the Reformed Society of Israelites of Charleston, S.C. 1824–1833.* Central Conference of American Rabbis, 1931.

OATES, STEPHEN B. *With Malice Toward None: The Life of Abraham Lincoln.* New York, 1977.

OREN, DAN A. *Joining The Club: A History of Jews and Yale.* New Haven, 1985.

OWSLEY, FRANK L. *King Cotton Diplomacy.* Chicago, 1931.

PEASE, T. C., and JAMES G. RANDALL (eds.). *The Diary of Orville Hickman Browning.* 2 vols. Springfield, Ill., 1925, 1933.

PEMBER, PHOEBE YATES. *A Southern Woman's Diary: Life in Confederate Richmond.* Ed. Bell I. Wiley. Jackson, Tenn., 1959.

POORE, BEN PERLEY. *Perley's Reminiscences: Or Sixty Years in the National Metropolis.* 2 vols. Philadelphia, 1886.

PRYOR, SARA. *My Day: Reminiscences of Peace and War.* New York, 1904.

PUTNAM, SALLIE ANN BROCK. *Richmond During The War: Four Years of Personal Observation.* New York, 1867.

RANDALL, G., and DAVID DONALD. *The Civil War and Reconstruction.* Rev. Ed. Boston, 1969.

REAGAN, JOHN H. *Memoirs: With Special Reference to Secession and the Civil War.* New York, 1906.

REZNIKOFF, CHARLES, and URIAH ENGELMAN. *The Jews of Charleston.* Philadelphia, 1950.

ROSS, ISHBEL. *First Lady of the South: The Life of Mrs. Jefferson Davis.* New York, 1958.

RUSSELL, WILLIAM HOWARD. *My Diary North and South.* New York, 1954.

SACHAR, ABRAM. *A History of the Jews.* 5th Ed., Rev. New York, 1967.

SANDBURG, CARL. *Abraham Lincoln: The War Years.* 4 vols. New York, 1939.

SASSON, B. H. (ed.). *A History of the Jewish People.* Cambridge, 1976.

SEARS, LOUIS M. *John Slidell.* Durham, N.C., 1925.

SCOTT, ANNE FIROR. *The Southern Lady: From Pedestal to Politics, 1830–1930.* Chicago, 1970.

SHERMAN, WILLIAM TECUMSEH. *Memoirs.* New York, 1875.

STOKES, ANSON PHELPS. *Memorials of an Eminent Yale Man.* New Haven, 1914.

THOMAS, EMORY M. *The Confederate Nation, 1861–1865.* New York, 1979.

———. *The Confederate State of Richmond: A Biography of the Capital.* Austin, Tex., 1971.

———. *Bold Dragoon: The Life of J. E. B. Stuart.* New York, 1986.

TURNER, THOMAS REED. *Beware the People Weeping: Public Opinion and the Assassination of Abraham Lincoln.* Baton Rouge, 1982.

VANDIVER, FRANK. *Mighty Stonewall.* New York, 1957.

———. *Their Tattered Flags: The Epic of the Confederacy.* New York, 1970.

WILLIAMS, T. HARRY. *P. G. T. Beauregard: Napoleon in Gray.* Baton Rouge, 1955.

WILLSON, BECCLES. *John Slidell and the Confederates in Paris: 1862–1865.* New York, 1932.

WISE, ISAAC M. *Reminiscences.* Cincinnati, 1901.

WISE, JOHN S. *The End of an Era.* Boston, 1902.

WOODWARD, C. VANN (ed.). *Mary Chesnut's Civil War.* New Haven, 1981.

Acknowledgments

✺✺

In the beginning, I did not expect that this book would require nine years of research and writing, but Judah P. Benjamin's life is filled with endless tributaries of interest and I was soon swept into rivers and seas which led to an inquiry on two continents. Because he burned his papers, there were mysteries about Benjamin which required a thorough search for his letters to others; I have been the grateful beneficiary of the kindness and cooperation of many members of the community of scholars in America and Europe.

I would first like to pay tribute to two men who preceded me as Judah P. Benjamin biographers and who shared my fascination, and in some ways obsession, with this extraordinary figure in American history. Every scholar builds on the work of those who have gone before, but this book could never have been written without the previous collection of material that would have been otherwise lost and the timely interviewing of associates and friends of Benjamin by Pierce Butler of Tulane University, who wrote the first biography of Benjamin in 1907, and Robert Douthat Meade of Randolph Macon College in Lynchburg, Virginia, whose work was published in 1943. Professor Meade's widow, Lucy Boyd Meade, was also his research associate over the course of his twelve-year effort. She told me how they worked in the New York Public Library on their honeymoon, of their trips to London and Paris, and she was most gracious in welcoming me to the task of analyzing her husband's notes. Edmund

Berkeley, the Curator of Manuscripts at the University of Virginia, where the Meade papers are collected, and his staff were extremely well organized. In New Orleans, I was both assisted and encouraged by the interest and enthusiasm of Wilbur F. Meneray, head of Rare Books and Manuscripts at Tulane University, where the Pierce Butler papers are located, and by Joseph Cohen, the head of the Jewish Studies Program at Newcomb College and Tulane, who time and again made special efforts to check sources.

I also owe an intellectual debt to the pioneering work of Bertram Korn, author of *American Jewry and the Civil War,* who brought the ordeal of American Jews, North and South, to public attention. As comprehensive as his book was, it was surprising to me how much more there was to uncover, especially when reading the primary sources and complete references about Judah P. Benjamin.

Many others—professional archivists and colleagues—were more generous than I ever expected and, in many cases, than their jobs required: Rabbi Malcolm Stern has served as my intellectual mentor in Southern Jewish history for almost twenty years, and it was he who first suggested to me that Benjamin's postwar reticence might have been connected in some way to his fears from the madness loosed by the Lincoln assassination. His wife, Louise, tolerated my many phone calls and discussions; together they were the first friends to visit Benjamin's grave in Paris.

Gary J. Kohn, former staff member of the Library of Congress, volunteered his list of more than eighty references to Benjamin, which several years later appeared in his book *The Jewish Experience: A Guide to Manuscript Sources of the Library of Congress.* His map of previously untapped treasures yielded much material about Benjamin that has not been published before.

Lynda Lasswell Crist, editor of *The Papers of Jefferson Davis* project at Rice University, allowed me to pepper the project staff with questions for several years and always went beyond first steps for answers; Constance Cooper, Manuscript Librarian at the Historical Society of Delaware, was most helpful with the Bayard family papers; Delanie Ross, Curator and Director of the Mississippi Valley Collection at Memphis State University, was of great assistance regarding the Jefferson Davis letters discovered in 1978; Kip Campbell, then director of the Museum of the Confederacy in Richmond, provided many details of life in the Confederate White House. I would also like to thank Abraham Peck, Administrative Director of the American Jewish Archives at Hebrew Union College, and its founder, Jacob Marcus;

Ralph Draughn, Jr., Curator of Manuscripts at the Historic New Orleans Collection; Nathan Kaganoff, Librarian of the American Jewish Historical Society; Louis Manarin of the Virginia State Library; Linda P. Lerman, Judaica Bibliographer of the Yale University Library; Kathy Griffin of the Massachusetts Historical Society; Stephen Whitfield of Brandeis University; John O'Brien of New Haven, Connecticut, for allowing the use of original negatives and photographs from his private collection; Ruth Cooke of the Louis A. Warren Lincoln Library and Museum; William Lee Frost of the Lucius N. Littauer Foundation; the staffs of the New York Public Library and the Southern Historical Collection at the Library of the University of North Carolina at Chapel Hill; Oliver Orr, Lincoln scholar, and other staff members of the Library of Congress and the National Archives.

Two university presidents—John Brademas of New York University and Terry Sanford of Duke University—extended the courtesies of their institutions over several summers. I am indebted to Jay Oliva, Chancellor of New York University, and Joel Fleishman, Vice Chancellor of Duke University, for arrangements; and to Eric Meyers, director of the Cooperative Program of Judaic Studies at Duke University and the University of North Carolina; Mattie Russell, former curator of manuscripts, and many other staff members of the Perkins Library at Duke University.

A number of people have assisted me in cities where Benjamin lived: in Charleston, Solomon Breibart and Rabbi William Rosenthall; in New Orleans, Shepard Samuels; in Washington, D.C., Karen and Barry Jagoda; in Richmond, Saul Viener; in London, Mrs. Elizabeth Murray; and in Paris, Anne Dominique Rives and Blandine Girard.

Every biographer faces the problem of maintaining objectivity because of the intimacy and long interaction with a life relived. Several friends have kept me detached, and I have been immensely enriched by their sensitive reading of the manuscript in its many stages. Avery Russell was generous beyond the call of friendship as a thoughtful editor and creative sounding board, willing for years to talk through the deeper questions and assumptions in every aspect of the book. She knows how far this book has come. I am also indebted to Lisa Goldberg, Pat Irving, and Sheila Schwartz for reading the early versions of the manuscript and for their insights into Benjamin and Jefferson Davis.

There are others who sustained me in different ways over the long course of writing: Morris B. Abram, Nancy Ehle, Jack Nessel, Lois Stark, Roy Hoffman, Nancy Schwartz, Hugh Holman, Doris Betts,

David Geffen, Rollin Osterweis, Betsy Holloway, Matthew Hodgson, Judge John Minor Wisdom, Jim Luetze, Gretchen Dykstra, Barbara Babcock, Dottie and Steve Bernholz, Ann and Walter Dellinger, and Nina and Jimmy Wallace. For their hospitality in allowing me to live and write in their homes during many summers in Chapel Hill and Durham, North Carolina, I thank Anne and Andy Scott, Caro Mae Russell, and Trish and Robbie Robinson.

I will always be grateful to Pam Bernstein of the William Morris Agency for her advice all along the way and to Erwin Glikes, editor in chief of The Free Press of Macmillan. Erwin has an uncanny ability to empathize with a writer and his subject, and had many hunches about Benjamin that sent me back to sources to dig deeper. I am very fortunate to have found an editor who loves words and ideas and was willing to take a chance on a book that needed several years of work.

Throughout the many drafts, I called on the superb secretarial talents, patience, and good humor of Rue Canvin, Mary Hlavaty, Debbie Francis, and Diane Schiumo. I also want to express my gratitude to the members of the Board of Directors of the Charles H. Revson Foundation who, as individuals, have been so personally supportive of this effort.

From members of my own family, I have received the continuing tolerance for the consuming preoccupation of biographical writing and research. I want to express my deep appreciation to my parents and my special gratitude for the affectionate understanding of my brother Bob Evans, his wife, Gail, and their children, Jason, Jeffrey, and Julie. They all believed.

Finally, my wife, Judith, had the misfortune of living with piles of Civil War books and research all these years, but it was her faith, her nurturing patience, and her determination to see it through that has helped me to sustain this dream through publication. I want also to acknowledge the inspiration of my son, Joshua, born on March 30, 1985, who helped me type. Sages tell us that if possible, every man should have a child, write a book, and plant a tree. I hope that this book will someday enable him to understand better his roots as a Jew, a Southerner, and an American.

Index

✖

About the Author

❃❃❃

Eli N. Evans was born and raised in Durham, North Carolina. He graduated from the University of North Carolina in 1958 and spent two years in the U.S. Navy, stationed in Japan. After graduating from Yale Law School in 1963, he served on the White House staff from 1964 to 1965 and was a speech writer for political candidates in North Carolina. From 1965 to 1967, he was staff director at Duke University of a nationwide study of the future of the states that was headed by former North Carolina Governor Terry Sanford. From 1967 to 1977, he traveled extensively in the South as a senior program officer for the Carnegie Corporation of New York, the national educational foundation.

He is the author of *The Provincials: A Personal History of Jews in the South* (Atheneum, 1973). Since 1977, he has been president of the Charles H. Revson Foundation, which makes grants for programs in urban affairs, education, and Jewish philanthropy. Mr. Evans currently lives with his wife and son in New York City.